About Pearson

Pearson is the world's learning company, with presence across 70 countries worldwide. Our unique insights and world-class expertise come from a long history of working closely with renowned teachers, authors and thought leaders, as a result of which, we have emerged as the preferred choice for millions of teachers and learners across the world.

We believe learning opens up opportunities, creates fulfilling careers and hence better lives. We hence collaborate with the best of minds to deliver you class-leading products, spread across the Higher Education and Test Preparation spectrum.

Superior learning experience and improved outcomes are at the heart of everything we do. This product is the result of one such effort.

Your feedback plays a critical role in the evolution of our products and you can contact us at reachus@pearson.com. *We look forward to it.*

NTA—UGC

Teaching and Research Aptitude Paper 1

PREVIOUS YEARS' SOLVED PAPERS (2014–2026)

NET | SET | JRF

2026

KVS MADAAN

Pearson

To
my revered gurus, my parents
Smt. Devika Rani and Late Shri Prem Singh Madaan

ISBN 978-93-713-6310-5

First Impression

Published by Pearson India Education Services Pvt. Ltd, CIN: U72200TN2005PTC057128.

Head Office: 1st Floor, Berger Tower, Plot No. C-001A/2, Sector 16B, Noida - 201 301, Uttar Pradesh, India.

Registered Office: 6th Floor, Tower A, Unit A and B International Tech Park, CapitaLand Chennai, 200 Feet Radial Road, Zamin Pallavaram, Old Pallavaram Chennai – 600117, Tamil Nadu India

Website: in.pearson.com, Email: companysecretary.india@pearson.com

Compositor: Saksham Printographics, Delhi
Printed in India.

Contents

Preface

I am deeply thankful to all of you for giving tremendous response to *NTA-UGC NET/SET/JRF Paper I—Teaching and Research Aptitude,* published by Pearson Education. The title has helped thousands of aspirants to become Assistant Professors and Researchers in the valuable institutions. *NTA-UGC NET/SET/JRF Paper I—Teaching and Research Aptitude: Previous Years' Solved Papers 2026* has been written with a very clear objective to help the aspirants to achieve excellent score in Paper 1. Net aspirants, as is the case with other exams, also want to get closer to the actual exam pattern. The better performance in Paper 1 helps students to qualify JRF.

The basic strategy of candidates should be—*Prepare, Practice and Perform.* This title helps in this endeavour.

This book in it's new edition is updated with January 2026 and June 2025 papers, along with solutions. The book tries to cover the gap between main course book and actual exam pattern. It has been a very challenging task as some questions have become more complicated. Certain changes were introduced in January 2019 notification of NET Paper 1 syllabus. These changes can also be termed as the better specification of syllabus, but still they are part of continuity. As has been the case with main course book, pragmatism has been kept as the main theme in this book.

Hints and solutions for previous years' papers' questions have been put in such a manner that aspirants get some idea about pattern of questions for upcoming examinations. This title rather helps them to enter into the context of questions. It put candidates on the right track to qualify the exam. The language of solutions has been kept very simple. Net aspirants may become more innovative for future questions while exploring hints and solutions of the present text.

For suggestions and feedback, you may write to: kvsm2003@yahoo.co.in.

KVS Madaan

Acknowledgement

As we roll out the new edition of *NTA-UGC NET/SET/JRF Paper I—Teaching and Research Aptitude: Previous Years' Solved Paper 2025.* I thank each of you who provided suggestions to enrich this book. This edition reflects the advice and wisdom of many dedicated reviewers and instructors. This product has been created to provide right choice to qualify the exam.

The style of the book has been kept lively that focuses to the changing education needs. I feel indebted to Prof. Priya Gupta, Research Scholar for her valuable inputs to the title. I would like to extend my gratitude to Ruchira Dash and Bhupesh Sharma from Pearson's Editorial team. They have been the main motivation behind the whole project. My Assistant Nidhi have been a valuable support. My wife, Anshu Bala and children Jiya, Srijan and Jappan have provided support that has always been instrumental as they made me work harder on the project.

About the Author

KVS Madaan, Author and Director, KVS Madaan Online Classes/KvsMadaan.com has been a Former Associate Director, Arni School of Business Management, Arni University, Himachal Pradesh is a renowned author and academician. He is post graduate in Business Administration from Haryana School of Business, GJUST, Hisar. He has helped thousands of career aspirants realize their goals. He worked at top positions in many Universities and institutions. He has been a keynote speaker at UGC and AICTE sponsored faculty development programmes. He has authored a book for Commerce, NTA UGC NET, Paper 2.

UGC NET Paper 1 January 2026

INSTRUCTIONS

Time Allowed: 1 hour *50 × 2 = 100 Marks*

- This paper consists of Fifty (50) objective type questions of Two (2) marks each.
- All questions are compulsory.
- Each item has four alternative responses marked (a), (b), (c) and (d). You have to darken the circle as indicated below on the correct response against each item.
- Example: ⓐⓑ●ⓓ where (c) is the correct response.
- Your responses to the items are to be indicated in the OMR Sheet given at the end of the book.
- Read instructions provided with each question carefully.
- There are no negative marks for incorrect answers.

Study carefully the table given below and answer the question asked here under.
A college has four programs B.A., B.Sc., B.Com and B.B.A. The results of the mid-semester and end-semester tests are shown in the table given below.

Results	Number of students			
	B.A.	B.Sc.	B.Com.	B.B.A.
Failed in both tests	28	23	17	27
Failed in mid-semester test but passed in end-semester test	14	12	8	13
Passed in mid-semester test but failed in end-semester test	6	17	9	15
Passed in both tests	64	55	46	76

1. If the number of students passing a test be considered a criterion for comparison of difficulty level of two tests, then mid-semester test of which of the following programs was the least difficult?
(a) B.A. (b) B.Sc.
(c) B.Com. (d) B.B.A.

2. Which program has the lowest passing percentage in end-semester test?
(a) B.A. (b) B.Sc.
(c) B.Com. (d) B.B.A.

3. Which program has the highest failure rate in the mid-semester test?
(a) B.A. (b) B.Sc.
(c) B.Com. (d) B.B.A.

4. How many students are there in the four programs?
(a) 420 (b) 430
(c) 320 (d) 330

5. What is the ratio of number of students in B.Sc. program to the number of students in B.Com. program?

(a) 80:107
(b) 107:131
(c) 107:80
(d) 80:131

6. Which of the following represents the ontological orientation of qualitative research strategies?
(a) Deductive
(b) Positivism
(c) Objectivism
(d) Constructionism

7. Which term is NOT related to computer hardware?
(a) Bus
(b) Switch
(c) Windows
(d) Mouse

8. Arrange the following pairs of standard deviation (σ) and total number of samples (n) pertaining to different sampling distributions in the decreasing order of their standard error.
A. $\sigma = 1.6, n = 16$
B. $\sigma = 1.5, n = 25$
C. $\sigma = 0.6, n = 36$
D. $\sigma = 1.4, n = 49$

Choose the correct answer from the options given below:
(a) A, B, C, D
(b) A, B, D, C
(c) D, C, B, A
(d) C, B, D, A

9. Given below are two statements: one is labelled as Assertion (A) and the other is labelled as Reason (R).

Assertion (A): The terms validity and invalidity do not apply to inductive arguments.

Reason (R): In an inductive argument, the conclusion does not have sufficient ground in the premises.

In light of the above statements, choose the most appropriate answer from the options given below:
(a) Both (A) and (R) are correct and (R) is the correct explanation of (A)
(b) Both (A) and (R) are correct but (R) is not the correct explanation of (A)
(c) (A) is correct but (R) is not correct
(d) (A) is not correct but (R) is correct

10. Given below are two statements: one is labelled as Assertion (A) and the other is labelled as Reason (R).

Assertion (A): People, who hold views contrary to those dominant in the media, keep those views to themselves.

Reason (R): Such people fear isolation or separation from those around them.

In light of the above statements, choose the most appropriate answer from the options given below:
(a) Both (A) and (R) are correct and (R) is the correct explanation of (A)
(b) Both (A) and (R) are correct but (R) is not the correct explanation of (A)
(c) (A) is correct but (R) is not correct
(d) (A) is not correct but (R) is correct

11. Arrange the following in the ascending order of adoption in terms of Diffusion of Innovation among the masses:
A. Opinion Followers
B. Opinion Leaders
C. Early Adopters
D. Change Agents
E. Laggards

Choose the correct answer from the options given below:
(a) A, D, C, B, E
(b) D, C, B, A, E
(c) C, D, B, A, E
(d) A, B, C, D, E

12. The theory that argues that media can have a strong influence in deciding the small number of public problems or issues that people will think about at any given point in time, is:
(a) Agenda-Setting Theory
(b) Knowledge-Gap Theory
(c) Limited Effects Theory
(d) Personal Influence Theory

13. Arrange the following in increasing order in terms of their coverage:
A. PAN
B. MAN
C. WAN
D. LAN

Choose the correct answer from the options given below:
(a) D, B, A, C
(b) A, B, D, C
(c) A, D, C, B
(d) B, A, D, C

14. Match List–I with List–II:

List–I (Departments of the Ashram)	List–II (Subjects)
A. Vishnu Sthana	I. Military education
B. Vikas Sthana	II. Astrology
C. Garg Sthana	III. Politics
D. Mahendra Sthana	IV. Travel and transportation

Select the correct answer from the options given below:
(a) A-II, B-IV, C-III, D-I
(b) A-I, B-III, C-II, D-IV
(c) A-III, B-II, C-IV, D-I
(d) A-I, B-II, C-III, D-IV

15. The issue related to 'traditional knowledge societies and their livelihood' is addressed in the National Mission for ________.
(a) Enhanced Energy Efficiency
(b) Sustaining the Himalayan Eco-system
(c) Sustainable Habitat
(d) A Green India

16. Which of the following are not true?
A. In the argument from ignorance fallacy, something is accepted as true because it is not proven false.
B. In Hasty generalization fallacy, a general truth is applied to a particular case ignoring its uniqueness.
C. In Begging the question fallacy, an event is wrongly accepted as the cause of some other event.
D. The fallacy of Amphiboly occurs in arguing from premises whose formulations are ambiguous because of their grammatical construction.

Choose the correct answer from the options given below:
(a) A, B and C only
(b) A, B and D only
(c) B and C only
(d) A and D only

17. Active Audience Theories focus on assessing what ________.
(a) people do with media
(b) media does with people
(c) administration does with media
(d) regulations impact media

18. As per the recommendations of National Education Policy, 2020, all standalone teacher education institutions will be required to convert into multidisciplinary institutions by:
(a) 2025 (b) 2030
(c) 2035 (d) 2040

19. Given below are two statements: one is labelled as Assertion (A) and the other is labelled as Reason (R).
Assertion (A): The projective techniques offer an approach to the measurement of the personality, which is different from the self-descriptive inventories.
Reason (R): Self-descriptive inventories require the subject to describe himself/herself while assessing personality.
In light of the above statements, choose the most appropriate answer from the options given below:
(a) Both (A) and (R) are correct and (R) is the correct explanation of (A)
(b) Both (A) and (R) are correct but (R) is not the correct explanation of (A)
(c) (A) is correct but (R) is not correct
(d) (A) is not correct but (R) is correct

20. Identify the correct mathematical statements:
A. The value of $\frac{1}{4}+\frac{1}{4\times 5}+\frac{1}{4\times 5\times 6}$ is equal to $\frac{37}{120}$.
B. $1+2\div\left\{1+2\div\left(1+\frac{1}{3}\right)\right\}$ is equal to $\frac{4}{5}$.
C. If the average of 6 numbers is 7, the average of 3 numbers of them is 5, then the average of remaining numbers is 9.
D. If 75% of a number is added to 75, then the result is number itself. Then the number is 300.
E. Largest fraction from $\frac{9}{31}, \frac{6}{23}, \frac{3}{17}, \frac{4}{11}$ is $\frac{9}{31}$.
Choose the correct answer from the options given below:
(a) A and B only (b) A, C and D only
(c) C and D only (d) C, E and D only

21. Which of the following explains the fallacy (hetvabha-s.a) of satpratipaks.a correctly?
(a) A fallacy where an inference is contradicted by perception or some other non-inferential pra-ma-n.a.
(b) A fallacy where one inference is contradicted by another inference.
(c) A fallacy that disproves the very proposition which it is meant to prove.
(d) A fallacy of the irregular middle

22. Match List – I with List – II.

List – I (Type of Development)	List – II (Related with)
A. Psycho-sexual Development	I. Identity vs. Role Confusion
B. Psycho-social Development	II. Anal Stage
C. Cognitive Development	III. Hypothetical-deductive reasoning
D. Moral Development	IV. Resolving ethical dilemma

Choose the correct answer from the options given below:

(a) A-II, B-III, C-I, D-IV
(b) A-III, B-I, C-IV, D-II
(c) A-I, B-IV, C-II, D-III
(d) A-II, B-I, C-III, D-IV

23. Identify the advantages of closed ended questions in survey research:

A. It is easy to process answers.
B. Respondents can answer in their own terms.
C. They are easy for the respondents to complete.
D. They allow unusual responses to be derived.

Choose the correct answer from the options given below:

(a) A and B only (b) A and C only
(c) A, B and C only (d) B, C and D only

24. Which of the following are application software?

A. Spreadsheet B. Word Processor
C. Operating system D. Database
E. Compiler

Choose the correct answer from the options given below:

(a) A, C and D only (b) B, C and E only
(c) A, D and E only (d) A, B and D only

25. Measurement validity primarily relates to:

(a) Qualitative research
(b) Quantitative research
(c) Interpretivism
(d) Constructionism

26. Match List – I with List – II.

List – I	List – II
A. Independent variable in true experimental design	I. Outcome variable
B. Dependent variable	II. Control variable
C. Intervening variable	III. Spurious variable
D. Confounding variable	IV. Stands between independent variable and dependent variable

Choose the correct answer from the options given below:

(a) A-IV, B-III, C-II, D-I
(b) A-II, B-I, C-IV, D-III
(c) A-I, B-II, C-III, D-IV
(d) A-II, B-III, C-IV, D-I

27. Match List – I with List – II.

List – I Successive discounts	List – II Equivalent discount
A. 10% and 15%	I. 28%
B. 20% and 30%	II. 32.5%
C. 10% and 20%	III. 23.5%
D. 10% and 25%	IV. 44%

Choose the correct answer from the options given below:

(a) A-I, B-II, C-IV, D-III
(b) A-II, B-III, C-I, D-IV
(c) A-III, B-IV, C-I, D-II
(d) A-IV, B-I, C-II, D-III

28. Given below are two statements: one is labelled as Assertion (A) and the other is labelled as Reason (R).

Assertion (A): National Education Policy, 2020 (NEP-2020) visualized 'Research-Intensive Universities'.

Reason (R): NEP-2020 envisioned university as a place which lays equal emphasis on teaching and research.

In light of the above statements, choose the most appropriate answer from the options given below:

(a) Both (A) and (R) are correct and (R) is the correct explanation of (A)
(b) Both (A) and (R) are correct but (R) is not the correct explanation of (A)
(c) (A) is correct but (R) is not correct
(d) (A) is not correct but (R) is correct

29. Match List – I with List – II.

List – I	List – II
A. Aesthetic/ Artistic	I. Considering communication as logical thinking in relation to dominant ideological forces
B. Symbol–science related (Semiotic approach)	II. Considering communication as the ability to experience reality through authentic dialogue
C. Event–process theory	III. Considering communication as a practical art
D. Critical	IV. Considering communication as the attainment of intersubjective meaning through symbols

Select the correct answer from the options given below:
(a) A-III, B-IV, C-II, D-I
(b) A-II, B-IV, C-III, D-I
(c) A-I, B-IV, C-II, D-III
(d) A-III, B-II, C-IV, D-I

30. Arrange the following greenhouse gases in increasing order of their lifetime in the Earth's atmosphere:
A. SF_6
B. N_2O
C. H_2O vapor
D. CH_4
Choose the correct answer from the options given below:
(a) C, D, B, A
(b) C, D, A, B
(c) A, B, C, D
(d) B, A, D, C

31. Arrange the following fractions in ascending order:
A. $\frac{2}{3}$
B. $\frac{7}{19}$
C. $\frac{9}{11}$
D. $\frac{8}{9}$
E. $\frac{7}{9}$

Choose the correct answer from the options given below:
(a) B, A, E, C, D
(b) B, E, A, D, C
(c) A, B, C, D, E
(d) B, C, A, E, D

32. Complete the following series:
N7V, K9T, H12R, ___?___, B21N
(a) E14R
(b) E13Q
(c) E16P
(d) F16R

33. Match List – I with List – II.

List – I (Types Categorical propositions)	List – II (Explanation)
A. A proposition	I. Distributes both subject and predicate terms
B. E proposition	II. Distributes only predicate term
C. I proposition	III. Distributes only subject term
D. O proposition	IV. Distributes neither subject nor predicate term

Choose the correct answer from the options given below:
(a) A-II, B-I, C-IV, D-III
(b) A-III, B-I, C-IV, D-II
(c) A-I, B-II, C-III, D-IV
(d) A-IV, B-III, C-II, D-I

34. Match List – I with List – II.

List – I	List – II
A. Phishing	I. Act of gaining unauthorized access
B. Hacking	II. Unsolicited email sent over the internet to a recipient on a mailing list
C. Spam	III. Small file or code stored on user's computer
D. Cookies	IV. The creator sends out legitimate-looking emails to target users

Choose the correct answer from the options given below:
(a) A-II, B-III, C-IV, D-I
(b) A-IV, B-I, C-III, D-II
(c) A-IV, B-I, C-II, D-III
(d) A-I, B-IV, C-II, D-III

35. Arrange the following senior functionaries of a central university in the correct hierarchical order:

A. Visitor
B. Dean of the faculty
C. Chancellor
D. Head of Department
E. Vice-Chancellor

Choose the correct answer from the options given below:

(a) A, C, E, D, B
(b) C, A, E, D, B
(c) A, C, E, B, D
(d) B, D, E, C, A

36. Which of the following is an example of biological motive?

(a) Achievement
(b) Hunger
(c) Power
(d) Affiliation

37. The smallest unit of information, a computer can understand and process is known as:

(a) Digit
(b) Byte
(c) Nibble
(d) Bit

38. Journals that prioritize self-interest at the expense of scholarship and are characterized by false or misleading information, deviation from best editorial/publication practices, lack of transparency and/or use of aggressive and indiscriminate solicitation practices, are known as:

(a) Open access journals
(b) Proprietary journals
(c) Professional journals
(d) Predatory journals

39. Arrange the steps of creative thinking process in correct sequence:

A. Preparation
B. Evaluation
C. Illumination
D. Revision
E. Incubation

Choose the correct answer from the options given below:

(a) A, B, C, D, E
(b) E, D, C, B, A
(c) D, C, B, E, A
(d) A, E, C, B, D

40. Match List – I with List – II.

List – I	List – II
A. Primary Air pollutant	I. Peroxyacyl nitrate
B. Secondary Air pollutant	II. Carbon monoxide
C. Ozone depleting substance	III. Aerosols
D. Cloud Condensation Nuclei	IV. Chlorofluorocarbons

Choose the correct answer from the options given below:

(a) A-I, B-II, C-III, D-IV
(b) A-II, B-I, C-IV, D-III
(c) A-I, B-II, C-IV, D-III
(d) A-II, B-I, C-III, D-IV

41. Given below are two statements: one is labelled as Assertion (A) and the other is labelled as Reason (R).

Assertion (A): A windmill will be more effective if it is placed at a higher elevation above the ground than a lower one.

Reason (R): Generally, the wind speed increases with altitude above the Earth's surface.

In light of the above statements, choose the most appropriate answer from the options given below:

(a) Both (A) and (R) are correct and (R) is the correct explanation of (A)
(b) Both (A) and (R) are correct but (R) is not the correct explanation of (A)
(c) (A) is correct but (R) is not correct
(d) (A) is not correct but (R) is correct

42. The oxygen consumed in the oxidation of an organic compound by microorganisms in the aquatic ecosystem is called ___________.

(a) Dissolved oxygen
(b) Chemical oxygen demand
(c) Theoretical oxygen demand
(d) Biochemical oxygen demand

43. Which of the following is/are true?

A. The conversion of an O proposition is valid.
B. The conversion of an A proposition is an A proposition.
C. The conversion of an E proposition is conversion by limitation.
D. The conversion of an I proposition is valid.

Choose the correct answer from the options given below:

(a) A and D only
(b) A and B only
(c) C only
(d) D only

44. Two cyclists cover the same distance at 15 km/hr and 16 km/hr, respectively. If one cyclist takes 16 minutes longer than the other, then the distance travelled by each cyclist is:

(a) 64 km
(b) 16 km
(c) 68 km
(d) 12 km

45. Which among the following is the most liberal Open Education Resource license?
(a) CC-BY (b) CC-BY-SA
(c) CC-BY-ND (d) CC-BY-NC

Read the following passage and answer the questions:

Organized endeavours directed by people responsible for planning, organizing, leading and controlling activities have existed for thousands of years. The Egyptian pyramids and the Great Wall of China, for instance, are tangible evidence that projects of tremendous scope, employing tens of thousands of people, were undertaken well before modern times. The pyramids are a particularly interesting example. The construction of a single pyramid occupied more than 100,000 workers for 20 years. Who told each worker what to do? Who ensured that there would be enough stones at the site to keep workers busy? The answer to such questions is managers. Regardless of what managers were called at the time, someone had to plan what was to be done, organize people and materials to do it, lead and direct the workers, and impose some controls to ensure that everything was done as planned.

Another example of early management can be seen during the 1400s in the city of Venice, Italy, a major economic and trade centre. The Venetians developed an early form of business enterprise and engaged in many activities common to today's organizations. For instance, at the arsenal of Venice, warships were floated along the canals, and at each stop materials and riggings were added to the ship. Doesn't that sound a lot like a car "floating" along an automobile assembly line while components are added to it? In addition to this assembly line, the Venetians also used warehouse and inventory systems to keep track of materials, human resource management systems to manage the labour force, and an accounting system to keep track of revenues and costs.

46. According to the passage, the role of a manager includes all of the following, except:
(a) Stacking stones for the pyramids
(b) Planning what is to be done
(c) Organizing people for the pyramids site
(d) Directing the pyramid work force

47. According to the passage, persons responsible for the control, organization and planning have been directing organized endeavors:
(a) Since 1400's (b) For 100,000 years
(c) For Twenty years (d) For Thousands of years

48. According to the passage, the ancient equivalent of the assembly line was used in:
(a) Egypt (b) China
(c) Venice (d) Giza

49. From the above passage, it is evident that:
(a) Management is a recent development
(b) Management degrees date backs to many years
(c) People with guided organised effort can be seen through ages
(d) Assembly line system was very popular in China, Egypt and Italy.

50. The passage documents that Egyptians involved in the construction of pyramids had:
(a) An inventory system to keep a record of the stones.
(b) A plan for what was to be done.
(c) An accounting system to keep a record of money.
(d) A warehouse system to manage materials.

ANSWER KEY

1. (d)	**2.** (b)	**3.** (a)	**4.** (b)	**5.** (c)	**6.** (d)	**7.** (c)	**8.** (b)	**9.** (a)	**10.** (a)
11. (b)	**12.** (a)	**13.** (c)	**14.** (a)	**15.** (b)	**16.** (c)	**17.** (a)	**18.** (b)	**19.** (a)	**20.** (b)
21. (b)	**22.** (d)	**23.** (b)	**24.** (d)	**25.** (b)	**26.** (b)	**27.** (c)	**28.** (a)	**29.** (a)	**30.** (a)
31. (a)	**32.** (c)	**33.** (b)	**34.** (c)	**35.** (c)	**36.** (b)	**37.** (d)	**38.** (d)	**39.** (d)	**40.** (b)
41. (a)	**42.** (d)	**43.** (d)	**44.** (a)	**45.** (a)	**46.** (a)	**47.** (d)	**48.** (c)	**49.** (c)	**50.** (b)

HINTS AND SOLUTIONS

1. (d)

Mid-semester pass =
(Passed mid-semester but failed end-semester) + (Passed both tests)

- **B.A.:** 6 + 64 = **70**
- **B.Sc.:** 17 + 55 = **72**
- **B.Com.:** 9 + 46 = **55**
- **B.B.A.:** 15 + 76 = **91**

The highest number of students passed the mid-semester test in **B.B.A.**

2. (b)

Total students in each program

Add all four categories for each program:

- B.A.: 28 + 14 + 6 + 64 = 112
- B.Sc.: 23 + 12 + 17 + 55 = 107
- B.Com.: 17 + 8 + 9 + 46 = 80
- B.B.A.: 27 + 13 + 15 + 76 = 131

Passing percentage (End-semester)

B.A.: $\frac{78}{112} \times 100 \approx 69.6\%$

B.Sc.: $\frac{67}{107} \times 100 \approx 62.6\%$

B.Com.: $\frac{54}{80} \times 100 \approx 67.5\%$

B.B.A.: $\frac{89}{131} \times 100 \approx 67.9\%$

3. (a)

Mid-semester failures =

(Failed in both tests) + (Failed in mid-semester but passed end-semester)

Count failures in mid-semester

- B.A.: 28 + 14 = 42
- B.Sc.: 23 + 12 = 35
- B.Com.: 17 + 8 = 25
- B.B.A.: 27 + 13 = 40

Failure percentage (Mid-semester)

B.A.: $\frac{42}{112} \times 100 \approx 37.5\%$

B.Sc.: $\frac{35}{107} \times 100 \approx 32.7\%$

B.Com.: $\frac{25}{80} \times 100 \approx 31.25\%$

B.B.A.: $\frac{40}{131} \times 100 \approx 30.5\%$

4. (b)

Total students in all four programs

= 112 + 107 + 80 + 131 = 430

5. (c)

Total students in each program:

B.Sc. = 23 + 12 + 17 + 55 = 107

B.Com. = 17 + 8 + 9 + 46 = 80

B.Sc. : B.Com.

107 : 80

6. (d)

Constructionism: This is the core orientation. Qualitative research assumes that reality is not a fixed, singular object waiting to be discovered. Instead, it views reality as socially constructed through human experiences, language, and interactions. This means there are multiple realities depending on the individual's perspective, rather than one objective truth.

Why not the following?

(c) Objectivism? Objectivism is the ontological position that social phenomena and their meanings have an existence that is independent of social actors. This is the foundation of Quantitative research, which seeks to measure a single, stable reality.

(b) Positivism? Positivism is an epistemological orientation (how we know what we know), not an ontological one. It relies on observable, measurable facts and is usually associated with objectivism and quantitative methods.

(a) Deductive? Deductive reasoning is a research strategy or style where you start with a theory and test it. Qualitative research typically uses Inductive reasoning, where theories are generated from the data collected.

7. (c)

Bus, Switch, and Mouse are hardware components, whereas Windows is an operating system (software), not hardware.

Hardware Components

Hardware refers to the physical parts of a computer system that you can touch.

(a) **Bus:** A communication system or set of parallel wires that transfers data between components inside a computer, such as between the CPU and memory.

(b) **Switch:** A networking device that connects multiple devices on a computer network and uses packet switching to forward data only to the specific destination device.

(d) **Mouse:** A handheld pointing device that detects two-dimensional motion relative to a surface, allowing users to control a graphical user interface (GUI).

8. (b)

We need to arrange the given pairs (σ, n) in decreasing order of standard error (SE).

Formula:

$$SE = \frac{\sigma}{\sqrt{n}}$$

A. $\sigma = 1.6, n = 16$

$$SE = \frac{1.6}{\sqrt{16}} = \frac{1.6}{4} = 0.40$$

B. $\sigma = 1.5, n = 25$

$$SE = \frac{1.5}{\sqrt{24}} = \frac{1.5}{5} = 0.30$$

C. $\sigma = 0.6, n = 36$

$$SE = \frac{0.6}{\sqrt{36}} = \frac{0.6}{6} = 0.10$$

D. $\sigma = 1.4, n = 49$

$$SE = \frac{1.4}{\sqrt{49}} = \frac{1.4}{7} = 0.20$$

9. (a)

Assertion (A): 'The terms validity and invalidity do not apply to inductive arguments.'

Correct. Validity/invalidity are terms used for deductive arguments only.

- Inductive arguments are judged by strength or weakness, not validity.

Reason (R): 'In an inductive argument, the conclusion does not have sufficient ground in the premises.' Inductive reasoning moves from specific cases to general conclusions, so the premises never guarantee the conclusion — they only provide probable support.

10. (a)

Assertion (A): People, who hold views contrary to those dominant in the media, keep those views to themselves.

Correct. This reflects the Spiral of Silence theory in communication, where individuals suppress minority opinions.

Reason (R): Such people fear isolation or separation from those around them.

Correct. The theory explains that fear of social isolation is the reason people remain silent.

11. (b)

D. Change Agents -Initiators, introduce innovation first.

C. Early Adopters - Quickly embrace new ideas after innovators.

B. Opinion Leaders - Influential people who spread adoption further.

A. Opinion Followers - Adopt later, influenced by leaders.

E. Laggards -Last group, resistant to change.

The Diffusion of innovation Theory

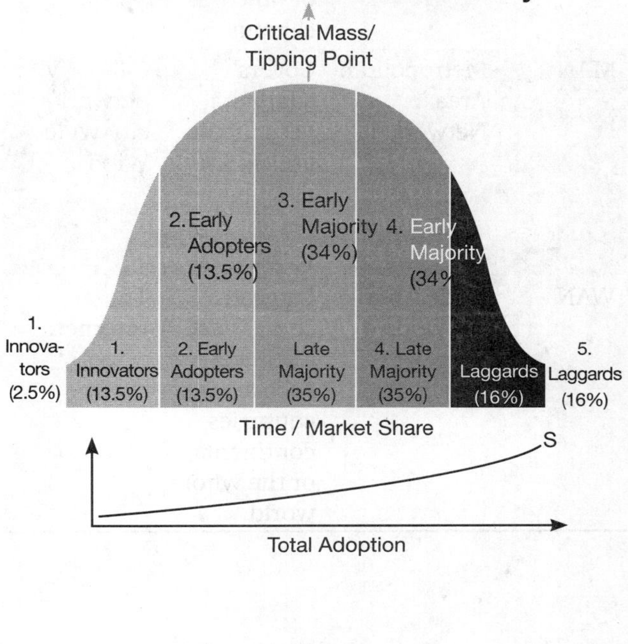

12. (a)

(a) Agenda-Setting Theory → It says media doesn't tell people what to think, but it tells them what to think about. The media highlights certain issues, making them appear more important in public discussion.

(b) Knowledge-Gap Theory → Focuses on differences in knowledge levels between groups.

(c) Limited Effects Theory → Suggests media has minimal influence compared to other factors.

(d) Personal Influence Theory → Emphasizes interpersonal communication, not media agenda.

13. (c)

There is a table summarizing the different types of computer networks based on their scale and coverage:

Network Type	Full Name	Coverage Area	Common Examples
PAN	Personal Area Network	Smallest; covers a few meters around an individual.	Bluetooth, wireless headphones, personal devices.
LAN	Local Area Network	Covers a small local area like a single building, home, or office campus.	Ethernet, Wi-Fi in a school or office.
MAN	Metropolitan Area Network	Covers a larger geographic area, such as an entire city or a large town.	Cable TV network, city-wide Wi-Fi.
WAN	Wide Area Network	Largest; covers vast distances such as countries, continents, or the whole world.	The Internet.

14. (a)

Each Ashram department was linked with a specific subject — Vishnu with astrology, Vivastra with travel, Garuda with politics, and Mahendra with military education.

15. (b)

The issue related to traditional knowledge societies and their livelihood is addressed in the National Mission for a Green India under India's National Action Plan on Climate Change (NAPCC).

16. (c)

(a) Argument from ignorance accepts something as true because it is not proven false.

(b) Hasty generalisation means drawing a general conclusion from too few cases, not applying a general truth to a particular case (that is fallacy of accident).

(c) Begging the question means assuming the conclusion in the premise, not wrongly accepting one event as the cause of another (that is false cause).

(d) Amphiboly arises due to grammatical ambiguity.

17. (a)

Active Audience Theories emphasize that audiences are not passive consumers.They study how people interpret, use, and interact with media content in their daily lives.So the focus is on what people do with media, not what media does to them.

18. (b)

NEP 2020 emphasizes integration of teacher education into multidisciplinary universities.The policy clearly sets the deadline as 2030 for this transition.

19. (a)

Assertion (A): Projective techniques (like Rorschach Inkblot, TAT) rely on indirect responses to ambiguous stimuli, unlike inventories.

Reason (R): Inventories (like MMPI, Big Five questionnaires) depend on self-reporting.

20. (b)

A. $\frac{1}{4}+\frac{1}{4\times5}+\frac{1}{4\times5\times6}=\frac{30+6+1}{120}=\frac{37}{120}$

B. $1+2\div\left\{1+2\div\left(1+\frac{1}{3}\right)\right\}$

$1+\frac{1}{3}=\frac{4}{3}, 2\div\frac{4}{3}=\frac{3}{2}$

$1+\frac{3}{2}=\frac{5}{2}, 2\div\frac{5}{2}=\frac{4}{5}$

$1+\frac{4}{5}=\frac{9}{5}\neq\frac{4}{5}$

C. Average of 6 numbers = 7 → Total = 42
Average of 3 numbers = 5 → Sum = 15
Remaining sum = 27 → Average = 9

D. Let number = x
75% of $x + 75 = x \Rightarrow 0.75x + 75 = x \Rightarrow x=300$

E. Convert the decimals:

$\frac{9}{31}\approx 0.29, \frac{6}{23}\approx 0.26, \frac{3}{17}\approx 0.18, \frac{4}{11}\approx 0.36$

Largest is $\frac{4}{11}$, not $\frac{9}{31}$

21. (b)

Satpratipaks.a (also called prakaran.asama in some texts) is a type of hetva-bha-sa (fallacy of inference) in Nya-ya logic. It occurs when the middle term (hetu) of an inference is counterbalanced or contradicted by another equally strong inference (with a different middle term) that proves the opposite conclusion (i.e., the negation of the original sa-dhya/proposition).

This is exactly 'a fallacy where one inference is contradicted by another inference.'

(a) A fallacy describes ba-dhita (contradicted by perception or other non-inferential prama-n.a).

(c) A fallacy is vague but points toward something like viruddha.

(d) A fallacy refers to savyabhica-ra (irregular/deviating middle).

22. (d)

A. This belongs to Freud's psychosexual theory, where the Anal Stage (approx. age 1–3 years) focuses on toilet training and control/expulsion themes.

B. This is from Erik Erikson's psychosocial theory (8 stages). Identity vs. Role Confusion is the key crisis during adolescence (stage 5), where teens form a stable sense of self.

C. This is a hallmark of Piaget's formal operational stage (from 11–12 years onward), where adolescents develop abstract thinking and can use hypothetical-deductive reasoning to solve problems logically.

D. This refers to Kohlberg's theory of moral development, where people progress through stages by reasoning about and resolving ethical/moral dilemmas (e.g., the famous Heinz dilemma).

23. (b)

C. They are easy for the respondents to complete. Respondents simply select from given options → quick, less effort, higher completion rates, and less respondent burden (widely supported in survey methodology sources like Nielsen Norman Group, SurveyMonkey, Qualtrics).

A. It is easy to process answers. Responses are standardized and quantifiable → easy to code, tabulate, statistically analyze, compare trends, and calculate percentages/metrics (a primary reason closed-ended questions dominate large-scale surveys).

B. Respondents can answer in their own terms. → This is an advantage of open-ended questions (respondents express freely in their own words), not closed-ended (limited to predefined choices).

D. They allow unusual responses to be derived. → Closed-ended questions restrict responses to listed options → they do not easily capture unusual/unexpected or novel responses (that's a strength of open-ended questions, which can reveal unanticipated insights).

24. (d)

A. Spreadsheet - Application software (e.g., MS Excel).

B. Word Processor - Application software (e.g., MS Word).

C. Operating System - System software, not an application.

D. Database - Application software (e.g., Oracle, MySQL front-end tools).

E. Compiler -System software, used to translate code.

25. (b)

Validity in measurement means: does the tool actually measure what it claims to measure?

(a) This concept is central to quantitative research because it relies on standardized instruments, scales, and numerical data.
(b) In qualitative research, the focus is more on credibility, trustworthiness, and interpretation rather than strict measurement validity.
(c,d) Interpretivism and constructionism are philosophical approaches, not directly tied to measurement validity.

26. (b)

A. It is the factor manipulated/controlled by the researcher.
B. It is the result or effect measured in the study.
C. It explains how/why the independent variable affects the dependent variable.
D. It creates false or misleading relationships by interfering with both independent and dependent variables.

27. (c)

To find equivalent discount for successive discounts, use the formula:

$$\text{Equivalent Discount} = x + y - \frac{xy}{100}$$

(where x and y are successive discounts)

A. 10% and 15% → 23.5%

$$10 + 15 - \frac{10 \cdot 15}{100} = 25 - 1.5 = 23.5\%$$

B. 20% and 30% → 44%.

$$20 + 30 - \frac{20 \cdot 30}{100} = 50 - 6 = 44\%$$

C. 10% and 20% → 28%

$$10 + 20 - \frac{10 \cdot 20}{100} = 30 - 2 = 28\%$$

D. 10% and 25% → 32.5%

$$10 + 25 - \frac{10 \cdot 25}{100} = 35 - 2.5 = 32.5\%$$

28. (a)

Assertion (A): NEP-2020 indeed visualized *Research-Intensive Universities* to strengthen India's research ecosystem.
Reason (R): NEP-2020 also emphasized that universities should balance *teaching and research equally.*

29. (a)

A. The aesthetic (artistic) view treats communication as a creative and organized art.
B. Symbol–science (semiotics) studies signs, symbols, and signals used in communication.
C. Event–process theory sees communication as a dynamic process through which reality is experienced.
D. The critical approach focuses on analysis, reflection, and reasoning.

30. (a)

C. H_2O vapour → Very short lifetime (a few days).
D. CH_4 → About 12 years.
B. N_2O → About 120 years.
A. SF_6 → Very long lifetime (~3,200 years).

31. (a)

This way, no decimals are needed

Compare A and B

Cross multiply: $2 \times 19 = 38$, $7 \times 3 = 21$.
$= 38 > 21$
So B < A

Compare A and E

$2 \times 9 = 18$, $7 \times 3 = 21$.
$= 18 < 21 = A < E$

Compare E and C

$7 \times 11 = 77$, $9 \times 9 = 81$
$= 77 < 81$
So E < C

Compare C and D

$9 \times 9 = 81$, $8 \times 11 = 88$.
$= 81 < 88$
$= C < D$.

So Final Order B, A, E, C, D

32. (c)

The first letters follow a pattern of moving backwards by 3 positions in the alphabet:

- $N \xrightarrow{-3} K$
- $K \xrightarrow{-3} H$
- $H \xrightarrow{-3} E$
- $E \xrightarrow{-3} B$ (Matches the last term)

The numbers increase by an increment that grows by 1 each time:

- $7 \xrightarrow{+2} 9$
- $9 \xrightarrow{+3} 12$
- $12 \xrightarrow{+4} 16$
- $16 \xrightarrow{+5} 21$ (Matches the last term)

The last letters follow a pattern of moving backwards by 2 positions in the alphabet:

- $V \xrightarrow{+2} T$
- $T \xrightarrow{+3} R$
- $R \xrightarrow{+4} P$
- $P \xrightarrow{+5} N$ (Matches the last term)

The correct answer is (c) E16P.

33. (b)

A-proposition (Universal Affirmative: 'All S is P'): It makes a claim about every member of the subject class but not every member of the predicate class. Therefore, it distributes only the subject terms.

E-proposition (Universal Negative: 'No S is P'): It states that every member of the subject class is excluded from the entire predicate class. Therefore, it distributes both subject and predicate terms.

I-proposition (Particular Affirmative: 'Some S is P'): It only claims that at least one member of S is also a member of P, making no claim about all members of either class. Therefore, it distributes neither subject nor predicate term.

O-proposition (Particular Negative: 'Some S is not P'): It claims that at least one member of S is excluded from the entire class of P. Therefore, it distributes only the predicate term.

34. (c)

A. **Phishing:** A deceptive technique where attackers send fraudulent emails that mimic trusted sources to steal sensitive information like passwords or credit card details.

B. **Hacking:** The process of identifying and exploiting weaknesses in a computer system or network to gain unauthorized access to data.

C. **Spam:** Irrelevant or unsolicited messages sent in bulk over the internet, typically for advertising or spreading malware.

D. **Cookies:** Data files saved on your device by a web browser that help websites remember your preferences, login status, and browsing activity.

35. (c)

A. Visitor – Highest authority (President of India)

C. Chancellor – Ceremonial head

E. Vice-Chancellor – Chief executive & academic head

B. Dean of the Faculty – Academic head of a faculty (below VC, above HOD in role but placed last as per options)

D. Head of Department – Head of a department

Visitor → Chancellor → Vice-Chancellor → Dean of Faculty → Head of Department

36. (b)

Hunger is a physiological need necessary for life, unlike achievement or power, which are social motives.

37. (d)

(a) Digit → refers to numbers (0–9), not the smallest computer unit.

(b) Byte → equals 8 bits, larger unit.

(c) Nibble → equals 4 bits, also larger.

(d) Bit → stands for *binary digit* (0 or 1). It is the smallest unit of information a computer can process.

38. (d)

(a) Open access journals → Legitimate journals that make content freely available, not necessarily harmful.

(b) Proprietary journals → Owned by organizations/publishers, but not defined by unethical practices.

(c) Professional journals → Scholarly and peer-reviewed, usually reputable.

(d) Predatory journals → Exploit authors, charge fees without proper peer review, use misleading practices, and prioritize profit over scholarship.

39. (d)

A. **Preparation:** The initial stage of gathering information, defining the problem, and conducting research to build a knowledge base.

E. **Incubation:** A passive period where you step away from the problem, allowing the subconscious mind to process information and make hidden connections.

C. **Illumination:** The sudden 'Aha!' moment or 'flash of insight' when a potential solution or new idea unexpectedly enters the conscious mind.

B. Evaluation: The critical phase of analyzing the newly formed idea to determine its validity, usefulness, and feasibility.

D. **Revision:** The final stage of refining, polishing, and making necessary adjustments to the idea based on the results of the evaluation.

40. (b)

A. Primary Air pollutant → Carbon monoxide
Directly emitted into the atmosphere, harmful gases.

B. Secondary Air pollutant → Peroxyacyl nitrate
Formed by chemical reactions in the atmosphere, not emitted directly.

C. Ozone depleting substance → Chlorofluorocarbons
CFCs break down ozone in the stratosphere.

D. Cloud Condensation Nuclei → Aerosols
Tiny particles on which water vapour condenses to form clouds.

41. (a)

Assertion (A): A windmill works better at a higher elevation.

Reason (R): Wind speed generally increases with altitude.

42. (d)

A. **Dissolved oxygen (DO):** Refers to the oxygen present in water, not specifically consumed.

B. **Chemical oxygen demand (COD):** Measures oxygen required to chemically oxidize organic matter, not biological.

C. **Theoretical oxygen demand (ThOD):** Calculated oxygen demand based on stoichiometry, not actual measurement.

D. **Oxygen Consumption:** The oxygen consumed by microorganisms to oxidize organic matter is called Biochemical oxygen demand (BOD).

43. (d)

A. (O proposition): Some S are not P → conversion is not valid.

B. (A proposition): All S are P → converts to I proposition, not A.

C. (E proposition): No S are P → converts to E proposition directly, not by limitation.

D. (I proposition): Some S are P → conversion is valid.

44. (a)

For the two cyclists (15 km/hr and 16 km/hr) where one takes 16 minutes longer.

$$\text{Distance} = \frac{S_1 \times S_2}{S_2 \times S_1} \times \text{Time} - \text{Difference:}$$

$$\text{Distance} = \frac{15 \times 16}{16 - 15} \times \frac{16}{60} = 240 \times \frac{16}{60} = 4 \times 16 = 64\text{km}$$

(OR)

Two cyclists at 15 km/hr and 16 km/hr; one takes 16 minutes (16/60 hours) longer.

- Let the distance be d.
- $\frac{d}{15} - \frac{d}{16} = \frac{16}{60}$
- $\frac{16d - 15d}{240} = \frac{16}{60} \Rightarrow \frac{d}{240} = \frac{16}{60}$
- $d = \frac{16 \times 240}{60} = 16 \times 4 = \mathbf{64km.}$

45. (a)

- CC-BY → Allows anyone to use, share, adapt, and build upon the work, even commercially, as long as attribution is given. This is the most liberal license.
- CC-BY-SA → Requires attribution and sharing under the same license (less flexible).
- CC-BY-ND → No derivatives allowed (restrictive).
- CC-BY-NC → Non-commercial use only (restrictive).

46. (a)

47. (d)

48. (c)

49. (c)

50. (b)

UGC NET Paper 1 June 2025

INSTRUCTIONS

Time Allowed: 1 hour **50 × 2 = 100 Marks**

- This paper consists of Fifty (50) objective type questions of Two (2) marks each.
- All questions are compulsory.
- Each item has four alternative responses marked (a), (b), (c) and (d). You have to darken the circle as indicated below on the correct response against each item.
- Example: ⓐⓑ●ⓓ where (c) is the correct response.
- Your responses to the items are to be indicated in the OMR Sheet given at the end of the book.
- Read instructions provided with each question carefully.
- There are no negative marks for incorrect answers.

The following table shows the number of students (Boys and Girls) and the percentage of girls who passed in a 10+2 examination from six different schools (A-F) in the year 2023 and 2024. Based on the data in the table, answer the questions that follow.

School-wise Details of Students Passing in a 10+2 examination

School	Year			
	2023		2024	
	Number of Passed Students	Percentage of Passed Girls	Number of Passed Students	Percentage of Passed Girls
A	500	46%	550	44%
B	600	42%	640	40%
C	650	56%	560	45%
D	720	60%	800	48%
E	600	54%	840	55%
F	650	50%	750	36%

1. What is the average number of boys who passed in the 10+2 examination in the year 2024 from all the six schools (A-F) together?

(a) 376 (b) 377
(c) 378 (d) 379

2. What is the ratio of the number of boys who passed from School A in 2023 to the number of girls who passed from School E in the year 2023?

(a) 4:3 (b) 5:4
(c) 5:6 (d) 6:7

3. For School F, the number of boys who passed in the year 2024 is approximately ________ % more than that in 2023.
(a) 42.5 (b) 47.7
(c) 52.8 (d) 57.5

4. The average number of girls who passed in the year 2024 from all the six schools is ________ % of the number of students who passed from School A in the year 2023.
(a) 61.1 (b) 62.2
(c) 63.3 (d) 64.4

5. Number of boys who passed in the examination is more than 300 in the year 2023 as well as in 2024 in only ________ schools.
(a) two (b) three
(c) four (d) five

6. The role of a teacher in supporting experiential learning can't be of a/the ________.
(a) Coach (b) Mentor
(c) Tutor (d) Technology

7. Which of the following is not considered as self-generated feedback?
(a) Assurance (b) Previewing
(c) Retracing (d) Observation

8. Arrange the level of Bloom's Taxonomy from lower to higher order in the cognitive domain.
A. Analyzing B. Understanding
C. Applying D. Evaluating
E. Remembering

Choose the correct answer from the options given below:
(a) B, E, C, A, D (b) E, B, C, A, D
(c) E, B, C, D, A (d) E, B, D, A, C

9. What among the following are known as Assessment Instruments?
A. Tests B. Examinations
C. Rubrics D. Worksheets
E. Quizzes

Choose the correct answer from the options given below:
(a) A, B and E Only (b) B, C, D and E Only
(c) D and E Only (d) A, B, D and E Only

10. Match List – I with List – II.

List – I (Principle)	List – II (Implication)
A. Encouraging student's deep approaches to learning objectives	I. Feedback should be embedded within assessment practices.
B. The summative and formative assessments to be learning oriented	II. Task design should be approached from a program-wide perspective.
C. Facilitating dialogic forms of feed back	III. Greater sense of ownership by students
D. Involving some personal student investment	IV. A variety of assessment for student motivation.

Choose the correct answer from the options given below:
(a) A-I, B-II, C-III, D-IV
(b) A-II, B-IV, C-I, D-III
(c) A-IV, B-II, C-III, D-I
(d) A-III, B-I, C-II, D-IV

11. What is not a Research?
(a) Research is a careful and exhaustive investigation of a phenomenon with an objective of advancing knowledge.
(b) It is a systematic and objective attempt to study a problem for the purpose of deriving general principles.
(c) Research is based on common sense knowledge, based on the accumulated experiences and beliefs of the people.
(d) It is a systematic investigation to find solutions to a problem.

12. Scientific Observations are based on ________.
(a) Verifiable evidence or systematic body of proof that can be cited.
(b) Accumulated experiences
(c) Prejudices
(d) Beliefs of the people

13. For different sets of datasets X and Y, correlation coefficient between X and Y, that is R and standard deviation of X and Y, that is, S(X) and S(Y) are given in A-D below. Estimate the covariance between X and Y for each dataset and arrange in ascending order.

A. R = 0.5, S(X) = 8, S(Y) = 10
B. R = 4/7, S(X) = 7, S(Y) = 9
C. R = 0.7, S(X) = 12, S(Y) = 5
D. R = 19/42, S(X) = 14, S(Y) = 6

Choose the correct answer from the options given below:

(a) B, A, D, C (b) C, B, A, D
(c) B, D, A, C (d) A, C, D, B

14. Criteria for Hypotheses construction are

A. It should describe one issue only.
B. It should describe many issues.
C. It should specify variables between which the relationship is to be established.
D. It should be specific and precise.
E. It should be empirically testable, whether it is right or wrong.

Choose the correct answer from the options given below:

(a) B Only (b) A, B and C Only
(c) A, C, D and E Only (d) A, B, C and D Only

15. Match List – I with List – II.

List – I (Concepts)	List – II (Meanings)
A. Theory	I. Generalized representations of a system or an object, that is constructed to some aspects of that system or the system as a whole.
B. Model	II. Research problem is represented by a mathematical model.
C. Survey	III. It is a set of systematically interrelated propositions that explain and predict a phenomenon or a fact.
D. Modeling	IV. It is a data collection technique using a questionnaire.

Choose the correct answer from the options given below:

(a) A-I, B-II, C-III, D-IV
(b) A-IV, B-III, C-II, D-I
(c) A-II, B-III, C-IV, D-I
(d) A-III, B-I, C-IV, D-II

16. When a person is talking to himself/herself or contemplating or dreaming while in sleep, then this type of communication is known as

(a) Inter-personal (b) Intra-personal
(c) Inter-cultural (d) Inter-national

17. If the sender has not formulated the idea, thought or message in proper manner, it can result into a barrier in communication. The barrier occurs at what level?

(a) Transmission stage
(b) At the end of the decoder
(c) At the level of the encoder
(d) Technical stage

18. As of February 28, 2025, write the highest grossing Indian films starting from highest grossing to the lowest grossing.

A. Bahubali-2 B. RRR
C. Pushpa-2 D. KGF- Chapter 2
E. Dangal

Choose the correct answer from the options given below:

(a) E, A, C, B, D (b) A, B, C, D, E
(c) B, A, D, E, C (d) D, B, C, A, E

19. What among the following are some media organizations?

A. Registrar of Newspaper for India (RNI)
B. National Institute of Fashion Technology (NIFT)
C. The Press Council of India (PCI)
D. Audit Bureau of Circulation Ltd (ABC)
E. University School of Mass Communication (USMC)

Choose the correct answer from the options given below:

(a) B and E Only (b) A and B Only
(c) A, C and D Only (d) A, B and C Only

20. Match List – I with List – II.

List – I (Films)	List – II (Year of release)
A. Mugle Azam	I. 1975
B. Sholay	II. 1973
C. Bobby	III. 1989
D. Maine Pyar Kiya	IV. 1960

Choose the correct answer from the options given below:
(a) A-I, B-II, C-III, D-IV
(b) A-IV, B-I, C-II, D-III
(c) A-IV, B-III, C-II, D-I
(d) A-III, B-II, C-IV, D-I

21. Find the wrong term in the series given below: 3, 12, 36, 144, 432, 1738, 5184
(a) 12 (b) 432
(c) 1738 (d) 5184

22. In a certain code language 'GERMANY' is coded as 9, 7, 20, 15, 3, 16, 27. How 'FRANCE' will be coded in this language?
(a) 7, 19, 2, 15, 4, 6 (b) 8, 20, 30, 16, 5, 7
(c) 8, 20, 3, 16, 5, 7 (d) 6, 18, 1, 14, 3, 5

23. The interest earned on ₹ 8000 when invested in some scheme for 2 years at 7% simple interest, per annum is half of the interest earned on another amount P invested for five years in the same scheme at the same rate of interest. Find the value of P.
(a) ₹ 6200 (b) ₹ 6000
(c) ₹6400 (d) ₹ 5000

24. Which of the following statement(s) is/are true?
A. Speed of x m/sec is equal to $x\frac{5}{18}$ km/hr.
B. If a train runs at $\frac{5}{6}$ of its usual speed, it gets late by 10 minutes. The usual time of the train to cover the journey is 40 minutes.
C. A car moves at the speed of 80 Km/hr. The speed of the car in meters per second is $22\frac{2}{9}$.
D. A person crosses a 600 m long street in 5 minutes. The speed of the person in Km per hour is 7.2.

Choose the correct answer from the options given below:
(a) A, B and C Only (b) A and B Only
(c) B, C and D Only (d) C and D Only

25. A person takes a loan of ₹ 5000 at 5% simple interest. He returns ₹3000 at the end of one year.

How much he would have to pay, in order to clear his dues, at the end of 2 years?
(a) ₹ 2450 (b) ₹2500
(c) ₹2350 (d) ₹ 2400

26. Which fallacy is committed in the following statement— I can expect that you would not find any moral issue in making abortion illegal, since your ability to feel sympathy for the rights of women in general is very limited?
(a) Begging the question
(b) Ad Hominem
(c) Hasty generalization
(d) Slippery slope

27. Which of the following statements are logically equivalent?
A. No soaps are writing-tools.
B. All soaps are non-writing-tools.
C. No non-writing-tools are soaps.
D. No writing-tools are soaps.

Choose the correct answer from the options given below:
(a) A and D Only (b) A, B and D Only
(c) B and C Only (d) A and C Only

28. Which of the following propositions are so related that they cannot both be false, though they can both be true?
A. Some poems are artworks.
B. All poems are artworks.
C. Some poems are not artworks.
D. Some artworks are poems.

Choose the correct answer from the options given below:
(a) A and D Only (b) A and C Only
(c) B and C Only (d) A and B Only

29. Arrange the following terms in order of increasing denotation.
A. Chess
B. Board games
C. Sports
D. Indoor games
Choose the correct answer from the options given below:
(a) A, B, C, D (b) C, D, A, B
(c) C, D, B, A (d) A, B, D, C

30. 'The world is an effect and hence it must have an efficient and intelligent cause. That efficient and

intelligent cause is God.' Which means of knowledge is used in this argument as per classical Indian School of Logic (Nya-ya)?
(a) Perception (b) Inference
(c) Analogy (d) Verbal authority

31. In ________, each communicating device is connected with every other device in the computer network.
(a) Star topology (b) Mesh topology
(c) Bus topology (d) Ring topology

32. Which of the following is not a web browser?
(a) Opera (b) Safari
(c) Firefox (d) Google

33. Identify the sequence of appropriate words A-D that correctly fills the blanks in the following paragraph:
Radio ________ Identification Systems use radio waves to read and capture information stored on a tag, which can be read from several metres away. The ________ is made up of a(n) ________ to store and process data, and a(n) ________ to receive and transmit data.
A. tag B. frequency
C. antenna D. microchip
Choose the correct answer from the options given below:
(a) B. D. A. C (b) C, A, D, B
(c) B, A, D, C (d) A, C, B, D

34. Which of following statements are correct?
A. Worm can be hardware and software.
B. Cookies are used to store browsing information.
C. Sandbox detection is malware identification method.
D. HTTP has better security than HTTPS.
E. Trojan is an antivirus.
Choose the correct answer from the options given below:
(a) A, B and C Only (b) C and E Only
(c) B and C Only (d) B and D Only

35. Match List – I with List – II.

List – I (Recognition System)	List – II (Application)
A. MICR	I. Reading the car number plates
B. OCR	II. Capturing product information so that it. can be added to the customer's purchase total
C. OMR	III. Reading the numbers found on a bank cheque
D. Barcode Reader	IV. Reading marks written using pencil or pen on a specially printed paper.

Choose the correct answer from the options given below:
(a) A-IV, B-I, C-III, D-II
(b) A-II, B-I, C-IV, D-III
(c) A-III, B-IV, C-I, D-II
(d) A-III, B-I, C-IV, D-II

36. What is the correct sequence, from initial to final, of blue baby disease, methemoglobinemia, in human infants?
A. Conversion of nitrate ions to nitrite ions by microorganisms in human body
B. Oxidation of ions from Fe(II) to Fe(III) in hemoglobin by nitrite ions
C. Consumption of nitrate polluted water
D. Forming of abnormal hemoglobin called methemoglobin
Choose the correct answer from the options given below:
(a) C, B, A, D (b) C, A, B, D
(c) A, D, B, C (d) A. C. B. D

37. Electrostatic Precipitator is used in Thermal Power Plants to remove which of the following air pollutants?
(a) Polycycli Aromatic Hydrocarbons
(b) Gaseous Pollutants
(c) Fly ash
(d) Volatile Organic Compounds

38. Match List – I with List – II.

List – I (Types of water pollutant)	List – II (Example)
A. Disease Causing Agent	I. Fine particles of clay

B.	Oxygen Consuming Waste	II.	Coliform Bacteria
C.	Plant Nutrient	III.	Animals and Plants in aquatic habitat
D.	Suspended Solids	IV.	Phosphorous

Choose the correct answer from the options given below:

(a) A-II, B-III, C-I, D-IV
(b) A-II, B-III, C-IV, D-I
(c) A-I, B-II, C-III, D-IV
(d) A-I, B-II, C-IV, D-III

39. Match List – I with List – II.

List – I (Waste water treatment process)	List – II (Explanation)
A. Ozonation	I. Removal of excess ion and manganese
B. Aeration	II. Removal of large solids
C. Flocullation	III. Disinfection
D. Screening	IV. Very small particles are clustered together

Choose the correct answer from the options given below:

(a) A-II, B-III, C-I, D-IV
(b) A-II, B-III, C-IV, D-I
(c) A-I, B-II, C-III, D-IV
(d) A-I, B-II, C-IV, D-III

40. What is the correct increasing order of U-235 (fissile uranium) ratio in following?

A. Natural Uranium
B. Uranium Ore
C. Weapon grade uranium
D. Reactor grade uranium

Choose the correct answer from the options given below:

(a) B, A, C, D (b) B, A, D, C
(c) D, C, A, B (d) D, C, B, A

41. Which of the following are four guiding principles in the development of higher education in India?

(a) Access, Authority, Equity, Equality
(b) Accountability, Based on freedom, Access, Free
(c) Access, Equity, Accountability, Equality
(d) Assessment, Equality, Affordability, Research Oriented

42. The full form of AICTE is ________

(a) Academic Institutions Council of Teacher Education
(b) All India Council for Technical Education
(c) All India Constitution for Teacher Education
(d) All India Institute for Teacher Education

43. Arrange the following components in the context of 'Effective Learning Environment'.

A. Continuous Formative Assessment
B. Adequate Students Support
C. Appropriate Curriculum
D. Engaging Pedagogy
E. Providing suitable resources and infrastructure

Choose the correct answer from the options given below:

(a) E, B, A, C, D (b) B, A, C, D, E
(c) C, D, A, B. E (d) A, B, C, D, E

44. In the Buddha Period, which educational centres were established along with monasteries?

A. Ballabhi
B. Baba Mastnath University
C. Nalanda
D. Vikramshila
E. Taxila

Choose the correct answer from the options given below:

(a) B, C and E Only (b) A, B, C and D Only
(c) A, C, D and E Only (d) B, D and E Only

45. List – I with List – II.

List – I (Author)	List – II (Area)
A. Sankara	I. Vedanta Sutras
B. Ramanuja	II. Algebra and Astronomy
C. Vidyapati	III. Dialect of Behar
D. Bhaskara	IV. Vedanta Sutras and the Bhagavatgita

Choose the correct answer from the options given below:

(a) A-I, B-II, C-III, D-IV
(b) A-IV, B-I, C-III, D-II
(c) A-IV, B-III, C-II, D-I
(d) A-I, B-III, C-IV, D-II

Read the following passage carefully and answer the questions:

The capitalist system of society does not foster healthy relations among human beings. A few people own all the means of production and others-though nominally few have to sell their labour under conditions imposed upon them. The emphasis of capitalism being on the supreme importance of material wealth the intensity of its appeal is to the acquisitive intensity. It promotes worship of economic power with little regard to the means employed for its acquisition and the end that it serves. By its exploitation of human beings to the limits of endurance its concentration is on the largest profit rather than maximum production.

Thus the division of human family is done on the basis of economic circumstances. All this is injurious to division of human dignity. And when the harrowed poor turn to the founders of religion for succour, they rather offer a subtle defence of the established order. They promise future happiness for their present suffering and conjure up visions of paradise to redress the balance to soothe the suffering and the revolt of the tortured men. The system imposes injustice, the religion justifies it.

46. After going through the passage, it can be inferred that the capitalist system is

(a) Ambitious
(b) Biased
(c) Humane
(d) Realistic

47. The maximum control over the means of production is under

(a) All the stake holders
(b) Proletarial class
(c) Owners of the system
(d) Working class

48. In a capitalist system,

(a) the ends justify the means
(b) the means justify the ends
(c) the means leading to exploitation are strictly prohibited
(d) the religion decides the issue related to the means

49. Capitalism is detrimental to equality as it divides the society into the groups, namely,

(a) Working and non-working
(b) Buyers and Sellers
(c) Exploiters and Exploited
(d) Religious and Atheist

50. The capitalist system focuses on

(a) Maximum production
(b) Unusual benefits
(c) Investment on human resources
(d) Reduction of expenditure

ANSWER KEY

1. (d)	**2.** (c)	**3.** (b)	**4.** (b)	**5.** (a)	**6.** (d)	**7.** (a)	**8.** (b)	**9.** (a)	**10.** (b)
11. (c)	**12.** (a)	**13.** (c)	**14.** (c)	**15.** (d)	**16.** (b)	**17.** (c)	**18.** (a)	**19.** (c)	**20.** (b)
21. (c)	**22.** (c)	**23.** (c)	**24.** (d)	**25.** (c)	**26.** (b)	**27.** (b)	**28.** (b)	**29.** (d)	**30.** (b)
31. (b)	**32.** (d)	**33.** (c)	**34.** (c)	**35.** (d)	**36.** (b)	**37.** (c)	**38.** (b)	**39.** (a)	**40.** (b)
41. (c)	**42.** (b)	**43.** (c)	**44.** (c)	**45.** (b)	**46.** (b)	**47.** (c)	**48.** (a)	**49.** (c)	**50.** (b)

HINTS AND SOLUTIONS

1. (d)

In 2024, first find the number of boys in each school.

Formula:

Boys = Total Passed − Girls

School	Total (2024)	% Girls	Girls	Boys
A	550	44%	242	308
B	640	40%	256	384
C	560	45%	252	308
D	800	48%	384	416
E	840	55%	462	378
F	750	36%	270	480

Total boys = 308 + 384 + 308 + 416 + 378 + 480 = 2274

Average boys = 2274 ÷ 6 = 379

2. (c)

School A (2023): Boys

- Total students = 500
- Girls = 46% of 500 = 230
- Boys = 500 − 230 = 270

School E (2023): Girls

- Total students = 600
- Girls = 54% of 600 = 324

Required Ratio

Boys (A): Girls (E)

= 270 : 324

= 5 : 6

3. (b)

School F (2023):

- Total students = 650
- Girls = 50% of 650 = 325
- Boys (2023) = 650 − 325 = 325

School F (2024):

- Total students = 750
- Girls = 36% of 750 = 270
- Boys (2024) = 750 − 270 = 480

Percentage Increase in Boys

Increase = 480 − 325 = 155

Percentage increase = 155/325 × 100 = 47.7%

4. (b)

Step 1: Girls passed in 2024 (each school)

School	Total (2024)	% Girls	Girls
A	550	44%	242
B	640	40%	256
C	560	45%	252
D	800	48%	384
E	840	55%	462
F	750	36%	270

Total girls (2024)

= 242 + 256 + 252 + 384 + 462 + 270 = 1866

Step 2: Average number of girls (2024)

Average = 1866 ÷ 6 = 311

Step 3: Find the percentage of School A (2023 total = 500).

$$\frac{311}{500} \times 100 = 62.2\%$$

5. (a)

First, find the number of boys in both years.

Boys Passed in 2023

School	Total	% Girls	Boys
A	500	46%	270
B	600	42%	348
C	650	56%	286
D	720	60%	288
E	600	54%	276
F	650	50%	325

Boys Passed in 2024

School	Boys
A	308
B	384
C	308
D	416
E	378
F	480

Schools with boys > 300 in both 2023 and 2024

- School B
- School F

Total = 2 schools

6. **(d)**

In experiential learning, the teacher acts as a human facilitator.

- **Coach** – guides practice and reflection
- **Mentor** – supports growth and learning
- **Tutor** – helps with understanding
- **Technology** – is a tool, not a teacher's role

Therefore, the teacher's role cannot be of technology.

7. **(a)**

Assurance – self-confidence or self-check

Previewing – mentally checking future performance

Retracing – recalling and reviewing one's actions

Observation – feedback gained by watching others or external events

Observation is not self-generated feedback.

8. **(b)**

In Bloom's Taxonomy (Cognitive Domain), learning moves from simple to complex.
Correct order (Lower → Higher):

1. **Remembering (E) –** recalling facts
2. **Understanding (B) –** explaining ideas
3. **Applying (C) –** using knowledge
4. **Analyzing (A) –** breaking into parts
5. **Evaluating (D) –** judging and critiquing

9. **(a)**

A. **Tests** → Standard assessment instruments used to measure learning outcomes.

B. **Examinations (B)** → Formal, structured assessments to evaluate student knowledge and skills.

E. **Quizzes (E)** → Short, focused assessments to check understanding quickly.

C. **Rubrics (C)** → These are assessment tools or guidelines, not instruments themselves.

D. **Worksheets (D)** → Primarily learning/practice materials, not formal assessment instruments.

10. **(b)**

A. Deep learning requires well-structured tasks across the entire program, not just isolated activities.

B. Learning-oriented assessments use diverse methods to engage and motivate students.

C. Dialogic feedback means ongoing, interactive feedback integrated into assessment processes.

D. When students invest personally, they develop ownership and responsibility for their learning.

11. **(c)**

Research is not based merely on common sense, accumulated experiences, or beliefs. Instead, research relies on systematic inquiry, evidence, and rigorous methodology to test hypotheses and build reliable knowledge, moving beyond informal or anecdotal understanding.

12. **(a)**

Verifiable evidence refers to data or proof that can be systematically observed, tested, and confirmed by others, forming a foundational pillar of the scientific method.
In contrast, accumulated experiences, prejudices, and personal beliefs are subjective in nature and cannot be reliably tested or replicated; therefore, they do not qualify as bases for scientific observation.

13. **(c)**

Covariance is calculated using the formula:

$\text{Cov}(X,Y) = R \times S(X) \times S(Y)$

Computing for each dataset:

A: $0.5 \times 8 \times 10 = 40$

B: $\frac{4}{7} \times 7 \times 9 = 36$

C: $0.7 \times 12 \times 5 = 42$

D: $\frac{19}{42} \times 14 \times 6 = 38$

Arranging these in ascending order: 36 (B), 38(D), 40 (A), 42 (C).

14. **(c)**
A: A hypothesis should focus on one issue to maintain clarity and testability.
C: It must specify the variables involved to clearly define the relationship being examined.
D: It should be specific and precise to allow accurate testing.
E: It must be empirically testable, enabling verification or falsification through evidence.

15. **(d)**

Theory (A): As a theory consists of systematically interrelated propositions that explain and predict phenomena.
Model (B): Since a model is a generalized representation of a system or object, focusing on certain aspects.
Survey (C): As a survey is a data collection method using questionnaires.
Modelling (D): Modelling involves representing a research problem with a mathematical model.

16. **(b)**

Interpersonal communication refers to communication that occurs within an individual, such as self-talk, contemplation, internal reflection, or dreaming.

The other options refer to different forms of communication:
Interpersonal involves communication between two or more people.
Intercultural refers to communication between individuals from different cultural backgrounds.
International pertains to communication across nations.

17. **(c)**

If the sender fails to formulate the idea properly, the problem originates at the encoder's level, even before the message is sent. This constitutes an encoding barrier, as the message is not clearly or effectively constructed for the receiver.

18. **(a)**

Based on available data and typical rankings as of early 2025, the highest-grossing Indian film worldwide is **Dangal**, followed by **Baahubali 2, Pushpa 2, RRR, and KGF: Chapter 2.**

19. **(c)**

Media organizations are typically involved in the regulation, oversight, or operational aspects of media and journalism.

A. **Registrar of Newspapers for India (RNI) –** Government body responsible for registering newspapers and monitoring their circulation.
C. **Press Council of India (PCI) –** Statutory body that regulates the conduct of the print media and upholds journalistic ethics.
D. **Audit Bureau of Circulation Ltd (ABC) –** Organization that audits and verifies the circulation data of newspapers and magazines, serving the media and advertising industries.

B (NIFT) is a fashion institute, and **E (USMC)** is an academic department for mass communication studies, neither of which functions as a media organization in the regulatory or industry-auditing sense.

20. **(b)**

Mughal-e-Azam (A) was released in **1960.**

Sholay (B) was released in **1975.**

Bobby (C) was released in **1973.**

Maine Pyar Kiya (D) was released in **1989.**

21. **(c)**

The pattern in the series is alternating multiplication by 4 and 3:
$3 \times 4 = 12$
$12 \times 3 = 36$
$36 \times 4 = 144$
$144 \times 3 = 432$
$432 \times 4 = 1728$ (but 1738 is given)
$1728 \times 3 = 5184$
Thus, **1738** is the wrong term (should be 1728).

22. **(c)**

The code is generated by taking each letter's alphabetical position and adding 2.

- G (7) $\rightarrow 7 + 2 = 9$
- E (5) $\rightarrow 5 + 2 = 7$
- R (18) $\rightarrow 18 + 2 = 20$
- M (13) $\rightarrow 13 + 2 = 15$

- A (1) → 1 + 2 = 3
- N (14) → 14 + 2 = 16
- Y (25) → 25 + 2 = 27

Applying the same to FRANCE:
F (6) → 6 + 2 = 8
R (18) → 18 + 2 = 20
A (1) → 1 + 2 = 3
N (14) → 14 + 2 = 16
C (3) → 3 + 2 = 5
E (5) → 5 + 2 = 7

23. (c)

Calculate interest on 8000:

$$SI = \frac{P \times R \times T}{100} = \frac{8000 \times 7 \times 2}{100} = \frac{112000}{100}$$

$= ₹1120$

Relate the interests:
Given that this interest is half of the interest earned on amount P:

$$1120 = \frac{1}{2} \times SI_2 \Rightarrow SI_2 = 2 \times 1120 = ₹2240$$

Set up equation for P:
For P invested at 7% for 5 years:

$$SI = \frac{P \times 7 \times 5}{100} = \frac{35\ P}{100}$$

$$\frac{35\ P}{100} = 2240 \Rightarrow 35\ P = 224000 \Rightarrow P = \frac{224000}{35}$$
$= 6400$

24. (d)

A. $1\ m/sec = \frac{18}{5}\ km/hr$, not $\frac{5}{18}$.

So, $x\ m/sec = x \times \frac{18}{5}\ km/hr$.

B. If speed becomes $\frac{3}{6}$ time becomes $\frac{6}{5}$.

Delay $= \frac{1}{5}$ of usual time = 10 minutes

Usual time = 50 minutes, **not 40 minutes.**

C. $80km/hr = 80 \times \frac{5}{18} = \frac{200}{9} = 22\frac{2}{9}\ m/sec$

D. 600 m in 5 minutes

$= 600$ m in $\frac{1}{12}$ hour

Speed = 600 × 12 = 7200 m/hr = 7.2 km/hr

25. (c)

Interest for 1st year = 5% of 5000 as per $\frac{PRT}{100} = 250$

He pays 3000 at the end of 1 year.

MCQ is based on Simple interest ('no interest on interest' and total time is 2 years), remaining balance = 5000 − 3000 = 2000

Interest for the 2nd year = 5% of 2000 = 100

Total interest = 250 + 100 = 350

Total amount to be paid at the end of 2 years = 2000 + 350 = 2350

26. (b)

This statement commits the **Ad hominem fallacy** because it attacks the person's character (their 'ability to feel sympathy') rather than addressing the merits of the argument about making abortion illegal.

- Begging the question would involve assuming the truth of the conclusion without evidence.
- Hasty generalization would involve making a broad claim from limited examples.
- Slippery slope would involve arguing that one step will lead to an extreme chain of events.

Here, the speaker dismisses the other's view by criticizing their personal trait, which is irrelevant to the logical discussion of the issue.

27. (b)

Statement A: 'No soaps are writing tools.' → This means soaps and writing tools are completely separate sets.
Statement D: 'No writing tools are soaps.' → This is just the same idea expressed in reverse order. So, A and D are equivalent.
Statement B: 'All soaps are non-writing tools.' → Saying 'No soaps are writing tools' is the same as saying 'Every soap belongs to the category of non-writing tools.' So, **A and B are equivalent**.

Statement C: 'No non-writing tools are soaps.' → This is different. It wrongly suggests that soaps don't belong to non-writing tools, which contradicts B.

28. (b)

Proposition A: 'Some poems are artworks' (I-type, particular affirmative).

Proposition C: 'Some poems are not artworks' (O-type, particular negative).

In traditional categorical logic (assuming the subject 'poems' is not empty), A and C are **subcontraries.** This means:

They **cannot both be false:** If A is false, then no poems are artworks, which implies all poems are not artworks, making C true. Similarly, if C is false, then all poems are artworks, implying at least one poem is an artwork (since poems exist), making A true.

They **can both be true:** This occurs when some poems are artworks and some poems are not artworks.

29. (d)

A. **Chess** → Very specific game.
B. **Board games** → Broader category that includes chess and other similar games.
C. **Sports** → The broadest category, covering both indoor and outdoor games.
D. **Indoor games** → Wider category that includes board games, card games, etc.

30. (b)

This reasoning moves from **effect (world)** to **cause (God).**

Such cause-and-effect reasoning is a classic example of **Anumāna (Inference).**

It is not **Perception** (direct sensory knowledge), not **Analogy** (comparison), and not **Verbal authority** (scriptural testimony).

Therefore, the means of knowledge used here is **Inference.**

31. (b)

Star topology → Each device connects to a central hub, not to every other device.

Bus topology → All devices share a single communication line (bus).

Ring topology → Devices are connected in a circular manner, each to two neighbours.

Mesh topology → Every device is directly connected to every other device in the network. This ensures maximum redundancy and reliability.

32. (d)

Opera → A recognized web browser.

Safari → Apple's web browser.

Firefox → Mozilla's web browser.

Google → A search engine company, not a browser itself (though it develops Chrome, which is a browser).

33. (c)

A. **tag:** A device that stores data and communicates via radio waves.
B. **frequency:** The radio wave band used for RFID communication.
C. **antenna:** Transmits and receives signals between tag and reader.
D. **microchip:** The silicon chip inside a tag that holds data.

34. (c)

A. Worms are a type of malware that are software-based; they are not typically categorized as hardware.
B. Cookies are indeed used to store browsing information such as session data and preferences.
C. Sandbox detection is a method used to analyze and identify malware by running it in an isolated environment.
D. HTTPS provides encryption and is more secure than HTTP.
E. A Trojan is a type of malicious software, not an antivirus program.

35. (d)

A. **MICR** → Magnetic Ink Character Recognition is used by banks to read cheque numbers.
B. **OCR** → Optical Character Recognition is used to convert printed/handwritten text into machine-readable form, such as recognizing license plates.
C. **OMR** → Optical Mark Recognition is used in exams/surveys to read shaded bubbles or marks.

D. **Barcode Reader** → Barcode readers scan product codes at checkout counters.

36. (b)

Let's arrange the sequence step by step for blue baby disease **(methemoglobinemia)**:

A. **Conversion of nitrate ions to nitrite ions by microorganisms in the human body** → In the gut, bacteria reduce nitrates to nitrites.

B. **Oxidation of ions from Fe(II) to Fe(III) in haemoglobin by nitrite ions** → Nitrites oxidize haemoglobin's iron, impairing oxygen transport.

C. **Consumption of nitrate-polluted water** → Infants ingest water contaminated with nitrates.

D. **Forming of abnormal haemoglobin called methemoglobin** → This abnormal haemoglobin cannot carry oxygen efficiently, leading to cyanosis ('blue baby').

37. **(c)**

Electrostatic Precipitator (ESP) is a device used in thermal power plants to control air pollution.

It works by charging particles (like ash) with electricity and then collecting them on oppositely charged plates.

Fly ash is the fine particulate matter produced when coal is burned in power plants.

ESPs are specifically designed to remove fly ash from flue gases before they are released into the atmosphere.

Polycyclic Aromatic Hydrocarbons (PAHs) → Organic pollutants, not removed by ESP.

Gaseous pollutants → ESP is ineffective; scrubbers or catalytic converters are used instead.

Volatile Organic Compounds (VOCs) → Also gaseous, not removed by ESP.

38. **(b)**

A. Coliform bacteria are indicators of pathogenic microorganisms that cause waterborne diseases.

B. Organic matter from dead plants and animals consumes dissolved oxygen during decomposition.

C. Phosphorous is a key nutrient that promotes excessive algal growth (eutrophication).

D. Clay and silt remain suspended in water, reducing clarity and affecting aquatic life.

39. **(a)**

A. Ozone is a powerful oxidizing agent used to kill bacteria and viruses in water.

B. Aeration oxidizes dissolved iron and manganese, making them easier to remove.

C. Chemicals are added to form flocs, which bind fine particles into larger aggregates.

D. Screens physically block and remove large debris like sticks, plastics, and rags.

40. **(b)**

B. **Uranium Ore** → Contains the least concentration of U-235 (mostly U-238, only trace amounts of U-235).

A. **Natural Uranium** → About 0.7% U 235.

D. **Reactor grade uranium** → Enriched to around 3–5% U-235 for use in nuclear reactors.

C. **Weapon grade uranium** → Highly enriched, typically >90% U-235.

41. **(c)**

Access → Ensuring opportunities for all sections of society to enter higher education.

Equity → Promoting fairness and inclusion, reducing disparities among different groups.

Accountability → Institutions must be responsible for quality, transparency, and outcomes.

Equality → Providing equal opportunities regardless of socio-economic background, gender, or region.

42. **(b)**

AICTE is the statutory body responsible for planning, formulation, and maintenance of norms and standards in technical education in India. The other options do not represent the correct expansion.

43. **(c)**

C. **Appropriate Curriculum** → Learning begins with a well-structured curriculum that defines what is to be taught.

D. **Engaging Pedagogy** → The curriculum must be delivered through effective and engaging teaching methods.

A. **Continuous Formative Assessment** → Regular assessment ensures learning progress and identifies gaps.

B. **Adequate Student Support** → Learners need guidance, mentoring, and emotional/academic support to succeed.

E. **Providing suitable resources and infrastructure** → Finally, proper facilities and resources sustain the learning environment.

44. (c)

Ballabhi (A) (also known as Vallabhi) was an important centre of Buddhist learning.

Nalanda (C) was a renowned Buddhist monastic university.

Vikramshila (D) was another major Buddhist monastic university.

Taxila (E) was an ancient centre of learning that existed during the Buddha's time and was associated with Buddhist studies.

45. (b)

A. Adi Shankara wrote commentaries on the Vedanta Sutras and the Bhagavad Gita, establishing Advaita Vedanta.

B. Ramanuja is known for his commentary on the Vedanta Sutras, promoting Vishishtadvaita philosophy.

C. Vidyapati was a poet who wrote in Maithili, a dialect of Bihar.

D. Bhaskara (Bhaskaracharya) made significant contributions to mathematics and astronomy, especially algebra.

46. (b)

47. (c)

The owners of the system dominate decision-making, profit distribution, and production processes.

48. (a)

49. (c)

The passage describes capitalism as creating a division based on economic power, where a few owners exploit the labour of others. This aligns with the division between exploiters and the exploited.

50. (b)

UGC NET Paper 1 January 2025

INSTRUCTIONS

Time Allowed: 1 hour — *50 × 2 = 100 Marks*

- This paper consists of Fifty (50) objective type questions of Two (2) marks each.
- All questions are compulsory.
- Each item has four alternative responses marked (a), (b), (c) and (d). You have to darken the circle as indicated below on the correct response against each item.
- Example: ⓐⓑ●ⓓ where (c) is the correct response.
- Your responses to the items are to be indicated in the OMR Sheet given at the end of the book.
- Read instructions provided with each question carefully.
- There are no negative marks for incorrect answers.

Read the passage carefully. The questions 1 to 5 are based on this paragraph.

The following table shows the percent (%) profit earned by two companies A and B over the six years from 2018 to 2023. Based on the data in the table, answer the questions that follow:

Year-wise Profit Details of Two Companies		
Year	Percent (%) Profit Earned by Company	
	A	B
2018	40%	25%
2019	25%	30%
2020	30%	50%
2021	60%	45%
2022	45%	30%
2023	50%	40%

Note: $\text{Profit \%} = \frac{\text{Income} - \text{Expenditure}}{\text{Expenditure}} \times 100$

1. For Company B, if the income in the year 2018 was equal to the expenditure in the year 2020, then what was the ratio of income of B in 2018 to that in 2020?

(a) 2 : 3 (b) 3 : 2
(c) 2 : 5 (d) 5 : 2

2. In the year 2022, if the income of Company B was ₹52 Crore and the expenditures of both the companies A and B were same, then what was the average of income of both the companies A and B?

(a) ₹22 Crore (b) ₹33 Crore
(c) ₹55 Crore (d) ₹44 Crore

3. If in the year 2021, the expenditure of Company A was equal to the expenditure of Company B, then what was the ratio of their respective incomes?

(a) 3 : 2 (b) 32 : 29
(c) 2 : 5 (d) 7 : 5

4. In the year 2023, if the income of Company B was ₹70 Crores, then what was the expenditure of the Company B in that year?

(a) ₹20 Crore (b) ₹30 Crore
(c) ₹40 Crore (d) ₹50 Crore

5. If the ratio of expenditures of Company A in 2019 and 2023 is 4 : 3, then the income of Company A in 2019 is ________ % more than the income of Company A in 2023.

(a) $\frac{70}{9}\%$ (b) $\frac{80}{9}\%$

(c) $\frac{40}{9}\%$ (d) $\frac{100}{9}\%$

6. If $(L)_M$ represents a number L in base-M number system, then identify the correct ascending order of the following numbers A-D when converted to decimal number system:

A. $(11111.11)_2$
B. $(102.3)_6$
C. $(42.5)_8$
D. $(32.6)_{16}$

Choose the most appropriate answer from the options given below:

(a) B, A, C, D (b) A, C, B, D
(c) C, A, D, B (d) D, C, B, A

7. What is the correct sequence of Global Warming Potential (GWP) of following Greenhouse Gases from lowest to highest?

A. CH_4 (Methane)
B. CO_2 (Carbon dioxide)
C. CFC-11 (Chlorofluoro carbon-11)
D. N_2O (Nitrous oxide)

Choose the most appropriate answer from the options given below:

(a) C, A, B, D
(b) A, D, B, C
(c) B, A, C, D
(d) B, A, D, C

8. Identify the figure and mood of the following:

"All sodium salts are water-soluble substances. All soaps are sodium salts.
Therefore, all soaps are water soluble substances."

Codes:

(a) AEI; IInd Figure
(b) AAA; IIIrd Figure
(c) IIA; IVth Figure
(d) AAA; I[st] Figure

9. The Smog of great London smog disaster was composed of high concentrations of

A. Nitrogen dioxide
B. Sulphur dioxide
C. Peroxy Acetyl Nitrate (PAN)
D. Particulate matters

Choose the most appropriate answer from the options given below.

(a) A and B only
(b) A and C only
(c) C and D only
(d) B and D only

10. Which of the following was a pertinent observation of the Indian Education Commission, 1964-66?

(a) Pyramid type of organization being replaced by a flat organization.
(b) Indian universities are global in character.
(c) Foreign universities are heavily funding Indian students.
(d) All university graduates are guaranteed jobs in India.

11. Which of the following are the elements of observational learning?

A. Retention
B. Attention
C. Adaptation
D. Production
E. Motivation

Choose the most appropriate answer from the options given below:

(a) A, B, D and E only
(b) C and E only
(c) A, B, C and E only
(d) B and D only

12. Which of the following are National Missions of National Action Plan on climate change?

A. National Ozone Mission
B. National Solar Mission
C. National Water Mission
D. National Air Mission
E. National Mission for Green India

Choose the most appropriate answer from the options given below:

(a) A, B and D only
(b) A, D and E only
(c) B, C and E only
(d) C, D and E only

13. Which of the following are the benefits of metacognition?

A. Metacognitive practices help learners to plan, monitor and evaluate their own progress.
B. Metacognitive practices make a unique contribution to learning over and above the influence of cognitive ability.
C. Metacognitive practices help to improve academic achievements of learners.
D. Metacognitive skills help students to transfer what they have learnt from one context to the next.

Choose the most appropriate answer from the options given below:

(a) A and D only
(b) B and C only
(c) A, B, C and D
(d) C only

14. Consider the following MS-EXCEL spreadsheet:

	A	B	C	D	E
1	Item	Quantity	Price	Revenue	
2	A-11	12	5	60	
3	B-32	31	9	279	
4	C-44	24	12	288	

If the formula = B2 × C2 is entered into cell E2, and the formula is then copied to cells E3 and E4, then the values in cells E2, E3 and E4 will be

(a) 60, 60 and 60 respectively.
(b) 60, 279 and 288 respectively.
(b) 0, 0 and 0 respectively.
(b) 60, 40 and 36 respectively.

15. Match the List – I with List – I

List – I Population Mean (μ) and $\left(\frac{1}{N}\sum x_i^2\right)$	List – II Population Standard Deviation (σ)
A. $\mu = 7, \frac{1}{N}\sum x_i^2 = 85$	I. 9
B. $\mu = 3, \frac{1}{N}\sum x_i^2 = 58$	II. 8
C. $\mu = 7, \frac{1}{N}\sum x_i^2 = 113$	III. 7
D. $\mu = 6, \frac{1}{N}\sum x_i^2 = 117$	IV. 6

Choose the correct answer from the options given below:

(a) A-I, B-II, C-III, D-IV
(b) A-II, B-III, C-IV, D-I
(c) A-III, B-IV, C-I, D-II
(d) A-IV, B-III, C-II, D-I

16. Match the List-I with List-II

List – I (Toxic Substance Group)	List – II (Level of Carcinogenicity)
A. Group A	I. Probable Human Carcinogen
B. Group B	II. Not Classified
C. Group C	III. Human Carcinogen
D. Group D	IV. Possible Human Carcinogen

Choose the correct answer from the options given below:

(a) A-II, B-IV, C-I, D-III
(b) A-II, B-I, C-IV, D-III
(c) A-III, B-IV, C-I, D-II
(d) A-III, B-I, C-IV, D-II

17. The speed of a boat in still water is 10 Km/hr (10 Kmph). If it can travel 26 Km downstream and 14 Km upstream in the same time, the speed of the stream is:

(a) 4.5 Km/hr
(b) 5 Km/hr
(c) 3 Km/hr
(d) 4 Km/hr

18. Which of the following text readings were identified by Stuart Hall?

A. Complex reading
B. Continuous reading
C. Dominant reading
D. Oppositional reading
E. Negotiated reading

Choose the most appropriate answer from the options given below:

(a) A, B, C only (b) C, D, E only
(c) B, C, D only (d) A, D, E only

19. According the Naiyāyikās, words mean
(a) Universals only (Jāti)
(b) Particular only (Vyakti)
(c) Configuration only (Ākṛti))
(d) Universal, particular and configuration (Jāti, Vyakti and Ākṛti)

20. Match the List-I with List-II

List – I (Cooperative Learning Strategy)		List – II (Meaning)	
A.	Round Robin Brain Storming	I.	Observing and listening to a core group discussion
B.	Numbered Heads Together	II.	Students teaching a specific topic to others
C.	Fishbowl	III.	Discussing a topic in turn within a small group
D.	Peer Teaching	IV.	Assigning roles and rotating group representatives

Choose the correct answer from the options given below:
(a) A-IV, B-III, C-II, D-I
(b) A-III, B-IV, C-I, D-II
(c) A-II, B-III C-I, D-IV
(d) A-III, B-II, C-IV, D-I

21. The degree to which two or more observers agree in their coding and scoring of behaviours, they are observing and recoding, relates to
(a) Observer bias
(b) Observer drift
(c) Subject reactivity
(d) Inter-observer reliability

22. The cultural meaning of a text is known as:
(a) Notification (b) Denotation
(c) Connotation (d) Closed text

23. The chronological sequence of the following chair-persons of UGC is:
A. Armaity S. Desai
B. G. Ram Reddy
C. Manmohan Singh
D. Yashpal
E. Madhuri R. Shah

Choose the most appropriate answer from the options given below:
(a) A, E, B, D, C
(b) B, C, E, A, D
(c) C, D, A, E, B
(d) E, D, C, B, A

24. In a certain code language:
'617' means "Sweet and hot",
'735' means "Coffee is sweet",
'263' means "Tea is hot",

What is the code for "Coffee is hot" in that language?
(a) '675' (b) '537'
(c) '536' (d) '573'

25. Find the number that can replace the question mark (?) in the series given below:

4, 27, 16, 125, 36, ?, 64, 729
(a) 343 (b) 81
(c) 49 (d) 161

26. A study meant to discover whether variables covary, relates to
(a) case study
(b) longitudinal research
(c) correlational research
(d) archival research

27. Which of the following are chemical parameters of water quality?
A. pH
B. Hardness
C. Turbidity
D. DO
E. BOD

Choose the most appropriate answer from the options given below:
(a) A, B, C and D only
(b) A, B, D and E only
(c) B, C, D and E only
(d) A, C and E only

28. With reference to digital communication, which of the following statements A-D are true?

A. A radio broadcast is an example of automatic type of transmission mode.

B. A keyboard communicating with a computer is an example of simplex type of transmission mode.

C. Walkie-talkies operate on half-duplex transmission mode.

D. Telephone calls are an example of full-duplex transmission mode.

Choose the most appropriate answer from the options given below:

(a) A and B only
(b) B and C only
(c) A and C only
(d) B, C and D only

29. Find out the inter-connected psychodynamics of oral thoughts sequentially, according to Walter J. Ong:

A. Additive
B. Aggregative
C. Copious
D. Traditionalist
E. Close to the human life

Choose the most appropriate answer from the options given below:

(a) A, B, C, D, E
(b) B, C, D, E, A
(c) C, D, E, A, B
(d) D, E, A, B, C

30. A set of rules governing the use of visual and linguistic signs within a particular culture is referred to as:

(a) Media rule
(b) Text frame
(c) Technical norms
(d) Code

31. Match the List-I with List-II

	List – I Scholar		List – II Work
A.	Boudhayana	I.	Rasaratnakara
B.	Nagarjuna	II.	Arthashastra
C.	Brahma Gupta	III.	Sulva Sutra
D.	Vishnu Gupta	IV.	Brahma Sputa Siddanthika

Choose the correct answer from the options given below:

(a) A-I, B-IV, C-II, D-III
(a) A-IV, B-II, C-III, D-I
(c) A-III, B-I, C-IV, D-II
(d) A-II, B-III, C-I, D-IV

32. Identify the sampling techniques that are for studying hidden populations.

A. Simple random sampling
B. Snowball sampling
C. Stratified random sampling
D. Key informant sampling

Choose the most appropriate answer from the options given below:

(a) A and B only
(b) A and C only
(c) B and D only
(d) C and D only

33. A woman walks 100 metres towards north. Then she turns to her left and walks 50 metres. Again turns left and walks 120 metres. Finally she turns to her right at an angle of 45 degrees and starts walking. In which direction is the woman walking now?

(a) North
(b) South-West
(c) West
(d) North-West

34. If 'Z' represents the standard normal variate, then arrange the following probabilities in increasing order:

A. $P(0 \leq Z \leq 1)$
B. $P(-\infty \leq Z \leq 0)$
C. $P(1 \leq Z \leq 3)$
D. $P(2 \leq Z \leq +\infty)$

Choose the most appropriate answer from the options given below:

(a) A, B, C, D
(b) B, C, D, A
(c) C, D, A, B
(d) D, C, A, B

35. Match the List-I with List-II

List – I (Concept)		List – II (Description)	
A.	Chirographic Culture	I.	Print
B.	Typographic Culture	II.	Speaking to experience the word
C.	Oral Culture	III.	Spatial understanding through images
D.	Visual Culture	IV.	Writing

Choose the correct answer from the options given below:

(a) A-I, B-II, C-III, D-IV
(b) A-II, B-III, C-IV, D-I
(c) A-III. B-IV, C-I, D-II
(d) A-IV, B-I, C-II, D-III

36. Which of the following subjects were taught in ancient Indian Universities?

A. Journalism
B. Environmental Science
C. Logic
D. Medicine
E. Philosophy

Choose the most appropriate answer from the options given below:

(a) A, B, C only
(b) B, C, D only
(c) C, D, E only
(d) A, B, E only

37. When a car passes you on the road and appears to shrink as it gets farther away, which phenomenon permits you to realize that car is not in fact getting smaller?

(a) Self-actualization
(b) Transitivity
(c) Perceptual constancy
(d) Similarity

38. The previous nomenclature of Ministry of Education was

(a) Ministry of Youth Affairs
(b) Ministry of Human Resource Development
(c) Ministry of Education and Research
(d) Ministry of Central Affairs

39. Match the List-I with List-II

List – I (Malware Type)		List – II (Definition)	
A.	Polymorphic Virus	I.	A seemingly useful program that contains hidden harmful program code
B.	Metamorphic Virus	II.	Changes its signature with each copy made during replication
C.	Trojan Horse	III.	A malware that spreads copies of itself through a network without user interaction
D.	Worm	IV.	Completely rewrites itself each time it is replicated, sometimes changing its behaviour

Choose the correct answer from the options given below:

(a) A-II, B-I, C-IV. D-III
(b) A-III, B-IV, C-I, D-II
(c) A-II, B-IV, C-I, D-III
(d) A-I, B-III, C-IV, D-II

40. A fallacy in which an opponent's position is depicted as being more extreme or unreasonable than is justified by what was actually asserted, is the fallacy of

(a) Appeal to Pity
(b) The Strawman
(c) The Red Herring
(d) The Appeal to the Populace

41. A teacher is looking for a Learning Management System (LMS) that can integrate with multiple assessment tools and track student progress. Which platform is best suitable for this?

(a) Moodle (b) Zoom
(c) Grammarly (d) Turnitin

42. When two propositions with same subject and predicate terms agree in quality but differ in quantity are known as

(a) Contraries
(b) Sub-contraries
(c) Contradictory
(d) Corresponding

43. Arguments by Analogy are
(a) Classified as valid
(b) Classified as invalid
(c) Claimed to follow from their premises with logical necessity
(d) Probable

44. The age of the father is twice that of the elder son. Ten years hence the age of the father will be three times the age of the younger son. If the difference of ages of the two sons is 15 years, what is the age of the father?
(a) 50 yrs
(b) 45 yrs
(c) 43 yrs
(d) 40 yrs

45. Rita's smartphone uses an open source operating system. Which of the following best describes the source code in an open source operating system?
(a) It is owned by the company who developed it.
(b) It is made available to users.
(c) It is more secure.
(d) It uses less processing power.

Read the passage carefully. The questions 46 to 50 are based on this paragraph.

Ayurveda defines health as a dynamic balance of the internal environment that positively impacts the sense organs, mind and the self. Each individual is unique and has a specific mental and physical constitution, which defines the vulnerability to disease and the scope for achieving higher levels of health. Ayurveda has also been at the forefront of advocating an approach to personalized medicine form historical times. Advances in human genetics and medical genetics have heralded the emergence of a personalized approach to medicine today that tailors medical intervention to suit individual needs.

Ayurveda points out that the balance of the inner environment can be maintained only by establishing harmony with the external environment. Ayurveda proclaims that the human being is an epitome of the universe. The microcosm is a miniature representation of the macrocosm and the human being is made up of the same elements that make up nature. Thus, it is that Ayurveda developed into an ecology-conscious system of healthcare. For the people of a locality, the plants growing around them are the most suited. Each individual has to carve a lifestyle that considers the geographical region as well as the changing seasons.

46. Ayurveda advocates
(a) A personalized treatment
(b) A similar treatment for all individuals
(c) Only a preventive approach to diseases
(d) Allopathic treatment

47. A suitable title for the passage would be:
(a) Dynamic Balance
(b) Disease Treatment in India
(c) Ayurveda
(d) Internal and External Environment

48. According to Ayurveda, the lifestyle of each individual needs to be carved out considering ______________.
(a) the things they like
(b) sticking to a diet of fruits
(c) their particular region and the changing seasons
(d) what is cheaply available

49. According to Ayurveda maintaining the balance of the internal environment of the body ______________.
(a) has no connection with the external environment
(b) is negligibly related to the external environment
(c) is closely related to the external environment
(d) is sometimes dependent on the external environment

50. Ayurvedic system of health ______________.
(a) does not care about the environment
(b) believes in destroying the environment
(c) is ecology conscious
(d) pollutes the environment

ANSWER KEY

1. (a)	**2.** (c)	**3.** (b)	**4.** (d)	**5.** (d)	**6.** (c)	**7.** (d)	**8.** (d)	**9.** (d)	**10.** (a)
11. (a)	**12.** (c)	**13.** (c)	**14.** (d)	**15.** (d)	**16.** (d)	**17.** (c)	**18.** (b)	**19.** (d)	**20.** (b)
21. (d)	**22.** (c)	**23.** (d)	**24.** (c)	**25.** (a)	**26.** (c)	**27.** (b)	**28.** (d)	**29.** (b)	**30.** (d)
31. (c)	**32.** (c)	**33.** (b)	**34.** (d)	**35.** (d)	**36.** (c)	**37.** (c)	**38.** (b)	**39.** (c)	**40.** (b)
41. (a)	**42.** (d)	**43.** (d)	**44.** (a)	**45.** (b)	**46.** (a)	**47.** (c)	**48.** (c)	**49.** (c)	**50.** (b)

HINTS AND SOLUTIONS

1. (a)

Assume that for Company B: Given: Income 2018 = Expenditure 2020 = P

For 2018:

Profit % = [(Income – Expenditure)/Expenditure] × 100
25% = [(Income 2018 – Expenditure 2018)/Expenditure 2018] × 100
Income 2018 = 1.25 × Expenditure 2018
P = 1.25 × Expenditure 2018
Therefore, Expenditure 2018 = P/1.25

For 2020:

Profit% = [(Income 2020 – Expenditure 2020)/Expenditure 2020] × 100
50% = [(Income 2020 – P)/P] × 100
Income 2020 = 1.5 × P
Now, to find ratio of Income 2018 : Income 2020
= P : 1.5 P
= 1 : 1.5
= 2 : 3
Therefore, the ratio of income of B in 2018 to that in 2020 is 2 : 3.
Thus, (a) is the correct answer.

2. (c)

First find the expenditure of Company B in 2022:
Let the expenditure of Company B in 2022 be 'x' Crore.
Profit% = (Income – Expenditure)/Expenditure × 100
$30 = [(52 - x)/x] \times 100$
$30x = 5200 - 100x$
$130x = 5200$
$x = 5200/130$
$x = 40$ Crore
Since the expenditures of both companies are the same, Company A's expenditure in 2022 is also 40 Crore.
Let the income of Company A in 2022 be 'y' Crore.
$45 = (y - 40)/40 \times 100$
$45 \times 40 = 100y - 4000$
$1800 = 100y - 4000$
$100y = 5800$
$y = 58$ Crore
Now finally, find the average income of both companies in 2022:
Average Income = (Income of A + Income of B) / 2
= (58 + 52) / 2 = 110 / 2 = 55 Crore
Thus, (c) is the correct answer.

3. (b)

Assume the expenditure for both companies in 2021 is 'x'.
Calculate the income of Company A in 2021:
Profit% = (Income – Expenditure)/Expenditure × 100
$60 = [(\text{Income A} - x) / x] \times 100$
$0.6x = \text{Income A} - x$
$\text{Income A} = 1.6x$
Calculate the income of Company B in 2021:
$45 = (\text{Income B} - x) / x * 100$
$0.45x = \text{Income B} - x$
$\text{Income B} = 1.45x$
Find the ratio of their respective incomes:
Income A : Income B = $1.6x : 1.45x$ = 32 : 29
Thus, (b) is the correct answer.

4. (d)

Again, Profit % = (Income – Expenditure)/Expenditure × 100

For Company B in 2023:

Profit % = 40%

Income = 70 Crore

Let Expenditure = x

$40 = [(70 - x) / x] \times 100$

$40x = (70 - x) \times 100 = 7000 - 100x$

$140x = 7000$

$x = 7000/140 = 50$ Crore

Thus, the expenditure of Company B in 2023 was 50 Crore.

Thus, (d) is the correct answer.

5. (d)

Let the expenditure of Company A in 2019 be $4x$ and in 2023 be $3x$.

Firstly, calculate the income of Company A in 2019:

Profit% = (Income – Expenditure)/Expenditure × 100

$25 = (\text{Income } 2019 - 4x) / 4x \times 100$
$100x = 100 \times \text{Income } 2019 - 400x$
$500x = 100 \times \text{Income } 2019$
$\text{Income } 2019 = 5x$

Now, calculate the income of Company A in 2023:

$50 = [(\text{Income } 2023 - 3x) / 3x] \times 100$
$150x = 100 \times \text{Income } 2023 - 300x$
$450x = 100 \times \text{Income } 2023$
$\text{Income } 2023 = 4.5x$

Calculate the percentage increase in income:

% increase = [(Income 2019 – Income 2023)/ Income 2023] × 100

$= [(5x - 4.5x) / 4.5x] \times 100$
$= (0.5x / 4.5x) \times 100 = 1/9 \times 100 = 100/9\%$

Thus, (d) is the correct answer.

6. (c)

A $(11111.11)_2$

Integer part: $1 \times 2^4 + 1 \times 2^3 + 1 \times 2^2 + 1 \times 2^1 + 1 \times 2^0 = 16 + 8 + 4 + 2 + 1 = 31$

Fractional part: $1 \times 2^{-1} + 1 \times 2^{-2} = 0.5 + 0.25 = 0.75$

Decimal equivalent: **31.75**

B $(102.3)_6$

Integer part: $1 \times 6^2 + 0 \times 6^1 + 2 \times 6^0 = 36 + 0 + 2 = 38$

Fractional part: $3 \times 6^{-1} = 3 \times 0.1667 = 0.5$

Decimal equivalent: **38.5**

C $(42.5)_8$

Integer part: $4 \times 8^1 + 2 \times 8^0 = 32 + 2 = 34$

Fractional part: $5 \times 8^{-1} = 5 \times 0.125 = 0.625$

Decimal equivalent: **34.625**

D $(32.6)_{16}$

Integer part: $3 \times 16^1 + 2 \times 16^0 = 48 + 2 = 50$

Fractional part: $6 \times 16^{-1} = 6 \times 0.0625 = 0.375$

Decimal equivalent: **50.375**

Thus, the correct order is (c). A, C, B, D

Thus, (c) is the correct answer.

7. (d)

Global Warming Potential (GWP): GWP measures how much heat a greenhouse gas traps in the atmosphere over a specific period (usually 100 years) compared to CO_2 (GWP = 1).

GWP helps to compare the impact of different greenhouse gases. GWP guides climate policies and emission reduction strategies such as Kyoto Protocol and Paris Agreement.

A. CO_2 (Carbon dioxide) → GWP = 1 (Standard Baseline)
B. CH_4 (Methane) → GWP ≈ 25 – 30
C. N_2O (Nitrous oxide) → GWP ≈ 298
D. CFC-11 (Chlorofluorocarbon-11) → GWP ≈ 4600

Thus, the correct ascending order (d). B, A, D, C

Note: There was one MCQ, linked with 20 years and 100 years spans of GWP.

Thus, (d) is the correct answer.

8. (d)

Mood and Figures are basically found in the case of syllogism statements.

Mood: We need to explore the types of categorical propositions – A, E, I, O

Premise 1: All sodium salts are water-soluble substances: **A** (Universal Affirmative)

Premise 2: All soaps are sodium salts: **A** (Universal Affirmative)

Conclusion: All soaps are water-soluble substances: **A** (Universal Affirmative)

Thus, the mood is **AAA**.

Figure:

Figure depends on the arrangement of the middle term in the premises. The middle term is the term that appears in both premises but not in the conclusion. Thus, Sodium Salts is the Middle Term.

In this case, the middle term is 'sodium salts.'

Premise 1: M - P (Middle term - Major term)
Premise 2: S - M (Minor term - Middle term)
Conclusion: S - P (Minor term - Major term)

Comparing this arrangement with the four figures:

1st Figure: M - P, S - M, S - P
2nd Figure: P - M, S - M, S - P
3rd Figure: M - P, M - S, S - P
4th Figure: P - M, M - S, S - P

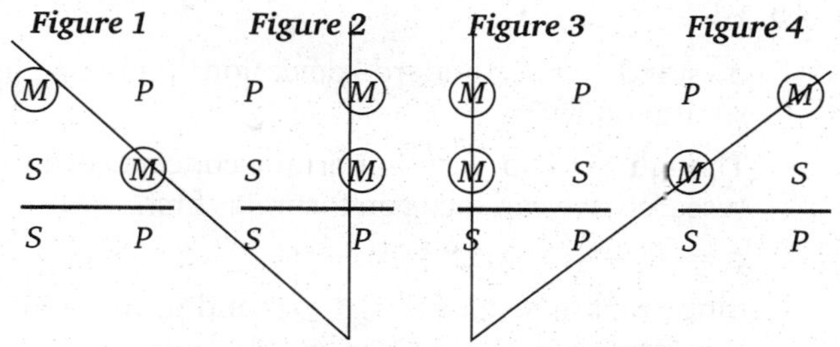

The given syllogism matches the 1st Figure.

Thus, (d) is the correct answer.

9. **(d)**

The Great London Smog of 1952 was primarily caused by high levels of sulphur dioxide (SO_2) and particulate matter from the burning of coal.

A. Nitrogen dioxide (NO_2) – Incorrect. While NO_2 is a major pollutant, it was not a primary component of the London Smog.

B. Sulphur dioxide (SO_2) – Correct. SO_2 was released in large amounts from coal combustion and played a crucial role in forming the smog.

C. Peroxyacetyl Nitrate (PAN) – Incorrect. PAN is a photochemical pollutant, commonly associated with modern urban smog rather than the coal-based smog of 1952.

D. Particulate matter – Correct. The smog was thick due to high concentrations of particulate pollutants from burning coal.

Thus, (d) is the correct answer.

10. **(a)**

(a) Pyramid type of organisation being replaced by a flat organization: Kothari Commission meant more equitable and accessible education system, where base is broad. Higher education means elevated structure on that broad base.

(b) and (c) were linked with global or foreign that was not the scenario at that point of time.

(d) All university graduates are guaranteed jobs in India: The focus was on vocational education and skill development to enhance employability.

Thus, (a) is the correct answer.

11. **(a)**

Albert Bandura's observational learning theory, also known as social learning theory, focuses on how we learn by watching others. Adaptation (C) is a result of learning, not a step in observational learning itself.

A. **Retention:** Remembering the observed behaviour.

B. **Attention:** Noticing the model's behaviour.

D. **Production:** Replicating the behaviour.

E. **Motivation:** Having a reason to perform the behaviour.

Thus, (a) is the correct answer.

12. **(c)**

NAPCC is an integral part of India's engagement with global efforts to address climate change. It reflects the country's commitment to international agreements, incorporates global best practices, promotes technology transfer and collaboration, and contributes to the achievement of sustainable development goals.

Main Domains of NAPCC:

Mitigation: Actions taken to reduce the sources of greenhouse gases and enhance their carbon sinks, thus lessening the impact of climate change.

Adaptation: As per IPCC, adaptation is in the form of adjustments in natural or human systems in response to actual or expected climatic stimuli or their effects, which moderate harm or exploit beneficial opportunities.

Sustainable Development: Development that meets the needs of the present without compromising the ability of future generations to meet their own needs. The main examples are MDGs and SDGs.

Now coming specifically to the question:

The Original Eight missions (launched in 2008):

1. **National Solar Mission:** To promote solar energy.
2. **National Mission for Enhanced Energy Efficiency:** To reduce energy consumption.
3. **National Mission on Sustainable Habitat:** To promote sustainable cities and settlements.
4. **National Water Mission:** To focus on water conservation and management.
5. **National Mission for Sustaining the Himalayan Ecosystem:** To protect the Himalayan region.

6. **National Mission for a Green India:** To enhance forest cover and ecosystems.
7. **National Mission for Sustainable Agriculture:** To promotes climate-resilient agriculture.
8. **National Mission on Strategic Knowledge for Climate Change:** To build knowledge and capacity.

Thus, National Ozone Mission, National Air Mission are missing from the list. National Hydrogen Mission was started in 2021.

Thus, (c) is the correct answer.

13. **(c)**

Meta means about or beyond. Cognition means thinking. Metacognition is thinking about thinking. It refers to the awareness, understanding, and control of one's own cognitive processes. It's about being aware of how you learn, what you know, and how you can improve your thinking and learning strategies.

Thus, (c) is the correct answer.

14. **(d)**

Cell E2: The formula is =B2*C2.

- B2 is an absolute reference, so it always refers to cell B2 (value 12).
- C2 is a relative reference, so it refers to the cell to the left of E2 (value 5).
- The result is $12 \times 5 = 60$.

Cell E3: When the formula is copied down, the relative reference C2 changes to C3.

- B2 remains an absolute reference (value 12).
- C3 is a relative reference (value 9).
- The result is $12 \times 9 = 108$. There is a typo in the original question here. It should be 108, not 40.

Cell E4: When the formula is copied down again, C2 changes to C4.

- B2 remains an absolute reference (value 12).
- C4 is a relative reference (value 12).
- The result is $12 \times 12 = 144$. Again, there is a typo in the original question. It should be 144, not 36.

Thus, (d) is the correct answer.

15. **(d)**

σ stands for standard deviation and ∑ for summation.

Though SD is a very important concept, even in research, we can focus on formulas first.

$\sigma = \sqrt{[(1/N) \times \sum(x_i^2 - \mu^2)]}$

Since we are given (1/N) * $\sum xi^2$ and μ, we can use this form:

$\sigma = \sqrt{[(1/N) \times \sum x_i^2 - \mu^2]}$

The calculations are

A. $\mu = 7, (1/N)\sum x_i^2 = 85$

$\sigma = \sqrt{(85 - 7^2)} = \sqrt{(85 - 49)} = \sqrt{36} = 6$

B. $\mu = 3, (1/N)\sum x_i^2 = 58$

$\sigma = \sqrt{(58 - 3^2)} = \sqrt{(58 - 9)} = \sqrt{49} = 7$

C. $\mu = 7, (1/N)\sum x_i^2 = 113$

$\sigma = \sqrt{(113 - 7^2)} = \sqrt{(113 - 49)} = \sqrt{64} = 8$

D. $\mu = 6, (1/N)\sum x_i^2 = 117$

$\sigma = \sqrt{(117 - 6^2)} = \sqrt{(117 - 36)} = \sqrt{81} = 9$

On matching, the correct answer is (d). A-IV, B-III, C-II, D-I

16. **(d)**

Carcinogenicity: The ability of a substance or agent to cause cancer.

Group A: Human Carcinogen (Highest evidence level)

Group B: Probable Human Carcinogen

Group C: Possible Human Carcinogen

Group D: Not Classified/Substances with Limited or Insufficient Evidence (possibly not carcinogenic).

Thus, (d) is the correct answer.

17. **(c)**

Let '*b*' be the speed of the boat in still water (10 km/hr).

We need to find out '*s*' that is the speed of the stream.

'*t*' is the time taken for both trips (which is the same).

Downstream:

Speed = Distance / Time

$(b + s) = 26 / t$

Upstream:

Speed = Distance / Time

$(b-s) = 14 / t$

$t = 26 / (b+s)$ ...(1)

$t = 14 / (b-s)$ ...(2)

From (1) and (2)

$26 / (b+s) = 14 / (b-s)$

Substitute the value of $b = 10$ km/hr

$26/(10+s) = 14 / (10-s)$

$s = 3$

Thus, (b) is the correct answer.

18. (b)

Stuart Hall's encoding/decoding model specifically identifies Dominant, Oppositional, and Negotiated readings as the three positions when interpreting media messages.

C. Dominant: Accepting the intended meaning.

D. Oppositional: Rejecting the intended meaning.

E. Negotiated: Partially accepting and modifying the meaning.

Thus, (b) is the correct answer.

19. (d)

Naiyayika Terms	Explanation	Example (Simplified)
Jāti (Universal/Class)	The general property shared by all members of a category.	"Human" (the quality of being human)
Vyakti (Particular/Individual)	A specific instance of a Jāti.	Any individual human being (e.g., "You")
Ākṛti (Configuration/Form)	The shape or structure that allows us to recognize a Vyakti as a Jāti.	Your specific appearance (face, height, etc.)
Jāti, Vyakti & Ākṛti (Universal, Particular & Configuration)	Refers to the general class, specific individuals and their forms, which are all necessary for complete understanding.	Humans as a species, and all individual humans, with their individual appearances.

Thus, (d) is the correct answer.

20. (b)

A. **Round Robin Brainstorming** involves discussing in turn (III).

B. **Numbered Heads Together** uses numbered roles and rotating representatives (IV).

C. **Fishbowl** involves observing a core group discussion (I).

D. **Peer Teaching** involves students teaching others (II).

Thus, (b) is the correct answer.

21. **(d)**

(a) **Observer Bias:** A researcher has his own experience or beliefs which can influence their observations. Thus, they may ignore the reality, and report what they want to say.

(b) **Observer Drift:** Over time, an observer may unintentionally change how they apply a coding system. This gradual shift can lead to inconsistencies in their observations.

(c) **Subject Reactivity:** Individuals may alter their behaviour when they are aware of being observed. This is also known as the 'Hawthorne' effect.

(d) **Inter-observer Reliability:** This refers to the extent to which different observers agree on their coding or scoring of the same behaviours or events. High reliability indicates consistency between observers.

Thus, (d) is the correct answer.

22. **(c)**

(a) Notification is formal in nature.

(d) Closed text is not associated with culture that is actually meant to be shown.

(b) Denotation is the literal, dictionary definition of a word. It's the objective meaning without any added emotional or cultural baggage. For example, denotation of 'home' is the physical structure where one lives.

The following is the correct answer.

(c) Connotation is the cultural or emotional association connected to a word or text. Connotation is subjective, so its meanings depend on cultural context, personal experiences, and societal values. These connotations can vary across cultures and individuals. Home may mean warmth, comfort, family, belonging, safety, etc.

Thus, (c) is the correct answer.

23. (d)

1. E (Madhuri R. Shah): 1981 – 1986
2. D (Yashpal): 1986 – 1991
3. C (Manmohan Singh): 1991 – 1991
4. B (G. Ram Reddy): 1991 – 1995
5. A (Armaity S. Desai): 1995 – 1999

Thus, (d) is the correct answer.

24. (c)

'617' means "Sweet and hot"

'735' means "Coffee is sweet"

'263' means "Tea is hot"

1. 'sweet' is common to the 1st and 2nd codes, AND 'so is '7'. So 'sweet' equates 7
2. Similarly, 'hot' equates '6'.
3. Similarly, 'is' equates '3'.

Interpreting, 1 and 2, Coffee equates 5.

Thus, "Coffee is hot" is 536.

Thus, (c) is the correct answer.

25. (a)

The pattern can be taken singly or divided into two parts:

4, 27, 16, 125, 36, ? , 64, 729 – it's the squares and cubes of 2, 3, 4, 5, 6, 7, 6, 9 ....

$= 2^2, 3^3, 4^2, 5^3, 6^2, 7^3, 8^2, 9^3$

Thus, the correct answer $7^3 = 343$.

Thus, (a) is the correct answer.

26. (c)

(c) **Correlational research** is specifically designed to examine the relationship between two or more variables. It aims to determine if and how these variables covary (change together).

Other Options:

(a) **Case Study:** A case study is an in-depth investigation of a single individual, group, event, or even a hypothetical scenario. While it *can* examine multiple variables, its primary goal is to understand the complexities of *that specific case*. It's often subjective and focuses on rich descriptions rather than discovering general patterns of how variables change together (covariation).

(b) **Longitudinal research:** This research tracks the same variables in the same subjects over time. It's about change over time, not specifically about how things change *together*.

(d) **Archival research:** Archival research uses existing data that has been collected for other purposes (historical records, census data).

Thus, (c) is the correct answer.

27. (b)

A, B, D and E refer to the chemical properties of water.

A. **pH:** pH is a measure of the acidity or alkalinity of water.

B. **Hardness:** Hardness refers to the concentration of dissolved minerals (usually calcium and magnesium) in water.

D. **DO (Dissolved Oxygen):** DO is the amount of oxygen gas present in water, that is vital for aquatic life.

E. **BOD (Biochemical Oxygen Demand):** BOD measures the amount of oxygen consumed by microorganisms while decomposing organic matter in water. It's a biological process influenced by chemical factors.

C. **Turbidity** is a physical property (appearance) of water, it refers to its cloudiness or lack of clarity due to suspended particles. It can be influenced by chemical factors.

Thus, (b) is the correct answer.

28. **(d)**

A. **Radio Broadcast:** It sends signals in one direction only—from the station to the listener. Therefore, it's NOT described as 'automatic' transmission, but as 'simplex' (one-way).

The true options are:

B. **Keyboard-Computer:** While a keyboard sends information to the computer, the vice versa is not true through the same connection. This one-way communication is 'simplex.'

C. **Walkie-talkies:** Walkie-talkies allow two-way communication, but only one person can talk at a time. You press a button to talk and release it to listen. This is 'half-duplex' communication.

D. **Telephone Calls:** During a phone call, both people can talk and listen at the same time. This two-way simultaneous communication is 'full duplex.'

Thus, (d) is the correct answer.

29. (b)

Walter J. Ong, in his book "Orality and Literacy," described the characteristics of oral thought. The following characteristics are interconnected and reflect the nature of oral cultures' thought processes.

B. **Aggregative:** There is a grouping of related ideas together rather than breaking them down. Oral thought is more aggregative than analytic.

C. **Copious:** It uses repetition and elaboration for memory and engagement. There's a 'more is more' aesthetic.

D. **Traditionalist:** Oral cultures preserve existing knowledge, valuing tradition over innovation.

E. **Close to human life:** Oral thought focuses on concrete, everyday experiences rather than abstract ideas.

A. **Additive:** Oral thought strings ideas together, it doesn't organize them into hierarchies and complex structures.

Thus, (b) is the correct answer.

30. (d)

A code, in semiotics and cultural studies, is a system of signs and symbols governed by rules and conventions shared by members of a culture or subculture. These codes dictate how meanings are assigned to visual and linguistic elements, shaping communication and understanding within that group.

Thus, (d) is the correct answer.

31. **(c)**

A. **Boudhayana - III. Sulva Sutra:** It deals with geometric constructions used in the design of Vedic altars.

B. **Nagarjuna - I. Rasaratnakara:** It is associated with Indian alchemy (rasayana), linked with Chemistry.

C. **Brahma Gupta - IV. Brahma Sputa Siddhantika:** It is a major work on astronomy and mathematics.

D. **Vishnu Gupta - II. Arthashastra:** It is an ancient Indian treatise on statecraft and political economy. The names of Kautilya and Chanakya are also linked to this work.

Thus, (c) is the correct answer.

32. **(c)**

Snowball sampling (B): It helps find hidden groups. The researcher establishes contact with one person in a group. He tells about another person, and so on. Thus, a chain may be established, thus, a snowball gets bigger, a researcher reaches more people in the hidden group. Insurance industry can be taken as an example.

Key informant sampling (D) uses experts. A researcher talks to key informants to learn about the group and find more people in it.

The reasons that the other options don't work:

Simple random sampling (A) needs a list of everyone. If the group is hidden, you can't have that list. So, you can't pick people randomly.

Stratified random sampling (C) also needs a list. You need to divide the list into smaller groups (strata) first. But you can't do that without knowing who is in the hidden group.

So, the best ways to study hidden groups are snowball sampling and key informant sampling. They don't need a full list of the group.

Thus, (c) is the correct answer.

33. (b)

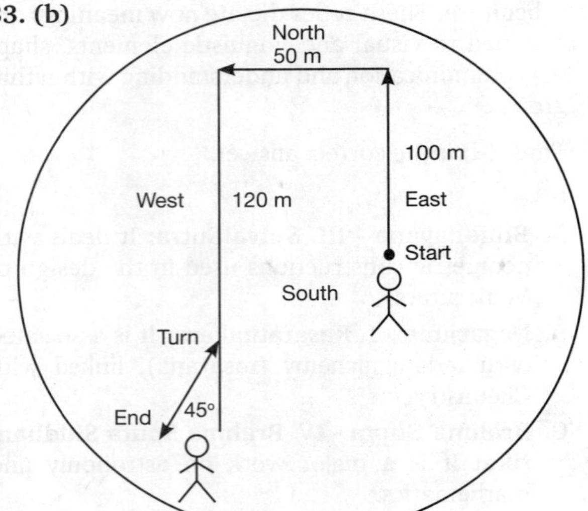

Key steps to know the direction

1. She starts by walking 100 metres towards the north.
2. She then turns left (west) and walks 50 metres.
3. Next, she turns left again (south) and walks 120 metres.
4. Finally, she turns to her right at an angle of 45 degrees and starts walking.

When she turns right at 45 degrees from the south, she will be walking in the south-west direction.

Thus, (b) is the correct answer.

34. (d)

We have one solved question in our book, under null hypothesis.

We see in a test to see if something is likely due to chance (a null hypothesis test):

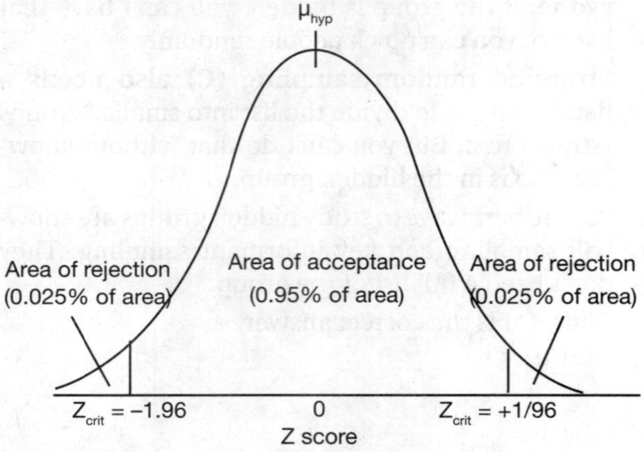

Normal Distribution

1. **z-score:** It tells us how far away our data is from the average. It is measured in standard deviations (sigma). Think of it like a measure of 'how unusual' (different from mean) our data is.

Z Test is used in the following situation:

- The sample size is large (usually $n > 30$).
- The population variance is known.
- The data is approximately normally distributed.

2. **p-value:** Tells you the probability of getting data as extreme as ours (or even more extreme) if the null hypothesis were actually true. A small p-value means our data is unlikely if the null hypothesis is true.

We calculate the z-score first. Then, we use the z-score to find the p-value. The p-value helps us decide whether to reject the idea that our results are just due to chance.

Ordering the Probabilities: There is use of word approximation in the question statement itself, so, accordinlgy, we are trying to find the answer.

B: $P(-\infty \le Z \le 0) = 0.5$. This is the largest probability as it covers half of the distribution.

A: $P(0 \le Z \le 1)$: This is a substantial portion of the area under the curve, but less than 0.5.

C: $P(1 \le Z \le 3)$: This area is smaller than $P(0 \le Z \le 1)$ as it's further out on the tail of the distribution.

D: $P(2 \le Z \le \infty)$: This area is the smallest as it is in the far tail of the distribution.

Therefore, the correct increasing order is (d). D, C, A, B.

Thus, (d) is the correct answer.

35. (d)

List-I (Concept)	List-II (Description)
A. Chirographic Culture	IV. **Writing** – Primary form to communicate and preserve knowledge.
B. Typographic Culture	I. **Print** - movable type - mass production of written materials.
C. Oral Culture	II. **Speaking to experience the word** – also for knowledge transmission and cultural preservation.

D. Visual Culture	III. **Spatial understanding through images** – to interpret visual elements

The answer is A-IV, B- I, C-II, D-III

Thus, (d) is the correct answer.

36. (c)

C. Logic – Its equivalents such as tarka or hetu-vidya in ancient India were highly developed. Dignaga and Dharmakirti made immense contributions towards logic.

D. Medicine – Ayurveda is becoming popular again - the important texts on medicine and surgery were created by Sushruta and Charaka.

E. Philosophy (Darshan Shastra (दर्शनशास्त्र)- Samkhya, Yoga, Nyaya, Vaisheshika, Mimamsa, and Vedanta are the main parts of Vedic system. These were central to the curriculum at universities like Nalanda and Taxila.

Thus, (c) is the correct answer.

37. (c)

(c) Perceptual constancy: It is actually the tendency to perceive an object as the same even when the sensory information we receive about it changes. For example, a car appears to be same in our perception, though the retina of our eyes supports it as some medical issue develops in our eyes.

Some explanations of incorrect options are

(a) **Self-actualization:** This is a concept from Maslow's hierarchy of needs, it refers to the realisation of one's full potential. It's not related to visual perception.

(b) **Transitivity:** This refers to the logical property that if A = B and B = C, then A = C. It's not relevant to how we perceive size.

(d) **Similarity:** This is the principle that we tend to group similar things together. While it's a perceptual principle, it doesn't explain why we perceive the car's size as constant.

Thus, (c) is the correct answer.

38. (b)

The Ministry of Education in India was previously known as the Ministry of Human Resource Development (MHRD). his change was made in 2020. Earlier education was part of MHRD, 2020 onwards it was given independent status while New Education Policy was also announced simultaneously. That indicated broader reforms. The change was not for the sake of name only.

Thus, (b) is the correct answer.

39. (c)

A **Polymorphic Virus-II. Changes its signature with each copy made during replication.** It alters its code slightly to avoid detection.

B **Metamorphic Virus-IV. Completely rewrites itself each time it is replicated, sometimes changing its behaviour:** This is what makes metamorphic viruses more advanced. They don't just tweak their code; they rewrite it entirely.

C **Trojan Horse-I. A seemingly useful program that contains hidden harmful program code:** Trojans hide malicious functionality within seemingly legitimate programs.

D **Worm-III. A malware that spreads copies of itself through a network without user interaction:** Worms are self-propagating and don't need a host program.

Thus, (c) is the correct answer.

40. **(b)**

(b) **The Strawman:** This fallacy involves misrepresenting an opponent's argument to make it easier to attack. This is done by creating a weaker, exaggerated, or distorted version of the argument – the 'strawman' – and then refuting that weaker version instead of the actual argument.

Though such questions are subjective, the not correct options are:

(a) Appeal to Pity: This fallacy tries to persuade by evoking feelings of pity or sympathy, rather than through logical reasoning.

(c) Red Herring: A red herring is a distraction, an irrelevant topic introduced to divert attention away from the main issue being discussed.

(d) Appeal to the Populace (Ad Populum): This fallacy argues that something must be true because many people believe it or want it to be true. It's based on popularity, not evidence or logic.

Thus, (b) is the correct answer.

41. **(a)**

Moodle: Moodle is a robust, open-source Learning Management System (LMS) specifically designed for educators. It excels at integration, tracking and customization as per a teacher's needs.

Other options for specific needs are

(b) Zoom: It is excellent for video conferencing and online meetings, it's not a full-fledged LMS.

(c) Grammarly: This writing assistance tool helps with grammar and style, specifically in course management, assessment integration, and progress tracking.

(d) Turnitin: Turnitin is primarily a plagiarism detection software. While it's a valuable assessment tool, it's focused on originality checking, not the broader range of assessment and tracking that a teacher needs in an LMS.

Thus, (a) is the correct answer.

42. **(d)**

When two propositions with the same subject and predicate terms agree in quality but differ in quantity, they are known as corresponding propositions. This means the propositions maintain the same quality (either affirmative or negative) but differ in quantity (universal vs. particular).

For example:

Universal Affirmative: 'All men are friendly.'

Particular Affirmative: 'Some men are friendly.'

Thus, (d) is the correct answer.

43. (d)

An analogy is a type of comparison. Specifically, an analogy compares two things that are generally different from each other but have similar aspects in certain ways. The purpose of an analogy is often to explain a concept or idea by comparing it to something more familiar. For example, we compare a computer with a brain.

Arguments by 'analogy' are generally considered to be probable rather than classified as definitively valid or invalid. They are reasoning by comparison, where the conclusion is likely but not logically necessary based on the premises. Comparison is after all probable, it is not deductive - certain or deterministic.

Thus, (d) is the correct answer.

44. **(a)**

Let the age of the elder son be x, the father's present age = $2x$ years.

Younger son present age = $x - 15$ years

After 10 years, father's age = $2x + 10$ years

After 10 years, younger son's age = $(x - 15) + 10 = x - 5$.

According to the question $2x + 10 = 3(x - 5)$

Solving, $x = 25$, that is the age of elder son.

Thus, father's present age = $2 \times 25 = 50$ years.

(**NOTE:** The facts may be verified by the candidate to check the accuracy of answer, depending upon time available in the exam).

Thus, (a) is the correct answer.

45. **(b)**

The correct answer is 'It is made available to users.'

Open-source operating systems make their source code available to users, allowing them to access, modify, and distribute the software freely. This enables greater transparency, collaboration, and community involvement in the development of the operating system.

The incorrect options are

(a) Open-source code is not being owned or controlled solely by the company that developed it.

(c) While the open nature allows for community scrutiny and faster bug fixes, it can also mean vulnerabilities are more readily exposed.

(d) Now coming to the point – it uses less processing power. Performance depends on the specific code, features, and optimizations, not the licensing model.

Thus, (b) is the correct answer.

46. (a)

47. **(c)**

48. **(c)**

49. **(c)**

50. **(b)**

UGC NET Paper 1 August 2024

INSTRUCTIONS

Time Allowed: 1 hour — *50 × 2 = 100 Marks*

- This paper consists of Fifty (50) objective type questions of Two (2) marks each.
- All questions are compulsory.
- Each item has four alternative responses marked (a), (b), (c) and (d). You have to darken the circle as indicated below on the correct response against each item.
- Example: ⓐⓑ●ⓓ where (c) is the correct response.
- Your responses to the items are to be indicated in the OMR Sheet given at the end of the book.
- Read instructions provided with each question carefully.
- There are no negative marks for incorrect answers.

Read the passage carefully. The questions 1 to 5 are based on this paragraph.

The following table embodies the details about the profits (in Rupees Lakhs) earned by five Retail Stores A-E during the years 2018–2023. Based on the data in the table, answer the questions that follow.

Store-wise Details of Profit

Store	Profit (in ₹ Lakh) earned in the year					
	2018	2019	2020	2021	2022	2023
A.	12	18	24	21	15	30
B.	9	15	18	12	21	24
C.	27	33	24	21	30	36
D.	15	12	18	9	21	9
E.	18	21	15	15	12	24

Note: Profit = Income – Investment

1. Consider the percentage change in profit for the stores A, B, D and E for the pair of years {2018 and 2019}, {2018 and 2019}, {2018 and 2022} and {2018 and 2022}, respectively. Which store has maximum percentage change in profits for the pair of years mentioned?
   (a) A (b) B
   (c) D (d) E

2. Owner of store C invests ₹9 lakh in 2021. What should be the investment of D in the same year to get an income which is double than that of store C?
   (a) ₹51 lakh (b) ₹6 lakh
   (c) ₹50000 (d) ₹33 lakh

3. In the year 2019, to earn a profit of 20% by each of the stores C and E, what is the ratio of investments made by C to that of E?
   (a) 7:11 (b) 1:5
   (c) 5:1 (d) 11:7

4. The profit earned by Store A in 2023 is approximately ____________ % more than that in 2019.
   (a) 40 (b) 66.67
   (c) 266 (d) 33.33

5. What should be the income of store D in 2020, so that its profit per cent is 30%?

(a) ₹33 lakh (b) ₹42 lakh
(c) ₹60 lakh (d) ₹78 lakh

6. What cannot be held as the correct motive of Question-Answer technique in teaching?

(a) To test the knowledge
(b) To locate the difficulty
(c) To intimidate and hamper self-confidence
(d) To promote thinking and originality

7. A 200 m long train is travelling at a constant speed of 20 m/s. How long will it take to completely cross a 1000 m long railway platform?

(a) 1 minute
(b) 1.5 minute
(c) 2 minutes
(d) 2.5 minutes

8. If (L)M represents a number L in base-M number system, then which of the following equalities are true?

A. $(512.125)_{10} = (1000000000.001)_2$
B. $(512.125)_{10} = (1000.1)_8$
C. $(512.125)_{10} = (200.2)_{16}$
D. $(512.125)_{10} = (2000.02)_4$

Choose the correct answer from the options given below:

(a) A and B only
(b) A and C only
(c) B, C and D only
(d) A, B and C only

9. Match the List-I with List-II

	List – I (Kinds of Classroom Resources)		List – II (Description)
A.	Simple Resources	I.	Resources which are not easily bought, measured or adjusted, e.g., instructional approaches and teaching philosophies.
B.	Compound Resources	II.	Resources difficult to discern and measure and often embedded via web of relationships and practices, decision making, teacher accountability, etc.
C.	Complex Resources	III.	Physical object and can be directly bought, adjusted and measured e.g. text-books, blackboards and chalks, etc.
D.	Abstract Resources	IV.	Use of two or more than two resources such as class, size reduction and use of technology.

Choose the correct answer from the options given below:

(a) A-I, B-II, C-III, D-IV
(b) A-IV, B-III, C-II, D-I
(c) A-IV, B-III, C-I, D-II
(d) A-III, B-IV, C-II, D-I

10. Match the List-I with List-II

	List – I (Fallacy)		List – II (Description)
A.	Strawman	I.	When an arguer tries to side track his audience by raising an irrelevant issue and the claims that the original issue is settled.
B.	Red Herring	II.	When an arguer states or assumes as a premise the very thing he/she is trying to prove as a conclusion.
C.	Equivocation	III.	When arguer distorts an opponents claim to make it easier to attack.
D.	Begging the question	IV.	When a key word is used in two or more senses in the same argument.

Choose the correct answer from the options given below:

(a) A-IV, B-I, C-III, D-II
(b) A-II, B-III, C-IV, D-I
(c) A-I, B-II, C-IV, D-III
(d) A-III, B-I, C-IV, D-II

11. Match the List-I with List-II

List – I (Word)		List – II (Unique Code)	
A.	PRIME	I.	NPGKC
B.	SIGHT	II.	QGEFR
C.	QUITE	III.	OSGRC
D.	RHYME	IV.	PFWKC

Choose the **correct** answer from the options given below:

(a) A-I, B-II, C-III, D-IV
(b) A-II, B-III, C-IV, D-I
(c) A-III, B-IV, C-I, D-II
(d) A-IV, B-I, C-II, D-III

12. Which one of the following ancient sites in India is known from the oldest forms of human communication?

(a) Dholavira
(b) Bhimbetka
(c) Ropar
(d) Sinauli

13. Qualitative research is generally associated with-

(a) Inductive approach
(b) Deductive approach
(c) Positivism
(d) Objectivism

14. According to UGC Regulations 2018 on Plagiarism, a student will have to submit a revised thesis for which of the following similarities of thesis?

A. 12%
B. 27%
C. 46%
D. 66%
E. 70%

Choose the correct answer from the options given below:

(a) A, B and C only
(b) B, C and D only
(c) C, D and E only
(d) A and B only

15. Qualitative content analysis of documents relating to different time periods corresponds to which of the following research designs?

(a) Cross-sectional
(b) Longitudinal
(c) Case study
(d) Comparative

16. In ancient India, Ujjain was famous for the study of:

(a) Anthropology
(b) Astronomy
(c) Archaeology
(d) Geology

17. Which of the following is NOT a fallacy of Relevance?

(a) Ad Hominem (Personal Attack)
(b) Attacking the Motive
(c) Tu Quoque (Look who's talking)
(d) False Alternatives

18. A webpage displays the following information, in which underlined word is a link to another webpage.

For digital devices, the bandwidth is usually expressed in bits per second (bps). For analog devices, the bandwidth is expressed in Hertz (Hz).

Which method of data organization is being used?

(a) HTML
(b) Hypertext
(c) Storyboard
(d) Data Scheme

19. Which of the following are the correct definitions of communication?

A. Process of ideating, searching and telling.
B. Process of sending, receiving, and interpreting the message.
C. Communication is social interaction through messages.
D. Process of thinking, writing, and channelizing the messages.

Choose the correct answer from the options given below:

(a) A and B only
(b) A and C only
(c) B and D only
(d) B and C only

20. Arrange the datasets with the following pairs of mean ($\bar{x}$) and standard deviation (σ) in increasing order of their coefficient of variation:

A. $\bar{x} = 25, \sigma = 9$
B. $\bar{x} = 40, \sigma = 12$
C. $\bar{x} = 30, \sigma = 10$
D. $\bar{x} = 35, \sigma = 11$

Choose the correct answer from the options given below:

(a) A, B, C, D
(b) B, C, D, A
(c) A, C, D, B
(d) B, D, C, A

21. According to the NEP-2020, which is/are not under curriculum framework of adult education?

A. Critical Life Skills
B. Vocational Skills Development
C. Continuing Education
D. Art in Education
E. Basic Education

Choose the correct answer from the options given below:

(a) A only (b) B and C only
(c) D only (d) A, D and E only

22. Which of the following can be considered as the component of development of ability of critical and logical thinking?

A. To identify the problems
B. To analyze the problems
C. To establish subjective truths
D. To select relevant facts and principles
E. To draw inferences and conclusions

Choose the correct answer from the options given below:

(a) A and C only
(b) A, B and C only
(c) A, B and D only
(d) A, B, D and E only

23. Identify the numbers that occur in the series 0, 7, 26, 63, 124 ....

A. 344
B. 511
C. 215
D. 730

Choose the correct answer from the options given below:

(a) A and B only
(b) B and C only
(c) C and D only
(d) A and D only

24. Match the List-I with List-II

List – I (ICT Term)		List – II (Description)	
A.	Authentication	I.	Identifies which device is connected at a given IP address.
B.	Biometrics	II.	Relies on certain unique characteristics of human beings such as retina scans.
C.	IP Address	III.	Verifies that data comes from a secure and trusted source and works with encryption to strengthen internet security.
D.	MAC Address	IV.	Identifies where on the network a device in located.

Choose the correct answer from the options given below:

(a) A-I, B-II, C-IV, D-III
(b) A-III, B-II, C-IV, D-I
(c) A-II, B-III, C-I, D-IV
(d) A-IV, B-III, C-II, D-I

25. The Sanskrit Commission (1956–57) was headed by

(a) Sukumar Sen
(b) U.N. Dhebar
(c) Suniti Kumar Chatterji
(d) V.T. Krishnamachari

26. Indigenous Knowledge and Resource Management System is at best can be considered as

(a) Mitigation Response
(b) Adaptation Response
(c) Decarbonization Response
(d) Ethical Response

27. Which of the following agencies launched the "International Environmental Education Programme"?

(a) UNESCO
(b) UNEP
(c) IUCN
(d) GEF

28. Match the List-I with List-II

	List – I (Communication Term)		List – II (Examples)
A.	Formal Communication	I.	Religious discourses
B.	Informal Communication	II.	Questioning oneself after doing a mistake
C.	Group Communication	III.	Taking part in meeting
D.	Intra-personal Communication	IV.	Conservation in canteen

Choose the correct answer from the options given below:

(a) A-I, B-II, C-III, D-IV
(b) A-II, B-III, C-I, D-IV
(c) A-III, B-IV, C-I, D-II
(d) A-IV, B-I, C-II, D-III

29. A shopkeeper first increases the price of an item by 12% and then announces a discount of 20%. The actual discount on the original price is:

(a) 12.6% (b) 10.4%
(c) 14.2% (d) 12%

30. Without whom the communication process cannot be completed?

(a) Receiver
(b) Media
(c) Writer
(d) Expert

31. Arrange the following four stages of communication in a proper sequence:

A. Transmission
B. Encoding
C. Sender
D. Feedback

Choose the correct answer from the options given below:

(a) C, B, A, D
(b) B, A, C, D
(c) D, C, B, A
(d) A, B, C, D

32. In the light of Nyaya's Syllogism, which of the following are correct?

A. 'Sādhya' is the major term
B. 'Linga' is the minor term
C. 'Hetu' is the middle term
D. 'Paksa' is the minor term
E. 'Anumāna' is the inferential knowledge

Choose the correct answer from the options given below:

(a) A, B and C only
(b) A, C, D and E only
(c) B and D only
(d) B, D and E only

33. Arrange the following fractions in decreasing order.

A. $\frac{17}{21}$ B. $\frac{15}{19}$

C. $\frac{13}{16}$ D. $\frac{14}{17}$

Choose the correct answer from the options given below:

(a) D, C, B, A
(b) A, B, C, D
(c) C, D, B, A
(d) D, C, A, B

34. Match the List-I with List-II

	List – I (Sustainable Development Goals – SDG)		List – II (Goal Number)
A.	Zero Hunger	I.	SDG-13
B.	Sustainable Cities and Communities	II.	SDG-7
C.	Affordable and Clean Energy	III.	SDG-2
D.	Climate Action	IV.	SDG-11

Choose the correct answer from the options given below:

(a) A-III, B-IV, C-II, D-I
(b) A-I, B-II, C-IV, D-III
(c) A-II, B-III, C-I, D-IV
(d) A-IV, B-I, C-III, D-II

35. Cloudless night with low wind speed indicates:
(a) Turbulent Atmosphere
(b) Unstable Atmosphere
(c) Neutral Atmosphere
(d) Stable Atmosphere

36. What can be inferred correctly from the following?
"Science is based on experiment, on a willingness to challenge old dogma, on an openness to see the Universe as it really is. Accordingly, science sometimes requires courage at the very least the courage to question the conventional wisdom."

A. Premise: Science sometimes requires courage.
B. Premise: Science is based on experiment, as a willingness to see the universe as it really is.
C. It is merely an illustration.
D. Conclusion: Science sometimes requires courage.
E. Conclusion: Science is based on experiment, on a willingness to see the universe as it really is.

Choose the correct answer from the options given below:
(a) A, B and D only
(b) A and D only
(c) B and D only
(d) B, C and E only

37. Match the List-I with List-II

	List – I (Type of Variables)		List – II (Example)
A.	Nominal	I.	Anger level
B.	Ordinal	II.	Crop yield
C.	Interval	III.	Type of forest
D.	Ratio	IV.	Temperature in Fahrenheit

Choose the correct answer from the options given below:
(a) A-I, B-II, C-IV, D-III
(b) A-I, B-II, C-III, D-IV
(c) A-III, B-I, C-IV, D-II
(d) A-III, B-IV, C-I, D-II

38. In MS-EXCEL, a formula = B$1 + C$3 + 5 in cell D9 when copied to cell F12 will become:

Choose the correct answer from the options given below:
(a) = D1 + E3 + 5
(b) = B$2 + C$4 + 5
(c) = C$1 + D$3 + 5
(d) = D$1 + E$3 + 5

39. Arrange the following institutions according to their year of establishment (from earliest to the most recent)
A. National Council of Rural Institutes (NCRI)
B. Indian Council of Social Science Research (ICSSR)
C. Indian Institute of Advanced Study (IIAS)
D. Indian Council of Historical Research (ICHR)
E. Indian Council of Philosophical Research (ICPR)

Chose the correct answer from the options given below:
(a) A, B, C, D, E
(b) C, D, B, E, A
(c) B, E, A, C, D
(d) C, B, D, E, A

40. Match the List-I with List-II

	List – I (Myers Briggs Type Learner)		List – II (Indicator)
A.	Judging learners	I.	Depend on outside simulation and interaction for engaging in learning.
B.	Extrovert learners	II.	They choose to decide things impersonally based on analysis, self discipline, logic, prefer clear course and outcomes.
C.	The intuitors	III.	Concerned with knowing the essentials and take actions quickly, intolerant to ambiguity.
D.	The thinkers	IV.	Seek out patterns and relationships among the facts they gather inferences and guesses from context.

Choose the correct answer from the options given below:

(a) A-II, B-III, C-I, D-IV
(b) A-IV, B-I, C-III, D-II
(c) A-III, B-I, C-IV, D-II
(d) A-I, B-II, C-III, D-IV

41. Identify the correct logical sequence of the following four randomly-ordered sentences A–D about the discovery of Computer Mouse.

A. We use the mouse today because it is the pointing device that is easiest to use compared to others such as joysticks, trackballs, etc.
B. Doug Engelbart was bored at a conference and started thinking about tracking movement of a plane using two sets of wheels moving in orthogonal directions.
C. Doug Engelbart remembered these notes when he was trying to come up with a device to select objects on a computer screen.
D. Doug Engelbart tells the story of how he invented the mouse.

Choose the correct answer from the options given below:

(a) D, C, B, A
(b) A, B, C, D
(c) B, C, D, A
(d) D, B, C, A

42. Arrange the following Indian States in descending order according to their climate vulnerability. (Starting from most vulnerable to least vulnerable)

A. Uttar Pradesh
B. Jharkhand
C. Maharashtra
D. Manipur
E. Punjab

Choose the correct answer from the options given below:

(a) D, B, C, A, E
(b) C, E, A, D, B
(c) B, A, D, E, C
(d) A, E, B, C, D

43. The Acronym 'SWAYAM' represents:

(a) Scopus Web of Attentive Learning for Youth and Apt Minds
(b) Social Web of Agent Learning for Youth and Adult Minds
(c) Study Webs of Active Learning for Young Aspiring Minds
(d) Science Web of Aspirants and Young Active Minds

44. Observe the following argument and find the correct form:

'A' has characteristics of 'X' and 'Y'.
'B' has characteristics of 'X' and 'Y'.
'A' has a characteristics of 'Z'.
Therefore 'B' has the characteristics of 'Z'.

Choose the correct answer from the options given below:

(a) Statistical Argument
(b) An argument from Authority
(c) Mathematical Argument
(d) Argument from Analogy

45. Which among the following are the renewable energy resources?

A. Biodiesel
B. Nuclear Energy
C. Solar Energy
D. Hydroelectric Energy
E. Wind Energy

Choose the correct answer from the options given below:

(a) A, B, C, D only
(b) B, C, D, E only
(c) C, D, E, A only
(d) E, A, B only

Read the passage carefully. The questions 46 to 50 are based on this paragraph.

Stone carvings are other impressive pieces of visual art of Gujarat. The State is also a repository of numerous places of historical importance, which attract thousands of people from all over the world. The city Junagadh is adorned with beautiful shrines of Hindus, Jains and Muslims. In Junagarh caves, a huge boulder preserves to this day the fourteen rock edicts inscribed by Emperor Ashoka in the 3rd century BCE. Besides, one can also see here classic examples of rock cut architecture in the Chitya Halls and the sculpted pillars of the caves. Maru-Gurjara or Chalukyan style architecture can also be seen in the Sun Temple of Modhera. Similarly, one can see architecture belonging to the Chalukya (Solanki) period at Adalaj, a heritage site protected by the Archaeological Survey of India in the Gandhinagar district. Hence an interesting depiction of 'Ami Khumbor' (symbolic pot with water of life) and 'Kalp Vriksha' (tree of life) carved from a single block of stone present a marvellous example of the State's sculptural heritage.

Copper has been in use in Gujarat since the times of the Chalcolithic Age. Its traces are found in the ruins of the Indus Valley Civilization at Lothal and Dholavira, The town of Shihor is still continuing that glorious tradition of metal craft with its 'Kansa' (Bell metal) works especially pots and pitchers of various sizes.

46. Which style of architecture is seen in the Sun Temple of Modhera?
(a) Maru-Gurjara (b) Solanki
(c) Cholan (d) Khamboj

47. A heritage site, protected by ASI in Gandhinagar district is known as:
(a) Adalaj (b) Khumbor
(c) Dholevira (d) Shihor

48. How many edicts of Ashoka are preserved on a boulder inside the Junagarh caves?
(a) Ten (b) Twelve
(c) Fourteen (d) Thirteen

49. Junagarh is known for beautiful shrines of which of the following combination of religions?
(a) Hinduism, Buddhism, Christianity
(b) Christianity, Hinduism, Jainism
(c) Hinduism, Buddhism, Islam
(d) Islam, Hinduism, Jainism

50. Which one of the following places is not associated with either traces of copper or with copper works?
(a) Shihor (b) Lothal
(c) Dholevira (d) Modhera

ANSWER KEY

1. (b)	**2.** (d)	**3.** (d)	**4.** (b)	**5.** (c)	**6.** (c)	**7.** (a)	**8.** (d)	**9.** (d)	**10.** (d)
11. (a)	**12.** (b)	**13.** (a)	**14.** (b)	**15.** (b)	**16.** (b)	**17.** (d)	**18.** (b)	**19.** (d)	**20.** (d)
21. (c)	**22.** (d)	**23.** (a)	**24.** (b)	**25.** (c)	**26.** (b)	**27.** (a)	**28.** (c)	**29.** (b)	**30.** (a)
31. (a)	**32.** (c)	**33.** (d)	**34.** (a)	**35.** (d)	**36.** (d)	**37.** (c)	**38.** (d)	**39.** (d)	**40.** (a)
41. (c)	**42.** (a)	**43.** (c)	**44.** (d)	**45.** (c)	**46.** (a)	**47.** (a)	**48.** (c)	**49.** (d)	**50.** (d)

HINTS AND SOLUTIONS

1. **(b)**

The given data represents the profit earned by five retail stores A, B, C, D, and E from 2018 to 2023.

Percentage change in profit:

A: (18 – 12)/12 × 100 = 50%

B: (15 – 9)/9 × 100 = 66.67%

D: (9 – 15)/15 × 100 = –40%

E: (21 – 18)/18 × 100 = 16.67%

Thus, store B has the maximum percentage change in profits.

2. **(d)**

Investment for store D:

Profit of store C in 2021 = ₹21 lakh

Double the profit = ₹42 lakh

Investment of store D = 42 lakh – 9 lakh = ₹33 lakh

Thus, the investment for store D should be ₹33 lakh.

3. **(d)**

Ratio of investments for C and E in 2019:

Profit of store C in 2019 = ₹33 lakh

Investment of store C = 33 lakh / 1.2 = ₹27.5 lakh

Profit of store E in 2019 = ₹21 lakh

Investment of store E = 21 lakh / 1.2 = ₹17.5 lakh

Ratio of investments = 27.5 lakh :17.5 lakh
= ₹11:7

Thus, the ratio of investments made by C to that of E is 11:7.

4. **(b)** Percentage increase in profit for store A:

Profit increase = (30 lakh –18 lakh) / 18 lakh × 100 = 66.67%

Thus, the profit earned by Store A in 2023 is approximately 66.67% more than that in 2019.

5. **(c)**

Income of store D in 2020 for 30% profit:

Let the income of store D in 2020 be x.

Profit = ₹18 lakh (given)

Profit percentage = 30%

Therefore, ₹18 lakh = 30% of x

x = 18 lakh / 0.3 = 60 lakh

Thus, the income of store D in 2020 should be ₹60 lakh.

6. **(c)** Intimidating students or hampering their self-confidence is counterproductive and not a valid educational objective.

Let's look at different options:

- **Test knowledge:** Assess students' understanding of the subject matter. It is part of learning – how much learning has taken place. Usually, exam is conducted as per syllabus.
- **Locate difficulties:** It may be done with formative, summative assessments.
- **Promote thinking and originality:** Encourage students to think critically and creatively.

7. **(a)**

The train has to cover the two parts to cross over the platform in a complete manner:

Length of Platform + Length of Train
= 1000 m + 200 = 1200 m

Time = Distance / Speed = 1200 m / 20 m/s
= 60 seconds = 1 minute

The correct answer is (a).

8. **(d)**

Options A, B and C are true because the decimal number $(512.125)_{10}$ correctly converts to the following values in the respective bases:

- **A:** $(512.125)_{10} = (1000000000.001)_2$ in binary.
- **B:** $(512.125)_{10} = (1000.1)_8$ in octal.
- **C:** $(512.125)_{10} = (200.2)_{16}$ in hexadecimal.

These conversions match the corresponding representations in the different base systems.

9. **(d)**

Let's do the matching:

Matching List I with List II

	List-I (Kinds of Classroom Resources)		List-II (Description)
A.	Simple Resources	III.	Physical objects (textbooks, blackboards, chalks)
B.	Compound Resources	IV.	Combination of resources (class size reduction, technology)

C.	Complex Resources	II.	Difficult to measure, embedded in practices (relationships, decision-making)
D.	Abstract Resources	I.	Not easily bought, measured, or adjusted (instructional approaches, philosophies)

Thus, correct matching is A-III, B-IV, C-II, D-I.

10. (d)

Here is the correct matching of the fallacies with their descriptions:

A. **Strawman → III.** When an arguer distorts an opponent's claim to make it easier to attack.

B. **Red Herring → I.** When an arguer tries to sidetrack the audience by raising an irrelevant issue and claims the original issue is settled.

C. **Equivocation → IV.** When a keyword is used in two or more senses in the same argument.

D. **Begging the question → II.** When an arguer states or assumes as a premise the very thing they are trying to prove as a conclusion.

11. (a)

- **A-I:** PRIME – NPGKC
- **B-II:** SIGHT – QGEFR
- **C-III:** QUITE – OSGRC
- **D-IV:** RHYME – PFWKC

So, the correct answer is (a) A-I, B-II, C-III, D-IV.

12. (b)

Bhimbetka is 'Bhim + bhetka' that is sitting place of Bhim who is associated with 'Mahabharata'. Bhimbetka is known for its ancient rock paintings and cave art, which show how early humans communicated through visuals. They depict scenes of hunting, gathering, and religious rituals.

That was the period between Paleolithic (Old Stone Age) and Mesolithic period (Middle Stone Age).

- **Paleolithic** was a nomadic lifestyle, simple tools, and early artistic expressions.
- **Mesolithic** era shows a transition to semi-sedentary life, specialized tools, and greater adaptability to changing environments.

Other places:

- **Dholavira (Gujarat):** Advanced urban center of the Indus Valley Civilization that is also called as Harappan Civilization.
- **Ropar (Punjab):** An ancient Harappan site with evidence of later cultures.
- **Sinauli:** Late Harappan site, notable for burials and copper-bronze artifacts.

13. (a)

(a) **Inductive Approach:** Starts with specific observations and develops broader theories. Common in qualitative research.

(b) **Deductive Approach:** Begins with a general theory or hypothesis and tests it with specific data. Often used in quantitative research.

(c) **Positivism:** Focuses on objective observation and measurement of phenomena. More associated with quantitative methods.

(d) **Objectivism:** Believes reality exists independently of the observer. Recognizes the subjective nature of human experience in qualitative research.

14. (b)

According to UGC Regulations 2018 on Plagiarism, the levels of plagiarism and the corresponding actions are as follows:

- **Level 0:** Similarities up to 10% – Minor similarities, no penalty.
- **Level 1:** Similarities above 10% to 40% – The student will have to submit a revised thesis.
- **Level 2:** Similarities above 40% to 60% – The student will have to submit a revised thesis and may face other penalties.
- **Level 3:** Similarities above 60% – The student may face severe penalties, including cancellation of registration.

Based on these regulations, a student will have to submit a revised thesis for similarities of **27% (Level 1), 46% (Level 2),** and **66% (Level 3).**

Thus, the correct answer is (b) B, C and D only.

15. (b)

Longitudinal: This design examines the same subjects or documents over an extended period. It is appropriate for analyzing changes in content across different time periods. It is the most fitting answer.

(a) Cross-sectional focuses on one point in time.
(c) Case study analyzes specific instances in detail.
(d) Comparative looks at differences between groups rather than changes over time.

16. (b)

Ujjain is an ancient city in Madhya Pradesh, India. It is famous for its expertise in astronomical observatories. It is famous for Jantar Mantar that is a set of astronomical instruments built by Maharaja Jai Singh II in 18th century. It is famous for its contributions to mathematical studies also which actually became the base for astronomy.

17. (d)

What is 'Fallacy of Relevance': Errors where the argument is irrelevant to the issue. Here, attacking the person is more important than the issue itself.

(d) False Alternatives: A fallacy of presumption, not relevance, presenting limited choices when more exist.

(a) Ad Hominem (Personal Attack): Attacks the person instead of the argument.

(b) Attacking the Motive: Questions the motives rather than the argument.

(c) Tu Quoque: It basically focuses on 'Look who's talking'. It dismisses an argument by accusing the person of the same behaviour.

18. (b)

Hypertext is a method of linking to additional content via clickable text. The underlined "another webpage" in the text indicates such a link, which is a key feature of hypertext for non-linear navigation.

The correct answer is (b) Hypertext.

19. (d)

The correct answer is B and C only:

(B): Communication involves sending, receiving, and interpreting messages.

(C): It is social interaction through message exchange.

Options A and D focus on parts of communication but do not capture its full essence.

20. (d)

The coefficient of variation (CV) = $(\sigma/x) \times 100$.

A. CV = $(9/25) \times 100 = 36\%$
B. CV = $(12/40) \times 100 = 30\%$
C. CV = $(10/30) \times 100 = 33.33\%$
D. CV = $(11/35) \times 100 = 31.43\%$

The increasing order of their CV: B, D, C, A

Thus, (d) is the answer.

21. (c)

Following are the parts of the curriculum framework for adult education under NEP 2020.

A. Critical Life Skills,
B. Vocational Skills Development,
C. Continuing Education, and E. Basic Education are part of the curriculum framework for adult education under NEP 2020.
D. Art in Education is not listed under the framework of adult education, making it the correct option that does not fit.

22. (d)

A: Identify the problems: to define issues.

B: Analyze the problems: into smaller manageable parts for better understanding.

D: Select relevant facts and principles: appropriate information.

E: Draw inferences and conclusions: through logical deductions.

C: Establishing subjective truths is not part of critical and logical thinking. Truth is always objective.

23. (a)

0, 7, 26, 63, 124 ....

The series follows the pattern $n^3 - 1$, where n is a consecutive integer:

For $n = 1 : 1^3 - 1 = 0$
For $n = 2 : 2^3 - 1 = 7$
For $n = 3 : 3^3 - 1 = 26$
For $n = 4 : 4^3 - 1 = 63$
For $n = 5 : 5^3 - 1 = 124$

Continuing the pattern:

For $n = 7 : 7^3 - 1 = 344$
For $n = 8 : 8^3 - 1 = 511$

Thus, (a) is the correct answer.

24. (b)

A-III: Authentication – Verifies data source.

B-II: Biometrics – Identifies via unique human traits.

C-IV: IP Address – Locates device on the network.

D-I: MAC Address – Identifies connected device at IP.

The correct answer is (b) A-III, B-II, C-IV, D-I.

25. (c)

The Sanskrit Commission (1956–57) was chaired by Suniti Kumar Chatterji, a renowned linguist who promoted Sanskrit language and culture.

26. (b)

Adaptation Response: Indigenous Knowledge and Resource Management Systems (IKRMS) are developed by indigenous communities. IKRMS focus on sustainable resource management. They help adapt to environmental changes or say climate change impacts.

27. (a)

Let's look at their full forms first:

UNESCO: United Nations Educational, Scientific and Cultural Organization

UNEP: United Nations Environment Programme

IUCN: International Union for Conservation of Nature

GEF: Global Environment Facility

The International Environmental Education Programme (IEEP) was launched by UNESCO in collaboration with UNEP. Therefore, the correct answer is (a) UNESCO.

28. (c)

A-III: Formal Communication – Taking part in a meeting. This happens in a professional or official setting and follows established rules and protocols.

B-IV: Informal Communication – Conversation in a canteen. This is casual and relaxed communication, usually happening between friends, family, or colleagues.

C-I: Group Communication–Religious discourses. This is communication between multiple people, like in a team or group. An example is religious discourses.

D-II: Intra-personal Communication–Questioning oneself (self-talk) after making a mistake.

Thus, the correct answer is (c) A-III, B-IV, C-I, D-II.

29. (b)

Let's assume that the original price = ₹100

Increase in price = 12%

New increased price = 100 + 12 = ₹112

After applying 20% discount, the price = 112×0.8 = ₹89.6

The actual discount on original price = 100 – 89.6 = ₹10.4

Thus, the correct answer is (b) 10.4%.

30. (a)

Communication involves the sender, message, medium, and receiver. Without the receiver, the process can't be completed as there's no one to interpret the message. The receiver's role is crucial for providing feedback and closing the communication loop.

31. (a)

Sender(C): The process starts with the sender who has a message.

Encoding (B): The sender converts the message into a suitable form.

Transmission (A): The encoded message is sent through a chosen channel.

Feedback (D): The receiver decodes the message and provides feedback.

Thus, the correct answer is (a) C, B, A, D.

32. (c)

In Nyāya Syllogism, the term "linga" is not used. It is a logical concept that refers to the middle term or the reason for the inference.

The correct terms used in Nyāya Syllogism are:

- **Pakṣa (minor term):** The subject of the inference.
- **Hetu (middle term):** The reason or ground for the inference.
- **Sādhya (major term):** The conclusion or the thing to be inferred.
- **Anumāna (inference):** The process of drawing a conclusion based on the relationship between the pakṣa, hetu, and sādhya.

The correct answer is B and D, that is (c).

33. **(d)**

We can solve this question by comparing the fractions using one of the following methods:

Converting them into decimals for easy comparison.

Comparing the differences between numerators and denominators. If the differences are the same, the fraction with the larger numerator is the larger fraction.

Cross-multiplication to compare two fractions at a time. The fraction with the larger product is the larger fraction.

Compare $\frac{14}{17}$ (D) and $\frac{13}{16}$ (C):

Cross-multiply: $14 \times 16 = 224$ and $13 \times 17 = 221$.

Since $224 > 221$, $\frac{14}{17} > \frac{13}{16}$.

Compare $\frac{13}{16}$ (C) and $\frac{17}{21}$ (A):

Cross-multiply: $13 \times 21 = 273$ and $17 \times 16 = 272$.

Since $273 > 272$, $\frac{13}{16} > \frac{17}{21}$.

Compare $\frac{17}{21}$ (A) and $\frac{15}{19}$ (B):

Cross-multiply: $17 \times 19 = 323$ and $15 \times 21 = 315$.

Since $323 > 315$, $\frac{17}{21} > \frac{15}{19}$.

From the comparisons, the fractions in decreasing order are:

(D) $\left(\frac{14}{27}\right)$, C $\left(\frac{13}{26}\right)$, A $\left(\frac{17}{21}\right)$, B $\left(\frac{15}{19}\right)$.

Thus, the correct answer is (d).

34. **(a)**

We need to match SDGs with their corresponding goal numbers:

A. **Zero Hunger:** This is SDG-2.

B. **Sustainable Cities and Communities:** This is SDG-11.

C. **Affordable and Clean Energy:** This is SDG-7.

D. **Climate Action:** This is SDG-13.

Thus, the correct answer is (a) A-III, B-IV, C-II, D-I.

35. **(d)**

Stable Atmosphere: A cloudless night with low wind speed generally indicates a stable atmosphere. In such conditions, air masses are arranged in layers, with colder, denser air at the bottom and warmer, less dense air at the top. This stability prevents vertical movement, leading to clear skies and calm weather.

Thus, the correct answer is (d).

36. **(d)**

Premise (B): "Science is based on experiment, on a willingness to see the universe as it really is." This is a foundational statement supporting the argument.

Illustration (C): The passage provides an example to support the premise.

Conclusion (E): "Science sometimes requires courage." This is the conclusion drawn from the premises.

Therefore, options B, C, and E are correct. Option A is incorrect because "Science sometimes requires courage" is the conclusion, not a premise.

37. **(c)**

A. Nominal – III. Type of forest: Nominal variables categorize data without any order. "Type of forest" fits this category as it classifies forests into types without any inherent ranking.

B. Ordinal – I. Anger level: Ordinal variables have a clear, ordered relationship. "Anger level" can be ranked (e.g., low, medium, high).

C. Interval – IV. Temperature in Fahrenheit: Interval variables have ordered categories with equal intervals between them but no true zero point. "Temperature in Fahrenheit" is an example because the difference between temperatures is meaningful, but 0°F does not mean 'no temperature'.

D. Ratio – II. Crop yield: Ratio variables have all the properties of interval variables, plus a true zero point. "Crop yield" is a ratio variable because it can be measured from zero upwards, and the ratios are meaningful (e.g., twice the yield).

The correct answer is (C) A-III, B-I, C-IV, D-II.

38. **(d)**

The relative references will adjust based on the new position.

- **B$1:** The column B is relative, and the row 1 is absolute.
- **C$3:** The column C is relative, and the row 3 is absolute.

When moving from D9 to F12:

- The column reference for B will shift by 2 columns to the right, becoming D.
- The column reference for C will shift by 2 columns to the right, becoming E.
- The row references $1 and $3 remain unchanged.

So, the formula in F12 will be = D$1 + E$3 + 5.

Therefore, the correct answer is (d).

39. **(d)**

C. Indian Institute of Advanced Study (IIAS) - 1965 - This is the earliest one

B. Indian Council of Social Science Research (ICSSR) - 1969

D. Indian Council of Historical Research (ICHR) - 1972

E. Indian Council of Philosophical Research (ICPR) - 1977

A. National Council of Rural Institutes (NCRI) - 1995 - This is the latest one

Therefore, the correct answer is (d) C, B, D, E, A.

40. (a)

The breakdown of each Myers Briggs Type Learner and its corresponding indicator is as follows:

Judging learners (A): These learners prefer structure and organization. They like to make decisions and plan ahead.

Extrovert learners (B): These learners are energized by interacting with others and prefer group work.

The intuitors (C): These learners are focused on the big picture and prefer to explore possibilities and possibilities.

The thinkers (D): These learners are logical and analytical. They prefer to make decisions based on facts and evidence.

Therefore, the correct match is A-II, B-III, C-I, and D-IV.

41. (c)

The breakdown of the logical sequence is:

B: Doug Engelbart's initial idea for the mouse stemmed from his observations of a plane's movement using two sets of wheels.

C: This idea resurfaced when he sought a device to select objects on a computer screen.

D: Doug Engelbart shared the story of his invention, highlighting its origins.

A: The mouse's widespread adoption is attributed to its ease of use compared to other pointing devices.

The correct sequence is B, C, D and A thus, (c) is the answer.

42. (a)

Based on recent reports, the correct order of Indian states from most vulnerable to least vulnerable to climate change is D, B, C, A, E.

Manipur and Jharkhand are among the most vulnerable due to their geographical and socio-economic conditions. Punjab is the least vulnerable. Manipur is the most vulnerable state due to its geographical location and susceptibility to natural disasters like floods, earthquakes, and landslides.

43. **(c)**

SWAYAM (Study Webs of Active-Learning for Young Aspiring Minds) is an initiative by the Government of India designed to achieve the three cardinal principles of education policy, namely, access, equity, and quality. The objective is to provide the best teaching-learning resources to everyone, including the most disadvantaged.

44. (d)

Argument from Analogy: This type of argument compares two or more things that share similar characteristics. In the given example, 'A' and 'B' are compared based on their shared characteristics 'X' and ‘Y’. Since ‘A’ has the characteristic ‘Z’, the argument concludes that ‘B’ must also have the characteristic ‘Z’.

The other options are not applicable:

(a) Statistical Argument: This type of argument relies on statistical data to support a claim.

(b) Argument from Authority: This type of argument relies on the credibility of a source or expert.

(c) Mathematical Argument: This type of argument uses mathematical reasoning to prove a claim.

45. **(c)**

Renewable energy sources are natural resources that can be replenished at a faster rate than they are consumed. Examples include sunlight, wind, and water. These sources are constantly available and can be used to generate clean energy. On the other hand, non-renewable fossil fuels may take millions of years to form and have harmful emissions when burned.

A: Biodiesel: A renewable fuel made from vegetable oils or animal fats.

C: Solar Energy: Energy obtained from sunlight.

D: Hydroelectric Energy: Energy obtained from the flow of water.

E: Wind Energy: Energy obtained from the wind.

B: Nuclear Energy is not a renewable energy source because it relies on a finite resource (uranium) and produces radioactive waste.

The correct answer is: (c) C, D, E, A only.

46. (a)

47. **(a)**

48. **(c)**

49. **(d)**

50. **(d)**

and Y. Since X has the characteristic Z, the argument concludes that Y must also have the characteristic Z.

The other options are not applicable:

(a) **Statistical Argument**: This type of argument relies on statistical data to support a claim.

(b) **Argument from Authority**: This type of argument relies on the credibility of a source or expertise.

(c) **Mathematical Argument**: This type of argument uses mathematical reasoning to prove a claim.

45. (d)

Renewable energy sources are natural resources that can be replenished at a faster rate than they are consumed. Examples include sunlight, wind, and water. These sources are constantly available and can be used to generate clean energy. On the other hand, non-renewable fossil fuels may take millions of years to form and have harmful emissions when burned.

A: **Biodiesel**: A renewable fuel made from vegetable oils or animal fats.

C: **Solar Energy**: Energy obtained from sunlight.

D: **Hydroelectric Energy**: Energy obtained from the flow of water.

E: **Wind Energy**: Energy obtained from the wind.

B: **Nuclear Energy** is not a renewable energy source because it relies on a finite resource (uranium) and produces radioactive waste.

The correct answer is A, C, D, E Only.

46. (a)

47. (a)

48. (c)

49. (d)

50. (d)

CHAPTER

1

Teaching Aptitude

TOPICS OF IMPORTANCE

- Education: Basic Elements
- Teaching: Concept, Objectives, Levels of Teaching (Memory, Understanding and Reflective), Characteristics and Basic Requirements.
- Learner's Characteristics: Characteristics of Adolescent and Adult Learners (Academic, Social, Emotional and Cognitive), Individual Differences.
- Factors Affecting Teaching Related to: Teacher, Learner, Support Material, Instructional Facilities, Learning Environment and Institution.
- Methods of Teaching in Institutions of Higher Learning: Teacher-Centred vs. Learner-Centred Methods; Off-line vs. Online Methods (Swayam, Swayamprabha, MOOCs, etc.).
- Teaching Support System: Traditional, Modern and ICT Based.
- Evaluation Systems: Elements and Types of Evaluation, Evaluation in Choice Based Credit System in Higher Education, Computer Based Testing, Innovations in Evaluation Systems.

1. Which one of the following is considered a sign of motivated teaching? **[Jun 2014]**
(a) Students asking questions.
(b) Maximum attendance of the students.
(c) Pin drop silence in the classroom.
(d) Students taking notes.

2. Which one of the following is the best method of teaching? **[Jun 2014]**
(a) Lecture (b) Discussion
(c) Demonstration (d) Narration

3. Classroom communication is normally considered as **[Jun 2014]**
(a) Effective (b) Cognitive
(c) Affective (d) Selective

4. Identify the category of evaluation that assesses the learning progress to provide continuous feedback to the students during instruction. **[Jun 2014]**
(a) Placement (b) Diagnostic
(c) Formative (d) Summative

5. Dyslexia is associated with **[Jun 2014]**
(a) Mental disorder (b) Behavioural disorder
(c) Reading disorder (d) Writing disorder

6. A smart classroom is a teaching space which has **[Dec 2014]**
(i) Smart portion with a touch panel control system.
(ii) PC/Laptop connection and DVD/VCR player.
(iii) Document camera and specialized software.
(iv) Projector and screen.

Select the correct answer from the codes given below.
(a) (i) and (ii) only
(b) (ii) and (iv) only

(c) (i), (ii) and (iii) only
(d) (i), (ii), (iii) and (iv)

7. MOOC stands for [Dec 2014]
(a) Media Online Open Course
(b) Massachusetts Open Online Course
(c) Massive Open Online Course
(d) Myrind Open Online Course

8. 'Education is the manifestation of perfection already in man' was stated by [Dec 2014]
(a) M. K. Gandhi
(b) R. N. Tagore
(c) Swami Vivekanand
(d) Sri Aurobindo

9. Which of the following is not a prescribed level of teaching? [Dec 2014]
(a) Memory (b) Understanding
(c) Reflective (d) Differentiation

10. Maximum participation of students during teaching is possible through [Dec 2014]
(a) Lecture method
(b) Demonstration method
(c) Inductive method
(d) Textbook method

11. Diagnostic evaluation ascertains [Dec 2014]
(a) Students performance at the beginning of instructions.
(b) Learning progress and failures during instructions.
(c) Degree of achievement of instructions at the end.
(d) Causes and remedies of persistent learning problems during instructions.

12. Instructional aids are used by the teacher to [Dec 2014]
(a) Glorify the class (b) Attract the students
(c) Clarify the concepts (d) Ensure discipline

13. The attitude of the teacher that affects teaching pertains to [Dec 2014]
(a) Affective domain
(b) Cognitive domain
(c) Connative domain
(d) Psychomotor domain

14. When academicians are called to deliver lecture or presentation to an audience on certain topics or a set of topics of educational nature, it is called [Dec 2014]
(a) Training program (b) Seminar
(c) Workshop (d) Symposium

15. Which of the following is the highest level of cognitive ability? [Jun 2015]
(a) Knowing (b) Understanding
(c) Analysing (d) Evaluating

16. Which of the following factors does not impact teaching? [Jun 2015]
(a) Teacher's knowledge.
(b) Class room activities that encourage learning.
(c) Socio-economic background of teachers and students.
(d) Learning through experience.

17. Which of the following statements about teaching aids are correct? [Jun 2015]
(i) They help in retaining concepts for longer duration.
(ii) They help students learn better.
(iii) They make teaching learning process interesting.
(iv) They enhance rote learning.

Select the correct answer from the codes given below:
(a) (i), (ii), (iii) and (iv)
(b) (i), (ii) and (iii)
(c) (ii), (iii) and (iv)
(d) (i), (ii) and (iv)

18. Techniques used by a teacher to teach include [Jun 2015]
(i) Lecture
(ii) Interactive lecture
(iii) Group work
(iv) Self study

Select the correct answer from the codes given below:
(a) (i), (ii) and (iii) (b) (i), (ii), (iii) and (iv)
(c) (ii), (iii) and (iv) (d) (i), (ii) and (iv)

19. Achievement tests are commonly used for the purpose of [Jun 2015]
(a) Making selections for a specific job.
(b) Selecting candidates for a course.
(c) Identifying strengths and weaknesses of learners.
(d) Assessing the amount of learning after teaching.

20. A good teacher is one who **[Jun 2015]**
(a) Gives useful information.
(b) Explains concepts and principles.
(c) Gives printed notes to students.
(d) Inspires students to learn.

21. Greater the handicap of the students coming to the educational institutions, greater the demand on the **[Dec 2015]**
(a) Family (b) Society
(c) Teacher (d) State

22. What are the characteristics of continuous and comprehensive evaluation? **[Dec 2015]**
(i) It increases the workload on students by taking multiple tests.
(ii) It replaces marks with grades.
(iii) It evaluates every aspect of the student.
(iv) It helps in reducing examination phobia.

Select the correct answer from the codes given below:
(a) (i), (ii), (iii) and (iv) (b) (ii) and (iv)
(c) (i), (ii) and (iii) (d) (ii), (iii) and (iv)

23. Which of the following attributes denote great strengths of a teacher? **[Dec 2015]**
(i) Full-time active involvement in the institutional management.
(ii) Setting examples.
(iii) Willingness to put assumptions to the test.
(iv) Acknowledging mistakes.

Select the correct answer from the codes given below.
(a) (i), (ii) and (iv)
(b) (ii), (iii) and (iv)
(c) (i), (iii) and (iv)
(d) (i), (ii), (iii) and (iv)

24. Which one of the following statements is correct in the context of multiple-choice type questions? **[Dec 2015]**
(a) They are more objective than true–false type questions.
(b) They are less objective than essay type questions.
(c) They are more subjective than short answer type questions.
(d) They are more subjective than true–false type questions.

25. As Chairman of an independent commission on education, Jacques Delors' report to UNESCO was titled **[Dec 2015]**
(a) International Commission on Education Report
(b) Millennium Development Report
(c) Learning : The Treasure Within
(d) World Declaration on Education for All

26. What is required for good teaching? **[Dec 2015]**
(i) Diagnosis (ii) Remedy
(iii) Direction (iv) Feedback

Select the correct answer from the codes given below:
(a) (i), (ii), (iii) and (iv)
(b) (i) and (ii)
(c) (ii), (iii) and (iv)
(d) (iii) and (iv)

27. The main objectives of student evaluation of teachers are **[Dec 2015]**
(i) To gather information about student weaknesses.
(ii) To make teachers take teaching seriously.
(iii) To help teachers adopt innovative methods of teaching.
(iv) To identify the areas of further improvement in teacher traits.

Identify the correct answer from the codes given below.
(a) (i) and (ii) only
(b) (ii), (iii) and (iv) only
(c) (i), (ii) and (iii) only
(d) (i) only

28. Using the central point of the classroom communication as the beginning of a dynamic pattern of ideas is referred to as **[Dec 2015]**
(a) Systemization (b) Problem-orientation
(c) Idea protocol (d) Mind mapping

29. A college-level assistant professor has planned his/her lectures with an intent to develop cognitive dimensions of students centred on skills of analysis and synthesis. Below, given are two sets of items, Set–I consisting of levels of cognitive interchange and Set–II comprising basic requirements for promoting them. Match the two sets and indicate your answer by choosing the correct alternative from the codes given below. **[Jul 2016]**

	Set–I (Levels of cognitive interchange)		Set–II (Basic requirements for promoting cognitive interchange)
A.	Memory level	I.	Giving opportunity for discriminating examples and non-examples of a point.
B.	Understanding level	II.	Recording the important points made during the presentations.
C.	Reflective level	III.	Asking the students to discuss various items of information.
		IV.	Critically analysing the points to be made and discussed.

Codes:

	A	B	C
(a)	II	IV	I
(b)	III	IV	II
(c)	II	I	IV
(d)	I	II	III

30. Which set of learner characteristics may be considered helpful in designing effective teaching–learning systems? Select the correct alternative from the codes given below. **[Jul 2016]**

(A) Prior experience of learners in respect of the subject.

(B) Interpersonal relationships of learner's family friends.

(C) Ability of the learners in respect of the subject.

(D) Student's language background.

(E) Interest of students in following the prescribed dress code.

(F) Motivational-orientation of the students.

Codes:

(a) (A), (B), (C) and (D)

(b) (A), (C), (D) and (F)

(c) (B), (C), (D) and (E)

(d) (C), (D), (E) and (F)

31. *Assertion (A):* The purpose of higher education is to promote critical and creative thinking abilities among students.

Reason (R): These abilities ensure job placements.

Choose the correct answer from the following code. **[Jul 2016]**

(a) Both (A) and (R) are true and (R) is the correct explanation of (A).

(b) Both (A) and (R) are true but (R) is not the correct explanation of (A).

(c) (A) is true but (R) is false.

(d) (A) is false but (R) is true.

32. Match the items of the first set with that of the second set in respect of evaluation system. **[Jul 2016]**

Choose the correct code.

	Set–I		Set–II
A.	Formative evaluation	I.	Evaluating cognitive and co-cognitive aspects with regularity.
B.	Summative evaluation	II.	Tests and their interpretations based on a group and certain yardsticks.
C.	Continuous and comprehensive evaluation	III.	Grading the final learning outcomes.
D.	Norm and criterion referenced tests	IV.	Quizzes and discussions.

Codes:

	A	B	C	D
(a)	IV	III	I	II
(b)	I	II	III	IV
(c)	III	IV	II	I
(d)	I	III	IV	II

33. Select the alternative which consists of positive factors contributing to effectiveness of teaching. **[Jul 2016]**

List of factors:
(A) Teacher's knowledge of the subject.
(B) Teacher's socio-economic background.
(C) Communication skill of the teacher.
(D) Teacher's ability to please the students.
(E) Teacher's personal contact with students.
(F) Teacher's competence in managing and monitoring the classroom transactions.

Codes:
(a) (B), (C) and (D) (b) (C), (D) and (F)
(c) (B), (D) and (E) (d) (A), (C) and (F)

34. The use of teaching aids is justified on the grounds of **[Jul 2016]**
(a) Attracting students' attention in the classroom.
(b) Minimising indiscipline problems in the classroom.
(c) Optimizing learning outcomes of students.
(d) Effective engagement of students in learning tasks.

35. As a teacher, select the best option to ensure your effective presence in the classroom. **[Jul 2016]**
(a) Use of peer command.
(b) Making aggressive statements.
(c) Adoption of well-established posture.
(d) Being authoritarian.

36. Which of the following set of statements represents acceptable propositions with respect to teaching–learning relationships? Choose the correct code to indicate your answer. **[Jan 2017]**
(i) When students fail in a test, it is the teacher who fails.
(ii) Every teaching must aim at ensuring learning.
(iii) There can be teaching without learning taking place.
(iv) There can be no learning without teaching.
(v) A teacher teaches but learns also.
(vi) Real learning implies rote learning.

Codes:
(a) (ii), (iii), (iv), and (v)
(b) (i), (ii), (iii), and (v)
(c) (iii), (iv), (v), and (vi)
(d) (i), (ii), (v), and (vi)

37. *Assertion (A):* Learning is a lifelong process.
Reason (R): Learning to be useful must be linked with life processes. **[Jan 2017]**

Choose the correct answer from the following code.
(a) Both (A) and (R) are true and (R) is the correct explanation of (A).
(b) Both (A) and (R) are true, but (R) is not the correct explanation of (A).
(c) (A) is true, but (R) is false.
(d) (A) is false, but (R) is true.

38. Effectiveness of teaching has to be judged in terms of **[Jan 2017]**
(a) Course coverage.
(b) Students' interest.
(c) Learning outcomes of students.
(d) Use of teaching aids in the classroom.

39. In which teaching method, the learner's participation is made optimal and proactive? **[Jan 2017]**
(a) Discussion method
(b) Buzz session method
(c) Brainstorming session method
(d) Project method

40. One of the most powerful factors affecting teaching effectiveness is related to the **[Jan 2017]**
(a) Social system of the country.
(b) Economic status of the society.
(c) Prevailing political system.
(d) Educational system.

41. *Assertion (A):* Formative evaluation tends to accelerate the pace of learning.
Reason (R): As against summative evaluation, formative evaluation is highly reliable. **[Jan 2017]**

Choose the correct answer from the following code.
(a) Both (A) and (R) are true and (R) is the correct explanation of (A).
(b) Both (A) and (R) are true, but (R) is not the correct explanation of (A).
(c) (A) is true, but (R) is false.
(d) (A) is false, but (R) is true.

42. Which of the following set of statements best represents the nature and objective of teaching and learning? **[Nov 2017]**
(A) Teaching is like selling and learning is like buying.
(B) Teaching is a social act while learning is a personal act.

(C) Teaching implies learning whereas learning does not imply teaching.

(D) Teaching is a kind of delivery of knowledge while learning is like receiving it.

(E) Teaching is an interaction and is triadic in nature, whereas learning is an active engagement in a subject domain.

Codes:

(a) (A), (D) and (E) (b) (B), (C) and (E)

(c) (A), (B) and (C) (d) (A), (B) and (D)

43. From the list given below identify the learner characteristics which would facilitate teaching-learning system to become effective. Choose the correct code to indicate your answer. **[Nov 2017]**

(A) Prior experience of learner

(B) Learner's family lineage

(C) Aptitude of the learner

(D) Learner's stage of development

(E) Learner's food habits and hobbies

(F) Learner's religious affiliation

Codes:

(a) (A), (C) and (D) (b) (D), (E) and (F)

(c) (A), (D) and (E) (d) (B), (C) and (F)

44. *Assertion (A):* All teaching implies learning.

Reason (R): Learning to be useful must be derived from teaching. **[Nov 2017]**

Choose the correct answer from the following.

(a) Both (A) and (R) are true, and (R) is the correct explanation of (A).

(b) Both (A) and (R) are true, but (R) is not the correct explanation of (A).

(c) (A) is true, but (R) is false.

(d) (A) is false, but (R) is true.

45. On the basis of summative tests, a teacher is interpreting his/her students, performance in terms of their wellness life style evident in behaviour. This will be called **[Nov 2017]**

(a) Formative testing

(b) Continuous and comprehensive evaluation

(c) Norm-referenced testing

(d) Criterion-referenced testing

46. Which one of the following is a key behaviour in effective teaching? **[Nov 2017]**

(a) Using student ideas and contribution

(b) Structuring

(c) Instructional variety

(d) Questioning

47. It is truism to say that no one was there when life first appeared on earth. Any assertion about life's origin, thus, should be treated as a theory. **[Nov 2017]**

The above two statements constitute:

(a) A historical explanation

(b) A narrative

(c) An argument

(d) A conjecture

48. In which of the following arrangements a wider spectrum of ideas and issues may be made possible? **[Nov 2017]**

(a) Research article (b) Workshop mode

(c) Conference (d) Symposium

49. The interaction between a teacher and students creates a zone of proximal **[Nov 2017]**

(a) Difference (b) Confusion

(c) Development (d) Distortion

50. Which of the following set of statements best describes the nature and objectives of teaching? **[Jul 2018]**

(A) Teaching and learning are integrally related.

(B) There is no difference between teaching and training.

(C) Concern of all teaching is to ensure some kind of transformation in students.

(D) All good teaching is formal in nature.

(E) A teacher is a senior person.

(F) Teaching is a social act whereas learning is a personal act.

Select the correct answer from the codes given below:

(a) (A), (B) and (D) (b) (B), (C) and (E)

(c) (A), (C) and (F) (d) (D), (E) and (F)

51. Which of the following learner characteristics is highly related to effectiveness of teaching? **[Jul 2018]**

(a) Prior experience of the learner.

(b) Educational status of the parents and the learner.

(c) Peer groups of the learner.

(d) Family size from which the learner comes.

52. In the two sets given below, Set–I indicates the methods of teaching while Set–II provides the basic requirements for success/effectiveness. Match the two sets and indicate your answer by choosing from the code. **[Jul 2018]**

Set–I (Method of teaching)		Set–II (Basic requirements for success/effectiveness)	
(A)	Lecturing	(i)	Small step presentation with feedback provided.
(B)	Discussion in groups	(ii)	Production of large number of ideas.
(C)	Brainstorming	(iii)	Content delivery in a lucid language.
(D)	Programmed instructional procedure	(iv)	Use of teaching aids.
		(v)	Theme-based interaction among participants.

	(A)	(B)	(C)	(D)
(a)	(i)	(ii)	(iii)	(iv)
(b)	(ii)	(iii)	(iv)	(v)
(c)	(iii)	(v)	(ii)	(i)
(d)	(iv)	(ii)	(i)	(iii)

53. From the list of evaluation procedures given below identify those which will be called 'formative evaluation'. **[Jul 2018]**

Indicate your answer by choosing from the code.

(A) A teacher awards grades to students after having transacted the course work.

(B) During interaction with students in the classroom, the teacher provides corrective feedback.

(C) The teacher gives marks to students on a unit test.

(D) The teacher clarifies to doubts of students in the class itself.

(E) The overall performance of a student is reported to parents at every three months interval.

(F) The learner's motivation is raised by the teacher through a question-answer session.

Select the correct answer from the codes given below:

(a) (A), (B) and (C) (b) (B), (C) and (D)
(c) (A), (C) and (E) (d) (B), (D) and (F)

54 *Assertion (A):* All teaching should aim at ensuring learning.
Reason (R): All learning results from teaching. **[Jul 2018]**

Choose the correct answer from the following codes.

(a) Both (A) and (R) are true, and (R) is the correct explanation of (A).
(b) Both (A) and (R) are true, but (R) is not the correct explanation of (A).
(c) (A) is true, but (R) is false.
(d) (A) is false, but (R) is true.

55. In which of the following activities, potential for nurturing creative and critical thinking is relatively greater? **[Jul 2018]**

(a) Preparing research summary.
(b) Presenting a seminar paper.
(c) Participation in research conference.
(d) Participation in a workshop.

56. Which among the following is a cognitive characteristic of learner? **[Dec 2018]**

(a) Sensory perception
(b) Belief
(c) Academic self-concept
(d) Level of visual literacy

57. As a teacher you wish to predict the capacity and potential success in your subject. Your main purpose is to predict or to identify individuals who have the greatest potential for development along special lines or who are likely to profit most by special training. Which test you would apply to accomplish that? **[Dec 2018]**

(a) Aptitude test (b) Intelligence test
(c) Personality test (d) Prognostic test

58. According to Jean Piaget, there are ______ stages of cognitive development. **[Dec 2018]**

(a) 2 (b) 4
(c) 6 (d) 8

59. John Dewey explained school as a/an ______ institution and education as a ______ process. **[Dec 2018]**

(a) Social, philosophical
(b) Social, social
(c) Economical, philosophical
(d) Environmental, psychological

60. Who among the following proposed the theory of 'Multiple Intelligences'? **[Dec 2018]**

(a) Sigmund Freud (b) Howard Gardner
(c) Albert Einstein (d) Jean Piaget

61. Computer-assisted language learning is called **[Dec 2018]**

(a) Aided learning
(b) Communicative call
(c) Language logic
(d) Electronic mediation

62. Which among the following best describes emotional intelligence as a learner characteristic? **[Dec 2018]**

(i) Recognize their own and other people's emotions.
(ii) Expressing their emotions strongly.
(iii) Use emotional information to guide thinking and behaviour.
(iv) Good observation, scientific drinking and deductive reasoning.
(v) Adjusting emotions to adapt to environments.
(vi) Being creative and open to diverse viewpoints.

Options:

(a) (iii), (v) and (vi) (b) (i), (iv) and (vi)
(c) (i), (iii) and (v) (d) (ii), (iv) and (v)

63. In a school, in which there are large number of failures, you may like to develop test for eliminating those who are likely to have substantial difficulties in meeting the academic goals of teaching. For this you need to develop test which should be able to predict the individual's ability or readiness to undertake the study of a school subject successfully. What is the name of such tests? **[Dec 2018]**

(a) Prognostic tests (b) Attitude tests
(c) Achievement tests (d) Analytical tests

64. The goal of formative assessment is to **[Dec 2018]**

(a) Promote student to next level.
(b) Form a group of students on the basis of their learning.
(c) Compare student learning against a standard or benchmark.
(d) Monitor student learning to provide ongoing feedback.

65. In a research setting, participants may act differently because they think they are getting special attention. This reaction of treatment group to the special attention rather than the treatment itself is known as **[Dec 2018]**

(a) Jung effect (b) Hawthorne effect
(c) Attention deficit (d) Markov effect

66. Which among the following can best be used as an asynchronous teaching aid? **[Dec 2018]**

(i) Skype
(ii) Blog
(iii) Facebook post
(iv) Online chat
(v) Email
(vi) Google Hangout

Options:

(a) (i), (iii) and (vi) (b) (iii), (v) and (vi)
(c) (i), (ii) and (iii) (d) (ii), (iii) and (v)

67. In teaching learning context, the results of an evaluation are useful to teachers in various ways. Which among the following is most important use for a teacher? **[Dec 2018]**

(a) To decide placement of students in other institutions.
(b) Planning instruction and knowing the effectiveness of the teaching strategies used by them.
(c) Getting information about student's study interests.
(d) To identify home influence on students.

68. Match the following. **[Dec 2018]**

Set–I	Set–II
(A) Swayam Prabha	(i) FM education radio network.
(B) GIAN (Global Institute of Academic Network)	(ii) Internet audio counselling service.
(C) Gyan Vani	(iii) Free DTH channel for education.
(D) Gyan Darshan	(iv) Talent pool of scientists and entrepreneurs for engagement with Indian higher education institution.
(E) Gyandhara	(v) Educational Television Channel

Code:

	(A)	(B)	(C)	(D)	(E)
(a)	(i)	(ii)	(v)	(iv)	(iii)
(b)	(ii)	(iii)	(iv)	(i)	(v)

(c) (iii) (iv) (i) (v) (ii)
(d) (v) (iii) (ii) (iv) (i)

69. In classroom communication, analogies are considered as **[Dec 2018]**
(a) Supporting evidence
(b) Unwanted information
(c) Control devices
(d) Attention-breakers

70. The field of study which uses role playing, simulation and self-evaluation as strategies for adult learners is known as **[Jun 2019]**
(a) Pedagogy (b) Andragogy
(c) Anthropology (d) Psychology

71. 'Cone of Experience' related to reaching-learning was suggested by **[Jun 2019]**
(a) John Dewey (b) Kilpatrick
(c) Froebel (d) Edgar Dale

72. Which of the following is a social characteristic of a learner? **[Jun 2019]**
(a) Power of sensory perception
(b) Thinking ability
(c) Power of synthetic imagination
(d) Ability to relate oneself with others

73. Which is the characteristic of formative evaluation? **[Jun 2019]**
(a) Evaluation occurs at the terminal point
(b) Evaluation is used before programme design
(c) Evaluation relates to indicating learning outcome of teaching
(d) Evaluation is conducted during teaching

74. Which among the following is a non-cognitive characteristic of learner? **[Jun 2019]**
(a) Recalling
(b) Problem solving
(c) Identifying important sensory inputs
(d) Believing what is true

75. SWAYAM refers to **[Jun 2019]**
(a) Study World of Action-Learning for Young Aspiring Minds
(b) Study Webs of Active-Learning for Young Aspiring Minds
(c) Student World of Action-Learning for Young Ailing Minds
(d) Study Web of Active-Learning for Youth Awareness Models

76. What is the main objective of formative evaluation? **[Jun 2019]**
(a) To promote students to the next class
(b) To enhance students learning
(c) To enhance co-operation in class
(d) To understand the learning difficulties

77. Student-centric classroom is meant for **[Jun 2019]**
(a) Addressing the individual differences
(b) Reducing teacher-oriented lectures
(c) Recalling the previous knowledge
(d) Engaging the entire class

78. A teacher intends to find out the learning difficulties of students. Which of the following tests can be used? **[Jun 2019]**
(a) Summative test (b) Formative test
(c) Performance test (d) Diagnostic test

79. The following teaching aids can be used by a teacher in the classroom as a live interactive device: **[Jun 2019]**
(i) E-mail (ii) Skype
(iii) Online chat (iv) Tele-conferencing
(v) Facebook (vi) Blog
Select your answer from the options given below:
(a) (i), (ii) and (iii) (b) (ii), (iii) and (iv)
(c) (iii), (v) and (vi) (d) (i), (ii) and (iv)

80. Below are given two Columns. Column-A presents the methods of teaching and Column-B presents the focus of a method. Match the two Columns. **[Jun 2019]**

Column-A (Methods of Teaching)	Column-B (Focus of a Method)
(A) Collaborative Method	(i) When expertise of teachers are used in teaching
(B) Cooperative Method	(ii) When emphasis is given on students as creator of knowledge
(C) Constructivist Method	(iii) When students share different aspects of a learning activity
(D) Team Teaching	(iv) When students help each other to learn

Select your answer from the options given below :

	(A)	(B)	(C)	(D)
(a)	(i)	(ii)	(iii)	(iv)
(b)	(iii)	(iv)	(ii)	(i)
(c)	(iv)	(iii)	(ii)	(i)
(d)	(ii)	(iv)	(iii)	(i)

81. Below is given a list of teaching methods and approaches. Which among them are individualized approach? **[Jun 2019]**

(A) Demonstration method
(B) Modular approach based teaching
(C) Programmed learning
(D) Personalized teaching
(E) Collaborative method

Select your answer from the options given below:

(a) (A), (B) and (C)
(b) (B), (C) and (D)
(c) (C), (D) and (E)
(d) (A), (D) and (E)

82. As per the cognitive development theory of Jean Piaget, adolescent students are in which stage of development? **[Jun 2019]**

(a) Sensory motor stage
(b) Concrete operational stage
(c) Operational stage
(d) Formal operational stage

83. Which of the following statements best explains the concept of team teaching? **[Jun 2019]**

(a) More than two teachers teach
(b) More than two teachers plan and teach together the same class
(c) More than two teachers plan and teach the same class as per their expertise
(d) A team of teachers who are ready and available to teach the students

84. Which among the following bases can be counted to judge the effectiveness of teaching? **[Jun 2019]**

(A) Marks obtained by students in overall subjects
(B) Level of realization of instructional objectives
(C) Time taken by the students to learn
(D) Resources used by the teacher in teaching
(E) Regularity of students in class

Select your answer from the options given below:

(a) (A), (B) and (C) (b) (A), (B) and (D)
(c) (C), (D) and (E) (d) (B), (C) and (D)

85. Think aloud procedure is **[Jun 2019]**

(a) A part of secondary source of data
(b) A technique used to investigate learner strategies and performance
(c) A strategy of testing learner's aptitude by providing primary sources
(d) A necessary method in scientific research

86. Which teaching aids enhance the skills like reading, listening and pronunciation? **[Jun 2019]**

(a) Audio-lingual teaching aids
(b) Scientific teaching aids
(c) General knowledge teaching aids
(d) Theoretical based teaching aids

87. In the two sets given below, Set–I provides the different level according to Bloom's Taxonomy, while Set–II gives their example and concerns. Match the two sets and select from the options to indicate your answer: **[Jun 2019]**

Set–I (Level of Learning)	Set–II (Examples)
(A) Memory level	(i) Identifying examples of a given concept
(B) Understanding level	(ii) Generating new ideas
(C) Analysing level	(iii) Recalling information
(D) Creating level	(iv) Isolating information into parts

Option:

	(A)	(B)	(C)	(D)
(a)	(ii)	(i)	(iii)	(iv)
(b)	(i)	(ii)	(iii)	(iv)
(c)	(iv)	(iii)	(i)	(ii)
(d)	(iii)	(i)	(iv)	(ii)

88. Diagnostic evaluation ascertains **[Jun 2019]**

(a) Students performance at the beginning of instructions
(b) Cause and remedies of persistent learning problems during instructions

(c) Degree of achievement of instructional objectives at the end
(d) Learning progress and failure after instructions

89. From the list given below identify the instructional events which form part of the structure of a lesson plan. Select your answer from the options given below the list: **[Jun 2019]**

List of instructional events:
(i) Gaining attention of students
(ii) Prior knowledge of students
(iii) Informing the learner about the objectives
(iv) Stimulating recall of pre-requisite learning
(v) Checking the availability of reading material in the library.
(vi) Eliciting the desired response

(a) (i) (ii) (iii) (iv) (b) (i) (iii) (iv) (vi)
(c) (ii) (iii) (v) (vi) (d) (i) (iii) (iv) (v)

90. Among the following which one is an examples of instructional software? **[Jun 2019]**
(a) Audio podcast (b) Printed material
(c) Radio talk (d) Edusat

91. Inclusive education implies **[Jun 2019]**
(a) Ensuring learning outcome of every child to be the same
(b) Including the disabled in the main stream
(c) Provides compulsory education for children below 14 years
(d) Ensuring that no child is left behind in education

92. When the learning outcomes of students are ensured with employment of less resources and effort on the part of a teacher and more initiative for self-learning is evident, which of the following expression will describe the teacher most appropriately? **[Jun 2019]**
(a) Teacher is successful
(b) Teacher is effective
(c) Teacher is intelligent
(d) Teacher is practical

93. Reflective practice implies use of one's **[Jun 2019]**
(a) Cognition
(b) Metacognition
(c) Metacognition on cognition
(d) Reinforcement of learning

94. Brain storming as a method can be used for **[Jun 2019]**
(a) Out-of-box thinking
(b) Coherent thinking
(c) Generate new ideas in the area of interest
(d) Critical thinking

95. Learning objectives mean **[Jun 2019]**
(a) Learning experience
(b) Concise outcomes
(c) Academic achievement
(d) Intended learning outcomes

96. For optimizing self-leraning which of the following motivational principles will be most helpful? **[Jun 2019]**
(a) Using reward and punishment
(b) Creating scope for fulfilling relatedness need
(c) Providing scope for satisfying need for competence
(d) Promoting concerns for meeting status needs

97. Which of the following is an example of maximum performance test? **[Jun 2019]**
(a) Personality tests
(b) Projective personality tests
(c) Aptitude tests
(d) Interest and attitude scales

98. Which of the strategies in the list given below will be associated with direct teaching? **[Jun 2019]**
(i) Providing example and explanation
(ii) Promoting inquiry
(iii) Focusing on concepts
(iv) Giving review and recapitulation
(v) Offering practice and feedback
(vi) Problem raising and problem-solving

Codes:
(a) (i), (iii) and (iv) (b) (i), (ii) and (iii)
(c) (i), (iv) and (v) (d) (iv), (v) and (vi)

99. The performance of a student is compared with another student in which type of testing? **[Jun 2019]**

(a) Criterion referenced testing
(b) Diagnostic testing
(c) Summative testing
(d) Norm-referenced testing

100. From the list given below identify those question which are called process rather than content based questions? **[Jun 2019]**
(i) Convergent questions
(ii) Divergent questions
(iii) Fact-based questions
(iv) Concept-based questions
(v) Open-ended questions
(vi) Closed questions
Choose the correct answer from the options given below:
(a) (i), (ii) and (iii)
(b) (ii), (iii) and (iv)
(c) (iv), (v) and (vi)
(d) (ii), (iv) and (v)

101. Which of the learner characteristics will influence his/her perspective in a course of study? **[Jun 2019]**
(i) Learner's commitment
(ii) Parents interest in the learner
(iii) Prior knowledge of the learner
(iv) Skill of the learner in the concerned area
(v) Family size of the learner
(vi) Socio-economic background of the family to which the learner belongs
Choose the correct answer from the options given below:
(a) (i), (iii) and (iv) (b) (i), (ii) and (iii)
(c) (iii), (iv) and (v) (d) (iv), (v) and (vi)

102. Which among the following best describes the emotional intelligence of learners? **[Jun 2019]**
(i) Understand the emotions of other people and your own
(ii) Express oneself very strongly
(iii) Being rational in thinking
(iv) Adjusting one's emotion as per situation
(v) Being creative and open to criticism
(vi) Accepting other people as they are
Choose your answer from the options given below:
(a) (i), (iv) and (v) (b) (iv), (v) and (v)
(c) (i), (ii) and (iii) (d) (ii), (iii) and (iv)

103. Who developed the theory of 'Multiple Intelligence'? **[Jun 2019]**
(a) Alfred Binet (b) L. Thurstone
(c) Charles Spearman (d) Howard Gardner

104. Which of the following statement explain the concepts of inclusive teaching? **[Jun 2019]**
(a) Teacher facilitates the learning of the gifted students
(b) Teacher facilitates the learning of the weak students
(c) Teacher takes support of parents of the student to make them learn
(d) Teacher makes the student of different background to learn together in the same class

105. To organize discussion method in teaching effectively, which of the following conditions should be met? **[Jun 2019]**
(i) Topic be easy
(ii) Topic be declared in advance
(iii) Topic of common interest
(iv) Availability of more than one teacher
(v) Language facility of participants
Select appropriate answer from the options given below:
(a) (ii), (iii) and (v) (b) (i), (ii) and (iii)
(c) (i), (ii) and (v) (d) (iii), (iv) and (v)

106. From the list of the effective teaching behaviours, identify those which are called key behaviours. **[Jun 2019]**
(i) Direct, audible and oral delivery to all students
(ii) Encouraging students to elaborate on an answer
(iii) Warm and nurturnig relationships with learners
(iv) Varying modes of presentation
(v) Preventing misbehaviour with a minimum of class disruption
(vi) Organizing what is to come and summarizing what has gone before
Select your answer from the options given below:
(a) (i), (iv) and (v) (b) (i), (ii) and (iii)
(c) (ii), (iii) and (iv) (d) (iv), (v) and (vi)

107. Below are listed some activities performed by a teacher. Which activities are of the nature of formative evaluation? **[Jun 2019]**
(a) Giving a mastery test
(b) Conducting quiz session
(c) Evaluating student in grading system
(d) Providing feedback while teaching
(e) Encouraging student reflect more

Select your answer from the options given below:
(1) (a), (b) and (c) (2) (b), (c) and (d)
(3) (b), (d) and (e) (4) (b), (c) and (e)

108. A teacher gives lot of positive and negative examples to support his/her presentation in the classroom, this will be related to which of teaching? **[Jun 2019]**
(a) Autonomous development level
(b) Memory level
(c) Understanding level
(d) Reflective level

109. Below given are two columns. Column–A lists methods of teaching and Column–B lists the focus of a method. Match Column–A with Column–B. **[Jun 2019]**

Column–A	Column–B
(a) Lecture method	(i) Emphasizing the participative procedure
(b) Demonstration method	(ii) Experience-based learning
(c) Project method	(iii) Imparting large amount of knowledge
(d) Collaborative method	(iv) Student engages in different activities together and learn

Select your answer from the options given below:
(1) (a)–(i); (b)–(iii); (c)–(ii); (d)–(iv)
(2) (a)–(ii); (b)–(iv); (c)–(i); (d)–(iii)
(3) (a)–(iii); (b)–(i); (c)–(ii); (d)–(iv)
(4) (a)–(iii); (b)–(ii); (c)–(iv); (d)–(i)

110. Below are listed some learners' characteristics. Identify those that help in effective teaching. **[Jun 2019]**
(i) Learner's respect for teacher
(ii) Learner's level of mental ability
(iii) Learner's previous experiences
(iv) Learner's level of interest to relation
(v) Learner's level of interpersonal relation
(vi) Learner's view about the society

Select your answer from the options given below:
(a) (i), (ii), (iii) and (vi)
(b) (iii), (iv), (v) and (vi)
(c) (i), (ii), (iii) and (vi)
(d) (ii), (iii), (iv) and (vi)

111. From the list given below, identify those teaching methods which have a great scope for dialogic discourses. **[Jun 2019]**
(i) Lecture with audio–visual aids
(ii) Team teaching
(iii) Tutorials
(iv) Problem-solving methods
(v) Chalk and talk method
(vi) Group discussions

Select your answer from the options given below:
(a) (i), (ii) and (iii) (b) (iii), (iv) and (vi)
(c) (ii), (iii) and (v) (d) (iv), (v) and (vi)

112. A workshop is meant for **[Jun 2019]**
(a) Hands-on-experience
(b) Listening to scholarly lectures
(c) Learning with interaction
(d) Discussing over one's own work

113. What is SWAYAM? **[Jun 2019]**
(a) Non-Governmental Organization
(b) Digital programme to achieve the principles of education
(c) Online platform
(d) Name of a web site

114. Which one of the following instructional designs is not a part of SWAYAM lauched by Government of India? **[Jun 2019]**
(a) E-tutorial (b) E-content
(c) Physical interaction (d) Discussion forum

115. Which of the following not correctly matched? **[Jun 2019]**
(i) Gyan Darshan – Satellite based educational T.V. channel
(ii) Gyan Vani – Educational FM Radio network
(iii) MOOCs – Massive Open Online Credits

Choose the correct answer from the options given below:

(a) Only (i) and (ii) (b) Only (ii) and (iii)
(c) Only (iii) (d) Only (i) and (iii)

116. Which of the following is an online store house of all academic award like certificates, diplomas, degrees, marksheet, etc? **[Jun 2019]**

(a) SWAYAM
(b) National Digital Library
(c) National Academic Library
(d) National Academic Depository

117. Which of the following instructional designs is part of SWAYAM launched by Goverment of India? **[Jun 2019]**

(i) E–Tutorial (ii) E–Content
(iii) Assessment (iv) Dissussion Forum
(v) Classroom Teaching

Choose the correct option from below:

(a) (i) and (ii) only
(b) (i), (iii), (iv) and (v) only
(c) (i), (ii), (iii) and (iv) only
(d) (iii) and (v) only

118. The introduction of MOOC in open and distance learning programmes is justified because of its **[Jun 2019]**

(a) Low cost considerations
(b) Accessibility considerations
(c) Speed considerations
(d) Novelty considerations

119. Match List I with List II.

List I (Behaviour modification techniques)	List II (Example)
(A) Positive reinforcement	(i) Withdrawal of a pleasant stimulus or application of an aversive stimulus to stop the behaviour
(B) Negative reinforcement	(ii) Painful or aversive stimulus is presented to stop the occurrence of behaviour
(C) Punishment	(iii) The behaviour increases in frequency after the removal of a stimulus
(D) Extinction	(iv) The behaviour increases in frequency after the presentation of a stimulus

Choose your answer from the following options. **[Dec 2019]**

Code:

	(A)	(B)	(C)	(D)
(a)	(i)	(ii)	(iii)	(iv)
(b)	(ii)	(i)	(iii)	(iv)
(c)	(iv)	(iii)	(ii)	(i)
(d)	(iii)	(i)	(ii)	(iv)

120. The emphasis in memory level teaching is on which of the following? **[Dec 2019]**

(A) Organisation of thoughts and ideas
(B) Seeing of relationships among facts
(C) Systematic presentations to enable quick reproduction
(D) Critical thinking
(E) Mastery of correct sequencing of facts
(F) Segregating one feature from another

Choose the answer from the following options.

(a) (A), (B) and (C) (b) (A), (C) and (E)
(c) (B), (C) and (D) (d) (D), (E) and (F)

121. The most characteristic feature of an adolescent learner, which determines his/her social and moral development is the: **[Dec 2019]**

(a) tendency to be away from parents
(b) concern for hero worshipping for emulating values and standards
(c) mixing up with peers in the neighbourhood
(d) identify crisis

122. Which of the following teaching methodologies are contributive to direct learning? **[Dec 2019]**

(A) Team teaching and lecturing.
(B) Simulation and role playing.
(C) Lecture with or without the use of audiovisuals.
(D) Participation in workshop and assignments.
(E) MOOCs and heuristics.
(F) Interactive presentations.

Choose the correct option.

(a) (B), (D) and (E) (b) (A), (B) and (C)
(c) (C), (D) and (F) (d) (D), (E) and (F)

123. Which of the following is an example of maximum performance test? **[Dec 2019]**
(a) Projective personality test
(b) Interest inventory
(c) Aptitude test
(d) Attitude scales

124. Match List I with List II.

List I (Study skills)	List II (Learning techniques)
(A) Elaborative interrogation	(i) Mixing different kinds of problems together when studying
(B) Practice testing	(ii) Explaining what a section of text or an example problem means to you
(C) Self-explanation	(iii) Testing yourself on the material you are trying to learn
(D) Interleaved practice	(iv) Answering why a fact is true

Choose the correct option. **[Dec 2019]**

Code:

	(A)	(B)	(C)	(D)
(a)	(iv)	(iii)	(ii)	(i)
(b)	(i)	(ii)	(iv)	(iii)
(c)	(ii)	(iv)	(i)	(iii)
(d)	(iii)	(i)	(ii)	(iv)

125. Choose the person who has control over self, mode of communication and method of delivery in classroom from the following. **[Dec 2019]**
(a) Student (b) Teacher
(c) Audience (d) Visitor

126. Which among the following is NOT a component of effective teaching? **[Dec 2019]**
(a) Questioning to check for the understanding of students
(b) Providing students with feedback
(c) Being flexible about how long it takes to learn
(d) Reactive mode of student's behaviour

127. Which among the following factors doesn't contribute to assessment bias? **[Dec 2019]**
(a) When language of the test and the tester is different from the languages of the students
(b) Answers that support middle class values
(c) Its assessment procedures are flexible and diverse to make disadvantaged students comfortable
(d) Objective test for assessing abstract reasoning of the student

128. Choose two factors that do NOT affect the academic performance of students adversely. **[Dec 2019]**
(i) Low self-efficacy belief
(ii) Belief in God
(iii) Indifferent attitude towards politics
(iv) Teacher's low expectation from students

Choose the correct option.
(a) (i) and (ii) only (b) (ii) and (iii) only
(c) (iii) and (iv) only (d) (ii) and (iv) only

129. Identify the factors that do not contribute to the effectiveness of teaching from the options given below. **[Dec 2019]**
(i) Socioeconomic background of teacher
(ii) Teacher's skill in pleasing the students
(iii) Teacher's subject knowledge
(iv) Teacher's personal contact with students

Choose the correct option.
(a) (i), (iii) and (iv) (b) (ii), (iii) and (iv)
(c) (i), (ii) and (iii) (d) (i), (ii) and (iv)

130. Given below are two statements—one is labelled as Assertion (A) and the other is labelled as Reason (R).
Assertion (A): Through online teaching, a large number of students can be taught by a very competent faculty.
Reason (R): Online teaching helps students in developing critical thinking more than the offline teaching can do.
In the light of the above statements, choose the correct option. **[Dec 2019]**
(a) Both (A) and (R) are true and (R) is the correct explanation of (A)
(b) Both (A) and (R) are true and (R) is not the correct explanation of (A)
(c) (A) is true but (R) is false
(d) (A) is false but (R) is true

131. The compositional skills and creativity in presentation of students can be most effectively evaluated by which of the following tests? **[Dec 2019]**

(a) Objective type tests
(b) Essay type tests
(c) Short answer tests
(d) Projective type tests

132. Identify the sequence which correctly indicates the order for ensuring teaching-learning activities in a constructivist approach. **[Dec 2019]**
(a) Explore, explain, engage, extend and evaluate
(b) Evaluate, extend, engage, explain and explore
(c) Explain, engage, explore, evaluate and extend
(d) Engage, explore, explain, evaluate and extend

133. Which of the following factors have been labelled as 'social competence' in influencing learning? **[Dec 2019]**
(a) Socioeconomic status
(b) Motivation
(c) Intelligence-general and specific
(d) Emotional well-being
(e) Inability to translate thoughts into action
Choose the correct answer from the options given below.
(a) Only (a), (b) and (c)
(b) Only (b), (c) and (d)
(c) Only (a), (b) and (d)
(d) Only (c), (d) and (e)

134. Which of the following will be considered as key teaching behaviour belonging to the category of effectiveness? **[Dec 2019]**
(a) Making ideas clear to learners who may be at different level of understanding.
(b) Showing enthusiasm and animation through variation in eye contact, voice and gestures.
(c) Using student ideas by acknowledging and summarising.
(d) Probing through general questions and shifting a discussion to some higher thought level.
(e) Using meaningful verbal praise to get and keep students actively participating in the learning process.
Choose the correct answer from the options given below.
(a) Only (a), (b) and (c)
(b) Only (a), (b) and (e)
(c) Only (b), (c) and (d)
(d) Only (c), (d) and (e)

135. Given below are two statements—one is labelled Assertion (A) and the other is labelled as Reason (R).
Assertion (A): Pedagogy and social interaction are two major result-oriented activities of a teacher.
Reason (R): Communication has a limited role in both these activities. **[Dec 2019]**
In the light of the above statements, choose the correct option from the following.
(a) Both (A) and (R) are true and (R) is the correct explanation of (A)
(b) Both (A) and (R) are true but (R) is not the correct explanation of (A)
(c) (A) is true but (R) is false
(d) (A) is false but (R) is true

136. From the list given below, identify those competencies of an effective teacher which relate to the domain of personality and attitude? **[Dec 2019]**
(i) Locus of control
(ii) Communicating
(iii) Managing
(iv) Self-efficacy
(v) Teacher enthusiasm
(vi) Being organised and orderly
Select the correct answer from the options given below.
(a) (i), (ii) and (iii) (b) (i), (iv) and (v)
(c) (ii), (iii) and (iv) (d) (iv), (v) and (vi)

137. In which level of teaching, lower level learning outcomes get focussed? **[Dec 2019]**
(a) Memory level
(b) Understanding level
(c) Reflective level
(d) Autonomous development level

138. In the spectrum of teaching methods, which of the following will be called 'dialogic'? **[Dec 2019]**
(i) Demonstration method
(ii) Problem-solving method
(iii) Chalk and talk method
(iv) Team teaching based method
(v) Interactive presentation
(vi) Tutorials
Select your answer from the options given below.
(a) (a), (b) and (c) (b) (b), (c) and (d)
(c) (c), (d) and (e) (d) (b), (e) and (f)

139. Which of the following evaluation systems belongs to the category of being an innovative practice? **[Dec 2019]**
(a) Semesterised examinations
(b) Performance evaluation
(c) Portfolio-based evaluation
(d) Learning outcome-based evaluation

140. Identify the distinctive feature of traditional method of Indian education from the following list. **[Dec 2019]**
(a) 'Direct perception of truth'—both as means and ends
(b) Making everything on trust
(c) Evolving own ways' of learning
(d) Following nyāya philosophy with deductive and inductive process

141. Non-traditional teaching and learning strategies lay emphasis on: **[Dec 2019]**
(i) students' need-based resource materials and learning standards
(ii) developing skills, attitude and values
(iii) promoting inbox thinking process
(iv) lecture-based model
(v) acquiring knowledge necessary to respond creatively

Select your answer from the following options.
(a) (i), (ii) and (v) (b) (ii), (iii) and (iv)
(c) (iii), (iv) and (v) (d) (i), (iv) and (v)

142. Given below are two statements—one is labelled as Assertion (A) and the other is labelled as Reason (R).

Assertion (A): If a teacher wants to improve his/her abilities as an effective classroom communicator, then he/she should first understand the students.

Reason (R): The ability to understand students and intended listening are disjointed propositions.

In the light of the above two statements, choose the correct option from the following. **[Dec 2019]**
(a) Both (A) and (R) are true and (R) is the correct explanation of (A)
(b) Both (A) and (R) are true but (R) is not the correct explanation of (A)
(c) (A) is true but (R) is false
(d) (A) is false but (R) is true

143. In the two sets given below, Set I provides levels of teaching, while Set II gives their focus of concern.

Set I (Levels of Teaching)	Set II (Focus of Concern)
(A) Autonomous development level	(i) Problem raising and problem-solving
(B) Memory level	(ii) Affects and feelings
(C) Understanding level	(iii) Recall of facts and information
(D) Reflective level	(iv) Seeing of relationship among facts and their examples
	(v) Peer learning

Select the correct answer from the options given below. **[Dec 2019]**

Code:

	(A)	(B)	(C)	(D)
(a)	(i)	(ii)	(iv)	(v)
(b)	(i)	(iv)	(iii)	(ii)
(c)	(ii)	(iii)	(iv)	(i)
(d)	(v)	(iv)	(iii)	(ii)

144. From the list of learning outcomes indicated below, identify those which are said to be high-level outcomes. **[Dec 2019]**
(i) Learning of facts and rules
(ii) Showing the ability to analyse and synthesise
(iii) Awareness, responding and valuing
(iv) Imitation, manipulation and precision
(v) Articulation and naturalisation
(vi) Organisation and characterisation

Select the correct answer from the options given below.
(a) (ii), (v) and (vi)
(b) (i), (ii) and (iii)
(c) (ii), (iii) and (iv)
(d) (i), (iii) and (vi)

145. In the context of classroom teaching, the foundation on which a warm and nurturing relationship with learners can be built is called: **[Dec 2019]**
(a) probing (b) teacher affect
(c) structuring (d) feedback

146. Match List I with List II. **[Dec 2019]**

List I	List II
(A) Ontology	(i) Ideographic
(B) Epistemology	(ii) Realism
(C) Methodology	(iii) Survey
(D) Method	(iv) Positivism

Choose the correct option.

Code:

	(A)	(B)	(C)	(D)
(a)	(ii)	(iv)	(iii)	(i)
(b)	(ii)	(i)	(iii)	(iv)
(c)	(iv)	(ii)	(i)	(iii)
(d)	(ii)	(iv)	(i)	(iii)

147. Given below are two statements—one is labelled as Assertion (A) and the other is labelled as Reason (R). **[Dec 2019]**

Assertion (A): Defining the objectives of the topic of discussion is not necessarily the first step in classroom communication.

Reason (R): Clear definitions of objectives make students understand the topic well.

In the light of the above stated statements, choose the correct option from the choices given below.

(a) Both (A) and (R) are true and (R) is the correct explanation of (A)
(b) Both (A) and (R) are true and (R) is not the correct explanation of (A)
(c) (A) is true but (R) is false
(d) (A) is false but (R) is true

148. When a large number of students with different performance levels are there in the class, for uniform imparting of educative interactions, a teacher should opt for a communication, which is: **[Dec 2019]**

(a) top-down and linear
(b) technology-enabled
(c) individual-centric
(d) self-projected

149. In Social Sciences, a central issue is the question of whether the social world can be studied using the methods of natural sciences. This statement refers to the issue of: **[Dec 2019]**

(a) ontology (b) axiology
(c) epistemology (d) etymology

150. Which among the following is a Massive Open Online Course (MOOC) platform created by the Ministry of Human Resource Development, Government of India? **[Dec 2019]**

(a) Pratham (b) Swayam
(c) FutureLearn (d) OpenLearn

151. Which of the following are indicators of external accountability for an institution of higher learning? **[2020]**

(A) Provision for profession development of teachers.
(B) Utilization pattern of library and technical resources.
(C) Relevance of courses to the societal needs.
(D) Performance of students in public examination.
(E) Employment pattern of pass-out students.

Choose the correct answer from the options given below:

(a) (A), (B), (C) only
(b) (B), (C), (D) only
(c) (C), (D), (E) only
(d) (D), (E), (A) only

152. Which of the following have been identified as the key behaviours contributing to effective teaching? **[2020]**

(A) Lesson clarity
(B) Instructional variety
(C) Using student ideas and contribution
(D) Engagement in learning process
(E) Structuring

Choose the correct answer from the options given below:

(a) (A), (B) and (D) only
(b) (A), (B) and (C) only
(c) (B), (C) and (D) only
(d) (C), (D) and (E) only

153. Given below are two statements: **[2020]**

Statement I: 'SWAYAM' an initiative of the Government of India, aims at providing affordable and quality education to the citizens.

Statement II: 'SWAYAM' aims at promoting the education and health of adolescent girls.

In the light of the above statements, choose the most appropriate from the options given below:
(a) Both Statements I and Statement II are true.
(b) Both Statements I and Statement II are false.
(c) Statement I is correct but Statement II is false.
(d) Statement I is incorrect but Statement II is true.

154. In which of the following the direction of influence is mainly one way: **[2020]**
(a) Counselling (b) Guiding
(c) Teaching (d) Learning

155. Given below are two statements: **[2020]**

Statement I: In order to be effective, teaching and testing must go together.

Statement II: Feedback does not form an essential component of formative assessment.

In the light of the above statements, choose the most appropriate from the options given below:
(a) Both Statements I and Statement II are correct
(b) Both Statements I and Statement II are incorrect.
(c) Statement I is correct but Statement II is incorrect.
(d) Statement I is incorrect but Statement II is correct.

156. Which of the following are objectives of a performance appraisal system? **[2020]**
(A) To help an employee in finding out his/her own strengths and weaknesses.
(B) To help in creating desirable organizational ethos.
(C) To help in identifying people for the purpose of motivating and training them for new roles.
(D) To help in distinguishing the non-performers from performers.
(E) To enable learners to understand the weakness in the system.

Choose the correct answer from the options given below:
(a) (A), (B), (C) only
(b) (B), (C), (D) only
(c) (C), (D), (E) only
(d) (E), (D), (A) only

157. In the cognitive domain of teaching-learning objectives, which will be categorized as a higher type of learning outcomes? **[2020]**
A. Knowledge and comprehension
B. Analysis of conceptual elements
C. Application of acquired knowledge and skills
D. Synthesis involving the creative organization of ideas
E. Evaluation involving judgment using internal or external standards.

Choose the correct answer from the options given below:
(a) A, B and C only
(b) B, C and D only
(c) C, D and E only
(d) B, D and E only

158. A teacher uses a question-answer session to ensure desired learning outcomes in his/her classroom. In this process, he/she offers the following type of comment to a few answers given by a student: **[2020]**
"Yes, you are right, good'
This will be considered as an example of
(a) Positive feedback
(b) Negative feedback
(c) Confirmatory feedback
(d) Corrective feedback

159. Match List I with List II. **[2020]**

List 1 Behavioural teaching competencies	List II Description
(A) Instructing	(I) Optimizing 'on task' and minimizing 'off task' activities
(B) Communicating	(II) Watching groups, behaviors and pace etc. and reacting quickly
(C) Managing	(III) Using methods and activities by the teacher to promote learning
(D) Monitoring	(IV) Transmitting thoughts and ideas verbally and non-verbally

Choose the correct answer from the options given below:

(a) A - I, B - II, C - III, D- IV
(b) A - IV, B - III, C - II, D - I
(c) A - III, B - IV, C - I, D - II
(d) A - II, B - I, C - IV, D - III

160. Given below are two statements, one is labelled as Assertion (A) and the other is labelled as Reason (R). **[2020]**

Assertion (A): Evaluation is said to be formative when the intention is to identify scope and potential for improvement of teaching-learning system.

Reason (R): The form of such evaluation is informal and has to take place during instruction/ teaching.

In light of the above statements, choose the correct answer from the options given below

(a) Both A and R are true and R is the correct explanation of A
(b) Both A and R are true but R is NOT the correct explanation of A
(c) A is true but R is false
(d) A is false but R is true

161. Given below are two statements **[2020]**

Statement I: Maximum performance tests are designed to assess the upper limits of the examinees' knowledge and ability.

Statement II: Typical response tests are designed to measure specific behaviors and characteristics of examinees.

In light of the above statements, choose the most appropriate answer from the options given below:

(a) Both Statement I and Statement II are true
(b) Both Statement I and Statement II are false
(c) Statement I is correct but Statement II is false
(d) Statement I is incorrect but Statement II is true

162. Given below are two statements: **[2020]**

Statement I: Persuasive communication by a teacher in the classroom is intended to make his/her version of information acceptable to students.

Statement II: If it happens at the institutional level, the purpose behind it is image building.

In light of the above statements, choose the most appropriate answer from the options given below:

(a) Both Statement I and Statement II are true
(b) Both Statement I and Statement II are false
(c) Statement I is true but Statement II is false
(d) Statement I is false but Statement II is true

163. Which of the following 'need strengths' in Maslow's hierarchy are related to higher order learning? **[2020]**

(A) Physiological needs
(B) Safety needs
(C) Social needs
(D) Esteem needs
(E) Needs for self actualization

Choose the correct answer from the options given below:

(a) (A) and (B) only
(b) (B) and (C) only
(c) (C) and (D) only
(d) (D) and (E) only

164. Given below are two statements, one is labelled as Assertion A and the other is labelled as Reason R **[2021]**

Assertion A: In classroom communication, teachers should acknowledge and take into account students' views.

Reason R: In a classroom, the probability of message reception can be enhanced by establishing a viewpoint.

In light of the above statements, choose the correct answer from the options given below

(a) A is false but R is true
(b) A is true but R is false
(c) Both A and R are true and R is the correct explanation of A
(d) Both A and R are true but R is NOT the correct explanation of A

165. mooKIT platform uses, an open source content management system. **[2021]**

(a) DRUPAL
(b) JOOMLA
(c) Moodle
(d) SAKAI

166. Given below are two statements **[2021]**

Statement I: According to Piaget, the ability to solve conservation problems depends on having an understanding of three basic aspects of reasoning: identity, compensation, and reversibility.

Statement II: The stage of classification does not depend on a student's ability to focus on a single characteristic of objects in a set and group the objects according to that characteristic.

In light of the above statements, choose the most appropriate answer from the options given below:

(a) Both Statement I and Statement II are correct
(b) Both Statement I and Statement II are incorrect
(c) Statement I is correct but Statement II is incorrect
(d) Statement I is incorrect but Statement II is correct

167. Given below are two statements: **[2021]**

Statement I: Personal competencies determine how we manage ourselves

Statement II: Social competencies determine how we handle relationships

In light of the above statements, choose the most appropriate answer from the options given below

(a) Both Statement I and Statement II are correct
(b) Both Statement I and Statement II are incorrect
(c) Statement I is correct but Statement II is incorrect
(d) Statement I is incorrect but Statement II is correct

168. The dynamics of classroom interaction can be effectively managed through **[2021]**

(a) Interpreting perceived meanings
(b) Language complexity
(c) Repetitive symbolism
(d) Verbosity

169. Which of the following level of teaching lays stress on critical sifting of ideas at the highest cognitive level? **[Dec 2021]**

(a) Memory level
(b) Understanding level
(c) Reflective level
(d) Autonomous development level

170. Which of the following are the highest taxonomic categories in the cognitive, affective, and psychomotor domains of learning? **[Dec 2021]**

(A) Analysis (B) Evaluation
(C) Awareness (D) Characterization
(E) Naturalization

Choose the correct answer from the options given below:

(a) (A), (B), and (C) only
(b) (B), (D), and (E) only
(c) (B), (C), and (D) only
(d) (C), (D), and (E) only

171. Match List I with List II **[Dec 2021]**

List I (Helping behavior of effective teaching)	List II (Description)
(A) Using student ideas of contributions	(i) Warm and nurturing relationship with learners
(B) Structuring	(ii) Teacher statements to encourage students to elaborate on an answer
(C) Probing	(iii) Teacher comments for the purpose of organizing what is to come
(D) Teacher affect	(iv) Taking a student's response and repeating or applying it

Choose the correct answer from the options given below :

Code:

	(A)	(B)	(C)	(D)
(a)	(iv)	(iii)	(ii)	(i)
(b)	(i)	(ii)	(iii)	(iv)
(c)	(ii)	(i)	(iv)	(iii)
(d)	(iii)	(iv)	(i)	(ii)

172. Given below are two statements: **[Dec 2021]**

Statement I: In norm-referenced testing of students, test data helps us determine a students place or rank.

Statement II: In Criterion-referenced testing, the test data tells us about a student's level of proficiency.

In the light of the above statements, choose the correct answer from the options given below:

(a) Both Statement I and Statement II are true
(b) Both Statement I and Statement II are false
(c) Statement I is true but Statement II is false
(d) Statement I is false but Statement II is true

173. Given below are two statements : One is labelled as Assertion (A) and the other is labelled as Reason (R): **[Dec 2021]**

Assertion (A): Modern and ICT based teaching support requires some technical knowledge on the part of the teacher and learner.

Reasons (R): Both teachers and learners have to be provided orientation in use of the various support tools and techniques in an intelligent way.

In the light of the above statements, choose the most appropriate answer from the options given below :

(a) Both (A) and (R) are true and (R) is the correct explanation of (A)
(b) Both (A) and (R) are true but (R) is NOT the correct explanation of (A)
(c) (A) is true but (R) is false
(d) (A) is false but (R) is true

174. Metacognition comprises which of the following skills? **[Dec 2021]**

A. Planning B. Developing
C. Monitoring D. Costing
E. Evaluation

Choose the correct answer from the options given below:

(a) A, B, and C only (b) A, C, and E only
(c) B, D, and E only (d) A, D, and E only

175. Match List List I with List II **[Dec 2021]**

List I (Learning Strategy)	List II (Action taken)
(A) Planning and focusing attention	(i) Creating example
(B) Organising and remembering	(ii) Self-questioning and self-testing
(C) Comprehension	(iii) Setting goal and timetables
(D) Cognitive monitoring	(iv) Using mnemonics, imagery

Choose the correct answer from the options given below:

Code:

	(A)	(B)	(C)	(D)
(a)	(i)	(ii)	(iii)	(iv)
(b)	(ii)	(iii)	(iv)	(i)
(c)	(iii)	(iv)	(i)	(ii)
(d)	(iv)	(i)	(ii)	(iii)

176. Which of the following are in the "Six Thinking Hats System", a form of parallel thinking? **[2021]**

A. Brown Hat B. White Hat
C. Violet Hat D. Red Hat
E. Black Hat

Choose the correct answer from the options given below:

(a) A, B and C only
(b) B, C and D only
(c) B, D and E only
(d) C, D and E only

177. Match List I with List II: **[2021]**

List I	List II
Thinking Hat System	Concepts and Ideas
A. White Hat	I. Judgement and caution-the logical negative
B. Red Hat	II. Data gathering-facts, figures, information needs and gaps
C. Black Hat	III. Provocations, alternatives and creativity-proposals
D. Green Hat	IV. Intuition and emotions

Choose the correct answer from the options given below:

(a) A -I , B -III , C -II , D -IV
(b) A -II , B -IV , C -I , D -III
(c) A -III , B -II , C -IV , D -I
(d) A -IV , B -I , C -III , D -II

178. What is the name for the technique which uses images that are often more evocative than words, and more precise and potent in triggering a wide range of associations and thinking? **[2021]**

(a) Brainstorming (b) Mind-mapping
(c) Story boarding (d) Synectics

179. The satellite used for the transmission and telecast of SWAYAMPRABHA is called **[2021]**

(a) EDUSAT Satellite
(b) GSAT-15 Satellite
(c) GSAT-3 Satellite
(d) SP-EDU-15 Satellite

180. Which of the following types of learners learn with the help of flow charts or diagrams? **[2022]**
(a) Tactile (b) Visual
(c) Auditory (d) Rote

181. Match List I with List II. **[2022]**

List I Concepts	List II Main proponent
A. Integral education	I. John Dewey
B. Focus on spiritual aspects of Indian philosophy	II. Sri Aurobindc
C. Learning to take place in nature and from nature	III. Dr. Sarvepalli Radhakrishar.
D. Experiential learning	IV. Rabindranath Tagore

Choose the correct answer from the options given below:
(a) A – II, B – IV, C – III, D – I
(b) A – I, B – II, C – III, D – IV
(c) A – III, B – II, C – I, D – IV
(d) A II, B – III, C – IV, D – I

182. In order to identify individual differences of learners in a class, which of the following can be used by a teacher? **[2022]**
(a) Summative Assessments
(b) Formative Assessments
(c) Diagnostic Assessments
(d) Peer Assessments

183. The e-content generated under e-PG Pathshala project for Non-Technical Post-Graduate courses in hosted on web by **[2022]**
(a) NPTEL (b) INFLIBNET
(c) SWAYAM (d) IGNOU

184. Which of the following is NOT an affective domain? **[2022]**
(a) Receiving (b) Analysing
(c) Valuing (d) Organizing

185. According to the revised Bloom's taxonomy, which of the following categories is considered to be highest for the learner? **[2022]**
(a) Understand (b) Apply
(c) Analyse (d) Create

186. Dynamic approach to teaching means **[2022]**
(a) Teaching should be lecture based.
(b) Teachers should be energetic.
(c) Teachers should be student friendly.
(d) Students should learn through activities.

187. Given below are two statements, one is labelled as **Assertion A** and the other is labelled as **Reason R** **[2022]**
Assertion A: MOOCs on the SWAYAM portal can be used for earning upto 40% credits per semester by students.
Reason R: All MOOCs on the SWAYAM portal are credit-based MOOCs.
In light of the above statements, choose the correct answer from the options given below
(a) Both **A** and **R** are true and **R** is the correct explanation of **A**
(b) Both **A** and **R** are true but **R** is NOT the correct explanation of **A**
(c) **A** is true but **R** is false.
(d) **A** is false but **R** is true

188. SWAYAM tries to take the best teaching-learning resources to all students through **[2022]**
(a) Seminars (b) Video lectures
(c) Classroom teaching (d) Conferences

189. Following are the characteristics of Non-Conventional learning: **[2022]**
A. It is teacher oriented.
B. It is for improvement of quality.
C. It is cost effective.
D. It is linked to employment.
E. It is on campus.

Choose the correct answer from the options given below:
(a) A, B and C only (b) B, C and D only
(c) A, C and D only (d) C, D and E only

190. Which of the following tools is used by learners and teachers for asynchronous interaction? **[June 2023]**
A. Web conferencing
B. E-mail
C. Wikis and collaborative documents
D. Discussion Boards
E. Live Streaming

Choose the correct answer from the options given below:
(a) B, C and D only
(b) C, D and E only

(c) A, C, D and E only
(d) A and B only

191. Which of the following are the strategies of Cognitive Apprenticeship to develop higher order skills among learners? **[June 2023]**

A. Mentoring, Collaboration and Socializing
B. Modelling, Coaching and Scaffolding
C. Augmentation, Retention and Explaining
D. Articulation, Reflection and Exploration
E. Memorization, Rehearsal and Identifying

Choose the correct answer from the options given below:

(a) A and D only
(b) A, C and E only
(c) B and D only
(d) B and C only

192. The stimulus which does not require any conditioning for desired behaviour is called **[June 2023]**

(a) Unconditional stimulus
(b) Conditioned stimulus
(c) Unconditioned response
(d) Conditioned response

193. Which of the following curriculum development models come under Technical Scientific models? **[June 2023]**

A. Taba's Model
B. Open Classroom Model
C. Weinstien and Fantini Model
D. Hunkin's Development Model
E. Goodlad's Model

Choose the correct answer from the options given below:

(a) B, C and D only
(b) A, C and E only
(c) A, D and E only
(d) A, B, D and E only

194. Match List I with List II. **[June 2023]**

List I (Swayam Prabha Channel Number)	List II (Name of the Channel)
A. Channel 01	I. Sanskriti
B. Channel 02	II. Prabodh
C. Channel 03	III. Saaraswat
D. Channel 04	IV. Vageesh

(a) A-I, B-III, C-II, D-IV
(b) A-III, B-II, C-IV, D-I
(c) A-IV, B-I, C-II, D-III
(d) A-II, B-III, C-IV, D-I

195. Given below are two statements: **[June 2023]**

Statement I: Learner-centerd approach is centerd on teacher needs.

Statement II : Learner-centered approach is centerd on cooperative determination of subject matter.

In the light of the above statements, choose the most appropriate answer from the option given below:

(a) Both Statement I and Statement II are correct.
(b) Both Statement I and Statement II are incorrect.
(c) Statement I is correct but Statment II is incorrect.
(d) Statement I is incorrect but Statement II is correct.

196. Which of the following is a technique to provide right kind of support in right amount at right time to increase child's competence? **[June 2023]**

(a) Scaffolding (b) Assistance
(c) Accommodation (d) Schemas

197. *SWAYAM PRABHA* is an education learning platform initiated by ____, that is available 24 × 7 through 34 DTH channels. **[June 2023]**

(a) Ministry of Human Resources and Development (Now Ministry of Education)
(b) University Grants Commission (UGC)
(c) Consortium for Educational Communication (CEC)
(d) All India Council of Technical Education (AICTE)

198. A learner combines her/his previous schemas or modifies them as per new experiences. The process of combining/modifying existing schemas and to arrive at new schemas is known as ____. **[June 2023]**

(a) Accommodation (b) Assimilation
(c) Adaptation (d) Equilibration

199. Which of the following curriculum development models come under Technical -Scientific Model? **[June 2023]**

(a) Open Classroom Model
(b) Taba's Model
(c) Weinstein and Fantini Model
(d) Roger's Model of Interpersonal Relations

200. The learning, in which a new behaviour is acquired but is not demonstrated until reinforcement is provided, is known as **[Dec 2023]**
(a) Observational learning
(b) Social learning
(c) Latent learning
(d) Moral learning

201. Given below are two statements: **[Dec 2023]**

Statement (I): As per Dewey's vision of learning, learners should demonstrate their knowledge through creativity and collaboration.

Statement (II): According to Piaget, learning is independent of the developmental stages of learner.

In light of the above statements, choose the most appropriate answer from the options given below:
(a) Both Statement (I) and Statement (II) are correct.
(b) Both Statement (I) and Statement (II) are incorrect.
(c) Statement (I) is correct but Statement (II) is incorrect.
(d) Statement (I) is incorrect but Statement (II) is correct.

202. In Charlotte Danielson's framework for teaching, the domain of 'Planning and Preparation' has the following components: **[Dec 2023]**
A. Organising physical space in classroom
B. Setting instructional outcomes
C. Designing student assessments
D. Demonstrating knowledge of content and pedagogy
E. Demonstrating knowledge of resources

Choose the correct answer from the options given below:
(a) C and E only
(b) A, B and D only
(c) B, C, D and E only
(d) A, B, C, D and E

203. A teacher wants to assess the student's performance and wants to give immediate feedback. Which software you will select for the assessment? **[Dec 2023]**
A. Kahoot
B. Plotagon
C. Screen-casto-matic
D. Animaker
E. Quizziz

Choose the correct answer from the options given below:
(a) A, B and D only (b) C, D and E only
(c) B and C only (d) A and E only

204. Given below are two statements: **[Dec 2023]**

Statement (I): The non-directive model of teaching nurtures students rather than controlling the sequence of learning.

Statement (II): In the non-directive model of teaching the teacher's role is that of a facilitator who has counselling relationship with students and who guides their growth and development.

In light of the above statements, choose the most appropriate answer from the options given below:
(a) Both Statement (I) and Statement (II) are correct.
(b) Both Statement (I) and Statement (II) are incorrect.
(c) Statement (I) is correct but Statement (II) is incorrect.
(d) Statement (I) is incorrect but Statement (II) is correct.

ANSWER KEY

1. (a)	2. (c)	3. (b)	4. (c)	5. (c)	6. (d)	7. (c)	8. (c)	9. (d)	10. (b)
11. (d)	12. (c)	13. (a)	14. (b)	15. (d)	16. (c)	17. (b)	18. (a)	19. (d)	20. (d)
21. (c)	22. (c)	23. (b)	24. (a)	25. (c)	26. (a)	27. (b)	28. (d)	29. (c)	30. (b)
31. (b)	32. (a)	33. (d)	34. (c)	35. (c)	36. (b)	37. (b)	38. (c)	39. (d)	40. (d)
41. (c)	42. (b)	43. (a)	44. (c)	45. (d)	46. (c)	47. (c)	48. (c)	49. (c)	50. (c)
51. (a)	52. (c)	53. (d)	54. (c)	55. (c)	56. (d)	57. (a)	58. (b)	59. (a)	60. (b)
61. (b)	62. (c)	63. (a)	64. (d)	65. (b)	66. (d)	67. (b)	68. (c)	69. (a)	70. (b)
71. (d)	72. (d)	73. (d)	74. (d)	75. (b)	76. (b)	77. (a)	78. (d)	79. (b)	80. (b)
81. (b)	82. (d)	83. (c)	84. (d)	85. (b)	86. (a)	87. (d)	88. (b)	89. (b)	90. (c)
91. (d)	92. (b)	93. (b)	94. (c)	95. (d)	96. (c)	97. (c)	98. (c)	99. (d)	100. (d)
101. (a)	102. (a)	103. (d)	104. (d)	105. (a)	106. (a)	107. (c)	108. (c)	109. (d)	110. (d)
111. (b)	112. (a)	113. (b)	114. (c)	115. (c)	116. (d)	117. (c)	118. (b)	119. (c)	120. (b)
121. (b)	122. (a)	123. (c)	124. (a)	125. (b)	126. (d)	127. (c)	128. (b)	129. (d)	130. (c)
131. (b)	132. (d)	133. (c)	134. (b)	135. (c)	136. (b)	137. (a)	138. (d)	139. (d)	140. (a)
141. (a)	142. (c)	143. (c)	144. (a)	145. (b)	146. (d)	147. (d)	148. (b)	149. (c)	150. (b)
151. (c)	152. (a)	153. (c)	154. (d)	155. (c)	156. (a)	157. (d)	158. (a)	159. (c)	160. (a)
161. (a)	162. (a)	163. (d)	164. (c)	165. (a)	166. (c)	167. (a)	168. (a)	169. (c)	170. (b)
171. (a)	172. (a)	173. (a)	174. (b)	175. (c)	176. (d)	177. (b)	178. (b)	179. (b)	180. (b)
181. (d)	182. (b)	183. (b)	184. (b)	185. (d)	186. (d)	187. (c)	188. (b)	189. (b)	190. (a)
191. (c)	192. (a)	193. (c)	194. (c)	195. (b)	196. (a)	197. (a)	198. (c)	199. (c)	200. (c)
201. (c)	202. (c)	203. (d)	204. (a)						

HINTS AND SOLUTIONS

1. **(a):** All of the methods given in the question are important, but (a) seems to be more important than other methods.

   (a) Actually, the learners are motivated in the same manner and feelings as an adult is motivated in the same way. If the students are asking questions in the classroom, they have instantaneous yearn and motivation to learn, the topic is being taught by the teacher in an interesting manner. That are teaching in such a manner that all the senses of the learner are involved in the learning process, so they may be asking relevant and innovative questions from the teacher. Moreover, there is sense of community in the classroom, every human being wants to feel part of the group, and they participate in the activities. It gives an opportunity to the teacher to identify the talent in the classroom in a unique and customised manner. That passion improves the overall environment of the classroom.

   (b) The maximum attendance may be seen as a compulsive active, the students have to be in the class to avoid shortage of lectures.

   (c) The pin drop silence during certain parts of the lecture may be required as the teacher may specifically require this.

   (d) The students are taking notes in the classroom means that they are jotting down all the points being discussed by the teacher. The learners may not have all the understanding of the topics.

2. **(c): (a) Lecture** – A lecture is considered to be the most pedagogical conventional approach. A lecture means a specialised talk on a topic that must be done in systematic manner. Teachers make use of various types of teaching-learning materials and instructional strategies.

   (b) Discussion – Discussion means to get focused on a topic. Learners come up with new ideas, participate in a group activity, develop articulation skills, try to come up with a common agreeable solution. There are 8-10 students in this activity. This leaderless activity is a learner centric approach, rather than teacher centric. This activity creates a vibrant class environment and inculcates a positive feeling among students.

   (c) Demonstration – This can be defined as an integration of lecture cum lab method, this is practical and pragmatic approach. The article or objective to be taught is shown to the students. This method combines theory with practical aspects, thus, it develops deep rooted understanding among the students.

   (d) Narration – The teacher exposes students to the content through storytelling. This develops a context in the minds of the students. The students may narrate that content to others. Thus students get actively engaged with the content. This helps in better learning, memorization and their reflection at desired times.

3. **(b):** If we put terms in a formal perspective, we get the following diagram as given by Bloom in 1956.

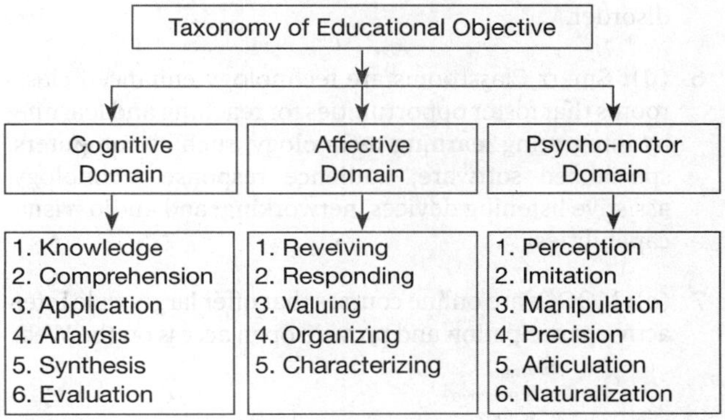

   Cognitive is basically the thought process, over which others lie.

4. **(c): (a) Placement Evaluation** – This technique is important when the aptitude of students seeking admission in a course is evaluated. So, this can be taken as a 'prior' approach.

   (b) Diagnostic Evaluation – This helps in gauzing students' knowledge, skills, strength and weaknesses, usually before a teacher starts imparting instructions. Thus, a teacher gets valuable information about students, and he can try to solve their issues. This makes the learning process more effective. The different sources that help in diagnostic evaluation are Journals, Quiz, Test, Conference/Interview, Poster, Performance Tasks, Mind Maps, Gap-Closing, Student Surveys, Parallel Activity etc., that help in this type of evaluation. A small detailed test and MCQs can be conducted for this.

   (c) Formative Evaluation – Formative assessment provides information and support during the learning. This evaluation takes places at the 'formative' stage of learning, the continuous interaction with the teacher is important. This evaluation monitors the progress of the students, so that a teacher could ensure that students are learning in the right direction. This evaluation happens without grading.

(d) **Summative Evaluation** – In this evaluation, the focus is on the outcome of a program. The students receive a grade, marks, percentage, percentile etc., that indicates their level of performance. This becomes important as the student can be shifted to next class or course on the basis of summative evaluation.

5. **(c):** Dyslexia is the most common learning disability in children and it is characterized by trouble with reading despite normal intelligence persists throughout the life.

   Steve Jobs, the founder of Apple also suffered from this disorder.

6. **(d):** Smart Classrooms are technology enhanced classrooms that foster opportunities for teaching and learning by integrating learning technology, such as computers, specialized software, audience response technology, assistive listening devices, networking, and audio/visual capabilities.

7. **(c):** MOOCs are online courses that offer large-scale interactive participation and provide open access on the Web.

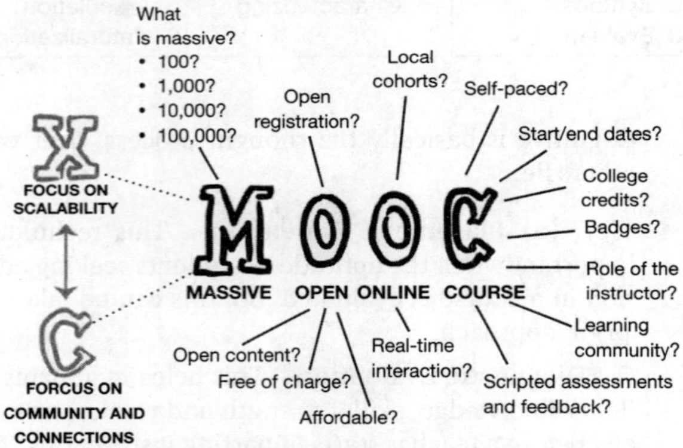

This poster explores explores the meaning of 'Massive Open Online Courses.'

8. **(c):** Education is the manifestation of perfection already existing in man was quoted by Swami Vivekananda. Education basically carries forward the existing knowledge to the present generation. It builds up new knowledge also. This happens through informal (parents and society) and formal (through teaching) manners. Thus, education does the act of socialization also.

9. **(d):** There is no differentiation level. Reflective level of teaching is considered to be the highest level at which teaching is carried out. A student can attain this level only after going through memory level and understanding level. Teaching at the reflective level enables the students to solve the real problems of life.

10. **(b):** Demonstration is a teaching method used to communicate an idea with the aid of visuals such as flip charts, posters, power point, etc. Such visual ideas generate interest among students.

11. **(d):** During the teaching-learning process, you have to locate and identify the areas where the learner commits mistakes. It is the crucial stage of the teaching-learning process where you have to diagnose and prepare instructional material for remedial teaching to ensure the desired quality of learning.

12. **(c):** Instructional aids are used in the classroom for clarity of concepts, they encourage active learning as the students can make use of multiple senses. The charts, maps, models, concrete objects, film strips, projector, radio, television etc. are the main instructional aids. Albert Duret rightly said, "It is easier to believe what you see than what you hear; but if you both see and hear, then you can understand more readily and retain more lastingly".

13. **(a):** We may refer to solution to question number 3.

    (a) Affective domain basically deals with the behavioural and motivational aspects. The learner's beliefs, values and interests are also linked with affective domain.

    (b) Cognitive domain deals with the intellectual aspects, how does information get into our minds.

    (c) Connotative meaning of a word includes the feelings and ideas that people may connect with that word. Connotation refers to the wide array of positive and negative associations that most words naturally carry with them. Denotative is more precise direct meaning.

    (d) Psychomotor domain reflects learning achieved through physical movement, coordination, and use of the motor-skill areas.

14. **(b): (a) Training Program**: The main objective of training is to enhance the practical skills of the participants. Training is well structured in nature, it is imparted by specific people for a set duration.

    (b) Seminar: This is the broadest of all these categories. This is a form of academic instruction, either at an academic institution or offered by a commercial or professional organization. This brings together small groups for recurring meetings. In each such meeting, we focus on some particular subject. The members are requested to participate. For example, the academicians are called to deliver a lecture on National Educational Policy, 2020.

    (c) Workshop: This group share a common interest or problem, some individual skills of a topic or subject. They tend to be pragmatic, as they add hands on experience to the participants. This may be conducted for ten to twenty people. They may do this through intensive study, research, practice and discussion.

(d) **Symposium**: They are more focused on a particular subject or issue. Here, people give presentations on different aspects of a topic. For example–The role of Mahatma Gandhi in freedom struggle.

15. (d): Cognitive functioning is connected with thinking or conscious mental processes. It is defined as 'the ability of an individual to perform the various mental activities most closely associated with learning and problem solving'.

Bloom identified six levels within the cognitive domain from Bloom Taxonomy in 1956.

(1) Knowledge 'involves the recall of specifics and universals, the recall of methods and processes, or the recall of a pattern, structure, or setting.'

(2) Comprehension 'refers to a type of understanding or apprehension such that the individual knows what is being communicated and can make use of the material or idea being communicated without necessarily relating it to other material or seeing its fullest implications'.

(3) Application refers to the 'use of abstractions in particular and concrete situations.'

(4) Analysis represents the 'breakdown of a communication into its constituent elements or parts such that the relative hierarchy of ideas is made clear and/or the relations between ideas expressed are made explicit.'

(5) Synthesis involves the 'putting together of elements and parts so as to form a whole.'

(6) Evaluation engenders 'judgments about the value of material and methods for given purposes.'

Additional fact—Intelligence Quotient (IQ) is one of the cognitive ability tests.

16. (c): Teaching is based upon a teacher's cognitive and affective domains.

(a) The subjective knowledge of teachers is important as the prime objective is to cover syllabus also. This may be linked with cognitive domain.

(b) Learners are engaged intellectually, emotionally, socially, and physically which produces a perception that the learning task is authentic. These can be counted as motivational factors.

(c) The socio economic background of teachers are usually personal attributes and may be important if channelized properly.

(d) Learning through experience: In experiential learning, students 'learn by doing' that includes laboratory experiments, internships, practicums, field exercises, research, apprenticeship. This also includes interdisciplinary learning, cultural awareness, leadership, participatory management, study abroad (for cultural immersion), decision making, innovation and creativity, career development etc.

Kolb's (1984) cycle of experiential learning includes the integration of knowledge (concepts, facts, and information), activity (the application of knowledge to a "real world" setting) and reflection (the analysis and synthesis of knowledge).

This cycle includes the following as well

1. **Active experimentation** – new ideas, new skills
2. **Concrete experience** – engaging directly in authentic situation
3. **Reflective observation** – noticing what happened
4. **Abstract conceptualization** – concretization of abstract ideas that includes analysis, critical thinking, and synthesis.

Experiential learning is linked with John Dewey also, then with Froebel's self activity, Maria Montessori's self-education, Rabindranath Tagore's learning with nature and so on.

17. (b): A good teacher never tries to enhance rote learning. The focus is on enhancing basic cognitive learning.

The main objective of teaching is to communicate an idea. The sender of information, message/information and receiver are the three parts of this process where it is important to generate a student's interest. If student's interest is built properly, the learning process can take place effectively and for a longer duration. Richard (1981), in his study found that a normal human being remembers 10% of what they read, 50% of what they saw and heard, above 70% of what they heard, seen and written and 90% what they do. Teaching aids are tool and equipment used in teaching as a supplement in class room instruction to enhance the interest of students. In teaching language, teaching aids/ materials are important because every individual has tendency to forget but proper use of these aids, help to remember lessons permanently. All teachings aids can be effectively used in class to motivate the students to learn better.

18. (a): (i) Lecture is a talk on a specialised topic by the teacher.

(ii) Interactive lectures are didactic learning sessions in which the teacher uses an activity that is also called as engagement trigger. That promotes learner engagement with the course material.

(iii) Group work is basically a collaborative learning environment where students work through the problems and assessments together. The help of teacher can be sought for mentoring. The students delegate roles and responsibilities, pool their knowledge and skills and receive support from one another.

(iv) Self-study depends upon the learner and is not a technique used by the teacher.

19. (d): An achievement test is a test of developed skill or knowledge. The most common type of achievement test is a standardized test developed to measure skills and knowledge learned in a given grade level, usually through planned instruction, such as training or classroom instruction. High achievement scores usually indicate a mastery of grade-level material, and the readiness for advanced instruction.

20. (d): Learning is a lifelong process, through formal or informal means. A good teacher should always inspire students to learn.

21. (c): Handicap is the mental or physical disadvantage which disable you in someway or another. Disability is one of most serious barriers to education across the globe. The Department of Empowerment of Persons with Disabilities in the Ministry of Social Justice & Empowerment facilitates empowerment of the persons with disabilities. This department is called as the 'divyanganjan'. No doubt, if a student has the issues of accessibility, less interest and distraction etc., a teacher has to deal with them. The expectations of parents and society are also there.

22. (c): Continuous and Comprehension Evaluation system was introduced by the Central Board of Secondary Education (CBSE) in 2009 with the enactment of the Right to Education (RTE) Act to bring about a holistic development among students. It is basically linked with process of assessment, that is school-based evaluation of students.

Firstly, the student's evaluation is done on continuous basis. It is a total teaching-learning process and spread over the entire span of academic session. It means regularity of assessment, frequency of unit testing, diagnosis of learning gaps, use of corrective measures, refreshing and feed back to evidence to teacher and students for their self evaluation. Secondly, it is comprehensive as it covers both the scholastic and the co-scholastic aspects. Through a paradigm shift in evaluation, it shifts the focus from testing to holistic learning.

It reduces phobia among students to face the exam.

23. (b): (i) Full time active involvement of a teacher in institutional management will take a teacher away from active teaching.

(ii) Setting examples, putting people in practical situations. The learners are usually highly impressionable. They always seek out role models whose actions they will learn, understand and reflect in life (or even avoid bad examples).

(iii) Assumption means to accept or believe that something is true even though you have no proof; to expect something to be true. Putting assumptions to the test means evaluating innovativeness, practicality and decision making skills of the people.

(iv). Acknowledging mistakes shows accepting the mistakes in public domain. This shows the humbleness of the person that makes him more acceptable in future behaviours.

24. (a): MCQs are mostly specific type of questions, and they are more objective as they require us to get more focused on the exam. Subjective or essay type means that we express our ideas in the form of words and sentences. Subjective helps us in better power of expression.

25. (c): The Delors Report titled - Learning: The Treasure with in. The Delors Report was a report created by the Delors Commission in 1996. It proposed an integrated vision of education based on two key concepts, `learning throughout life' and the four pillars of learning, to know, to do, to be and to live together.

Learning to know – a broad general knowledge with the opportunity to work in depth on a small number of subjects.

Learning to do – to acquire not only occupational skills but also the competence to deal with many situations and to work in teams.

Learning to be – to develop one's personality and to be able to act with growing autonomy, judgment and personal responsibility.

Learning to live together – by developing an understanding of other people and an appreciation of interdependence.

The idea of the integrated approach to education reflected in the four pillars of learning has had significant influence on policy debates, teacher training and curriculum development in a range of countries worldwide.

(For full text, please refer to www.unesco.org/education/pdf/15_62.pdf can be visited).

26. (a): Diagnosis is an approach that works through helping students to learn, to detect, to understand and to correct misconceptions in their own and their fellow student work. It is also called learning from mistake.

Remedial learning is a well designed learning environment that helps to maintain pupils' attention and interest in learning and facilitates the achievement of teaching aims. It also helps to achieve the aims of teaching. The teaching environment should be designed to support remedial teaching and group activities.

Direction means guiding the efforts of students in the right direction.

Feedback is to get response of the students.

27. (b): The students are basically the product of teaching – learning process. The quality of a product depends upon the quality of teachers. This can be taken as feedback of students about the teachers.

(i) The question is about the evaluation of teachers.

(ii) As evaluation of students makes students to take study seriously, the same sort of evaluation of teachers will prompt teachers to teach students seriously.

(iii) To stand good in the perception of students, teachers will adopt innovative methods of teaching.

(iv) The teaching is mostly a behavioural activity, so scope of improvement in the traits of teachers is always there.

28. (d): Mind mapping is a highly effective way of getting information in and out of your brain. Mind mapping is a creative and logical means of note-taking and note-making that literally 'maps out' your ideas. All mind maps have some things in common.

We can take the following perspective also for mind mapping:

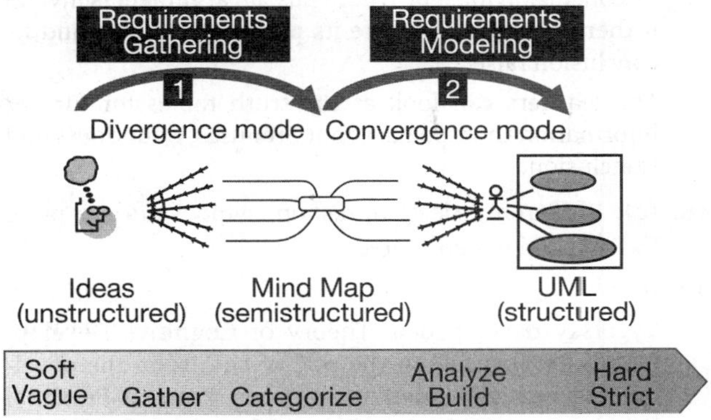

29. (c): Memory, Understanding and Reflective levels can be linked in the life form of sequence

30. (b): (B) pertains to family friends. (E) deals with dress code. These are not linked with teaching learning systems. Learning basically means bringing about change in behaviour. The mention of family friends and interest in dress code are not relevant.

31. (b): The main objective of higher education is to develop the critical and creative thinking abilities among students, that is basically reflective level of understanding that enhances their decision making skills in a complex society. These abilities enhance possibilities of getting a job but do not 'ensure' a job.

32. (a): A. Formative means during process of learning. Quizzes and discussions help in some feedback and evaluation.

B. Summative means final exams.

C. Continuous and comprehensive evaluation means to focus upon 'thought levels' on regular basis.

D. Norms and criterion referenced tests: They are different tests. Criterion-referenced means the test relates to some sort of established unit of measure. Norm-referenced is a percentage ranking compared to an average population.

33. (d): Effectiveness of teaching means requisite feedback to know whether objectives of teaching has been achieved or not. A teacher's socio-economic back ground, his ability to please students and his maintaining personal contacts with student's are not directly relevant in achieving his objectives.

34. (c): A teaching aid is anything used by a teacher to help teach a lesson or make it more interesting to students. Teaching aids are an integral component in any classroom. The benefits of teaching aids include helping learners improve reading comprehension skills, illustrating or reinforcing a skill or concept, differentiating instruction and relieving anxiety or boredom by presenting information in a new and exciting way.

35. (c): Adoption of well-established posture helps to create congenial environment for communication.

36. (b): There is learning without teaching, it can be even self-learning.

37. (b): For a reason, learning can be transcendentalism. The process of education is the understanding the world around us, the cultivation of good reasoning and judgment, and the development of an identity.

38. (c): Effectiveness is basically denoted by quality and feedback. Learning outcome for students means holistic development of their personality, to make them good citizens, increase their knowledge, intellectual and decision making skills so that they can help in the jobs and professional avenues.

39. (d): Optimal means being result oriented without minimum cost. Proactive means we need to be associated from the very beginning.

40. (d): Education system aims at our overall personality development. All factors mentioned here affect the teaching effectiveness but 'educational system' is the most direct.

41. (c): Evaluation is an educational program that aims to measure all three areas of cognitive, affective and psychomotor learning. To reach a final conclusion, process as well as product is evaluated.

Considering Assertion (A), formative evaluation is linked with process or 'during the stage of formation'. The goal of formative evaluation is to monitor student learning to provide ongoing feedback. This way a teacher can improve his own teaching and can help students to improve their learning. The students identify their strengths and weaknesses (SWOT analysis), they identify the areas which need harder work. The faculty also identifies areas where students are struggling, they try to find immediate solutions. This evaluation may have some nominal or no score or point value.

Summative assessments are used to evaluate student learning, skill acquisition, and academic achievement at the conclusion of a defined instructional period. This basically means to evaluate a learner/student learning at the end of an instructional unit by comparing it against some standard or benchmark. This stage carries high stakes – scores or points. This may include midterm exam, final project, paper etc.

For comparison, it is actually the formative evaluation that leads to better summative evaluation. Thus, both supplement each other. As summative evaluation carries point value that helps a learner to get a certificate and shift to next level of education, this may be counted as more valuable but still formative evaluation may act as a base. Moreover, summative evaluation is more systematic than formative evaluation, that may make it more valuable.

42. (b): Learning is basically a psychological concept, so depends upon individual to a great extent. It is active engagement in a subject domain.

In (a) and (d), teaching is being described as a kind of commodity, so they are to be eliminated. Teaching is triadic in nature as shown in the diagram below.

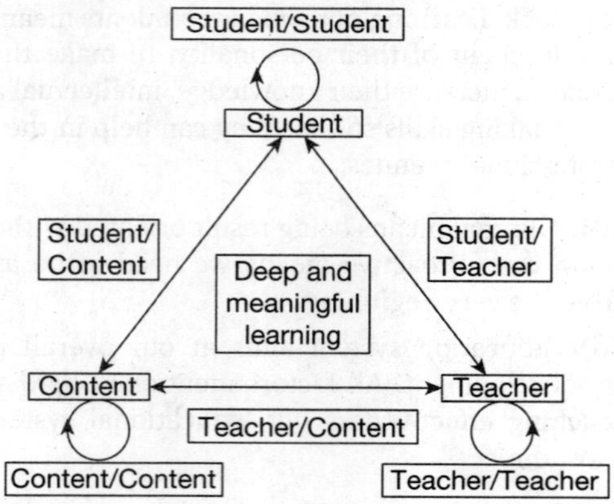

43. (a): Family lineage, food habits, religious functions, etc., are not linked with teaching learning system to become effective.

Experience, aptitude and stage of development are directly related with teaching learning system to be effective.

44. (c): *Assertion (A)* is right, as the ultimate objective of teaching is to make students learn.

Reason (R) is false as learning is a lifelong process and not all of it takes place in classroom. In a broader perspective, a great deal of learning takes place in actual life situations as well.

45. (d): Summative tests are usually conducted by external agencies with well-defined criteria. These are tests that measure a particular student's performance against a standard or criterion. They should not be confused with the norm-referenced assessments that measure a student's performance against that of other students. The content and skills in a criterion-referenced assessment are more specific.

46. (c): The main objective of using instructional variety is to ensure optimum involvement of all senses so that understanding and retention is better, for example, multimodal teaching.

47. (c): An argument is more likely to use the words such as truism.

Looking at validity, we can say that the validity of an argument guarantees that if its premises are true, then its conclusion must be true. Thus, an argument is invalid if there is any case where its premises are true and its conclusion false.

The learners can look at the truth tables for further information that speaks about Premises, Soundness and Conclusion.

48. (c): Research article, workshop, symposium are more focused and workoriented.

49. (c)

Vygotsky developed a 'Theory of Cognitive Development' that focused on the role of culture in the development of higher mental functions. Zone of Proximal Development (ZPD) is defined as the range of tasks that a child can perform with the help and guidance of others but cannot yet perform independently. Within ZPD, there are two levels, such as actual development level and potential development level.

For future exams, NET aspirants must remember that closely related to ZPD is the concept of 'scaffolding' where a teacher should provide clues about how to proceed through the problem.

50. (c): We need to look at the statements one by one:

(A) Under objectives of teaching, the last line clearly mentions that the objectives of teaching and learning must integrate.

(B) Teaching is a wider concept than training.

(C) Transformation through making students is the main target of all teaching.

(D) Teaching is through both formal, informal means - it mainly depends upon the stage in life also.

(E) 'Maxims of Teaching' do not indicate that a teacher is to be a senior person.

(F) Learner's characteristics are mainly about individual differences reflect that learning is a personal act. Types of learners also reflect upon this point.

51. (a): Under, Effective Teaching Practices/Maxims of Teaching, 'Known to Unknown' that retention is always better if new knowledge can be linked with the known one that is basically prior experience of learner.

52. (c): We have already discussed lecture method and discussion in groups.

Brainstorming—This permits people to think more freely, without any fear of judgment, they tend to think `out of box'. This encourages open and ongoing collaboration with an objective to solve problems and generate innovative ideas. Thus, a large number of ideas are generated quickly. These ideas can be refined and merged to create the ideal solution. The students build on or develop higher order thinking skills.

Programmed Instructional Procedure—In this method, new subject matter is presented to the students in a graded sequence of controlled steps. Students work at their own speed. The feedback is in the form of set of questions or comprehension knowledge.

53. (d): Formative means judging while the program activities are forming or under progress. The goal of formative evaluation is to monitor student learning to provide on going feedback that can be used by teachers to improve teaching learning environment.

For future exams, NET aspirants should refer to ADDIE process also:

(1) Analysis

(2) Design

(3) Development

(4) Implement

(5) Evaluate

It is considered a part of the ISD (Instructional System Design).

54. (c): Teaching definitions refer to learning as main objective.

Under Gagne and Griggs Classification of Teaching Objectives, there is mention of learning outcomes.

Thus, Assertion (A) is right.

Learning is the modification of behaviour, it is not necessarily through teaching. Under concept of teaching, it is mentioned that there are informal agencies such as family that teach in an informal manner, so reason (R) is wrong.

Learning objectives should be brief, clear, specific statements of what learners will be able to do at the end of a lesson as a result of the activities, teaching and learning that has taken place. They are sometimes called learning outcomes. The learning objective or objectives that you use can be based on three areas of learning: knowledge, skills and attitudes. Learning objectives define learning outcomes and focus teaching. They help to clarify, organize and prioritize learning. They help you and your students evaluate progress and encourage them to take responsibility for their learning.

55. (c): A research paper is an essay in which one explains what has been learnt after exploring some topic in-depth. The information can be included from sources, such as books, articles, interviews, and internet sites. One can also use one's own ideas, knowledge and opinions. It should be in one's own words.

A workshop is a period of discussion or practical work on a particular subject in which a group of people share their knowledge or experience.

56. (d): Cognitive learning is a type of learning that is active, constructive, and long-lasting. It engages students in the learning processes, teaching them to use their brains more effectively to make connections when learning new things.

Visual literacy is the ability to interpret, negotiate, and make meaning from information presented in the form of an image, extending the meaning of literacy, which commonly signifies interpretation of a written or printed text.

Sensory perception—An individual or organism must be capable of performing neurophysiological processing of the stimuli in their environment for them to possess for learning.

Academic self-concept—construct refers to self-perception and evaluation of a student on his or her self-regulation, general intellectual abilities, motivation, and creativity. Belief is a state or habit of mind in which trust or confidence is placed in some person or thing.

57. (a): An aptitude test, by meaning, is any type of assessment that evaluates the talent/ability/potential to perform a certain task, with no prior knowledge and/or training. Bottom line, there are many different types of aptitude tests used by employers during the recruitment process.

Intelligence tests are psychological tests that are designed to measure a variety of mental functions, such as reasoning, comprehension, and judgment

Personality test—The test usually helps measure one's interpersonal skills, thought process and their emotional capabilities. These traits may be used to evaluate if you are right fit for a certain job position.

Prognostic test is used to predict a patient's likelihood of developing a disease or experiencing a medical event. Therefore, the 'reference test' for a prognostic test is the observed proportion of the population who develop what is being predicted.

58. (b): Jean Piaget proposed that humans progress through four developmental stages of cognitive development.

(1) Sensorimotor
(2) Preoperational
(3) Concrete operational
(4) Formal operational period.

The sensorimotor stage begins at birth and lasts through age 2. During this period child learns about the world using there senses to interact with their surroundings. The main feature of the stage is object permanence.

59. (a): According to John Dewey, school is an essential social and psychological institution where children learns from their own experiences.

Education, according to John Dewey, is a philosophical process by which man is able to regulate his environment and realize his potential to learn. This is social aspect of his philosophy.

60. (b): The multiple intelligences theory differentiates human intelligence into specific modalities, rather than seeing intelligence as dominated by a single general ability. Howard Gardner (1983) proposed this model in his 1983 book '*Frames of Mind the Theory of Multiple Intelligences*'. According to the theory, an intelligence 'modality' must fulfil eight criteria.

Jean Piaget's theory says that thinking was different during each stage of development. His theory includes how children perceive, think, understand, and learn about their world. There are four stages and as you age your intelligence goes into deeper thinking.

Sigmund Freud emphasized the importance of the unconscious mind, and a primary assumption of Freudian theory is that the unconscious mind governs behaviour to a greater degree than people suspect. Indeed, the goal of psychoanalysis is to make the unconscious conscious. Freud produced the following model:

Id: Instincts | **Ego:** Reality | **Superego:** Morality

61. (b): Computer-assisted language learning is briefly defined in a seminal work by Levy (1997) as 'the search for and study of applications of the computer in language teaching and learning'. They help through texting and picture sharing, and thus, called up as communicative call.

It helps in the study or implementation of computer programs capable of discovering or checking proofs of formal expressions or segments.

62. (c): The term emotional intelligence was created by two researchers, Peter Salavoy and John Mayer in their article 'Emotional Intelligence'. Emotional intelligence (EI) as learner characteristic takes into account the following things.

Self awareness—People with high EI understand their emotions and they don't let their feelings rule them. They help guide our thinking and behaviour on continuous basis.

Self regulation—This is the ability to control emotions and impulses.

Motivation—People with a high EI are willing to defer immediate results for long-term success. It helps in adapting to environment.

63. (a): Prognostic assessments act as a means of estimation and prediction of the future career. Prognostic assessment combines basic aspects taken from an assessment of learning processes and an assessment of learning achievements and tries to formulate a diagnosis for the student's future.

64. (d): Formative assessment is a process used by teachers and students during instruction that provides feedback to adjust ongoing teaching and learning to improve students' achievement of intended instructional outcomes. It is usually a 'low stakes' or non-graded type of assessment.

65. (b): Howthorne effect—It means that workers participating in a study might, for example, temporarily become more productive as a result of being observed. The effect generally refers to alterations in behaviour by participants in a research study. In general, Hawthrone experiments were conducted in the area of management.

Jung theory was basically founded by Carl Gustav Jung. He actually founded analytic psychology, in some aspects a response to Sigmund Freud's psychoanalysis. Jung proposed and developed the concepts of the extraverted and the introverted personality, archetypes, and the collective unconscious. His work has been influential in psychiatry and in the study of religion, literature, and related fields.

Attention deficit disorder (ADD) is a neurological disorder that causes a range of behaviour problems such as difficulty attending to instruction, focusing on schoolwork, keeping up with assignments, following instructions, completing tasks and social interaction.

The Markov property refers to the memory less property of a stochastic process. A stochastic process has the Markov property if the conditional probability distribution of future states of the process depends only upon the present state, not on the sequence of events that preceded it.

66. (d): Asynchronous learning is a student-centered teaching method that uses online learning resources to facilitate information sharing outside the constraints of time and place among a network of people. Asynchronous learning is based on constructivist theory, a student-centered approach that emphasizes the importance of peer-to-peer interactions.

For future questions, we can add this information. The online learning resources used to support asynchronous learning include email, electronic mailing lists, threaded conferencing systems, online discussion boards, wikis, and blogs. Course management systems such as Campus Cruiser LMS, Desire2Learn, Blackboard, WebCT, Moodle, and Sakai, have been developed to support online interaction, allowing users to organize discussions, post and reply to messages, and upload and access multimedia. These asynchronous forms of communication are sometimes supplemented with synchronous components, including text and voice chat, telephone conversations, videoconferencing, and even meetings in virtual spaces such as *Second Life*, where discussions can be facilitated among groups of students.

67. (b): Teaching and learning is a process that includes many variables. These variables interact as learners work toward their goals and incorporate new knowledge, behaviours, and skills that add to their range of learning experiences.

We should also keep in mind that over the past century, various perspectives on learning have emerged, among them—cognitive (learning as a mental operation); and constructivist (knowledge as a constructed element resulting from the learning process).

68. (c): SET–II offers kind of direct definitions of SET–I elements which are quite direct.

69. (a): Analogy is a cognitive process of transferring information or meaning from a particular subject (the analog, or source) to another (the target). It is a linguistic expression. Supporting evidence is a crucial part in body paragraphs and it is important to be discerning in the evidence chosen. Supporting evidence proving claims.

70. (b): In nutshell, andragogical approach is identified as the 'adult learning'.

Though no directly related with the question, adult learning have specifically been mentioned in Chapter 1 of new NTA syllabus. There are some important points for adult learning. Adult education found a rightful place in the Report of the Education Commission (1964–66). The Commission accepted the new concept of 'life-long education'.

A national adult education programme (NAEP) was launched on 2 October 1978 to cover 65 million (650 lakhs) illiterate persons, in the age- group 15–35.

With the objective of promoting adult education, a series of programmes have been introduced since the First Five Year Plan, the most prominent being the National Literacy Mission (NLM), that was launched in 1988 to impart functional literacy to non-literates in the age group of 15-35 years in a time bound manner.

There can be question relating to census 2011 education data also that is also somewhat dependent upon adult education. The five top literate states in India are

(1) Kerala (94%)

(2) Lakshadweep (91.85%)

(3) Mizoram (91.33%)

(4) Goa (88.70%)

(5) Tripura (87.22%)

71. (d): The cone of experience is a pictorial device use to explain the interrelationships of the various types of audio-visual media, as well as their individual 'positions' in the learning process—from the concrete to the abstract. It was given by Edgar Dale in 1969.

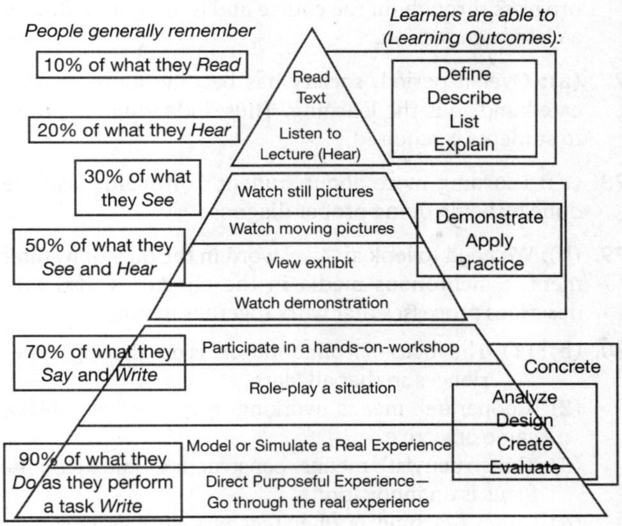

72. (d): Power of sensory perception is mainly psychological in nature.

Thinking ability is cognitive development.

Power of synthetic imagination is kind of artificial simulation by general or special purpose computers, it's about human imagination.

73. (d): Formative evaluation is not before or after learning process but it's in between, it means during the formative stage of course, that's why it is called as formative evaluation.

74. (d): Choice (d) is more about believing, it's not characteristically confirmed. Thus, it is non cognitive and is the answer.

75. (b): SWAYAM stands for Study Webs of Active-Learning for Young Aspiring Minds - Sikshit Bharat Unnat Bharat. This MOOC Platform was developed indigenously by AICTE in 2016 to facilitate hosting of online courses which could be accessed by anyone, anywhere at any time, free of cost to achieve three cardinal principles of Education Policy viz. access, equity and quality. The current SWAYAM platform is developed by the Ministry of Education, NPTEL,and IIT Madras with the help of Google Inc. and Persistent Systems Ltd.

The courses hosted on SWAYAM are in 4 quadrants – (1) video lectures, (2)specially prepared reading material that can be downloaded/printed, (3) self-assessment tests through tests and quizzes, and (4) an online discussion forum for clearing the doubts.

There are nine verticals - NPTEL, CEC, AICTE, IGNOU, IIMB, NITTTR, UGC, NIOS, NCERT.

76. (b): Formative evaluation is used to determine student progress throughout the course and is often used during a classroom session.

77. (a): Over a period, society has become more complicated and so is the learning. Thus, individual attention to students is required.

78. (d): Learning more about student's difficulties can be done by being doing proper diagnose.

79. (b): We need to look at 'Live' word in the question statement. Synchronous media in the chapter 4 also that describes processes that work together in time.

80. (b): (1) The focus of 'collaboration' is on 'sharing' experiences so that all learn.
(2) 'Cooperate' means working together to achieve same objective.
(3) 'Constructivist' means constructing knowledge—focus is on innovation.
(4) 'Team Teaching' is when teachers work as a team.

81. (b): (1) A demonstration is the process of teaching someone how to make or do something in a step-by-step process. This can be done with the aid of visuals such as flip charts, posters, power point, etc.
(2) Modular approach is a self contained package dealing with one specific subject in the convenient form, so that a learner can complete it as his own pace or independently or in small groups.
(3) Programmed learning received its major impetus from B. F. Skinner and is based on his theory of operant conditioning, according to which learning is best accomplished in small, incremental steps with immediate reinforcement, or reward, for the learner.
(4) Personalized learning refers to instruction in which the pace of learning and the instructional approach are optimized for the needs of each learner.
(5) Collaborative method means grouping students to work together towards a common academic goal.

82. (d): Piaget proposed four stages of cognitive development which reflect the increasing sophistication of children's thought:
(1) Sensorimotor stage (birth to age 2)
(2) Pre-operational stage (from age 2 to age 7)
(3) Concrete operational stage (from age 7 to age 11)
(4) Formal operational stage (age 11+ – adolescence and adulthood).

Schemas are the building blocks of the knowledge.

83. (c): Team teaching means when teachers as experts work as a team to complete the various topics in a subject to the same class.

84. (d): The core bases for 'effectiveness of teaching' are reflected by options (b), (c) and (d), though 'marks obtained' and 'regularity' are also important.

85. (b): The think aloud procedure asks students to say out loud what they are thinking about when reading, solving math problems, or simply responding to questions posed by teachers or other students. Effective teachers think out loud on a regular basis to model this process for students.

Thus, both students and learners show the practical ways of approaching difficult problems while bringing to the surface the complex thinking processes that underlie reading comprehension, mathematical problem solving, and other cognitively demanding tasks.
(1) Here, the students learn to monitor their thinking as they read and improve their comprehension.
(2) It teaches students to re-read a sentence, read ahead to clarify, and/or look for context clues to make sense of what they read.
(3) It slows down the reading process and allows students to monitor their understanding of a text.

86. (a): The audio-lingual teaching method is the right answer. Let's go into some historical perspective.

With the outbreak of World War II armies needed to become orally proficient in the languages of their allies and enemies as quickly as possible. This teaching technique was initially called the army method, and was the first to be based on linguistic theory and behavioural psychology.

Based on Skinner's behaviourism theory, it assumed that a human being can be trained using a system of reinforcement. Correct behaviour receives positive feedback, while errors receive negative feedback.

This approach to learning is similar to the direct method, in that the lesson takes place entirely in the target language.

Emphasis is on the acquisition of patterns in common everyday dialogue.

Some characteristics of this method are:

(1) Drills are used to teach structural patterns
(2) Set phrases are memorized with a focus on intonation
(3) Grammatical explanations are kept to a minimum
(4) Vocabulary is taught in context
(5) Audio-visual aids are used
(6) Focus is on pronunciation
(7) Correct responses are positively reinforced immediately

Focus–Sentence and sound patterns

Characteristics–Listening and speaking drills and pattern practice only in English

Supporters–B. F. Skinner, Leonard Bloomfield, Robin Callan

87. **(d): Memory level of teaching:** In this level emphasis is laid down on the presentation of the facts and information's and its cramming.

Understanding level: In understanding level of teaching, teacher stresses to make understand to the pupils the generalizations, principles and facts.

Reflective level of teaching means 'problem-centered' teaching.

Analysing level: Separates material or concepts into component parts so that its organizational structure may be understood. Distinguishes between facts and inferences.

Creating level: Builds a structure or pattern from diverse elements. Put parts together to form a whole, with emphasis on creating a new meaning or structure.

According to Bloom's taxanomy: Revised Bloom's taxonomy by Anderson and Krathwohl.

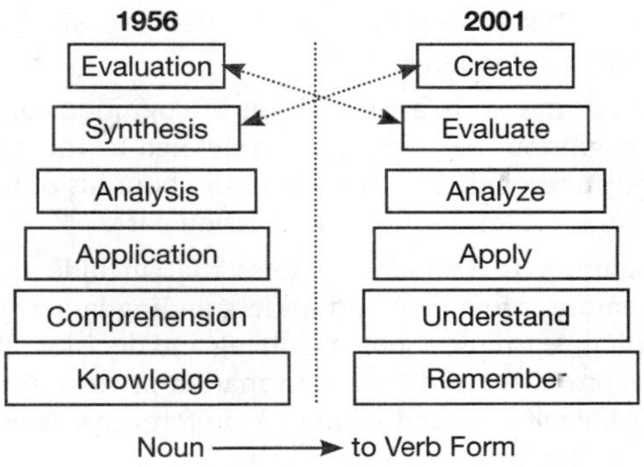

88. (b) Diagnostic evaluation is concerned with evaluation of pupils learning difficulties during instruction. A diagnostic test used to diagnose or to reveal an individual's weakness and strengths in a certain course of study. It tries to discover the specific area of weakness of a student in a given course of instruction and then suggest remedial measures.

Diagnostic tests are designed to analyze individual's performance and provide information on the causes of difficulty.

The purpose of the diagnostic evaluation is to enquire into the nature of the difficulties faced by a pupil in his subject, so that proper remedial instructions may be applied.

89. **(b):** A lesson plan is the instructor's road map of what students need to learn and how it will be done effectively during the class time. Then, you can design appropriate learning activities and develop strategies to obtain feedback on student learning. A successful lesson plan addresses and integrates three key components:

(1) Learning objectives
(2) Learning activities
(3) Assessment to check for student understanding

Before the class	During the class	After the class
• Identify the learning objectives • Plan the specific learning activities, assessments, and the sequence of the lesson • Create a realistic timeline • Plan for a lesson closure	• Share the lesson plan with your students helps keep them more engaged and on track	• Reflect on what worked well and why, and what you could have done differently

A good lesson plan that is simple yet powerful is based on behavioural research that characterizes well-structured lessons.

(1) Start lessons by reviewing prerequisite learning. This can include a type of formative assessment.
(2) Provide a short statement of goals.
(3) Present new material in small steps, with student practice after each step. This practice is in the form of formative assessments to get fair idea about student's level of mastery. This also shows how a teacher should modify instruction, if required.
(4) There is need to give clear and detailed instructions and explanations.
(5) There is need to provide a high level of active practice for all students.
(6) We can ask a large number of questions, check for understanding, and obtain responses from all students. Thus, using formative assessments to determine student mastery.

(7) The information should undergo systematic feedback and corrections. This phase requires that the teacher provide detailed information to the student. Simply telling the student the answer is incorrect and not enough.

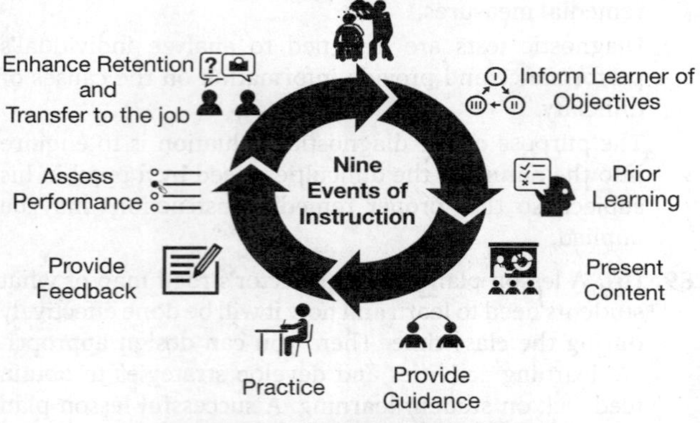

Gagne's: Nine events of instructions

90. (c): Instructional Software (IS) programs include pictures, sounds, animations, and other various stimuli used to enhance the development of skills such as reading, writing and problem solving. IS programs provide individualized experiences used to enhance the general curriculum and mastery of skills through extra practice, simulations, and problem solving opportunities. For example, Radio Talk (Broadcast Talks) that combines radio broadcasts with active learning to improve educational quality and teaching practices. Radio programs may include educational and scientific topics, current affairs, discussions, etc.

The three categories of classification for IS programs are as follows.

(1) Drills and Practice Programs provide opportunities to master skills previously taught while providing corrective feedback. These types of programs teach a skill and then give multiple opportunities to practice this skill.

(2) Simulations provide practice for decision-making in cause and effect situations.

(3) Games provide opportunities to reinforce skills through activities that motivate the students. These can be successful for students with various types of learning or cognitive disabilities.

91. (d): Global and local prioroties are shaped by changing conditions in a fast-moving world. Inclusive education responds to education, underachievement and diminished social opportunities of vulnerable student identities—indigenous and First Nations children, the girl child, children displaced by conflict or natural disasters, children from minority, ethnic, religious or tribal groups, inclusive education must develop a practical understanding of exclusive; its structures and cultures. In essence, inclusive education ought to provide a principled and systematic approach to identifying and dismantling barriers for vulnerable populations.

The central message of inclusive education is quite simple—Every learner matters and matters equally. (UNESCO–2017).

This approach has been incorporated in Indian education policy in the form of 'The Right to Education Act, 2009'.

92. (b): Teaching is usually described as effective when teachers get desired feedback from the learners. A teacher is automatically considered successful or practical or say intelligent when he/she is effective also.

93. (b): Let's look at the concept of reflective practices first.

Reflective practice has huge benefits in increasing self-awareness, which is a key component of emotional intelligence. It also helps in developing a better understanding of others. Reflective practice can also help you to develop creative thinking skills, and encourages active engagement in work processes.

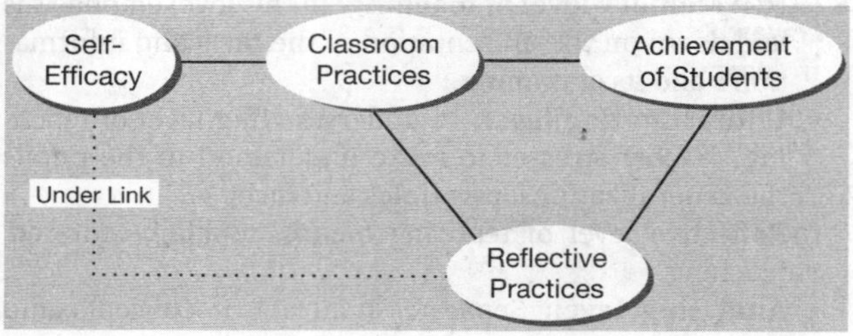

Now coming to concepts of cognition and metacognition. It is often difficult to distinguish the difference between cognition and metacognition. They are closely related and can often overlap. Flavell described an example such as 'Asking yourself questions about the chapter might function either to improve your knowledge (a cognitive function) or to monitor it (a metacognitive function).' This quote shows how different, yet similar these two concepts can be.

Metacognition is a subdivision of cognition, or a type of cognition. Metacognition is defined as the scientific study of an individual's cognitions about his or her own cognitions. It is basically application part.

Cognition is a mental process that include memory, attention, producing and understanding language, reasoning, learning, problem-solving and decision-making. It is often referred to as information processing, applying knowledge, and changing preferences. It is something that is more basic.

Thus, relating these with reflective practices we can say that metacognition should be the answer as both talk about 'self-awareness' and 'individual awareness'.

Reinforcement of learning means strengthening of one's knowledge by repeated trials and maximizing the rewards.

94. (c): Brainstorming is a group creativity technique by which efforts are made to find a conclusion for a specific problem by gathering a list of ideas spontaneously contributed by its members. All the ideas are noted down and those ideas are not criticized and after brainstorming session the ideas are evaluated.

95. (d): Intended learning outcomes should be about student performance. They basically aim at changing human behaviour.

Learning objectives are statements that define the expected goal of a curriculum, course, lesson or activity in terms of demonstrable skills or knowledge that will be acquired by a student as a result of instruction. Learning objectives can be tied to competence maps, also known as instructional, objectives, learning outcomes, learning goals.

96. (c): They are self-motivated learners who are constantly looking for new ways to improve their performance and deepen their understanding of the world around them. In a general learning situation, self-motivation without rewards will not succeed. Students must find satisfaction in learning based on the understanding that the goals are useful to them or, less commonly, based on the pure enjoyment of exploring new things.

97. (c): Maximum Performance Tests: These assess the individual's ability to perform effectively under standard conditions. Performance on these tests, which includes ability and aptitude tests, can be judged as right or wrong.

98. (c): Direct teaching is the use of straightforward, explicit teaching techniques, usually to teach a specific skill. In teacher-directed method, the teacher stands in front of a classroom and presents the information. It is mostly used for the languages where there is no need to make use of native language.

Here, a teacher gets focused on explanations, reviews and feedback.

99. (d): A criterion-referenced test is a style of test which uses test scores to generate a statement about the behaviour that can be expected of a person with that score. Most tests and quizzes that are written by our teachers can be considered criterion-referenced tests.

The goal of summative assessment is to evaluate student learning at the end of an instructional unit by comparing it against some standard or benchmark. Summative assessments are often high stakes, which means that they have a high point value.

Diagnostic assessment is a form of pre-assessment that allows a teacher to determine students' individual strengths, weaknesses, knowledge, and skills prior to instruction. It is primarily used to diagnose student difficulties and to guide lesson and curriculum planning.

The exact definition of norm-referenced is given in the question statement itself. In this a percentage ranking is compared to an average population.

100. (d): Divergent questions allow students to explore different avenues and create many different variations and alternative answers or scenarios. Correctness may be based on logical projections, may be contextual, or arrived at through basic knowledge, conjecture, inference, projection, creation, intuition, or imagination. answering these types of questions may be aided by higher levels of affective thinking.

An open-ended question is a question that cannot be answered with a 'yes' or 'no' response, or with a static response. Open-ended questions are phrased as a statement which requires a response. The response can be compared to information that is already known to the questioner. For example, how do you feel today? What is your favourite past time memory?

Closed-ended questions can be answered in fast manner, less complicated and easy to find (say by use of internet).

Concept questions are questions designed to check learners' understanding of a particular concept.

101. (a): Socio-economic background, parent's interest and family background are indirect factors. We need to be clear about definition of learning and look for pragmatic approach.

102. (a): Emotional intelligence is different from general or common intelligence. It's the ability of an individual to monitor their own emotions, to monitor the emotions of others, to understand the differences between them, and to use all of this information in order to guide their actions. This is about accurately understanding the emotions of oneself and others, as well as expressing emotions in a way that's accessible.

A high level of emotional intelligence is an essential aspect of learning. The ability to develop the skill of emotional understanding is a driver not only in the realm of relationships but also in the realm of education. The following four dimensions of emotional intelligence can help teachers and administrators to better understand and support student learning.

(1) Understanding

(2) Management

(3) Empathy

(4) Relationships

Thus, other choices are automatically eliminated.

103. (d): The theory of multiple intelligences differentiates human intelligence into specific 'modalities', rather than seeing intelligence as dominated by a single general ability. Howard Gardner proposed this model in his 1983 book *Frames of Mind: The Theory of Multiple Intelligences*.

104. (d): Inclusive teaching describes the range of approaches to teaching that consider the diverse needs and backgrounds of all students to create a learning environment where all students feel valued and where all students have equal access to learn. It is our social and ethical responsibility as well.

105. (a): Topic should not be necessarily easy. The role of a teacher is more of moderator or facilitator.

Topic is always announced in advance and should be of common interest so that all participants can speak on it. The people should have language skills that others are familiar with for the sake of participation.

106. (a): Based on the research conducted by the T. Good and J. Brophy in 1987 , there are five key behaviour for effective teaching and some indicators pertaining to them are the following:

(1) **Lesson clarity:** Logical, step-by-step order; clear and audible delivery free of distracting mannerisms.

(2) **Instructional variety:** Variability in instructional materials, questioning, types of feedback, and teaching strategies.

(3) **Task orientation**: Achievement (content) orientation as opposed to process orientation, maximum content coverage, and time devoted to instruction.

(4) **Student engagement:** Limiting opportunities for distraction and getting students to work on, think through, and inquire about the content.

(5) **Student Success rate:** 60% to 70% of time spent on tasks that afford moderate-to-high levels of success, especially during expository or didactic instruction.

107. (c): Formative evaluation is basically a continuous evaluation in classroom sessions.

A mastery test that is used to decide whether individuals have attained some particular level of performance, is called as a mastery test.

'Evaluating students in a grading system' is also done at the end of some academic session and is a part of Summative evaluation.

108. (c): Autonomous level means not exactly in the classroom.

Memory level is the first and thoughtless level of teaching.

Understanding level explains pupils about the relationship between principles and facts, may be through positive and negative examples. Kindly look at the words 'presentations in classroom'.

Reflective means dealing with 'real life problems'.

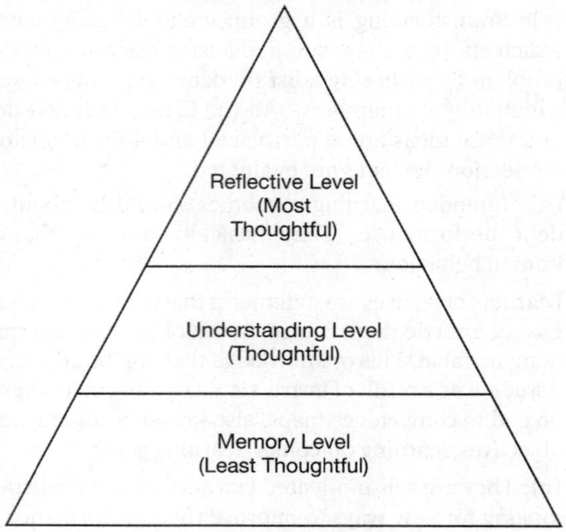

Hierarchical order of the levels of teaching

109. (d): Lecture method mainly focuses on 'cognitive' objectives, it helps in forming generalization.

Demonstration method of teaching is a traditional classroom strategy used in technical and training colleges and in teacher education. As you show how, you 'tell' what you are doing. A demonstration always has a finished product.

Project method is based on the philosophy of pragmatism and the principle of 'Learning by doing'. It demands work from the pupils.

Collaborative method basically involves grouping students to work together towards a common academic goal.

110. (d): Effective teaching should result in effective learning. Options (a) and (e) are important but more on emotional and social grounds.

111. (b): Here 'dialogic' means having a dialogue. Dialogue is defined as 'any negotiated exchange of ideas and opinions'. It is kind of having dialogical approach to learning.

Lecture is usually one-sided and passive for students. Lecturing is sometimes described as 'chalk and talk method.

Team teaching involves a group of instructors working purposefully, regularly, and cooperatively to help a group of students of any age learn.

Choices (c), (d) and (f) carry close interaction between teachers and participants.

112. (a): A workshop is a period of discussion or practical work on a particular subject in which a group of people share their knowledge or experience. A workshop is a building which contains tools or machinery for making or repairing things, especially using wood or metal.

There is no lecture, interaction or specific group discussion.

113. (b): SWAYAM (Study Webs of Active–Learning for Young Aspiring Minds) is a programme initiated by Government of India and designed to achieve the three cardinal principles of Education Policy viz., access, equity and quality. The objective of this effort is to take the best teaching learning resources to all, including the most disadvantaged. SWAYAM seeks to bridge the digital divide for students who have hitherto remained untouched by the digital revolution and have not been able to join the mainstream of the knowledge economy. This is done through an indigenous developed IT platform that facilitates hosting of all the courses taught in classrooms to be accessed by anyone, anywhere at any time. All the courses are interactive, prepared by the best teachers in the country and are available, free of cost to the residents in India.

114. (c): Ministry of Education has embarked on a major and new initiative called 'Study Webs of Active Learning for Young Aspiring Minds' (SWAYAM), which provides one integrated platform and MOOCs (Massive Open Online Courses) portal for online courses, using Information and Communication Technology (ICT) and covering all higher education subjects and skill sector courses. It's all digital and there is no physical interaction at any level.

Credit transfer facility up to 20% is enabled through the notification issued by UGC/AICTE—'Credit Framework for online learning courses through SWAYAM Regulation 2016'. It is the endeavour of MHRD to align the courses on the SWAYAM portal with the curriculum of universities.

115. (c): MOOCs is Massive Open Online Courses. The basic idea is given in the diagram below.

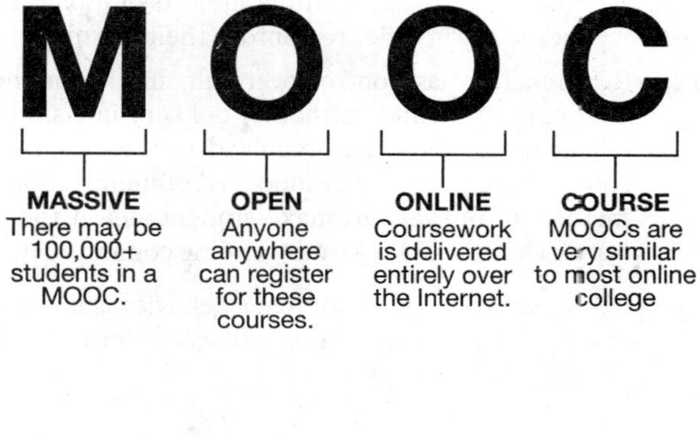

116. (d): Government has set-up National Academic Depository (NAD) which is a 24 × 7 online store house of academic awards digitally lodged by various academic institutions/school boards/eligibility assessment bodies.

UGC has been designated as authorized body to operationalize NAD. NAD covers degrees, diplomas, certificates, mark-sheets including awards issued for skill development. The framework of NAD includes various Central Universities, Central Higher Educational Institutions, State Universities, Deemed to be Universities, Central Board of Secondary Education (CBSE), State School Education Boards, etc., located in various States/Union Territories including the State of Maharashtra.

NAD comprises two interoperable digital depositories viz., NSDL Database Management Limited (NDML) and CDSL Ventures Limited (CVL).

Maintenance of academic awards in a digital depository also helps eliminating fraudulent practices such as forging of certificates and mark-sheets, etc.

CBSE has introduced 'Parinam Manjusha' for the purpose.

117. (c): The courses hosted on SWAYAM are in four quadrants:

(1) video lecture,

(2) specially prepared reading material that can be downloaded/printed,

(3) self-assessment tests through tests and quizzes, and

(4) an online discussion forum for clearing the doubts. Steps have been taken to enrich the learning experience by using audio-video and multi-media and state-of-the-art pedagogy/technology.

118. (b): The term MOOC was coined by Canadian academician David Cormier in 2008. MOOCs are next big thing in the technological development of higher education. They are of two types—cMOOCs (innovactive–active learning) and xMOOCs (conventional-well-structured courses).

NPTEL (2003), mmoKIT (by IIT, Kanpur in 2012), IITBX (by IIT Bombay in 2014), SWAYAM (2016), SWAYAM Prabha (2016) are the major platforms developed so far. Coursera, EdX, Udacity are the other names.

119. (c): Positive reinforcement: Positive reinforcement works by presenting a motivating or reinforcing stimulus to the person after the desired behaviour is presented, making the behaviours more likely to happen in the future.

For example, a father gives his daughter chocolate for doing homework.

Negative Reinforcement: Negative reinforcement occurs when a certain stimulus is removed after a particular behaviour is exhibited. For example, Bob does the dishes (behaviour) in order to stop his mother's nagging.

Punishment: It is simply a stimulus that is used to discourage or decrease an undesirable behaviour.

Extinction: Extinction refers to the gradual weakening as a conditioned response that causes behaviour decreasing. Conditioned behaviours eventually stop.

120. (b): Memory level is the first and the thoughtless level of teaching. It induces the habit of rote memorisation of facts and allows the learner to retain and to reproduce the learnt material whenever required.

In memory level teaching, the subject material is well organised and also delivered in a definite and structured way.

121. (b): Learning can be described as the process of acquiring new or modifying existing knowledge, skill values, behaviours and preferences.

There are many characteristics of an adolescent learner, which determine his/her social and moral development.

Social Values

A. Modeling behaviour (imitate behavior) after that of older students not necessarily that of parents and other adults.

B. Experimenting with ways of talking and acting as a part of searching for a social position with their peers.

C. Seeking approval of peers and other with attention—getting behaviours.

Moral Values

A. The new ability to think abstractly helps youth to recognise that rules are simply created by other people.

B. Some youths, those have reached the highest level of moral development may feel passionate about their moral code, as such they may choose to participate in activities that demonstrate their moral convictions.

122. (a): A. **Simulation and Role playing**

Simulation refers to the imitation of real world activities and processes in a safe environment. Simulation aims to provide an experience as close to the very helpful to direct learning.

For example, medical simulators allow students to practice diagnosis and treatment on dummies that can react in sophisticated and fairly realistic ways.

Role playing: Role playing is a technique that allows the students to explore the realistic situations by interacting with other people in a managed way in order to develop experience and trial different strategies in a supported environment.

B. **Workshop and Assignment**

Workshop: A workshop is a great way for someone to learn about a particular subject by learning new projects and methods in order to better you. Attending workshops can help the students achieve success in their academic environment by utilising these skills into practice.

Assignment: Assignment is also important for direct learning because it helps you research on your own and teach yourself.

C. **MOOCs and Heuristics**

MOOCs: Massive Open Online Courses (MOOCs) allow participants free access and unrestricted participation to any course of their choice. It is helpful to direct learning.

Heuristics method: Heuristics method is a pure discovery method of learning independent of teacher. In this, the teacher sets a problem for the students and then stands aside while the students discover the answer.

123. (c): Example of maximum performance test is an aptitude test. Because, it is the ability test such as measures of cognitive ability or test of a particular knowledge or skill as like in the aptitude test we test a job candidate's abilities to perform specific task and react to a range of different situations.

124. (a): a. Elaborative interrogation: It is a strategy for enhancing memory during the process of learning. In this method, the learner reads the fact to be remembered and generates an explanation for it. The learner uses questions like why? and How?, to understand the meaning of the information.

b. Practice testing refers to any form of testing for learning, which a student is able to do on their own. Examples of this technique include practicing, recall through flash cards or completing practice problems or tests.

c. Self-explanation keeps an eye on the process of working out a solution to a problem.

d. Interleaving practice is a process where, students mix or interleave, multiple subjects or topics, while they study in order to improve their learning.

125. (b): Teacher has control over self, his/her mode of communication and method of delivery in classroom. A teacher needs to be organized in classroom. They should have control over mode of communication and method of delivery to make students learn the concepts. They should transmit genuine commitment.

126. (d): Reactive mode of student's behavior is not a component of effective teaching as reaction does take place during extreme situations.

127. (c): Assessment bias unfairly penalizes students on the basis of race, ethnicity, socioeconomic status, religion, etc.

Here, we need to work on one assumption that every learner is unique and some flexible mechanism may help.

128. (b): (i) The concept of self efficacy was given by Albert Bandura. **Self-efficacy** reflects confidence in the ability to exert control over one›s own motivation, behavior, and social environment. Self efficacy means looking into one's potential.

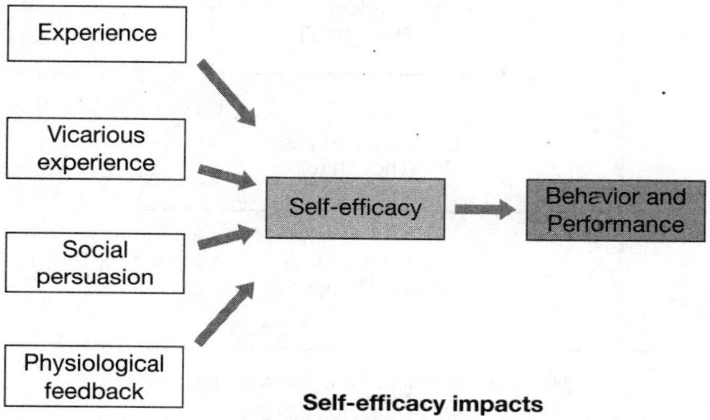

Self-efficacy impacts behaviour and performance

(ii) Belief in God – It is one's personal issue.

(iii) We may not be interested in politics but it is part of democracy. So some interest in politics is desirable.

(iv) Teacher's low expectation from students is not good for the confidence of a teacher himself or herself.

129. (d): We need to focus on objective criteria as teaching is both art and science. Teachers are trained also for the purpose.

Thus subject knowledge matters.

130. (c): Assertion addresses the issues of 'access to education'.

In Reason, it's difficult to assess the difference between online and offline for this.

131. (b): 1. Essay type test is a test that requires the student to compose responses, usually lengthy up to several paragraphs. Distinctive features of 'Essay Type Test' is the "Freedom of responses". Pupils are free to select, relate and present idea in their own words.

The compositional skills and creativity in presentation of students can be most effectively evaluated by assessing the ability to recall, organized and integrate idea.

2. Assess the ability to express oneself in writing
3. Ability to supply information
4. Assess student understanding of subject matter,
5. Measures the knowledge of factual information.

132. (d): Learning is an 'active' process which allows students to construct new idea or concept based upon their current and past knowledge. Students develop a cognitive structure, making meaning out of experience. This means the student can develop ideas beyond what he or she has been given.

Process / sequence of teaching, learning activities in a constructivist approach

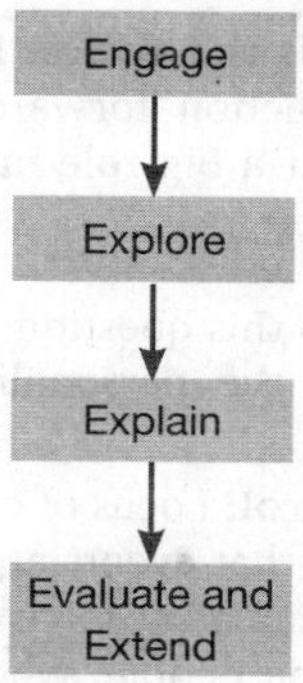

133. (c): Following factors have been labeled as social competence in influencing learning.

Socio – economic status – SES influences academic achievement and cognitive development variables such as parents educational expectations, parenting ideas and behaviors and the parent – child relationship

Motivation – Motivation has several effects on students learning and behaviors towards particular goal. Motivation determines whether a student will pursue a task with enthusiasm or with lackluster attitude.

Emotional Factors – Emotional factors like happiness and anger and sadness. Happiness has a positive effect on learning memory and social behaviour. Negative emotional states such as anger and sadness have been shown to have a negative impact on learning and motivation.

134. (b): Following factors will be considered key teaching behaviour belonging to the category of effectiveness.

(a) Making ideas clear to learners who may be at different level of understanding.

(b) Showing enthusiasm and animation through variation in eye contact, voice and gestures.

(c) Using meaningful verbal praise to get and keep students actively participating in the learning process.

135. (c): Pedagogy and social interaction are indeed two major result oriented activities of a teacher. Pedagogy is the method and practice of teaching, to get result. If the teacher takes into account the various factors involved such as the availability of resources, learner's characteristics, individual differences etc., and plan the instruction with the most suitable teaching method and resources available to ensure equality of opportunity to every learner, teaching is effective. Teaching is also effective when the teacher interacts and communicates well not only with the learner but also with the other members of the teaching staff, school management / administration and parents. Hence A is true.

Communication is the vehicle that carries pedagogy and social interaction forward. So it doesn't play a limited role but a big role in both these activities. Hence (R) is false.

136. (b): According to this question, there are three traits, which influence the personality and attitude of a teacher.

1. **Locus of control:** Locus of control refer to an individual's belief that events are either in one control or are determined by force beyond one's control. There are some people, who have the courage to face and control every type of situations. Thus, it refers to that attribute of personality, which shows the extent to which people consider themselves as architect of their fate. Locus of control is of following types.
   (1) Internal locus of control
   (2) External locus of control
2. **Self-efficacy:** Refer to an individual's confidence in their ability to complete a task or achieve a goal. It also effect the personality and attitude of the teacher.
3. **Teacher enthusiasm:** Teacher enthusiasm is considered to be a special mode of delivering information to students. A teacher is perceived as being enthusiastic, when he/she succeeds in communicating the excitement about the subject to the students.

137. (a):

Memory level is the first and thoughtless level of teaching. It induces the habit of rote memorisation of facts and bites of information. It enables the learner to retain and also to reproduce the learnt material, whenever required. Understanding level of teaching is more thoughtful and useful. In this level of teaching the relationships between principles and facts are explained.

Autonomous level means not exactly in the classroom. Reflective means dealing with real life problems understanding level. It is memory plus insight as it goes beyond just memorising of facts it focus on mastery of the subject.

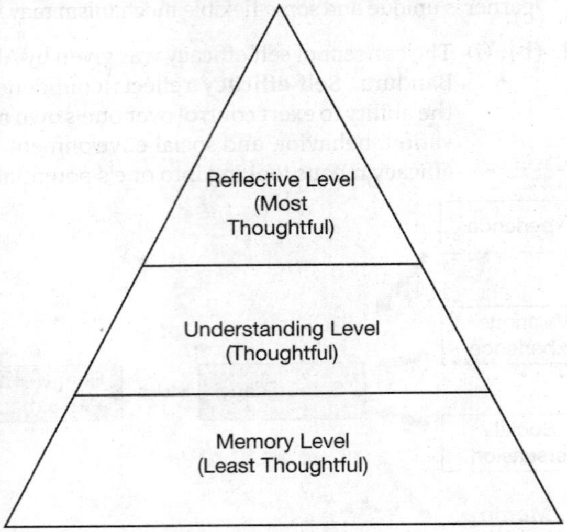

Hierarchical order of the levels of teaching

138. (d): Dialogic teaching involves ongoing talk between teacher and students and not just teacher presentation. Through dialogue, teacher can elicit student's everyday common sense perspectives, engage with their developing ideas and help them overcome misunderstandings in the spectrum of teaching method, which include problem-solving method interactive presentation and tutorials.

139. (d): Out of the four choices, the learning outcome-based evaluation assumes the learning process to be dynamic and it aims at improving our future performance.

140. (a): Traditional method of teaching is, when a teacher directs students to learn through memorisation and recitation techniques, thereby not developing their critical thinking, problem-solving and decision-making skills.

141. (a): Non-traditional teaching and learning strategies lay emphasis on students' need-based resource materials and learning standards and developing skills, attitude and values and also acquiring knowledge necessary to respond creatively.

142. (c): If a teacher wants to improve his/her abilities as an effective classroom communication then he/she should first understand the students strengths, weakness and interests, and thus guide them to success. First statement is true. So, the Assertion is right.

The reason is wrong as the word disjointed means anything with no common elements but here both understanding and intended listening are interrelated. They help the teacher in effective classroom communication.

143. (c):

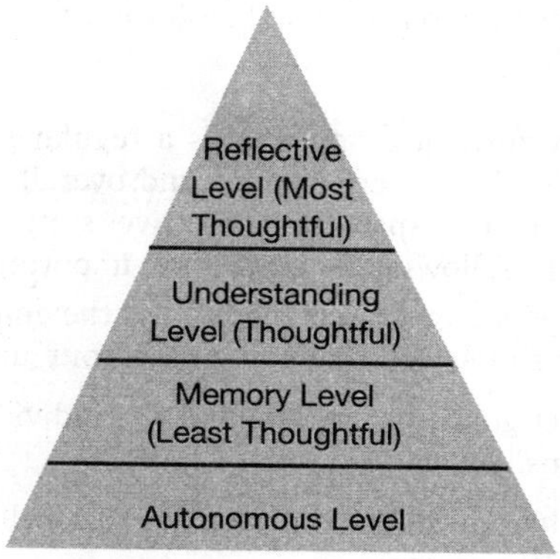

Souce: www.learningclassesonline.com,

Memory level is the first and thoughtless level of teaching. Good memory includes rapidity in learning, stability of retention, rapidity in recalling and the ability to bring only desirable contents to the conscious level. The main objective is imparting knowledge and information to the learner. Simple memorable things are taught to students.

Understanding Level of Teaching: Explains pupils the relationship between principles and facts may be through positive and negative examples.

Kindly look at the words "presentations in classroom."

Reflective Level: Deals with real life problem. It is also termed as the introspective level. It also means thinking deeply about something. At this level, the students is made to face a real problematic situation. Here the problem is identified, defined and then a solution is found.

Autonomous Level: In this there is the development of a feeling of autonomy with little or no scope for teacher intervention thats why it is a kind of negative education.

144. (a): There are following outcomes which are said to be high level outcomes:

(1) Showing the ability to analyse and synthesise.
(2) Articulation and naturalisation.
(3) Organisation and characterisation.

145. (b): In the context of class room teaching, the foundation on which a warm and nurturing relationship with learner can be built is called teacher affect.

The results show that teacher affects are dominant factors affecting student academic gain and improving student self esteem with increased motivation and learning.

146. (d): Ontology, in Greek, means *study, theory, or science of being*, that is, which exists. Ontology is a fundamental branch of philosophy and one of the oldest after metaphysics. ontology divides all things into two large groups:

1. **Concrete Entities:** like trees or stones.
2. **Abstract Entities:** such as God or ideas.

Logically, it is not possible to study the two types of entities in the same way because they have different characteristics.

Epistemology means *study of knowledge.* However, we must bear in mind that for the Greeks there were two types of knowledge:

1. ***doxa:*** is based on subjective observance and opinion. For example: If I look out the window, I **know** it rains.
2. ***episteme:*** rigorous knowledge, which is acquired from objective analysis and study. For example: After studying, I **know** what causes the rain.

Epistemology deals with the second type of knowledge. That is why it is sometimes said that epistemology is the branch of philosophy that studies science.

Methodology is the justification for using a particular research method thus it is ideographic.

Method is simply a research tool, a component of research – say for example, a qualitative method such as observations and interviews.

147. (d)

If we go by the objectives of management, setting objectives is the foremost task so that financial and other resources can be developed. Setting objectives is the part of planning function of management. The other functions are organising, staffing, directing and controlling.

148. (b): Technology enabled communication can therefore be defined as the transfer of message or information with the help of various technological tools.

Communication has also become faster and less tedious. With the help of group SMS services and email facility, the students and faculty members can share news and information easily among each other at a fraction of time and least cost.

149. (c): (a) **Epistemology** is the study of nature and scope of knowledge and justified belief.

(b) **Ontology** is part of metaphysics, a branch of philosophy that looks at the very nature of things, their being, cause or identity.

(c) **Axiology** is the branch of philosophy that considers the nature of value and what kinds of things have value. Axios means value.

(d) **Etymology:** The study of the origin of words and the way in which their meanings have changed throughout history.

150. (b): SWAYAM is a massive open online course platform which is world's largest online e-learning platform. Free E-learning platform portal designed to achieve the three cardinal principles of Education policy viz, access, equity and quality by covering School / Vocational, Under-Graduates, Post Graduate, Engineering and other professional courses.

151. (c): External accountability means contribution towards the society while dealing with external environment. Points A and B are meant for internal purposes.

152. (a): As per question, the most important have been mentioned below.

1. **Lesson Clarity**: Logical, step-by-step order; clear and audible delivery free of distracting mannerisms.
2. **Instructional Variety**: Variability in instructional materials, questioning, types of feedback, and teaching strategies.
3. **Engagement in Learning Process**: Limiting opportunities for distraction and getting students to work on, think through, and inquire about the content.

153. (c): SWAYAM is a programme initiated by Government of India and designed to achieve the three cardinal principles of Education Policy viz., access, equity and quality. The objective of this effort is to take the best teaching learning resources to all, including the most disadvantaged. SWAYAM seeks to bridge the digital divide for students who have hitherto remained untouched by the digital revolution and have not been able to join the mainstream of the knowledge economy.

The courses hosted on SWAYAM are in 4 quadrants:

1. Video lecture
2. Specially prepared reading material that can be downloaded/printed
3. Self-assessment tests through tests and quizzes
4. An online discussion forum for clearing the doubts.

SWAYAM was launched on 9th july 2017 and is facilitated by National Programme on Technology Enhanced Learning (NPTEL). It is a project of MHRD initiated by seven Indian Institutes of Technology (Bombay, Delhi, Kanpur, Kharagpur, Madras, Guwahati and Roorkee) along with the Indian Institute of Science, Bangalore in 2003.

154. (d): There can be multiple ways of teaching/counseling/ guiding for the sole purpose of learning. The answer is reflected through choices as well.

155. (c): Testing is important for a teacher as it enables him to give feedback to learners. In the second statement, feedback option is denied so (c) becomes the correct answer.

156. (a): Performance appraisal is a regular review of an employee's job performance and overall contribution to a company. Apart from objectives stated in the question, the following six aspects are important.

1. Reflect on what is required of the employee to do their job well (including behaviour and results)
2. Set goals that will benefit the individual and the business
3. Share feedback on great work as well as areas for improvement
4. Identify opportunities to develop performance through ongoing education, training and learning
5. Formally review performance after a specific period
6. Reward a job well done

157. (d): According to Bloom's taxonomy, cognitive domain is represented by six different domain levels in ascending order are (1) knowledge, (2) comprehension, (3) application, (4) analysis, (5) synthesis, and (6) evaluation. All of the Bloom domains focused on the knowledge and cognitive processes.

158. (a): The following can be identified as the factors which contributes towards positive feedback:

- It should be educative in nature.
- It should be given in a timely manner.
- Be sensitive to the individual needs of the student.
- It should reference a skill or specific knowledge.
- Feedback should be given to keep students 'on target' for achievement.
- There should be scope for one-on-one conference to make it more effective.

159. (c): Answer is clear from the question itself.

160. (a): Formative evaluations are often informal and ungraded. Their aim is to provide both the students and teacher with a gauge of where their level of understanding is at the current moment, and enable the teacher to adjust accordingly to meet the emerging needs of the class.

Let us learn the important concepts about evaluation before coming to question. Evaluation is a part of everyday life. In education, it is basically a decision making about performance of students, it is linked with teaching and learning. Through evaluation, a teacher judges the growth and development of students, the changes taking place in their behaviour, the progress they are making in the class and also the effectiveness of her/ his own teaching in the class.

The National Curriculum Framework for School Education, 2000, observes, "Teaching for successful learning cannot occur without high quality evaluation." A teacher must be properly trained for this job as it is linked with the career of the students. After the announcement of New Education Policy, 2020, the new National Curriculum Framework is in progress as per announcement made by our Prime Minister, Sh Narender Modi in April, 2022.

The word 'evaluation' is often confused with testing and measurement. Testing is only a technique to collect evidence regarding pupil behaviour. Measurement on the other hand, is limited to quantitative description of the pupil behaviour.

Evaluation is a more comprehensive term which includes testing and measurement and also qualitative description of the student's behaviour. It also includes value judgment regarding the worth or desirability of the behaviour measured or assessed.

We can try to indicate these aspects with the help of an equation.

Evaluation = quantitative description of pupils (measurement) + value judgment

Evaluation = qualitative description of pupils (non-measurement) + value judgment

A students' achievement may be viewed at three different levels:

1. Self-referenced how the student is progressing with reference to himself/herself.
2. Criterion-referenced how the student is progressing with reference to the criteria set by the teacher.
3. Norm-referenced how the student is progressing with reference to his/her peer group.

Tyler defined evaluation as "a systematic process of determining the extent to which educational objectives are achieved by pupils". This definition indicates that evaluation is a systematic process, and it omits the casual, informal or uncontrolled observation of the pupils. The definition also implies that objectives of education have to be identified in advance.

Thus, evaluation is a systematic process of collecting evidence about students' achievement in both cognitive and non-cognitive areas of learning on fie basis of which judgments are formed and decisions are made. It is a continuous process. Evaluation is an integral part of any teaching and learning programme. Whenever a question is asked and answered evaluation takes place. Thus, both teaching and evaluation overlap and merge into each other. In fact, it is not possible to have teaching and learning without evaluation.

Now after discussing main aspects of evaluation, let us look at the types of evaluation as given in the question. Specifically, there are four types of evaluation used in the classroom – placement evaluation, summative evaluation, formative evaluation and diagnostic evaluation.

Placement Evaluation: This is primarily meant for admission purpose. One gets to know how well he has prepared. We get to know how well we can perform under performance pressure and time constraints. We get to know your weak spots as well as your strengths.

Summative Evaluation: This is most common type of evaluation. It comes at the end of the term, course or programme of teaching. The examples are formal testing of pupil's achievement. Annual examinations and half yearly examinations in schools, public examinations are the example of such evaluation. Tile purpose of this kind of evaluation is to grade, rank, classify, compare and promote the pupils. It is also used for the purpose of certification. Summative evaluation is also used for selecting students for scholarships or for admission to particular courses. Prediction regarding the success of students in their future endeavours can also be made on its basis.

Formative Evaluation: This type of evaluation is inbuilt with the process of teaching and learning. It is done during the course of instruction with a view to improving students' learning. The purpose of this evaluation is to provide feedback regarding the students' progress, by finding out the learning gaps and the weak points. The teacher can then organize remedial programmes for them. Formative evaluation also provides the teacher feedback regarding the efficiency of the teaching methods, so that the teaching can be improved. It can also provide clues to the effectiveness of the course content and teaching materials. Formative evaluation is done continuously throughout the course period. It can be done by means of unit tests which can be given after teaching each unit, informal class tests, assignments and other class room activities.

This evaluation is less formal in nature in comparison to summative evaluation.

Diagnostic Evaluation: This is more closely related to formative than the summative evaluation. In fact, it is to be carried out along with formative evaluation in the class. Sometimes, even the summative evaluation may be used for diagnostic purpose. The main purpose of diagnostic evaluation is to find out the underlying cause of weaknesses in a student's learning, but it is also needed even prior to instruction in order to place the student properly by looking at higher level of achievement. Thus, diagnostic evaluation provides a starting point to carry out the instruction.

Diagnostic evaluation helps in ascertaining entry behaviour of the students, it helps in knowing the level to which students have learnt so far. Diagnosis helps the teacher classify students according to their level of mastery and this in turn will help him / her to work out a remedial instruction programme for the low achievers and slow learners.

161. (a): Cronbach (1949/1960) classified personnel selection tests into two broad categories, tests of maximum and tests of typical performance. The distinguishing feature of maximum performance tests is that they seek to assess how much or how well people can perform at their best. Hence, candidates are encouraged to do well in order to earn the best score they can.

On the other hand, 'Tests of typical performance' assess how the ability of a job candidate is evident on a day-to-day basis.

In short, these two types of tests assess what the candidate chooses to do. Hence, they assess a candidate's motivation rather than his or her ability.

162. (a): The basic style of communication should remain the same. Persuasive communication is a form of communication that involves the act of convincing or guiding listeners or readers towards the adoption of certain attitudes, actions, and ideas through emotional or rational means. Persuasive skills include emotional intelligence, active listening, interpersonal skills, negotiation, logic and reasoning, etc.

163. (d): There are five sets of needs – physiological needs (lower order needs), safety needs, social needs, esteem needs and self-actualization needs (higher order needs).

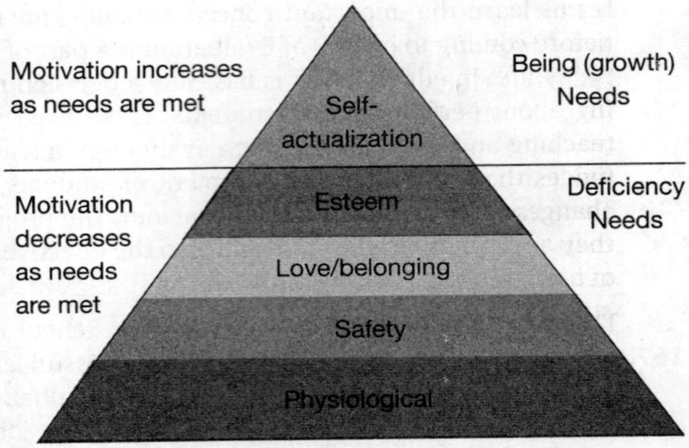

Higher order learning means that we need to be reflective. The reflective needs are depicted through needs for self-actualization and inwardly directed esteem needs.

164. (c): This question is linked with feedback in the classroom to make it effective communication. A teacher should be proficient in all four modes of communication – listening, speaking, reading, and writing – and should know how to utilize this proficiency effectively in an educational institute environment. Being able to do this has been proven to impact the success students achieve in their academic lives, as well as the teacher's own career success.

165. (a): DRUPAL: Drupal is a free software package that allows an individual or a community of users to easily publish, manage and organize a wide variety of content on a website.

Drupal is used by mooKIT platform for open source content management system.

JOOMLA: This uses to build, organize, manage and publish content for websites, blogs, Intranet and mobile applications.

Moodle: Moodle is a free and open–source learning management system (LMS) written in PHP and distributed under GNU (General Public licence). Moodle is used for blended learning, distance education, flipped classroom and other e–learning projects in schools, universities, workplaces and other sectors

SAKAI: Sakai is a free, community source, educational software platform designed to support teaching, research and collaboration. Systems of this type are also known as Course Management Systems (CMS), Learning Management Systems (LMS), or Virtual Learning Environments (VLE).

166. (c): According to Piaget, the ability to solve conservation problems depends on having an understanding of three basic aspects of reasoning: identity, compensation and reversibility.

Jean Piaget mentioned the following stages for cognitive development:

(i) Sensory Period (0–2 years)
(ii) Pre – operational period (2–7 years)
(iii) Concrete operational period (7 – 11 years)
(iv) Formal operation period (11 – 15 years)

The stage of classification depends on students' ability to focus on a single characteristic of objects in a set and group of objects according to that characteristic. Thus, statement II is incorrect.

167. (a): Competencies refer to skills or knowledge that led to superior performance.

Personal competencies determine how we manage ourselves while the social competencies determine how we handle relationships. Thus, both the statements are correct.

168. (a): The dynamic of classroom interaction can be effectively managed through interpreting perceived meanings.

Effective teaching: teaching is a planned activity and effective teaching depends on the following factors:

(a) How clearly the students understand what they are expected to learn?
(b) How accurately their learning can be measured?

Thus, the dynamics of interactions in the classroom can be effectively related to the interpretation of understood meanings.

169. (c): Memory Level: Memory level is the first and thoughtless level of teaching. Good memory includes swift learning, stability of retention, rapidity in recalling and the ability to bring only desirable contents to the conscious level. The main objective is imparting knowledge and information to the learner. Simple, memorable things are taught to students.

Understanding Level of Teaching: This level explains to pupils that the relationship between principles and facts may be through positive and negative examples.

Reflective Level: This level deals with real-life problems. It is also termed as the introspective level, which means thinking deeply about something. At this level, the students are made to face a real-life situation that is problematic.

The problem is identified, defined and then a solution is found. Thus, the reflective level of teaching lays stress on the critical sifting of ideas at the highest cognitive level.

Autonomous Development Level: In this level there is the development of a feeling of autonomy with little or no scope for teacher intervention thats why it is a kind of negative education.

170. (b): According to Bloom (1956), teaching or instructional objectives are divided into three categories: which are also called the 3 H of the English language-

(A). Cognitive Domain

Cognitive domain involves the development of intellectual ability. This domain is divided into six levels:

I. **Knowledge:** This level involves remembering information or material.
II. **Comprehension:** This level refers to the ability to understand the meaning of the material.
III. **Application:** This level is concerned with bringing abstract knowledge into tangible or practical form.
IV. **Analysis:** This level involves the division of the received information into components in such a way that its meaning can be understood properly.
V. **Student Synthesis:** It level is concerned with assimilating the components, so that a holistic approach is developed. It is also considered an antonym of analysis level.
VI. **Evaluation:** This level refers to the decision made regarding the assessment of the teaching method and the material used for those particular purposes.

(B). Affective Domain

This domain mainly includes attitude, motivation, participation of students in the learning process, knowing the importance of what we learn, how to incorporate values like discipline in life, etc. It includes the following levels:

I. **Receiving:** The willingness to listen
II. **Responding:** The willingness to participate
III. **Valuing:** Understanding the importance of what we are learning
IV. **Organizing**
V. **Characterization**

(C). Psychomotor Domain

This domain can also be referred to as functional domain. It mainly deals with the acquisition of technical skills. The following five levels of instructional objectives are described within the Mind Driven Learning Area:

I. **Imitation:** In this level, an attempt is made to adopt the skill of a skilled person or learner.
II. **Manipulation:** A learner tries to experiment with machinery, equipment, etc., so as to increase self-confidence in this level.
III. **Precision:** This level involves doing the same work over and over again so that it brings improvement and purity. The learner's skills become more exact with practice.

IV. **Articulation:** This level also depends on continuous practice.

V. **Naturalization:** In this level, skills are imbibed, and the learner learns the qualities of adapting, modifying, designing new techniques, etc.

Therefore, the highest-graded categories are assessment, characterization and facilitation in the fields of cognitive, emotional and motor learning. Analysis and cognition are not the highest categories.

171. (a): The two types of teaching behaviours are as follows:

(A). Key Teaching Behaviours of Effective Teaching

The following are the five key behaviours for effective teaching and some indicators pertaining to them:

I. **Lesson Clarity:** Logical, step-by-step order; clear and audible delivery that is free of distracting mannerisms

II. **Instructional Variety:** Variability in instructional materials, questioning, types of feedback and teaching strategies

III. **Task Orientation**: Achievement (content) orientation as opposed to process orientation, maximum content coverage and time devoted to instruction

IV. **Student Engagement:** Limiting opportunities for distraction and getting students to work on, think through and enquire about the content

V. **Student Success Rate:** 60–70% of time spent on tasks that afford moderate-to-high levels of success, especially during expository or didactic instruction

(B). Helping Behaviour of Effective Teaching

I. **Using Student Ideas and Contributions:** Taking a student's response and repeating or applying it

II. **Structuring:** The teacher comments for the purpose of organizing what is to come

III. **Probing:** The teacher makes statements to encourage students to elaborate on an answer

IV. **Teacher Effect:** Having a warm and nurturing relationship with learners.

V. Questioning: Use a variety of questions, and be sure to include questions that require more thinking and problem solving.

172. (a): Norm-Referenced Testing: A norm-referenced test is used to ascertain an individual's status with respect to the performance of other individuals on that test. In norm-referenced testing of students, test data helps teachers determine a student's place or rank. It is normally used in competitive exam. Thus, statement I is true.

Criterion-Referenced Testing: Glasser (1963) first used the term 'criterion-referenced test' to describe the learner's achievement on a performance continuum. A criterion-referenced test is used to ascertain an individual's status with respect to a defined achievement domain. It determines an individual's status with reference to a well-defined criterion behaviour. Therefore, in criterion-referenced testing, the test data tells teachers about a student's level of proficiency. Thus, both the statements are correct.

173. (a): ICT-based teaching support is an approach to facilitate and enhance learning through both computer and communication technology. It refers to the use of computer-based electronic technologies of the internet, websites, emails, etc. in order to deliver, facilitate and enhance both formal and informal learning and knowledge sharing at any place and at any time. The communication devices can also include digital television, Personal Digital Assistants (PDA) and mobile phones – these require some technical knowledge on the part of the teacher and learners. The advantage of modern and ICT-based learning is that it permits learners to have the convenience of flexibility. Both teachers and learners must be provided orientation in use of the various support tools and techniques in an intelligent way. Thus, both (A) and (R) are true, and (R) is the correct explanation of (A).

174. (b): Metacognition is basically the evaluation of one's own thinking. It is a useful mechanism to enhance student learning and mastery over the subject matter. It enhances problem-solving and critical thinking ability among students.

Reflective learning is a part of metacognition. It helps students become independent learners and develop lifelong divergent-thinking skills.

Metacognitive strategies are as follows:

i. Self-Questioning: Self-questioning involves pausing throughout a task to consciously check your own actions

ii. Meditation and Reflection

iii. Awareness of Strengths and Weaknesses

iv. Awareness of Learning Styles and the Use of Mnemonic Aids

These techniques help students focus with greater intention, reflect on their existing knowledge versus information they still need to learn, recognize errors in their thinking and develop practices for effective learning. Thus, metacognition comprises of developing, monitoring and evaluation of your own thinking.

175. (c): Metacognitive strategies are what you design to monitor your progress related to your learning and the tasks at hand. It is a mechanism for controlling your thinking activities and to ensure that you are meeting your goals.

Learning Strategies	Actions taken
Planning and Focusing Attention	• Setting goals and timetables • Underlining and highlighting • Skimming, looking for headings and topic sentences
Organizing and Remembering	• Making organizational charts • Creating flowchartsCreating Venn diagrams • Using mnemonics, imagery
Comprehension	• Using concept mapping, webs • Summarizing, outlining and role-taking • Creating examples • Explaining to a peer
Cognitive Monitoring	• Making predictions • Self-questioning and self-testing • Identifying what doesn't make sense
Practice	• Using part practice • Using whole practice

176. (d): Qualitative research methods mostly use open-ended techniques (such as interviews), to collect data. They may use non-statistical techniques to analyze the data.

The first statement uses the word 'inductively' that is mostly used in qualitative research. The third statement reflects use of words or pictures and not exactly the quantitative data. The fifth statement reflects that data is better collected in 'natural settings'.

177. (b): These basically reflect our thought processes, they guide our direction as well, where should we move and what should be our approach. We may refer to solution of question number 147.

178. (b)

Mind mapping: A mind map is a diagram used to visually organize information. A mind map is hierarchical and shows relationships among pieces of the whole. It is often created around a single concept, drawn as an image in the centre of a blank page, to which associated representations of ideas such as images, words and parts of words are added. Major ideas are connected directly to the central concept, and other ideas branch out from those major ideas.

Thus, mind mapping is the technique which uses images that are often more evocative than words and are precise and potent in triggering a wide range of associations and thinking patterns.

179. (b): SAWAYAM PRABHA satellite: The SWAYAM PRABHA is a group of 34 DTH channels devoted to telecasting high-quality educational programmes across the country on 24 × 7 basis using the GSAT-15 satellite. Every day, there will be new content for at least (4) hours which would be repeated 5 more times in a day, allowing the students to choose the time of their convenience. The channels are up linked from BISAG, Gandhinagar. The contents are provided by NPTEL, IITs, UGC, CEC, IGNOU, etc. The INFLIBNET Centre maintains the web portal.

180. (b): A flowchart is a diagram that depicts a process, system or computer algorithm. It is used for visual representation of data flow. Flowcharts use rectangles, ovals, diamonds and potentially numerous other shapes to define the type of step, along with connecting arrows to define flow and sequence. Flowcharts were used to document business, specifically by Frank and Lillian Gilbreth. They are used in any field such as education, business, manufacturing, engineering, architecture, etc. Few examples have been shown below

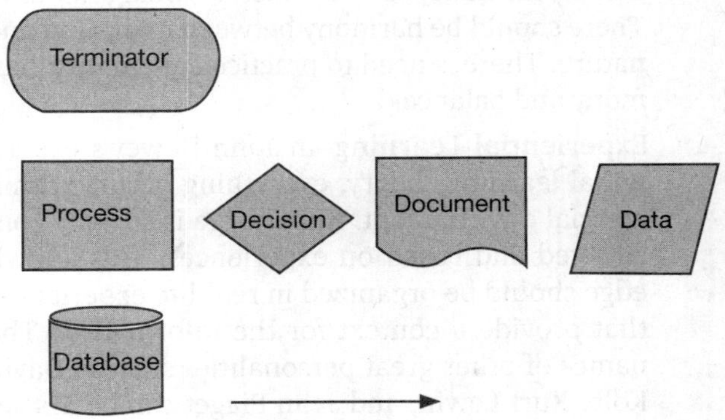

181. (d): Integral Education–The concept of Integral Education was given by Sri Aurobindo that is based on the belief that the education of a human being should begin at birth and continue throughout his life. The main objective of any kind of education is to ensure the realization of the inner potential of the learner. Thus, this concept is quite dynamic and flexible, it takes into account the whole personality of the learner, through the concept of dealing with the 'whole child'. This takes into account the individual curiosity, passion and compassion, and this applies to all situations in a beautiful manner. There are integral schools at many places in India as enunciated by Sri Aurobindo and his spiritual companion Mirra Alfassa – known as mother.

Focus on spiritual aspects of Indian philosophy–This is associated with Dr. Sarvapalli Radhakrishnan's metaphysics that is based on Sankara's Advaita (non-dual) Vedanta tradition (sampradaya). He was associated with Prasthanatraya (main primary texts of Vedanta), Upanishads, Brahma Sutra, and the Bhagavad Gita. He was greatly influenced by the writings and work of Swami Vivekananda.

Dr. Sarvapalli Radhakrishnan was actively involved in the works of UNESCO. He was known for being a bridge between eastern and western philosophies to promote world unity and universal fellowship. To Dr Radhakrishnan – 'The idea of God is an interpretation of experience'.

Learning to take place in nature and from nature–Sri Rabindranath Tagore believed in complete freedom of every kind for the students in terms of his intellectual level, decision making, feelings, knowledge, etc. The independence means normalcy or the fact of being natural. There should be harmony between man, God and nature. There is need to practice equanimity, harmony and balance.

Experiential Learning–In John Dewey's experiential learning theory, everything occurs within a social environment. Knowledge is socially constructed and based on experiences. This knowledge should be organized in real-life experiences that provide a context for the information. The names of other great personalities such as David Kolb, Kurt Lewin, and Jean Piaget can be associated with experiential learning.

182. (b): Every learner (in fact, an individual) is unique. This also gives rise to the concept of 'individual differences'. Every learner **has her**/his own characteristics. For a teacher, the individual differences in the form of variables such as physical characteristics, intelligence, perception, gender, ability, learning styles are important. A more effective and productive learning-teaching process can be planned by a teacher with this kind of knowledge.

Assessments are a useful way of maintaining quality. Assessments assess students' understanding, knowledge, and takeaways from the educational experience. Assessments make learning process more effective and enhance student development. Usually, the assessments make use of empirical data.

Summative Assessment–This evaluates the overall learning of the students at the end of a unit or course. This assessment compares against some standardized criteria or benchmark. These are basically formal in nature which help in awarding a certificate also. This assessment can be written assessment (writing an original piece, such as a narrative or analytical essay), performance assessment (to do an activity or task that will showcase the abilities of the learners), standardized assessment (an exam created for a given curriculum) or oral assessment (such as a speech or presentation).

Formative Assessment–This assessment measures how a student is learning during a course of study. The goal is to monitor student learning to provide ongoing feedback that can be used by instructors to improve their teaching and by students to improve their learning. This word can be linked with actual formation of career of a student in the class.

Diagnostic Assessment–A diagnostic assessment is an evaluation of a child's knowledge and skill level of a certain topic. These assessments are done at the start of the topic to understand how much students already know about the subject.

Peer Assessment: This assessment provides a structured learning process for students to critique and provide feedback to each other on their work. Thus, students develop lifelong skills. It equips them with skills to self-assess and improve their own work.

183. (b): e-PG Pathshala–The UGC has launched an e-PG Pathshala Project for standardizing the textbook materials for MA, MSc and MCom courses in different universities of India. In India, e-PG Pathshala is such an innovation maintained by UGC-INFLIBNET and funded by Ministry of Education. As part of its National Education Mission through ICT (NME-ICT), it is a wide e-learning platform in terms of its subject material and breadth of use as well.

On the other hand, Ministry of Education (earlier MHRD) launched 'e-pathshala' web portal to host educational resources for students, teachers, parents, researchers and educators. This is a single point repository of e- resources containing NCERT text-books and various other learning resources.

184. (b): The affective domain is one of the three domains in Bloom's Taxonomy. The affective domain as described by Krathwohl, Bloom, Masia in the year 1973, includes the manner in which we deal with things emotionally, such as feelings, values, appreciation, enthusiasms, motivations, and attitudes. As per question, they have been put in the following five categories (for future questions):

1. **Receiving**
   (a) awareness of the action
   (b) desire to achieve action
   (c) controlled attention to action
2. **Response (responding)**
   (a) In response to an agreement
   (b) Desire to respond
   (c) Response Contentment
3. **Evaluation (valuing)**
   (a) Acceptance of value (valuing)
   (b) Priority of value
   (c) Commitment
4. **Organizing (managing)**
   (a) Concept of values
   (b) Price system organization
5. **Specialization**
   (a) Higher evaluation by peers to do
   (b) Normal group
   (c) Specialization

In option (b), analysing means dividing a topic into parts for the sake of understanding and also synthesising means integrating the parts into a consolidated form.

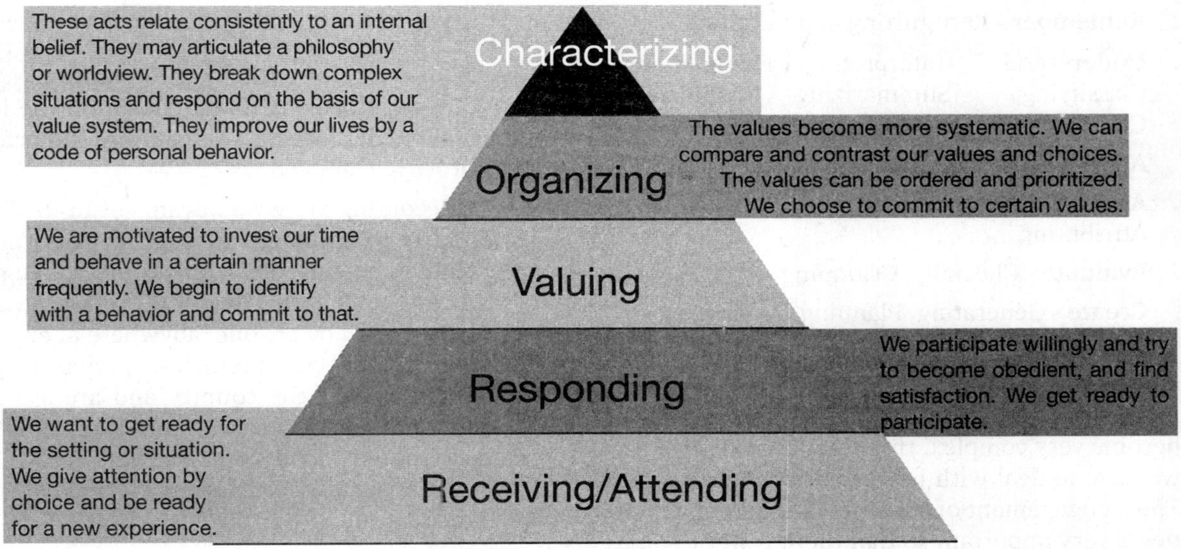

185. (d): There are different phases of human learning:

1. **Cognitive** - knowing, or head
2. **Affective** - emotions, feelings, or heart and
3. **Psychomotor** - doing, or kinesthetic, tactile, haptic or hand/body

Bloom's Cognitive Taxonomy in 1956 had remained an essential element in teacher training. The updated version was done by Anderson and Krathwohl in 2001. Affective skills were added in 1961 by David Krathwohl.

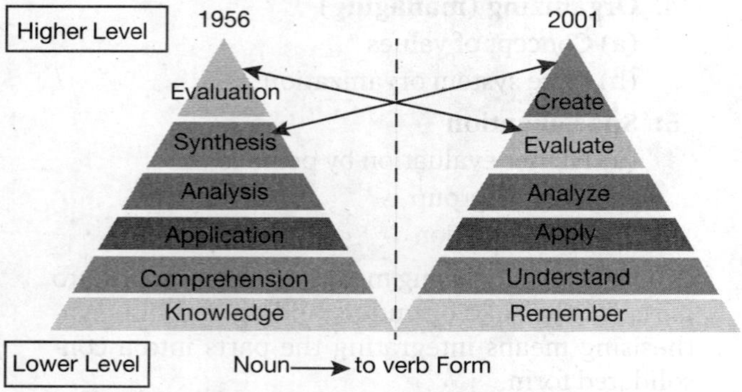

The revised taxonomy has these elements –

1. **Remember** - Recognizing and Recalling
2. **Understand** - Interpreting, Exemplifying, Classifying, Summarizing, Inferring, Comparing, Explaining
3. **Apply** - Executing, Implementing
4. **Analyze** - Differentiating, Organizing, Attributing
5. **Evaluate** - Checking, Critiquing
6. **Create** - Generating, Planning, Producing

186. (d): Learning allows us to make sense of the world around us, the world inside of us, and where we fit within the world. The life and society have become very complex, the situations are diverse, we have to deal with new situations every time. Thus, engagement of students in different activities is very important so that there is wholesome development of personality. Education helps us get exposure to new ideas and concepts.

187. (c): Assertion (A): According to government sources, courses offered through SWAYAM (Study Webs of Active Learning for Young Aspiring Minds) are fully recognized and eligible for credit transfer as per the UGC (Credit Framework for Online Learning Courses through Study Webs of Active Learning for Young Aspiring Minds) Regulations, 2021. These regulations, now facilitate an institution to allow upto 40% of the total courses being offered in a particular programme in a semester, through the online learning courses offered through the SWAYAM platform. The credits/marks obtained by the candidate enrolled in universities for SWAYAM Certificate will be counted in the transcript of the candidate, only if the University has adopted MOOCs (Massive Open Online Course) offered on SWAYAM Platform for Credit Transfer as per the UGC (Credit Framework for Online Learning Courses through Study Webs of Active Learning for Young Aspiring Minds) Regulations, 2021.

Reason (R): SWAYAM is a part of MOOC. SWAYAM is India's own MOOCs platform, which offers free online courses on almost all the discipline to students/learners. The objective is to ensure access to the best teaching learning resources to all, including the most disadvantaged. The courses delivered on SWAYAM are expected to reduce the digital divide by providing access to best content to all. These courses are developed by reputed teachers in the country and available free of cost. By integrating SWAYAM MOOCs with conventional education the learning outcomes of the students are expected to improve in coming days.

188. (b): According to www.swayam.gov.in - SWAYAM conducts programmes through a platform that facilitates hosting of all the courses, taught in the classrooms from Class 9 till post-graduation to be accessed by anyone, anywhere at any time. All the courses are interactive, prepared by the best teachers in the country and are available, free of cost to any learner. More than 1,000 specially chosen faculty and teachers from across the country have participated in preparing these courses.

The courses hosted on SWAYAM are in 4 quadrants

1. video lecture
2. specially prepared reading material that can be downloaded/printed
3. self-assessment tests through tests and quizzes and
4. an online discussion forum for clearing the doubts. Steps have been taken to enrich the

learning experience by using audio-video and multi-media and state of the art pedagogy / technology.

For future questions - In order to ensure that best quality content is produced and delivered, nine National Coordinators have been appointed. They are the following

1. AICTE (All India Council for Technical Education) for self-paced and international courses
2. NPTEL (National Programme on Technology Enhanced Learning) for Engineering
3. UGC (University Grants Commission) for non technical post-graduation education
4. CEC (Consortium for Educational Communication) for under-graduate education
5. NCERT (National Council of Educational Research and Training) for school education
6. NIOS (National Institute of Open Schooling) for school education
7. IGNOU (Indira Gandhi National Open University) for out-of-school students
8. IIMB (Indian Institute of Management, Bangalore) for management studies
9. NITTTR (National Institute of Technical Teachers Training and Research) for Teacher Training programme

189. (b): Non Conventional Learning Programmes-

The education system in which teaching-learning activities is offered other than the on-campus with fixed time classrooms. For examples, evening learning, distance learning, vocational studies, skill-based courses, online learning, etc.

Non-conventional education is inspired by the P.H. Coombs, and Ahmed who has worked on non-formal education for the poor.

Characteristics of Non-conventional learning

- Learners oriented
- No fixed curriculum
- Cost-effective
- Linked to employment
- Continuous
- For improvement of Quality

Target groups of non-conventional education are unemployed youths, the school dropped out, underprivileged group, women and girls, Tribal and Minority population. This type of education is also for literacy programmes.

190. (a): Asynchronous interaction refers to communication that does not occur in real time, so that participants, learners and teachers need not to be engaged at the same moment.

A. **Web conferencing:** This is typically synchronous, as it involves real-time communication.

B. **E-mail:** This is asynchronous. Participants can send and receive emails at different times.

C. **Wikis and Collaborative Documents:** These are asynchronous. Participants can contribute at different times without needing real-time interaction.

D. **Discussion Boards:** These are also asynchronous. Users can post messages and respond to them at their convenience.

E. **Live Streaming:** This is synchronous, as it involves real-time broadcasting and viewing.

Thus, B, C, and D refer to asynchronous situations, (a) is the correct answer.

191. (c): Under Cognitive Apprenticeship, a learner acquires knowledge and skill under the guidance of an expert. Thus, the role of an expert is important. The objective is to develop higher-order skills like problem-solving, critical thinking, and metacognition. Cognitive Apprenticeship prioritizes deep understanding and application of knowledge. The answer is combination of techniques.

A. **Mentoring:** Mentoring, though not a central strategy in cognitive apprenticeship, serves as a crucial support mechanism. It provides learners with guidance, feedback, and motivation. The learner learns from the real-world experience of mentor. It helps in knowledge transfer and it demonstrates the desired behaviours, thus it increases the reflective learning.

B. **Collaboration and socializing** are general practices that can be applied in various learning contexts.

C. **Modelling:** The expert demonstrates a task so that the student can observe and learn.

Coaching: The expert provides feedback and support as the student practices.

Scaffolding: The expert provides support structures to aid the student's learning.

D. **Augmentation:** This typically focuses on passive exposure or reinforcement, which doesn't directly align with the core principles. This is not a core principle.

Retention: This refers to the ability to remember and recall information over time. This is again a basic general skill, and not a specific skill for cognitive apprenticeship.

Explaining: This term refers to the ability to articulate one's understanding of a concept or process.

E. **Articulation:** This encourages students to 'verbalize' their knowledge and reasoning.

Reflection: This helps students to compare their problem-solving skills with those of an expert, peer, this may be in context of their previous performance.

Exploration: This encourages students to pose and solve problems on their own.

F. **Memorization:** This is basic to all kinds of learning.

Rehearsal: This refers to repeating information or practising skills to reinforce learning.

Identifying: This refers to recognizing or recognizing patterns that is construction of knowledge.

Thus, mainly B and D applies, and (c) is the correct answer.

192. (a): Unconditional Stimulus (US or UCS): Always remember that unconditional stimulus is a natural trigger for a natural response. It is a kind of reflex action like when we touch a hot stove and instantly pull away our hand. No prior learning is required for this action, our mind is actually not conditioned for this.

In a similar manner, in Pavlov's experiment, the food was the unconditional stimulus and a natural response (salivation) without any prior conditioning (or simply say training). Later, a bell was added before placing the food, that was the conditioned stimulus. It only started triggering salivation after being repeatedly paired with the unconditional stimulus (food).

- **Conditioned Stimulus (CS):** This is previously neutral stimulus that, after becoming associated with the unconditioned stimulus, eventually comes to trigger a conditioned response.
- **Unconditioned Response (UR or UCR):** The unlearned response that occurs naturally in reaction to the unconditioned stimulus.
- **Conditioned Response (CR):** The learned response to the previously neutral stimulus.

The stimulus which does not require any conditioning for the desired behaviour is called as the Unconditional stimulus. So, the answer is (a).

193. (c): Technical-Scientific Models: These focus on systematic planning, logical analysis and rigor. They help in curriculum development.

A. **Taba's Model:** This is a specific technical-scientific model which focus on a systematic manner to develop curriculum.

B. **Open Classroom Model:** This is more learner-centred and flexible, thus, not a specific technical-scientific models.

C. **Weinstien and Fantini Model:** This is more focused on multicultural education. This is strictly not a technical-scientific approach.

D. **Hunkin's Development Model:** This is a practical, procedural model that fits into the definition of technical-scientific approach.

E. **Goodlad's Model:** This also fits into the technical-scientific concept as it has the systematic approach.

Thus, A, D and E apply, the correct answer is (c).

194. (c)

A. Channel 01– Vageesh - Language and Literature - IV

B. Channel 02– Sanskriti - History, Culture, and Philosophy - I

C. Channel 03– Prabodh - Social Science-1-II

D. Channel 04 - Saaraswat - Music and Fine Arts-III

Thus, A – IV, B – I, C – II, D – III

The correct answer is (c).

195. (b)

Statement 1: Actually, the learner-centred approach focuses on the needs and interests of the learner, not the teacher. It aims to make them active participants in their learning process, not passive recipients of information. Therefore, Statement I is incorrect.

Statement 2: Though the learner input is valuable, but through 'cooperative determination of the subject matter' things are not left over to the sole discretion of learners only. Educators and curriculum guidelines are always given the authority over decisions of subject matter. Therefore, Statement II is also incorrect.

196. (a): Scaffolding: This concept is often attributed to the educational psychologist Lev Vygotsky. The Zone of Proximal (ZPD) is also linked with it. It is basically a structured support to the learner which can take the forms of explanations, prompts, modelling, or hints. It is a gradual approach to build the confidence of learner with an objective of making them independent and self-reliant.

Accommodation: Modifying existing knowledge or mental frameworks to incorporate new information or experiences.

Schemas: Mental frameworks or organized structures that help individuals process and understand new information and experiences.

197. (a): *SWAYAM PRABHA* is an education learning platform initiated by the Ministry of Human Resources and Development (now Ministry of Education), so the correct answer is (a)

198. (c): Let's compare all the options so that such MCQs can be solved in the future exams also.

(a) **Accommodation:** This involves modifying existing schemas to fit new experiences.

(b) **Assimilation:** This involves fitting new experiences into existing schemas without changing the schemas themselves.

(c) **Adaptation:** Adaptation is the broader process that includes both assimilation and accommodation. The new information is integrated into existing schemas.

(d) **Equilibration:** This shows a kind of dynamism in the Piaget's theory of cognitive development. Equilibration suggests that learning and intellectual growth occur as individuals continually move between states of equilibrium and disequilibrium. Disequilibrium is an issue linked with fitting them into existing schemas that is a stage of cognitive conflict or confusion. Equilibrium is linked with accommodation. Thus, they integrate new information into existing knowledge in a harmonious manner. That results in more effective learning.

199. (c): (Hilda) Taba's Model focus on the development of cognitive skills and processes through a problem-solving approach.

Open Classroom Model: This philosophical model focuses on student autonomy and flexible learning spaces, not specifically technical and scientific education.

Weinstein and Fantini Model: This model focuses on social and cultural factors in curriculum development, not technical and scientific content.

Roger's Model of Interpersonal Relations: This education philosophy focuses on communication and relationships, not curriculum development.

200. (c): The answer is 'latent learning' which was developed by psychologist Edward C. Tolman. This learning happens in a hidden manner, and the learner realises this kind only at the moment when it is exhibited. Thus, this type of learning suggests that much of learning is internal and cognitive, rather than just behavioural and based on external reinforcements. Tolman conducted famous rat maze experiment for this. We specially as children often pick up on new words and grammar rules long before they actively use them in conversation.

201. (c): Statement (I) aligns with Dewey's views on learning: Dewey emphasized active learning, hands-on experiences, and collaboration as crucial for meaningful learning. He believed that learners should demonstrate their understanding through creative expression and collaborative projects, not just rote memorization and passive reception of information.

Statement (II) contradicts Piaget's theory of cognitive development: Piaget proposed that learning is inherently tied to a child's developmental stage. Each stage has specific cognitive abilities and limitations that shape how children learn and understand the world. Therefore, learning cannot be entirely independent of these stages.

Thus, (c) is the correct answer.

202. (c): In Charlotte Danielson's Framework for Teaching, the components that fall under the domain of 'Planning and Preparation' are as follows:

- **B. Setting Instructional Outcomes:** This involves establishing clear, measurable objectives for student learning.
- **C. Designing Student Assessments:** This includes planning how to assess student understanding and progress effectively.
- **D. Demonstrating Knowledge of Content and Pedagogy:** This requires understanding the subject matter and the methods of teaching it.
- **E. Demonstrating Knowledge of Resources:** This involves effectively using various teaching resources available.

The component **A. Organizing Physical Space in Classroom** is not included in the 'Planning and Preparation' domain but is rather part of the 'Classroom Environment' domain.

The (c) is the correct answer.

203. (d): The question is about performance of a student and immediate feedback.

A. Kahoot: While Kahoot is great for engaging assessments, it doesn't offer immediate individual feedback unless using specific features like 'Blind Kahoot' which might not be ideal for detailed feedback.

E. Quizizz: This online quiz platform allows teachers to create interactive quizzes and receive immediate feedback on student responses. Students can see their individual results and explanations while the teacher can identify areas for improvement and provide individual feedback in real-time.

Therefore, option (d) is the correct answer. B, C and D are meant for other purposes.

204. (a): Statement (I): This statement appropriately summarises the non-directive teaching model. Unlike traditional methods in which a teacher manages the learning sequence, this approach values student autonomy and allows them to investigate concepts at their own pace.

Statement (II): This statement is also consistent with the core principles of non-directive teaching. The teacher serves as a facilitator, offering advice and support rather than prescribing facts. The use of 'counselling relationship' emphasises the focus on student-centred learning and discovery.

Here, (c) is the correct answer.

CHAPTER 2

Research Aptitude

TOPICS OF IMPORTANCE

- Research: Meaning, Types and Characteristics
- Positivism and Post-positivistic Approach to Research
- Methods of Research: Experimental, Descriptive, Historical
- Qualitative and Quantitative Methods
- Steps of Research
- Thesis and Article Writing
- Format and Styles of Referencing
- Application of ICT in Research
- Research Ethics

1. Who among the following propounded the concept of paradigm? **[Jun 2014]**
(a) Peter Haggett (b) Von Thunen
(c) Thomas Kuhn (d) John K. Wright

2. In a thesis, figures and tables are included in **[Jun 2014]**
(a) The appendix
(b) A separate chapter
(c) The concluding chapter
(d) The text itself

3. A thesis statement is **[Jun 2014]**
(a) An observation (b) A fact
(c) An assertion (d) A discussion

4. The research approach of Max Weber to understand how people create meanings in natural settings is identified as **[Jun 2014]**
(a) Positive paradigm
(b) Critical paradigm
(c) Natural paradigm
(d) Interpretative paradigm

5. Which one of the following is a non-probability sampling? **[Jun 2014]**
(a) Simple random (b) Purposive
(c) Systematic (d) Stratified

6. The research stream of immediate application is **[Jun 2014]**
(a) Conceptual research
(b) Action research
(c) Fundamental research
(d) Empirical research

7. When planning to do as social research, it is better to **[Dec 2014]**
(a) Approach the topic with an open mind.
(b) Do a pilot study before getting stuck into it.
(c) Be familiar with literature on the topic.
(d) Forget about theory because this is very practical.

8. The core elements of a dissertation are **[Dec 2014]**
(a) Introduction; Data Collection; Data Analysis; Conclusions and Recommendations.

(b) Executive Summary; Literature Review; Data Gathered; Conclusions; Bibliography.
(c) Research Plan; Research Data; Analysis; References.
(d) Introduction; Literature Review; Research Methodology; Results; Discussion and Conclusion.

9. What is a research design? **[Dec 2014]**
(a) A way of conducting research that is not grounded in theory.
(b) The choice between using qualitative or quantitative methods.
(c) The style in which you present your research findings, for example, a graph.
(d) A framework for every stage of the collection and analysis of data.

10. 'Sampling cases' means **[Dec 2014]**
(a) Sampling using a sampling frame.
(b) Identifying people who are suitable for research.
(c) Literally the researcher's brief case.
(d) Sampling of people, newspapers, television programmes, etc.

11. The frequency distribution of a research data which is symmetrical in shape similar to a normal distribution but centre peak is much higher, is **[Dec 2014]**
(a) Skewed (b) Mesokurtic
(c) Leptokurtic (d) Platykurtic

12. Which of the following statements regarding the meaning of research are correct? **[Jun 2015]**
(i) Research refers to a series of systematic activity or activities undertaken to find out the solution of a problem.
(ii) It is a systematic, logical and an unbiased process wherein verification of hypothesis, data analysis, interpretation and formation of principles can be done.
(iii) It is an intellectual enquiry or quest towards truth.
(iv) It leads to enhancement of knowledge.

Select the correct answer from the codes given below:
(a) (i), (ii) and (iii) (b) (ii), (iii) and (iv)
(c) (i), (iii) and (iv) (d) (i), (ii), (iii) and (iv)

13. A good thesis writing should involve **[Jun 2015]**
(i) Reduction of punctuation and grammatical errors to a minimum.
(ii) Careful checking of references.
(iii) Consistency in the way the thesis is written.
(iv) A clear and well-written abstract.

Select the correct answer from the codes given below.
(a) (i), (ii), (iii) and (iv)
(b) (i), (ii) and (iii)
(c) (i), (ii) and (iv)
(d) (ii), (iii) and (iv)

14. Jean Piaget gave a theory of cognitive development of humans on the basis of his **[Jun 2015]**
(a) Fundamental research
(b) Applied research
(c) Action research
(d) Evaluation research

15. 'Male and female students perform equally well in a numerical aptitude test'. This statement indicates a **[Jun 2015]**
(a) Research hypothesis
(b) Null hypothesis
(c) Directional hypothesis
(d) Statistical hypothesis

16. The conclusions/findings of which type of research cannot be generalized to other situations? **[Jun 2015]**
(a) Historical research
(b) Descriptive research
(c) Experimental research
(d) Causal comparative research

17. Which of the following steps are required to design a questionnaire? **[Jun 2015]**
(i) Writing primary and secondary aims of the study.
(ii) Review of the current literature.
(iii) Prepare a draft of questionnaire.
(iv) Revision of the draft.

Select the correct answer from the codes given below:
(a) (i), (ii) and (iii)
(b) (i), (iii) and (iv)
(c) (ii), (iii) and (iv)
(d) (i), (ii), (iii) and (iv)

18. Which of the following statements is not true in the context of participatory research? **[Dec 2015]**
(a) It recognizes knowledge as power.
(b) It emphasises on people as experts.
(c) It is a collective process of enquiry.
(d) Its sole purpose is production of knowledge.

19. Which of the following statements is true in the context of the testing of a hypothesis? **[Dec 2015]**
(a) It is only the alternative hypothesis that can be tested.
(b) It is only the null hypothesis that can be tested.
(c) Both the alternative and the null hypotheses can be tested.
(d) Both the alternative and the null hypotheses cannot be tested.

20. Which of the following are the basic rules of APA style of referencing format? **[Dec 2015]**
(i) Italicize titles of shorter works such as journal articles or essays.
(ii) Invert authors' names (last name first).
(iii) Italicize titles of longer works such as books and journals.
(iv) Alphabetically index reference list.

Select the correct answer from the codes given below:
(a) (i) and (ii) (b) (ii), (iii) and (iv)
(c) (iii) and (iv) (d) (i), (ii), (iii) and (iv)

21. Which of the following are the characteristics of a seminar? **[Dec 2015]**
(i) It is a form of academic instruction.
(ii) It involves questioning, discussion and debates.
(iii) It involves large groups of individuals.
(iv) It needs involvement of skilled persons.

Select the correct answer from the codes given below:
(a) (ii) and (iii) (b) (ii) and (iv)
(c) (ii), (iii) and (iv) (d) (i), (ii) and (iv)

22. A researcher is interested in studying the prospects of a particular political party in an urban area. What tool should he prefer for the study? **[Dec 2015]**
(a) Rating scale (b) Interview
(c) Questionnaire (d) Schedule

23. Ethical norms in research do not involve guidelines for **[Dec 2015]**
(a) Thesis format (b) Copyright
(c) Patenting policy (d) Data sharing policies

24. The format of thesis writing is the same as in **[Jul 2016]**
(a) Preparation of a research paper/article.
(b) Writing of seminar presentation.
(c) A research dissertation.
(d) Presenting a workshop/conference paper.

25. In qualitative research paradigm, which of the following features may be considered critical? **[Jul 2016]**
(a) Data collection with standardized research tools.
(b) Sampling design with probability sample techniques.
(c) Data collection with bottom-up empirical evidences.
(d) Data gathering to take place with top-down systematic evidences.

26. From the following list of statements, identify the set which has negative implications for 'research ethics'. **[Jul 2016]**
(A) A researcher critically looks at the findings of another research.
(B) Related studies are cited without proper references.
(C) Research findings are made the basis for policy making.
(D) Conduct of practitioner is screened in terms of reported research evidences.
(E) A research study is replicated with a view to verify the evidences from other researches.
(F) Both policy making and policy implementing processes are regulated in terms of preliminary studies.

Codes:
(a) (A), (B) and (C) (b) (B), (C) and (D)
(c) (B), (D) and (F) (d) (A), (C) and (E)

27. In a research on the effect of child-rearing practices on stress-proneness of children in completing school projects, the hypothesis formulated is that 'child rearing practices do influence stress-proneness'. At the data-analysis stage, a null hypothesis is advanced to find out the tenability of research hypothesis. On the basis of the evidence available, the null hypothesis is rejected at 0.01 level of significance. What decision may be warranted in respect of the research hypothesis? **[Jul 2016]**

(a) The research hypothesis will also be rejected.
(b) The research hypothesis will be accepted.
(c) Both the research hypothesis and the null hypothesis will be rejected.
(d) No decision can be taken in respect of the research hypothesis.

28. A researcher intends to explore the effect of possible factors for the organization of effective mid-day meal interventions. Which research method will be most appropriate for this study? **[Jul 2016]**

(a) Historical method
(b) Descriptive survey method
(c) Experimental method
(d) *Ex post facto* method

29. Which of the following is an initial mandatory requirement for pursuing research? **[Jul 2016]**

(a) Developing a research design.
(b) Formulating a research question.
(c) Deciding about the data analysis procedure.
(d) Formulating a research hypothesis.

30. The principal of a school conducts an interview session of teachers and students with a view to explore the possibility of their enhanced participation in school programmers. Which type of research does this endeavour be related to? **[Jan 2017]**

(a) Evaluation research
(b) Fundamental research
(c) Action research
(d) Applied research

31. In doing action research, what is the usual sequence of steps? **[Jan 2017]**

(a) Reflect, Observe, Plan, Act
(b) Plan, Act, Observe, Reflect
(c) Plan, Reflect, Observe, Act
(d) Act, Observe, Plan, Reflect

32. Which sequence of research steps is logical in the following list? **[Jan 2017]**

(a) Problem formulation, Analysis, Development of research design, Hypothesis making, Collection of data, Arriving at generalizations and conclusions.
(b) Development of research design, Hypothesis making, Problem formulation, Data analysis, Arriving at conclusions and Data collection.
(c) Problem formulation, Hypothesis making, Development of a research design, Collection of a data, Data analysis and formulation of generalizations and Conclusions.
(d) Problem formulation, Deciding about the sample and data collection tools, Formulation of hypothesis, Collection and interpretation of research evidence.

33. The following are two sets, such as research methods (Set-I) and data collection tools (Set-II). Match the two sets and indicate your answer by selecting the correct code. **[Jan 2017]**

Set-I	Set-II
A. Experimental method	(i) Using primary secondary sources
B. *Ex post facto* method	(ii) Questionnaire
C. Descriptive survey method	(iii) Standardized tests
D. Historical method	(iv) Typical characteristics tests

Codes:

	A	B	C	D
(a)	(ii)	(i)	(iii)	(iv)
(b)	(iii)	(iv)	(ii)	(i)
(c)	(ii)	(iii)	(i)	(iv)
(d)	(ii)	(iv)	(iii)	(i)

34. The issue of 'research ethics' may be considered pertinent at which stage of research? **[Jan 2017]**

(a) At the stage of problem formulation and its definition.
(b) At the stage of defining the population of research.
(c) At the stage of data collection and interpretation.
(d) At the stage of reporting the findings.

35. In which of the following, reporting format is formally prescribed? **[Jan 2017]**

(a) Doctoral-level thesis
(b) Conference of researchers
(c) Workshops and seminars
(d) Symposia

36. Among the following, identify the continuous type of data. **[Jan 2017]**
(a) Number of languages a person speaks.
(b) Number of children in a household.
(c) Population in cities.
(d) Weight of students in a class.

37. Which of the following research types focuses on ameliorating the prevailing situations? **[Nov 2017]**
(a) Fundamental research
(b) Applied research
(c) Action research
(d) Experimental research

38. A researcher attempts to evaluate the effect of method of feeding on anxiety-proneness of children. Which method of research would be appropriate for this? **[Nov 2017]**
(a) Case study method
(b) Experimental method
(c) *Ex post facto* method
(d) Survey method

39. In finalizing a thesis writing format which of the following would form part of supplementary pages? **[Nov 2017]**
(a) List of tables and figures.
(b) Table of contents.
(c) Conclusions of the study.
(d) Bibliography and appendices.

40. Which of the following is susceptible to the issue of research ethics? **[Nov 2017]**
(a) Inaccurate application of statistical techniques.
(b) Faulty research design.
(c) Choice of sampling techniques.
(d) Reporting of research findings.

41. There are two sets given below: **[Jul 2018]**
Set–I specifies the types of research, while Set–II indicates their characteristics. Match the two and given your answer by selecting the appropriate code.

Set-I (Research types)	Set-II (Characteristics)
A. Fundamental research	(i) Finding out the extent of perceived impact of an intervention.
B. Applied research	(ii) Developing an effective explanation through theory building.
C. Action research	(iii) Improving an existing situation through use of interventions.
D. Evaluative research	(iv) Exploring the possibility of a theory for use in various situations.
	(v) Enriching technological resources.

	(A)	(B)	(C)	(D)
(a)	(ii)	(iv)	(iii)	(i)
(b)	(v)	(iv)	(iii)	(ii)
(c)	(iii)	(ii)	(iii)	(iv)
(d)	(ii)	(iii)	(iv)	(v)

42. Which of the sets of activities best indicate the cyclic nature of action research strategy? **[Jul 2018, Jun 2019]**
(a) Reflect, Observe, Plan, Act
(b) Observe, Act, Reflect, Plan
(c) Act, Plan, Observe, Reflect
(d) Plan, Act, Observe, Reflect

43. Which of the following sequence of research steps is nearer to scientific method? **[Jul 2018]**
(a) Suggested solution of the problem, deducing the consequences of the solution, perceiving the problem situation, location of the difficulty and testing the solutions.
(b) Perceiving the problem situation, locating the actual problem and its definition, hypothesizing, deducing the consequences of the suggested solution and testing the hypothesis in action.
(c) Defining a problem, identifying the causes of the problem, defining a population, drawing a sample, collecting data and analysing results.
(d) Identifying the causal factors, defining the problem, developing a hypothesis, selecting a sample, collecting data and arriving at generalization and conclusions.

44. The problem of 'research ethics' is concerned with which aspect of research activities? **[Jul 2018]**
(a) Following the prescribed format of a thesis.
(b) Data analysis through qualitative or quantitative technique.
(c) Defining the population of research.
(d) Evidence-based research reporting.

45. Empirical research in social sciences is associated with [Dec 2018]
(a) Fictional narratives (b) Positivist philosophy
(c) Historical artifacts (d) Religious practices

46. The purpose of review of literature includes [Dec 2018]
(i) To understand the subject background.
(ii) To formulate research questions.
(iii) To find out relevant methodology.
(iv) To debate the ethical aspects of research.
(v) To carry out meta-analysis of bibliography.
(vi) To identify the data sources code.
Options:
(a) (i), (ii), (iii) and (iv)
(b) (ii), (iii), (iv) and (v)
(c) (i), (ii), (iii) and (vi)
(d) (iii), (iv), (v) and (vi)

47. If you are to calculate Spearman's rho, then what kind of data you would enter? [Dec 2018]
(a) Actual scores (b) Ranks
(c) Dichotomous data (d) Nominal data

48. A variable that measures the effect of a manipulated variable is known as [Dec 2018]
(a) Independent variable
(b) Dependent variable
(c) Confounding variable
(d) Controlled variable

49. Poster sessions in research conferences provide better opportunities for [Dec 2018]
(a) Focus group discussions
(b) Interpersonal interactions
(c) Formal speeches
(d) Display of common interest

50. The characteristics of scientific method of research are [Dec 2018]
(i) Empiricism
(ii) Objectivity
(iii) Systematic
(iv) Secretive
(v) Security' related
(vi) Predictive
Options:
(a) (i), (ii), (iii) and (vi)
(b) (i), (ii), (iv) and (v)
(c) (iv), (v), (vi) and (i)
(d) (iii), (iv), (v) and (vi)

51. The kind of numbers which do not represent amounts but instead represent kind (different qualities, types or categories) are known as [Dec 2018]
(a) Absolute (b) Ordinal
(c) Prime (d) Nominal

52. When a reviewer reviews a research article without knowing the authors name, it is referred to as [Dec 2018]
(a) Anonymous review
(b) Uncategorized review
(c) Blind review
(d) Behind-the-curtain review

53. A good review of research literature aims at [Jun 2019]
(a) Subjective analysis of the content
(b) Provide information about the authors and their affiliations
(c) Generates research question and validating those questions
(d) Conducts multiple task-based screening

54. Which of the following action sets best represent an action research cycle? [Jun 2019]
(a) Reflect, act, plan and observe
(b) Plan, act, observe and reflect
(c) Observe, plan, reflect and act
(d) Act, plan, observe and reflect

55. Which of the following research formats focuses on hypothesis testing and generalizations? [Jun 2019]
(a) Experimental and *ex post facto* research
(b) Intervention based action research
(c) Phenomenalogical and narrative research
(d) Case study research

56. Which one of the following is the main feature of qualitative research? [Jun 2019]
(a) Avoids positivist assumptions and data analysis
(b) Subscribes to pre-existing categories
(c) Collects data in numerical form
(d) Uses empirical method of data analysis

57. A researcher fails to reject the null hypothesis (Ho) in his/her research. What implications will it carry for his/her principle research hypothesis? [Jun 2019]
(a) Accepting the research hypothesis
(b) Rejecting the research hypothesis

(c) Not taking any decision on the research hypothesis
(d) Improving the research hypothesis

58. ERIC, MEDLINE and ABI/INFORM are instances of **[Jun 2019]**
(a) Citation services (b) Electronic databases
(c) Printed databases (d) Libraries

59. In which of the following research paradigms the focus of concern is on interpreting reality in terms of participants perspective? **[Jun 2019]**
(a) Experimental Research
(b) *Ex post facto* Research
(c) Ethnographic Research
(d) Survey Research

60. Snowball sampling is the process of selecting a sample using **[Jun 2019]**
(a) Networks (b) Groups
(c) Snowballs (d) Computer Programs

61. Research design that needs to collect factual information on a continuing basis is classified as **[Jun 2019]**
(a) Longitudinal Study Design
(b) Pre and Post Study Design
(c) Cross-Sectional Study Design
(d) Double-Control Study Design

62. A tentative proposition with unknown validity that specifies a relationship between two or more variables is called **[Jun 2019]**
(a) Research problem (b) Research proposal
(c) Research design (d) Research hypothesis

63. When the researcher does not know the identity of the experimental and placebo groups, the study is termed as **[Jun 2019]**
(a) Blind (b) Double-blind
(c) Panel (d) Cohort

64. In the research method, generalizations may be made that will be applicable to other situations of the same type. What is it the called? **[Jun 2019]**
(a) Cohort study (b) Case study
(c) Panel study (d) Blind study

65. Quantitative research is also called the **[Jun 2019]**
(a) Ethnographic approach
(b) Unstructured approach
(c) Descriptive approach
(d) Structured approach

66. Research that focusses on social inequality between men and women is called **[Jun 2019]**
(a) Comparative research
(b) Longitudinal research
(c) Action research
(d) Feminist research

67. The easiest attitudinal scale which is a summated rating scale is the **[Jun 2019]**
(a) Guttman scale (b) Likert scale
(c) Thurstone scale (d) MLA scale

68. Plagiarism in research is **[Jun 2019]**
(a) Creative use of previous data
(b) Copying unscrupulously and making use of it
(c) Quoting someone and citing him/her
(d) Referring to previous data and working over it with new objectives

69. A university teacher plans to study the effect of level of aspiration of students in terms of their socio-economic background on their scholastic performance at the term end evaluation conducted by an external testing agency. What is the dependent variable in this study? **[Jun 2019]**
(a) Level of aspiration of students
(b) Socio-economic background of students
(c) Scholastic performance of students
(d) Term end evaluation

70. Participant observation is a part of **[Jun 2019]**
(a) Philosophical research
(b) Mentalist theory of language
(c) Mathematical research
(d) Ethnographic research

71. The study of 'why does stressful living result in heart attack'. Can be classified as **[Jun 2019]**
(a) Descriptive research
(b) Explanatory research
(c) Correlational research
(d) Feasibility research

72. Mailed questionnaire, observation, interview and collective questionnaire are instances of **[Jun 2019]**
(a) Secondary sources (b) Personal sources
(c) Primary sources (d) Tertiary sources

73. A hypothesis should be conceptually **[Jun 2019]**
(a) Convoluted, complex and generic
(b) Complex, tough and general

(c) Simple, clear and specific
(d) Obscure, complicated and simple

74. The formulation of a research problem can be compared to **[Jun 2019]**
(a) Laying the foundation of a building
(b) Building the walls of a home
(c) Polishing the doors of a building
(d) Constructing the ceiling of a house

75. During research, while recording observations, if an observer rates an individual based on the rating given in another aspect of the interaction, this is termed as the **[Jun 2019]**
(a) Evaluation effect
(b) Error of central tendency
(c) Halo effect
(d) Categorical effect

76. A pilot study is also called a **[Jun 2019]**
(a) Descriptive study (b) Feasibility study
(c) Correlational study (d) Explanatory study

77. Which of the following research types has a potential for enhancing teaching competencies? **[Jun 2019]**
(a) Fundamental research
(b) Applied research
(c) Impact assessment research
(d) Action research

78. The fishbowl draw is a method of drawing a/an **[Jun 2019]**
(a) Independent sample (b) Structured sample
(c) Non-random sample (d) Random sample

79. A questionnaire that offers no scope for any respondent's own view is called **[Jun 2019]**
(a) Closed-ended (b) Schedule
(c) Open-ended (d) Unstructured

80. In experimental research based studies the observations derived from which of the following variables are considered for statistical analysis? **[Jun 2019]**
(a) Independent variable
(b) Dependent variable
(c) Moderator variable
(d) Control variable

81. In research, reliability is that quality of a measurement procedure which provides **[Jun 2019]**
(a) Repeatability and accuracy
(b) Punctuality and accuracy
(c) Accuracy and speed
(d) Speed and repeatability

82. A shift in attitude in respondents between two points during collection is called **[Jun 2019]**
(a) Reactive effect (b) Maturation effect
(c) Regression effect (d) Conditioning effect

83. The time frame in which a study explore a situation or problem is also called the **[Jun 2019]**
(a) Reference period (b) Age
(c) Longitudinal (d) Retrospective time

84. The major characteristic of correlation analysis is to seek out **[Jun 2019]**
(a) Difference among variables
(b) Variations among variables
(c) Association among variables
(d) Regression among variables

85. The conceptual frame work in which a research is conducted is called a **[Jun 2019]**
(a) Synopsis of research
(b) Research design
(c) Research hypothesis
(d) Research paradigm

86. From the list given below identify those which are called 'Non-probability sampling procedures': **[Jun 2019]**
(i) Simple random sampling
(ii) Dimensional sampling
(iii) Snowball sampling
(iv) Cluster sampling
(v) Quota sampling
(vi) Stratified sampling
Choose the correct option
(a) (i), (ii) and (iii) (b) (ii), (iv) and (v)
(c) (i), (iii) and (iv) (d) (ii), (iii) and (v)

87. The research design is a specifically related to which of the following features in research? **[Jun 2019]**
(i) Sample selection
(ii) Formulation of a plan
(iii) Deciding about the tool for data collection
(iv) Hypothesis making
(v) Choice of a field of inquiry
Select your answer from the options given below:
(a) (ii), (iii) and (iv)
(b) (i), (ii) and (iii)

(c) (ii), (iv) and (v)
(d) (iii), (iv) and (v)

88. Which of the following is a plagiarism checking website? **[Jun 2019]**
(a) http://go.turnitin.com
(b) http://www.researchgate.com
(c) http://www.editorial.elsevier.com
(d) http://www.grammarly.com

89. In which of the following research studies, interpretation and meaning get more attention than formulation of generalizations? **[Jun 2019]**
(i) Historical studies
(ii) Survey studies
(iii) Philosophical studies
(iv) Ethnographic studies
(v) Hypothetico–deductive studies
(vi) *Ex post facto* studies
Choose your answer from the options given below:
(a) (i), (ii) and (iii)
(b) (iv), (v) and (vi)
(c) (ii), (iv) and (v)
(d) (i), (iii) and (iv)

90. Bibliograpy given in a research report **[Jun 2019]**
(a) Helps those intersted in further research
(b) Shows the vast knowledge of the researcher
(c) Makes the report authentic
(d) Is an optional part of the report

91. Through which research method, the manipulation of an independent variable and its effect on dependent variable is examined with reference to a hypothesis under controlled conditions? **[Jun 2019]**
(a) *Ex post facto* research
(b) Descriptive research
(c) Case study research
(d) Experimental research

92. Reference serve the purpose of **[Jun 2019]**
(a) Lending authenticity to the given content
(b) Insightful decision-making
(c) Giving ornamental value to the research
(d) Exhibiting the great achievement

93. Supervisor's certification on the thesis **[Jun 2019]**
(a) Gives name and fame to the supervisor
(b) Clears different bottlenecks in the system
(c) Gives weightage to the scholar's work
(d) Ensure originality of the work

94. After identifying the different variables and establishing the logical reasoning in the theoretical framework, the next step in the research process is to **[Jun 2019]**
(a) Conduct survey
(b) Generate hypothesis
(c) Focus on the group discussion
(d) Use experiment in the investigation

95. Participation in which type of research has the great potential for ensuring the improvement of the professional as well as work situation? **[Jun 2019]**
(a) Fundamental research
(b) Applied research
(c) Evaluative research
(d) Action research

96. Which stage in research creates a working thesis for the research paper by specifying and organizing the category of information? **[Jun 2019]**
(a) Research design
(b) Developing a hypothesis
(c) Review of literature
(d) Analysis of data

97. Critical language testing in a research report is **[Jun 2019]**
(a) Testing language from an ethical point of view, revealing its misuses
(b) Evaluating the stylistic characteristics of language
(c) Critiquing the ideology of the author
(d) Observing the gender role played by language

98. A college teacher does research with a view to depict the reality situations relating to home conditions of students and hostels provided for. Which of the following research format will be helpful to do so? **[Dec 2019]**
(a) Experimental research
(b) Descriptive research
(c) Participant observation based research
(d) Ethnographic research

99. In case the population of research is heterogeneous in nature, which of the following sampling techniques will ensure optimum representativeness of sample units? **[Dec 2019]**
(a) Simple random sampling
(b) Stratified random sampling
(c) Cluster sampling
(d) Systematic sampling

100. Which of the following statistical technique will be appropriate for data analysis, when the observations are available in the form of frequencies? **[Dec 2019]**
(a) Parametric 't' test
(b) Non-parametric 'u' test
(c) Non-parametric 'chi-square' test
(d) Parametric correlated 't' test

101. In which of the following steps of research, the scope for creativity and imagination is utmost? **[Dec 2019]**
(a) Identifying the research problem and defining it
(b) Figuring out the related studies and the techniques used by other researchers
(c) Identifying variables and hypothesising
(d) Data analysis and presentation of results

102. Which one of the following represents the correct order of sequence for reading skills in the context of research? **[Dec 2019]**
(a) Read, question, recall, review, survey
(b) Questions, survey, read, recall, review
(c) Recall, review, survey, question, read
(d) Survey, question, read, recall, review

103. Which among the following is not the outcome of grounded theory research? **[Dec 2019]**
(a) Concepts (b) Narratives
(c) Categories (d) Hypotheses

104. Identify the correct statements from the following. **[Dec 2019]**
(i) Sampling related error is subsumed under the category non-sampling error.
(ii) Sampling error doesn't occur in multistage cluster sampling.
(iii) Inaccurate sampling frame and non-response are examples of sampling related error.
(iv) There is an inverse relation between heterogeneity of population and sampling error.

Choose the correct option.
(a) (i) and (iii) only
(b) (i) and (iv) only
(c) (ii) and (iv) only
(d) (ii) and (iii) only

105. Arrange the steps of research in the sequence in which they are presented in the thesis. **[Dec 2019]**
(a) Discussion, review of literature, result, conceptual framework, problem
(b) Review of literature, problem, conceptual framework, result, discussion
(c) Problem, review of literature, conceptual framework, result, discussion
(d) Problem, review of literature, conceptual framework, discussion, result

106. Which among the following is NOT related to qualitative research? **[Dec 2019]**
(a) Thematic analysis
(b) Case study
(c) Discourse analysis
(d) Survey method

107. Which among the following is the usually recommended sequence in an intervention-based action research process? **[Dec 2019]**
(a) Plan, act, observe and reflect
(b) Observe, plan, act and reflect
(c) Reflect, plan, act and observe
(d) Observe, act, reflect and plan

108. A college teacher presents a research paper in a seminar. The research paper cites references which are pretty old. This situation will be described as the case of: **[Dec 2019]**
(a) technical lapse
(b) ethical lapse
(c) academic ignorance
(d) inability of updating research source

109. At the stage of data analysis, which quantitative techniques have been used by a researcher, the evidence warrants the rejection of Null Hypothesis (*Ho*). Which of the following decisions of the researcher will be deemed appropriate? **[Dec 2019]**
(a) Rejecting the (H_0) and also the substantive research hypothesis

(b) Rejecting the (H_0) and accepting the substantive research hypothesis
(c) Rejecting the (H_0) without taking any decision on the substantive research hypothesis
(d) Accepting the (H_0) and rejecting the substantive research hypothesis

110. Match List I with List II. **[Dec 2019]**

List I (Research Tools)	List II (Measurement Scale)
(A) Questionnaire and interview	(i) Ratio scale of measurement
(B) Intelligence and aptitude tests	(ii) Ordinal scale of measurement
(C) Attitude and value tests	(iii) Interval scale of measurement
(D) Speed and frequency tests	(iv) Nominal scale of measurement

Choose the correct answer from the following.

Code:

	(A)	(B)	(C)	(D)
(a)	(i)	(ii)	(iii)	(iv)
(b)	(iii)	(i)	(iv)	(ii)
(c)	(iv)	(iii)	(ii)	(i)
(d)	(ii)	(iii)	(i)	(iv)

111. Which of the following sequences represent the most logical sequence in doing research? **[Dec 2019]**
(a) Identifying and defining a research problem, formulating a hypothesis, testing of hypothesis and reporting the results
(b) Identify a research problem, defining the population and sample, collecting and analysis of data
(c) Survey of research, defining the research problem, collecting data and presenting the outcomes
(d) Defining research variables, hypothesising, testing of research and reporting of research outcomes

112. Hypothesis testing is the main concept of which type of research? **[Dec 2019]**
(a) Experimental research
(b) Historical research
(c) Survey research
(d) Exegetic research

113. A university teacher intends to study the relationship between level of aspiration and achievement of rural children. Which design of research will be most appropriate in this context? **[Dec 2019]**
(a) Experimental research design
(b) Ex post facto research design
(c) Historical research design
(d) Survey research design

114. In the post positivistic approach to research, which of the following types of researches got emphasised? **[Dec 2019]**
(i) Experimental research
(ii) Phenomenological research
(iii) Ethnographic research
(iv) Ex post facto research
(v) Action research

Choose the correct answer from the options given below.
(a) (i), (ii) and (iii) (b) (ii), (iii) and (iv)
(c) (ii), (iii) and (v) (d) (iii), (iv) and (v)

115. In which of the following formats, 'research abstract' is must? **[Dec 2019]**
(i) Research article
(ii) Seminar paper presentation
(iii) Thesis
(iv) Research synopsis

Choose the most appropriate option from those given below.
(a) (i), (iii) and (iv) (b) (i), (ii) and (iv)
(c) (i), (ii) and (iii) (d) (ii), (iii) and (iv)

116. In which type of qualitative research designs, individual stories to describe the lives of people are explored? **[Dec 2019]**
(a) Ethnography
(b) Grounded theory research
(c) Symbolic interaction
(d) Narrative research

117. Match the two sets given below, in which Set I mentions the level of measurement and Set II mentions their properties. **[Dec 2019]**

Set I (Level of Measurement)	Set II (Properties)
(A) Nominal	(i) Classification, order, equal units and absolute zero
(B) Ordinal	(ii) Classification, order and equal units
(C) Interval	(iii) Classification
(D) Ratio	(iv) Classification and order

Select the correct answer from the options given below.

Code:

	(A)	(B)	(C)	(D)
(a)	(i)	(ii)	(iii)	(iv)
(b)	(ii)	(iii)	(iv)	(i)
(c)	(iii)	(i)	(ii)	(iv)
(d)	(iii)	(iv)	(ii)	(i)

118. In which of the following sampling methods employed in research, the units comprising the sample are given equal and independent chance? **[Dec 2019]**
(a) Stage sampling
(b) Cluster sampling
(c) Dimensional sampling
(d) Snowball sampling

119. The issue of research ethics becomes relevant in which of the following stages of research? **[Dec 2019]**
(i) Problem selection
(ii) Hypothesis formulation
(iii) Hypothesis testing
(iv) Data analysis and interpretation
(v) Defining of research population
Select the correct answer from the following options.
(a) (i) and (ii) (b) (iii) and (iv)
(c) (ii) and (v) (d) (iii) and (v)

120. From the list given below, identify the tests which are maximum performance tests in the context of research. **[Dec 2019]**
(i) Personality tests
(ii) Projective personality tests
(iii) Achievement tests
(iv) Attitude tests
(v) Intelligence tests
(vi) Aptitude tests
Choose the correct answer from the options given below.
(a) (i), (ii) and (iii)
(b) (ii), (iii) and (v)
(c) (iii), (v) and (vi)
(d) (i), (iv) and (vi)

121. Which of the following research is cyclic in nature? **[Dec 2019]**
(a) Fundamental research
(b) Applied research
(c) Action research
(d) Evaluative research

122. Given below are two statements: **[2020]**
Statement I: Chance or accidental errors in research will cause obtained results to depart from the true value as often in one direction or in another
Statement II: Systematic error causes obtained results in research to vary in a particular direction and is far more likely to catch the researcher by surprise than is chance error.
In the light of the above statements, choose the most appropriate from the options given below:
(a) Both Statements I and Statement II are correct.
(b) Both Statements I and Statement II are incorrect.
(c) Statement I is correct but Statement II is incorrect.
(d) Statement I is incorrect but Statement II is correct.

123. List I mentions various methods of research while List II offers their description. Match List I with List II **[2020]**

List 1	List II
(A) Experimental method	(I) A detailed description of the way people believe and act in a particular society.
(B) Ex-post facto method	(II) Studies designed to obtain information concerning the current status of phenomena.

List 1	List II
(C) Descriptive survey method	(III) Studying the effect of manipulating independent variable on dependent variable under appropriate control imposed.
(D) Ethnographic method	(IV) Conducting a probe into casual factors on the basis of evidenced manifest now.

Choose the correct answer from the options given below:

(a) (A) -(I), (B) - (II), (C) - (III), (D) - (IV)
(b) (A) -(IV), (B) - (III), (C) - (II), (D) - (I)
(c) (A) -(II), (B) - (I), (C) - (IV), (D) - (III)
(d) (A) -(III), (B) - (IV), (C) - (I), (D) - (II)

124. Which of the following features best describe an independent variable in research? **[2020]**

(A) It is cause in the cause-effect relationship.
(B) It is the effect in the cause-effect relationship.
(C) It is condition or characteristic which is manipulated in the experimental study.
(D) It is the variable which is placed under control.
(E) It is kind of response variable.

Choose the correct answer from the options given below:

(a) (A) and (B) only (b) (B) and (C) only
(c) (A) and (C) only (d) (D) and (E) only

125. When a particular 'statistics' in a research situation is evidently declared to be significant, which of the following decisions will be considered tenable? **[2020]**

(A) Null hypothesis is rejected
(B) Alternative hypothesis is accepted
(C) Null hypothesis is accepted
(D) Alternative hypothesis is rejected
(E) Null hypothesis along with the alternative hypothesis are accepted.

Choose the correct answer from the options given below:

(a) (B) and (C) only (b) (C) and (D) only
(c) (D) and (E) only (d) (A) and (B) only

126. Match List I with List II. **[2020]**

List 1 Research concepts	List II Description
(A) Hypothesis	(I) It is statistical test that does not make assumptions about the parameters
(B) Sample	(II) Device using which data are collected in research
(C) Research tool	(III) A subset drawn from a larger set to represent it
(D) Non-parametric tests	(IV) A tentative statement indicating relationship between two or more than two variables

Choose the correct answer from the options given below:

(a) A -IV, B - III, C - II, D - I
(b) A - I, B - II, C - III, D - IV
(c) A - II, E - I, C - IV, D - III
(d) A - III, B - IV, C - I, D - II

127. In quantitative research paradigm, which of the following sampling methods are given preference? **[2020]**

A. Simple random sampling
B. Stratified sampling
C. Quota sampling
D. Snowball sampling
E. Systematic sampling

Choose the correct answer from the options given below:

(a) A, B and C only
(b) A, B and E only
(c) B, C and D only
(d) C, D and E only

128. In which research method manipulation of 'independent variable' and control of 'extraneous variables' are neither possible nor desirable? **[2020]**

(a) Experimental method
(b) Ex post facto method
(c) Historical method
(d) Descriptive survey method

129. Identify those statements which describe the characteristic features of qualitative research paradigm **[2020]**

A. Researchers tend to analyze their data inductively
B. The substantive research hypothesis is tested via Null hypothesis
C. Data take the form of words or pictures
D. Actual settings are the direct source of data
E. It assumes that there are social facts with a single objective reality. Choose the correct answer from the options given below:

(a) A, B and C only (b) A, B and E only
(c) B, C and E only (d) A, C and D only

130. Given below are two statements, one is labelled as Assertion (A) and the other is labelled as Reason (R). **[2020]**

Assertion (A): A cross break is a numerical tabular presentation of data usually in frequency or percentage form in which variables are cross-partitioned to study relations between them.

Reason (R): The categories are set up according to the research hypothesis.

In light of the above statements, choose the most appropriate answer from the options given below

(a) Both A and R are correct and R is the correct explanation of A
(b) Both A and R are correct but R is NOT the correct explanation of A
(c) A is correct but R is not correct
(d) A is not correct but R is correct

131. Given below are two statements: One is labeled as Assertion (A) and the other is labeled as Reason (R): **[2020]**

Assertion (A): Data must be authentic before it can be of any value in a historical research, yet proof of authenticity does not establish its value, it must also be accurate.

Reason (R): External criticism is therefore referred to as lower criticism of the data.

In the light of the above statements, choose the correct answer from the options given below:

(a) Both (A) and (R) are correct and (R) is correct explanation of (A)
(b) Both (A) and (R) are correct and (R) is NOT the correct explanation of (A)
(c) (A) is correct but (R) is not correct
(d) (A) is not correct but (R) is correct

132. Given below are two statements **[2021]**

Statement I: Exploration is particularly useful when researchers lack a clear idea of the problems they will meet during the study.

Statement II: Through exploration, researchers develop concepts more clearly, establish priorities, develop operational definitions, and improve the final research design.

In light of the above statements, choose the correct answer from the options given below:

(a) Both Statement I and Statement II are false
(b) Both Statement I and Statement II are true
(c) Statement I is false but Statement II is true
(d) Statement I is true but Statement II is false

133. Which one of the following is an important characteristic of the researchers involved in qualitative study? **[2021]**

(a) Enthusiasm (b) Non-partisan
(c) Reflexivity (d) Transparency

134. Survey research is based on which of the following? **[2021]**

(a) Constructivism (b) Hermeneutics
(c) Interpretivism (d) Positivism

135. Which among the following are non-parametric statistics? **[2021]**

A. t-test
B. F-test
C. Spearman's rank order correlation
D. Mann-Whitney-Wilcoxon test
E. Kendall coefficient of concordance

Choose the correct answer from the options given below:

(a) A, B and C only (b) B, C and D only
(c) B, D and E only (d) C, D and E only

136. Some of the types of hypothesis are as follows: **[2021]**

A. Descriptive B. Null
C. Confounding D. Intervening
E. Explanatory (Causal)

Choose the correct answer from the options given below:

(a) A, B and D only (b) A, B and E only
(c) A, B and C only (d) B, C and D only

137. The characteristics of a normal distribution curve are: **[2021]**

A. It reflects an asymmetrical distribution
B. It is bell-shaped
C. It does not show standard deviations
D. The mean, mode and median coincide at the centre of the distribution
E. The curve is based on an infinite number of observations

Choose the correct answer from the options given below:

(a) A, B and C only
(b) B, C and D only
(c) B, D and E only
(d) C, D and E only

138. Match List I with List II: **[2021]**

List I	List II
Types of Design	Characteristics
A. Solomon Four Group Design	I. It is a cross-sectional design
B. Post-test only Control Group Design	II. Contains an additional set of control and experimental groups
C. One-shot Case Study	III. Omits the pre-tested groups altogether
D. Correlational Design	IV. Observation of a single group at one point of time to observe the change

Choose the correct answer from the options given below:

(a) A -I , B -II , C -III , D -IV
(b) A -II , B -III , C -IV , D -I
(c) A -III , B -IV , C -I , D -II
(d) A -IV , B -I , C -II , D -III

139. An extraneous variable is also known as **[2021]**

(a) Artifact
(b) Contiguous factor
(c) Dependent variable
(d) Intervener

140. Given below are two statements: **[2021]**

Statement I: A variable measured at the nominal level can be used in higher-level statistics if it is converted into another form.

Statement II: The result of the conversion process is called dummy variable.

In light of the above statements, choose the correct answer from the options given below:

(a) Both Statement I and Statement II are false
(b) Both Statement I and Statement II are true
(c) Statement I is false but Statement II is true
(d) Statement I is true but Statement II is false

141. Which of the following is an example of qualitative research? **[Dec 2021]**

(a) Experimental research
(b) Ex post facto research
(c) Descriptive survey research
(d) Grounded theory research

142. Identify from the list below the threats to internal validity of research. **[Dec 2021]**

(A) Interaction of selection and independent variable (X)
(B) Statistical regression
(C) Interaction of pretesting and X
(D) Differential selection of subjects
(E) Experimental mortality

Choose the correct answer from the options given below:

(a) (B), (D), and (E) only
(b) (A), (B), and (C) only
(c) (B), (C), and (D) only
(d) (C), (D), and (E) only

143. Match List I with List II **[Dec 2021]**

List I (Research Steps)	List II (Characteristics)
(A) Research problem definition	(i) Appropriateness of techniques and their application
(B) Formulation of research hypothesis	(ii) Development of a conceptual framework which is in accord with hypothesis of research
(C) Design of research	(iii) Defining the variables to be related in unambiguous terms
(D) Data Analysis	(iv) Academic and social value of the research question to be weighed

Choose the correct answer from the options given below:

Code:

	(A)	(B)	(C)	(D)
(a)	(iii)	(iv)	(i)	(ii)
(b)	(iv)	(iii)	(ii)	(i)
(c)	(i)	(ii)	(iii)	(iv)
(d)	(ii)	(i)	(iv)	(iii)

144. Given below are two statements: **[Dec 2021]**

Statement I: Scientific research is systematic, controlled, empirical, and critical investigation of hypothetical propositions.

Statement II: Population of research need not be defined in qualitative and quantitative researches.

In the light of the above statements, choose the correct answer from the options given below:

(a) Both Statement I and Statement II are true
(b) Both Statement I and Statement II are false
(c) Statement I is true but Statement II is false
(d) Statement I is false but Statement II is true

145. Given below are two statements : One is labelled as Assertion (A) and the other is labelled as Reason (R): **[Dec 2021]**

Assertion (A) : Actual settings are the direct source of data and the researcher is the key instrument in qualitative research.

Reasons (R) : The purpose underlying qualitative researches is relatively more directed at depiction of reality rather than arriving at context-free generalizations.

In the light of the above statements, choose the most appropriate answer from the options given below :

(a) Both (A) and (R) are true and (R) is the correct explanation of (A)
(b) Both (A) and (R) are true but (R) is NOT the correct explanation of (A)
(c) (A) is true but (R) is false
(d) (A) is false but (R) is true

146. Given below are two statements: **[Dec 2021]**

Statement I: Reliability refers to whether a test measures what it says it measures.

Statement II: Validity refers to whether a test consistently yields the same or similar scores.

In light of the above statements, choose the *most appropriate* answer from the options given below:

(a) Both Statement I and II Statement are correct
(b) Both Statement I and Statement II are incorrect
(c) Statement I is correct but Statement II is incorrect
(d) Statement I is incorrect but Statement II is correct

147. The kind of sample that is simply available to the researcher by virtue of its accessibility is known as: **[Dec 2021]**

(a) Quota sampling
(b) Snowball sampling
(c) Convenience sampling
(d) Web sampling

148. Which among the following is the names for validity whereby researcher uses a future criterion measure, rather than a contemporary one? **[Dec 2021]**

(a) Convergent validity
(b) Predictive validity
(c) Construct validity
(d) Concurrent validity

149. Given below are two statements: **[Dec 2021]**

Statement I: If we are interested in the worldview of members of a certain social group, a qualitative research strategy that is sensitive to how participants interpret their social world may be preferable.

Statement II: If a researcher is interested in a topic on which little or no research has been done in the past, quantitative research may be easy to employ because there is little prior literature from which to draw leads.

In light of the above statements, choose the most *appropriate* answer from the options given below:

(a) Both Statement I and Statement II are correct
(b) Both Statement II and Statement I are incorrect
(c) Statement I is correct but Statement II is incorrect
(d) Statement I is incorrect but Statement II is correct

150. Match List I with List II. **[Dec 2021]**

List I (Research Design)	List II (Type of study)
(A) Sampling design	(i) Pre-planned design for analysis
(B) Statistical design	(ii) Structured or well thought out instruments for collection of data
(C) Observational design	(iii) Advanced decisions about operational procedures
(D) Operational design	(iv) Probability sampling design

Choose the correct answer from the options given below:

Code:

	(A)	(B)	(C)	(D)
(a)	(iv)	(i)	(ii)	(iii)
(b)	(i)	(iii)	(iv)	(ii)
(c)	(iii)	(ii)	(i)	(iv)
(d)	(ii)	(iv)	(iii)	(i)

151. Given below are two statements: **[Dec 2021]**

Statement I: In the before-and-after without control' design, a single test group or area is selected and the dependent variable is measured before the introduction of the treatment.

Statement II: In the 'before-and-after with control' design, two areas are selected but the dependent variable is not measured in both the areas for an identical time-period before the treatment.

In light of the above statements, choose the most *appropriate* answer from the options given below

(a) Both Statement I and Statement II are correct
(b) Both Statement I and Statement II are incorrect
(c) Statement I is correct but Statement II is incorrect
(d) Statement I is incorrect but Statement II is correct

152. Which of the following are advantages of observation as a tool of data collection? **[2021]**

A. Observation takes place only in natural settings
B. Observation methods demand the active participation of subjects in the programme
C. Observations are known for directness
D. Artificiality can be minimised in observational studies
E. Recording devices can be used in observational studies for accuracy

Choose the correct answer from the options given below:

(a) A, B and C only
(b) A, B and E only
(c) B, C and D only
(d) C, D and E only

153. When a variable leads to a spurious interpretation of research results, it is called **[2022]**

(a) Control variable
(b) External variable
(c) Conflicting variable
(d) Confounding variable

154. The 'Age' of a respondent is an example of **[2022]**

(a) Parallel variable
(b) Monadic variable
(c) Dyadic variable
(d) Simple variable

155. Which of the following are disadvantages of qualitative research? **[2022]**

A. Too sensitive to the context
B. Open to debate
C. Too subjective
D. Difficult to generalize
E. Issue of replication

Choose the correct answer from the options given below:

(a) A, D and E only
(b) B, C and D only
(c) C, D and E only
(d) A, B and C only

156. Which of the following factors influence the sample size for a project? **[2022]**

A. Type of project
B. Purpose of project
C. Previous research in the area
D. Researcher's personality
E. His/her standing as a researcher

Choose the correct answer from the options given below:

(a) A, B and C only
(b) B, C and D only

(c) C, D and E only
(d) A, C and E only

157. Match List I with List II. **[2022]**

List I Research method	List II Characteristic
A. Content analysis	I. Summarization
B. Social network analysis	II. Use of bipolar adjectives
C. Semantic differential	III. Focus on dyadic relations
D. Meta analysis	IV. Context unit

Choose the correct answer from the options given below:
(a) A – II, B – III, C – IV, D – I
(b) A – IV, B – III, C – II, D – I
(c) A – I, B – II, C – III, D – IV
(d) A – III, B – IV, C – I, D - II

158. Which of the following have been considered as threat to internal validity in research? **[2022]**
A. Randomisation B. Generalisability
C. Maturation D. History
E. Instrumentation

Choose the correct answer from the options given below:
(a) A, B and C only (b) B, C and D only
(c) C, D and E only (d) A, B and E only

159. The term 'Hermeneutics' is drawn from **[2022]**
(a) Sociology (b) Theology
(c) Anthropology (d) Economics

160. Which of the following is NOT characteristic of a good question paper? **[2022]**
(a) Objectivity (b) Subjectivity
(c) Reliability (d) Validation

161. Given below are two statements **[2022]**

Statement I: The qualitative data are powerful because they are collected from very sensitive social, historical and temporal context

Statement II: Context sensitivity cannot be completely removed from the qualitative data.

In light of the above statements, choose the correct answer from the options given below
(a) Both Statement I and Statement II are true
(b) Both Statement I and Statement II are false
(c) Statement I is true but Statement II is false
(d) Statement I is false but Statement II is true

162. Historical research has the limitation of **[2022]**
(a) Problem identification
(b) Analytical synthesis
(c) Universal generalisation
(d) Probable conclusions

163. Match List I with List II **[2022]**

List I Research Perspective	List II Discipline
A. Phenomenology	I. Anthropology
B. Ethnography	II. Sociology
C. Ethnomethodology	III. Social psychology
D. Symbolic interactionism	IV. Philosophy

Choose the correct answer from the options given below:
(a) A – I, B – II, C – III, D – IV
(b) A – II, B – III, C – IV, D – I
(c) A – III, B – IV, C – I, D – II
(d) A – IV, B – I, C – II, D – III

164. When a researcher has no control over the variables; he/she can only report what has happened or what is happening. Such research is called **[June 2023]**
(a) Clinical Research
(b) Diagnostic Research
(c) Ex post facto research
(d) De facto research

165. Which of the following relates mainly to the issue of causality? **[June 2023]**
(a) Measurement validity
(b) Construct validity
(c) Internal validity
(d) External validity

166. A sampling technique in which units are randomly sampled from a population that has been divided into categories, is called: **[June 2023]**
(a) Simple Random Sampling
(b) Stratified Random Sampling

(c) Cluster Random Sampling
(d) Systematic Random Sampling

167. Given below are two statements: **[June 2023]**

Statement-I: Debriefing involves revealing the purposes of the research to the participants.

Statement-II: Debriefing of participants takes place at the beginning of a study.

In the light of the above statements, choose the most appropriate answer from the options given below:

(a) Both Statement I and Statement II are correct.
(b) Both Statement I and Statement II are incorrect.
(c) Statement I is correct but Statement II is incorrect.
(d) Statement I is incorrect but Statement II is correct.

168. In which of the following scales of measurements ranking of observations is not possible? **[June 2023]**

(a) Nominal (b) Ordinal
(c) Interval (d) Ratio

169. Survey research is one of the key methods in **[June 2023]**

(a) Physics
(b) History
(c) Sociology
(d) Hermeneutics

170. Methods of social research are directly linked to different visions of **[June 2023]**

(a) Social reality
(b) Laboratory experiments
(c) Simulations
(d) Virtual reality

171. Grand theories of social sciences operate at a **[June 2023]**

(a) ower level
(b) Simplistic level
(c) Categorical level
(d) Higher level of abstraction

172. Which of the following are considered major types of qualitative research questions? **[June 2023]**

A. Non-purposive
B. Causes and consequences
C. Predictive
D. Evaluative
E. Descriptive

(a) A, B and C only
(b) A, C and D only
(c) A, D and E only
(d) B, C, D and E only

173. Given below are two statements: **[June 2023]**

Statement I: Time and cost are not relevant in determining the sample size.

Statement II: Unit non-response do not matter in deciding the sampling error.

In the light of the above statements, choose the correct answer from the options given below :

(a) Both Statement I and Statement II are true.
(b) Both Statement I and Statement II are false.
(c) Statement I is true but Statement II is false.
(d) Statement I is false but Statement II is true.

174. Given below are two statements: **[Dec 2023]**

Statement (I): Qualitative research lays emphasis on contextual understanding.

Statement (II): Quantitative research is typically highly unstructured.

In light of the above statements, choose the most appropriate answer from the options given below.

(a) Both Statement (I) and Statement (II) are correct.
(b) Both Statement (I) and Statement (II) are incorrect.
(c) Statement (I) is correct but Statement (II) is incorrect.
(d) Statement (I) is incorrect but Statement (II) is correct.

175. In academic writing, the abbreviation 'fn.' is used to represent **[Dec 2023]**

(a) forenoon
(b) footnote
(c) Forward page number
(d) Following page number

176. Quantitative research can be construed as a research strategy that usually **[Dec 2023]**
   (a) Entails a deductive approach to the relationship between theory and research
   (b) Emphasizes an inductive approach to the relationship between theory and research.
   (c) Rejects the practices and norms of natural scientific model, and of positivism in particular.
   (d) Embodies a view of social reality as a constantly shifting emergent property of individual's creation

177. A variable that has a causal impact on another variable, is called **[Dec 2023]**
   (a) Dependent variable
   (b) Independent variable
   (c) Confounding variable
   (d) Extraneous variable

ANSWER KEY

1. (c) **2.** (d) **3.** (c) **4.** (d) **5.** (b) **6.** (b) **7.** (c) **8.** (d) **9.** (d) **10.** (d)
11. (c) **12.** (d) **13.** (a) **14.** (a) **15.** (b) **16.** (a) **17.** (d) **18.** (d) **19.** (b) **20.** (b)
21. (d) **22.** (c) **23.** (a) **24.** (c) **25.** (c) **26.** (c) **27.** (b) **28.** (d) **29.** (b) **30.** (c)
31. (b) **32.** (c) **33.** (b) **34.** (c) **35.** (a) **36.** (d) **37.** (c) **38.** (c) **39.** (d) **40.** (d)
41. (a) **42.** (d) **43.** (b) **44.** (d) **45.** (b) **46.** (c) **47.** (b) **48.** (b) **49.** (b) **50.** (a)
51. (d) **52.** (c) **53.** (c) **54.** (b) **55.** (a) **56.** (a) **57.** (b) **58.** (b) **59.** (c) **60.** (a)
61. (a) **62.** (d) **63.** (b) **64.** (b) **65.** (d) **66.** (d) **67.** (b) **68.** (b) **69.** (c) **70.** (d)
71. (b) **72.** (c) **73.** (c) **74.** (a) **75.** (c) **76.** (b) **77.** (d) **78.** (d) **79.** (a) **80.** (b)
81. (a) **82.** (c) **83.** (a) **84.** (c) **85.** (b) **86.** (d) **87.** (b) **88.** (d) **89.** (d) **90.** (a)
91. (d) **92.** (a) **93.** (d) **94.** (b) **95.** (d) **96.** (c) **97.** (a) **98.** (c) **99.** (b) **100.** (c)
101. (c) **102.** (d) **103.** (b) **104.** (a) **105.** (c) **106.** (d) **107.** (a) **108.** (d) **109.** (b) **110.** (c)
111. (a) **112.** (a) **113.** (b) **114.** (c) **115.** (c) **116.** (d) **117.** (d) **118.** (b) **119.** (b) **120.** (c)
121. (c) **122.** (a) **123.** (d) **124.** (c) **125.** (d) **126.** (a) **127.** (b) **128.** (b) **129.** (d) **130.** (a)
131. (a) **132.** (b) **133.** (c) **134.** (d) **135.** (d) **136.** (b) **137.** (c) **138.** (b) **139.** (a) **140.** (b)
141. (d) **142.** (a) **143.** (b) **144.** (c) **145.** (a) **146.** (b) **147.** (c) **148.** (b) **149.** (c) **150.** (a)
151. (c) **152.** (d) **153.** (d) **154.** (b) **155.** (c) **156.** (a) **157.** (b) **158.** (c) **159.** (b) **160.** (b)
161. (a) **162.** (c) **163.** (d) **164.** (c) **165.** (c) **166.** (b) **167.** (c) **168.** (a) **169.** (c) **170.** (a)
171. (d) **172.** (d) **173.** (d) **174.** (c) **175.** (b) **176.** (a) **177.** (b)

HINTS AND SOLUTIONS

1. **(c):** A paradigm shift, a concept identified by the American physicist and philosopher Thomas Kuhn, is a fundamental change in the basic concepts and experimental practices of a scientific discipline.

   Paradigm shifts can occur at any of level of domain, discipline and field, and this may cut across these levels. For example, we may say that a paradigm shift in economy has taken place after economic reforms in 1991.

2. **(d):** Thesis is basically topic plus claim to prove the topic. A thesis statement is the main idea of an essay. The thesis usually appears at the end of the introduction, often as the last sentence. This builds up the expectations of the reader. The thesis places the argument to prove the claim. We may study null hypothesis also in this context.

   The figures and tables are required in the thesis to make the manuscript more readable as they highlight trends or patterns in the data. They remove the numeric data from the text. Thus, figures and tables are primarily included in the text itself so as to make the discussion more relevant.

   Tables may be used to synthesize existing literature, explain variables, or present the wording of survey questions.

   The figures must be included in the centre of the page, preferably immediately below the paragraph where the data was mentioned. All figures must be identified with a number and followed by a brief but intelligible statement that describes the data provided.

   (a). The appendix is a section that is placed at the end of the thesis and may contain material such as tables, figures, maps, photographs, raw data, computer programs, musical examples, interview questions, sample questionnaires, CDs, and many other types of material.

   Appendix is something attached. As the appendix is attached to the intestines, the appendix is attached to the end of a book.

   (b). A separate chapter for figures and tables is not a very relevant idea.

   (c). The concluding chapter summarizes the book's main arguments.

   Thus, (d) is the right answer that has been explained earlier.

3. **(c):** The thesis statement is the main assertion of the thesis. Our thesis should tell your reader the main point or idea of our thesis. A good thesis will be clearly identifiable within the paper and will be narrow, purposeful, and specific. A thesis statement must always be a complete sentence.

4. **(d):**There are basically two paradigms in research – positivism and post positivism.

   Positivism: This approach is based on the technique used to study basic or natural sciences. This follows the scientific methodological principles of empirical observation, deductive reasoning, and formulation of laws or universal generalizations. Positivism took sociology more in the form of science, that gives a more objective (away from caste, creed, colour etc.) and professional look to sociology. So that we can reconstruct our society, and create a better world.

   Post Positivism: The post positivism shifted its focus towards human aspects. If it was on 'reality' in positivism earlier, it was on 'critical reality' that was focused more on human aspect that indicates interpretation. It is mostly qualitative. As post positivism is not exactly given as answer choice, we can pick interpretative paradigm as the answer. That has been explained in greater details in Pearson title for UGC NET Paper 1.

5. **(b):** Sampling is basically of two types–probability and non-probability.

   1. Probability Sampling: This is based on the fact that every member of a population has a known and equal chance of being selected. This is also known as the random sampling. For example, if we have a population of 50 people, each member stands equal chance of 1/50 of being selected. These can be taken as types of probability sampling - simple random sampling, systematic sampling, stratified sampling, and cluster sampling. Cluster sampling works better if population is homogeneous.

   2. Non-probability Sampling: This subjective approach selects units from a population by using a subjective method. That method is basically non-random. This is also known as convenience sampling. This does not require a complete survey frame, it is a fast, easy and cost effective way of getting data. This method may be biased also, as a researcher may rather pick people from own neighbourhood, than following a sampling framework where each member has equal chance of being selected.

6. **(b):** Action research is for solution of our professional problems and their application is immediate. Action research can only be applied in organized, planned programme where every part related to programme are well prepared.

7. **(c):** The question is about 'when planning'. Social research means to observe behaviour-how do we see the world. So, it is important to look at the 'theory'. All approaches are important, but stages differ.

(a) Having an 'open mind' is mandatory while analysing our data, but that data will not be available at planning stage.

(b) A pilot study is highly recommended as the research should be basically qualitative, we can do this once we establish a research plan, not before.

(c) First of all, we need to be familiar with literature on the topic that will help us to figure out our research questions and consequently, the kind of data we need.

(d) The social research should be subjective to begin with, and it should be qualitative as well.

8. **(d):** A research student is expected to describe in desired detail, all the phases of the research in a dissertation. This is basically meant for guides and examiners. This includes the purpose and significance of research, the rationale behind it, the review of the literature, a detailed information of the research tools and the procedures, an interpretation of the results in the form of conclusions, implications and recommendations.

9. **(d):** Research design can be defined as a basic framework, or the set of methods and procedures that is used to collect and analyse data on variables specified in a particular research problem. This is mostly linked with data and its collection. This takes into account the nature of question, the goal of research, and the availability of resources. It is important to understand the different types of study designs and their strengths and limitations as they are going to impact the final outcome of the research.

10. **(d):** The process of selecting a small number of important cases that are likely to 'yield the most information and have the greatest impact on the development of knowledge'. A 'case' is the general, collective word used for the unit of analysis. We know that social research is mostly conducted on people, though it may not be done in an exclusive manner.

Newspapers, television programmes, etc., supply us with useful research data for the purpose.

Sampling frames is mostly for probability sampling, it means that each member of the population has an equal chance of being selected for the sample.

11. **(c):**

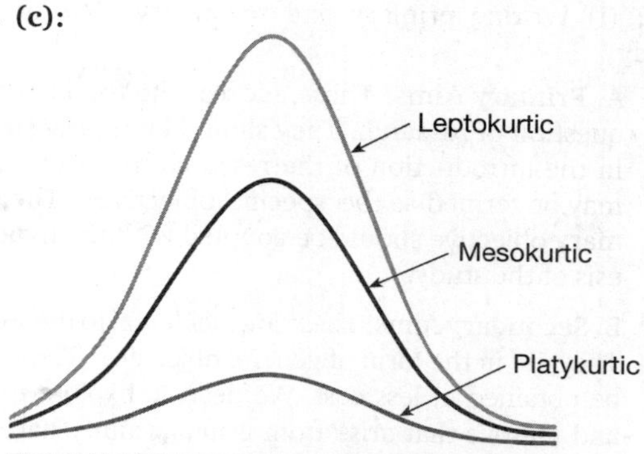

12. **(d):** Research is a careful and detailed study into a specific problem, concern, or issue using the scientific method. This is best accomplished by turning the issue into a question, with the intent of the research to answer the question.

13. **(a):** (i) Reduction of punctuation and grammatical errors to a minimum – so as to comprehend the whole idea in a lucid manner.

(ii) Careful checking of references – this allows us to acknowledge the contribution of other writers and researchers in our work. We need to avoid the possibility of being termed as plagiarized.

(iii) Consistency in the way the thesis is written – Consistency in research means the logical alignment of the title, purpose, problem, and research question. We need to be reliable in research, and consistency helps in that.

(iv) A clear and well-written abstract - Abstracts are basically being summarised in our research, we need to be self-contained, concise, brief and clear to the desired extent. The language should be kept simple.

14. **(a):** Fundamental research aim to improve scientific theories for improved understanding or prediction of fundamental things. Piaget (1936) was the first psychologist to make a systematic study of cognitive development. His contributions include a stage theory of child cognitive development, detailed observational studies of cognition in children, and a series of simple but ingenious tests to reveal different cognitive abilities is a kind of fundamental research.

15. **(b):** Here, null means no difference. Thus, null hypothesis means no difference between the two sets of students here, such as one as a male and other as a female. Then, we collect data to test the null hypothesis.

16. **(a):** Historical research is a qualitative technique. Historical research studies the meaning of past events in an attempt to interpret the facts and explain the cause of events, and their effect in the present events.

17. (d): (i) Writing primary and secondary aims of the study

A. **Primary Aims**: These address the fundamental question of research. They should be clearly stated in the introduction of the research protocol. They may be termed as the 'specific' objectives. The primary objective should be coupled with the hypothesis of the study.

B. **Secondary Aims**: These are incidental to the study. They are in the form of general objectives. These can be obtained at less cost. We need to explore issues and reasons that arise from primary aim. That may be done with help from secondary aims. They may be multiple in nature (more than one).

(ii) **Review of the Current Literature:** This helps in taking a more pragmatic viewpoint of research. The literature review helps to identify gaps in research, that identifies conflicts in previous studies, and we try to open questions left from previous research.

(iii) **Prepare a Draft of Questionnaire**: A research questionnaire is typically a mix of close-ended questions and open-ended questions to gather information from respondents. In case of qualitative studies, we can try to prepare a draft of questionnaire for this. This may be refined with the use of exploratory or pilot studies.

(iv) **Revision of the Draft**: This again is important in case of exploratory or pilot study, where it is difficult to set null hypothesis.

18. (d): The production of knowledge is not the sole objective of any kind of research. That may happen in case of a type of research that is called as the fundamental research. We need to focus on the word 'sole purpose' in this statement.

19. (b): Null Hypothesis (H_0) and Alternative Hypothesis (H_1). The null hypothesis is the statement which asserts that there is no difference between the sample statistic and population parameter and is the one which is tested, while the alternative hypothesis is the statement which stands true if the null hypothesis is rejected.

We assume that coaching helps students. But in null hypothesis, we assume that coaching does not help. Here null means no. Alternative hypothesis states that coaching helps. If null is accepted then alternative is rejected or vice versa.

When we collect data and find that marks of students who take coaching are same as are of average or not different from past. It means that null hypothesis is accepted and coaching actually does not help. If actual marks of students are very different, then we assume that null hypothesis is rejected, and coaching makes a difference—positive or may be negative.

For testing of hypothesis, level of significance, *z*-test, *t*-test, etc., also come into picture.

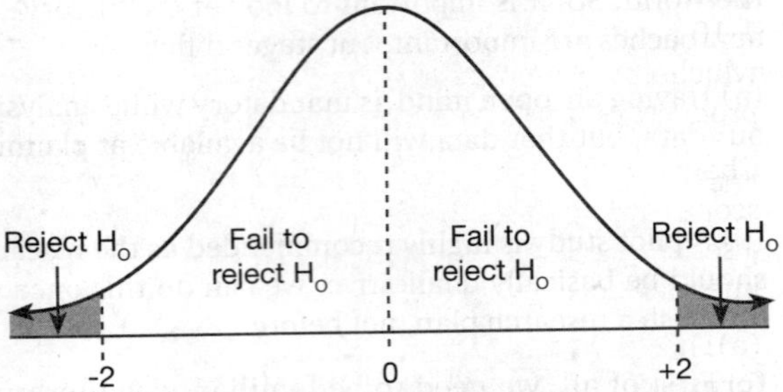

20. (b): APA (American Psychological Association) is an 'author date' system, for all formats (book, journal, article, web documents) consists of the author(s) surname and year of publication.

The basics of an in-text reference in APA:

(1) Include author or authors and year of publication.

(2) Use round brackets.

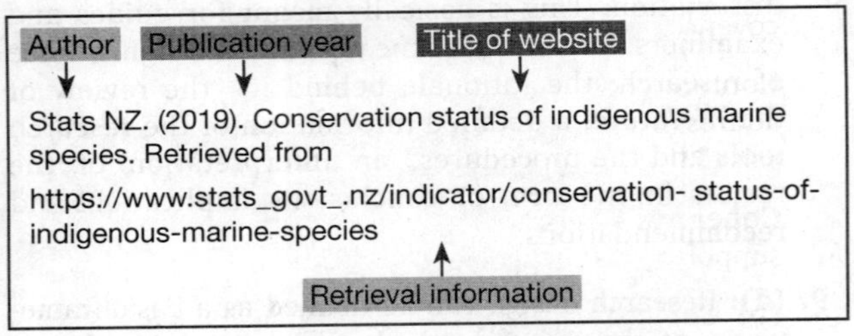

21. (d): A seminar is a form of academic instruction, either at an academic institution or offered by a commercial or professional organization. It has the function of bringing together small groups for recurring meetings, focussing each time on some particular subject, in which everyone present is requested to participate. This is often accomplished through an ongoing Socratic dialogue with a seminar leader or instructor, or through a more formal presentation of research. It is essentially a place where assigned readings are discussed, questions can be raised and debates can be conducted.

22. (c): Electoral politics itself is a complex game. Exceptions can always be there. Urban areas are a complex phenomenon, people don't open up so easily, as there are chances of easy identity. But urban people are literate. So, questionnaire tool should be preferred for the study, they can be close ended or open ended or a mix of both. A questionnaire is a research instrument that consists of a set of questions or other types of prompts that aims to collect information from a respondent.

The rating scale is a good tool, but it can be used if any political party has done some work, this may not be used for new parties. A rating scale is a set of categories designed to elicit information about a quantitative or a qualitative attribute. There are Likert response scale and 1-10 rating scales in which a person selects the number which is considered to reflect the perceived quality of a product (or say party here).

Channels do conduct the interviews, but there is always scope for biased approach. A schedule is a structure of a set of questions on a given topic that are asked by the interviewer or investigator personally.

23. (a): In ethical norms, we 'tend' to be pure in case of thesis format, that is the essence of the research. No researcher would like that fingers are raised if there is an attempt to manipulate the thesis format.

(a) Thesis Format: This is linked most directly with the research. A thesis statement summarizes the central points of our paper or essay. This tells about the argument being in the research. The following points about the essence of the research:

Concise: A good thesis statement is short and lucid. We cover our points clearly and directly.

Contentious: A good thesis statement basically addresses a claim that requires further evidence or analysis to back it up.

Coherent: The whole idea of thesis statement must be supported and explained clearly in the rest of our paper.

(b) Copyright: This is somewhat linked with plagiarism. According to WIPO–copyright is a legal term used to describe the rights that creators have over their literary and artistic works.

(c) Patenting Policy: They are meant to secure invention relating either to a product or process that is new which is capable of having industrial application.

(d) Data Sharing Policies: There are government policies for both human readable and machine readable forms.

24. (c): A thesis or dissertation is a document submitted in support of candidature for an academic degree. In the India, we write a dissertation at the end of a bachelor's or master's degree, and we write a thesis to complete a PhD. In the US, it's the other way around: you may write a thesis at the end of a bachelor's or master's degree, and you write a dissertation to complete a PhD.

25. (c): The terms standardized research tools, probability random sampling, systematic evidences apply to quantitative researches. In qualitative research, we need to work at ground level, it looks at bottom-up empirical evidences.

26. (c): Research that involves human subjects or participants raises unique and complex ethical, legal, social, and political issues. Research ethics specifically deals with the analysis of ethical issues that are raised when people are involved as participants in research.

There are three objectives in research ethics. The first and broadest objective is to protect human participants. The second objective is to ensure that research is conducted in a way that serves interests of individuals, groups, and/or society as a whole. Finally, the third objective is to examine specific research activities and projects for their ethical soundness, looking at issues such as the management of risk, protection of confidentiality, and the process of informed consent.

27. (b):

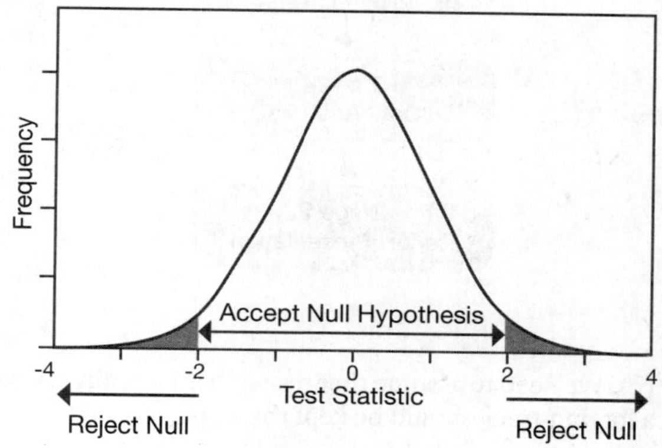

Null hypothesis, as per its nature will say 'no impact' or 'no relationship' between two variables - Child Rearing Practices (CRP) and Stress Proneness (SP). And CRP does not influence SP. That situation will arise if null hypothesis, and sample data (evidence) convey the same idea. Then the region will be Acceptance Region.

But what should happen in case of evidence falling in Rejection region.

Thus, if the null hypothesis is rejected at whatever level (0.01, 0.05, 0.10), it indicates that there is relation between CRP and SP. It means that Child Rearing Practices do influence Stress Proneness.

With some understanding of diagram, we can say that one thing rejected and one thing will be accepted. Thus, (b) is the right answer.

28. (d): *Ex post facto* design is a quasi-experimental study examining how an independent variable, present prior to the study in the participants, affects a dependent variable. In the question we need to identify – dependent and independent variables. Here, 'possible factors' are independent variables and 'meal interventions' is dependent variable.

29. **(b):** The following diagram gives us some basic idea. Even formulation of hypothesis is done once we are clear about concepts for the research purpose.

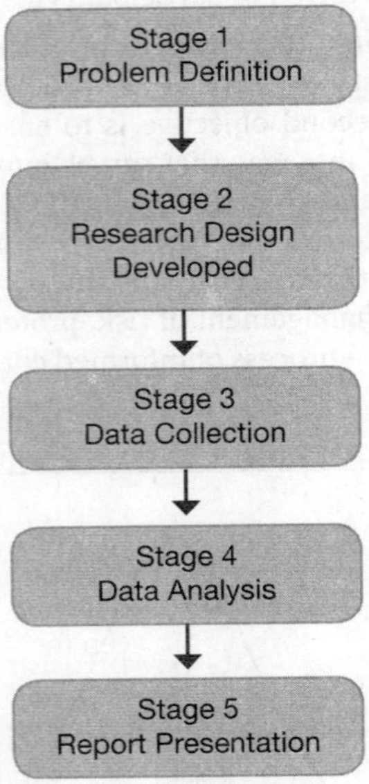

30. **(c):** Action research is an enquiry conducted by the self into the self. It is a self reflection process. It helps in professional development—both formally and informally.

Action research is specifically applicable in education sector. Action research and professional development help to create better classrooms and teachers, which should be of great importance to both learners and the educators themselves.

According to Rabat, 'The emergence of action research has been considered a key element to the development and improvement of learning and teaching in the classroom'.

31. **(b):** A commonly known cycle is that of the influential model of Kemmis and McTaggart (1988) mentioned earlier plan, act, observe, reflect; then, in the light of this, plan for the next cycle. It is also generally held that action research is participative, though writers differ on how participative it is.

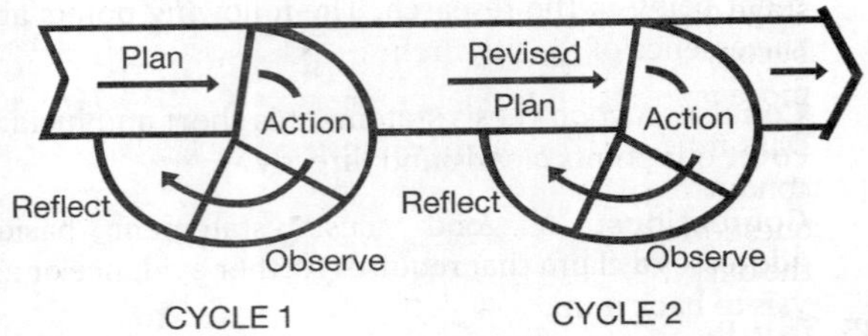

32. **(c):** We need to assume that research is basically scientific quantitative or qualitative or mix of both. The methods may vary a lot, but track should be kept the same.

Rearch Process–A snapshot

Step 1: Formulation of Research Problem	**Step 2: Preparing Research Design**	**Step 3: Developing Data Collection Instrument (Research Instrument)**	**Step 4: Selecting Samples Types of samples**
• Literature review • Formulation of objectives • Identifying research variables and measuring scales • Formulating hypothesis	• Problem structure • Study design • Experimental study • Non-experimental study	• Types of data • Methods of data collection • Designing research tool	• Probability • Non-probability • Determining sample design
Step 5: Writing a Research Proposal	**Step 6: Collecting Data**	**Step 7: Processing and Analyzing Data**	**Step 8: Writing a Research Report**
Main elements – Need – Benefits – Types of data – Justification for funds and other resources	• Observations • Interviews • Questionnaire • Schedules	• Editing and Coding • Classification of data • Tabulation • Analysis • Hypothesis testing • Generalizations	• Title page • Table of contents • Chapters • Appendices

33. (b): The following diagram gives better idea as per NTA exam syllabus where experiment is part of it.

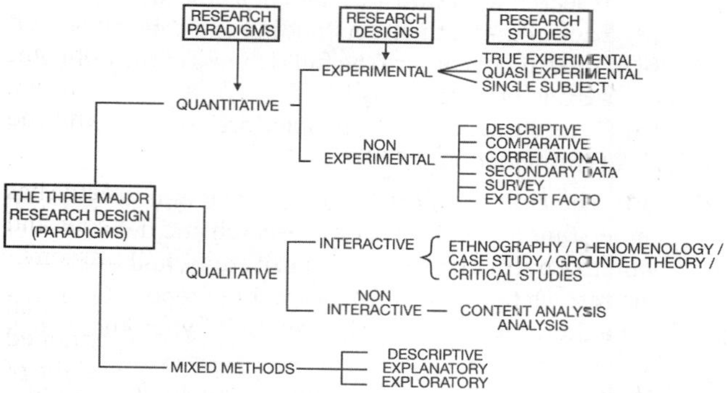

34. (c): Though research ethics issues may erupt at any stage. Formulation right kind of questions is at the initial stage of research. For the sake of data collection, when it becomes a question of easiness and cost, we may become more unethical. This will impact interpretation.

Data interpretation and presentation is a crucial stage in conducting research, what were your original research questions, how you collected the data, what eventually was the data that went into this particular study, and so on.

35. (a): Research thesis takes lots of efforts and lead to a degree also, they require research format.

36. (d): There are two types of variables:

(i) **Discrete:** Definite values such as 1, 2... 4, 5 and so on. For example, number of chairs can only be 1, 2, 3 ..... and not value 1.2357, etc.

(ii) **Continuous Variables:** Take possible value with in a range. For example, weight, the weight of a boy can be anything such as 5.23125.....kg.

37. (c): Action research is usually conducted by the professionals such as teachers, administrators, policy makers themselves. They face some issues in their related area and take help of the action research to find the solution. The researcher is usually from concerned area. This research consists of following four steps which may be cyclical in nature if the desired results are not obtained.

1. Plan–for the sake of improvement
2. Act–for implementation of plan
3. Observe–to monitor and evaluate the action effects
4. Reflect–the outcome of action.

38. (c): Ex-post-facto method would be appropriate to evaluate the effect of the method of feeding on anxiety - proneness of children.

Case Study: Case study is basically a qualitative study. In the question statement, we speak about anxiety – proneness of children. Case study approach applies in single case study, in case of children, we need to go for multiple case studies.

Experimental Method: This involves the manipulation of variables to establish cause and effect relationship/s. We use the features of controlled methods and the random allocation of participants into controlled and experimental groups. Scientifically tested hypothesis should preferably be used in this method.

Ex Post Facto Research: This is also called as after-the-fact research. Here, the investigation starts after the fact has occurred without interference from the researcher. The majority of social research, in contexts in which it is not possible or acceptable to manipulate the characteristics of human participants, is based on ex post facto research designs. This research shares many features of true experimental research, we try to get the cause effect relationship, but without any kind of manipulation.

Survey Method: This approach is the collection of information from a sample of individuals through their responses to questions. So, the whole exercise becomes difficult from the beginning, even for sample selection.

39. (d): Appendices are always supplementary to the research paper. As such, your study must be able to stand alone without the appendices and the paper must contain all information including tables, diagrams, and results necessary to understand the research problem. The key point to remember when including an appendix is that the information is non-essential; if it were removed, the reader would still be able to comprehend the significance, validity, and implications of your research.

40. (d): Research findings, specifically, in social sciences are prone to subjective interpretation.

41. (a): Basic research, also called pure research or fundamental research, has the scientific research aim to improve scientific theories for improved understanding or prediction of natural or other phenomena. Applied research, in turn, uses scientific theories to develop technology or techniques to intervene and alter natural or other phenomena. Though often driven by curiosity, basic research fuels applied science's innovations. The two aims are often coordinated in research and development. Action research is a form of investigation designed for use by teachers to attempt to solve problems and improve professional practices in their own. Action research involves a systematic process of examining the evidence. The results of this type of research are practical, relevant, and can inform theory. Action research is different than other forms of research as there is less concern for universality of findings, and more value is placed on the relevance of the findings to the researcher and the local collaborators.

Evaluative research is a type of research used to evaluate a product or concept, and collect data to help improve your solution

42. (d):
Action research process may move in the cycles.
It is like a heuristic method as the next action is based on the previous result.

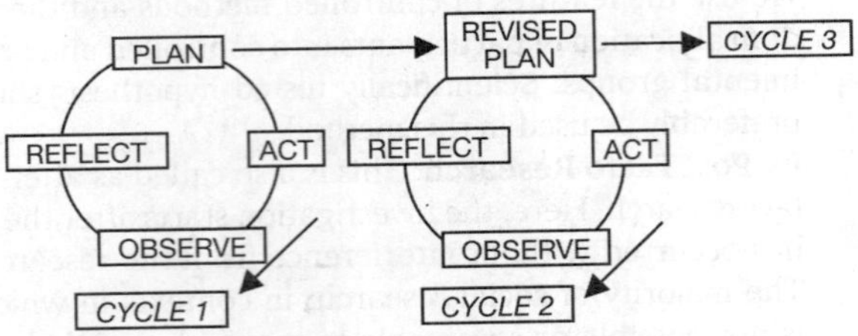

Kolb (1984) extended this model to offer a conception of the action research cycle as a learning process, whereby, people learn and create knowledge by critically reflecting upon their own actions and experiences, forming abstract concepts, and testing the implications of these concepts in new situations. Practitioners can create their own knowledge and understanding of a situation and act upon it, thereby, improving practice and advancing knowledge in the field.

43. (b): Research is always scientific, whether it is of social science or pure science or any other field. We can solve them only in a systematic manner.

The scientific method has the following basic steps:
(1) Make an observation.
(2) Ask a question.
(3) Form a hypothesis, or testable explanation.
(4) Make a prediction based on the hypothesis.
(5) Test the prediction.
(6) Iterate (if required): use the results to make new hypotheses or predictions.

44. (d): Evidence-based approach to ethics. What is remarkable is that there should be a debate in academia about whether or not to take a scholarly, evidence-based approach to ethics. While there is much reason to be skeptical of relying solely on well-controlled research studies that does not mean that we should abandon such studies. A case in point is our attempts to provide education in research ethics. There is mention of 'avoiding bias' and other points under ethical issues relating to the researcher that emphasize 'objectivity' or 'evidence-based research reporting'.

45. (b): Positivism is a philosophical theory stating that certain (positive) knowledge is based on natural phenomena and their properties and relations. Thus, information derived from sensory experience, interpreted through reason and logic, forms the exclusive source of all certain knowledge.

From a researcher's perspective, the following points must be noted down.

(1) Gives validity and objectivity to a research.
(2) It is based on precise methods and can support a research with statistical and objective data.
(3) Lack of in-depth understanding of a context.
(4) 'You cannot capture the full richness of the individuals and environments.'
(5) Deterministic view, people are social products (Wotherspoon, 1998).

46. (c): The purpose of a literature review is to gain an understanding of the existing research and debates relevant to a particular topic or area of study, and to present that knowledge in the form of a written report. Conducting a literature review helps you build your knowledge in your field.
An introduction should announce our topic, it should provide context and a rationale for our work, before stating our research questions and hypothesis. Well-written introductions set the tone for the paper, catch the reader's interest, and communicate the hypothesis or thesis statement.

47. (b): Spearman's Rho is basically for ranks, it is a non-parametric test used to measure the strength of association between two variables, where the value $r = +1$ means a perfect positive correlation and the value $r = -1$ means a perfect negative correlation.

48. (b): Scientists make changes in experiments to see if those changes will cause an effect in something they observe. The thing that is changed on purpose is called the manipulated variable. Sometimes it is also called the independent variable.

49. (b): A poster session advertises your research. It combines text and graphics to make a visually pleasing presentation. Typically, a professional poster involves showing your work to numerous researchers at a conference or seminar. This can take place in one large room, several smaller rooms, or even on a balcony.

Basically, interpersonal interaction is a communication process that involves the exchange of information, feelings and meaning by means of verbal and non-verbal messages, between two or more persons.

A focus group is a gathering of deliberately selected people who participate in a planned discussion intended to elicit consumer perceptions about a particular topic or area of interest in an environment that is non-threatening and receptive. Focus groups are collective on a purpose.

A formal speech is a speech presented without visual aids. The purpose of the formal speech is to inform, to persuade, to entertain, to stimulate action or further interest in a topic of community concern.

Display of common interest is the purpose of every such activity.

50. (a): Scientific method involves making conjectures (hypotheses), deriving predictions from them as logical consequences, and then carrying out experiments or empirical observations based on those predictions Scientists then test hypotheses by conducting experiments or studies.

Empiricism is a theory that states that knowledge comes only or primarily from sensory experience. It is one of several views of epistemology, the study of human knowledge, along with rationalism and skepticism. Empiricism emphasizes the role of empirical evidence in the formation of ideas, rather than innate ideas or traditions.

Being objective means being unbiased towards achievement of goals.

Being systematic in scientific research, means an observation of relationships that is carefully structured, so you can learn about cause and effect relations between them.

Being predictive means, we can tell about the future events with more certainty.

51. (d): Absolute number means that to remove any negative sign in front of a number, and to think of all numbers as positive (or zero).

A nominal number, for example, a telephone number, a player on a team. Nominal numbers do not show amount or quantity or rank. They are used only to identify something.

Ordinal refers to the sequence in which something is in relation to others of its kind. Examples of ordinal numbers are first, third, 11th, and 123rd. Ordinal numbers can be contrasted to cardinal numbers.

Prime number is a natural number greater than 1 that cannot be formed by multiplying two smaller natural numbers. The smallest prime natural number is 2.

52. (c): A research article is basically a primary source of information. It reports the methods and results of an original study performed by the authors. The kind of study may vary (it could have been an experiment, survey, interview, etc.), but in all cases, raw data have been collected and analysed by the authors, and conclusions drawn from the results of that analysis.

Single-blind peer review means that the identity of the reviewer is anonymous, but the author's name and affiliation are on the paper. Like the other forms of reviewing, there are advantages and disadvantages to single-blind.

53. (c): The main objective of research literature is identifying 'gaps' in the research—what has been done so far and what should be done next.

54. (b): Action research process may move in the cycles. It is like a heuristic method as the next action is based on the previous result. This PAOR approach is reflected through the diagram of 'action research', and specifically mentioned in NTA-UGC NET/SET/JRF Paper I—Teaching and published by Pearson Education.

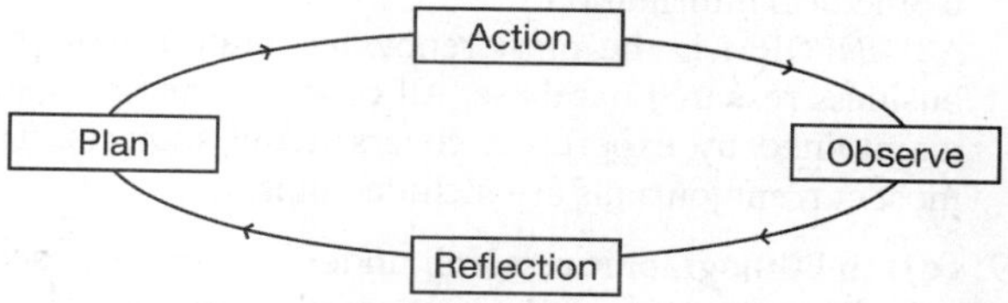

55. (a): Intervention based action research, phenomenological and narrative research and case study research—all are basically qualitative researches. Experimental and *ex post facto* are basically quantitative researches and specifically aims at hypothesis testing and generalizations.

56. (a): Option (a) talks about avoiding positivist approach and data analysis, thus, it indicates post-positivist approach that itself is qualitative in nature. In (b), subscribing to old categories is contradictory in nature. (c) and (d) indicate positivist approach.

Positivist	Non–Positivist
Quantitative	Qualitative
Objectivist	Subjectivist
Scientific	Humanistic
Experimentalist	Interpretivist
Traditionalist	Reflexive/reactive

57. (b): Null hypothesis means no change in values. We safely assume that coaching impact our performance, mostly for betterment. According to question, this can be assumed as principal assumption.

Coaching has zero impact as shown in diagram. Null is set at 0, but can decrease or increase to a level of + / – 1.96 (again a limit). When we collected data from students, we 'fail to reject the null hypothesis'. It means we accept it. Accepting means saying that null is true and coaching actually does not make any impact. That is actually rejecting our principal knowledge (about coaching).

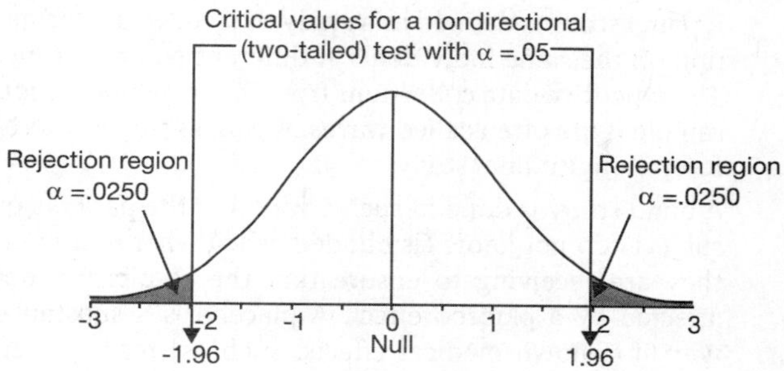

58. (b): ERIC is an online library of education research and information, sponsored by the Institute of Education Sciences (IES) of the US Department of Education.

MEDLINE is a bibliographic database of life sciences and biomedical information.

ABI/INFORM is the most renowned multidisciplinary business research database. All content is indexed and maintained by experts. It covers many subjects. The most current journals are included in it.

59. (c): In Ethnographic research understanding the socio-cultural prospective of a society can be understood better by being participant of that society. It is mentioned in Research unit.

60. (a): Refer 'Types of sampling' in research. As 'snowball' moves from one hand to another, it attaches more and more snow (or participants) with it.

61. (a): Again mentioned in research unit—longitudinal and cross-section studies. In question statement 'continuing' means when data is being collected from same variables (say people) repeatedly over a period of time and is done in longitudinal studies.

62. (d): Tentative proposition means 'tentative solution' and researchers start working on that.

63. (b): NTA has added the concept of experimental research in our syllabus. Sometimes, it is also called as the 'double-blind, placebo-controlled study', it is termed as the best and most reliable form of research. The main objective is to prevent biasedness. It is a kind of 'comparative study'—comparison of a new drug to another that is already known to work.

'Double-blind' is closely linked to randomization, where participants are allocated to groups in a random manner.

64. (b): Cohort is basically linked with health sciences. It is the best available scientific method for measuring the effects of a suspected risk factor. It is a longitudinal and panel study.

In social sciences and life sciences, a case study is a research method involving an up-close, in-depth, and detailed examination of a subject of study (the case), as well as its related contextual conditions. Case studies can be produced by following a formal research method.

A panel study is defined as a study that collects information on the same individuals at different points in time. The repetitive data collections from the same population sample is are often called waves. A panel study is, therefore, a longitudinal study.

A blind study is done in such a way that the patients or subjects do not know (is blinded as to) what treatment they are receiving to ensure that the results are not affected by a placebo effect. A placebo is a substance with no known medical effects, such as sterile water, saline solution, or a sugar pill. It is due to patient's belief in that treatment.

65. (d): Primarily we know that ethnographic and unstructured are basically qualitative research approaches. Where as descriptive approach doesn't fit into definition of either quantitative or qualitative research methodologies, instead it can utilize elements of both within the same study. A structured approach is a quantitative research method that is commonly employed in a 'survey research', where each interview is presented with exactly the same questions in the same order to the each interviewer.

66. (d): The question statement does not guarantee longitudinal studies that ask for continuous or repeated measures to follow particular individuals over prolonged periods of time—often years or decades. Action research is basically for improvement in one's profession such as in education. One answer can be 'comparative research', but specifically it is feminist research.

67. (b): A Likert scale is a rating scale, often found on survey forms, that measures how people feel about something. It includes a series of questions.

Guttman scale also called cumulative scaling or scalogram analysis and is created with elements that can possibly be ordered in a hierarchical manner. It is representative of the extreme 'attitude' of respondents, i.e., extremely positive or negative, about the subject in-hand.

The Thurstone scale was the first formal method of measuring attitude both in psychology and sociology.

68. (b): Plagiarism is presenting someone else's work or ideas as your own, with or without their consent, by incorporating it into your work without full acknowledgement. All published and unpublished material, whether in manuscript, printed or electronic form, is covered under this definition.

Plagiarism is unscrupulous; something that is dishonest or immoral, i.e., copying someone's work behind his back and then take credit for it.

69. (c): An independent variable is the variable that is changed or controlled in a scientific experiment to test the effects on the dependent variable.

A dependent variable is the variable being tested and measured in a scientific experiment.

The dependent variable is 'dependent' on the independent variable. As the experimenter changes the independent variable, the effect on the dependent variables observed and recorded.

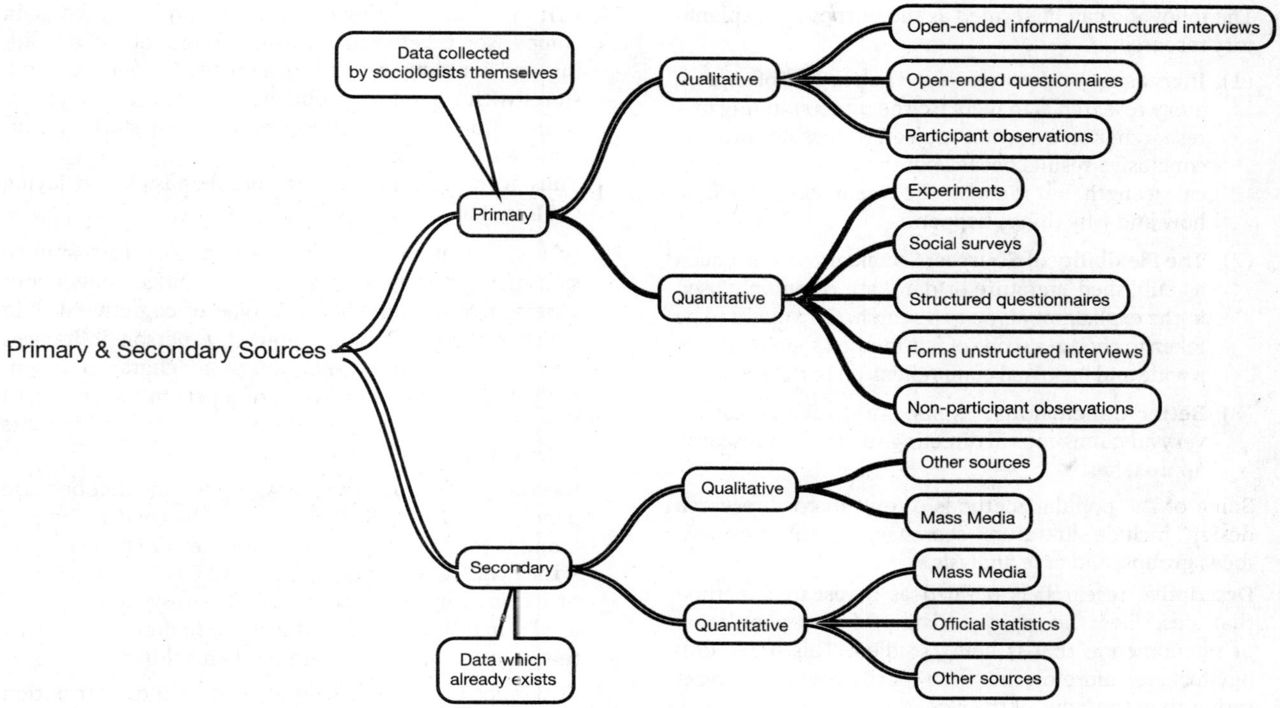

Figure 1

(1) The independent variable is the one that the experimenter controls. The dependent variable is the variable that changes in response to the independent variable.

(2) The two variables may be related by cause and effect. If the independent variable changes, then the dependent variable is affected.

The independent and dependent variables may be viewed in terms of cause and effect. If the independent variable is changed, then an effect is seen in the dependent variable. Remember, the values of both variables may change in an experiment and are recorded. The difference is that the value of the independent variable is controlled by the experimenter, while the value of the dependent variable only changes in response to the independent variable.

In the given question, level of aspiration is an independent variable and scholastic performance is dependent variable.

70. (d): Ethnographic research is a qualitative method where researchers observe and/or interact with a study's participants in their real-life environment.

Ethnography is a study through direct observation of users in their natural environment rather than in a lab. The objective of this type of research is to gain insights into how users interact with things in their natural environment.

71. (b): We should focus on the word 'why' in the question statement. Explanatory research is the research whose primary purpose is to explain why events occur to build, elaborate, extend or test theory.

The coding scheme for the explanatory model of heart attack may include four main domains: physiologic (high blood pressure, cholesterol, diabetes, etc.), psychosocial (stress, depression, etc.), behavioural (high fat diet, not exercising, smoking, etc.), and spiritual (God, fate). They may be compared with biomedical results also. In addition to qualitative data analysis, descriptive statistics were calculated for the socio-demographic characteristics of the participants.

Detailed Description

Explanatory research is conducted for a problem which was not well researched before, demands priorities, generates operational definitions and provides a better-researched model. It is actually a type of research design which focusses on explaining the aspects of your study in a detailed manner. The researcher starts with a general idea and uses research as a tool which could lead to the subjects that would be dealt within (one word) the incoming future. This conducts the research in a more efficient manner.

The following can be termed as the purpose of explanatory research:

(1) **Increasing Understanding:** The purpose of explanatory research is to increase the understanding of a researcher on a certain subject. It does not provide conclusive results because of the lack of its statistical strength, but it makes the researcher determine how and why things happen.

(2) **The Flexibility of Sources:** Secondary sources, such as published literature or data, are commonly used in the explanatory type of research. Care ought to be taken to choose a scope of fair-minded sources to give a wide and balanced comprehension of the subject.

(3) **Better Conclusions:** Explanatory research can be very advantageous in directing subsequent research approaches.

Some of the popular methods of explanatory research design include literature searches, depth interview, focus groups, and case analysis.

Descriptive research is defined as a research method that describes the characteristics of the population or phenomenon that is being studied. This methodology focusses more on the 'what' of the research subject rather than the 'why' of the research subject.

A correlational study is a type of research design where a researcher seeks to understand what kind of relationships naturally occurring variables have with one another. In simple terms, correlational research seeks to figure out if two or more variables are related and, if so, in what way.

Feasibility study is the initial design stage of any project, which brings together the elements of knowledge that indicate if a project is possible or not.

72. (c): We need to look at definition of 'primary sources'. The question is mainly about knowing the differences between primary and secondary sources.

In this diagram, we have tried to go into bit detail so that some future questions can also be attempted. (See Figure 1)

73. (c): Here we need to look at the meanings of words.

Convoluted sentences, explanations, arguments, etc., are unreasonably long and difficult to understand. It has a negative connotation.

Generic means characteristic of a class or group of things; it is not very specific.

Obscure not discovered or known about, that it is uncertain.

The third choice fully applies—simple means that concepts and variables are properly understood. We are clear and specific on approach adopted. They should become part of research hypothesis.

74. (a): In the formulation of a research problem, the main comparison is between 'laying the foundation of a building' and 'building the walls of a home'. As every research starts with a kind of 'problem', so working towards its formulation is the foremost step that may start with literature survey, etc.

Thus, formulation of research problem is akin to 'laying the foundation of a house'.

75. (c): To put it simply, halo effect means 'first impression matters' in making subsequent judgements about a person. The halo effect is a type of cognitive bias in which our overall impression of a person influences how we feel and think about his or her character. Essentially, your overall impression of a person ('He is nice!') impacts your evaluations of that person's specific traits ('He is also smart!').

It is the phenomenon whereby, we assume that because people are good at doing A, they will be good at doing B, C and D (or the reverse—because they are bad at doing A they will be bad at doing B, C and D). The phrase was first coined by Edward Thorndike, a psychologist who used it in a study published in 1920 to describe the way that commanding officers rated their soldiers.

Evaluation effect is basically evaluating the contribution that research makes to society and the economy, future funding can be allocated where it is perceived to bring about the desired impact.

Error of central tendency refers to the phenomenon where raters assign scores to most subjects that are average regardless of the differences in performance between subjects.

76. (b): A pilot study is a small-scale preliminary study conducted in order to evaluate feasibility, time, cost, adverse events, and improve upon the study design prior to performance of a full-scale research project. This puts us in the context of a research project.

Feasibility study is the initial design stage of any project, which brings together the elements of knowledge that indicate if a project is possible or not. A feasibility study is an assessment of the practicality of a proposed project or system. A feasibility study aims to objectively and rationally uncover the strengths and weaknesses of an existing business or proposed venture, opportunities and threats present in the natural environment, the resources required to carry through, and ultimately the prospects for success. In its simplest terms, the two criteria to judge feasibility are cost required and value to be attained.

77. (d): First we can have a look at teacher competencies. Teacher competencies facilitate physical, intellectual, social, and emotional development of the students. The teaching competency of a teacher is determined by various aspects. Teaching competency is mainly measured on five dimensions—induction, content, pedagogy, organization and assessment. The findings revealed that there is a continuous improvement in all the dimensions of teaching competency.

It further shows that every teacher needs to review/update his/her potential in all possible novel/new/innovative strategies, so as to modify and improve his/her teaching competency in accordance with the changes envisaged in the educational system. Here, the 'action research' comes into play. It enhances the professional skills of a teacher.

78. (d): We know that sampling has the purpose to gain information about the population. The researcher may get random sampling (unbiased) by using 'fishbowl' method.

Let's learn more about fishbowl method for future questions.

Fishbowl technique is also termed as 'Lottery Method',—that is simply writing the names or numbers of all the individual members in a small rolled pieces of papers, then placed in container.

In addition to fishbowl, there can be another method, called as 'Table of Random Numbers'—the tables show sets of random digits arranged in groups. Under this, there are two methods:

(1) Direct selection method

(2) The remainder method

Students can go through them also for future questions. There is non-probability sampling, called as 'chunk sampling' that consider one area only.

In teaching, fishbowl is also defined as an engaging and student-centered strategy that builds comprehension of complex texts while developing group discussion skills. In the inner circle—or 'fishbowl' for students' practice responding to multiple viewpoints.

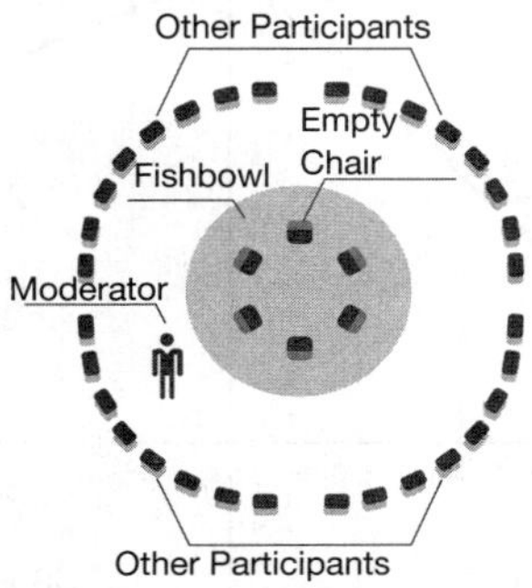

Source: unicef.org

Fishbowl method can help in the following ways:

(1) It helps us to generate many ideas and point of views.

(2) This method can reach variety of topics.

(3) It can help in dealing with different social skills.

(4) This type of discussion can work at all ages in life.

(5) This works well for group discussions.

79. (a): A closed-ended question is made up of pre-populated answer choices for the respondent to choose from; while an open-ended question asks the respondent to provide feedback in their own words.

80. (b): In experimental research based studies, the dependent variables refer to that type of variable that measures the affect of the independent variable(s) on the test units. Usually when one is looking for a relationship between two things, one is trying to find out what makes the dependent variable change the way it does.

81. (a): In the context of an experiment, repeatability measures the variation in measurements taken by a single instrument or person under the same conditions. Accuracy in a (survey) research refers to the match between the target population and the sample.

There are many other features of a good research that have been mentioned below:

(1) **Objective, Unbiased, and Logical**–All findings are logically based on empirical findings.

(2) **Reliability and consistency**–For confirmation of findings.

(3) **Empirical**–Based on observations and experimentation on theories.

(4) **Systematic**–Follows orderly and sequential procedure.

(5) **Controlled**–All variables except those that are tested/experimented upon are kept constant.

(6) **Formulation of hypothesis**–Guides the investigation process.

(7) **Analytical**–There is critical analysis of all data used so that there is no error in their interpretation.

(8) **Use of quantitative or statistical methods**–Data are transformed into numerical measures and are treated statistically.

82. (c): This question is about study design in research. We need to focus on the limitation of a design that is called as the 'total change'.

Maturation Effect: If the study population is very young and if there is a significant time lapse between the before and after sets of data collection, changes in the study population may be seen because it is maturing. This is particularly true when you are studying young children.

Reactive Effective: Sometimes the instrument itself educates the respondents. This is known as the reactive effect of the instrument. For example, suppose you want to ascertain the impact of a programme designed to create awareness of drugs in a population. To do this, you design a questionnaire listing various drugs and asking respondents to indicate whether they have heard of them.

Regression Effect: Sometimes people who place themselves at the extreme positions of a measurement scale at the pre-test stage may, for a number of reasons, shift towards the mean at the post-test stage. They might feel that they have been too negative or too positive at the pre-test stage. Therefore, the mere expression of an attitude in response to a questionnaire or interview has caused them to think about and alter their attitude at the time of the post-test. This type of effect is known as the regression effect.

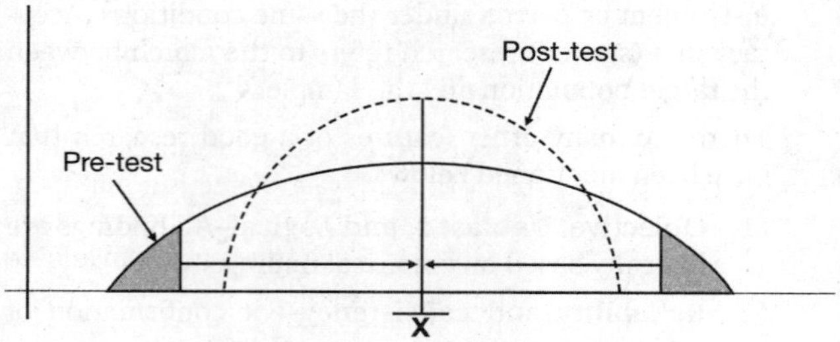

The regression effect

Conditioning Effect: This describes a situation where, if the same respondents are contacted frequently, they begin to know what is expected of them and respond to questions without thought, or they may lose interest in the enquiry, with the same result.

83. (a): The answer is reference period but it is closely linked with the longitudinal studies. During reference period, the study population is visited a number of times at regular intervals.

Reference period are not fixed so their length may vary from study to study. Intervals might be as short as a week or longer than a year.

Longitudinal studies helps in exploring a situation or problem on continuous basis.

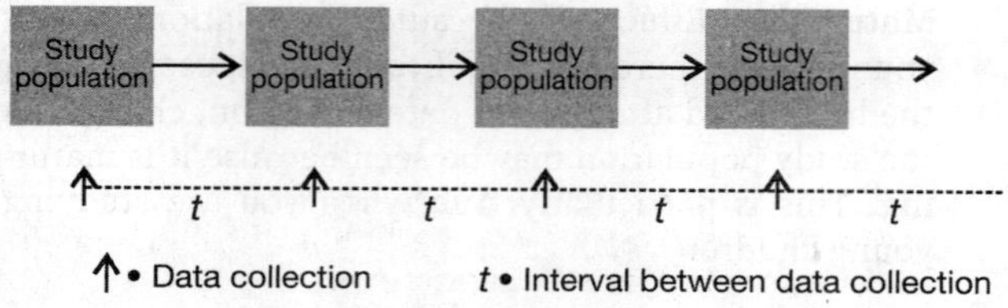

Retrospective time means when study is done for some past event. Here prospective study designs and retrospective-prospective study designs are also mentioned for future questions.

Retrospective Study Design

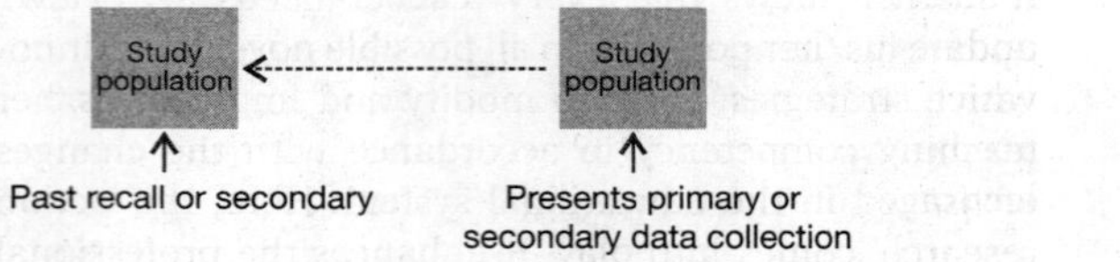

Prospective Study Design

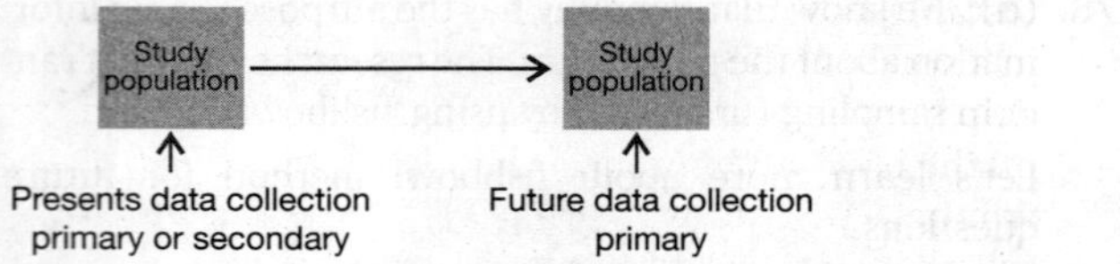

Retrospective-prospective Study Design

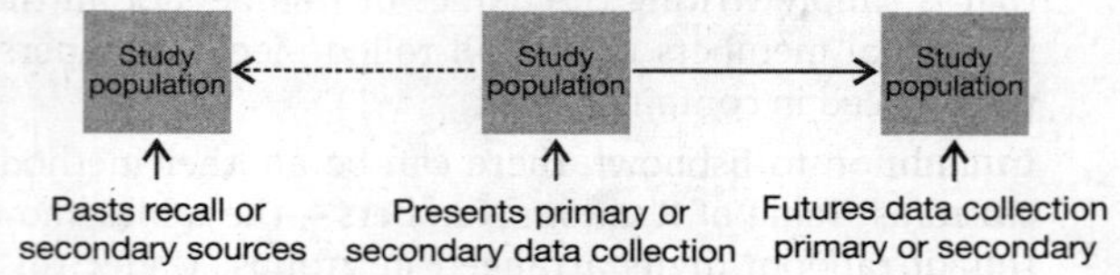

84. (c): The word correlation is used in everyday life to denote some form of association. In statistical terms we use correlation to denote association between two quantitative variables. The degree of association is measured by a correlation coefficient, denoted by r. The correlation coefficient is measured on a scale that varies from + 1 through 0 to –1. Complete correlation between two variables is expressed by either + 1 or –1. When one variable increases as the other increases the correlation is positive; when one decreases as the other increases it is negative.

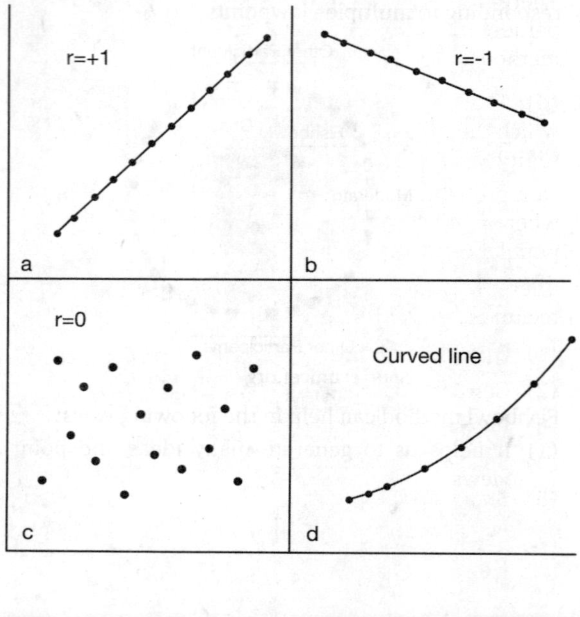

85. (b): The synopsis of research is a short outline of what your research thesis is and all the steps you propose to follow in order to achieve them. It gives you and your supervisor a clear view of what the research aims at achieving and within what time frame.

A research is valid when a conclusion is accurate or true and research design is the conceptual blueprint within which research is conducted. A scholar for his research, prepare an action plan, it constitutes the outline of collection, measurement and analysis of data.

A hypothesis is a tentative statement about the relationship between two or more variables. It is a specific, testable prediction about what you expect to happen in a study. For example, we want to study the relationship between sleep deprivation and test performance might have a hypothesis that states. The hypothesis will be—This study is designed to assess the hypothesis that sleep-deprived people will perform worse on a test than individuals who are not sleep deprived. Hypothesis is more than a guess.

In the title '*The Structure of Scientific Revolutions*' American philosopher Thomas Kuhn (1962) first used the word research paradigm to mean a philosophical way of thinking. It can be defined in different ways—paradigm means a worldview, a paradigm is an epistemological stance, a paradigm is a set of shared beliefs among members of a specialty area and, a paradigm as a model example of research.

There are three major paradigms currently operating in the social sciences:

(1) Positivism /postpositivism
(2) Interpretivism/constructivism
(3) Critical theory

There are four components of a research paradigm: ontology, epistemology, methodology, and methods.

86. (d): Probability sampling is a sampling technique, in which the subjects of the population get an equal opportunity to be selected as a representative sample.

Non-probability sampling is a method of sampling wherein, it is not known that which individual from the population will be selected as a sample.

There are five types of non-probability sampling techniques:

(1) Quota sampling
(2) Convenience sampling
(3) Purposive sampling
(4) Self-selection sampling
(5) Snowball sampling.

Dimensional sampling is an extension to quota sampling. The researcher takes into account several characteristics, e.g., gender, age, income, residence and education. The researcher must ensure that there is at least one person in the study representing each of the chosen characteristics.

87. (b): A research design is the logical and systematic planning and directions for the activities regarding data collection, analysis and presentation of fact in a research. It guides not only for the data collection methods but also supplies the essential tools to be used for data analysis and criteria for decision-making. There are three main sections of research design: Data collection, measurement, and analysis.

88. (d): Plagiarism is presenting someone else's work or ideas as your own, with or without their consent, by incorporating it into your work without full acknowledgement. All published and unpublished material, whether in manuscript, printed or electronic form, is covered under this definition.

In India, Shodhganga tries to overcome the serious problem of duplication of research and poor quality resulting from the 'poor visibility' and the 'unseen' factor in research output. Two plagiarism detection platform, namely, 'iThenticate' and 'Turnitin' are being made accessible to 100 universities with funds made available by the University Grants Commission.

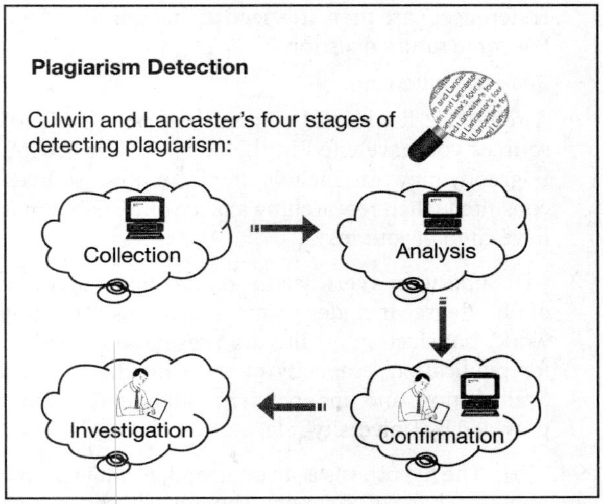

89. (d): In case we look at the question statement, it is about deductive–qualitative research. Thus, option (d) is the right answer. We want to focus on 'specific' interpretations rather than on generalizations.

In *ex post facto* study or after-the-fact research is a category of research design in which the investigation starts after the fact has occurred without interference from the researcher. Thus, it is a quantitative.

To put it simply, philosophy explains an individuals or a groups worldview in general or in a specific context. Such questions as the nature of knowledge, reality, and existence are questions that philosophy tries to answer. Survey is also more about focus on present situation.

90. (a): Bibliography helps those people who are interested in further research. In addition, for any research paper, writing a bibliography is essential to preventing any accusations of plagiarism, and to give fair credit to the work of previous authors in the field.

91. (d): Question statement can directly be taken as the definition of experimental research. We can look at the following points also for experimental research:

(1) manipulate the independent variable
(2) compares the groups in terms of the dependent variable
(3) assures that only the IV causes the change in the DV if this is accomplished then the experiment has internal validity
(4) minimizes confounding variables any variable that varies along with the IV
(5) uses randomization
(6) uses experimente control

92. (a): Reference lists (and Bibliographies) are placed at the end of your essay, assignment or thesis. Citations (references) are then arranged alphabetically by author. For some future question,

Read the following:

A reference list should contain only the details of the sources you have cited in the body of your text. A bibliography may also include details of other sources you consulted when researching a piece of work but may not have cited in your text.

93. (d): Supervisor's certification on the thesis for the award of PhD degree includes points such as 'results of original work', 'satisfaction for literary presentation', 'suitability for publication', 'capacity of the candidate for critical examination and independent judgment', 'guidelines provided by University', etc.

94. (b): The hypothesis is an educated, testable prediction about what will happen. Though while being generated, it is based on inductive logical reasoning. A good hypothesis is written in clear and simple language. A null hypothesis is a hypothesis that says there is no statistical significance between the two variables. It is usually the hypothesis a researcher or experimenter will try to disprove or discredit. An alternative hypothesis is one that states there is a statistically significant relationship between two variables.

95. (d): Action research is a formative study of progress commonly practiced by professional such as teachers in schools. Basically an action research is a spiral process that includes problem investigation, taking action and fact-finding about the result of action.

96. (c): It can be concluded from the above-mentioned points that a review of research literature helps in creating a working thesis for the research paper by specifying and organizing the category of information. Research design is defined as a framework of methods and techniques chosen by a researcher to combine various components of research in a reasonably logical manner so that the research problem is efficiently handled. The sketch of how research should be conducted can be prepared using research design.

The 'hypothesis' has already been discussed.

Analysis of data is deploying some statistical or mathematical technique after 'hypothesis'.

97. (a): Critical Language Testing (CLT) is a philosophical approach that states that there is widespread bias in language testing. CLT refers to the examination of the uses and consequences of tests in education and society.

CLT also signifies a paradigm shift in language testing. It introduces new criteria for the validity of language tests.

98. (c): Participant observation is a qualitative research method, in which the researchers not only observe the research participant but also actively engages in the activities as the research participants. This requires the research to become integrated into the participant environment, while also taking objective notes about what is going on.

99. (b): Stratified random sampling is a method of sampling that involves the division of a population into smaller subgroups.

In other words, divide the whole heterogeneous population into smaller groups or subpopulations such that the sampling units are homogeneous with respect to the characteristic under study between or among the subpopulation. Such population is termed as strata.

Treat each subpopulation as a separate population and draw a sample by SRS from each stratum.

Note: Stratum is singular and strata is plural.

100. (c): The chi square test is intended to test how likely it is that a reserved distribution as due to chance. It is also called a 'goodness of fit' statistic because it measures how well the observed distribution of data fits with the distribution that is expected, if the variables are independent.

101. (c): It is the third step of research, when we identifying variables and hypothesising. Working hypotheses is tentative assumption made in order to draw out and test its logical and empirical consequences. They also effect the manner, in which test must be conducted in the analysis of data and indirectly the quality of data which is required for the analysis.

102. (d): First survey is decided as data collection technique. Questions are asked and read. Some recall may be necessary for error minimisation. The last step here is review.

103. (b): Grounded theory is a systematic methodology in the social sciences involving the construction of theories through methodical gathering and analysis of data. This research methodology uses inductive reasoning.

104. (a): We don't collect data from every member of population to save time and money. The negative impact is sampling errors. They happen in any kind of research.

In (i), we need to focus on the words 'related' and 'subsumed'. Non-sampling error is 'catch-all' term.

(ii) Sampling error do occur in every kind of sampling whether single stage or multistage.

(iii) Inaccurate sampling frame and non-response are examples of sampling related error.

(iv) Rather, the more homogenous is the population, less will be the sampling error.

105. (c): This is direct question of sequence of steps.

106. (d): Quantitative research focuses more on the ability to complete statistical analysis. With quantitative studies, each respondent is asked to respond to the same questions: Surveys and questionnaires are the most common technique for collecting quantitative data.

107. (a):

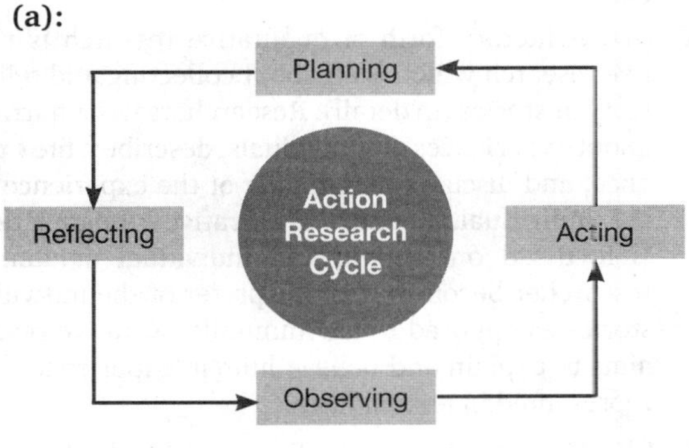

Action research process may move in the cycles. It is like a heuristic method as the next action is based on the previous result. This PAOR approach is reflected through the diagram of action research

108. (d): Research studies are meant not only to answer research questions but also stand as reference/ guidance for further research in the same or related area(s). A research must be able to produce results which are contemporary and relevant. For this it is imperative to use updated data and resources by citing old reference the academic/ scholar, researcher show that they have not cared to update the materials/resources used for their research study and thereby has committed the serious lapse of carelessness which will undermine the relevance of the study.

109. (b): Like any hypotheses a substantive hypothesis is an assumption about the relation between two or more variables. It is called substantive hypothesis, the purpose of distinguishing it from the statistical hypothesis (Null, Alternative) because it is not operationalised. An operationalised hypothesis phrased clearly to show how the variables are manipulated or measured or how the main concepts were put into effect.

In the eventuality of rejection of the Null hypothesis after quantitative data analysis, the substantive research hypothesis should be accepted.

110. (c): Nominal Scale of Measurement

A nominal scale is a measurement scale in which numbers serve as "tags" and "labels" only to indentify and classify an object. A nominal scale measurement normally deal only with non-numeric variables or where number have no value. It is good research tool for questionable and interview.

Interval Scale of Measurement

The interval scale is defined as a quantitative measurement scale where the difference between 2 variables is meaningful. Interval scale is the 3rd level of measurement. This means that the difference between two variables on a scale is an actual or equal distance. It is used for intelligence and aptitude test.

Ordinal Scale of Measurement

Ordinal scale is the 2nd level of measurement that reports the ranking and ordering of the data without actually establishing the degree of variation between them. Ordinal indicates 'Orders'. Ordinal data is quantitative data which have naturally occurring orders and the difference between is unknown.

Ratio Scale

Ratio scale refers to the level of measurement in which the attributes composing variables are measured on specific numerical scores or values that have equal distances between attributes or points along the scale and based on a zero point.

111. (a):

Research process flowchart

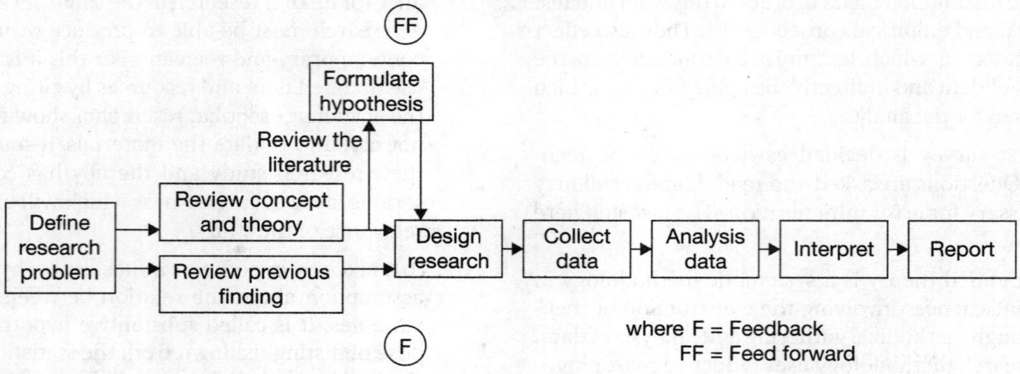

With the help of this, we can find the logical sequence of research.

112. (a): In experimental research, the researcher develops one or more hypothesis to state the nature of expected relationship. Experimental research is designed for establishing casual relationships and testing hypothesis is the main concept. It begins with a question concerning the relationship between two or more variables.

1. An independent variable is manipulated.
2. All other variables except the independent variables are held constant.
3. The effect of manipulation of the dependent variable is observed. The dependent variable is so named because its value is hypothesised to depend upon and vary with the value of the independent variables.

113. (b): Ex post facto research: This research is also known as after the fact research. In this study, investigation starts after the fact has occurred. Manipulation is not possible in this study. In this research, the researcher identifies the event that has already occurred.

For example, we will record the effects of an earthquake after the earthquake hit an area. Similarly, after the achievement of rural children, a teacher intends to study the relationship between the level of aspiration and the achievement of rural children.

114. (c): In the post positivistic approach to research, three types of researches got emphasised.

(1) **Phenomenological research:** It is an approach to qualitative research that focuses on the commonality of a lived experience within a particular group.

For example, studying the green flash, that sometimes happens just after the sunset.

(2) **Ethnographic research:** Is a qualitative method for collecting data often used in the social and behavioral sciences. Data are collected through observations and interviews, which are then used to draw conclusions about how societies and individuals function. Ethnographers observe life as it happens instead of trying to manipulate it in a lab.

(3) **Action research:**

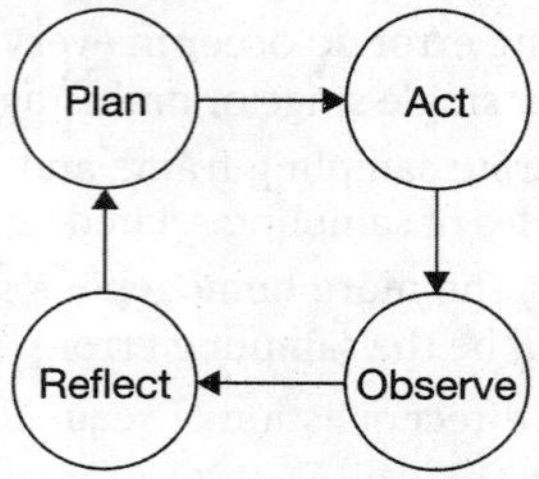

115. (c): An abstract research is a brief summary of a research article thesis review, conference proceeding or any in depth analysis of a particular subject and it is often used to help the reader quickly ascertain the paper's purpose.

116. (d): A literary form of qualitative research is narrative research which is all about collecting and telling a story or stories (in detail). Researchers write narratives about experiences of individuals, describe a life experience, and discuss the meaning of the experience with the individual. Usually, a narrative research design is focussed on studying an individual person. The researcher becomes the interpreter of the individuals' stories as opposed to a community. Narative research aims to explain and believe human experience as it is represented in textual form.

117. (d): Nominal Scale: Nominal scale is the least powerful level of measurement. It indicates no order or distance relationship and has no arithmetic origin. A nominal scale simply describe differences between things by assigning them to categories. In other words, Nominal Scale is simply a system of assigning number, symbols to events in order to label them.

Example – The assignment of numbers of basketball players to label them.

Ordinal Scale: The ordinal scale places events in order, but there is not any attempt to make the intervals of the scale in terms of some rules. Rank orders represent ordinal scales and are frequently used in research relating to qualitative phenomena. A students' rank in his graduation class involves the use of an ordinary scale. Example - If Ram's position is 10 and Mohan's position is 40, it cannot be said that Ram's position is four times good as that of Mohan's.

Interval Scale: The intervals are adjusted in terms of some rule that have been established as a basis for making the units equal. Interval scales can have an arbitrary zero, but it is not possible to determine for what may be called an absolute zero or the unique origin.

Ratio Scale: Ratio Scale have an absolute or true zero of measurement. We can conceive of an absolute zero of length and similarly we can conceive of an absolute zero of time. Example – the zero point on a centimetre scale indicates the complete absence of length or height.

118. (b):

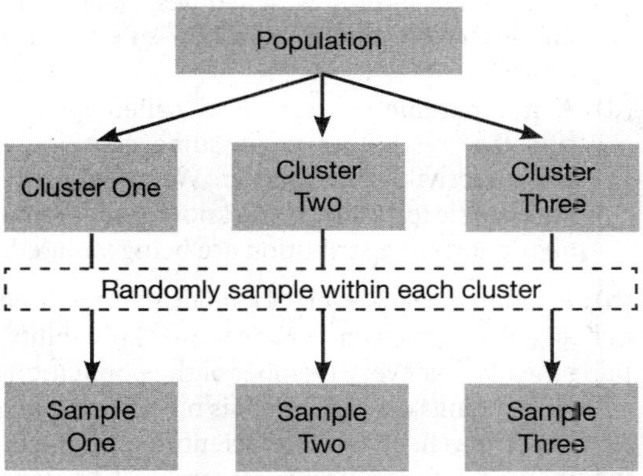

Cluster sampling refer to a type of probability sampling method. With cluster sampling, the researcher divides the population into separate groups, called clusters, then, a simple random sample of cluster is selected from the population. The researcher conducts his analysis on data from the sampled clusters.

The main advantage is equal sample sizes. Cluster sampling usually provides less precision than either simple random sampling as stratified sampling.

119. (b): The issue of research ethics becomes relevant in Hypothesis and data analysis and interpretation.

(1) **Hypothesis Testing:** A statiscal hypothesis test is a method of statistical inference commonly, two stastical data sets are compared, as a data set obtained by sampling is compared, against a synthetic data set from an idealized model. A hypothesis is proposed for the statistical relationship between the two data sets, and this is compared as an alternative to an idealized null hypothesis that proposes no relationship between two data sets would be an unlikely realization of the null hypothesis according to a threshold probability – the significance level.

(2) **Data Analysis and Interpretation:** It is the process of assigning meaning to the collected information and determining the conclusion, significance and implications of the findings. It is an important and exciting step in the process of research. In all research studies, analysis follows data collection.

120. (c): (1) **Achievement Test:** An achievement test is a test of developed skill of knowledge. The most common type of achievement test is a standardized test developed to measure skill and knowledge learned in a grade level, usually through planned instruction, such as training or classroom instruction.

Example of familiar, formal achievement test include the American college test, the lowest test of basic skill.

Informal achievement tests are used by class room teachers to evaluate student learning and assign grade.

(2) **Aptitude Test:** An aptitude test is a systematic means of testing a job candidate's ability to perform specific tasks and react to a range of different situations. Each test have a standardised method of administration.

Example of Aptitude tests – A test assessing "an individual's aptitude to become a fighter pilot.

(3) **Intelligence Tests:** These psychological tests are designed to measure a variety of mental functions, such as reasoning, comprehensions and judgement. The two main individuals intelligence tests are

1. Stanford-Binet Intelligence Test
2. Wechsler Tests: Wechsler intelligence for children and Wechsler Adult intelligence scale for adults.

121. (c): Action Research Cycle

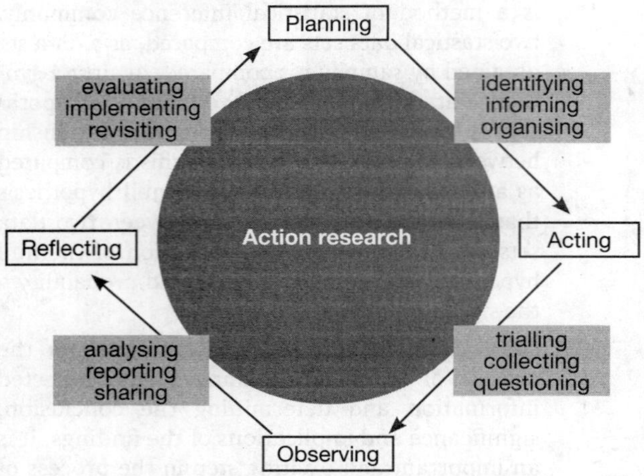

Action research is a process by which change and understanding can be pursued at one time. It is usually described as cyclic, with action ad critical reflection taking place in turn. The reflection is used to review the previous action and plan the next one. It is commonly done by a group of people, though sometimes individuals use it to improve their practice.

122. (a): Random error describes errors that fluctuate due to the unpredictability or uncertainty inherent in the researcher's measuring process. They may occur due to variation in the quantity the researcher is trying to measure.

A systematic error mostly results from a persistent issue. It leads to a consistent error in the measurements. For example, if the measuring tape got elongated without our knowledge, the results will always be lower than the true value.

Random errors are essentially unavoidable, while systematic errors are not. Systematic errors are difficult to spot.

123. (d): This question is basically about definitions.

124. (c): We may think of independent and dependent variables in terms of cause and effect: an independent variable is the variable can be identified with the cause, while a dependent variable is the effect. In an experiment, we manipulate the independent variable and measure the outcome in the dependent variable.

B and E indicate dependent variables. Point D may be applied in certain situation but its partner E does not go with the right answer.

Thus, C is the right answer.

125. (d): In case, the observed value falls in the rejection region, then it is said to be statistically significant. It tells us that difference between points in acceptance region and rejection region is not due to random chance factor, and that difference is statistically significant. Thus, null hypothesis is rejected and alternative hypothesis is accepted. If we take 5% significant level, it means that we are 95% confident that the observed results are real and not an error caused by randomness. It also means that there is a 5% chance that you could be wrong.

126. (a): These concepts are important in research process.

(a) Hypothesis testing in statistics is a way for the researcher to test the results of a survey or experiment to see, whether we can have meaningful results.

(b) A sample refers to a smaller, manageable version of a larger group. It is a subset containing the characteristics of a larger population. Samples are used in statistical testing when population sizes are too large for the test to include all possible members or observations.

(c) Anything that becomes a means of collecting information for your study is called a research tool or a research instrument. For example, observation forms, interview schedules, questionnaires, and interview guides are all classified as research tools.

(d) A non-parametric test (also called as distribution free test) does not assume anything about the underlying distribution. We should use non-parametric tests only if you know that assumptions about normal distribution are being violated.

127. (b): Random means every member has equal chance of being elected as member of sample. Probability sampling means that every member of the population has a chance of being selected which is mostly used in quantitative research. It is more scientific approach. It is mainly used in quantitative research. These sampling means are preferred as they help in being unbiased and objective.

128. (b): In Ex post facto study (or say after-the-fact research), the investigation starts after the fact has occurred without interference from the researcher. Here, the groups with qualities that already exist are compared on some dependent variable. The assignment of subjects to different groups is based on whichever variable is of interest to the researchers.

129. (d): The substantive research hypothesis is tested via null hypothesis is the main characteristic of quantitative research, so by eliminating 'b' from the options we can get the right answer.

130. (a): To describe a single categorical variable, we use frequency tables. To describe the relationship between two categorical variables, we use a special type of table called a cross-tabulation (or crosstab). In a cross-tabulation, the categories of one variable determine the rows of the table, and the categories of the other variable determine the columns. The cells of the table contain the number of times that a particular combination of categories occurred.

The table dimensions are reported as as R × C, where R is the number of categories for the row variable, and C is the number of categories for the column variable. Tables of dimensions 2 × 2, 3 × 3, 4 × 4, etc., are called as square crosstabs.

Basis for Comparison		Do you drink coffee?		
		No	Yes	Total
Gender	Male	13	33	46
	Female	13	32	45
Total		26	65	91

131. (a): Many people don't appreciate statistics for the same reasons but that is also valuable. Getting right data and authentic data is not an easy task but still research must be carried on.

132. (b): Statement II is the solution for Statement I. For this purpose, we conduct exploratory study that is more useful in qualitative research.

In Statement II, there is list of steps in exploratory study.

Research is a continuous process that needs improvement with the passage of time, thus it is non–exhaustive. Exploratory research mostly deals with qualitative data. Most of the researchers work on existing theories or formulations and build on them. Some researchers are motivated to work on a problem that has not been studied very clearly to establish priorities, develop operational definitions and improving the final research design.

Much time is spent on exploring the problem so that better insights are built for the future. It usually doesn't lead to a conclusive result. It starts on a general idea and we try to specify the related issues with the topic of the research.

Exploratory research is inexpensive, highly interactive and open–ended in nature. There is usually no prior relevant information available from past researchers. Since there is no standard for carrying out exploratory research, it is usually flexible and scattered.

133. (c): Reflexivity: Research should be classified as a "Mission', the researchers get in this mission and their own personalities become part of it. Conducting qualitative research, such as fieldwork, changes a researcher in many ways. Through reflexivity, researchers acknowledge the changes brought about in themselves as a result of the research process and how these changes have affected the research process. Thus, this reflexivity is an iterative and empowering process. Reflexivity should be recognized as a significant part of the research findings. Thus, it is an analytic attention to the researcher's role in qualitative research", it is both a concept and a process. As a concept, it refers to a certain level of consciousness.

There are the few basic principles in the linked qualitative research:

(i) **Feminist Principle**

(ii) **Rights–based Research:** the respect of human rights of participants during the research process.

(iii) **Participatory Research Principles:** It recognizes that people have expert knowledge and deep insight into their own lives and communities.

134. (d): Survey Research

Survey research a research method involving the use of standardized questionnaires or interviews to collect data about people and their preferences, thoughts, and behaviors in a systematic manner. As surveys are used to collect data from a predefined subject(s), they have been counted under **'positivism'** approach.

The survey as a formal research method was pioneered in the 1930–40s by sociologist Paul Lazarsfeld to examine the effects of the radio on political opinion formation of the United States. This method has since become a very popular method for quantitative research in the social sciences.

The survey method can be used for descriptive, exploratory, or explanatory research.

Survey research has several inherent strengths compared to other research methods due to following reasons.

(i) Survey is an excellent vehicle to measure a wide variety of data – people's preferences (political orientation), traits (self–esteem), attitudes (toward immigrants), beliefs (about a new law), behaviors (smoking), or factual information (income).

(ii) It is ideally suited for remotely collecting data about a population. For example, a large nation such as India or its state UP, MP, Maharashtra that can be covered using mail–in, electronic mail, or telephone surveys. Researches can use well planned sampling to ensure that the population is adequately represented in a small sample.

(iii) Interviews may be the only way of reaching certain population groups such as the homeless or illegal immigrants for which there is no sampling frame available.

(iv) Survey research is economical in terms of researcher time, effort and cost than most other methods such as experimental research and case research.

At the same time, survey research also has some unique disadvantages. It is subject to a large number of biases such as non–response bias, sampling bias, social desirability bias, and recall bias, etc.

Depending on data collection techniques, survey research can be divided into two broad categories:

(i) **Questionnaire surveys** – mail–in, group–administered, or online surveys), and

(ii) **Interview surveys** – personal, telephone, or focus group interviews (These have been discussed in detail in second unit of Pearson title for NTA–NET exam).

Constructing a survey questionnaire (or interviewing) is an art. For the benefit of research students, the following responses to structured questions have been suggested.

(i) Dichotomous response – responses such as true/ false, yes/no, or agree/disagree. Is MSP required for crops – Yes / No

(ii) Nominal response – more than two unordered options. What is your industry of employment: manufacturing / supply chain / consumer services / retail / education.

(iii) Ordinal Response: more than two ordered options. What is your highest level of education: high school / college degree / graduate studies/ PG / PhD.

(iv) Interval–level Response: When respondents are presented with a 5–point or 7–point Likert scale, semantic differential scale, or Guttman scale etc.

(v) Continuous Response: When respondents enter a continuous (ratio–scaled) value with a meaningful zero point, such as their age or tenure in a firm. These responses generally tend to be of the fill–in–the blanks type.

The survey questions should be stated in a very simple language, preferably in active voice, and without complicated words or jargon so that they are clearly understandable by a typical respondent. Questions must not be biased and too much detailed.

Double–barreled questions are those that can have multiple answers. For example, are you satisfied with the hardware and software provided for your work?

Question should not be presumptuous such as on taxes – too high or too low. Avoid questions with built–in presumptions.

'**Question sequencing**' should be proper, such as questions should flow logically from one to the next.

Role of interviewer should be motivational for respondents. They should make a good questionnaire.

Just pausing and waiting (without going into the next question) may suggest to respondents that the interviewer is waiting for more detailed response. It is called as '**silent probe**'.

The interviewer can try the psychotherapist's trick of repeating what the respondent said is called as '**Reflection**'.

Five common biases in survey research are non–response bias, sampling bias (excluding some people who don't have some resources such as mobile phone), social desirability bias (avoid negative opinions), recall bias (subjects' motivation, memory, and ability to respond). Common method bias refers to the amount of spurious covariance shared between independent and dependent variables that are measured at the same point in time such as in a cross–sectional survey, using the same instrument, such as a questionnaire.

135. (d): Non–parametric (and Parametric tests): First, we need to look at some basic difference between parametric and non–parametric tests.

In parametric tests, the parameters are assumed and the population distribution is always known. To calculate the central tendency, a mean value is used. In such tests, we assume normal distribution curve (bell shaped curve). For example, if we were to measure the height of people (in a population), we take some sample, we would see a typical bell–shaped curve. This distribution is also called the Gaussian distribution.

In statistics, nonparametric tests are methods of statistical analysis that do not require a distribution to meet the required assumptions to be analyzed (especially if the data is not normally distributed). Due to this reason, they are sometimes referred to as distribution–free tests.

Parametric tests are generally more powerful than the non–parametric tests, where smaller sample sizes are required in parametric tests.

Types of Non–Parametric Tests

- 1 Sample Sign Test
- 1 Sample Wilcoxon Signed Rank Test
- Friedman Test
- Goodman Kruska's Gamma
- Kruskal–Wallis Test
- The Mann–Kendall Trend Test
- Mann–Whitney Test
- Mood's Median Test
- Spearman Rank Correlation

136. (b): Descriptive Hypothesis: This contains only one variable so it is called a univariate hypothesis. This typically states the existence, size, form or distribution of some variable. It describes the situation or collects the data, the same as it has happened without adding our own assumptions as a researcher.

Null Hypothesis: the null hypothesis (often denoted H_0) is that two possibilities are the same. The null hypothesis is that the observed difference is due to chance alone. Using statistical tests, it is possible to calculate the likelihood that the null hypothesis is true.

Explanatory Hypothesis: This hypothesis guides the cause and effect relationship between two variables. For example, when salaries increase, then spending on food items also increase.

Intervening and confounding variables add to the impact of independent variables on dependent variables.

137. (c): The normal distribution curve is mostly used in hypothesis testing in research. There are basically two types of hypothesis—Null hypothesis and Alternative hypothesis. The null hypothesis is generally considered to be the 'accepted fact' that there is no difference between dependent and independent variables or else we may assume that the population parameter and the sample statistic. The null hypothesis is often an initial claim that is based on previous analysis or special knowledge. The null hypothesis is considered the opposite of the alternative hypothesis.

Researchers also come up with an alternative hypothesis that they think explains a phenomenon. Researchers try to reject or disprove the null hypothesis by means of sampling, so that the alternative hypothesis is accepted as true. For this work, researchers also take the help of confidence level / level of significance, which can be 1%, 5% or 10%. The area under the entire normal distribution curve is 1, or is 100 percent. The Z-table or T-table helps by telling us what percentage is under the curve at a particular point.

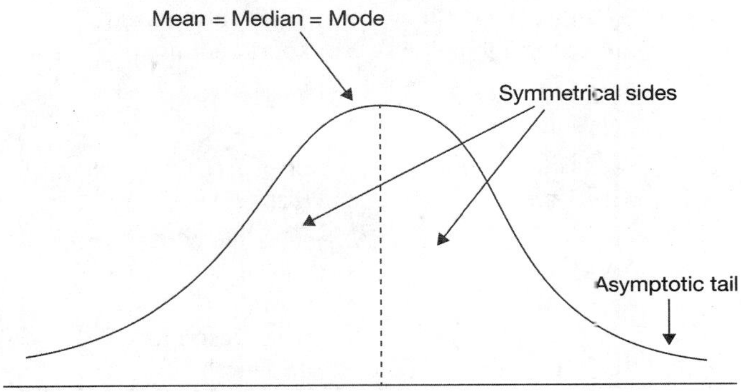

The characteristics of the normal distribution curve are given as under:

1. It is bell shaped curve and symmetrical in its appearance.
2. The height of normal distribution curve is at its maximum at the mean. Hence the mean, mode and median coincide at the centre of the distribution.
3. The curve is a based on an infinite number of observations.
4. Since, there is only one maximum point, the normal curve is unimodal, i.e., has only one mode.
5. The first and third quarter are equidistant from mean.

138. (b): Solomon four Group Design: The Solomon four group test is a standard pretest-posttest two-group design and the post-test only control design. The various combinations of tested and untested groups with treatment and control groups allows the researcher to ensure that confounding variables and extraneous factors have not influenced the results.

The Post-test Only Control Design: It is a research design in which there are at least two groups, one of which does not receive a treatment or intervention and data are collected on the outcome measure after the treatment. The group does not receive the treatment of interest is the control group.

The main features of post-test are as follows:

- This type of design has two randomly assigned groups an experimental group and a control group.
- Neither group is pretested before implementing the treatment.
- The treatment is applied only to the experimental group.

One-shot Case Study: It is difficult to draw conclusions as there is no typical cause and effect relationship between the intervention and the outcome.

Correlational Design: As the name indicates, the purpose of correlational studies is to explore whether there is any relationship or interdependence between two variables or characteristics and to ascertain the degree of such relationships. The value of correlational research is to discover relationships among different phenomena with a view to predict and in some situations control their occurrence.

139. (a): Extraneous Variable: An extraneous variable is also known as artifact. In real life situations, there can be many factors or variables that may affect the outcome. These variables are termed as extraneous variables. Extraneous variables are also affecting the dependent variable, although these are not manipulated by the researcher.

They may mask the relationship between independent variable and dependent variable. Extraneous variable may directly affect the dependent variable or may combine with the independent variable to produce an affect.

Therefore, extraneous variables must be controlled so that the experimenter can determine whether or not the dependent variable changes in relation to a variation in the independent variable.

If an extraneous variable is the real reason for an outcome instead of the independent variables, then it is also known as a confounding variable because it has confused or confounded the relationship, we are interested in.

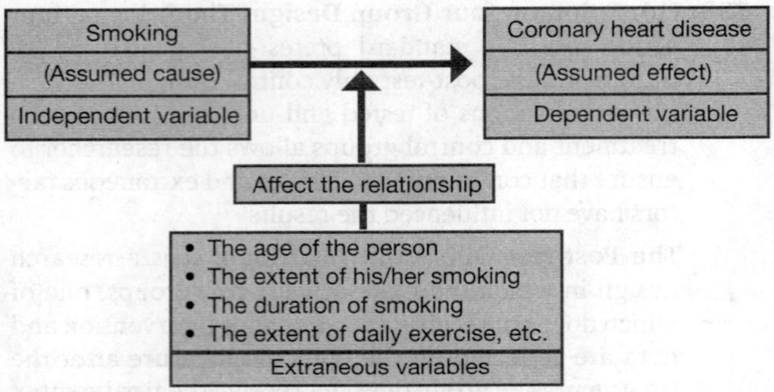

Relationship between Independent, Dependent and Extraneous Variables

140. (b): The nominal scale is also called the classification scale. It allows variables to be measured in one, two, and three subcategories according to their diversity. For example, gender can be classified into two subcategories, male and female. A variable measured at the nominal level can be used in higher–level statistics if it is converted into another form.

The result of the conversion process is called dummy variable. So, both the statements are right.

141. (d): Grounded Theory Research: It is a qualitative approach to generate and develop a theory from data that the researcher collects. Role play, simulation and diary methods are also used in qualitative research.

Descriptive Theory Research: Descriptive theory research is all about describing the phenomenon, observing and drawing conclusions from it. It is a quantitative research method. It includes surveys and fact-finding enquiries with adequate interpretation. Survey research, correlational studies and casual comparative studies are the main types of descriptive research.

Ex Post Facto Research: This type of research is used in the social sciences and in business organizations. It is conducted in context of a phenomenon after it has occurred or at the time of its occurrence. It basically deals with non-manipulated variables of a phenomenon.

Experimental Research: Experimental research is designed to establish casual relationships. It begins with a question concerning the relationship between the two variables.

142. (a): Validity in research mainly stands for the accuracy of procedures, research instruments, tests etc. Validity means that the research must be unbiased and free from any systematic errors as they impact the applicability of research. Without validity, research goes in a wrong direction.

With higher internal validity, a researcher can establish a better causal relationship between two or more variables. This is specifically true in the case of laboratory experiments where the cause-and-effect relationship is supposed to be more clearly established. The threats of internal validity are statistical regression, differential selection of subjects and experimental mortality.

143. (b): Research Problem Identification: Academic and social value of the research question should be weighed
Formulation of Research Hypothesis: Defining the variables in unambiguous terms
Design of Research: Development of a conceptual framework which is in accordance with the hypothesis of research
Data Analysis: Appropriateness of techniques and their application

144. (c): Statement I: Scientific research is systematic, controlled, empirical and a critical investigation of hypothetical prepositions. Thus, statement I is true.

Scientific research done with the aim of contributing to science in a methodical manner by systematic collection, interpretation and evaluation of data is called. The results obtained from a small group are generalized through scientific studies, and the reliability of diagnosis, treatment and applications is ascertained.

Under this, the problem should be selected first, and following that, the plan and methodology should be specified.

Classification of scientific research can be explained as the following:

Based on Data Collection Techniques	• Observation-Based • Experimental
Based on Causal Relationship	• Descriptive • Analytical
Based on Relationship with Time	• Retrospective • Prospective • Cross-Sectional
Based on the Application	• Clinical • Laboratory • Social Descriptive Research

Statement II: Population of research should be defined in qualitative and quantitative researches. Thus, statement II is false.

145. (a): Qualitative research is essentially an approach and not just a method to conduct research. It is inductive or spiral in nature and has a very different structure. The researcher starts with tentative ideas or questions, and these questions become more specific as the research progresses. The main objective of qualitative research is to develop an understanding of human beings/social sciences to know what people feel and think. Actual settings are the direct source of data, and the researcher is the key instrument in qualitative research. This type of research uses verbal data, such as words and images, in-depth interviews, focus group discussion, observation and document reviews. In qualitative research, a subjective and holistic approach is followed to understand patterns. It generally explores to know questions like 'How' and 'When'. Reports of qualitative research are narratives that include direct quotations from the participants. The purpose underlying qualitative research is directed relatively more at the depiction of reality rather than arriving at context-free generalizations.

Thus, both (A) and (R) are true, and (R) is the correct explanation of (A).

146. (b):

Reliability: In the context of research, consistency is reliability. Reliability refers to the extent to which an investigation produces consistent results. It can also be termed as verifiability. If the research yields similar results each time it is undertaken with a similar population in the given context and via similar procedures, it is said to be reliable research. The more similarity there is in the results, the more reliable is the research. The coefficient of determination is also termed as reliability coefficient.

Validity: Validity in research mainly stands for the accuracy of procedures, research instruments, tests, etc. The concept of validity is also understood by posing the question, 'Are we measuring what we originally intended to measure?'. It means that research must be unbiased and free from any systematic errors, as they may impact the applicability of the research. Without validity, research goes in the wrong direction.

The different types of validity are as follows:

(a) Internal Validity: Through high internal validity a researcher is able to establish better causal relationship between two or more variables. Internal validity is more appropriate for experiments in the laboratory where the cause-and-effect relationship is more pronounced. The extent to which a measurement is consistent with itself is called internal reliability. A variant of this, called the 'half split method', measures the extent to which all parts of the test contribute equally to the material being measured.

(b) External Validity: External validity refers to the extent to which a research result can be 'generalized' and applied to other subjects that are not under study. External factors influencing the study should be controlled. For example, in social science surveys, the response of a respondent may be influenced only by the presence of a non-participating observer.

(c) Face Validity: By face validity, we mean that surveys and questionnaires measure exactly what they should measure. For example, all participants who filled out questionnaires to measure certain personality traits agreed that the exercise appeared to be appropriate for measuring those traits.

(d) Content Validity: Content validity is the indicator measures all aspects of the construction or concept and not just a part of it.

(e) Criterion Validity: Criterion validity measures how well one measure (or indicator) predicts the outcome of another measure. It is of three types:

i. Predictive Validity: The test should make an accurate prediction of what it should predict i.e., the purpose for which the test was conducted.

ii. Concurrent Validity: When the predictor and criterion data are collected at the same time, it is called concurrent validity. For example, when one test takes the place of another test because it costs less.

iii. Post-Directive Validity: If the test is a valid measurement of something that happened earlier it is called progressive validity. For example, childhood events serve as a test for adult memories.

(f) Construct Validity: Construct validity measures the indicator hypothesis in such a way that it converges with other measures in terms of direction. For example, education level and income level converge. This indicator also allows discrimination in the opposing hypothesis.

147. (c): Convenience Sampling: The type of sampling that is simply available to the researcher by virtue of its accessibility is known as convenience sampling. Simply put, the researcher selects the easiest population members from whom to obtain information.

148. (b): Predictive Validity: In predictive validity, the researcher uses a future criterion measure, rather than a contemporary one. It is a type of criterion validity that refers to how well the measurement of one variable can predict the response of another variable.

149. (c): Statement I: The ethnographic research method is used to learn about the lives of others. It helps us understand how and why people behave differently in various societies or cultures. If we are interested in the worldview of members of a certain social group, a qualitative research strategy that is sensitive to how participant interpret their social world may be preferable.

Ethnographic research is the process of collecting data about a group of people. It's a popular technique used by anthropologists, sociologists and others who study human behaviour. It's mainly a qualitative research method, which means that it allows us to study subjects that don't lend themselves to numerical data. But it can be used to collect quantitative data as well. Thus, statement I is correct.

Statement II: Exploratory research is the process of investigating a problem that has not been studied or thoroughly investigated in the past. This type of research is usually carried out for a better understanding of the current problem, but it usually does not produce any conclusive results.

Researchers use exploratory research when trying to become familiar with an existing phenomenon and gain new insight into it to create a more precise problem. It begins on the basis of a general idea, and the results of the research are used to explore issues related to the topic of research.

In exploratory research, the process of research varies according to the discovery of new data or insights. Also known as explanatory research or the foundational theory approach, the results of this research provide answers to questions such as 'What', 'How' and 'Why'. If a researcher is interested in a topic on which little to no research has been done in the past, qualitative research may be easy to employ because there is little prior literature from which to draw leads. Thus, statement II is incorrect.

150. (a): 1. Sampling design: It is a probability sampling design. Designing the sample calls for three decisions:

i. The Sample: Who will be surveyed? It further depends upon what type of information is required.

ii. Sample Size: How many people should ideally be surveyed?

iii. Sampling Method: How should the sample be chosen? Sampling can be done by adopting either the probability or non-probability method.

Statistical Design: Pre-planned design for analysis

Observational Design: Structured or well-thought-out instruments for collection of data

Operational Design: Advanced decisions about operational procedures.

151. (c): Before and After Without Controls Design: In this design, first, a single test group or region is selected, and the dependent variable is measured before starting treatment. Then, treatment commences, and the dependent variable is measured once more after treatment.

Effect of treatment = Level of event after treatment – Level of event before treatment

This design can be represented as follows:

Test area: Level of phenomenon before treatment (X) → Treatment introduced → Level of phenomenon after treatment (Y)

Treatment Effect = (Y) – (X)

The disadvantage of such a design is that its healing effect may undergo considerable external changes over time. Thus, statement I is true.

Before and After With Control Design: In this design, two regions are selected, and the dependent variable is measured in both regions for the same time period before treatment. The treatment is then presented only in the test area, and the dependent variable is measured in both regions for a similar time period after the start of the treatment. So, the statement II is incorrect.

Treatment effect = Change in dependent variable in test area – Change in dependent variable in controlled area

This design can be represented as follows:

	Time Period I		Time Period II
Test area:	Level of phenomenon before treatment (X)	Treatment introduced →	Level of phenomenon after treatment (Y)
Control area:	Level of phenomenon without treatment (A)		Level of phenomenon without treatment (A)
	Treatment Effect = (Y – X) – (Z – A)		

152. (d): The advantages of observation as a tool of data collection are:

1. Observations are known for directness.
2. Artificiality can be minimised in observation studies.
3. Recording devices can be used in observational studies for accuracy.

153. (d): A variable is any quantity that a researcher is able to measure in some way. This could be temperature, height, age, etc. Basically, a variable is anything that contributes to the outcome or result of your experiment in any way.

Control Variable–A control variable is anything that is held constant or limited in a research study. It's a variable that is not of interest to the study's aims, but is controlled because it could influence the outcomes. For example, one control variable in the plant growth experiment could be temperature. Assume that this should be kept uniform at 25° C, so it is the duty of researcher to keep it at this uniform level.

External variable–These variables are factors that are not manipulated as part of an experiment, but they may exert some influence on the dependent variable under study.

Confounding Variable–This is an unmeasured third variable that 'confounds' (or influences) the relationship between an independent and a dependent variable. It actually suggests the presence of a spurious correlation. Confounding is a causal concept, and as such, cannot be described in terms of correlations or associations.

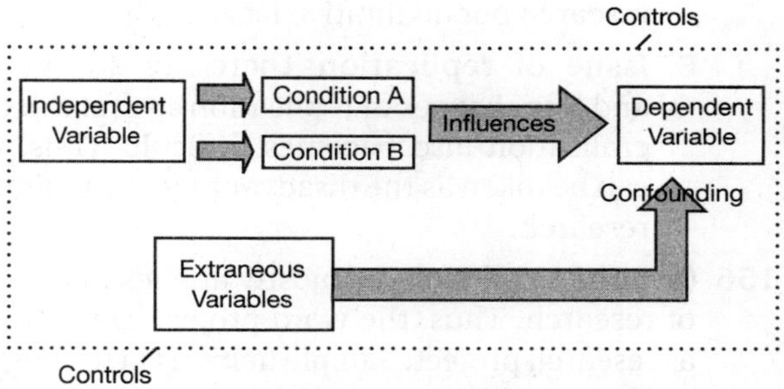

154. (b): Monadic variable is basically used in the survey research that offers individual concepts to survey respondents in isolation–one at a time. The independent findings are required for each stimulus. They provide clear detailed feedback. This is available with every automated tool. This can be compared with polyadic variables. In comparison testing several stimuli are tested simultaneously.

155. (c): There are two kinds of variables-Qualitative and Quantitative

Qualitative Variables–This is also called as a categorical variable. As the name indicates, it is not numerical. This describes data that fits into categories. These are all qualitative variables as they have no natural order.

The examples are

Skin colours–White, Yellow, Brown, Black

States–Haryana, Punjab, Manipur, Kerala

Quantitative variables–They have a value and they can be added, subtracted, divided or multiplied.

Now look at the detailed discussion in context of its disadvantages.

A. **Too sensitive to context**–The main objective of qualitative or any kind of research is to connect with the theme or basic idea. It is basically behavioural in nature.

B. **Open To Debate**–It is also positive reflection as it is linked with the transparency.

C. **Too subjective**–Qualitative can always be somewhat subjective but being too much subjective is its negative characteristic as the personal viewpoint becomes very important.

D. **Difficult to generalise**–Though generalisation is the main objective of any kind of research but qualitative lacks in that.

E. **Issue of replication**–There are always less and less chances of replication so that the generalisation also becomes difficult. Thus, this can be taken as the disadvantage of qualitative research.

156. (a): The word 'sample' mostly applies in the case of research. Thus, the word project can be taken as research project. Sample helps us in finding the truth or getting us very close to the truth. Sample size calculation and determination are imperative to the researcher to determine the right number of respondents, keeping in mind the research study's quality.

The sample is the miniature version of the population that reflects the desired features. That helps us in saving time and associated costs.

In qualitative studies, the study is mostly subjective, and the sample size may have to be kept small as we want to do their detailed analysis.

Thus, the population size matters, so is the confidence level (90%, 95% or 99% to reflect upon the accuracy and confidence of results), the margin of error (confidence interval), standard deviation from mean (also called as sigma that reflects upon the variability of a distribution of population) – all these things matter to a researcher.

Necessary Sample Size = (Z-score)2 * StdDev*(1-StdDev) / (margin of error)2

The precision of obtaining the results from population may ask for changing the sample size. Thus, the population variability is important. If the population is homogeneous, a researcher can manage with smaller sample and vice versa. We have to determine if the increased accuracy is more important than the cost.

There can be probability (random and objective) or non-probability (non random and more subjective) sampling techniques.

The choices D and E are not or least important for a researcher as research should always be objective.

157. (b): Meta-analysis intends to take a quick review of multiple research studies on basically the same or closely related problem or issue. combines the results of multiple scientific studies. It is basically a quantitative, formal, epidemiological study design that is based on randomized, controlled trials.

Content Analysis–this is basically used in qualitative studies where the answers may be subjective which are based on the personal opinion. The language used by the respondents in the qualitative research (such as case studies) may be different and a researcher need to find the basic idea or description. This is called content analysis.

Semantic Differential–A semantic differential can be used for the structuring of attitudes, most likely in qualitative studies. This survey or questionnaire rating scale asks people to rate a product, event, or any 'entity' within the frames of a multi-point rating option. These survey answering options are grammatically on opposite adjectives at each end. As they are opposite to each other on the two ends of a continuum, this may be called as bipolar adjective.

Social Network Analysis–The dyad definition is the close relationship of two people over a long period with many interactions in different settings. The most basic requirement for dyad sociology is that there are two members of the group. The dyadic communication definition pertains to how the two group members interact with each other. German sociologist Georg Simmel studied how group dynamics changed based on the size of the group.

158. (c): Internal validity is concerned with correctly concluding that an independent variable and not some extraneous variable is responsible for a change in the dependent variable.

External validity refers to the generalizability and also to randomisation of the treatment/condition outcomes.

A. **Randomisation** - We need unbiased and objective in our research, and randomisation helps in that. In simple terms, randomization eliminates predictability. It follows the theory of probability. This removes the possibility of any kind of human interruption by the researcher. Randomization eliminates accidental bias, including selection bias.

   Assume that a teacher has to select 10 students out of 100 for a research purpose, they can be any ten. Everyone in the class stands 1/100 chance of selection which are equal for anyone. This equal chance of being selected is called as randomisation.

B. **Generalisation** – It means that results of a research study are applicable to the outer world. That is called as the external validity.

C. **Maturation** – The processes within subjects act as a function of the passage of time. This happens when study is conducted on people which are base of research findings. If that element changes over a period of time, it threatens the internal validity of the research.

D. **History** – This refers to any event other than the 'independent variable'. History--the specific events which occur between the first and second measurement.

E. **Instrumentation** – The reliability of the instrument used to gauge the dependent variable or manipulate the independent variable may change in the course of an experiment. Thus, internal validity may be threatened.

Both A and B facilitate the objectivity, unbiasedness and validity of research. The question is about the threat to internal validity in research. In this case, these factors also matter for future questions.

1. **Testing** - first test affecting the subsequent tests
2. **Statistical regression** - candidates with extreme scores, for example, choosing the poorest or the most intelligent students in the class
3. **Experimental mortality** - that is the loss of subjects
4. **Selection of subjects** - the biases which may result in selection of comparison groups. Randomisation can help in minimisation of this effect.

When the sample size is small, randomization may lead to Simpson Paradox. Similarly, the students can study John Henry effect for additional knowledge that is not conducive to internal validity.

The NET aspirants may remember the following aspects which apply on external validity for future questions.

1. Reactive or interaction effect of testing
2. Interaction effects of selection biases and the experimental variable
3. Reactive effects of experimental arrangements
4. Multiple treatment interference

159. (b): Hermeneutics is the art of understanding and interpretation of texts, specifically religious ones. Hermeneutics is philosophical and theological in nature. The history of hermeneutics stretches across epochs, methods and all the disciplines in the humanities, social sciences, and even the natural sciences. It can be identified with four major strands: conservative, critical, radical, and moderate.

Sociology is linked with society, groups and social institutions. Anthropology is the study of human beings in its entirety. Economics deals with wealth related issues in the form of micro and macro- economics.

160. (b): The question papers are made with the perspective of evaluation and assessment of candidates.

Objectivity – This can be taken as the main element of a good question paper. They should be constructed for the sake of qualifying an exam or the ranking of candidates.

Subjectivity – This means that question paper setter may be biased so that a particular set of candidates get benefited from this.

Reliability – This refers to the consistency of a measure (whether the results can be reproduced under the same conditions).

Validition – This refers to the accuracy of a measure (whether the results really do represent what they are supposed to measure).

From a research perspective, objectivity, reliability and validity are important characteristics.

161. (a): Statement I – Qualitative data is powerful as the most of this is to be collected from human resources whose behaviour is always complex and dynamic. Even the social context is so dynamic and changeable. The behavioural context may even change from one point of time to another. Qualitative data is basically non numeric, and it holds conceptual information. We use their feedback or response to capture their themes and patterns. The answering research questions is difficult. Thus, the whole scene is based on sensitive social, historical and temporal (time based) context.

Statement II – Obtaining right kind of information in a set of complex situations through customer interviews, surveys, and feedback. Context sensitivity takes the surroundings into consideration while planning for the research. It takes into account community values and assets.

We can look at the following types of approaches to deal with the qualitative data so that we get the right kind of information. This may be useful for the future questions.

1. **Content analysis** – This element examines and quantifies the presence of certain words, subjects, and concepts in text, image, video, or audio messages. The method transforms qualitative input into quantitative data to help you make reliable conclusions. This can be used for quantitative data as well.
2. **Thematic analysis** – This can only be applied to qualitative data, and focuses on identifying patterns and 'themes'. This can be done with innovative tools such as Dovetail and Thematic.
3. **Narrative analysis** – This method used to interpret research participants' stories—things like testimonials, case studies, interviews, and other text or visual data.
4. **Grounded theory analysis** – This is a method of conducting qualitative research to develop theories by examining real-world data.
5. **Discourse analysis** – This is the act of researching the underlying meaning of qualitative data. It involves the observation of texts, audio, and videos to study the relationships between the information and its context.

162. (c): Historical research is basically a descriptive study, which mostly is a qualitative study.

The problem identification is the first thing that should be done in any research. So, this can be taken as the main objective.

Analytical synthesis means first probing all the aspects of research study and then integrating them in a desirable manner.

Universal Generalisation is an act of reasoning that involves drawing broad inferences from particular observations. It is widely-acknowledged as a quality standard in quantitative research. The chances of generalisation are limited in qualitative research.

163. (d): Phenomenology - This is a qualitative research approach that seeks to understand and describe the universal essence of a phenomenon. The approach investigates the everyday experiences of human beings while suspending the researchers' preconceived assumptions about the phenomenon.

Ethnography – In this qualitative research, a researcher or an ethnographer study a particular social/cultural group with the aim to understand it better. They actively participate in the group in order to gain an insider's perspective of the group. He may try to get the equivalent experience that is similar to the group members. There are experiences relating to process, participation, data collection, interviews, and the analysis of documents and artifacts.

Ethnomethodology – This is the study of how social order is produced in and through processes of social interaction. It generally seeks to provide an alternative to mainstream sociological approaches.

Symbolic interactionism – This counsels us that a complex social situation like triangulated research involves much more than simply forging a rational design among fairly like-minded colleagues, since participants must work hard to create a working, shared understanding of their research.

164. (c): When a researcher cannot control variables and can only report what has happened or is happening, this type of research is known as Ex post facto research.

165. (c): Assume that we check that a new fertilizer (the independent variable) makes plants grow taller (the dependent variable). We also make an assumption that other factors, like sunlight, water, or soil quality, are not influencing the plant's growth. We are focused only on the fertilizer variable. The concept that mainly relates to the issue of causality in research is internal validity. We try to avoid other confounding variables.

166. (b): The stratified sampling provides a more accurate and comprehensive picture, specifically, if population is 'diversified'. And also, the researcher is more interested to make inferences about specific subgroups within a larger population. They may also want to ensure that important subgroups are adequately represented in the sample. This stratified sampling approach fits better into diversified Indian population than that of Japan.

167. (c): Statement I is correct but Statement II is incorrect.

Debriefing is crucial in research for ethical integrity and participant understanding. Debriefing is not an 'informed consent' which is taken before the study. Informing the participants earlier may make the participants unwilling to cooperate in the research due to some reasons or manipulate the research, so debriefing becomes important. For instance, in a medical study on a new pain medication, participants are informed post-study about the use of placebos (instead of actual medications). This clarifies the study's purpose and methodology. This enhances transparency, trust, and the validity of the research. The participants may cooperate at a later stage also.

168. (a): Scales of measurement without ranking is not possible in the nominal scale. This is used for categorizing or labelling variables without any quantitative value. For example, gender (male, female), nationality, or hair colour. Since it is purely for categorization, there is no inherent order or ranking in the nominal scale.

169. (c): Sociology: Survey research involves collecting data through questionnaires or interviews, which is a common method used in sociology to understand various social phenomena like demographics, attitudes, and behaviours. We need to recall that positivism was also started in Sociology by Auguste Comte.

Physics, History, and Hermeneutics primarily rely on different methods like observation, analysis of historical documents, and interpretation of texts, respectively.

170. (a): Social reality is basically the set of shared beliefs, norms, and constructs which are collectively accepted by individuals in a society. With this, they try to interpret and understand their social world. The caste system in India is an example of this concept. The surveys, interviews, or ethnographic studies are the examples of social research that is done for the sake of social reality.

171. (d): Higher level of abstraction: The abstraction focuses on essentials and underlying principles. It manages complexity and it fosters on creative and innovative thinking. This may take place in art, education philosophies, mathematics, social sciences and so on.

Abstraction is basically cognitive and thus, automatically happens at the highest level of thinking. Grand theories in social sciences, like functionalism or conflict theory, aim to explain broad patterns and dynamics in societies. This requires operating at a level of abstraction that transcends specific contexts and focuses on general principles.

Other lower options may be used for specific hypotheses or research questions within a broader theoretical framework.

172. (d): This includes B, C, D and E.

A. **Non-purposive:** Non-purposive usually means non probability. Non-purposive sampling can still be used in certain qualitative research scenarios, especially in exploratory or preliminary phases.

B. **Causes and consequences:** We try to understand the relationships between phenomena.

C. **Predictive:** Making predictions is mainly the duty of quantitative research.

D. **Evaluative:** This is often linked with subjective elements and involves content analysis and interpretation.

E. **Descriptive:** They aim to provide detailed descriptions and understandings of phenomena, behaviours, experiences, or social contexts.

Here, A, D and E appeal to qualitative research questions. (Though there is scope of subjective differentiations in this question).

173. (d)

Statement I: This states that 'Time and cost are not relevant in determining the sample size' is false. The researchers often need to balance the desired accuracy of the results with the available time and resources

Statement II: Unit non-response (persons, organisations etc) does not matter in deciding the sampling error).

Item non response means partial availability of information. The non-response can be biased also and thus contribute to sampling error.

Thus, the correct answer is (b). Both Statement I and Statement II are false.

174. (c): Qualitative research is highly dependent upon contextual understanding, so we have to make high level of efforts to get meaning and data. Researchers must carefully sift through the data to identify patterns, themes, and insights, which can be subjective and complex.

On the other hand, quantitative research deals with measurable data, it provides us the data in a structured form, we simply need to apply some statistical technique to get the data.

175. (b): Footnotes are used to provide additional information, citations, or clarifications to the text without interrupting the main flow of the document. They are typically numbered and appear at the bottom of the page where the reference is made.

176. (a): We need to keep in mind that Quantitative is mainly about deductive, scientific and experimental research, we are in better position to apply null hypothesis here that is based on numerical data.

177. (b): Independent variable is a variable that is manipulated or controlled by the researcher and causes changes in another variable (the dependent variable). It has a causal effect on the dependent variable.

CHAPTER 3

Comprehension

TOPICS OF IMPORTANCE

- Comprehension Passages from 2014 to 2021

Read the following passage carefully and answer the questions from 1 to 5:

Traditional Indian values must be viewed both from the angle of the individual and from that of the geographically delimited agglomeration of people or groups enjoying a common system of leadership which we call the 'State'. The Indian 'State's' special feature is the peaceful, or perhaps mostly peaceful, coexistence of social groups of various historical provenances that mutually adhere in a geographical, economic, and political sense, without ever assimilating to each other in social terms, in ways of thinking, or even in language. Modern Indian law will determine certain rules, especially in relation to the regime of the family, upon the basis of how the loincloth is tied, or how the turban is worn, for this may identify the litigants as members of a regional group and therefore, as participants in its traditional law, though their ancestors left the region three or four centuries earlier. The use of the word 'State' above must not mislead us. There was no such thing as a conflict between the individual and the State, at least before foreign governments became established, just as there was no concept of state 'sovereignty' or of any church-and-state dichotomy.

Modern Indian 'secularism' has an admittedly peculiar feature as it requires the state to make a fair distribution of attention and support amongst all religions. These blessed aspects of India's famed tolerance (Indian kings so rarely persecuted religious groups that the exceptions prove the rule) at once struck Portuguese and other European visitors to the West Coast of India in the sixteenth century, and the impression made upon them in this and other ways gave rise, at one remove, to the basic constitution of Thomas More's Utopia. There is little about modern India that strikes one at once as Utopian. However, the insistence upon the inculcation of norms and the absence of bigotry and institutionalized exploitation of human or natural resources are two very different features that link the realities of India and her tradition with the essence of all Utopians.

1. Which of the following is a special feature of the Indian State? **[Jun 2014]**

(a) Peaceful coexistence of people under a common system of leadership.

(b) Peaceful coexistence of social groups of different historical provenances attached to each other in a geographical, economic and political sense.

(c) Social integration of all groups.

(d) Cultural assimilation of all social groups.

2. The author uses the word 'State' to highlight **[Jun 2014]**
   (a) Antagonistic relationship between the state and the individual throughout the period of history.
   (b) Absence of conflict between the state and the individuals up to a point in time.
   (c) The concept of state sovereignty.
   (d) Dependence on religion.
3. Which one is the peculiar feature of modern Indian 'secularism'? **[Jun 2014]**
   (a) No discrimination on religious considerations.
   (b) Total indifference to religion.
   (c) No space for social identity.
   (d) Disregard for social law.
4. The basic construction of Thomas More's Utopia was inspired by **[Jun 2014]**
   (a) Indian tradition of religious tolerance.
   (b) Persecution of religious groups by Indian rulers.
   (c) Social inequality in India.
   (d) European perception of Indian state.
5. What is the striking feature of modern India? **[Jun 2014]**
   (a) A replica of utopian State.
   (b) Uniform laws.
   (c) Adherence to traditional values.
   (d) Absence of bigotry.

Read the following passage carefully and answer questions 6 to 10.

The literary distaste for politics, however, seems to be focussed not so much on the largely murky practice of politics in itself as a subject of literary representation but rather more on how it is often depicted in literature, i.e., on the very politics of such representation. A political novel often turns out to be not merely a novel about politics but a novel with a politics of its own, for it seeks not merely to show us how things are but has fairly definite ideas about how things should be and precisely what one should think and do in order to make things move in that desired direction. In short, it seeks to convert and enlist the reader to a particular cause or ideology; it often is (in an only too familiar phrase) not literature but propaganda. This is said to violate the very spirit of literature which is to broaden our understanding of the world and the range of our sympathies rather than to narrow them down through partisan commitment. As John Keats said, 'We hate poetry that has a palpable design upon us'.

Another reason why politics does not seem amenable to the highest kind of literary representation seems to arise from the fact that politics by its very nature is constituted of ideas and ideologies. If political situations do not lend themselves to happy literary treatment, then political ideas present perhaps an even greater problem in this regard. Literature, it is argued, is about human experiences rather than about intellectual abstractions; it deals in what is called the 'felt reality' of human flesh and blood, and in sap and savour *(rasa)* rather than in arid and lifeless ideas. In an extensive discussion of the matter in her book *Ideas and the Novel,* the American novelist Mary McCarthy observed that 'ideas are still today felt to be unsightly in the novel' though that was not so in 'former days', i.e., in the 18th and 19th centuries. Her formulation of the precise nature of the incompatibility between ideas on the one hand and the novel on the other betrays perhaps a divided conscience in the matter and a sense of dilemma shared by many writers and readers, 'An idea cannot have loose ends, but a novel, I almost think, needs them. Nevertheless, there is enough in common for the novelists to feel... the attraction of ideas while taking up arms against them—most often with weapons of mockery.'

6. According to the passage, a political novel often turns out to be a **[Dec 2014]**
   (a) Literary distaste for politics.
   (b) Literary representation of politics.
   (c) Novel with its own politics.
   (d) Depiction of murky practice of politics.
7. A political novel reveals **[Dec 2014]**
   (a) Reality of the things.
   (b) Writer's perception.
   (c) Particular ideology of the readers.
   (d) The spirit of literature.
8. The constructs of politics by its nature is **[Dec 2014]**
   (a) Prevalent political situation.
   (b) Ideas and ideologies.
   (c) Political propaganda.
   (d) Understanding of human nature.

9. Literature deals with **[Dec 2014]**
(a) Human experiences in politics.
(b) Intellectual abstractions.
(c) Dry and empty ideas.
(d) Felt reality of human life.

10. The observation of the novelist, Mary McCarthy reveals **[Dec 2014]**
(a) Unseen felt ideas of today in the novel.
(b) Dichotomy of conscience on political ideas and novels.
(c) Compatibility between idea and novel.
(d) Endless ideas and novels.

Read the following passage carefully and answer the questions from 11 to 16.

Storytelling is not in our genes. Neither it is an evolutionary history. It is the essence of what makes us human.

Human beings progress by telling stories. One event can result in a great variety of stories being told about it. Sometimes those stories differ greatly. Which stories are picked up and repeated and which ones are dropped and forgotten often determine how we progress. Our history, knowledge and understanding are all the collections of the few stories that survive. This includes the stories that we tell each other about the future and how the future will turn out depends partly, possibly largely, on which stories we collectively choose to believe.

Some stories are designed to spread fear and concern. This is because some storytellers feel that there is a need to raise some tensions. Some stories are frightening and they are like totemic warnings, 'Fail to act now and we are all doomed'. Then, there are stories that indicate that all will be fine so long as we leave everything up to a few especially able adults. Currently, this trend is being led by those who call themselves 'rational optimists'. They tend to claim that it is human nature to compete and to succeed and also to profit at the expense of others. However, the rational optimists, do not realize how humanity has progressed overtime through amiable social networks and how large groups work in less selfishness and in the process accommodate rich and poor, high and low alike. This aspect in storytelling is considered by the 'Practical Possibles', who sit between those who say all is fine and cheerful and be individualistic in your approach to a successful future, and those who ordain pessimism and fear that we are doomed.

What the future holds for us is which stories we hold on to and how we act on them.

Answer the following questions.

11. Our knowledge is a collection of **[Jun 2015]**
(a) All stories that we have heard during our lifetime.
(b) Some stories that we remember.
(c) A few stories that survive.
(d) Some important stories.

12. Story-telling is **[Jun 2015]**
(a) An art
(b) A science
(c) In our genes
(d) The essence of what makes us human

13. How the future will turn out to be, depends upon the stories **[Jun 2015]**
(a) We collectively choose to believe in.
(b) Which are repeatedly narrated.
(c) Designed to spread fear and tension.
(d) Designed to make prophecy.

14. Rational optimists **[Jun 2015]**
(i) Look for opportunities.
(ii) Are sensible and cheerful.
(iii) Are selfishly driven.

Identify the correct answer from the codes given below:
(a) (i), (ii) and (iii)
(b) (i) only
(c) (i) and (ii) only
(d) (ii) and (iii) only

15. Humans become less selfish when **[Jun 2015]**
(a) They work in large groups.
(b) They listen to frightening stories.
(c) They listen to cheerful stories.
(d) They work in solitude.

16. 'Practical possibles' are the ones who **[Jun 2015]**
(a) Follow midway path
(b) Are doom-mongers
(c) Are self-centre
(d) Are cheerful and carefree

Read the following passage carefully and answer the questions from 17 to 21.

I did that thing recently where you have to sign a big card—which is a horror unto itself, especially as the keeper of the Big Card was leaning over me at the time. Suddenly I was on the spot, a rabbit in the headlights, torn between doing a fun message or some sort of in-joke or a drawing. Instead overwhelmed by the myriad options available to me, I decided to just write 'Good luck, best, Joel'.

It was then that I realized, to my horror, that I had forgotten how to write. My entire existence is 'tap letters into computer'. My shopping lists are hidden in the notes function of my phone. If I need to remember something I send an e-mail to myself. A pen is something I chew when I am struggling to think. Paper is something I pile beneath my laptop to make it a more comfortable height for me to type on.

A poll of 1000 teens by the stationers, Bic found that one in 10 do not own a pen, a third have never written a letter, and half of 13 to 19 years old have never been forced to sit down and write a thank you letter. More than 80% have never written a love letter, 56% do not have letter paper at home, and a quarter have never known the unique torture of writing a birthday card. The most a teen ever has to use a pen is on an exam paper.

Bic, have you heard of mobile phones? Have you heard of e-mail, Facebook, and snap chatting? This is the future. Pens are dead. Paper is dead. Handwriting is a relic.

'Handwriting is one of the most creative outlets we have and should be given the same importance as other art forms such as sketching, painting or photography'.

Answer the following questions:

17. When confronted with signing a big card, the author felt like 'a rabbit in the headlight'. What does this phrase mean? **[Dec 2015]**

(a) A state of confusion
(b) A state of pleasure
(c) A state of anxiety
(d) A state of pain

18. According to the author, which one is not the most creative outlet of pursuit? **[Dec 2015]**

(a) Handwriting
(b) Photography
(c) Sketching
(d) Reading

19. The entire existence of the author revolves round **[Dec 2015]**

(i) Computer
(ii) Mobile phone
(iii) Typewriter

Identify the correct answer from the codes given below.

(a) (ii) only
(b) (i) and (ii) only
(c) (i), (ii) and (iii)
(d) (ii) and (iii) only

20. How many teens, as per the Bic survey, do not own a pen? **[Dec 2015]**

(a) 800 (b) 560
(c) 500 (d) 100

21. What is the main concern of the author? **[Dec 2015]**

(a) The teens use social networks for communication.
(b) The teens use mobile phones.
(c) The teens use computer.
(d) The teens have forgotten the art of handwriting.

Read the following passage carefully and answer question numbers from 22 to 27.

In terms of labour, for decades, the relatively low cost and high quality of Japanese workers conferred considerable competitive advantage across numerous durable goods and consumer electronics industries (For example, machinery, automobiles, televisions, radios). Then labour-based advantages shifted to South Korea, then to Malaysia, Mexico and other nations. Today, China appears to be capitalizing best on the basis of labour. Japanese firms still remain competitive in markets for such durable goods, electronics and other products, but the labour force is no longer sufficient for competitive advantage over manufacturers in other industrializing nations. Such shifting of labour-based advantage is clearly not limited to manufacturing industries. Today, a huge number of IT and service jobs are moving from Europe and North America to India, Singapore, and other countries with relatively well-educated, low-cost workforces possessing technical skills. However, as educational levels and technical skills continue to rise in other countries, India, Singapore and other nations enjoying labour-based competitive advantage today are likely to find such advantage cannot be sustained through emergence of new competitors. In terms of capital, for centuries, the days of gold coins and later even paper money restricted financial flows. Subsequently, regional concentrations were formed where large banks, industries and markets coalesced. But today, capital flows internationally at rapid speed. Global commerce no longer requires regional interactions among business players. Regional capital concentrations in places, such as New York, London and Tokyo still persist, of course, but the capital concentrated there is no longer sufficient for competitive advantage over other capitalists distributed worldwide. Only if an organization is able to combine, integrate and apply its resources (For example, land, labour, capital, IT) in an effective manner that is not readily imitable by competitors can such an organization enjoy competitive advantage sustainable overtime. In a knowledge-based theory of the firm, this idea is extended to view organizational knowledge as a resource with at least the same level of power and importance as the traditional economic inputs. An organization with superior knowledge can achieve competitive advantage in markets that appreciate the application of such knowledge. Semiconductors, genetic engineering, pharmaceuticals, software, military warfare and like knowledge-intensive competitive arenas provide both time-proven and current examples. Consider semiconductors (For example, computer chips), which are made principally of sand and common metals. These ubiquitous and powerful electronic devices are designed within common office buildings, using commercially available tools and fabricated within factories in many industrialized nations. Hence, land is not the key competitive resource in the semiconductor industry.

Based on the passage answer the following questions.

22. How can an organization enjoy competitive advantage sustainable overtime? **[Jul 2016]**
- (a) Through regional capital flows.
- (b) Through regional interactions among business players.
- (c) By making large banks, industries and markets coalesced.
- (d) By effective use of various instrumentalities.

23. What is required to ensure competitive advantages in specific markets? **[Jul 2016]**
- (a) Access to capital
- (b) Common office buildings
- (c) Superior knowledge
- (d) Common metals

24. The passage also mentions about the trend of **[Jul 2016]**
- (a) Global financial flow.
- (b) Absence of competition in manufacturing industry.
- (c) Regionalization of capitalists.
- (d) Organizational incompatibility.

25. What does the author lay stress on in the passage? **[Jul 2016]**
- (a) International commerce
- (b) Labour-intensive industries
- (c) Capital resource management
- (d) Knowledge-driven competitive advantage

26. Which country enjoyed competitive advantages in automobile industry for decades? **[Jul 2016]**
- (a) South Korea
- (b) Japan
- (c) Mexico
- (d) Malaysia

27. Why labour-based competitive advantages of India and Singapore cannot be sustained in IT and service sectors? **[Jul 2016]**
- (a) Due to diminishing levels of skill.
- (b) Due to capital-intensive technology making inroads.
- (c) Because of new competitors.
- (d) Because of shifting of labour-based advantage in manufacturing industries.

Read the following passage carefully and answer questions from 28 to 33.

The last Great War, which nearly shook the foundations of the modern world, had little impact on Indian literature beyond aggravating the popular revulsions against violence and adding to growing disillusionment with the 'humane pretensions' of the Western World. This was eloquently voiced in Tagore's poems and his last testament, 'Crisis in Civilization'. The Indian intelligentsia was in a state of moral dilemma. On the one hand, it could not help sympathizing with the England's dogged courage in the hour of peril, with the Russians fighting with their backs on the wall against ruthless Nazi hordes, and with the China groaning under the heel of Japanese militarism. On the other hand, their own country was practically under the military occupation of their own soil and the Indian army under Subhas Bose was trying from the opposite camp to liberate their country. No creative impulse could issue from such confusion of loyalties. One would imagine that the achievement of Indian independence in 1947, which came in the wake of the Allies victory and was followed by collapse of colonialism in the neighbouring countries of South East Asia, would have released an upsurge of the creative energy. No doubt it did, but it was soon submerged in the great agony of partition with the inhuman slaughter of innocents and the uprooting of the millions of the people from their homeland followed by the martyrdom of Mahatma Gandhi. These tragedies along with Pakistan's invasion of Kashmir and its later atrocities in Bangladesh, did indeed provoke a pregnant writing, particularly in the languages of the regions most affected, Bengali, Hindi, Kashmiri, Punjabi, Sindhi and Urdu. Both poignant or passionate writing does not by itself make great literature. What reserves of enthusiasm and confidence served these disasters have been mainly absorbed in the task of national reconstruction and economic development. Great literature has always emerged out of chains of convulsions. Indian literature is richer today in terms of volume, range and variety than it ever was in the past.

28. What was the impact of the last great war on Indian literature? **[Jan 2017]**
(a) It had no impact.
(b) It aggravated popular revulsion against violence.
(c) It shook the foundations of literature.
(d) It offered eloquent support to the Western World.

29. What did Tagore articulate in his last testament? **[Jan 2017]**
(a) Offered support to Subhas Bose.
(b) Exposed the humane pretensions of the Western World.
(c) Expressed loyalty to England.
(d) Encouraged the liberation of countries.

30. What was the stance of Indian intelligentsia during the period of great war? **[Jan 2017]**
(a) Indifference to Russia's plight.
(b) They favoured Japanese militarism.
(c) They prompted creativity out of confused loyalties.
(d) They expressed sympathy for England's dogged courage.

31. Identify the factor responsible for the submergence creative energy in Indian literature. **[Jan 2017]**
(a) Military occupation of one's own soil.
(b) Resistance to colonial occupation.
(c) Great agony of partition.
(d) Victory of allies.

32. What was the aftermath that survived tragedies in Kashmir and Bangladesh? **[Jan 2017]**
(a) Suspicion of other countries
(b) Continuance of rivalry
(c) Menace of war
(d) National reconstruction

33. The passage has the message that **[Jan 2017]**
(a) Disasters are inevitable.
(b) Great literature emerges out of chains of convulsions.
(c) Indian literature does not have a marked landscape.
(d) Literature has no relation with war and independence.

Read the following passage carefully and answer Questions from 34 to 38.

Climate change is considered to be one of the most serious threats to sustainable development with adverse impacts on the environment, human health, food security, economic activity, natural resources and physical infrastructure. Global climate varies naturally. According to the Intergovernmental Panel on Climate Change (IPCC), the effects of climate change have already been observed, and scientific findings indicate that precautionary and prompt action is necessary. Vulnerability to climate change is not just a function of geography or dependence on natural resources, whereas it also has social, economic and political dimensions which influence how climate change affects different groups. Poor people rarely have insurance to cover loss of property due to natural calamities, i.e., drought, floods, super cyclones, etc. The poor communities are already struggling to cope with the existing challenges of poverty and climate variability and climate change could push many beyond their ability to cope or even survive. It is vital that these communities are helped to adapt to the changing dynamics of nature. Adaptation is a process through which societies make themselves better able to cope with an uncertain future. Adapting to climate change entails taking the right measures to reduce the negative effects of climate change (or exploit the positive ones) by making appropriate adjustments and changes. These range from technological options such as increased sea defences or flood-proof houses on stilts to behavioural change at the individual level, such as reducing water use in times of drought. Other strategies include early warning systems for extreme events, better water management, improved risk management, various insurance options and biodiversity conservation. Because of the speed at which climate change is happening due to global temperature rise, it is urgent that the vulnerability of developing countries to climate change is reduced and their capacity to adapt is increased and national adaptation plans are implemented. Adapting to climate change will entail adjustments and changes at every level from community to national and international. Communities must build their resilience, including adopting appropriate technologies while making the most of traditional knowledge, and diversifying their livelihoods to cope with current and future climate stress. Local coping strategies and knowledge need to be used in synergy with government and local interventions. The need of adaptation interventions depends on national circumstances. There is a large body of knowledge and experience within local communities on coping with climatic variability and extreme weather events. Local communities have always aimed to adapt to variations in their climate. To do so, they have made preparations based on their resources and their knowledge accumulated through experience of past weather patterns. This includes times when they have also been forced to react to and recover from extreme events, such as floods, drought and hurricanes. Local coping strategies are an important element of planning for adaptation. Climate change is leading communities to experience climatic extremes more frequently, as well as new climate conditions and extremes. Traditional knowledge can help to provide efficient, appropriate and time-tested ways of advising and enabling adaptation to climate change in communities who are feeling the effects of climate changes due to global warming.

34. Given below are the factors of vulnerability of poor people to climate change. Select the code that contains the correct answer. **[Nov 2017]**

(A) Their dependence on natural resources
(B) Geographical attributes
(C) Lack of financial resources
(D) Lack of traditional knowledge

Codes:

(a) (A), (B) and (C) (b) (B), (C) and (D)
(c) (A), (B), (C) and (D) (d) (C) only

35. Adaptation as a process enables societies to cope with **[Nov 2017]**

(A) An uncertain future
(B) Adjustments and changes
(C) Negative impact of climate change
(D) Positive impact of climate change

Select the most appropriate answer from the following code.

(a) (A), (B), (C) and (D)
(b) (A) and (C)
(c) (B), (C) and (D)
(d) (C) only

36. To address the challenge of climate change, developing countries urgently require **[Nov 2017]**

(a) Imposition of climate change tax.
(b) Implementation of national adaptation policy at their level.
(c) Adoption of short-term plans.
(d) Adoption of technological solutions.

37. The traditional knowledge should be used through **[Nov 2017]**

(a) Its dissemination.
(b) Improvement in national circumstances.
(c) Synergy between government and local interventions.
(d) Modern technology.

38. The main focus of the passage is on **[Nov 2017]**

(a) Combining traditional knowledge with appropriate technology.
(b) Coordination between regional and national efforts.
(c) Adaptation to climate change.
(d) Social dimensions of climate change.

Reading Comprehension: Read the following passage carefully and answer questions from 39 to 43.

If India has to develop her internal strengths, the nation has to focus on the technological imperatives, keeping in mind the three dynamic dimensions, such as the people, the overall economy and the strategic interests. These technological imperatives also take into account a 'fourth' dimensions, time, and offshoot of modern-day dynamism in business, trade and technology that leads to continually shifting targets. We believe that technological strengths are especially crucial in dealing with this fourth dimension underlying continuous change in the aspirations of the people, the economy in the global context and the strategic interests. The progress of technology lies at the heart of human history. Technological strengths are the key to creating more productive employment in an increasingly competitive market place and to continually upgrade human skills. Without a pervasive use of technologies, we cannot achieve overall development of our people in the years to come. The direct linkages of technology to the nation's strategic strengths are becoming more and more clear, especially since 1990s. India's own strength in a number of core areas still puts it in a position of reasonable strength in geopolitical context. Any nation aspiring to become a developed one needs to have strengths in various strategic technologies and also the ability to continually upgrade them through its own creative strengths. For people-oriented actions as well, whether for the creation of large-scale productive employment or for ensuring nutritional and health security for people, or for better living conditions, technology is the only vital input. The absence of greater technological impetus could lead to lower productivity and wastage of precious natural resources. Activities with low productivity or low value addition, in the final analysis hurt the poorest most important. India, aspiring to become a major economic power in terms of trade and increase in GDP, cannot succeed on the strength of turnkey projects designed and built abroad or only through large-scale imports of plant machinery, equipment and know-how. Even while being alive to the short-term realities, medium and long-term strategies to develop core technological strengths within our industry are vital for envisioning a developed India.

39. According to the above passage, which of the following are indicative of the fourth dimension? **[Jul 2018]**

(A) Aspirations of peo[illegible]
(B) Modern-day dynamism
(C) Economy in the global context
(D) Strategic interests

Select the correct ans[illegible]er from the codes given below:

(a) (A), (B) and (C) only
(b) (B), (C) and (D) only
(c) (A), (C) and (D) only
(d) (A), (B) and (D) only

40. More productive employment demands **[Jul 2018]**

(a) Pervasive use of technology
(b) Limiting competitive market place
(c) Geopolitical considerations
(d) Large industries

41. Absence of technology would lead to **[Jul 2018]**

(A) Less pollution
(B) Wastage of precious natural resources
(C) Low value addition
(D) Hurting the poorest most

Select the correct answer from the codes given below:

(a) (A), (B) and (C) only
(b) (B), (C) and (D) only
(c) (A), (B) and (D) only
(d) (A), (C) and (D) only

42. The advantage of technological inputs would result in **[Jul 2018]**

(a) Unbridled technological growth.
(b) Importing plant machinery.
(c) Sideling environmental issues.
(d) Lifting our people to a life of dignity.

43. Envisioning a developed India requires **[Jul 2018]**

(a) Aspiration to become a major economic player.
(b) Dependence upon projects designed abroad.
(c) Focus on short-term projects.
(d) Development of core technological strengths.

Read the following passage carefully and answer questions from 44 to 48.

It has to be noted that, although certain overall results had been obtained in the matter of economic growth in the developing countries regarded as a group, little progress had been made towards the establishment of the new international economic order within the framework of negotiations among nations for the purpose of applying the principles adopted in 1974 by the United Nations General Assembly. The situation appeared to be marked by a slowing down at world level in the effort to find a solution to most of the major problems, due to certain inability to control the evolution of societies and economies, and a fairly widespread feeling of uncertainty as to the future. The changes which have occurred between 1978 and 1980 have only magnified the difficulties, so that today there is much talk of a deterioration in the international situation. This is immediately apparent in regard to inequalities between human beings, whether considered as individuals or groups or nations. Overall economic disparities have not been attenuated. In many countries, per capita gross national product remains less than $300, while in others it is situated at levels ten, twenty or even thirty times higher than this amount. In some rich countries, the average income is a hundred times higher than in the poorest countries. Particularly, drastic is the state of penury, destitution and all too often, homelessness of those populations that may be regarded as history's most recent rejects: tire disinherited masses of the poorest countries. In these countries, whose economic situation is particularly critical, the problems of hunger, disease and ignorance experienced by a large part of the population seem to all but paralyse efforts made to cope with them.

44. What was the purpose of principles adopted by the United Nations General Assembly? **[Dec 2018]**

(a) Considering developing countries as a group.
(b) Obtaining results in the economic growth of developing countries.
(c) Establishing a new international economic order.
(d) Permitting negotiations among nations.

45. What is the consequence due to the little progress made by nations during negotiations? **[Dec 2018]**

(a) Evolution of societies
(b) Control of economies
(c) UN intervention
(d) Uncertain future

46. What is apparent due to the changes occurred between 1978 and 1980? **[Dec 2018]**

(a) Plan adjustment
(b) Support of rich countries
(c) Reduction in poverty
(d) Inequality between human beings

47. How economic disparities are reflected? **[Dec 2018]**

(a) $300 per capita GNP as benchmark.
(b) Collectivizing individuals into groups or nations.
(c) Higher average income for poor countries.
(d) Average income of some countries is a hundred times higher than in the poor countries.

48. Whom do you call as history's recent rejects? **[Dec 2018]**

(a) Homeless population
(b) Ignorant population
(c) Large part of population
(d) Rich countries

Read the passage carefully and answer questions 49 to 53.

Today, in the digital age, who owns information owns the future. In this digital world, we face a fundamental choice between open and closed. In an open world, information is shared by all and it is freely available to everyone. In a closed world, information is exclusively owned and controlled by a few. Today, we live in a closed world a world of extraordinary and growing concentrations in power and wealth. A world where innovation is held back and distorted by the dead hand of monopoly, where essential medicines are affordable only to the rich, where freedom is threatened by manipulation, exclusion and exploitation; and each click you make, every step you take, they will be watching you. By contrast, in an open world, all of us would be enriched by the freedom to use, enjoy and build on everything from statistics and research to newspaper stories and books, from software and films to music and medical formulae. In an open world, we would pay innovators and creators more and more fairly, using market-driven remuneration rights in place of intellectual property monopoly rights. As they have improved, digital technologies have taken on ever more of the tasks that humans used to do, from manufacturing cars to scheduling appointments. And in the next few decades, artificial intelligence may well be not only driving our cars for us but drafting legal contracts and performing surgery. On the face of it, we have much to gain if machines can spare us tedious or routine tasks and perform them with greater accuracy. The danger, though, is that robots run on information-software, data algorithms and at present the ownership of this sort of information is unequal. And because it is protected by our closed system of intellectual property rights.

49. The crux of the passage contains the following statements. **[Dec 2018]**

(i) Digital technology is dangerous.
(ii) Those who own information will own the future.
(iii) Artificial intelligence will do the human tasks.
(iv) Monopoly of digital technology has led to unequal ownership of information.
(v) Intellectual property rights should be protected in an open world.

Options:

(a) (iv), (v) and (i) (b) (iii), (iv) and (v)
(c) (i), (ii) and (iii) (d) (ii), (iii) and (iv)

50. What is the impact of digital technologies on the present day world? **[Dec 2018]**

(a) Tedious tasks see an upward trend.
(b) Mechanical accuracy is distorted.
(c) Creativity is sidelined.
(d) Human tasks are performed by machines.

51. Which of these characteristics of a closed world? **[Dec 2018]**

(i) Concentration in power arid wealth increases.
(ii) Innovation is controlled.
(iii) Only the rich have access to medicines.
(iv) Freedom is manipulated.
(v) Information is shared by all.
(vi) Creativity is recognized.

Options:

(a) (iii), (iv), (v) and (vi)
(b) (i), (ii), (iii) and (iv)
(c) (iv), (v), (vi) and (i)
(d) (ii), (iii), (iv) and (v)

52. What is the status of intellectual property rights in an open world? **[Dec 2018]**

(a) Replaced by remuneration rights.
(b) They are monopoly rights.
(c) Protected proprietorial rights.
(d) Medical formulae are restricted.

53. How will an open world function? **[Dec 2018]**

(a) With limited choices.
(b) Information is available to everyone.
(c) Information is controlled.
(d) Information is exclusive.

Read the following passage carefully and answer questions from 54 to 58.

Read the following passage and answer question:

There is a common thread running through the unravelling of India's statistical system. A modern economy with sound institutions is characterized by timely dissemination of credible data. A long-term policy needs an empirical basis and issues of veracity of data will influence investment decisions. In a country with a large population of youth, data on national development, especially in core sectors like agriculture, industry, health, education and employment, will be critical. Here comes the role of National Statistical Commission, a body created to establish standards. Questioning the data veracity is a global phenomenon. The official narrative is always questioned by the people on the other side of the fence. Dissemination of economic data is essential to reach out to the public who lived their reality. Lack of data will adversely impact the quality of national policies. India must start strengthening institutions such as the Central Statistical Commission. These institutions must be granted autonomy and insulated from external interferences. Enhanced operational autonomy will make their work credible. An indicator of operational autonomy is their ability to stick to dissemination calendar regardless of what the data indicates.

54. What does the passage ultimately suggest to National Statistical Commission? **[Jun 2019]**

(a) Restricting policy decisions
(b) Critically examining data veracity
(c) Stick to a calendar of data dissemination
(d) Support development in core sectors

55. Investment decisions are impacted by **[Jun 2019]**

(a) Youth population
(b) National development
(c) Issues of data veracity
(d) Establishment of national institutions

56. What is the work of National Statistical Commission? **[Jun 2019]**

(a) Establishing standards
(b) Questioning data veracity
(c) Questioning official narrative
(d) Supporting the public perception

57. How can the quality of national policies be improved? [Jun 2019]
   (a) By living reality
   (b) By supporting external interferences
   (c) By controlling autonomous institutions
   (d) By enhanced operational freedom

58. What is important for a modern economy? [Jun 2019]
   (a) A common thread
   (b) Dissemination of credible data
   (c) Unravelling of statistical system
   (d) Selective distribution of data

Read the following passage carefully and answer questions from 59 to 63.

An important difference between human beings and animals is the property of language. Animals have a rudimentary information process but this process does not have the sophistication and complexity of human language. If two dogs communicate, they pass on information but they can't discuss details the way humans can. While humans are blessed to possess the language faculty, most of the time they don't utilize it to its greatest potential. Perhaps this is because human beings tend to react rather than respond. And a lot of the message of languages is lost in this reaction.

In the daily use of language, people forget the complex process involved in order to put even one word in place. The wonder of this process lies in the fact that it is involuntary in nature, the whole set of chain processes right from the command in the brain to the forming of words from the message required to the movement of the vocal chords and corresponding movements in the lungs and mouth takes place within seconds. Perhaps the whole suggestion of think before you speak may lead to a silent world!

In the world of daily interaction, language becomes a marker and a means of projecting identity. The people around us identify us with a certain style of using language and unknowingly, each language user follows this style by habit. It is not a bad idea to record one's spoken communication from time to time, as this will assist in removing any unwanted elements that the speech may be expressing. Similarly, it is a good idea to step back once in a while and read one's written communication objectively.

59. The process of language is a wonder because it is [Jun 2019]
   (a) a reaction (b) a response
   (c) smooth (d) involuntary

60. Which of the following forms is assumed by the language style of a person? [Jun 2019]
   (a) a reaction (b) a habit
   (c) a response (d) a thought

61. Animals do not possess language because [Jun 2019]
   (a) the power of speech is missing
   (b) the life breath is missing
   (c) the level of complexity is missing
   (d) the information-sharing is missing

62. When human beings react rather than respond [Jun 2019]
   (a) They lose the message
   (b) They lose control
   (c) They become emotional
   (d) They can't speak

63. The world will become a silent place if people will think [Jun 2019]
   (a) too much (b) before listening
   (c) before responding (d) before speaking

Read the following passage carefully and answer questions from 64 to 68.

Intelligence is associated with academic achievement by most people. The various theories of intelligence created by psychologists hold that there are two kinds of academic intelligence, verbal and mathematical or logical intelligence is an inherited trait that impacts individual behaviour and performance according to most experts. But many research studies have revealed that the environment greatly impacts the development of intelligence. Since one property of intelligence is analytical and reasoning skills, people with high intelligence quotient will understand the problem at hand better than people with a low IQ.

Many organizations consider intelligence as an important criterion while recruiting. For instance, in many management schools, a lot of weightage is given to high IQ while admitting students or recruiting faculty members. The qualities of intelligent people are high energy drive, achievement and competitiveness. Very intelligent employees learn job-related skills and other organization practices quickly and organizations have to spend less time training them. People with high intelligence have good decision-making ability due to their good analytical and reasoning skills with a high achivement drive, they are mostly by very productive. As the saying goes. 'A wise enemy is better than a foolish' friend.

Even with such a high IQ very intelligent people may not always be very happy. The high IQ makes them dysfunctional leading to anxiety and depression. Generally speaking, people with at high intelligence quotient are often dissatisfied people.

64. Dissatisfaction is often witnessed in people with **[Jun 2019]**
   (a) Creative skills
   (b) High expectations
   (c) Good decision-making ability
   (d) High education qualifications

65. When a student stands first in the class, the general credit is given to **[Jun 2019]**
   (a) Contacts (b) Intelligence
   (c) Hard work (d) Attractive features

66. Another word for 'Weightage' is **[Jun 2019]**
   (a) Credit (b) Mass
   (c) Weight (d) Freedom

67. Those who understand a problem in a short span of time will be people with **[Jun 2019]**
   (a) High IQ (b) Low IQ
   (c) Average IQ (d) Good IQ

68. High energy drive, achievements and competitiveness are valued during **[Jun 2019]**
   (a) Admission
   (b) Recruitment
   (c) Promotion
   (d) Admission and recruitment

Read the following passage carefully and answer questions from 69 to 73.

Unquestionably, a literary life is for the most part an unhappy life, because if you have genius, you must suffer the penalty of genius; and if you have only talent, there are so many cares and worries incidental to the circumstances of men of letters, as to make life exceedingly miserable. Besides the pangs of composition, and the continuous disappointment which a true artist feels at his inability to reveal himself, there is the ever-recurring difficulty of gaining the public ear. Young writers are buoyed up by the hope and the belief that they have only to throw that poem at the world's feet to get back in return the laurel-crown; that they have only to push as a new light in literature. You can never convince a young author that the editors of magazines and the publishers of books are practical body of men, who are by no means frantically anxious about placing the best literature before the pubic. Nay, that for the most part they are mere brokers, who conduct their business on the hardest lines of a profit and loss account. But supposing your book fairly launches, its perils are only beginning you have to run the gauntlet of the critics. When you are a little older, you will find that criticism is not much more serious than the bye-play of clowns in a circus, when they beat around the ring, the victim with bladders stung at the end of long poles. A time comes they comes in the life of every author when he regards critics as comical rather than formidable, and goes his way unheeding. But there are sensitive souls that yield under the chastisement and perhaps after suffering much silent torture abandon the profession of the pen forever.

69. The effective way of tackling criticism is **[Jun 2019]**
   (a) To defend oneself through print media
   (b) To be vocal about one's craft
   (c) To become a critic of one's own art and start analysing its merit
   (d) To be gracefully glued to the artistic exercise

70. Experience and age of an author **[Jun 2019]**
   (a) Makes the author stoic to criticism
   (b) Makes the author angry and lovely
   (c) Turns the author to a buffoon
   (d) Drives the author to cynicism

71. The perception towards the publishers and critics in the above passage is **[Jun 2019]**
   (a) That of a scathing attack
   (b) That of sympathy
   (c) That of generosity
   (d) That of cynicism

72. Literary life is unhappy because **[Jun 2019]**
   (a) One has to carry the load of being a genius while not being one
   (b) The genius can still remain a genius and be amidst misery in the face of adversity
   (c) Talent brings pseudo happiness
   (d) There is constant desire to outshine others

73. Young authors aspire to **[Jun 2019]**
   (a) Equate themselves to the established authors
   (b) Remain content in their work only
   (c) Achieve glory by their merit yet always in a hurry
   (d) Become critics subsequently

Read the following passage carefully and answer questions from 74 to 78.

A business will usually go through a clear set stages that will make up its organizational life cycle. These stages include introduction, early growth, continuous growth, maturity and decline. The first stage, the introduction stage, is the start-up phase where a business decides what its core strengths and capabilities are and starts selling its product of service. At this early stage, the founder or founders will be a part of every aspect of the daily precess of the business. The main goal at this stage is to take off to a good start and make a place in the market.

The next stage, the early growth phase, aims at increased sales and more development. The focus at this stage remains on the original product or service but the effort is to increase the market share and venture into related products or services. The main goal is to move founder to a more managerial role so more time is spent on managing and building the business. At this stage, documents and policies need to be developed so any member of the organization can see the business any time.

The third stage, the continuous growth stage, requires a systematic structure and more formal relationships among its participants. At this stage, the resource requirements of the business need careful handling. The focus is on the expansion of the business, keeping in mind its core strength and capability. A formal organizational structure and a clear delegation plan are important at this stage.

At the fourth stage of maturity, a business often slows down as the level of innovative energy may have become weak and the formal structures may have become obstacles. A lot of care is required to prevent decline.

74. The slowing down of a business can happen if, **[Jun 2019]**

(a) There is decline in the market share
(b) The level of innovative energy weakens
(c) The managerial roles are not clear
(d) The level of investment declines

75. When will a business create its place in the market? **[Jun 2019]**

(a) At maturity
(b) At introduction
(c) At early growth
(d) At later growth

76. The founder of a business does not move to a more managerial role at which stage? **[Jun 2019]**

(a) Early growth stage (b) Maturity stage
(c) Decline stage (d) Start-up stage

77. Venturing into related products and services does not mean that a business will **[Jun 2019]**

(a) Ignore the original product
(b) Move the founder to a more managerial role
(c) Delegate more responsibilities
(d) Ignore the related product and services

78. The resource requirement of a business need careful handling at which stage? **[Jun 2019]**

(a) Fourth (b) First
(c) Third (d) Second

Indian organizations have traditionally not considered their human resource as a means of distinct competitive advantage. Rather, people management has been a big challenge for the Indian business head. This situation is undergoing a rapid change today; because as Indian organizations are recognizing the need for professional human resource management, simultaneously there is a growing demand for trained human resource professional. At most universities, business schools have begun to offer specialized, customized courses to train the human resource professional. Increasingly, organizations are encouraging line managers to handle human resource responsibilities.

Ancient India was known for its occupation based hierarchy. The ancient Indian test, the *Arthashastra* refer to the job description of a supervisor and performance linked pay for artisans.

It was only after the year 1850 that formal industrial organizations emerged in India. But it was only after India became an independent country in 1947 that significant improvement was witnessed in the personnel management policy of business organizations.

After independence, when a mixed economy was encouraged as the Indian growth model, industrial organizations were broadly classified into public sector and private sector. Since the public sector units were the recipients of large investment and became the biggest employers, their approach towards personnel management received a lot of attention. The goal of a socialistic society enshrined within the constitution of India implied that the protection of human resource became a significant objective. Many constitutional provisions were created in order to protect workers.

Organizations had to appoint welfare officers to take care of all personnel.

The next phase of development saw the rise of the trade unions, and manager unions in the Indian business organization. This further boosted the growth of personnel offices in most organizations.

79. Significant improvement was seen in the personnel management policy of business organizations after **[Jun 2019]**

(a) 1850 (b) 1857
(c) 1940 (d) 1947

80. Personnel offices in many organizations witnessed an increase because of **[Jun 2019]**

(a) Independence of India
(b) Industrial development
(c) The rise of unions
(d) Work-friendly policies

81. More and more organizations are encouraging their line managers to handle **[Jun 2019]**

(a) The whole organization
(b) The responsibilities of human resource
(c) The offices of juniors
(d) The public relations

82. The hierarchy system in ancient India was based on **[Jun 2019]**

(a) The job you did
(b) The family you belonged to
(c) The place you lived in
(d) The year of your birth

83. The competitive advantages of human resource has not been **[Jun 2019]**

(a) Understood in the past
(b) Realized in the present
(c) Ignored in the past
(d) Planned for the future

Read the following passage carefully and answer questions from 84 to 88.

Geography seeks to understand the physical and human organization of the surface of the Earth. In the field of geography, inter-related themes are frequently seen. These are scale, pattern and process. Scale is defined as the level of structure on organization at which a phenomenon is studied. Pattern is defined as the variation observed in a phenomenon studied at a particular scale. The third theme, process, further connects the first two. Process is defined as the description of how the factors that affect a phenomenon act to product a pattern at a particular scale. For instance, when a passenger on an aircraft looks out of the window, the view changes according to the scale. At the global scale when the aircraft maintains its height, he can see the chunks of clouds in all their pattern, the sun or the moon, as per the time. When the aircraft loses a little height, passengers can see the land and water masses in their different colours and the shape of land masses. At the continental scale, the passengers can see the shapes of the land features and how they are distributed. The pattern emerges as the variation of land and water and the proportion of each. Looking carefully, passengers can note how each land mass aligns with the others and how each mountain bears the signs of the process through which it emerged.

The processes in a geography change in a regular manner. One instance of this is the annual solar cycle of the sun and the earth. Most systems in nature display time cycles that are organized in a rhythm of their own. As these time cycles and natural processes are always active, the environment of the earth is always in a state of dynamism. This environmental change is not only the result of natural process but also the result of human activity. Physical geography works towards understanding the interaction between man and nature and also the results of this interaction in order to manage global climate change better.

84. The alignment of landmass with other elements can be seen by a passenger on a flight on a **[Jun 2019]**

(a) Global scale (b) Continental scale
(c) Local scale (d) Time scale

85. Physical geography studies the results of the interaction between man and nature in order to **[Jun 2019]**

(a) Understand global climate change
(b) Study the impact of man's activities on nature
(c) Address the issue of global climate change
(d) Reduce man-animal conflict

86. The time cycle of the system of nature follow their own **[Jun 2019]**

(a) Path (b) Rhythm
(c) Process (d) Cycle

87. In geography, pattern studies the variation observed in a phenomenon at [Jun 2019]
(a) A particular scale
(b) Any scale
(c) Every scale
(d) Most scale

88. The view seen by a passenger looking out of the window of an aircraft will be affected by the [Jun 2019]
(a) Process (b) Pattern
(c) Scale (d) Rhythm

Read the following passage carefully and answer questions from 89 to 93.

Michelangelo is famous for having successfully interpreted the human body. His great achievement is that of painting of David whose hands reach out as a sign of human capability and potential. It is assumed that the time he lived was ripe for exchange of knowledge, development in science and matured enough to advance the horizon of investigation in all fields. Renaissance humanism stressed on a serious rethink on the nature of art that focused on accurate details. In painting and sculpture, artists focussed on not so casual but verifiable and minute details. Michelangelo's paintings are no exception to it. In a study published in the Journal of the Royal Society of Medicine, a group of surgeons are of the opinion that the great master was 'afflicted by an illness involving his joints'.They have used his portraits as evidence to argue their view. During his life, he complained of what he felt to be 'gout'. Later he complained of his sore and stiff hands which the doctors would find to be natural for someone who was engage in handmade art. The doctors found corroboration of those claims in portraits of the artist that show a hanging left hand with both degenerative and non-degenerative changes. They attribute the pain not just to arthritis, but to the stress of hammering and chiseling and note that though the master was seen hammering days before his death at an old age, he did not write or sign his own letters before his death. In recent times, there have been attempts to diagnose famous artists with diseases that were not known during their time. This practice has raised many questions especially on the issue of ethics in research. It is also inferred from authentic analysis that Michelangelo persisted in his work until his last days. This theory would emphasize that his artistic subject defied his physical infirmities.

89. Renaissance painting in Europe was sceptical of [Jun 2019]
(a) The obsessive medieval method of accuracy
(b) The classical simplicity and lack of control
(c) The case and decorative excess of earlier art
(d) Expressionist technique

90. Michelangelo lived during a time that lets us know that [Jun 2019]
(a) Human aspirations are limitless and open to vistas of knowledge
(b) Cross-cultural exchange in ideas is the only way for human progress
(c) It is progress of science and anatomy that contributes to civilizations exclusively
(d) Human beings possess language which is the only key to knowledge

91. What actually may be concluded from the above passage? [Jun 2019]
(a) Physical infirmities do dissuade people with capabilities from excelling
(b) Excellence in any form triumphs over extraneous factors including physical ailments
(c) Michelangelo's gout and other ailments lessened his efficiency
(d) The diseases Michelangelo faced were due to constant hammering

92. The controversy that the passage above refers to is whether [Jun 2019]
(a) Michelangelo worked under duress
(b) Michelangelo could contain his physical infirmity by artistic excellence
(c) Michelangelo submitted to disease
(d) Michelangelo survived different diseases before pursuing art

93. What generalizations do people subscribe to? [Jun 2019]
(a) Establishing facts by DNA tests
(b) Inferring the essence of character from famous people's handwriting
(c) Carbon daring of the hair of celebrities to draw conclusions on their physical structure
(d) To retroactively diagnose famous artists and public figures of conditions that were not prevalent during their time

Read the following passage carefully and answer questions from 94 to 98.

All great thinkers live and move on a high plane of thought. It is only there, they can breathe freely. It is only in contact with spirits like themselves they can live harmoniously and attain that serenity which comes from ideal companionship. The studies of all great thinkers must range along the highest altitudes of human thought. I have always thought that the strongest argument in favour of the Baconian theory was, that no man, however, indubitable his genius, could have written the play and sonnets that have come down to us under Shakespeare's own name who had not the liberal education of Bacon. The magnificent ideals that have ever haunted the human mind and give us our highest proofs of a future immortality by reason of the impossibility of their here, are splintered into atoms by contact with life's realities. Hence, comes our sublime discontent. A habitual mediation on the vast problems that underline human life and are knit into human destinies–thoughts of immortality, of the littleness of mere man, of the greatness of man's soul, of the splender of the universe that are invisible to the ordinary traffickers in the street, as the vastness of St. Peter's is to the spinder that weaves her web in a corner of the the dome—these things do not fit men to understand the average human being, or tolerate with patience the sordid wretchedness of the unregenerated masses. It is easy to understand, therefore, why such thinkers fly to the solitude of their own thoughts, or the silent companionship of the immortals and if they care to present their views in prose or verse to the world, that these views take a sombre and melancholy setting from 'the pale caste of thought' in which they were engendered.

94. Great thinkers are content to live **[Jun 2019]**
- (a) Amidst crises of civilizations
- (b) In lofty thoughts with exceptional calm
- (c) At high altitudes in order to be away from society
- (d) With complexities of and find solutions to them

95. Why do great thinkers love solitude? **[Jun 2019]**
- (a) To be in pursuit of the ideal in the company of immortals
- (b) To spend time in peace
- (c) Because they are misanthropists
- (d) Because the world is unhealthy for them

96. Immortality is the crucial idea constantly being explored by **[Jun 2019]**
- (a) Ordinary traffickers
- (b) Great thinkers
- (c) Gods who appear to the thinkers
- (d) Scientists

97. Baconian liberal education is **[Jun 2019]**
- (a) A lofty and ideal fantasy
- (b) Instrumental in making human being rue over their destiny
- (c) An engagement with the intricacies of the day-to-day life
- (d) Equivalent to ancient ideas of sublimity

98. According to the passage, our sublime discontent is due to **[Jun 2019]**
- (a) Realization of our lack of contact with God
- (b) Acute sense of loneliness in a hostile world
- (c) Possibility of immortality through some channels to God and inability to get hold of it
- (d) The contrast between the ideals in great literature and their opposite in the real life

Read the passage and answer the questions from 99 to 103.

Anyone, who has ever been in a classroom, where the teacher's presentation was lifeless, static and without vocal variety can appreciate the commonsense value of the affective side of teaching. However, unlike the other behaviours, affect cannot be captured in transcripts of teaching or by classroom interaction instruments. Narrowly focussed research instruments often miss a teacher's affective nature, which emerges from a more holistic view of the classroom. This affective nature is the foundation on which, one can build a warm and nurturing relationship with his or her learness. What the instruments miss, the students see clearly. Students are good perceivers of the emotions and intentions underlying a teacher's actions and they often respond accordingly. A teacher, who is excited about the subject being taught and shows it by facial expressions, voice inflection, gesture and movement—thus communicating respect and caring for the learner—is more likely to hold the attention of students and motivate them to higher levels of achievement than one who does not exhibit these behaviours. Students take their cues from these affective signs and lower or heighten their engagement with the lesson accordingly. Enthusiasm is an important aspect of a teacher's affect. Enthusiasm is the teacher's vigour, power, involvement, excitement and interest during a classroom presentation and willingness to share this emotion with learners who will want to respond in kind.

99. When does one feel the need for the value of affective aspects of teaching? **[Dec 2019]**
(a) When a teacher has a vocal variety
(b) When a teacher makes a dynamic presentation
(c) When a teacher's presentation is monotonous
(d) When a teacher's lecture is beyond expectation

100. Students respect a teacher, who: **[Dec 2019]**
(a) is emotional
(b) displays concern for students
(c) has a powerful voice
(d) has narcissistic attitude

101. The affective nature of teaching is reflected in: **[Dec 2019]**
(a) deeper understanding of the classroom environment
(b) other behaviours of the teacher
(c) the recording of classroom interaction
(d) the limited reliance on research instruments

102. The affective signs will provide students: **[Dec 2019]**
(a) the basis for understanding contents
(b) exhibitional behaviours
(c) cues to hold attention
(d) a basis which triggers further enthusiasm

103. The passage focusses attention on: **[Dec 2019]**
(a) lifeless classroom presentation
(b) affective factors of teaching
(c) students as emotional learners
(d) measuring teacher's affective nature

Read the following passage and answer the questions from 104 to 108.

Even though globalisation is one of the most discussed topics in the contemporary world, it is not altogether a well defined concept. A multitude of global interactions are put under the broad heading of globalisation, varying from the expansion of cultural and scientific influences across borders to the enlargement of economic and business relations throughout the world. A wholesale rejection of globalisation would not only go against global business, it would also cut out movements of ideas, understanding and knowledge that can help all the people of the world, including the most disadvantaged members of the world population. A comprehensive rejection of globalisation can thus be powerfully counterproductive. There is a strong need to separate out the different questions that appear merged together in the rhetoric of the antiglobalisation protests. The globalisation of knowledge deserves particularly high profile recognition, despite all the good things that can be rightly said about the importance of 'local knowledge'.

Globalisation is often seen in both journalistic discussions and in remarkably many academic writings, as a process of westernisation. Indeed, some who take an upbeat view of the phenomenon even sees it as a contribution of Western civilisation to the world.

104. According to the passage, which one of the following is not a well defined concept? **[Dec 2019]**
(a) Multiculturalism (b) Identity
(c) Globalisation (d) Local knowledge

105. As per the passage, a wholesale rejection of globalisation would result in affecting: **[Dec 2019]**
(i) global businesses
(ii) movement of ideas
(iii) local knowledge systems
Choose the correct answer from the options given below.
(a) (i) and (ii) only (b) (i) and (iii) only
(c) (iii) and (ii) only (d) (i), (ii) and (iii)

106. According to the passage, which one of the following is counterproductive? **[Dec 2019]**
(a) Comprehensive support to globalisation
(b) Wholesale rejection of globalisation
(c) Comprehensive rejection of antiglobalisation protests
(d) Recognition of local knowledge systems

107. The attempt of the author in the passage is: **[Dec 2019]**
(a) unconditioned advocacy of globalisation
(b) unconditioned rejection of globalisation
(c) unconditioned rejection of local knowledge systems
(d) unbiased evaluation of globalisation

108. According to the passage, globalisation is perceived often by media and academia as: **[Dec 2019]**
(a) supporting local knowledge systems
(b) detrimental to local knowledge systems
(c) a process of westernisation
(d) a process of facilitating global business

Read the given passage and answer the questions from 109 to 113.

The motives for direct investments abroad are generally the same as earning higher returns, possibly resulting from higher growth rates abroad, more favourable tax treatment or greater availability of infrastructure and diversifying risks. Indeed, it has been found that firms with a strong international orientation, both through exports or through foreign production and/ or sales facilities, are more profitable and have a much smaller variability in profits than purely domestic firms. Although these reasons are sufficient to explain international investments they leave one basic question unanswered with regard to direct foreign investments. That is, they cannot explain why the residents of a nation do not borrow from other nations and themselves make real investments in their own nation; rather, than accept direct investments from abroad. After all, the residents of a nation can be expected to be more familiar with local conditions and thus to be at a competitive advantage with respect to foreign investors. There are several explanations for this. The most important is that many large corporations, usually in monopolistic and oligopolistic markets, often have some unique production knowledge or managerial skill that could easily and profitably be utilized abroad and over which the corporation wants to retain direct control. In such a situation, the firm will make direct investments abroad. This involves horizontal integration or the production abroad of a differentiated product that is also produced at home. This helps serve the foreign market better by adaption got local conditions than through exports.

109. In the case of direct foreign investments, which among the following factor remains unaddressed? **[Dec 2019]**
(a) Acceptance of foreign investment
(b) Non-acceptance of foreign investment
(c) Absence of competitive edge
(d) Role of monopolistic corporations

110. The passage focuses on which of the following aspects? **[Dec 2019]**
(a) Indirect control over investments
(b) International orientation of investment
(c) Sales facilities
(d) Risks involved in integration of production

111. The possible reasons for direct foreign investment can be: **[Dec 2019]**
(a) higher returns
(b) better tax regimes
(c) availability of infrastructure+
(d) risk mitigation
(e) financial support from local investors
Choose the correct answer from the following.
(a) Only (a), (d) and (e)
(b) Only (b), (c) and (d)
(c) Only (a), (b) and (c)
(d) Only (d), (e) and (f)

112. Purely domestic firms are affected by: **[Dec 2019]**
(a) low interest rates
(b) small variability of profits
(c) larger variability of profits
(d) export controls

113. What advantage do large corporations have in oligopolistic markets? **[Dec 2019]**
(a) Direct control over-profitability
(b) Large production of undifferentiated products
(c) Localisation of managerial skills
(d) Eliminating barriers to higher profits

Read the passage carefully and answer the questions from 114 to 118.

The pre-first world war era is really in a well-suited way for an in-depth evaluation of popular movements, as they were spontaneous and no more than, marginally affected intelligentsia ideologies, objectives or techniques. The limitations of such spontaneity are fairly clear. Popular movements were directed usually against the immediate Indian oppressor, rather than the distant white superior and so were often not consciously or subjectively anti-imperialist. They tended to be fairly widely scattered in both space and time and were extremely volatile with different social forms of articulation interpenetrating and passing over each other with bewildering ease. All this makes it rather difficult to accept without some qualification the concept of 'peasant nationalism' as a coherent alternative to elite patriotic ideologies and movements, popular initiative and autonomy were undoubted, even remarkable at times but unlike middle class nationalism which does have certain continuity, at the level of ideology at least, from the formulation of the drain of wealth theory in the 1870s onwards, the movement that have been considered were clearly fragmented. Yet despite such limitations and crudities, popular unrest did anticipate much of middle class nationalism in terms of issues and forms of struggle, while its specific gains were at times not inconsiderable. Forest rights, the burdens of rent, usury and land revenue, planter exploitation and labour grievances were all themes taken over by middle class nationalism later.

114. According to the passage, the issue with peasant nationalism was: **[Dec 2019]**
(a) a viable alternative to elite nationalism
(b) coherence and control
(c) lack of continuity
(d) quite timely

115. The popular movements were: **[Dec 2019]**
(a) against imperialists (b) against their masters
(c) consciously violent (d) time-bound

116. What is the author's assessment of the popular movements? **[Dec 2019]**
(a) Some of the popular issues were taken over by middle class nationalism
(b) It was bewildering and amusing
(c) It was remarkable and time tested
(d) Pre-war popular unrest was anti-imperialist

117. The pre-war popular movements were of: **[Dec 2019]**
(a) uniform social form
(b) insignificant value
(c) middle class nationalism
(d) specific gain at times

118. What does the analysis of pre-first world war popular movements reveal? **[Dec 2019]**
(a) Intelligentsia's influence on popular movement was less
(b) The movements were ideological
(c) The movements had clear objectives
(d) Limited spontaneity

Read the following passage carefully and answer the questions from 119 to 123.

Intra-industry trade arises in order to take advantage of important economies of scale in production. That is, international competition forces each firm or plant in industrial countries to produce only one or at most a few varieties and styles of the same product rather than many different varieties and styles. This is crucial in keeping unit costs low. With few varieties and styles, more specialised and faster machinery can be developed for a continuous operation and for a longer production run. The nation then imports other varieties and styles from other nations. Intra-industry trade benefits consumers because of the wider range of choices, i.e., the greater variety of differentiated products, available at the lower prices made possible by economies of scales in production. Due to this, large welfare gains arise from the ability of consumers to greatly increase the variety of goods that they can purchase through trade. The importance of intra-industry trade became apparent when tariffs and other obstructions to the flow of trade among the members of the European Union or common market were removed in 1958. It was found that volume of trade surged but most of the increase involved the exchange of differentiated products within each broad industrial classification.

119. Lower product price means: **[Dec 2019]**
(a) continued production run
(b) absence of choice
(c) increase in trade information exchange
(d) increased consumer purchasing power

120. Development and use of specialised machinery will lead to: **[Dec 2019]**
(a) more varieties of products
(b) decreased consumer welfare
(c) import of varieties of product
(d) hindered intra-industry trade

121. The impact of international competition on intra-industry trade can be seen in: **[Dec 2019]**
(a) the availability of wide varieties of products
(b) the limited varieties of the same product
(c) adverse effect on industrial production
(d) restrictive advantages of production

122. Mass production of a few varieties of products will result in: **[Dec 2019]**
(a) low cost of unit
(b) advantage to industrial economies of scale

(c) benefits to the customers of important economies
(d) increased cost of production

123. What was the consequence of removal of barriers to the flow of trade in European Union? **[Dec 2019]**
(a) Sluggish intra-industry trade
(b) Flow of uniform products
(c) Spurt in trade volume among member states
(d) Emphasis on differentiated products

Comprehension: Read the passage carefully and answer questions from 124 to 128.

The true role of our energy is to gain personal power and operate from it at all times. Today, in many situations, people loose their personal power in relationships between boss-subordinate, client-customer, colleague-colleague, teacher-student, husband-wife, parent-child, friend-friend, etc. Often in these relationships someone plays the role of the oppressor while the other plays the role of the oppressed. But this is a great weakness in the relationship and it undermines people's capacity to be their authentic sieves and accomplish what they want in their lives. We need personal power to hold our self-esteem and go forward to succeed in our pursuits. Human relationships often deteriorate through these power struggles and ultimately both, whether they are playing the role of an oppressor or the oppressed, lose their personal power. Personal power can be seen as the result of an interplay between masculine and feminine forms of power. Both these forms of power can co-exist in both men and women. Both feminine and the masculine forms of power need to be honoured and expressed for a beautiful presence and creation in the world. We have to gain a deeper understanding the characteristics of masculine and feminine forms of power.

124. Relationships of different types of power among people will lead to **[2020]**
(a) Social diversity
(b) Hierarchical structure
(c) Balance of power in society
(d) Subjugation of the weak and meek

125. Interplay of forms of power is **[2020]**
(a) The essence of success in our pursuits
(b) Distinguish gender-based
(c) Nothing but assertion of power
(d) Needed for the creation of world

126. Loss of personal power in the society is attributed to **[2020]**
(a) Rigid human relations
(b) Aggressiveness of the oppressors
(c) Weakness of the oppressed
(d) Power struggle in society

127 The passage focuses on the idea of **[2020]**
(a) Importance of power struggle
(b) Different forms and structures of power
(c) The need for power division in the society
(d) Harnessing personal power in the interest of co-existence

128. The power relations in a society tend to **[2020]**
(a) Hurt self-accomplishments by people
(b) Improve the people's abilities
(c) Increase self-esteem
(d) Have more oppressors than the oppressed

Comprehension Passage (for question numbers 129–133)

Much is still unknown about human behavior. Unanswered questions remain and further research is necessary. Knowledge about motivation, leadership, behavior, and change will continue to be of great concern to practitioners of management for several reasons: It can help improve the effective leadership of human resources; it can help in preventing resistance to change, restriction to output, and personnel disputes; and often it can lead to a more productive organization. Our intention has been to provide a conceptual framework that may be useful to you in applying the conclusions of the behavior sciences. The value that a framework of this kind has is not in changing one's knowledge, but in changing one's behavior in working with people.

We have discussed three basic competencies in influencing: diagnosing - being able to understand and interpret the situation you are attempting to influence; adapting - being able to adapt your behavior and the resources you control to the contingencies of the situation; and communicating - being able to put the message in such a way that people can easily understand and accept it. Each of these competencies is different and requires a different developmental approach. For example, diagnosing is cognitive or of the mind in nature and requires thinking skills; adapting is behavioral in nature and requires behavioral practice; and communicating is process-oriented and requires learning and interrelating the key steps in the process. Because these three competencies require different knowledge and skills, how do we continue the process that we started with

The key to starting the process of changing behavior is sharing what you have learned with other people in your own organization. Two things occur when people who work together all have a common language. First, they are able to give each other feedback and help in a very rational, unemotional way that effects behavior.

Second, when followers start to realize that if their manager is using situational leadership, it is not the manager, but their behavior, that determines the leadership style to be used with them.

129. What is the value outcome of applying a theoretical framework of behavioral science? **[2020]**
(a) Changes in one's own knowledge
(b) Change in one's behavior while working with others
(c) Not understandable human behavior
(d) Emergence of value-loaded framework

130. What prompts a change in a person's behavior? **[2020]**
(a) Leadership style
(b) Situational support to the managers
(c) Sharing of learning outcomes with others in the organization
(d) Segregation of competencies

131. The inferences that can be drawn from the passage are **[2020]**
A. Common language among people in an organization will ensure unbiased feedback
B. People are known for fluctuating behavior
C. People's behavior influences the leader
D. Emotions and human behavior are separate and easily explicable. Choose the correct answer from the options given below:

(a) A and B only (b) B and C only
(c) C and D only (d) A and C only

132. Which of the following prohibits resistance to change? **[2020]**
(a) Knowledge of leader behavior
(b) Removing restriction on output
(c) Personnel disputes
(d) Non-productive organization

133. Each of the basic competencies needs **[2020]**
(a) Exclusivity
(b) Situational contingency
(c) Inter-relation with others
(d) A different approach in acquiring it

Read the passage carefully and answer the questions 134-138:

Leadership studies are an emergent discipline, and the concept of leadership will continue to change. Leadership lore is defined as an influence relationship among leaders and followers who want real change and outcomes that reflect their shared purpose. Leadership involves influence. It occurs among people; those people who intentionally desire significant changes, and the changes reflect purpose shared by the leaders and their followers.

Influence means that the relationship among people is not passive; however, also part of this definition is that influence is multidirectional. It does not use orders or threats to make somebody do something. The basic cultural values in America make it easiest to think of leadership as something a leader does to a follower. However, leadership has an effect in both directions. In most organizations, superiors influence subordinates, but subordinates also influence superiors. The people involved in the relationship want real and important changes- leadership involves creating change, not maintaining what normally happens. In addition, the changes sought are not dictated by leaders, but reflect purposes that leaders and followers share. Moreover, change is toward an outcome that the leaders and follower both want; a desired future or shared purpose that motivates them toward this more preferable outcome. An important aspect of leadership is influencing others to come together around a common vision. Thus, leadership involves the influence of people to bring about change toward a desirable future.

134. What is the main theme of this passage? **[2021]**
(a) Argument about leadership
(b) Explanation of leadership construct
(c) Models of leadership
(d) Pros and cons of leadership

135. The concept of leadership discussed in this passage is **[2021]**
(a) Exceptional
(b) Horizontal
(c) Individualistic
(d) Verticle-topdown

136. "Leadership studies are an emerging discipline", means: **[2021]**
(a) Leadership studies are a valid field of research
(b) Leadership studies are an established field
(c) Leadership studies is an elaborate field
(d) Leadership studies is an evolving domain of scholarship

137. What should be the outcome of leadership actions? **[2021]**
(a) Movement towards common vision of the leader and the followers
(b) Movement towards the vision of the leader
(c) Movement towards the vision of the majority
(d) Strengthening of the authority of leaders

138. What variables are used for defining leadership? **[2021]**
(a) Power to affect relationship and desire for change in the true sense of the team
(b) Power to change and control
(c) Power to effect and desire for mandated change
(d) Power to get things done quickly by influence

Read the given passage and answer the questions 139-143:

Despite the fact that social security programmes in India are not responses to structural adjustment but have a long history of their own. Social expenditure in India is nevertheless particularly vulnerable to budget cuts. The social sector is a major spending area of the government, comprising poverty reduction interventions, health, education, nutrition, social assistance and social welfare. Most departments of government are in some way responsible for spending under this broad head.

The sector is highly divisible, thus facilitating incremental and piecemeal reductions in real expenditure. It has a weak political constituency, dominated by technical-expert persons, which the mass of evaluative research that has historically been critical of state interventionism has further weakened.

Such work has been put to uses other than those originally intended - not to reform the sector but as justification to abolish major components of it entirely. However, since 1991, social sector expenditure has not declined as much as had been anticipated. Despite, or because of, its departmental pervasiveness, it is an extremely-perhaps uncuttable-low proportion of GNP: 2.4 per cent as compared with 6.5 per cent in Malaysia, 12.2 per cent in Botswana and 15-25 per cent in OECD countries. Even though social sector expenditure is also flawed by spatial patchiness, conflicting time trends in expenditure levels and composition and patterns specific to each component of welfare, cuts have been widely resisted and certain Indian states have increased their current debt in order to protect social expenditure. There is, fortunately, and necessarily, speculative literature predicting, sometimes with illustrations drawn from elsewhere, the likely outcomes of cuts in various types of social expenditure. But it is far too early for these to be evidence of the actual impact on social welfare is a long-term project of several decades.

139. The government spending on poverty reduction programmes suffers from **[2021]**
(a) Down-sized expenditure in real terms
(b) High demand from prospective beneficiaries
(c) Several social welfare programmes competing for funds
(d) Too many divisible allocations

140. Social security programmes in India encounter the issue of **[2021]**
(a) Direct implementation
(b) Increased government intervention
(c) Indirect implementation
(d) Structural rearrangement

141. The social sector in India is experiencing **[2021]**
(a) A vast amount of speculative literature
(b) Change in composition and patterns of social welfare
(c) Increased current debt account by certain states to protect their social security measures
(d) Upward revision of budget allocations in a few specific areas

142. The expert evaluation reports are used to **[2021]**
(a) Justify banishing the social security system
(b) Reform the social welfare sector
(c) Strengthen the political constituency of social security
(d) Support the government spending on social sector

143. The gist of the passage is that **[2021]**
(a) In actuality, diversification funds to areas other than social welfare are justifiable
(b) The social security system in India should be strengthened

(c) The social welfare system must be abandoned
(d) There is no evidence as to the utility of social welfare measures in India

Read the passage carefully and answer the question that follow

The need for continuing and reinforcing value-oriented curriculum at the post-graduate level and level of professional studies may be considered even more important. Most of the students trained at these levels are likely to become leaders of business and industry, technocrats, leaders of thought, teachers and educationists, research workers, professionals, political leaders, and social workers, etc., besides playing their normal roles as citizens and family members like all other people. It appears that most of them at the time of leaving the college after 3-6 years of study may have a poor idea of the values of freedom and human dignity, the value of food, security and health care for millions of poor and disadvantaged people, the importance of correct public policies for managing societies and solving several problems, the importance of proper human relations and personal lifestyles, etc. A good technical knowledge of high standards, particularly in some of our institutions of excellence, is comparable to the best institutions in the developed countries. But the problem of inadequate access to this kind of modern knowledge for the poor and disadvantaged groups in our society constitutes a serious social and moral issue.

Curricular reform and reconstruction on proper lines should be an active concern of educationists and educational planners, because as pointed out in the national policy document 1986, it can be a forceful tool for the cultivation of social and moral values. In our culturally plural societies, education should foster universal and eternal values, oriented towards the unity and integration of our people. Such value education should eliminate obscurantism religious fanaticism, violence superstition, and fatalism.

144. In higher education, in the context of promoting strong value orientation, which of the following statement holds true? **[Dec 2021]**
(a) Provide opportunities to students to acquire scientific knowledge of high standards.
(b) A policy for development of values may be prepared.
(c) Offer courses related to interdisciplinary contemporary socio-economic problems.
(d) The universities should aim to enrich technological dimensions.

145. The higher education system as of now emphasizes on: **[Dec 2021]**
(a) Utilitarian values
(b) Human values
(c) Social and Political values
(d) Spiritual values

146. Value-oriented curriculum at professional studies level is important: **[Dec 2021]**
(a) To propagate the values further
(b) To have a glimpse of the issues of the poor and disadvantaged
(c) To balance other pedagogy-related deficiencies
(d) To train students as efficient resource agents

147. The most suitable Caption for the passage may be: **[Dec 2021]**
(a) Enforcing values in education
(b) Importance of values
(c) Value implementation
(d) Value basis for tertiary education and society

148. In order to cultivate values, the higher education system should concentrate on **[Dec 2021]**
(a) Plugging pedagogical deficiencies
(b) Integrating technology
(c) Integrating technology with pedagogy
(d) Curricular reforms

Comprehension

Read the given passage carefully and answer the following question.

Two factors have mainly caused the present disastrous conditions and events. One is the change in rainfall pattern resulting from climate change. The monsoon behaviour has changed, and rainfall that used to happen over many days occur in a day or even in hours, making it difficult for the soil in the plains and the hills and for many manmade structures to withstand the impact. The high altitude areas along the Western Ghats have been especially vulnerable, because of encroachments, destruction of forests, quarrying and mining, formation of human settlements, setting up of industries and other commercial enterprises, promotion of activities like tourism without checks, and regulations and diminution of biodiversity. All these have separately and collectively contributed to the present situation in the Western Ghats region which is ecologically very sensitive and valuable. A Western ghat State which has inflicted the most damage on the environment has come to suffer the most.

The report of the Madhav Gadgil Committee which studied the destruction caused to the Western Ghats environment and made sensible recommendations to remedy the situation was thrown into the dust bin, and another committee under Dr K Kasturirangan was setup to water down its proposals. The recommendations of the Kasturirangan Committee were also not implemented. Gadgil had prophetically warned in 2013 that the tragedy that is waiting to happen will not take ages but only four or five years to happen. The abnormal natural events and the huge devastation caused by them now may only be intimations of bigger calamities lying in wait in future. Lives which are lost now will not be regained, and nature which is lost will take several hundred years to rebuild itself. The greater tragedy is that the lessons of the tragedy are not learnt at all.

149. Man-made structures are unable to withstand the rain impact due to: **[Dec 2021]**
(a) The steepness of high altitude areas.
(b) Change in monsoon behaviour in recent times.
(c) Non-stop rains over a longer period.
(d) Soil accumulation in the plains.

150. Which of the following factors have affected the Western ghats? **[Dec 2021]**
(A) Sensitive bio-diversity
(B) Formation of human settlements
(C) Flora and Fauna of the area
(D) Promotion of unchecked tourism

Choose the correct answer from the options given below
(a) A and B only (b) B and C only
(c) C and D only (d) B and D only

151. A particular state in the Western Ghats has suffered the most because: **[Dec 2021]**
(a) It has caused most damage on the environment
(b) It has most of the biodiversity hotspots of the country
(c) The state has many hill stations
(d) The state has too many checks and regulations regarding environment

152. What is the real tragedy with respect to natural disasters in the Western ghats? **[Dec 2021]**
(a) Loss of human lives
(b) The abnormal natural events
(c) Not realising the gravity of the consequences of climate change
(d) Downgrading the disasters

153. The author of the passage regrets: **[Dec 2021]**
(a) Environmental ignorance on the part of policymakers
(b) Vulnerability of high altitude areas
(c) Impact of environmental disasters
(d) Non-implementation of reports of committees

Read the given passage carefully and answer the five questions that follow:

Many great inventions are initially greeted with ridicule and disbelief. The invention of the airplane was no exception. Although many people who heard about the first powered flight on December 17, 1903, were excited and impressed, others reacted with peals of laughter. The idea of flying an aircraft was repulsive to some people. Such people called Wilbur and Orville Wright, 'the inventors of the first flying machine', impulsive fools. Negative reactions, however, did not stop the Wrights. Impelled by their desire to succeed, they continued their experiments in aviation.

Orville and Wilbur Wright always had a compelling interest in aeronautics and mechanics. As young boys, they earned money by making and selling kites and mechanical toys. Later, they designed a newspaper-folding machine, built a printing press, and operated a bicycle repair shop. In 1896, when they read about the death of Otto Lilienthal, the brothers' interest in flight grew into a compulsion.

Lilienthal, a pioneer in hang-gliding, had controlled his gliders by shifting his body in the desired direction. This idea was repellent to the Wright brothers, however, they searched for more efficient methods to control the balance of airborne vehicles. In 1900 and 1901, the Wrights tested numerous gliders and developed control techniques. The brothers' inability to obtain enough lift power for the gliders almost led them to abandon their efforts.

After further study, the Wright brothers concluded that the published tables of air pressure on curved surfaces must be wrong. They set up a wind tunnel and began a series of experiments with model wings.

Because of their efforts, the old tables were repealed in time and replaced by the first reliable figures for air pressure on curved surfaces. This work, in turn, made it possible for the brothers to design a machine that would fly. In 1903, the Wrights built their first airplane, which cost less than $1,000. They even designed and built their own source of propulsion – a lightweight gasoline engine. When they started the engine on December 17, the airplane pulsated wildly before taking off. The plane managed to stay aloft for 12 seconds, however, and it flew 120 feet.

By 1905, the Wrights had perfected the first airplane that could turn, circle, and remain airborne for half an hour at a time. Others had flown in balloons and hang gliders, but the Wright brothers were the first to build a full-size machine that could fly under its own power. As the contributors of one of the most outstanding engineering achievements in history, the Wright brothers are accurately called the fathers of aviation.

154. The major interest of Wright brothers was in **[2022]**
(a) Making kites
(b) Producing mechanical toys
(c) Designing newspaper–folding machines
(d) Methods to control airborne vehicles

155. The Wright brothers succeeded in **[2022]**
(a) Testing numerous gliders
(b) Proving previous air pressure tables wrong
(c) Setting up a wind tunnel
(d) Finding desired direction for gliders

156. Which of the following was responsible for the invention of the first flying machine? **[2022]**
(a) People's support
(b) Negative reactions of the people
(c) Compelling desire of the inventors
(d) Previous experiments in aviation

157. The Wright brothers were ultimately successful in flying their plane when they built their own **[2022]**
(a) Air pressure system
(b) Model wings
(c) Gasoline engine
(d) Curved surfaces

158. The passage points out that **[2022]**
(a) Determination to succeed pays dividends
(b) People are always skeptical of inventors
(c) The due credit to gliders has not been given
(d) Small efforts in different sectors lead to a major invention in one sector

Read the given passage and answer the questions that follow:

Marie Curie was a Polish-born physicist and chemist and one of the most famous scientists of her time. Together with her husband, Pierre, she discovered radium, an element widely used for treating cancer, and studied uranium and other radioactive substances. Pierre and Marie's amicable collaboration later helped to unlock the secrets of the atom. Together with her husband Pierre, she was awarded the Noble Prize for Physics in 1903.

Marie was born in Warsaw, Poland on 7 November 1867, the daughter of a Physics teacher. At an early age, she displayed a brilliant mind and a blithe personality. Her great exuberance for learning prompted her to continue with her studies after high school. She became disgruntled, however, when she learned that the university in Warsaw was closed to women. Determined to receive a higher education, she defiantly left Poland and in 1891 entered the Sorbonne, a French University, where she earned her master's degree and doctorate in Physics.

Marie was fortunate to have studied at the Sorbonne with some of the greatest scientists of her day, one of whom was Pierre Curie. Marie and Pierre were married in 1895 and spent many productive years working together in the physics laboratory. A short time after they discovered radium, Pierre was killed by a horse-drawn wagon in 1906. Marie was stunned by the horrible misfortune and endured heartbreaking anguish. Despondently she recalled their close relationship and the joy that they had shared in scientific research. The fact that that she had two young daughters to raise by herself greatly increased her distress.

Curie's feeling of desolation finally began to fade when she was asked to succeed her husband as a Physics professor at the Sorbonne. She was the first woman to be given a professorship at the world-famous university. She received her second Noble Prize in Chemistry for isolating radium, in 1911. Curie's eldest daughter, Irene, was herself a scientist and winner of the Noble Prize for Chemistry.

Although Marie Curie eventually suffered a fatal illness from her long term exposure to radium, she never became disillusioned about her work. Regardless of the consequences, she had dedicated herself to science and to revealing the mysteries of the physical world.

159. At what age did Marie Curie receive her first Nobel prize? **[2022]**
(a) 36 years (b) 46 years
(c) 56 years (d) 44 years

160. After how many years of her marriage did Marie Curie lose her husband? **[2022]**
(a) 11 years (b) 39 years
(c) 28 years (d) 6 years

161. The passage shows Marie Curie to be a great scientist who **[2022]**
(a) was amiable in nature.
(b) had indomitable spirit and dedication to science.
(c) was emotionally vulnerable.
(d) became disillusioned after her husband's death.

162. Which of the following elements is widely used in treatment of Cancer? **[2022]**
(a) Uranium (b) Radium
(c) Thorium (d) Plutonium

163. What made Marie Curie study at Sorbonne University? **[2022]**
(a) University in Warsaw did not allow her admission.
(b) She wanted to work with Pierre Curie.
(c) She wanted to work on Radium.
(d) She did not enjoy learning at an early age in Warsaw.

Directions: Read the following passage and answer the question.

The idea of the 'White Man's Burden' was promoted and popularized by Rudyard Kipling through his similarly titled poem written in 1899. By 1860, the British expansion in India was complete. Carnoy uses the White Man's Burden as a motivating factor for British expansion in the eighteenth century, a century before is was even conceptualized. Contrary to Carnoy's assumption, missionaries often fought for the rights of the local population from the very beginning. Rev V. Taylor, after witnessing the execution of a Kannada peasant in Dharwar district, fought for the recognition of Kannada as a court language in the Bombay Presidency in 1836. This entirely Kannada-speaking district had Marathi village and district officers due to the pre-colonial Peshwa rule. The system was continued under the colonial rule. The execution took place because the peasant charged with the murder had given his testimonial in Kannada, which was recorded in Marathi by the native official, and the court proceeding was conducted in Hindustani. The prisoner, ignorant of both Marathi and Hindustani, unwillingly expressed assent to the confession. There was no circumstantial evidence against him. He was charged with murder and later executed. Taylor effectively fought for the introduction of Kannada as the language of administration and education. Within six months, Kannada was made a court language and twenty-seven Kannada primary schools were established in the district.

164. Given below are two statements: One is labelled as Assertion A and the other is labelled as Reason R: **[June 2023]**

Assertion A: The village and district officers in Dharwar district were Kannada.

Reason R: Dharwar district in the pre-colonial era was ruled by the Peshwa.

In the light of the above statements, choose the most appropriate answer from the options given below:
(a) Both A and R are correct and R is the correct explanation of A.
(b) Both A and R are correct but R is not the correct explanation of A.
(c) A is correct but R is not correct.
(d) A is not correct but R is correct.

165. The testimonial given by the peasant was recorded in: **[June 2023]**
(a) Hindustani (b) Kannada
(c) Marathi (d) English

166. Given below are two statements: **[June 2023]**

Statement-I: Carnoy was in favour of British expansion in India.

Statement-II: Carnoy believed in the supremacy of White Man.

In the light of the above statements, choose the correct answer from the options given below:
(a) Both Statement I and Statement II are correct.

(b) Both Statement I and Statement II are incorrect.
(c) Statement I is correct but Statement II is incorrect.
(d) Statement I is incorrect but Statement II is correct.

167. The peasant who was executed, was conversant in which of the following languages? **[June 2023]**

(a) Hindustani (b) English
(c) Marathi (d) Kannada

168. Identify those who were sympathetic to the rights of the local population: **[June 2023]**

A. Rudyard Kipling
B. V. Taylor
C. Carnoy

Choose the most appropriate answer from the options given below:

(a) A and B only (b) B only
(c) B and C only (d) C only

Directions: Read the following passage and answer the question given below.

Around the age of 2, children have a sense of intention, at least of their around intentions, They will announce, "I wanna peanut butter sandwich". As children develop a theory of mind, they also can understand that other people have intentions of their own. Older pre-schoolers who get along well with their peers can separate intentional from unintentional actions and react accordingly. For example, they will not get angry when another child accidently knocks over their block tower. But aggresive children have more trouble assessing intention. They are likely to attack anyone who topples their tower, even accidently. As children mature, they are more able to assess and consider the intentions of others.

With a developing theory of mind, children are increasingly able to understand that other people have different feelings and experiences and therefore may have a different viewpoint or perspective. This perspective-taking ability develops overtime until it is quite sophisticated in adults. Being able to understand how others might think and feel is important in fostering cooperation and moral development, reducing prejudice, resolving conflicts, and encouraging positive social behaviours in general. Some coaching in perspective taking from the teacher might help if children mistreat peers and the mistreatment is not part of a dipper emotional or behavioural disorder.

169. Children of which of the following ages would generally have the best perspective taking ability? **[June 2023]**

(a) 3 years (b) 8 years
(c) 13 years (d) 18 years

170. Given below are two statements: **[June 2023]**

Statement I: Aggressive children can assess intention of others with ease.

Statement II: Different persons may have diffrent view point.

In the light of the above statements, choose the most appropriate answer from the options given below :

(a) Both Statement I and Statement II are correct.
(b) Both Statement I and Statement II are incorrect.
(c) Statement I is correct but Statement II is incorrect.
(d) Statement I is incorrect but Statement II is correct.

171. Understanding how other feel is important in **[June 2023]**

A. Developing empathy
B. Reducing prejudice
C. Conflict resolution
D. Encouraging Selfishness
E. Enhancing cooperation

Choose the most appropriate answer from the options given below:

(a) A, B, C and D only
(b) A, B, C and E only
(c) B, C, D and E only
(d) A, B, D and E only

172. Given below are two statements : One is labelled as Assertion A and the other is labelled as Reason R. **[June 2023]**

Assertion A: Older pre-schoolers have better chances of getting along well with their peers as compared to young pre-schoolers.

Reason R: Older pre-schoolers generally have a better understanding of the intentions of others.

In the light of the above statements, the most appropriate answer from the options given below:

(a) Both A and R are correct and R is the correct explanation of A.
(b) Both A and R are correct but R is not the correct explanation of A.
(c) A is correct but R is not correct.
(d) A is not correct but R is correct.

173. Given below are two statements: **[June 2023]**

Statement I: A 2 years old child is likely to have a better understanding of his own intentions than those of others.

Statement II: It is always helpful to coach a child in perspective taking if the child has the habit of mistreating others becuase of some behavioural disorder.

In the light of the above statements, choose the most appropriate answer from the options given below:

(a) Both Statement I and Statement II are correct.
(b) Both Statement I and Statement II are incorrect
(c) Statement I is correct but Statement II is incorrect.
(d) Statement I is incorrect but Statement II is correct.

Directions: Read the passage given below and answer the following questions.

India became the first country to land near the Moon's uncharted south pole region at 6.03 pm after 18 nail-biting minutes of descent ended in a perfect touchdown, offering irrefutable evidence of the astronomical abilities and galactic ambitions of a nation that on Wednesday announced itself as one of the world's foremost space powers.

Chandrayaan-3's touchdown which completed an extraordinary arc of decades of scientific perseverance also opened new vistas for the country's space programme in the lucrative market of space exploration and commerce.

'India is on the Moon!' S. Somnath, the chief of Indian Space Research Organization (ISRO) said, as the Chandrayaan-3's lander Vikram, with the Pragyan rover contained within, made a safe and soft landing on the Moon.

The watershed moment came mere days after Russia - a space veteran - crashed its moon craft while attempting to reach the same territory. At an estimated budget of $75 million, Chandrayaan-3 was built at a fraction of the cost of not only previous American lunar missions but also this summer's cinema blockbusters Oppenheimer and Barbie. The Russian Luna-25 had cost $200 million.

'This is a victory cry of a new India,' said Prime Minister Narendra Modi, waving the Indian flag as he watched the landing from South Africa. Beaming scientists and officials burst into applause and hugged each other in joy at ISRO's mission operations complex at Bengaluru after Vikram lander finally came to a rest on the rugged lunar terrain after 18 minutes that pushed millions in India on the edge of their seats.

174. The words 'India is on the moon' were spoken by **[Dec 2023]**

(a) The Indian Prime Minister
(b) The Russian President
(c) The Chief of ISRO
(d) The American President

175. Which of the following represents the estimated cost of building Chandrayaan-3? **[Dec 2023]**

(a) 200 million dollars
(b) The same cost as the making of film *Barbie*
(c) More than the cost of making film *Oppenheimer*
(d) 75 million dollars

176. The success of India's moon mission is significant because **[Dec 2023]**

A. It will make India a manufacturing hub.
B. It has made India one of world's foremost space powers
C. It has opened new avenues for India's space exploration
D. It has opened new vistas in the lucrative market of space exploration and commerce.

Choose the correct answer from the options given below:

(a) B, C and D only
(b) A, B and C only
(c) C and D only
(d) A and D only

177. Given below are two statements: **[Dec 2023]**

Statement (I): Chandrayaan-3's success was a result of years of scientific efforts.

Statement (II): Russia's Luna-25 landed on the moon minutes after Chandrayaan-3.

In light of the above statements, choose the most appropriate answer from the options given below:

(a) Both Statement (I) and Statement (II) are true.
(b) Both Statement (I) and Statement (II) are false.
(c) Statement (I) is true but Statement (II) is false.
(d) Statement (I) is false but Statement (II) is true.

178. India became the first country in the world to **[Dec 2023]**

(a) Land on the moon.
(b) Land a man on the moon.
(c) Land near the south pole of the moon.
(d) Orbit the moon.

ANSWER KEYS

1. (b)	2. (b)	3. (a)	4. (a)	5. (d)	6. (c)	7. (b)	8. (b)	9. (d)	10. (a)
11. (c)	12. (d)	13. (a)	14. (a)	15. (a)	16. (a)	17. (a)	18. (d)	19. (b)	20. (d)
21. (d)	22. (d)	23. (c)	24. (a)	25. (d)	26. (b)	27. (c)	28. (b)	29. (b)	30. (d)
31. (c)	32. (d)	33. (b)	34. (a)	35. (a)	36. (b)	37. (c)	38. (c)	39. (c)	40. (a)
41. (b)	42. (d)	43. (d)	44. (c)	45. (d)	46. (d)	47. (d)	48. (a)	49. (d)	50. (d)
51. (b)	52. (a)	53. (b)	54. (c)	55. (c)	56. (a)	57. (d)	58. (b)	59. (d)	60. (b)
61. (c)	62. (a)	63. (d)	64. (c)	65. (b)	66. (a)	67. (a)	68. (d)	69. (d)	70. (a)
71. (d)	72. (b)	73. (c)	74. (b)	75. (b)	76. (d)	77. (a)	78. (c)	79. (d)	80. (c)
81. (b)	82. (a)	83. (a)	84. (b)	85. (c)	86. (b)	87. (a)	88. (c)	89. (c)	90. (a)
91. (b)	92. (b)	93. (d)	94. (b)	95. (a)	96. (b)	97. (c)	98. (d)	99. (c)	100. (b)
101. (a)	102. (d)	103. (b)	104. (c)	105. (a)	106. (b)	107. (d)	108. (c)	109. (b)	110. (b)
111. (c)	112. (c)	113. (a)	114. (c)	115. (b)	116. (a)	117. (d)	118. (a)	119. (d)	120. (c)
121. (b)	122. (a)	123. (c)	124. (b)	125. (b)	126. (d)	127. (d)	128. (a)	129. (b)	130. (c)
131. (d)	132. (a)	133. (d)	134. (b)	135. (b)	136. (d)	137. (a)	138. (a)	139. (a)	140. (d)
141. (c)	142. (a)	143. (b)	144. (c)	145. (a)	146. (d)	147. (d)	148. (d)	149. (b)	150. (d)
151. (a)	152. (c)	153. (d)	154. (c)	155. (d)	156. (b)	157. (c)	158. (a)	159. (a)	160. (a)
161. (b)	162. (b)	163. (a)	164. (c)	165. (c)	166. (b)	167. (d)	168. (b)	169. (d)	170. (d)
171. (b)	172. (a)	173. (c)	174. (c)	175. (d)	176. (a)	177. (c)	178. (c)		

CHAPTER 4

Communication

TOPICS OF IMPORTANCE

- Communication: Meaning, Characteristics of Communication
- Communication and its Types
- Effective Communication: Verbal and Non-verbal, Inter-cultural and Group Communications, Classroom Communication
- Barriers to Effective Communication
- Mass-media and Society

1. Breakdown in verbal communication is described as **[Jun 2014]**
(a) Short circuit (b) Contradiction
(c) Unevenness (d) Entropy

2. The Telephone Model of Communication was first developed in the domain of **[Jun 2014]**
(a) Technological theory
(b) Dispersion theory
(c) Minimal effects theory
(d) Information theory

3. The Dadasaheb Phalke Award for 2013 has been conferred on **[Jun 2014]**
(a) Karan Johar (b) Amir Khan
(c) Asha Bhonsle (d) Gulzar

4. Photographs are not easy to **[Jun 2014]**
(a) Publish (b) Secure
(c) Decode (d) Change

5. The grains that appear on a television set when operated are also referred to as **[Jun 2014]**
(a) Sparks (b) Green dots
(c) Snow (d) Rain drops

6. In circular communication, the encoder becomes a decoder when there is **[Jun 2014]**
(a) Noise (b) Audience
(c) Criticality (d) Feedback

7. The term 'Yellow Journalism' refers to **[Dec 2014]**
(a) Sensational news about terrorism and violence.
(b) Sensationalism and exaggeration to attract readers/viewers.
(c) Sensational news about arts and culture.
(d) Sensational news prints in yellow paper.

8. In a classroom, the teacher sends the message either as words or images. The students are really **[Dec 2014]**
(a) Encoders (b) Decoders
(c) Agitators (d) Propagators

9. Media is known as **[Dec 2014]**
(a) First estate (b) Second estate
(c) Third estate (d) Fourth estate

10. The mode of communication that involves a single source transmitting information to a large number of receivers simultaneously is called **[Dec 2014]**
(a) Group communication
(b) Mass communication
(c) Intrapersonal communication
(d) Interpersonal communication

11. Digital empowerment means **[Dec 2014]**

(i) Universal digit literacy.
(ii) Universal access to all digital resources.
(iii) Collaborative digital platform for participative governance.
(iv) Probability of all entitlements for individuals through cloud.

Choose the correct answer from the codes given below.

(a) (i) and (ii) only
(b) (ii) and (iii) only
(c) (i), (ii) and (iii) only
(d) (i), (ii), (iii) and (iv)

12. Effectiveness of communication can be traced from which of the following? **[Jun 2015]**

(i) Attitude surveys
(ii) Performance records
(iii) Students attendance
(iv) Selection of communication channel

Select the correct answer from the codes given below:

(a) (i), (ii), (iii) and (iv)
(b) (i), (ii) and (iii)
(c) (ii), (iii) and (iv)
(d) (i), (ii) and (iv)

13. *Assertion* (*A*): Formal communication tends to be fast and flexible. **[Jun 2015]**

Reason (*R*): Formal communication is a systematic and orderly flow of information.

(a) Both (*A*) and (*R*) are correct, and (*R*) is the correct explanation of (*A*).
(b) Both (*A*) and (*R*) are correct, but (*R*) is not the correct explanation of (*A*).
(c) (*A*) is correct, but (*R*) is false.
(d) (*A*) is false, but (*R*) is correct.

14. Which of the following are the characteristic features of communication? **[Jun 2015]**

(i) Communication involves exchange of ideas, facts and opinions.
(ii) Communication involves both information and understanding.
(iii) Communication is a continuous process.
(iv) Communication is a circular process.

Select the correct answer from the codes given below:

(a) (i), (ii), and (iii)
(b) (i), (ii), and (iv)
(c) (ii), (iii), and (iv)
(d) (i), (ii), (iii), and (iv)

15. The term 'grapevine' is also known as **[Jun 2015]**

(a) Downward communication
(b) Informal communication
(c) Upward communication
(d) Horizontal communication

16. Which of the following is not a principle of effective communication? **[Jun 2015]**

(a) Persuasive and convincing dialogue
(b) Participation of the audience
(c) One-way transfer of information
(d) Strategic use of grapevine

17. In communication, the language is **[Jun 2015]**

(a) The verbal code
(b) Intrapersonal
(c) The symbolic code
(d) The non-verbal code

18. Using the central point of the classroom communication as the beginning of a dynamic pattern of ideas is referred to as **[Dec 2015]**

(a) Systemization
(b) Problem-orientation
(c) Idea protocol
(d) Mind mapping

19. Aspects of the voice, other than the speech are known as **[Dec 2015]**

(a) Physical language
(b) Personal language
(c) Para language
(d) Delivery language

20. Every type of communication is affected by its **[Dec 2015]**

(a) Reception (b) Transmission
(c) Non-regulation (d) Context

21. Attitudes, actions and appearances in the context of classroom communication are considered as **[Dec 2015]**

(a) Verbal (b) Non-verbal
(c) Impersonal (d) Irrational

22. Most often, the teacher–student communication is **[Dec 2015]**
(a) Spurious
(b) Critical
(c) Utilitarian
(d) Confrontational

23. In a classroom, a communicator's trust level is determined by **[Dec 2015]**
(a) The use of hyperbole.
(b) The change of voice level.
(c) The use of abstract concepts.
(d) Eye contact

24. What are the barriers to effective communication? **[Jul 2016]**
(a) Moralizing, being judgemental and comments of consolation.
(b) Dialogue, summary and self-review.
(c) Use of simple words, cool reaction and defensive attitude.
(d) Personal statements, eye contact and simple narration.

25. The choice of communication partners is influenced by factors of **[Jul 2016]**
(a) Proximity, utility and loneliness.
(b) Utility, secrecy and dissonance.
(c) Secrecy, dissonance and deception.
(d) Dissimilarity, dissonance and deviance.

26. Every communicator has to experience **[Jul 2016]**
(a) Manipulated emotions.
(b) Anticipatory excitement.
(c) The issue of homophiles.
(d) Status dislocation.

27. Imagine you are working in an educational institution where people are of equal status. Which method of communication is best suited and normally employed in such a context? **[Jul 2016]**
(a) Horizontal communication
(b) Vertical communication
(c) Corporate communication
(d) Cross communication

28. Identify the important element a teacher has to take cognizance of while addressing students in a classroom. **[Jul 2016]**
(a) Avoidance of proximity
(b) Voice modulation
(c) Repetitive pause
(d) Fixed posture

29. Effective communication pre-supposes **[Jan 2017]**
(a) Non-alignment (b) Domination
(c) Passivity (d) Understanding

30. When verbal and non-verbal messages are contradictory, it is said that most people believe in **[Jan 2017]**
(a) Indeterminate messages
(b) Verbal messages
(c) Non-verbal messages
(d) Aggressive messages

31. The typical feature of information-rich classroom lecture is in the nature of being **[Jan 2017]**
(a) Sedentary (b) Staggered
(c) Factual (d) Sectoral

32. Expressive communication is driven by **[Jan 2017]**
(a) Passive aggression
(b) Encoder's personality characteristics
(c) External clues
(d) Encoder–decoder contract

33. Positive classroom communication leads to **[Jan 2017]**
(a) Coercion (b) Submission
(c) Confrontation (d) Persuasion

34. Classroom communication is the basis of **[Jan 2017]**
(a) Social identity (b) External inanities
(c) Biased passivity (d) Group aggression

35. The spatial audio reproduction in a classroom can reduce the students' **[Nov 2017]**
(a) Cognitive load in understanding
(b) Respect for the teacher
(c) Motivation for excellence
(d) Interest in technology-orientation

36. The classroom communication should essentially be **[Nov 2017]**
(a) Contrived (b) Empathetic
(c) Abstract (d) Non-descriptive

37. A good communicator begins his/her presentation with a **[Nov 2017]**
(a) Complex question
(b) Non-sequitur
(c) Repetitive phrase
(d) Ice-breaker

38. In a classroom, the probability of message reception can be enhanced by **[Nov 2017]**
(a) Establishing a viewpoint.
(b) Exposing the ignorance of students.
(c) Increasing the information load.
(d) Using high decibel audio tools.

39. Differentiation between acceptance and non-acceptance of certain stimuli in classroom communication is the basis of **[Jul 2018]**
(a) Selective expectation of performance.
(b) Selective affiliation to peer groups.
(c) Selective attention.
(d) Selective morality.

40. *Assertion (A):* The initial messages to students in the classroom by a teacher need not be critical to establish interactions later. **[Jul 2018]**
Reason (R): More control over the communication process means more control over what the students are learning.
(a) Both (A) and (R) are true, and (R) is the correct explanation of (A).
(b) Both (A) and (R) are true, but (R) is not the correct explanation of (A).
(c) (A) is true, but (R) is false.
(d) (A) is false, but (R) is true.

41. *Assertion (A):* To communicate well in the classroom is a natural ability.
Reason (R): Effective teaching in the classroom demands knowledge of the communication process. **[Jul 2018]**
(a) Both (A) and (R) are true, and (R) is the correct explanation of (A).
(b) Both (A) and (R) are true, but (R) is not the correct explanation of (A).
(c) (A) is true, but (R) is false.
(d) (A) is false, but (R) is true.

42. *Assertion (A):* Classroom communication is a transactional process. **[Jul 2018]**
Reason (R): A teacher does not operate under the assumption that students' responses are purposive.
(a) Both (A) and (R) are true, and (R) is the correct explanation of (A).
(b) Both (A) and (R) are true, but (R) is not the correct explanation of (A).
(c) (A) is true, but (R) is false.
(d) (A) is false, but (R) is true.

43. Which of the following set of statements is correct for describing the human communication process? **[Jul 2018]**
(A) Non-verbal communication can stimulate ideas.
(B) Communication is a learnt ability.
(C) Communication is not a universal panacea.
(D) Communication cannot breakdown.
(E) More communication means more effective learning by students.
(F) Value of what is learnt through classroom communication is not an issue for students.
Select the correct answer from the codes given below:
(a) (A), (C), (E) and (F)
(b) (B), (D), (E) and (F)
(c) (A), (B), (C) and (D)
(d) (A), (D), (E) and (F)

44. *Assertion (A):* Empathy is essential for effective communication between the communicator and the communicatee. **[Dec 2018]**
Reason (R): Empathy links the teacher and students.
(a) Both (A) and (R) are true.
(b) Both (A) and (R) are true, but R is the correct explanation of (A).
(c) (A) is true, but (R) is false.
(d) (A) is false, but (R) is true.

45. The word 'haptics' denotes **[Dec 2018]**
(a) Spatial communication
(b) Timely communication
(c) Staggered communication
(d) Tactile communication

46. Social media platforms have created a **[Dec 2018]**
(a) Society of reactionary opinions
(b) Society of consumables
(c) Society of negativity
(d) Society of networking

47. Modern educational communication is described as **[Dec 2018]**

(a) Telescopic (b) Teleologic
(c) Non-distributive (d) Unapproximate

48. In verbal communication, words act as **[Dec 2018]**
(a) Symbols (b) Decoratives
(c) Passive barriers (d) Fillers

49. Classroom communication has a basis in **[Dec 2018]**
(a) Audience fragmentation
(b) Intensive listener focus
(c) Attention diversion
(d) Non-informative cues

50. Effective classroom communication would help students internalize **[Dec 2018]**
(i) Knowledge
(ii) Subject matter
(iii) Articulation
(iv) Language felicity
(v) Non-responsiveness
(vi) Modalities of resistance

Options:
(a) (i), (ii), (iii) and (iv)
(b) (iii), (iv), (v) and (vi)
(c) (ii), (iii), (iv) and (v)
(d) (i), (iv), (v) and (vi)

51. The challenging behaviours of students as related to communication are **[Dec 2018]**
(i) Purposive challenges
(ii) Critical challenges
(iii) Procedural challenges
(iv) Evaluation challenges
(v) Practicality challenges
(vi) Power challenges

Options:
(a) (iii), (iv), (v) and (vi)
(b) (ii), (iii), (iv) and (vi)
(c) (i), (ii), (iii) and (iv)
(d) (iv), (v), (vi) and (i)

52. In a classroom, use of communication technology pre-supposes **[Jun 2019]**
(a) Inattentive audience
(b) Luxurious ambience
(c) Extrapolation of contents
(d) New forms of expression and applications

53. *Assertion(A):* The correlation function of mass media is vital for any society. **[Jun 2019]**

Reason (R): The interpretational aspect that include advertising and public relations shape and influence public opinion.

Choose the correct answer from the codes given below:

Codes:
(a) Both (A) and (R) are true and (R) is the correct explanation of (A)
(b) Both (A) and (R) are true but (R) is not the correct explanation of (A)
(c) (A) is true but (R) is false
(d) (A) is false but (R) is true

54. In a classroom, content produced for a specific user will lead to **[Jun 2019]**
(a) Personality development
(b) Content filtering
(c) Personalization
(d) General academic integration

55. Some of the barriers to effective communication are **[Jun 2019]**
(a) Polysemy
(b) Simply language
(c) Use of Cliche's
(d) Easy construction of sentences

Choose the correct answer from the codes given below:
(i) (a) and (b) (ii) (b) and (c)
(iii) (c) and (d) (iv) (a) and (c)

56. The sequential order of elements in classroom communication is **[Jun 2019]**
(a) Knowledge, interest, evaluation, awareness
(b) Awareness, interest, evaluation, knowledge
(c) Knowledge, awareness, knowledge, interest
(d) Interest, knowledge, evaluation, awareness

57. Which of the following elements a good classroom communication should adopt? **[Jun 2019]**
(i) Concreteness
(ii) Courtesy
(iii) Filibustering
(iv) Fictionalization
(v) Coherence

Choose the answer from the options given below:
(a) (i), (ii) and (iv) (b) (ii), (iv) and (v)
(c) (i), (ii) and (v) (d) (i), (iii) and (iv)

58. Non-verbal communication is mostly **[Jun 2019]**

(a) mechanical (b) organic
(c) unstructured (d) structured

59. Below are given two sets in which Set–I describes the types of listener involved in communication, while Set–II indicates their characteristics: **[Jun 2019]**

Set–I (Types of listener involved in communication)	Set–II (Characteristics)
(A) Non-Listener	(i) is engaged in information other than the one needed
(B) Marginal Listener	(ii) receives information without processing the significance in the context of communication
(C) Evaluative Listener	(iii) looks into the relevance of the information for understanding its implication
(D) Active Listener	(iv) pays heed to the communicated information occasionally

Match the two sets and give your answer by choosing from the options given below:

	(A)	(B)	(C)	(D)
(a)	(iv)	(iii)	(ii)	(i)
(b)	(iii)	(iv)	(i)	(ii)
(c)	(ii)	(i)	(iii)	(iv)
(d)	(i)	(iv)	(ii)	(iii)

60. In the context of a classroom teaching 'Smiles or Frowns' when used as non-verbal cues, tend to perform which of the following basic functions? **[Jun 2019]**

(a) contradicting the verbal cue function
(b) regulating the verbal cue function
(c) substitute function
(d) supplement function

61. Which of the following principles a good communicator should follow? **[Jun 2019]**

(i) He should stay organized.
(ii) He should avoid the use of visuals.
(iii) He should be authoritarian.
(iv) He must adjust to the medium.
(v) He should prefer the method of story-telling.

Choose the correct answer from the options given below:

(a) (i), (ii) and (iii) (b) (ii), (iii) and (iv)
(c) (ii), (iv) and (v) (d) (i), (iv) and (v)

62. In both mass communication and classroom communication, filtering of information and contents is referred to as **[Jun 2019]**

(a) Rationalization
(b) Gatekeeping
(c) Content correction
(d) One-way flow

63. The cognitive domain of communication involves matters related to **[Jun 2019]**

(a) Emotions (b) Knowledge
(c) Fantasy (d) Escapism

64. In a classroom, a student to be an effective listener, has to take note of **[Jun 2019]**

(a) The teacher appearance
(b) The peer group
(c) The academic content
(d) Communication distractions

Choose the correct answer from the options given below:

(a) (a), (b) and (c) (b) (b), (c) and (d)
(c) (a), (d) and (c) (d) (c) and (d) only

65. In a classroom, delayed feedback can happen due to **[Jun 2019]**

(a) Use of technology
(b) Expanded communication
(c) Semantic noise
(d) Participatory environment

66. Which of the following are barriers to effective communication? **[Jun 2019]**

(i) Physical noise
(ii) Semantic noise
(iii) Psychological noise
(iv) Non-semantic noise

Choose the correct answer from the options given below.

(a) (i), (ii) and (iv) (b) (i), (ii) and (iii)
(c) (i), (iii) and (iv) (d) (i) and (iv) only

67. Match the following: **[Jun 2019]**

Set–I (Communication Elements)	Set–II (Description of Process Part)
(A) Sender	(i) Brain
(B) Receiver	(ii) Electromagnetic impulses
(C) Message	(iii) The central nervous system
(D) Medium	(iv) Sensory organs

Choose the correct answer from the options given below:

	(A)	(B)	(C)	(D)
(a)	(i)	(iii)	(ii)	(iv)
(b)	(iii)	(i)	(iv)	(ii)
(c)	(iv)	(i)	(ii)	(iii)
(d)	(ii)	(iv)	(iii)	(i)

68. Peer group interaction in a classroom helps in **[Jun 2019]**

(a) Concept understanding
(b) Realization of one's misunderstanding
(c) Rapport building
(d) Questioning

69. Listening is important for a teacher to **[Jun 2019]**

(a) Address the requirement of the learner
(b) Gain knowledge
(c) Keep the learner in good humour
(d) Evaluate the learner for the progress made

70. Semantic barrier of communication is implied when the **[Jun 2019]**

(a) Signal is lost before reaching the receiver
(b) Message transmitted by the source is unclear
(c) Receiver's attention is diverted
(d) Receiver does not understand the meaning of the message

71. Which of the following is a characteristic of modern mass media? **[Jun 2019]**

(a) Capital intensive (b) Labour intensive
(c) Sustainable (d) Developmental

72. Which of the following signifies non-verbal communication in an essential way? **[Jun 2019]**

(a) Instructions written on a question paper
(b) Learner attending an online class
(c) The dress code followed by an individual
(d) Yoga instructor teaching yoga poses to the pupils

73. *Assertion(A)* Communication presupposes a shared, symbolic environment, a social relationship even among non-participants **[Jun 2019]**

Reason (R): It lead to social interaction, which in combination with other factors contributes to a sense of community.

Choose the correct option given below:

(a) Both (A) and (R) are true and R is the correct explanation of A
(b) Both (A) and (R) are true but R is not the correct explanation of A
(c) (A) is true but (R) is false
(d) (A) is false but (R) is true

74. Which of the following is a stage of intrapersonal communication? **[Jun 2019]**

(a) Phatic stage
(b) Intimate stage
(c) Personal stage
(d) Transcendental communication

75. *Assertion (A):* The 'arts' have grown out of the fundamental desire and need to communicate **[Jun 2019]**

Reason (R): Language is inseparable from culture which is its very source of sustenance and fundamental to communication

Choose the correct option:

(a) Both (A) and (R) are true and (R) is the correct explanation of (A)
(b) Both (A) and (R) are true but (R) is not the correct explanation of (A)
(c) (A) is true but (R) is false
(d) (A) is false but (R) is true

76. A teacher while offering feedback in a classroom transaction utters, 'No, you are incorrect'. **[Jun 2019]**

They will be called which type of feedback?

(a) Positive (b) Negative
(c) Confirmatory (d) Corrective

77. Gatekeeping by media to ensure what audiences consume is indicative of **[Jun 2019]**

(a) The audiences' voice in media programming
(b) Media's control on society

(c) Feedback received by the media
(d) Media's role in creating culture

78. We listen attentively to and favourably interpret messages which boost our self image and reject of misinterpret message which threaten that image. This is called: **[Jun 2019]**

(a) Communication selectivity
(b) Change resistance
(c) Image rationalization
(d) Communication distortion

79. Which of the following is a characteristic of interpersonal communication? **[Jun 2019]**

(a) It is both focused and unfocused.
(b) It is not participation friendly.
(c) It is philosophical.
(d) It is metaphorical.

80. A communication process can be considered complete when **[Jun 2019]**

(a) The sender transmits the message
(b) The message enters the channel
(c) The message leaves the channel
(d) The receiver understands the message

81. In the context of communication, usual sequence is **[Jun 2019]**

(a) Language → Communication → Society → Civilization
(b) Communication → Society → Language → Civilization
(c) Communication → Language → Society → Civilization
(d) Language → Society → Communication → Civilization

Choose the correct answer from the options given below:

	(a)	(b)	(c)	(d)
(a)	(iii)	(iv)	(ii)	(i)
(b)	(i)	(ii)	(iii)	(iv)
(c)	(iv)	(iii)	(i)	(ii)
(d)	(ii)	(i)	(iv)	(iii)

82. Match Set 'A' with Set 'B': **[Jun 2019]**

A (Media)	B (Transmission/ communication)
(A) Audio	(i) Bandwidth
(B) Advertising	(ii) Linear communication
(C) Internet	(iii) Non-personal communication
(D) Newspaper	(iv) Frequency modulation

Choose the correct answer from the options given below:

	(A)	(B)	(C)	(D)
(a)	(iii)	(iv)	(ii)	(i)
(b)	(i)	(ii)	(iii)	(iv)
(c)	(iv)	(iii)	(i)	(ii)
(d)	(ii)	(i)	(iv)	(iii)

83. Mass media do not have pre-determined functions for everyone and people use them the way they like. This is suggestive of the fact that, **[Jun 2019]**

(a) Audiences are active
(b) Content is of little significance
(c) Content lacks plurality
(d) Audience are homogeneous

84. A customer writes to a bank, 'Kindly send me a statement of my transactions in my savings bank account 'A' during the last three months'. In terms of communication it will be called **[Jun 2019]**

(a) Input (b) Message
(c) Output (d) Feedback

85. Choose the correct sequence of communication from the options given below: **[Jun 2019]**

(a) Information–exposure–persuasion–behavioural change
(b) Persuasion–information–behavioural change–exposure
(c) Exposure–information–persuasion–behavioural change
(d) Behavioural change–information–persuasion–exposure

86. Today's media-society equation is largely **[Jun 2019]**

(a) Mystical (b) Morally bound
(c) Consumer conscious (d) Tradition centric

87. Which of the following is a function of mass media? **[Jun 2019]**

(a) To transmit culture

(b) To formulate national policies
(c) To help the judiciary take its decisions
(d) To stabilize the share market

88. The dance of the honeybee conveying to other bees where nectar will be found is an example of **[Jun 2019]**
(a) Mass communication
(b) Group communication
(c) Interpersonal communication
(d) Intrapersonal communication

89. In a classroom situation, a teacher organizes group discussion to help arrive at a solution of a problem. In terms of a model of communication used, it will be called **[Jun 2019]**
(a) A transactional model
(b) An interaction model
(c) A horizontal model
(d) A linear model

90. A key element for effictive classroom communication is **[Jun 2019]**
(a) Passivity (b) Negativity
(c) Deflection (d) Advocacy

91. Local and face-to-face commuicaton is referred to as **[Jun 2019]**
(a) Clinical integration
(b) Demonstrative integration
(c) Social integration
(d) Spatial integration

92. A basic principle of effective classroom commuication is that one should adapt his or her own ___________ to the audience. **[Jun 2019]**
(a) Accent (b) Exterior
(c) Message (d) Mannerism

93. *Assertion (A):* Communication has the power to inform, persuade and misinform. **[Jun 2019]**
Reason (R): Propaganda blurs the thin line between truth and falsehood to be persuasive.
Choose the correct answer from the options given below:
(a) Both (A) and (R) are true and (R) is the correct explanation of (A)
(b) Both (A) and (R) are true but (R) is not the correct explanation of (A)
(c) (A) is true, but (R) is false
(d) (A) is false, but (R) is true

94. In communiation process, body language is associated with **[Jun 2019]**
(a) A culture
(b) A movie audience
(c) A classroom situation
(d) A subject taught

95. *Assertion (A):* No enculturisation takes place with resistance **[Jun 2019]**
Reason (R): People have their own values and self-interest that filter communicated messages
Choose the correct answer from the options given below:
(a) Both (A) and (R) are true and (R) is the correct explanation of (A)
(b) Both (A) and (R) are true, but (R) is not the correct explanation of (A)
(c) (A) is true but (R) is false
(d) (A) is false, but (R) is true

96. 'Non-content behaviours such as rate of speaking, loudness, tendency to interrupt and pronunciation peculiarities' are referred to as ___________ behaviour. **[Jun 2019]**
(a) Extrapersonal (b) Animated
(c) Extralinguistic (d) Involuntary

97. In analog communication, content is considered to be **[Jun 2019]**
(a) Convergent (b) Static
(c) Physical (d) Ethereal

98. Swapping of encoder-decoder roles in communication happens due to: **[Dec 2019]**
(a) cognitive disruptions
(b) semantic noise
(c) feedback analysis
(d) weak channelization

99. Classroom communication is: **[Dec 2019]**
(A) like a computer program
(B) dictatorial
(C) purposeful
(D) pragmatic
Choose the correct option from those given below.
(a) (A) and (C) (b) (B) and (C)
(c) (B)and (D) (d) (C) and (D)

100. Given below are two statements, one is labelled as Assertion (A) and the other is labelled as Reason (R). **[Dec 2019]**

Assertion (A): Classroom communication is pre-decided by social and institutional demands.

Reason (R): Positive educative actions should guide learners to acquire knowledge of social significance.

In the light of the above statements, choose the correct option.

(a) Both (A) and (R) are true and (R) is the correct explanation of (A)
(b) Both (A) and (R) are true and (R) is not the correct explanation of (A)
(c) (A) is true but (R) is false
(d) (A) is false but (R) is true

101. Classroom interactions are influenced largely by: **[Dec 2019]**

(a) students' commitment
(b) teacher-centric environment
(c) organizational oversight
(d) unsolicited interventions

102. Which of the following communication technologies employ only asynchronous communication? **[Dec 2019]**

(a) Video conferencing
(b) Email
(c) Forums
(d) Instant messaging

Choose the correct option.

(a) Only (a) and (c)
(b) Only (b) and (d)
(c) Only (b) and (c)
(d) Only (a) and (d)

103. Of the following options, select the advantage of feedback in the process of communication. **[Dec 2019]**

(a) It is beneficial in understanding of the subject matter.
(b) It diagnoses the defects in receiver.
(c) It clarifies the communication.
(d) It explores the defects in receiver.

104. Which of the following groups has the components of paralanguage communication? **[Dec 2019]**

(a) Voice, emphasis and impression
(b) Social space, voice and impression
(c) Voice, social space and expression
(d) Emphasis, social space and voice

105. Successful educational communication is dependent upon the skills of: **[Dec 2019]**

(a) understanding the negative characteristics of the audience
(b) verbal communication and body language
(c) estimating time for audience impact
(d) analysing the audience needs

Choose the correct answer from the following options.

(a) Only (a) and (b) (b) Only (b) and (c)
(c) Only (c) and (d) (d) Only (b) and (d)

106. Effective educational communication is: **[Dec 2019]**

(a) non-reciprocal (b) repetitive
(c) continuous (d) coercive

107. Which of the following will help overcome communication barriers? **[Dec 2019]**

(a) Focused listening
(b) Neglecting semantic noise
(c) Top-down command structure
(d) Use of clichéd idioms

108. If data has been recorded using technical media, which among the following is a necessary step on the way to its interpretation? **[Dec 2019]**

(a) Transcription
(b) Structural equation modelling
(c) Sequential analysis
(d) Sampling

109. Which of the following theories can be applied to classroom communication? **[Dec 2019]**

(a) Theory of social constructivism
(b) Audience marginalization theory
(c) Ritualistic theory
(d) Theory of hegemony

110. Learner communication has relatively high potential of challenging: **[Dec 2019]**

(a) teaching as profession
(b) innovative and creative ideas
(c) methods of evaluation
(d) long-held attitudes

111. Communication in the classroom takes place in which of the following levels? **[Dec 2019]**
(a) Opportunistic meaning
(b) Surficial meaning
(c) Noise level meaning
(d) Non-coded meaning

112. Which of the following are rhetorical techniques for structuring classroom communication? **[Dec 2019]**
(i) Relating the day's topic to student's interests
(ii) Providing scattered information to the target audience
(iii) Smooth transition from one idea to another
(iv) Avoiding the use of artifacts
(v) Using media to improve the quality aspect of reception of messages
(vi) Opting for one-way communication

Choose the correct option from the choices given below:
(a) (i), (ii) and (iii)
(b) (ii), (iii) and (vi)
(c) (i), (iii) and (v)
(d) (iv), (v) and (vi)

113. Effective classroom communication can transform: **[Dec 2019]**
(a) academic administration
(b) academic marketing
(c) teaching-learning process
(d) management strategies

114. Which of the following are essential for a good classroom communication? **[Dec 2019]**
(i) Over emphasise on certain words
(ii) Use of gobbledygook
(iii) Proper employment of redundancy
(iv) Immediacy of feedback
(v) Non-verbal cues
(vi) Sidelining student criticism
Choose the correct option from the following:
(a) (i), (ii) and (iii)
(b) (ii), (iii) and (vi)
(c) (iii), (iv) and (v)
(d) (iv), (v) and (vi)

115. Micro expressions, as a part of classroom communication are: **[Dec 2019]**
(a) negative
(b) positive
(c) manipulative
(d) fleeting

116. Mini-summaries at the end of each class is called: **[Dec 2019]**
(a) verbal break-up
(b) clichéd conclusion
(c) verbal signposting
(d) staggered conclusion

117. Pitch of the teacher's voice in the classroom is described as: **[Dec 2019]**
(a) linguistic
(b) paralinguistic
(c) non-linguistic
(d) macro-linguistic

118. Given below are two statements: **[2020]**
Statement I: Aggressive and inflammatory statements by the teacher make the classroom communication academically effective.
Statement II: Choice of appropriate words lends credence to classroom communication processes.
In the light of the above statements, choose the most appropriate from the options given below:
(a) Both Statements I and Statement II are true.
(b) Both Statements I and Statement II are false.
(c) Statement I is correct but Statement II is false.
(d) Statement I is incorrect but Statement II is true.

119. Which of the following can be the major communication barriers to online teaching? **[2020]**
(A) Technology
(B) Legalities
(C) Student community
(D) Culture
(E) Gender
Choose the correct answer from the options given below:
(a) (A), (B), (C) only
(b) (A), (D), (E) only
(c) (B), (C), (D) only
(d) (C), (D), (E) only

120. The communication process is active and interactive at a very high level in which of the following level of teaching? **[2020]**

(a) Reflective level
(b) Understanding level
(c) Memory level
(d) Autonomous development level

121. Identify the correct sequence of the media production process. **[2020]**

(A) Content Preparation
(B) Planning
(C) Production
(D) Transmission
(E) Feedback analysis

Choose the correct answer from the options given below:

(a) (A), (B), (C), (D), (E)
(b) (B), (C), (D), (A), (E)
(c) (D), (C), (B), (E), (A)
(d) (B), (A), (C), (D), (E)

122. Cognitive dissonance in classroom communication is the result of **[2020]**

(a) Filtering of message
(b) Student interest
(c) Student-based interaction
(d) Chaotic conditions

123. Which of the following can be considered as psychological barriers to effective communication? **[2020]**

A. Descriptive message
B. Inattentiveness
C. Too much reliance on the written word
D. Limited retention
E. Logical organization
F. Flow of thought

Choose the correct answer from the options given below:

(a) A, B and C only
(b) B, C and D only
(c) C, D and E only
(d) D, E and F only

124. Match List I with List II. **[2020]**

List I Type of communication	List II Characteristics
(A) Vertical	(I) Feedback oriented
(B) Horizontal	(II) Inter-personal
(C) Circular	(III) Top-down
(D) Transactional	(IV) Rumour-oriented

Choose the correct answer from the options given below:

(a) A - I, B - II, C - III, D - IV
(b) A - II, B - III, C - IV, D - I
(c) A - III, B - IV, C - I, D - II
(d) A - IV, B - I, C - II, D - III

125. Given below are two statements: **[2020]**

Statement I: Different communities exist independent of one another but jointly somehow, they give an idea of communitarian life of a society.

Statement II: Earth exists either through a blind chance or through an inner necessity or through an external cause.

In light of the above statements, choose the most appropriate answer from the options given below:

(a) Both Statement I and Statement II are true
(b) Both Statement I and Statement II are false
(c) Statement I is true but Statement II is false
(d) Statement I is false but Statement II is true

126. Given below are two statements, one is labelled as Assertion (A) and the other is labelled as Reason (R): **[2020]**

Assertion (A): Human touch in communication enables students to become participatory.

Reason (R): In a technology-driven classroom environment, the communicative role of a teacher is secondary.

In light of the above statements, choose the correct answer from the options given below

(a) Both A and R are true and R is the correct explanation of A
(b) Both A and R are true but R is NOT the correct explanation of A
(c) A is true but R is false
(d) A is false but R is true

127. When communication meets the aims and objectives of classroom teaching, it becomes **[2020]**
(a) Extra-ordinary
(b) Personal
(c) Functional
(d) Obligatory

128. Match List I with List II: **[2020]**

List 1 (Example of Communication)	List II (Types of Communication)
(A) Sending e-mail	(I) Semiotics.
(B) Verbal instruction	(II) Transactional
(C) Exchange of information between two groups of people	(III) Formal
(D) Traffic signals	(IV) Informal

Choose the correct answer from the options given below:
(a) (A)-(III), (B)-(IV), (C)-(II), (D)-(I)
(b) (A)-(II), (B)-(III), (C)-(I), (D)-(IV)
(c) (A)-(I), (B)-(II), (C)-(IV), (D)-(III)
(d) (A)-(IV), (B)-(I), (C)-(III), (D)-(II)

129. Given below are two statements, one is labelled as Assertion A and the other is labelled as Reason R: **[2021]**

Assertion A: In classroom communication, teachers should acknowledge and take into account students' views.

Reason R: In a classroom, the probability of message reception can be enhanced by establishing a viewpoint.

In light of the above statements, choose the correct answer from the options given below
(a) A is false but R is true
(b) A is true but R is false
(c) Both A and R are true and R is the correct explanation of A
(d) Both A and R are true but R is NOT the correct explanation of A

130. Marshall Mcluhan's name is associated with the assertion: **[2021]**
(a) A message is a message
(b) The medium is the message
(c) The message determines the medium accurately
(d) The message is the medium

131. The communication among persons working at different levels who have no direct reporting relationship is called: **[2021]**
(a) Diagonal communication
(b) Horizontal communication
(c) Intrapersonal communication
(d) Upward communication

132. Which one of the following is an example of a technological barrier in communication? **[2021]**
(a) Complexity of ideas
(b) Low bandwidth of internet
(c) Personal attitude towards technology
(d) Physical locations of communicators

133. Given below are two statements: **[2021]**

Statement I: One's perceptions and beliefs are the basis of generalization in communication.

Statement II: Generalizations of the environment develop through experiences.

In light of the above statements, choose the correct answer from the options given below:
(a) Both Statement I and Statement II are false
(b) Both Statement I and Statement II are true
(c) Statement I is false but Statement II is true
(d) Statement I is true but Statement II is false

134. Which of the following are myths about communication? **[2021]**
A. Good communicators are born, not made
B. Stage fright is not a communication apprehension
C. Communication skills have nothing to do with relationships
D. Communication has its own barriers
E. Practice leads to the right habits of communication

Choose the correct answer from the options given below:
(a) A, B and C only
(b) A, D and E only
(c) B, C and D only
(d) C, D and E only

135. According to Robbins et al, the sequence of barriers to effective communication in an organization is: **[2021]**

A. Language
B. Emotions
C. Selective perception
D. Information load
E. Filtering

Choose the correct answer from the options given below:

(a) A, B, D, E, C (b) B, C, D, A, E
(c) D, A, E, C, B (d) E, C, D, B, A

136. Match List I with List II. **[2021]**

List I	List II
Elements of Effective Communication	Description
A. Common frame of reference	I. Communications with people of similar background
B. Congruence	II. Use of understandable language
C. Language relevance	III. Messages of common interest between encoder and decoder
D. Compatible environment	IV. Compatibility between the receiver and the sender

Choose the correct answer from the options given below:

(a) A -I , B -II , C -III , D -IV
(b) A -II , B -III , C -IV , D -I
(c) A -III , B -IV , C -I , D -II
(d) A -IV , B -III , C -II , D -I

137. In describing elements of communication, a person or an event which provides verbal or non-verbal use to which someone can respond is known as: **[Dec 2021]**

(a) Message
(b) Source
(c) Channel
(d) Communication context

138. Given below are two statements : One is labelled as Assertion (A) and the other is labelled as Reason (R): **[Dec 2021]**

Assertion (A): Agenda building is a collective communication process in which media, government, and the citizens reciprocally influence one another.

Reasons (R): Agenda building presumes cognitive effects and inactive audience with less societal-level effects.

In the light of the above statements, choose the most appropriate answer from the options given below:

(a) Both (A) and (R) are true and (R) is the correct explanation of (A)
(b) Both (A) and (R) are true but (R) is NOT the correct explanation of (A)
(c) (A) is true but (R) is false
(d) (A) is false but (R) is true

139. Given below are two statements: **[Dec 2021]**

Statement I: The art of Mass Communication is much more simple than of face-to-face communication or any type of communication.

Statement II: Each of us uses 3S (Sight, Sound, and Smell) and 2T (Touch and Taste) when we communicate with others.

In the light of the above statements, choose the most appropriate answer from the options given below:

(a) Both Statement I and Statement II are correct
(b) Both Statement I and Statement II are incorrect
(c) Statement I is correct but Statement II is incorrect
(d) Statement I is incorrect but Statement II is correct

140. Feedback reflects the reactions of the audience when: **[Dec 2021]**

(A) One knows the effects of communication.
(B) One knows the quality of content the message.
(C) One knows the future prospect of the object of communication.
(D) One knows the financial implications of the communication.

Choose the most appropriate answer from the options given below:
(a) (A), (B), (D) only
(b) (B), (D), (C) only
(c) (A), (C), (D) only
(d) (A), (B), (C) only

141. The power which comes through connectedness of one's words matching one's feelings, body, and facial expression in communication process is known as: **[Dec 2021]**
(a) Conformity (b) Congruence
(c) Collaboration (d) Control

142. According to communication research findings, some amount of gossip is necessary for: **[Dec 2021]**
(a) Pro-social motivation
(b) Prevention of distortion
(c) Extending communication range
(d) Relocation of emotional affiliations

143. Which of the following are important in intercultural communication? **[Dec 2021]**
A. Valuelessness
B. Absence of respect
C. Power distance
D. Individualism
E. Gender roles
Choose the *correct* answer from the options given below:
(a) A, B, and C only (b) B, C, and D only
(c) C, D, and E only (d) A, B, and E only

144. Given below are two statements, one is labelled as Assertion A and the other is labelled as Reason R: **[Dec 2021]**
Assertion A: Smiles and laughter should be avoided when messages are serious.
Reason R: Non-verbal cues are always contextual like verbal communication
In light of the above statements, choose the correct answer from the options given below
(a) Both A and R are true and R is the correct explanation of A
(b) Both A and R are true but R is NOT the correct explanation of A
(c) A is true but R is false
(d) A is false but R is true

145. Identify the sequence of human communication skills. **[Dec 2021]**
A. Public speaking B. Group interaction
C. Relationship D. Feed forward
E. Self presentation
Choose the correct answer from the options given below:
(a) B, D, E, C, A
(b) A, C, D, B, E
(c) C, E, A, D, B
(d) E, C, B, A, D

146. Match List I with List II. **[Dec 2021]**

List I (Communication barriers)	List II (Examples)
(A) Psychological	(i) Use of technical language
(B) Organizational	(ii) Poor retention
(C) Personal	(iii) Functional specialization
(D) Semantic	(iv) Fear of challenge to authority

Choose the correct answer from the options given below:

	(A)	(B)	(C)	(D)
(a)	(i)	(ii)	(iii)	(iv)
(b)	(ii)	(iii)	(iv)	(i)
(c)	(iii)	(iv)	(i)	(ii)
(d)	(iv)	(i)	(ii)	(iii)

147. In a classroom, an effective listener **[2022]**
(a) Resists distractions
(b) Seeks diversions
(c) Prefers message filtering
(d) Judges the message delivery style

148. The two way, face-to-face communication is technically referred to as **[2022]**
(a) Level one (b) Level two
(c) Level three (d) Level four

149. From the communication perspective, which of the following variables distinguish one culture from another? **[2022]**
A. Learning skills
B. Time sense
C. Level of gratitude
D. Level of honesty

Choose the correct answer from the options given below:

(a) A and B only (b) B and C only
(c) C and D only (d) A and D only

150. Given below are two statements: **[2022]**

Statement I: Small group communication fulfills the relationship needs.

Statement II: However, small group communication does not serve task related needs.

In light of the above statements, choose the correct answer from the options given below:

(a) Both statement I and statement II are true
(b) Both statement I and statement II are false
(c) Statement I is true but statement II is false
(d) Statement I is false but statement II is true

151. Which of the following are the functions of media as related to their audiences? **[2022]**

A. Creation of passive longing for media products
B. Omnivorous devouring of media content
C. Compensation through identification
D. Vicarious wish fulfillment
E. Sources of suggestion for appropriate role

Choose the correct answer from the options given below:

(a) A, B and C only (b) B, C and D only
(c) A, B and E only (d) C, D and E only

152. Suggestions for communication with people from different cultures can be: **[2022]**

A. Emphasise your interpretation
B. Forget your own cultural identity
C. Promote an eco-system of mutual respect
D. Know the cultural context of other people
E. Always state facts

Choose the correct answer from the options given below:

(a) A, B and C only (b) C, D and E only
(c) B, C and E only (d) A, D and E only

153. Given below are two statements. **[2022]**

Statement I: The new system of communication has facilitated the emergence of an interactive society.

Statement II: The new system of communication is digital and has integrated multiple modes of communication through networks.

In light of the above statements, choose the correct answer from the options given below

(a) Both Statement I and Statement II are true
(b) Both Statement I and Statement II are false
(c) Statement I is true but Statement II is false
(d) Statement I is false but Statement II is true

154. In face-to-face communication, the non-verbal cues provided by the receiver, can be considered as **[2022]**

(a) Feedback
(b) Decoding
(c) Physical noise
(d) Symbolic representaion

155. Communication compatibility between individuals is rooted in **[2022]**

(a) Stewardship (b) Interest in media
(c) Empathy (d) External influence

156. Which of the following are the advantages of grapevine communication? **[2022]**

A. Smooth float of adverse comments
b. Knowing the morale in the organisation
C. Spead of propagandist views
D. To know the important issues faced by the employees
E. Assessment of employee anxities

Choose the correct answer from the options given below:

(a) A, B and C only (b) B, C and D only
(c) D, C and E only (d) B, D and E only

157. Critical readings in mediated communication are ______ in character. **[June 2023]**

(a) emotional (b) passive
(c) ineffectual (d) cognitive

158. The symbolic mode of communication is: **[June 2023]**

(a) Instrumental (b) Non- ritualistic
(c) Socio-cultural (d) Mechanical

159. Integrating communication with the educational system will **[June 2023]**

A. increase opportunities for teachers to go abroad.
B. increase public awareness of educational rights.
C. improve the quality of policy preparation.
D. improve the educational service delivery.
E. make teachers to have access to better perks.

Choose the correct answer from the options given below:

(a) A, B, C only (b) B, C, D only
(c) C, D, E only (d) A, D, E only

160. Given below are two statements: **[June 2023]**

Statement-I: The internet reflects the existence of techno-science world of cyber-space.

Statement-II: The cyberspace has necessitated the arrival of many sub-media like e-mail, www and many others.

In the light of the above statements, choose the correct answer from the given below:

(a) Both Statement I and Statement II are true.
(b) Both Statement I and Statement II are false.
(c) Statement I is true but Statement II is false.
(d) Statement I is false but Statement II is true.

161. Match List I with List II **[June 2023]**

List I (Communication Effect)	List II (Characteristic)
A. Instrumental effect	I. Increase in self-approval
B. Prestige effect	II. Experience from the specimens of art and literature
C. Aesthetic effect	III. Pleasant distraction
D. Respite effect	IV. Competence to deal with a practical problem.

Choose the correct answer from the options given below:

(a) A-I, B-II, C-III, D-IV
(b) A-II, B-III, C-IV, D-I
(c) A-III, B-IV, C-I, D-II
(d) A-IV, B-I, C-II, D-III

162. The science of studying the feedback systems in humans, animals and machines is described as **[June 2023]**

(a) Feedback science
(b) Experience study
(c) Message Hermeneutics
(d) Cybernetics

163. De Saussure labelled language as a **[June 2023]**

(a) Technical code (b) Profusion of signs
(c) Verbalism (d) Macro generaliser

164. Which of the following are the criteria for public service communication? **[June 2023]**

A. Personal bias
B. Ideological slant
C. Accuracy
D. Comprehensiveness
E. Separation of opinion and facts

Choose the correct answer from the options given below:

(a) A, B, C only (b) B, C, D only
(c) C, D, E only (d) A, D, E only

165. According to some experts like Marshal McLuhan, the following are considered hot media: **[June 2023]**

A. Telephone
B. Television
C. Radio
D. Cinema
E. Print

Choose the correct answer from the options given below:

(a) A, B, C only (b) B, C, D only
(c) C, D, E only (d) A, C, E only

166. Given below are two statements: **[June 2023]**

Statement I: Internet itself is a network and also a model for Cyberspace relations.

Statement II: Global interactive technologies, aided by the Internet, heralded the arrival of the 'second media age' by the end of the twentieth century.

In the light of the above statements, choose the correct answer from the options given below:

(a) Both Statement I and Statement II are true.
(b) Both Statement I and Statement II are false.
(c) Statement I is true but Statement II is false.
(d) Statement I is false but Statement II is true.

167. Given below are two statements: **[Dec 2023]**

Statement (I): Buddhists consider the language of communication as a divine gift.

Statement (II): Buddhists are of the view that the language for communication evolves according to social contexts and conditions.

In light of the above statements, choose the most appropriate answer from the options given below:

(a) Both Statement (I) and Statement (II) are true.

(b) Both Statement (I) and Statement (II) are false.
(c) Statement (I) is true but Statement (II) is false.
(d) Statement (I) is false but Statement (II) is true.

168. The concept of framing is used to tailor political issues in election campaigns as part of communication strategy by **[Dec 2023]**
(a) Media audience
(b) Security agencies
(c) The Election Commission
(d) The Spin doctors

169. Which of the following are the examples of explicit meta communication? **[Dec 2023]**
A. Silent remorse
B. Avoidance of eye contact
C. Apologies
D. Excuses
E. Explanations

Choose the correct answer from the options given below:
(a) A, B and C only (b) B, C and D only
(c) C, D and E only (d) A, B and E only

170. From the communication viewpoint, a completely predictable situation is considered to have **[Dec 2023]**
(a) Less fidelity (b) Negentrophy
(c) Fluidity (d) Less sensitivity

171 Which of the following are identified as roles of non-verbal communication in relation to verbal communication? **[Dec 2023]**
A. Accentuation
B. Supervision
C. Repetition
D. Substitution
E. Contradiction

Choose the correct answer from the options given below:
(a) A, B and C only
(b) B, C, D and D only
(c) A, C, D and E only
(d) A, B and E only

ANSWER KEY

1. (d)	**2.** (d)	**3.** (d)	**4.** (c)	**5.** (c)	**6.** (d)	**7.** (b)	**8.** (b)	**9.** (d)	**10.** (b)
11. (d)	**12.** (b)	**13.** (d)	**14.** (d)	**15.** (b)	**16.** (c)	**17.** (a)	**18.** (d)	**19.** (c)	**20.** (d)
21. (b)	**22.** (c)	**23.** (d)	**24.** (a)	**25.** (a)	**26.** (b)	**27.** (a)	**28.** (b)	**29.** (d)	**30.** (c)
31. (c)	**32.** (b)	**33.** (d)	**34.** (a)	**35.** (a)	**36.** (b)	**37.** (d)	**38.** (a)	**39.** (c)	**40.** (d)
41. (d)	**42.** (c)	**43.** (c)	**44.** (a)	**45.** (d)	**46.** (d)	**47.** (b)	**48.** (a)	**49.** (b)	**50.** (a)
51. (a)	**52.** (d)	**53.** (a)	**54.** (c)	**55.** (d)	**56.** (b)	**57.** (c)	**58.** (c)	**59.** (d)	**60.** (c)
61. (d)	**62.** (b)	**63.** (b)	**64.** (d)	**65.** (c)	**66.** (b)	**67.** (c)	**68.** (a)	**69.** (a)	**70.** (d)
71. (a)	**72.** (c)	**73.** (d)	**74.** (d)	**75.** (b)	**76.** (b)	**77.** (b)	**78.** (a)	**79.** (a)	**80.** (d)
81. (c)	**82.** (c)	**83.** (a)	**84.** (b)	**85.** (c)	**86.** (c)	**87.** (a)	**88.** (b)	**89.** (a)	**90.** (d)
91. (c)	**92.** (c)	**93.** (a)	**94.** (a)	**95.** (b/d)	**96.** (c)	**97.** (b)	**98.** (c)	**99.** (d)	**100.** (a)
101. (a)	**102.** (c)	**103.** (c)	**104.** (a)	**105.** (d)	**106.** (c)	**107.** (a)	**108.** (a)	**109.** (a)	**110.** (d)
111. (b)	**112.** (c)	**113.** (c)	**114.** (c)	**115.** (d)	**116.** (c)	**117.** (b)	**118.** (d)	**119.** (b)	**120.** (a)
121. (d)	**122.** (d)	**123.** (b)	**124.** (c)	**125.** (a)	**126.** (c)	**127.** (c)	**128.** (c)	**129.** (a)	**130.** (b)
131. (a)	**132.** (b)	**133.** (b)	**134.** (a)	**135.** (d)	**136.** (d)	**137.** (b)	**138.** (c)	**139.** (d)	**140.** (d)
141. (b)	**142.** (a)	**143.** (c)	**144.** (a)	**145.** (d)	**146.** (b)	**147.** (a)	**148.** (a)	**149.** (b)	**150.** (c)
151. (d)	**152.** (b)	**153.** (a)	**154.** (a)	**155.** (c)	**156.** (d)	**157.** (d)	**158.** (c)	**159.** (b)	**160.** (a)
161. (d)	**162.** (d)	**163.** (b)	**164.** (c)	**165.** (a)	**166.** (a)	**167.** (d)	**168.** (d)	**169.** (c)	**170.** (b)
171. (c)									

HINTS AND SOLUTIONS

1. (d)

Entropy has meanings in physics and in communications theory. More generally, entropy means a process in which order deteriorates with the passage of time. It has several special meanings in data communications.

In data communications, the term entropy refers to the relative degree of randomness. The higher the entropy, the more frequent are signaling errors. Entropy is also directly proportional to noise and bandwidth.

2. (d)

The basic model IT of was also known as Shannon's Communication Model, developed in 1940s. The focus was on science and technology instruments.

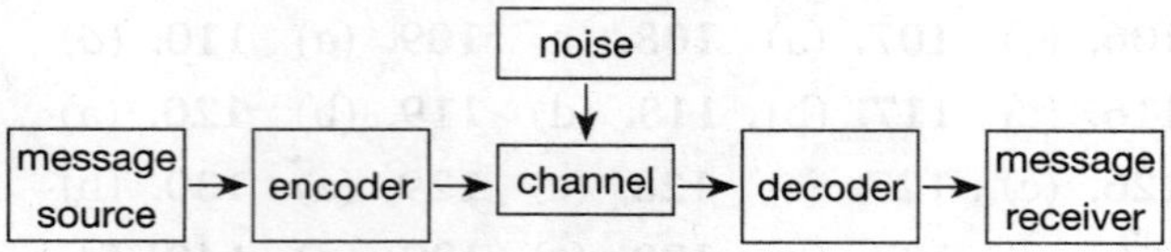

Consider a simple telephone conversation: A person (message source) speaks into a telephone receiver (encoder), which converts the sound of the spoken word into an electrical signal. This electrical signal is then transmitted over telephone lines (channel) subject to interference (noise). When the signal reaches the telephone receiver (decoder) at the other end of the line it is converted back into vocal sounds. Finally, the recipient (message receiver) hears the original message.

3. (d)

The Dadasaheb Phalke Awards is given annually at the National Films Awards, which is India's highest award in cinema. The award honours for their outstanding contribution to the growth and development of Indian cinema. The later awards have been offered to the following personalities:

Ceremonial year	Recipient	Film industry
2017 (65th)	Vinod Khanna	Hindi
2016 (64th)	Kasinathuni Viswanath	Telugu
2015 (63th)	Manoj Kumar	Hindi
2014 (62nd)	Shashi Kapoor	Hindi
2013 (61st)	Gulzar	Hindi

The first award was for Smt. Devika Rani in 1969.

4. (c)

There are many complexities involved in decoding the photograph as there are many pixels involved. Each pixel has its own characteristics.

5. (c)

The random pattern superimposed on the picture, visible as a random flicker of 'dots' or 'snow', is the result of electronic noise and radiated electromagnetic noise accidentally picked up by the antenna.

6. (d)

The given diagram shows a Circular Model, so that communication is something circular in nature. It is also termed as 'Osgood-Schramm model of communication'. It is not a traditional model. It is rather more practical.

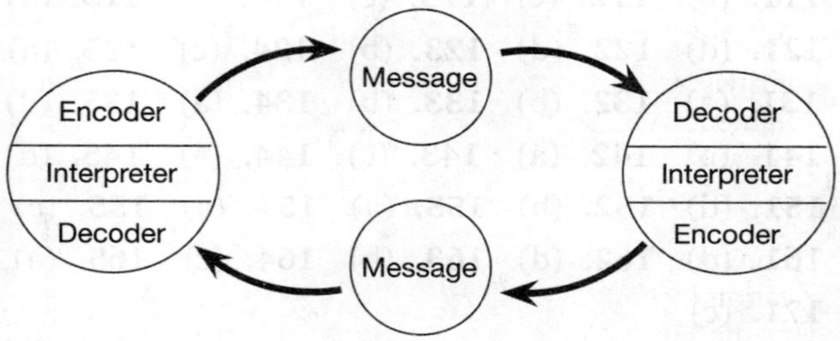

Encoder–Who does encoding or sends the message (message originates)

Decoder–Who receives the message

Interpreter–Person trying to understand (analyses, perceive) or interpret

7. (b)

Yellow journalism is a sensational style of newspaper reporting that emerged at the end of the 19th century when rival newspaper publishers William Randolph Hearst and Joseph Pulitzer competed for sales in the coverage of events leading up to and during the Spanish-American War, and it's a type of reporting that continues today.

8. (b)

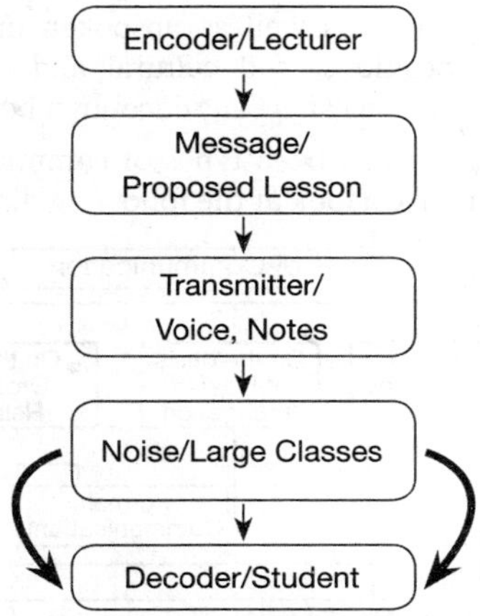

Shannon and Weaver's Communication Model

There is element of feedback also.

9. (d)

Fourth estate refers to the news media. The origin of the term is attributed to Edmund Burke, who used it in a parliamentary debate in 1787 in the House of Commons of Great Britain.

10. (b)

Common communication channels in mass communication include television, radio, social media, and print media. Examples of mass communication include commercial advertising, public relations, journalism, and political campaigning.

11. (d)

Digital empowerment basically deals with maximizing personal potential through digital technology.

12. (b)

Effectiveness of communication (specifically classroom communication) is guessed through enhancement in learning that further aims at permanent change in behaviour. Thus, options (i), (ii), and (iii) are applicable.

13. (d)

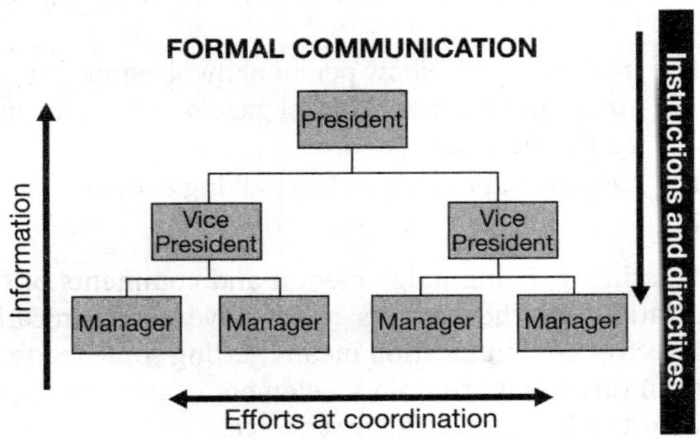

Formal communication may be faster due to internet but it is not flexible, there are rigid norms. Informal communication is 'grapevine' communication. So, it is flexible and not as per specifications.

14. (d)

This question actually covers the basic aspects of the communication. Communication is the sending and receiving of information. The communication can be
1. one-on-one
2. between groups of people
3. face-to-face
4. through communication devices.

Communication requires a sender who initiates communication so that thoughts or ideas can be communicated. For that a sender encodes a message.

The receiver of the message, decodes, or interprets the message.

Language uses symbols and signs that is distinct to the culture. That language is spoken and written between those people. There are translator options on apps that help communication between people from different languages. Effective communication requires a shared language and understanding of common concepts.

15. (b)

Grapevine communication is informal workplace dialogue in its purest form. It is characterized by conversations between employees and superiors that do not follow any prescribed structure or rule-based system. Grapevine communication spreads rapidly and likely touches each person throughout the organization.

16. (c)

Communication is basically sharing of information or ideas. Effective communication entails feedback by the receiver and is to be two way communication.

(a). The persuasive and convincing dialogue depends on the individual perceptions, theoretical perspectives, and subjective knowledge. It may be received or understood by the other persons.

(b). Participation of the audience is the direct indication of effective communication. The questions will be put by the audience who have understood or tried to understand the ideas by sender but may have further queries.

(c). One way transfer of information is conveyed by the sender but not been received or understood by the receiver.

(d). Grapevine means informal communication in a group situation.

17. (a)

Verbal communication means exchanging messages with one another and develop as individuals. The term verbal communication often evokes the idea of spoken communication, but written communication is also part of verbal communication.

18. (d)

Mind mapping is a highly effective way of getting information in and out of your brain. Mind mapping is a creative and logical means of note-taking and note-making that literally 'maps out' your ideas. All mind maps have some things in common.

We can take the following perspective also for mind mapping:

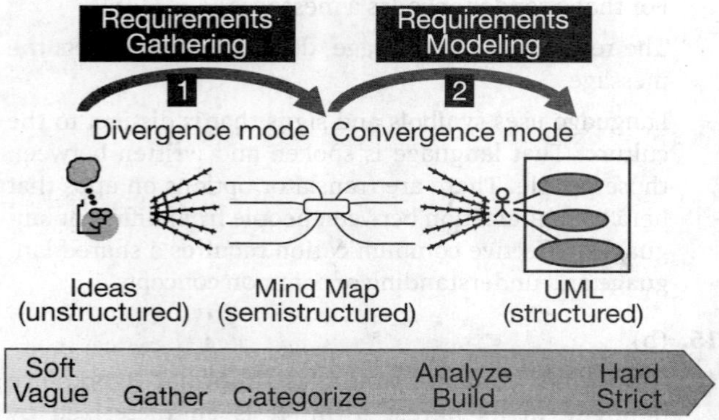

19. (c)

Among the forms of paralanguage, we find physical elements like facial expressions or gestures. There are also many vocal features that contribute to our interpretation of spoken language, such as voiced pauses or intonation.

20. (d)

Context in communication refers to the surrounding physical environment and the framework of related facts and events within which a communication takes place. These contextual factors affect the perception of a person which in turn influences the way a message is decoded understood by the recipient.

The context can be anyone or all of the following:

(1) Physical: actual setting, place and space

(2) Temporal: linked with time

(3) Social: psychological settings

(4) Technical

21. (b)

Non-verbal is a form of communication without the use of spoken or written language. It includes gestures, facial expressions, and body positions (known collectively as 'body language'), as well as unspoken understandings and presuppositions, and cultural and environmental conditions that may affect any encounter between people.

As many are asked from types of communication, students must have a look at the following diagram:

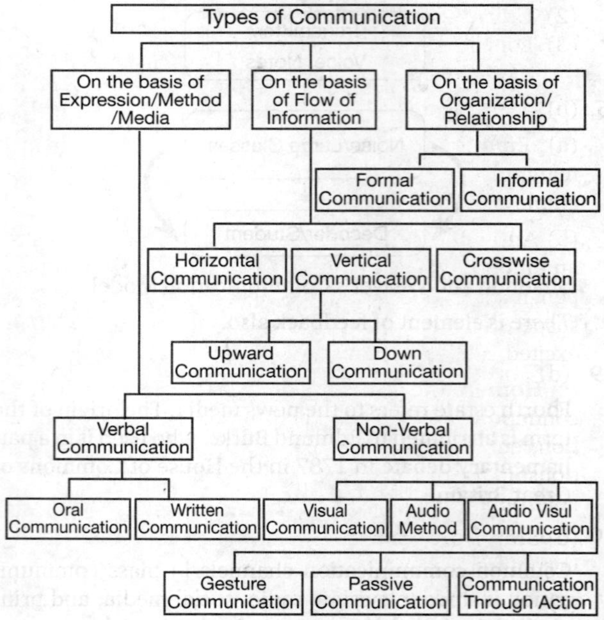

22. (c)

Classroom communication takes place with certain clear objectives, so it is utilitarian.

Jeremy Bentham (1748—1832) was the father of modern utilitarianism, a moral theory that argues that actions should be judged right or wrong to the extent they increase or decrease human well-being or 'utility'.

23. (d)

Eye contact is most important in a classroom, it reflects level of confidence.

(1) eye contact is form of non-verbal communication and is thought to have a large influence on social behaviour.

(2) It is believed to show personal involvemnet and create intimate bonds. Mutual gaze narrows the physical gap between humans.

(3) we can read one's mind by looking at eyes.

24. (a)

Moralizing, being judge-mental and comments of consolation are the barriers to effective communication. Effective communication means getting some feedback, even this should contain an element of motivation, this is best reflected through first choice.

25. (a)

The first choice is based on positivity as far as choice of partners is concerned.

Communication partners provide a kind of context for better communication and decision making.

(1) Proximity—remaining close
(2) Utility—useful
(3) Loneliness—one does feel isolated and therefore motivated to start communication.

26. (b)

(a) **Emotional manipulation:** This occurs when a manipulative person seeks power over someone else and employs dishonest or exploitive strategies to gain it.

(b) **Anticipatory Excitement**: This may be counted as an emotion when we are expecting something to happen, may be good or bad. We are left in a state of anxious suspense at that point of time. Some people may feel excited, and some may come under stress.

(c) **Homophilic Issues** – Such type of individuals share common characteristics such as beliefs, values, education, etc. That aspect makes communication and relationship formation easier. The opposite of it is called as heterophilic.

(d) **Status dislocation** – This can be counted as barrier in communication.

27. (a)

Kindly note down the following points for horizontal communication.

(1) In this communication, information flows between people holding same rank and status.
(2) Horizontal communication enjoys greater degree of informality.
(3) Horizontal communication is mostly done through oral media.
(4) Message of horizontal communication are usually free from distortion.
(5) Horizontal communication occurs in short line as it happens directly between sender and receiver.

28. (b)

Voice modulation means to generate more interest and break monotony while addressing students in a classroom.

29. (d)

Understanding means being empathetic towards each other.

'Effective' includes quality and feedback also.

30. (c)

Concept of kinesics with non-verbal behavior and it has been mentioned in the Mehrabian model that words account for 7%, tone of voice accounts for 38% and body language accounts for 55% of communication.

31. (c)

The answer is (c), in this question more facts are being delivered in the class.

We need to have some idea about the types of knowledge or information that should be shared with the learners in a classroom. A psychologist, David Krathwohl (2002) categorised knowledge into four types:

1. Factual Knowledge – deals with terminologies, glossaries, details and necessary building details of any professional domain
2. Conceptual Knowledge – deals with the interconnectedness of facts is what forms the body of conceptual knowledge stored in our minds. Conceptual knowledge allows us to collect facts and ideas and group them into clusters that represent connectivity.
3. Procedural Knowledge – it talks about every task or action required to attain any given goal.
4. Metacognitive Knowledge – it is seen as the 'mother' of all other knowledge types, discussed above. Metacognition represents your ability to use previously learned knowledge to plan a strategy, be self-reflective or understand the world around you.

32. (b)

Expressive communication is an assertive message to another person. This includes feelings, wants, likes, dislikes, gesturing (and facial expressions), writing, comments, intents, vocalizations (crying, yelling) etc. It can be thought of as the output. For effective communication, both expressive and receptive communication must occur.

33. (d)

Positive classroom communication creates healthy interactions between a teacher and students, and also in between students. This will improve the ambiance of the class. The learning becomes more effective. It improves the personality aspect of the students. The class becomes more innovative.

34. (a)

A social identity is the portion of an individual's self-concept derived from perceived membership in a relevant social group. Social identity has been explained in a way that makes it easy to explain intergroup behaviour.

35. (a)

It was developed by Sweller in late 1980s, Cognitive Load theory focuses on amount of mental effort being used in working memory and how instructional design can be used to reduce cognitive load in learners.

36. (b)

An empathetic teacher uses teachable moments in class to explain how one student or even a character in a story might be feeling during a certain situation. This will get your students thinking about things from the perspectives of others. Emphasize shared values and common interests. One diagrams regarding empathy have been placed under 2018 Papers also.

37. (d)

The main objective of ice-breaking questions/interactions is to create congenial, humorous and motivating environment for discussion.

38. (a)

When students move to higher classes, students tend to develop reflective understanding of the facts, they want to develop a thought process or opinion. The learners want to come with new innovative ideas.

39. (c)

Selective attention is a cognitive process in which a person attends to one or a few sensory inputs/stimuli while ignoring the other ones.

'Selective Expectation of Performance' is also seemingly right but it is not a standardized term. Students are aware of differential classroom treatment, where high achievers receive more frequent and challenging opportunities to participate in class, more appreciation, more trust and greater autonomy.

NET aspirants can refer to terms 'sensorybuffer', 'filtering of messages', 'selective perception', etc., for future exams.

40. (d)

Assertion (A): We use to say that the first impression is the last impression. Thus, initial dialogue has long term implications. That may be set as per syllabus, it creates clear cut goals among the students as a teacher tries to generate an initial approach, plan or strategy to deal with the things.

This assertion has been found to be false.

Reason (R): There is usually more control of teacher while delivering a lecture in the classroom.

This reason is true.

Thus, (d) is the correct answer.

41. (d)

Principles of Effective Classroom Communication. To communicate well in the classroom is more a learnt ability than a natural ability. So, option (A) is false.

Effective teaching is helped by the knowledge of communication process.

42. (c)

Refer to Classroom Communication Process: Classroom communication is basically a transactional model wherein a sender represents the individual who has important information that needs to reach someone else, and a feedback mechanism is very crucial to ensure its effectiveness.

Reason (R) is incorrect as teaching is effective only if there is some feedback mechanism and students' responses are to be taken seriously.

'Cole and Chan Model' is considered as two-way 'interactive' communication process.

43. (c)

(A) Non-verbal messages include all the Non-verbal aspects of our behaviour: facial expression, posture, tone of voice, hand movements, manner of dress, and so on.

(B) Communication is a learnt ability means that this can be learnt and improved further.

(C) It is clear that human communication occurs in several kinds of situation but is not a panacea always.

(D) Communication cannot breakdown; it merely changes. For instance, when you ignore someone, you are communicating to them that you do not wish to talk.

(E) Effective when a person gets his or her point across. This is but one measure of effectiveness.

(F) Communication is always with some objective.

There are various characteristic features of Communication chapter in NTA-UGC NET/SET/JRF Paper I—Teaching and Research Aptitude published by Pearson Education.

44. (a)

Empathy means getting into shoes of others.

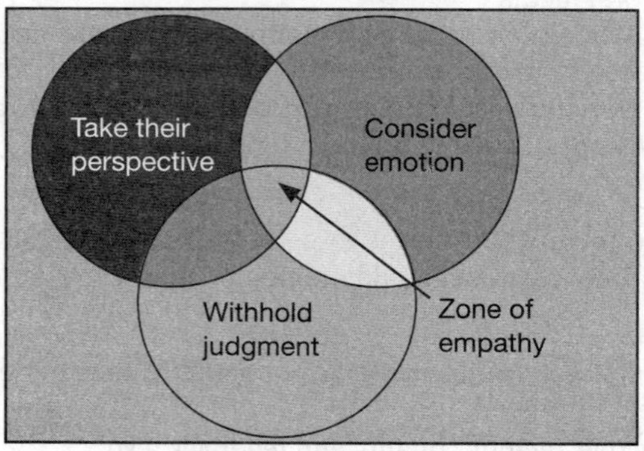

Empathy leads to strengthening of collaborative, negotiating, creative, safety, emotional connectivity, identifying needs of others and types of skills over a period. This can be linked with emotional intelligence also.

45. (d)

Tactile communication refers to what we communicate through the sense of touch through touching, or not touching each other in various ways. Touch may be the most primal or basic form of communication, since it's the way things are communicated to infants, way before infants has learned anything about other modes of communication. Tactile messages tend to convey aspects of emotional and attitudinal states.

Haptics is the science of applying touch (tactile) sensation and control to interaction with computer applications. The word derives from the Greek *haptein* meaning 'to fasten.'

46. (d)

The networking is basically through Web 2.0.

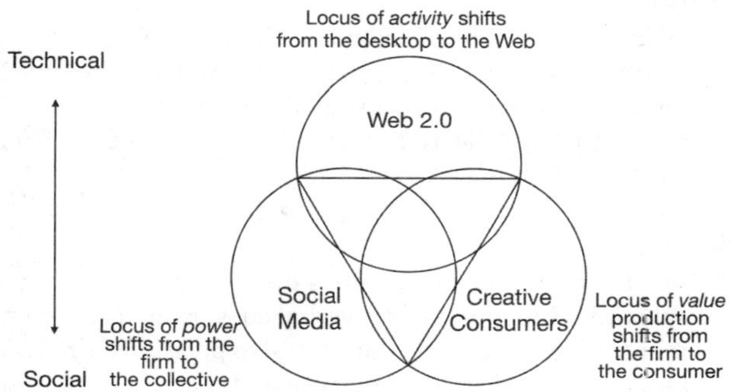

47. (b)

Telescopic means relating to or made with a telescope.

Teleology means a reason or explanation for something as a function of its end, purpose, or goal. It is derived from two Greek words: *telos* (end, goal, purpose) and *logos* (reason, explanation).

The modern trend is of distributive communication in education. It is an instructional model that allows instructor, students, and content to be located in different, non-centralized locations so that instruction and learning occurs independent of time and place.

The non-distributive communication is opposite of the distributive communication.

Unapproximate is a negative term to be attached with communication. With science, we tend to move towards accuracies.

48. (a)

We can look at the meanings.

(a). A symbol is a mark, sign or word that indicates, signifies, or is understood as representing an idea, object, or relationship.

(b). Decoratives may be images (or even emoticons should be put in the same sense, they may enhance communication but they are not words.

(c). Passive barriers are usually taken in the form of security. They limit access.

(d). Filler words, or discourse markers, are words, phrases or sounds that fill up space in writing or conversation without adding substance. They may happen when we are not confident, have no clarity or may use them for distraction. For example, we may use fillers such as um, uh, er, ah, okay, right etc. For example, saying okay is followed by a sentence. "Okay, I think we're ready to get started." Here, saying okay or the other part was enough.

49. (b)

Audience fragmentation takes us away from principle of equality. Attention diversion may be practiced occasionally. Cues are of no use if they don't provide information in the learning process. Intensive listener focus is the basis of classroom communication.

50. (a)

Knowledge is a familiarity, awareness, or understanding of someone or something, such as facts, information, descriptions, or skills, which is acquired through experience or education by perceiving, discovering, or learning. Knowledge can refer to a theoretical or practical understanding of a subject.

Subject Matter is to be used in a sentence noun. Subject matter is what something is about. An example of subject matter is a paper written about cows.

Articulation is the act of expressing something in a coherent verbal form, or an aspect of pronunciation involving the articulatory organs. Articulation comes from the Latin word for jointed or 'divided into joints.' The joints themselves can also be called articulations.

Felicity is great happiness and pleasure. If it is there, it means that even language has been falls in the definition of felicity.

51. (a)

Challenging behaviour is any behaviour that interferes with a child's learning, engagement, and social interactions with her peers or adults. As early as preschool, challenging behaviour can lead to fewer social interactions, lesser academic engagement, and the diagnosis of emotional or behavioural disorders.

Procedural challenge means a leaner is not able to understand the procedure set by the teacher as per his pedagogy.

Evaluation challenge—There is no one-size-fits-all approach for evaluating rural programs and interventions. Even a well-designed evaluation strategy may encounter challenge.

52. (d)

Use of communication Technology requires (presuppose) new forms of expression and applications.

(a) Inattentive audience may be dealt better by direct human involvement.

(b) Communication technology is required by all of us.

(c) Extrapolation of contents is to be done better by human involvement.

53. (a)

Mass media as communication correlate the aspects given in (R). Thus, (a) is the correct answer.

54. (c)

We need to focus on two terms specific user. In answers, our focus shifts to personalization in that context.

55. (d)

(a) and (c) are barriers to effective communication.

(a) Polysemy is an aspect of 'semantic ambiguity' that concerns the multiplicity of word meanings. For example, good day, good orange, good decision, etc.

(c) A cliché is a word or phrase that has been overused in writing. Clichés such as 'leave no stone unturned' have been used so much in writing that they have lost all their effectiveness. These phrases have become weak and meaningless.

56. (b)

Communication plays a crucial role in a classroom teaching-learning process. It takes place between teachers and learners as well as among learners. Classroom communication consists of four elements.

1. Awareness: Classroom communication starts when the teacher makes the learners aware of the lesson that he/she is about to teach. This involves telling them the objectives of the lesson before starting the lesson.
2. Interest: The second step is to get the learners engaged and interested in the lesson by making use of interesting techniques of teaching, connecting the lesson with real life, using appealing teaching aids, etc.
3. Evaluation: Once the lesson is taught, the learners are assessed on their learning. This can be done in many ways. Evaluation occurs during the lesson and also after the lesson.
4. Knowledge: Following the above steps successfully will lead to the gaining of new knowledge in the learners. It is the outcome of the communication process where the pre-set goal of gaining knowledge is achieved.

Thus, the classroom communication process follows the above-mentioned sequential order

57. (c)

Filibustering means 'to obstruct legislation by talking at great length', thus it's a kind of obstruction in legislative process.

Fictionalization means a narrative, explanation, or belief that may seem true but is false or fabricated.

So these don't apply in creating a good classroom communication.

58. (c)

Non-verbal communication happens through gestures, touch (haptic), body language, posture, facial expression and eye contact. It is mostly unstructured, and varies according to culture and context.

59. (d)

Listening is a skill of language. It is a combination of hearing what another person says and psychological involvement with the person who is talking. Active listening (or say reflective listening) comes at the top from learning point of view.

60. (c)

As per communication unit, 'smiles or frowns' perform substitute function as non-verbal cues. Non-verbal communication or cues includes facial expressions, eye contact, tone of voice, body posture and motions, and positioning within groups. It may also include the way we wear our clothes or the silence we keep.

According to G. W. Porter, non-verbal communication has four broad types:

Physical is the personal type that includes facial expressions, tone of voice, sense of touch, sense of smell, and body motions.

Aesthetic communication takes place through creative expressions: playing instrumental music, dancing, painting and sculpturing.

Signs is the mechanical type of communication, which includes the use of signal flags, gun salutations, horns, sirens etc.

Symbolic makes use of religious, status, or ego-building symbols.

Static Features in non-verbal cues includes distance, orientation, posture, and physical contact. The dynamic features include facial Expressions, gestures, looking etc.

61. (d)

(ii) It should be about optimum use of visuals, not for avoiding purpose. In (iii), if a person is authoritarian, he becomes inaccessible. Story telling is better for engaging the people.

62. (b)

Gatekeeping is the process through which information is filtered for dissemination, whether for publication, broadcasting, the Internet, or some other mode of communication.

63. (b)

Cognitive involves some conscious intellectual activity. Thus, answer is 'Knowledge'. Emotions and fantasy (to an extent) indicates affective domain. Escapism means tendency to seek distraction and relief from unpleasant realities towards some fantasy.

64. (d)

A student, in order to be effective listener, should focus on the academic content and to be away from communication distractions.

65. (c)

Semantic noise in communication is a type of disturbance in the transmission of a message that interferes with the interpretation of the message due to ambiguity in words, sentences or symbols used in the transmission of the message.

66. (b)

The following are some of the main barriers:

(1) Linguistic Barriers

(2) Psychological Barriers

(3) Emotional Barriers

(4) Physical Barriers

(5) Cultural Barriers

(6) Organizational Structure Barriers

(7) Attitude Barriers

(8) Perception Barriers

(9) Physiological Barriers

(10) Technological Barriers

(11) Socio-religious Barriers

(12) Semantic Barriers

67. (c)

According to the question, we have identified the following elements of communication.

Sender – He is the initiator of the idea or information that is to be sent to the other person. That message is encoded. The sender uses his sensory organs to send the message.

Message – This is a group of signs and symbols. This sensory output is carried as electromagnetic impulses by axons, neurons and dendrites. Then chemical reactions do take place in the brains also so that message is conveyed.

Receiver – The message is decoded in the brain of receiver.

Medium – The message is conveyed through Central Nervous System and spinal cord.

Feedback – In feedback, the receiver of the message assumes the role of sender of message. When feedback is there, it becomes two way communication.

68. (a)

A peer is someone at your own level. If you are a 10th grader, other high school students are your peers. Peer comes from the Latin par which means equal. When you are on par with someone, you are their peer. If kids of your age are pressuring you to do something you don't want to do, that's peer pressure.

Peer group interaction basically helps in better conceptual clarity. The members of peer group are likely to be more innovative. At a secondary level, they may help in realization of one's misunderstanding.

Rapport building is to develop mutual trust, empathy and understanding with students.

Questioning is usually done in the classroom.

69. (a)

Listening is an important aspect of effective communication. The following diagram reflects upon the importance of listening in the class communication.

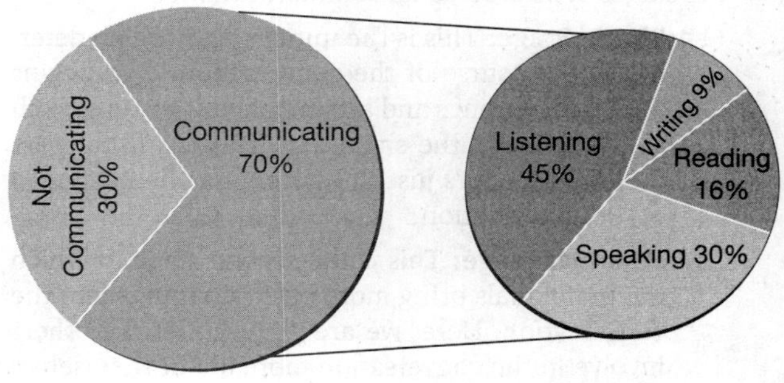

For a teacher, listening does mean that they learn more about the queries of the students. Their effective redress makes the teaching more effective. Gain knowledge, keep the learner in good humour and evaluating the learner for the progress made are also the secondary benefits.

70. (d)

Semantic barriers to communication are the symbolic obstacles that distorts the sent message in some other way than intended, making the message difficult to understand. The meaning of words, signs and symbols might be different from one person to another and the same word might have hundreds of meanings.

71. (a)

Modern mass media is part of globalization that makes it capital intensive also. For example, we can use the term, cultural hegemony that refers to the power of the dominant culture to overshadow and even overtake local cultures. Though internet has become a cheaper option throughout the world but economies of scale, experience good, switching costs are the various factors that make modern mass media an expensive venture.

72. (c)

Although no word is used in non-verbal communication, it can effectively communicate many human feelings more accurately than verbal methods of communication. The dress code followed in third choice indicates that it is part of our culture.

In other choices use of words such as instructions written, learner attending classes, and instructor teaching tells that they are verbal communication.

73. (d)

In the assertion, communication may not always be shared or pertains to symbolic environment. Participation is also required.
In reason, social interaction is an important aspect for any kind of communication to take place.

74. (d)

We can communicate effectively when we understand the stages of interpersonal communication:

(1) **Phatic Stage:** This is the initial stage, which determines the course of the conversation. This begins with the greetings and accompanying gestures such as eye contact, the smile, etc. There is usually no intention, but it's just the setting for the next level of the conversation.

(2) **Personal Stage:** This is the second stage in which the individuals bring more personal things into the conversation. Here, we are ready to let the others involve in the conversation more about themselves and the hesitation decreases.

(3) **Intimate Stage:** This stage is mainly meant for conversations between friends, family and relatives, where those involved in the conversation share a higher level of intimacy with each other.

The definition of transcendent is extraordinary or beyond human experience. Talking to God or even himself is an example of a transcendent experience.

75. (b)

Art is often considered the process or product of deliberately arranging gap elements in a way that appeals to the senses or emotions. It encompasses a diverse range of human activities, creations and ways of expression, including music, literature, film, sculpture and paintings. Arts help in communication, with or without use of words.

Here, language been taken in different context and perspective. So, both the assertion and reason are correct but are not interrelated.

76. (b)

Negative is the right word to explain the teacher's feedback in the statement. Other choices positive, confirmatory, corrective give us the almost the same meaning.

77. (b)

The role of a gatekeeper within communication is of extreme importance. Katz's in its 'Intermediary Model of Communication' talks about the role of gatekeepers or intermediaries or censor groups. These gatekeepers have some ability to shape the organization through their selective sharing of information. Katz talked about technical skills, human skills and conceptual skills in case of management.

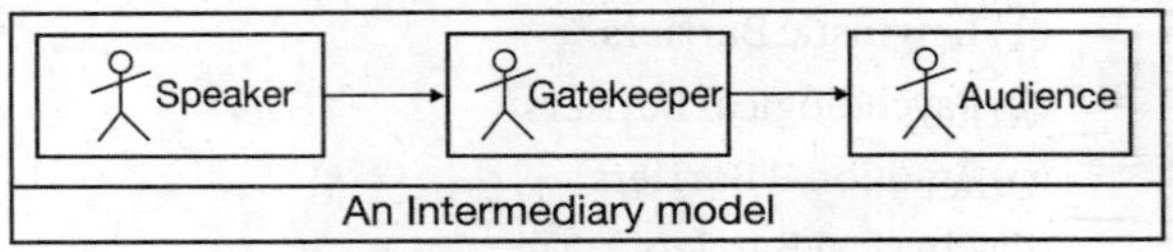

78. (a)

Here, definition of communication selectivity has been given in the question statement itself.

Communication selectivity is kind of communication barrier. If we were to consider the fault, it is of the receiver and not of the sender. This can be part of written communication also. It can be explained with the help of a diagram also.

Communication vehicles/messages

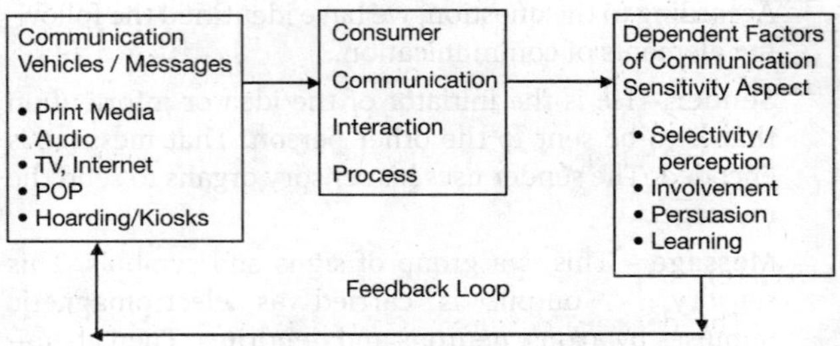

79. (a)

The answer is quite direct. Interpersonal can be focused and unfocused.

Let's understand metaphorical discussion also for such questions in future exams.

Metaphors help writers and poets make a point in a more interesting way. They also help the reader see something from a new perspective.

A metaphor is a figure of speech that is used to make a comparison between two things that aren't alike but do have something in common. Unlike a simile, where two things are compared directly using like or as, a metaphor's comparison is more indirect, usually made by stating something is something else. A metaphor is very expressive; it is not meant to be taken literally. You may have to work a little to find the meaning in a metaphor.

For example, a river and tears aren't very alike. One is a body of water in nature, while the other can be produced by our eyes. They do have one thing in common, though: both are a type of water that flows. A metaphor uses this similarity to help the writer make a point:

Her tears were a river flowing down her cheeks.

As a river is so much larger than a few tears, the metaphor is a creative way of saying that the person is crying a lot. There are so many tears that they remind the writer of a river.

Other examples are:

(1) The snow is a white blanket.

(2) He is a shining star.

(3) Her long hair was a flowing golden river.

80. (d)

The process of communication is complete and cyclic one as, it begins with the sender and ends with the sender in the form of feedback he receives.

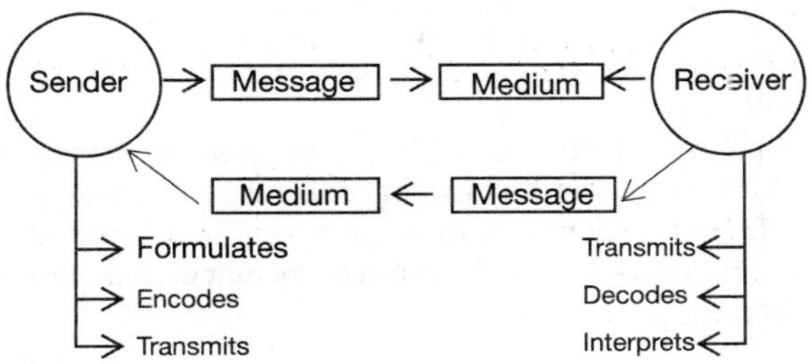

81. (c)

The desire of communication was the main cause of language making. Language is a constituent element of forming a society which creates civilization.

82. (c)

Frequency modulation (FM) is the encoding of information in a carrier wave by varying the instantaneous frequency of the wave. FM is used at audio frequencies to synthesize sound. This technique is called as FM synthesis.

Advertising is a non-personal communication that employs an openly sponsored to promote a product, service or idea. Sponsors of advertising are typically businesses wishing to promote their products or services. Advertising is differentiated from public relations in that an advertiser pays for and has control over the message.

Internet is the global system of interconnected computer networks through bandwidths. It uses internet protocol suite (TCP/IP) to link devices worldwide.

Newspaper is a linear communication that is printed on paper on a regular basis. It gives information and opinions about current events and news and many other topics such as political events, crime, business, sports, and opinions.

83. (a)

Mass media usually deal with a scope of an area, may be through changing contents. Thus, audience needs to be active to engage with them on continuous basis.

84. (b)

Here, the answer is message. Input and output are parts of a information system.

85. (c)

Exposure means we get some messages from surroundings, some information is generated as a result. Information leads to a kind of persuasion or motivation and ultimately, it should result in the change of our behaviour.

86. (c)

Media has become a popular vehicle for marketers in promoting their corporation, products and services, specifically in highly individualized and privatized society.

87. (a)

Mass communication is a process of disseminating messages to a large number of audiences through some forms of technology at a time. And some forms of technology used to disseminate messages is the mass media.

Mass media are the means of public communication reaching to the large, scattered, heterogeneous and anonymous audience at the same time. Mass media have been proved a boon to human society. Nothing has influenced the lives of modern men as the mass media have.

Mass media functions can be divided into following two parts: General and Specific.

Under general functions, the following are important:

(1) **Information:** Information is knowledge and knowledge is power. Mass media offers authentic and timely facts. Information provided by mass media can be opinionated, objective, subjective, primary and secondary. Informative functions of mass media also lets the audience knows about the happening around them and come to the truth.

(2) **Education:** Education is defined as a sort of cultural transmission. Media have been successful in eradicating various traditional and evil superstitious practices from society through continuous advocacy. Media tries to educate people directly or indirectly using different forms of content. Distance education program, for example, is a direct approach. Dramas, documentaries, interviews, feature stories and many other programs are prepared to educate people indirectly. Especially in the developing country, mass media is used as effective tools for mass awareness.

Then we have 'entertainment' and 'persuasion' functions. Persuasion involves making influence on others mind. Media content builds opinions and sets agendas in the public mind. It influences voters, changes attitudes and moderates behaviour. Using editorials, articles, commentaries and among others, mass media persuades audience.

The main specific functions of mass media are as follows:

(1) **Surveillance:** Surveillance denotes observation. Here observation means to watch the society closely. The function of mass media is to observe the society closely and continuously. Warning surveillance occurs when the media informs us about threats from hurricanes, erupting volcanoes, increasing deforestation, drug abuse, girls trafficking.

(2) **Interpretation:** Unlike reporting, interpretation functions provide knowledge. News analysis, commentaries, editorials, and columns are some examples of interpretative contents.

(3) **Linkage:** The function of mass media is to join together different elements of society that are not directly connected. For instance: mass advertising attempts to link the needs of buyers with the products of sellers.

(4) **Socialization:** Socialization is the transmission of culture. Media are the reflectors of society. They socialize people, especially children and new-comers. Socialization is a process by which, people are made to behave in ways that are acceptable in their culture or society. Through this process, we learn how to become a member of our society or human society in greater sense. Whenever a person reads newspaper or watches television, individual knows how people react on matters and what types of norms and values they perceive on particular event, issue or situation.

Through the process of socialization, media help to shape our behaviours, conducts, attitudes and beliefs. The process of socialization brings people close and ties them into single unity.

The four functions of mass media are: surveillance, correlation, cultural transmission and entertainment. In many ways, the four functions of mass media are still relevant and transferable to contemporary media.

88. (b)

'Dancing of honeybee' is a kind of group communication of members of same community.

89. (a)

The transactional model is a continuous model, it helps in solution of problems through discussions also as given in the diagram below:

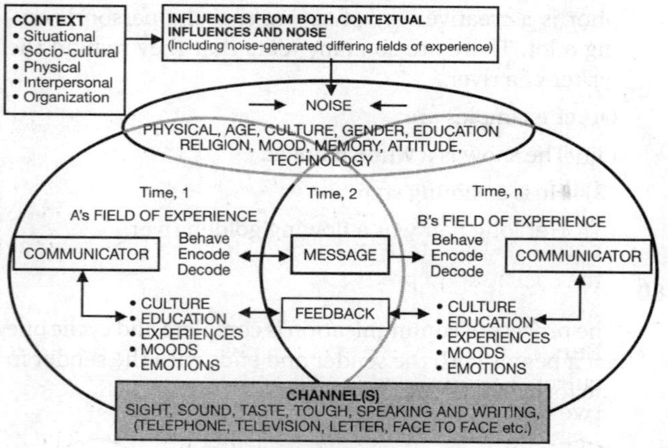

A transactional model of communication

90. (d)

Options (a), (b) and (c) carry negative meanings and don't fit in the context of 'effective communication'. Advocacy communication puts you in a position of 'standing for', or advocating a particular action, position or set of principles.

91. (c)

Communicating with someone face-to-face implies that you are both present in the same place with each other. Almost ditto is the explanation for local. Thus, these are examples of social integration.

92. (c)

When we use the word 'effective' in communication, the focus is always on effectiveness in conveying the message.

93. (a)

Here, in reason (R), propaganda is taken as the type of communication which spreads false or exaggerated information—inform is akin to truth, misinform is akin to falsehood and persuasion is again used in both assertion and reason.

94. (a)

Body language makes-up the largest part of our non-verbal communication—eye contact, gestures, and facial expressions can convey powerful messages. However, there are substantial cultural differences in how people use body language to communicate.

One example is given below:

95. (b/d)

As per NTA different answer key is provided for the same question, so possible explanations are as follows.

Culture refers to a distinctive way of living of a community including the shared customs, rituals, traditions and norms that are transmitted across generations through the socialisation process.

Assertion (A):

Enculturation: All human beings are raised within a cultural context, wherein their language and cognitive development occur. This process of engaging with one's own culture is known as enculturation. The key to enculturation is learning by observation, as it takes place without any direct or deliberate teaching. This process begins at childhood by conditioning to fundamental habits such as eating, sleeping, speaking, and personal hygiene.

Acculturation: It is the process of adaptation to a new cultural environment. It is the cultural and psychological changes resulting from contact with other cultures. It may be voluntary (e.g. one goes abroad for higher studies) or involuntary (through colonialism or invasion). For example, several individuals adopted the various aspects of the British lifestyle during the colonial period in India. Acculturation often generates or triggers some kind of conflict or resistance to change in both groups (the dominant as well as the non-dominant cultural group).

So, the assertion (A) that 'No enculturation takes place with resistance' is true.

Reason (R):

A message is essentially an idea that someone wants to convey to others. Filtering is a process of withholding or not communicating information to others. People see and hear through a filter made up of their own values, feelings, attitudes, self-interest and reaction patterns. Some people tend to filter messages that are not consistent with their views or that can harm their self-interest.

So, Reason (R) is true.

Hence, Both (A) and (R) are true but (R) is not the correct explanation of (A).

Alternative solution

Culture refers to a distinctive way of living of a community including the shared customs, rituals, traditions and norms that are transmitted across generations through the socialisation process.

Assertion (A):

According to Maslow's hierarchy of needs, self-actualization is the highest level in Maslow's hierarchy and refer to the realization of a person's potential or self-fulfillment. Self-actualizing people do not approve of and identify with their culture - i.e., they are not well-adjusted. They get along with the culture in various ways, at the same time in a more meaningful sense, they resist enculturation and detach themselves from the culture in which they are immersed, i.e. enculturation is encountered with some kind of resistance.

So, Assertion (A) is false.

Reason (R):

A message is essentially an idea that someone wants to convey to others. Filtering is a process of withholding or not communicating information to others. People see and hear through a filter made up of their own values, feelings, attitudes, self-interest and reaction patterns. Some people tend to filter messages that are not consistent with their views or that can harm their self-interest.

So, Reason (R) is true.

Hence, (A) is false, but (R) is true.

96. (c)

Extra-linguistic behaviours are the non-content aspects which includes temporal- such as rate of speaking and rhythm,verbal stylistic- such as pronunciation peculiarities, dialect and tendency to interrupt or dominate. Extralinguistic behaviour is also called as Para-language.

97. (b)

Analog communication is the process of conveying i.e. sending, receiving and processing of information including image, voice and video by using continuous signals or analog signals. Here the content can only be linear and static but not dynamic.

98. (c)

Feedback analysis is the process of setting up objective for yourself and reviewing how you performed.

It is about listening actively, taking the time to analyse and then thinking of the best possible solution to perform better. It produce positive criticism and allow to see what everyone can change to improve their focus and result. It brings people together and creates a healthy communication flow with the help of encoding and decoding.

Encoding means the creation of a message (which you want to communicate with other person

Decoding means interpreting the meaning of the message.

99. (d)

(i) Purposeful communication goes beyond just understanding the exchange of these ideas and hones in on why they exist. It allows an organization to think about the reason behind your communication, the most effective approach and the outcome you want to achieve.

(ii) Pragmatic communication refers to the way in which the children use language within the social situations.

- The ability to use language for different purposes.
- The ability to adapt language to meet the need of the listener of situation.

100. (a)

There is direct relation between societal demands and communication objectives.

101. (a)

Classroom interactions with teachers and peers are critical for learners academic, social and behavioral development. Students commitment is the key for classroom interaction to be effective. In constructivist classroom approach students active participation and commitment emphasizes collaboration and exchange of ideas.

102. (c)

Asynchronous communication is the exchange of message such as among the hosts on a network or devices in a computer by reading and responding as schedules permit, rather than according to some clock that is synchronized for both the sender and receiver or in real time.

Most communications between devices within computers (between the CPU and disk drives) and between computers and external devices (for example, modems and printers) are asynchronous. Asynchronous communications also include computer-based exchange of messages, for which the participants need not be available or online at the same time, rather read and respond as their schedules permit. For example, email, discussion board and text messaging over cell phones (forum).

103. (c)

Feedback is essential in communication so as to know whether the recipient has understood the message in the same terms as intended by the sender and whether he agrees to that message or not.

Feedback is essential for 'effective communication'.

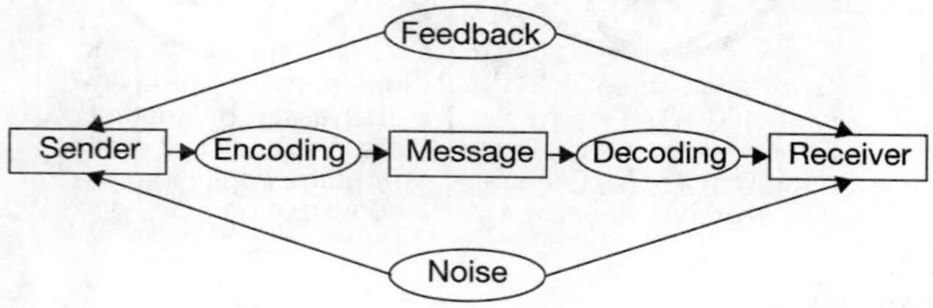

104. (a)

Paralanguage is the area of non-verbal communication that emphasizes body language and voice nuances as means of expressing thoughts and feelings.

105. (d)

Communication is a two way street. This means that both the person communicating and the person being communicated have to participate, so communication happens when information is shared between two people. Since communication is a two-way street, successful communication relies just as much on the person receiving the message as it does on the person sending the message.

When most people think of communication, they probably think of talking or verbal communication. However it is important to remember that talking is not the only form of communication. In addition to verbal communication, you communicate non-verbally with body movements and facial expressions. Good communication skills not only help to improve your personal relationship, but also our success in education.

So, successful educational communication is dependent upon the following skills:

1. Listening
2. Verbal communication
3. Non-Verbal communication
4. Emotional awareness
5. Written communication
6. Communication in different situation

106. (c)

Continuous educational communication is a consistent application of information flow from within the projects core community to its extremities and beyond into wild unknown beyond the core member's awareness horizon.

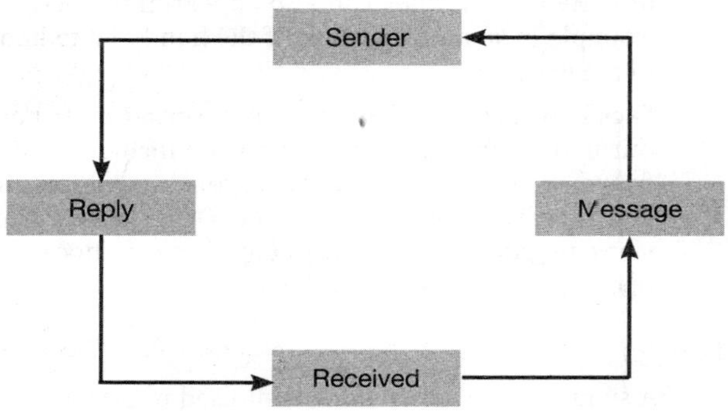

107. (a)

Focused listening will help overcome communication barriers

Focused listening is a strategy that guides students to listen closely to a text. It helps students listen attentively with no distractions and to identify key points and ideas.

108. (a)

Interpreting and analyzing the collected data is essential to make inference and arrive at conclusions. However, data should be in comprehensible form to be useful for the purpose. Qualitative data is generally descriptive and need to be coded for ease of analysis. Qualitative data collected through technical media such as audio or video recording first needs to be transcribed (Put though, speech or data in to written or printed form) only then can it be coded.

Data transcription refers to the process by which certain qualitative data is interpreted as translated into words that can be categorized as coded and studied. Structural equation modeling is a multivariate statistical analyses relationship between measured variables and latent constructs.

109. (a)

Theory of social constructivism can be applied to classroom communication because social constructivism is a sociological theory of knowledge according to which human development is socially situated and knowledge is constructed through interaction with other.

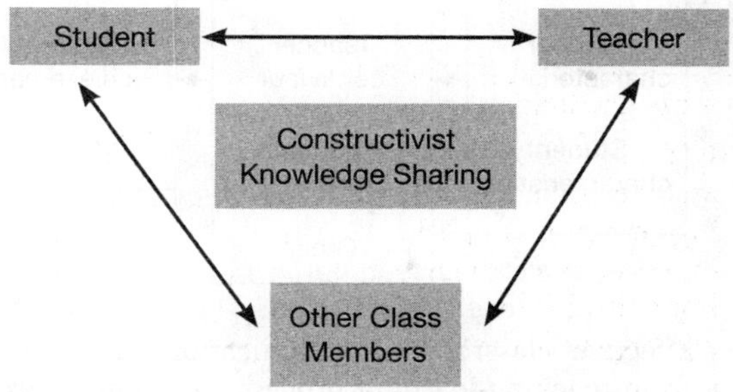

110. (d)

Long held attitude of learner communication has relatively high potential of challenging. A long held attitude is a disposition, feeling or manner that is not constructive, co-operative or optimistic. It can effect anyone just about anywhere for same of us. It is at home perhaps you know of someone, who had a bad attitude about doing chases or maybe it's happened to you at work.

111. (b)

Classroom communication exists in three categories namely, verbal, non-verbal and written. These are surficial levels. Verbal communication means anything that a teacher or a student speaks aloud. In a non-verbal language, the people express written communication directed at a specific audience. Teacher and students interact with one another in many different contexts.

112. (c)

There are different rhetorical techniques for structuring classroom communication.

(1) **Organise the class:**

Structure the class in a logical way. For example, frame the topic as a story, present a problem and then develop its solution, describe events and process chronologically or show the relationship of an interconnected idea to an overarching theme.

(2) **Get the students interested:**

Connect the day topic to the student interests, experience and prior knowledge to spark students' curiosity and explain why it is valuable and useful for them.

(3) **Clarify the purpose and the goal of the class**

Repeat key ideas and concepts to emphasise their importance to students and help students to understand them. For example, summarise.

113. (c)

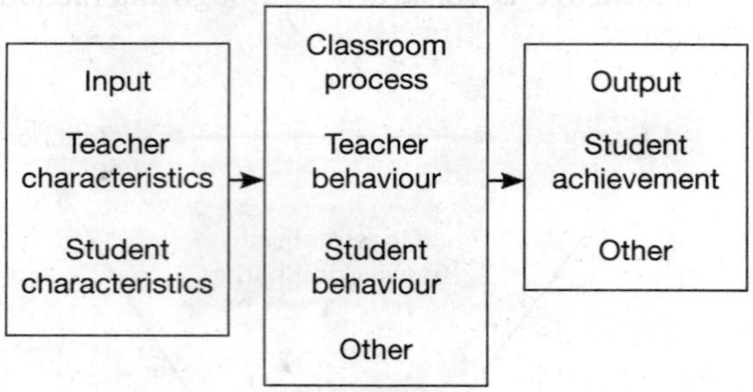

Effective classroom communication can transform from teaching-learning process. Learning is brought about through teaching. Teaching process is an arrangement of environment within which the students can interact and study how to learn. The process of teaching-learning aims at transmission of knowledge, imparting skills and formation of attitudes values and behaviours.

114. (c)

Prefer employment of redundancy, immediacy of feedback and non-verbal cues are essential for a good classroom communication.

1. Proper Employment of Redundancy

In classroom communication, redundancy is sometimes useful because it provides better understanding and remembering of same information. Pupils do not understand brief explanation easily. It is advisable for the teacher to develop the information. Students do not understand brief explanation easily. It is advisable for the teacher to develop the information and repeat it in a paraphrased form.

2. Immediacy of Feedback

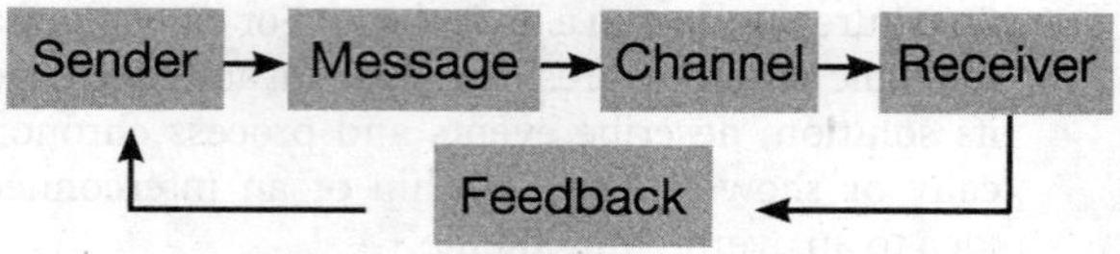

Feedback refers to the response or reaction of receiver to the senders' messages. When message reach to the receiver, he decodes the message and sends his response to the sender to complete the communication process. Feedback helps the sender to evaluate the effectiveness of his message.

3. Non-verbal Cues

Include "all the communication between people that do not have a verbal translation. They are body movements, body orientation, nuances of the voice, facial expressions, details of dress and choice and movement of objects that communicate."

115. (d)

Micro-expressions are feelings, facial expression that betray underlying emotions that the person may be trying to suppress. They mostly happen around the eyes and mouth and are very brief, typically lasting between 1/25 and 1/15 of a second. While micro expressions are often facial, they can also appear in the body for example in small movement of the hand and twitches of the legs.

Facial expressions and other non-verbal cues boost our understanding. Facial expression include smiling, frowning, eye rolling, making eye contact, scowling and appearing bored or interested. Other facial expressions might indicate excitement or even shock, like opening one's eyes or mouth widely.

116. (c)

A signpost is a verbal statement used to orientate the audience inside your speech or presentation or to show them where you are going. A signpost draws in the audiences attention and aims to maintain their attention through the presentation or public speech. Writing these regularly helps students to sustain attention to distinguish main idea from details to paraphrase succinctly and accurately and to create a record of what they have heard.

117. (b)

We need to be conscious about some important aspects of non-verbal communication to increase, loyalty and rapport.

Proxemics: We can use personal and physical space to communicate many non-verbal messages including intimacy, affection, aggression or dominance.

Paralanguage: When we speak, other people 'read' our voices in addition to listening to our words. They pay attention to our timing, pace, tone, loudness, pitch, volume rate, quality, intonation, inflection, vocalized pauses etc.

Kinesics: There are many body signals that amplify meaning between communicators. These include gestures, eye contact, facial expressions, posture, locomotion and haptics. In USA, a long eye contact may be to show respect while in Japan, a long eye contact is better to be averted, it shows disrespect.

Haptics: Haptics refers to how and what touch communicates. Reaction to unsolicited touch va-ries from person to person. This may vary according to culture. The examples are gentle touch on the forearm, a two-handed handshake, or a slight kiss on the cheek.

Phonemics: Phonemics is a linguistic ability. A phoneme is a unit of sound that distinguishes one word from another in a particular language.

Dress and Appearance: The meaning depends upon the situation.

Chromatics: Chromatics is communication through the use of color. Colors of clothing, products or gifts send intended or unintended messages to the recipient of message.

Iconic: These systems are used to represent words or linguistic concepts. We can take ex-amples of different types of 'emoticons' to represent the idea.

118 (d)

Aggressive and inflammatory statements by the teacher make the classroom communication academically ineffective. Statement I is incorrect.

Choice of appropriate words lends credence to classroom communication processes. Thus, statement II is correct. Hence option 'd' is the right answer.

119. (b)

Technology is largely used to mediate communication. Technological barriers occur in the form of lack of feedback and non verbal cues, polarization, generation gaps and socio-economic groupings (such as urban rural divide). Without non-verbal cues such as eye contact, facial expressions, and body language, people are more likely to misunderstand messages, causing the quality of communication to suffer.

There are no specific legalities as communication barriers to online teaching. Cultural barriers (such as in the form of linguistic, low context, high context) does exist.

Gender biasedness is an example of communication barrier. Usually gender stereotypes lead to men being deemed as 'competitive' and 'independent,' while women are deemed as 'cooperative'.

120. (a)

As per our discussion in the Unit 1, reflective means the capability to deal with the real problems in the society that also indicates that we are good citizens. Autonomous development level means self learning thereafter we progress through memory, understanding and reflective levels.

121. (d)

During media production process, the overall objectives are set as a part of planning. After planning, content preparation and transmission are undertaken. To see whether project was successful (or not), feedback is done.

122. (d)

Cognitive dissonance can be defined as a psychological phenomenon which occurs whenever we hold two contradicting cognitions such as behaviors, attitudes, values. This contradiction causes a feeling of discomfort that is termed as chaotic condition. This phenomenon was first studied by Leon Festinger.

123. (b)

There are various psychological barriers. These barriers are perception, homeostasis, conformity, commitment, and personality factors. There is selective perception. This is when the person only chooses to remember certain details about the change. They cannot look beyond the negative to see all the positives a change could make. Perception also is a barrier when the change agent may act in a way that someone in the organization may perceive as inappropriate.

Homeostasis simply wants to stay in an environment where it is comfortable. The key to this barrier is to understand what the organization is going through at each stage of the change and maintaining a certain level of comfort as much as possible for the people affected.

124. (c)

Vertical communication occurs across different hierarchies in social institutions such as family or management.

Horizontal communication means communication between the members at the same level. Grapevine communication (sort of informal also) may be a part of it.

Circular means 'effective' communication that needs some feedback mechanism.

Transactional Model of communication is the exchange of messages between sender and receiver where each take turns to send or receive messages. The model is mostly used for interpersonal communication. Some times, as the element of feedback is there, it is also called as circular model of communication.

125. (a)

(i) The human life should exist as independent but diversified form in the society.

(ii) The earth intends to provide an integrating opportunity for all.

126. (c)

The concept of human touch in communication means understanding different point of views shared in classroom, including the micro-dynamics of participation is always crucial at important stages. The teacher as a facilitator is challenged by a range of social contingencies.

The role of a teacher is to share understanding in an innovative manner, so the role of a teacher is never secondary.

127. (c)

Functional communication is the means by which an individual spontaneously and independently communicates his/her wants and needs and socializes with others. This communication can occur through a variety of forms, including speech, picture exchange, gestures, sign language and assistive devices.

128. (c)

This question is linked with feedback in the classroom to make it effective communication. A teacher should be proficient in all four modes of communication – listening, speaking, reading, and writing – and should know how to utilize this proficiency effectively in an educational institute environment. Being able to do this has been proven to impact the success students achieve in their academic lives, as well as the teacher's own career success.

129. **(a):**

1. The receiver is fixed in case of sending mails.
2. Verbal instruction may move into any direction, and anyone nearby can be a receiver.
3. Transactional model of communication is the exchange of messages between sender and receiver where each take turns to send or receive messages. The model is mostly used for interpersonal communication and is also called circular model of communication. The communicators generate social realities within social, relational, and cultural contexts.
4. The semiotic tradition explores the study of signs and symbols as a significant part of communications.

130. (b)

'**The medium is the message**' is an expression coined by Canadian educator Marshall McLuhan that is often interpreted to mean that the "media" used to communicate information have a significant impact on the messages they deliver. The form of a message (print, visual, musical, etc.) determines the ways in which that message will be perceived. Modern electronic communications (including radio, television, films, and computers) would have far–reaching sociological, aesthetic, and philosophical consequences, to the point of actually altering the ways in which we experience the world.

131. (a)

Diagonal communication: The communication among the persons at different levels who have no direct relationship is called diagonal relationship. This communication is effective as hierarchical bindings are removed and there is a free flow of information, cutting across different positions.

Horizontal communication: communication with people at the same level in a hierarchy of peers and colleagues is termed as horizontal communication.

This may combine both formal and informal communication.

Intrapersonal communication: it is a communication within an individual almost all the times, such as talking to oneself, listening to oneself and relating to oneself. It includes individual reflection, meditation, contemplation and praying to God.

Upward communication: This communication is the process of information flowing from the lower levels of a hierarchy to the upper levels. It is the process by which lower–level company employees can directly communicate with upper management to provide feedback, complaints or suggestions regarding the day–to–day operations of the company.

132. (b)

Technological barrier: low bandwidth of internet is example of technological barrier.

Psychological barrier: Complexity of ideas and personal attitude towards technology is an example psychological barrier.

Geographical barriers: physical locations of communicators is a geographical barrier.

Semantic barrier: communication barriers related to language and the meaning of the words.

133. (b)

One's perception and beliefs are the basis of generalization in communication.

Generalizations of the environment develop through experience.

Thus, both the statements are true.

134. (a)

These are myths about communications:

- Good communicators are born, not made.
- Stage fright is not a communication apprehension.
- Communication skills have nothing to do with relationships.

135. (d)

According to Robbins et. al, the sequence of barriers to effective communication in an organization is:

Filtering > Selective perception > Information load > language > Emotions.

Filtering: Filtering prevents the members of an organization from getting a complete picture of a situation. The main objective here is to manage the reactions of a person. During upward communication, people filter out bad news more. To maximize your chances of sending and receiving effective communication, it's helpful to deliver a message in a variety of ways and get information from multiple sources.

Selective perception: Selective perception refers to the filtering of what we see and hear according to our needs. This process is often unconscious. We are bombarded every day with a plethora of stimuli of information, whether we want them or not. That's why we choose the information we need. 'Selective perception' is a time-saving measure. This is an essential tool in a complex culture, but it can also lead to mistakes.

Information load: Every type of message reaches us in different ways every day. Some messages are social, some in the form of advertising, some are commercial, such as e-mail, memos, and voice mail, conversations with colleagues. There are other personal messages too, i.e., messages and conversations from our loved ones and friends. Dealing with all this becomes a very difficult task at times. This state of imbalance is known as information overload.

Emotions: An effective communication requires a sender and a receiver. They should be free to talk and listen to each other. There could be potential differences of opinion or personality between them. Both of them may have to separate themselves from the flow of emotions if they want to achieve the goal of communicating clearly. A receiver who is emotionally upset ignores or distorts what the sender is saying. A sender who is emotionally upset may be unable to effectively present thoughts or feelings.

Words may have different meanings to different people, or they may not mean anything to another person. This is called semantics.

Language Complexity: Effective communication is clear, factual and goal-oriented. This is also respectable. Referring to a person by an adjective (a brain, a diabetic) reduces the person to that one trait. Language that provokes or stereotypes a person poisons the communication process. Language that insults an individual (or group) on the basis of age, ethnicity, sexual preference, and vulgarity should be avoided.

Organizational barriers: These barriers develop when an organization evolves. They can be attributed to the following conditions.

1. Size of organization
2. Physical distance between employees
3. Specialization of jobs and activities
4. Organizational culture, which impacts freedom and trust
5. Organizational rules and regulations
6. Power structure in the organization
7. Complexity in organizational structure
8. Inadequate facilities and opportunities
9. Lack of cooperation between seniors and subordinates.

136. (d)

Elements of effective communication are:

Common frame of reference: Compatibility between the receiver and the sender. For example, common language develops better understanding between the sender and receiver of the message and makes communication more effective.

Congruence: Messages of common interest between encoder and decoder.

Language relevance: Use of understandable language.

Compatible environment: Communications with people of similar background.

137. (b)

In describing elements of communication, a person or an event that provides verbal or non-verbal use that someone can respond to is known as a source.

The source or sender is basically the origin of the message. Sources are the objects which encode, create and transmit the message through a channel or medium.

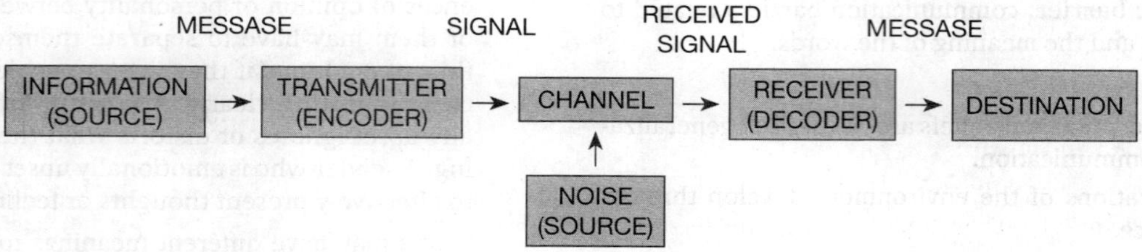

138. (c)

Agenda building is a collective communication process in which media, government and the citizenry reciprocally influence one another. (A) is true and (R) is false. The influence of media affects the presentation of reports and issues made in the news, which in turn influences the public mind. When a particular news report is given more importance and attention than other news, the audience automatically perceives it as the most important information that is being given to them. The media decides and sets which news report comes first based on how people think and how much influence it will have among the audience.

- Agenda-building is defined as 'a process through which the policy agendas of political elites are influenced by a variety of factors, including media agendas and public agendas' (Rogers & Dearing, 1988).
- Elite categories who engage in building and promoting policy promote agenda building.
- Government issues give priority to agenda building.

139. (d)

Statement I: The art of mass communication is much complex than face-to-face, or any other type of communication. Thus, statement I is incorrect. Mass media is not a mere physical transmission of information but a complex, integrated, intermixed and interactive system that has resulted in the seamless integration of data, text, images and sound. Whereas face-to-face communication is interactive. The feedback mechanism helps to determine whether the receiver has understood the message or not. In mass communication, the heterogeneity among audience, lack of feedback, semantic barriers and channel noise, decrease the viability of the transmitted message. Thus, the art of mass communication is more complex.

Statement II: Each of us uses 3S (Sight, Sound and Smell) and 2T (Touch and Taste) when we communicate with others. Thus, statement II is correct.

140. (d)

In communication, feedback is the sign that indicates whether the receiver has understood the message. It encourages further communication between the sender and receiver.

Feedback reflects the reactions of the audience when:

one knows the effects of communication, one knows the quality of content of the message, one knows the future prospect of the object of communication

141. (b)

The power which comes through the connectedness of one's words matching with their feelings, body and facial expression in the communication process is known as congruence.

Non-verbal congruence is the consistency among the cluster of non-verbal expressions that we are observing, which influence our understanding of what message is being conveyed.

142. (a)

Pro-social Motivation: According to A.M. Grant (2008), prosocial motivation is the desire to spend the effort that will serve to benefit others. Individuals may strive to benefit others to be agreeable, show empathy, exhibit a helpful attitude and show a general concern for others.

According to communication research findings, some amount of gossip is necessary for prosocial motivation.

There are four forms of prosocial motivation:

1. **Egoism:** 'I help others to benefit myself'
2. **Altruism:** 'I help others because it is the right thing to do'
3. **Collectivism:** 'I help others to benefit the group'
4. **Principlism:** 'I help others in order to uphold a moral principle'

143. (c)

In the intercultural communication power distance, individualism and gender roles are important.

Power Distance – This concept was given by Hofstede and the role of power distance in his cultural dimensions' theory. Power distance refers to the relationship between authority (high power) and subordinate individuals (lower power) that depends on how the latter react to the former. The less powerful members of organizations and institutions (including the family) accept and expect unequal power distributions.

Individualism – This concept of individualism / collectivism was given again by Hofstede. This concept focuses on the relationship between the individual and larger social groups. The cultures vary on degree of importance they give on encouraging individuality and uniqueness OR on conformity and interdependence. USA puts more focus on individualism and Japan on collectivism.

Gender roles: This kind of role in society means how the people in society are expected to act, speak, dress, groom, and conduct ourselves based upon our assigned gender.

144. (a)

Smiles and laughter should be avoided when messages are serious. Non-verbal cues are always contextual like verbal communication. Communication always takes place within a context. Without context, words and actions don not carry any meaning at all. There are four types of contexts in communication: physical context (place where communication takes place), social context (status of relationship between sender and receiver), psychological context (formal and informal communication), temporal context (time factor in communication). Thus, both (A) and (R) are true, and (R) is the correct explanation of (A).

145. (d)

The correct sequence of human communication skills is as follows:

Self-presentation, relationship, group interaction, public speaking, feed forward

146. (b)

Psychological Barriers: The term 'psychological' essentially refers to the 'mind' or 'psyche'. Poor retention, frame of reference, field of experience, cognitive dissonance, selective perception and filtering are the different types of psychological barriers.

Organizational Barriers: These barriers develop when an organization evolves. They can be attributed to the following conditions:

i. Size of organization
ii. Physical distance between employees
iii. Organizational culture, which impacts freedom and trust
iv. Functional specialization (power structure)
v. Lack of cooperation between seniors and subordinates

Personal Barriers: Personal barriers are personal factors related to the sender and receiver and act as a hindrance to the communication process. These factors include life experiences, emotions, attitudes, behaviour, etc. The fear of challenging authority is an example of personal barriers.

Semantic Barriers: The term 'Semantic' barriers occur when there is a disagreement about the words being used, which is a result of individuals being from different cultures. Use of technical language and jargon leads to semantic barriers.

147. (a): The word effective in communication means that a message has been sent and received properly with an understanding. That understanding is reflected by 'feedback'. In a classroom, an effective listener is completely focused and thus tries to resist any kind of distraction (or noise) that exists in the environment.

Message filtering in communication may actually be perceived as a communication, as some fact is kept hidden, distorted or manipulated with an objective to manage receiver's reaction. For example, a manager tries to hide the poor sales figures of his division so that the receiver (boss) does not get angry.

148. (a): This question is about face to face communication but different levels have been given by different authors. In two way communication, the sender of message gets the feedback from the receiver, that fulfils the basic objective of communication. The main objective of communication is understanding the message in the intended form.

Our answer is Level 1 as the communication is two way and Face to Face between two persons. There can be higher channels as per the channels involved.

The verbal, physical, auditory, emotional and energetic are also described as the five levels of communication.

149. (b): Time Sense–This is linked with temporal aspect linked with culture. Western cultures, even South East Asia tend to measure their time by the clock, keeping in view that each activity should have a precise beginning and end that may be termed as linear timing. To them, the word 'deadline' is very important. Westerners also see that time has a limited supply, so they structure that accordingly.

In India, there is a concept of rebirth (punrjanam), we assume that if something could not be completed in this birth, will be completed in next birth. India has the concepts of satya yug, dwapar yug, treta yug and kaliyug, according to different time spans and culture makes a shift accordingly. In most parts of India, Pakistan, Bangladesh. etc. a culture is event or personality-related. The culture also travels if we look at history. Some practices which were part of Greece travelled to India and vice versa. Thus, the institutions such as marraige become institutional.

Level of Gratitude–This is an integral part of culture According to Robert Emmons as he expressed in his book Thanks, 'Gratitude is literally one of the few things that can measurably change people's lives'. Gratitude can improve our health and relationships—making it one of the most well-studied and effective ways to increase our well-being in life. This level of gratitude varies according to our culture such as India, China, Russia, Japan, Germany, etc. There can be high context, low context, temporal context, emotive context, directive, phatic contexts of different cultures which have been mentioned in Pearson Unit 3.

They found some similarities across cultures, as well as some differences—an initial glimpse at how our early steps toward gratefulness might be shaped by larger societal forces. There can be Verbal or oral gratitude, concrete gratitude (offering toffee, chocolate, etc) and connective gratitude (offer of friendship or help, etc).

150. (c): Statement 1–Small group communication refers to interactions among three or more people who are connected through a common purpose, mutual influence, and a shared identity which indicate the relationship needs. The upper number of a small group is taken between 15 to 20.

Statement 2–A person who is well informed about the group's task and/or highly motivated as a group member may emerge as a leader and set into motion internal decision-making processes, such as recruiting new members or assigning group roles, that affect the structure of a group. Different members will also gravitate toward different roles within the group and will advocate for certain procedures and courses of action over others. External factors such as group size, task, and resources also affect group structure.

151. (d): The options seem to be very close ones so that we need to get some idea about all of them.

A. Creation of passive longing for media products–It has the word 'passive', otherwise we see the media and audience and products for audience as dynamic and active.

B. Omnivorous devouring of media content – Here, omnivorous means to consume all kinds of food and devouring means consuming them. Omnivorous devouring means that all types of media content is being taken in, but media has to show the contents to the audience or public also, so that it is appreciated (or depreciated).

C. Compensation through identification– Here, identification means connectivity with the audience or public so that some kind of rewards (through advertisements) can be generated. That is basically being done by YouTube, Facebook, Instagram, etc. They develop loyalty and CRM (Customer Relationship Management).

D. Vicarious Wish Fulfilment–Vicarious means a feeling developed or experienced by watching or reading about somebody else doing something, rather than by doing it yourself. An example of vicarious is when a mother who always wanted to be a dancer continually pushes her children to do ballet.

Freud's most well-known theory, wish fulfilment, is the idea that when wishes can't or won't be fulfilled in our waking lives, they are carried out in dreams. Even anxious or punishing dreams have their roots in wish fulfilment. Freud's dream theory is rooted in the idea that we all need a way to express or vicariously fulfil all of our wishes and desires.

Now, we see that people are led by their dreams and fantasies. The social media generates the need for product which were not felt by public till they see them on social media.

Sources of suggestion for appropriate roles–this point is vey important. Even the children of today want to empathize the roles of adult members. This role perception means that they are becoming more assertive and challenging. They have almost complete access to media that enables them to challenge the roles being played by elders.

152. (b):

A. Emphasize your interpretation approach indicates that we may be highly subjective. It is not relevant as we have to deal with open and diverse society. The globalization has happened all around. This type of approach also indicates the feeling of 'ethnocentrism'.

B. Forgetting your own culture means that we as a culture are not participating so that establishing contact with others may not be fruitful.

C. An ecosystem of mutual respect creates the feeling of trust so that one culture can communicate better with other cultures.

D. Knowing the cultural context of other people promotes the feeling of 'cultural relativism', so that we emphasize that every culture is equally important. This helps in better communication with other cultures.

E. Stating facts means that we believe in transparency and trustworthiness. We are not hiding anything.

Thus, (b) is the correct answer.

153. (a): Both statements are true.

Statement 1 - Here, we can speak about three models of communication – linear, transactional and interactive.

The linear model is transmission of communication - mostly one way communication. So, called as transmission model of communication.

Transactional Model takes into account social and relational aspects and thus social context.

Interactive Models talk about channel (the way messages are sent and received), field of experience, physical context and psychological context. We can take the examples of social media, interactive and online marketing, user generated contents, chat rooms etc. for interactive communication. We always look for immediate feedback. Here, the communication is a process where participants alternate positions as sender and receiver and generate meaning by sending messages and receiving feedback within physical and psychological contexts.

1. The continuous feedback is the main element in interactive communication. We are quickly able to understand if a message is received or understood. WhatsApp may be taken as an example.
2. There are continuous updates and communication with audiences.
3. There is more transparency in our interactive communication.
4. There are additional alignment opportunities. That was it seems to be extrovert as well.
5. We can share information with large audiences.

For statement 2 - The interested candidates may look for Bloom Taxonomy once again that comes for digital iconic communication.

154. (a): Let's discuss the main aspects of communication and feedback.

Communication is the main source of interaction between people by which they share their ideas, and thoughts with each other. Communication is important in every aspect of life. The communication can be verbal, nonverbal or through by the use of sign language or body language. Feedback can be referred as 'fed-back'. Feedback means that response is generated.

Feedback can be in the form of non-verbal cues provided by the receiver. Thus, feedback fulfils the basic objective of two-way communication. The importance of feedback can be gauzed from the following facts.

1. The element of feedback should always be there to make the communication effective.
2. Feedback is effective listening.
3. Feedback can motivate.
4. Feedback can improve performance.
5. Feedback is a tool for continued learning.

The feedback can be of following types:

1. **Negative feedback:** It reflects about mistakes, errors during the process of communication, the areas which have not been understood properly and improvements required.

2. **Positive feedback:** There is proper understanding of the message conveyed by sender.
3. **Negative feedforward:** These are basically corrective comments about future behaviour of the work and communication.
4. **Positive feedforward:** These affirm about the future events.

155. (c): The natural ability to live or work together in harmony because of well-matched characteristics is called as compatibility between individuals.

(a) Stewardship is an ethical value that embodies the responsible planning and management of resources.

(b) Interest in media for two individuals may not develop in compatibility. Between two individuals, one may be interested in football matches, and other one in serials.

(c) Empathy is shown in how much compassion and understanding we can give to another. Sympathy is more of a feeling of pity for another. Empathy is our ability to understand how someone feels while sympathy is our relief in not having the same problems.

(d) External influence may help in temporary association, and not in compatibility.

156. (d): Grapevine communication is basically informal in nature so that more and more people feel comfortable in it. They get connected in it, they feel connected to informal groups where they express themselves. Thus, informal communication boosts the morale of the employees.

In the grapevine, employees discuss various issues. The anxieties of the employees are also expressed.

The formal communication moves in a set direction, so employees are bound by rules and regulations.

157. (d): The term 'critical' in critical readings implies going beyond surface-level understanding. It involves deep analysis, problem-solving, and a thorough examination of information. This aligns perfectly with the meaning of 'cognitive'. Cognitive means 'thinking', that is the answer as well.

(a) **Critical:** These readings are objective rather than emotional.

(b) **Passive:** As critical readings need active engagement with the contents in a thoughtful manner.

(c) **Ineffectual:** Critical readings may raise relevant questions and issues so they are not ineffective.

158. (c): The symbolic mode of communication is typically socio-cultural. It involves the use of symbols that have meaning within a particular social and cultural context.

The answer is (c) Socio-cultural.

159. (b): Integrating communication with the educational system means that this should mostly benefit the learners. It offers us the following benefits:

(A) Going abroad is not the sole permanent objective of integrating communication.

(B) Increase public awareness of educational rights – So that public engagement is increased in a transparent manner through communication channels

(C) Improve the quality of policy preparation – By taking into account diverse perspectives and feedback from stakeholders.

(D) Improve educational service delivery – The system needs to become more efficient by information sharing, feedback mechanism. There needs to be collaboration between teachers, administrators, parents, and students.

(E) Better perks for teachers is again not in direct benefits of students.

Thus, (b) is the right answer.

160. (a): Statement I: This statement is generally true as the Internet is a part of the broader concept of cyberspace, which is the virtual computer world.

Statement II: This statement is also true, as cyberspace encompasses various digital communication platforms and media.

The correct answer is (a) Both Statement I and Statement II are true.

161. (d): Let's look at the communication effects:

A. **Instrumental effect (A) – (IV):** Instrumental is basically linked with achievement of goals.

B. **Prestige effect – (I):** Self-approval is linked with prestige effect.

C. **Aesthetic effect (II):** Aesthetic is linked with specimens of art and literature.

D. **Respite effect (III):** That means showing a sense of humour. It reflects a break or relief that is 'a pleasant distraction'.

With this A-IV, B-I, C-II, D-III, the correct answer is (d)

162. (d): Cybernetics is the study of feedback systems in complex systems, including humans, animals, and machines. It examines how information is used to control and regulate behaviour or processes.
(a) Feedback science is too general.
(b) Experience study is mostly experience-based.
(c) Message Hermeneutics focuses on interpretation of messages.

163. (b): Ferdinand de Saussure viewed language as a system of signs (words, sounds, symbols) that represent meanings and ideas. Profusion means dealing with vast variety or say complex network.
(a) Technical code suggests a focus on practical function.
(b) Verbalism is negative and implies excessive use of words.
(c) Macro generaliser doesn't reflect the intricate structure of language.

164. (c): Public service communication should be accurate, comprehensive, and objective. It should separate opinion and facts to avoid bias and misinformation. Other options are not acceptable.

165. (a): A, B, C Only
- Marshall McLuhan categorized media into 'hot' and 'cool' based on their level of emotional engagement and sensory involvement. Hot media, like telephone, television, radio, and cinema, are considered low in sensory involvement and require active participation from the audience to fill in gaps and create meaning.
- Print, on the other hand, is considered a 'cool' medium due to its high sensory involvement. The reader has more control over the pace and information they consume, leading to a less emotionally-charged experience.

166. (a): Both Statement I and Statement II are true.

Statement I: The internet physically consists of cables, routers, and servers and also interactions and communities.

Statement II: This concept by media scholars like Mark Poster highlights the shift from traditional, one-way media like television and radio to interactive platforms where users actively engage and contribute.

167. (d): Statement (I): This statement is not correct. There is no mention a language as the 'divine gift' in Buddhist literature. Rather, language is a powerful tool to reach to the masses. Buddha used common language 'Pali' to reach to the masses. Even Buddhism used Sanskrit words to some extent, but that is largely used for 'scholarly works'.

Statement (II): This statement is correct. The common language is actually impermanent, this evolves with changes with social contexts and conditions. There is lot of diversification in the population, and there connect through a common language. Buddhism focused more on nature of reality, suffering, and the path to enlightenment.

168. (d): In politics, a spin doctor is someone who controls and manages the public perception of a politician or political party. He uses the technique of framing to present information in a way that puts a particular interpretation on an issue, aiming to influence public perception and, ultimately, the outcome of elections.

169. (c): Metacommunication refers to the process of communicating about communication. It's the non-verbal cues, gestures, tone, context, and other factors that surround the primary message and help to interpret its meaning and intention. Keep that in view, (c) is the correct answer.

170. (b): Negentropy, or negative entropy, refers to situations of order and predictability, which are opposite to the concept of entropy that denotes disorder and unpredictability.

171. (c): This question is about the roles of non-verbal communication in relation to verbal communication.
A. **Accentuation:** Gestures, facial expressions, and tone enhance verbal messages.
B. **Supervision:** An organized and responsible task.
C. **Repetition:** Non-verbal cues reinforce verbal communication.
D. **Substitution:** Non-verbals can replace words to convey emotions or meanings.
E. **Contradiction:** Non-verbal cues may oppose verbal meanings, exposing true feelings or intentions.

CHAPTER

5

Mathematical Reasoning and Aptitude

TOPICS OF IMPORTANCE

- Concept of Reasoning
- Types of Reasoning
- Number Series, Letter Series, Codes and Relationships
- Mathematical Aptitude (Fraction, Time and Distance, Ratio, Proportion and Percentage, Profit and Loss, Interest and Discounting, Averages, etc.)

1. In a post office, stamps of three different denominations of ₹7, ₹8, and ₹10 are available. The exact amount for which one cannot buy stamps is **[Jun 2014]**

(a) 19 (b) 20 (c) 23 (d) 29

2. In certain coding method, the word QUESTION is encoded as DOMESTIC. In this coding, what is the code word for the word RESPONSE? **[Jun 2014]**

(a) OMESUCEM (b) OMESICSM
(c) OMESICEM (d) OMESISCM

3. If the series 4, 5, 8, 13, 14, 17, 22, ... is continued in the same pattern, then which one of the following is not a term of this series? **[Jun 2014]**

(a) 31 (b) 32
(c) 33 (d) 35

4. Complete the series BB, FE, II, ML, PP, ______ by choosing one of the following options given. **[Jun 2014]**

(a) TS (b) ST
(c) RS (d) SR

5. A man started walking from his house towards south. After walking 6 km, he turned to his left and walked 5 km. Then he walked further 3 km after turning left. He then turned to his left and continued his walk for 9 km. How far is he away from his house? **[Jun 2014]**

(a) 3 km (b) 4 km
(c) 5 km (d) 6 km

6. One writes all numbers from 50 to 99 without the digits 2 and 7. How many numbers have been written? **[Jun 2014]**

(a) 32 (b) 36
(c) 40 (d) 38

7. The next term in the series **[Dec 2014]**
2, 7, 28, 63, 126, ______ is

(a) 215 (b) 245
(c) 276 (d) 296

8. The next term in the series **[Dec 2014]**
AB, ED, IH, NM, ______ is

(a) TS (b) ST
(c) TU (d) SU

9. If STREAMERS is coded as UVTGALDQR, then KNOWLEDGE will be coded as **[Dec 2014]**

(a) MQPYLCDFD
(b) MPQYLDCFD
(c) PMYQLDFCD
(d) YMQPLDDFC

10. A is brother of B. B is the brother of C. C is the husband of D. E is the father of A. D is related to E as **[Dec 2014]**

(a) Daughter (b) Daughter-in-law
(c) Sister-in-law (d) Sister

11. Two numbers are in the ratio 3:5. If 9 is subtracted from the numbers, the ratio becomes 12:23. The numbers are **[Dec 2014]**

(a) 30, 50 (b) 36, 60
(c) 33, 55 (d) 42, 70

12. The mean of the ages of father and his son is 27 years. After 18 years, the father will be twice as old as his son. Their present ages are **[Dec 2014]**

(a) 42, 12 (b) 40, 14
(c) 30, 24 (d) 36, 18

13. The next term in the series is **[Jun 2015]**
2, 5, 9, 19, 37, ?

(a) 73 (b) 75 (c) 78 (d) 80

14. In certain code, MATHURA is coded as JXQEROX. The code of HOTELS will be **[Jun 2015]**

(a) LEQIBP (b) ELQBIP
(c) LEBIQP (d) ELIPQB

15. One day Prakash left home and walked 10 km towards south, turned right and walked 5 km, turned right and walked 10 km and turned left and walked 10 km. How many km will he have to walk to reach his home straight? **[Jun 2015]**

(a) 10 (b) 20
(c) 15 (d) 30

16. A girl introduced a boy as the son of the daughter of the father of her uncle. The boy is related to the girl as **[Jun 2015]**

(a) Brother (b) Uncle
(c) Nephew (d) Son

17. In an examination, 10,000 students appeared. The result revealed the number of students who have **[Jun 2015]**

Passed in all five subjects	=	5583
Passed in three subjects only	=	1400
Passed in two subjects only	=	1200
Passed in one subject only	=	735
Failed in English only	=	75
Failed in Physics only	=	145
Failed in Chemistry only	=	140
Failed in Mathematics only	=	200
Failed in Bioscience only	=	157

The number of students passed in at least four subjects is

(a) 6300 (b) 6900
(c) 7300 (d) 7900

18. At present, a person is 4 times older than his son and is 3 years older than his wife. After 3 years, the age of the son will be 15 years. The age of the person's wife after 5 years will be **[Jun 2015]**

(a) 42 (b) 48
(c) 45 (d) 50

19. Find the next term in the series
2, 5, 10, 17, 26, 37, ___?___. **[Dec 2015]**

(a) 50 (b) 57
(c) 62 (d) 72

20. A group of 210 students appeared in some test. The mean of $\frac{1}{3}$ rd of students is found to be 60. The mean of the remaining students is found to be 78. The mean of the whole group will be **[Dec 2015]**

(a) 80 (b) 76
(c) 74 (d) 72

21. Anil after travelling 6 km towards east from his house realized that he has travelled in a wrong direction. He turned and travelled 12 km towards west, turned right, and travelled 8 km to reach his office. The straight distance of the office from his house is **[Dec 2015]**

(a) 20 km (b) 14 km
(c) 12 km (d) 10 km

22. Find the next term in the series
B2E, D5H, F12K, H27N, ?. **[Dec 2015]**

(a) J56I (b) I62Q
(c) Q62J (d) J58Q

23. A party was held in which a grandmother, father, mother, four sons, their wives and one son and two daughters to each of the sons were present. The number of females present in the party is **[Dec 2015]**

(a) 12 (b) 14
(c) 18 (d) 24

24. P and Q are brothers. R and S are sisters. The son of P is brother of S. Q is related to R as **[Dec 2015]**
(a) Son (b) Brother
(c) Uncle (d) Father

25. Two railway tickets from city A to B and three tickets from city A to C cost ₹177. Three tickets from city A to B and two tickets from city A to C cost ₹173. The fare for city B from city A will be **[Jul 2016]**
(a) ₹25 (b) ₹27
(c) ₹30 (d) ₹33

26. A person walks 10 m in front and 10 m to the right. Then every time turning to his left, he walks 5, 15 and 15 m, respectively. How far is he now from his starting point? **[Jul 2016]**
(a) 20 m (b) 15 m
(c) 10 m (d) 5 m

27. A is the sister of B. F is the daughter of G. C is the mother of B. D is the father of C. E is the mother of D. A is related to D as **[Jul 2016]**
(a) Granddaughter (b) Daughter
(c) Daughter-in-law (d) Sister

28. In the series
AB, EDC, FGHI, ...?...., OPQRST, the missing term is **[Jul 2016]**
(a) JKLMN (b) JMKNL
(c) NMLKJ (d) NMKLJ

29. In certain code, SELECTION is coded as QCJCARGML. The code of AMERICANS will be **[Jul 2016]**
(a) YKCPGAYLQ (b) BNFSJDBMR
(c) QLYAGPCKY (d) YQKLCYPAG

30. In the series
3, 11, 23, 39, 59, ... **[Jul 2016]**
The next term will be
(a) 63 (b) 73
(c) 83 (d) 93

31. The missing term in the series 1, 4, 27, 16, ?, 36, 243, ... is **[Jan 2017]**
(a) 30 (b) 49
(c) 125 (d) 81

32. The next term in the series
YEB, WFD, UHG, SKI, _?_ will be **[Jan 2017]**
(a) TLO (b) QOL
(c) QLO (d) GQP

33. Ali buys a glass, a pencil box and a cup and pays ₹21 to the shopkeeper. Rakesh buys a cup, two pencil boxes, and a glass, and he pays ₹28 to the shopkeeper. Preeti buys two glasses, a cup, and two pencil boxes, and she pays ₹35 to the shopkeeper. Then, the cost of 10 cups will be **[Jan 2017]**
(a) ₹40 (b) ₹60
(c) ₹80 (d) ₹70

34. If A is coded as C, M as I, N as P, S as O, I as A, P as N, E as M, O as E, and C as S, then the code of COMPANIES will be **[Jan 2017]**
(a) SPEINMOAC (b) NCPSEIOMA
(c) SMOPIEACN (d) SEINCPAMO

35. In the series 1, 6, 15, 28, 45, ... the next term will be **[Nov 2017]**
(a) 66 (b) 76
(c) 56 (d) 84

36. The next term in the series ABD, DGK, HMS, MTB, ... is **[Nov 2017]**
(a) NSA (b) SBL
(c) PSK (d) RUH

37. In certain code, COVALENT is coded as BWPDUOFM. The code of ELEPHANT will be **[Nov 2017]**
(a) MFUIQRTW (b) QMUBIADH
(c) QFMFUOBI (d) EPHNTEAS

38. Ajay is a friend of Rakesh. Pointing to an old man Ajay asked Rakesh 'who is he?' and Rakesh said 'His son is my son's uncle'. The old man is related to Rakesh as **[Nov 2017]**
(a) Grandfather (b) Father-in-law
(c) Father (d) Uncle

39. A postman walked 20 m straight from his office, turned right and walked 10 m. After turning left he walked 10 m and after turning right walked 20 m. He again turned right and walked 70 m. How far he is from his office? **[Nov 2017]**
(a) 50 m (b) 40 m
(c) 60 m (d) 20 m

40. The next term in the series –1, 5, 15, 29, ______, is **[Jul 2018]**
(a) 36 (b) 47
(c) 59 (d) 63

41. Two numbers are in the ratio 2:5. If 16 is added to both the numbers, then their ratio becomes 1:2. The numbers are: **[Jul 2018]**
(a) 6, 40 (b) 20, 50
(c) 28, 70 (d) 32, 80

42. The next term in the series: ABD, DGK, HMS, MTB, SBL, ________, ... is **[Jul 2018]**
(a) ZKU (b) ZCA
(c) ZKW (d) ZKU

43. If VARANASI is coded as WCUESGZQ, then the code of KOLKATA will be **[Jul 2018]**
(a) LOQOZEH
(b) HLZEOOQ
(c) ZELHOQO
(d) LQOOFZH

44. Introducing, Rakesh to her husband a women said, 'His brother's father is the only son of my grandfather'. **[Jul 2018]**
The woman is related to Rakesh as
(a) Aunt (b) Mother
(c) Sister (d) Daughter

45. If DICE is coded as FLGJ, then the code for BITE will be **[Dec 2018]**
(a) DLXJ (b) DKYH
(c) DKVY (d) DICL

46. The next term in the series 7, 11, 19, 35, 67, ________ is **[Dec 2018]**
(a) 121 (b) 133 (c) 131 (d) 99

47. The next term in the letter series KB, JH, IM, HQ, GT, ________ is **[Dec 2018]**
(a) EY (b) FV (c) FU (d) EU

48. Pointing to a man, Abhijit said 'His granddaughter is the only daughter of my brother'. How is the man related to Abhijit? **[Dec 2018]**
(a) Father (b) Grandfather
(c) Uncle (d) Brother-in-law

49. Ram said to Shyam, 'That girl playing with the doll, is the younger of the two daughters of my father's wife'.
How is the girl playing with the doll is related to Ram? **[Dec 2018]**
(a) Cousin (b) Sister-in-law
(c) Sister (d) Aunty

50. The next number in the series 12, 15, 21, 33, 57, ____ is **[Dec 2018]**
(a) 97 (b) 95
(c) 107 (d) 105

51. Which of these words is different from the rest? **[Dec 2018]**
(a) Sharp (b) Thin
(c) Huge (d) Tall

52. If FACE is coded as HCEG, then the code for HIGH will be **[Dec 2018]**
(a) ZXYZ (b) KH1K
(c) BEFB (d) JKIJ

53. The next term in the letter series DY, JX, OW, SV, VU, ________ is **[Dec 2018]**
(a) XS (b) YT
(c) XT (d) VVV

54. On a map, 1 inch represents 250 miles. What is the actual distance between two cities if they are $4\frac{1}{2}$ inches apart on the map? **[Jun 2019]**
(a) 1100 miles (b) 1125 miles
(c) 1150 miles (d) 1200 miles

55. Choose the missing term out of the following: JAK, KBL, LCM, MDN, ________. **[Jun 2019]**
(a) OEP (b) NEO
(c) MEN (d) PFQ

56. What will be the ratio of simple interest earned by certain amount at the same rate of interest for 9 years and that for 12 years? **[Jun 2019]**
(a) 3:4 (b) 2:3
(c) 4:3 (d) Data inadequate

57. If the number $345\overline{x}y$ is divisible by 90, than $(x + y)$ = ? **[Jun 2019]**
(a) 9 (b) 8
(c) 7 (d) 6

58. A, B, C, D, E and F are six member in a family in which there are two married couples. E, a teacher is married to the doctor who is the mother of C and F. B, the lawyer is married to A, A has one son and one grandson. Of the two married ladies one is a housewife. There is also one student and one male engineer in the family. How is A related to C? **[Jun 2019]**
(a) Grandfather (b) Mother
(c) Sister (d) Grandmother

59. Six friends A, B, C, D, E and F are sitting in a closed circle facing the centre. The E is to the left of D. C is between A and B. F is between E and A. Who is to the right of C? **[Jun 2019]**

(a) A (b) B
(c) D (d) E

60. If 60% of $(a - b)$ = 40% of $(a + b)$,them what per cent of a is b? **[Jun 2019]**

(a) 20% (b) 25%
(c) 40% (d) 50%

61. In a class of 35 students, Rajan is placed seventh from the bottom where as Karan is placed ninth from the top. Divya is placed exactly in between the two. What is the differences in the positions of Rajan and Divya? **[Jun 2019]**

(a) 9 (b) 10
(c) 11 (d) 13

62. If DRIVER = 12, GOVERNMENT = 20, BELIEVED = 16, then BAT = ? **[Jun 2019]**

(a) 6 (b) 8
(c) 10 (d) 12

63. A person incurs 10% loss by selling a watch for ₹1,800. At what price should the watch be sold to earn 10% profit? **[Jun 2019]**

(a) ₹1980 (b) ₹2,160
(c) ₹2,200 (d) ₹2,360

64. Two cyclists start from the same place in opposite directions. One goes towards north at 9 kmph and the other goes towards south at 10 kmph. What time will they take to be 47.5 km apart? **[Jun 2019]**

(a) $2\frac{1}{2}$ hrs (b) $4\frac{1}{2}$ hrs
(c) $4\frac{1}{4}$ hrs (d) $2\frac{1}{4}$ hrs

65. The price of item A increases by 50 paise every year while the price of item B increases by 25 paise every year. If in 2008, the price of item A was ₹3.20 and that of B was ₹5.30 in which year item A will cost 40 paise more than the item B? **[Jun 2019]**

(a) 2016 (b) 2017
(c) 2018 (d) 2019

66. The average age of a class of 59 students is 18 years. If the age of the teacher is included, then the average increases by 3 months. The age of the teacher is **[Jun 2019]**

(a) 28 years (b) 30 years
(c) 33 years (d) 35 years

67. The product of two numbers a and b is twice the sum of the numbers. What is the sum of the reciprocals of a and b? **[Jun 2019]**

(a) 1/8 (b) 1/2
(c) 2 (d) 4

68. A group of 40 employees of Cadre A has a mean age of 31. A different group of 60 employees of Cadre B has a mean age of 28. What is the mean age of two employees of the two groups together? **[Jun 2019]**

(a) 29.8 (b) 29.5
(c) 29.2 (d) 29

69. An aeroplane flies along the four sides of a square field at the speed of 400, 600, 800 and 200 km/hr. Find the average speed of the plane around the field. **[Jun 2019]**

(a) 324 km/hr (b) 360 km/hr
(c) 384 km/hr (d) 396 km/hr

70. A retailer marks all his goods at 40% above the cost price and thinking that he will still make 20% profit, offers a discount of 20% on the marked price. What is his actual profit percentage on the sales? **[Jun 2019]**

(a) 20% (b) 18%
(c) 16% (d) 12%

71. If the simple interest on a certain sum for 1 year 3 months at $8\frac{1}{2}$ per annum exceeds the simple interest on the same sum for 8 months at 7% per annum by ₹45, then the sum is **[Jun 2019]**

(a) ₹600 (b) ₹800
(c) ₹6,000 (d) ₹8,000

72. If x and y two positive numbers and x is 25% greater than y, what is the value of the ratio $\frac{y}{x}$? **[Jun 2019]**

(a) 0.75 (b) 0.80
(c) 1.20 (d) 1.25

73. 5% of the inhabitants of a village having died of malaria, a panic set in. During this, 20% of the remaining inhabitants left the village. The population is then reduced to 4750. Find the number of original inhabitants. **[Jun 2019]**

(a) 5000 (b) 5250
(c) 6250 (d) 7500

74. A trader mixes three varieties of refined oil costing ₹100, ₹40 and ₹60 per litre in the ratio 2:4:3 in term of litre, and sells the mixture at ₹66 per litre. What percentage of profit does he make? **[Jun 2019]**

(a) 12% (b) 10%
(c) 9% (d) 8%

75. If $0.75\,x = 0.02\,y$, then the value of $\left(\frac{y-x}{y+x}\right)$ **[Jun 2019]**

(a) $\frac{73}{75}$ (b) $\frac{75}{77}$
(c) $\frac{73}{77}$ (d) $\frac{730}{75}$

76. A man travelled from the village to the railway station at the rate of 20 kmph and walked back at the rate of 5 kmph. If the whole journey took 5 hours, find the distance of the railway station from village **[Jun 2019]**

(a) 10 km (b) 15 km
(c) 20 km (d) 40 km

77. If the average of five number is 20 and the sum of three of the number is 32, then what is the average of the other two numbers? **[Jun 2019]**

(a) 66 (b) 33
(c) 34 (d) 132

78. After giving a discount of 10 per cent to the customer, at what percentage of the cost price should an item be fixed to get 8 per cent profit? **[Jun 2019]**

(a) 18% (b) 20%
(c) 28% (d) 10.8%

79. 40% of the employees in a factory are workers. All the remaining employees are executives. The annual income of each worker is ₹39,000. The annual income of each executive is ₹42,000 What is the average income annual of all employees in the factory together? **[Jun 2019]**

(a) ₹40,500 (b) ₹40,800
(c) ₹41,000 (d) ₹41,500

80. If E = 5 and HOTEL = 12, how will you code BALM? **[Jun 2019]**

(a) 28 (b) 26
(c) 16 (d) 7

81. Sameer walks a certain distance and rides back taking a total time of 40 minutes. He could walk both ways in 60 minutes. How long would it take for him to ride both ways? **[Jun 2019]**

(a) 15 min (b) 20 min
(c) 28 min (d) 30 min

82. Rohan gave 3/5th part of the amount he had, to Sahil. Rohan now has ₹2000 left. How much amount did he give Sahil? **[Jun 2019]**

(a) ₹1200 (b) ₹2000
(c) ₹3000 (d) ₹5000

83. If REASON is coded as 5 and GOVERNMENT as 9, then what is the code for ACCIDENT? **[Jun 2019]**

(a) 6 (b) 7 (c) 8 (d) 9

84. A train leaves Agra ar 5 a.m. and reaches Delhi at 9 a.m. Another train leaves Delhi at 7 a.m. and reaches Agra at 10:30 a.m. At what time do the two trains cross each other? **[Jun 2019]**

(a) 6:36 a.m. (b) 6:56 a.m.
(c) 7 a.m. (d) 7:56 a.m.

85. Which of the following fractions is the result of the sum of an integer and its reciprocal? **[Jun 2019]**

(a) $\frac{15}{8}$ (b) $\frac{26}{5}$
(c) $\frac{36}{7}$ (d) $\frac{37}{5}$

86. The average of 35 raw scores is 18. The average of first seventeen of them is 14 and the that of last seventeen is 20. Find the eighteenth raw score? **[Jun 2019]**

(a) 42 (b) 46 (c) 52 (d) 56

87. Sanjay sold an article at a loss of 25%. If the selling price had been increased by ₹175, there would have been a gain of 10%. What was the cost price the article? **[Jun 2019]**

(a) 350 (b) 400
(c) 500 (d) 750

88. In a new budget, the price of petrol rose by 25%. By how much per cent must a person reduce his consumption so that his expenditure on it does not increase? **[Jun 2019]**

(a) 10% (b) 15%
(c) 20% (d) 25%

89. For all integers $y > 1, \{y\} = 2y + (2y - 1) + (2y - 2) + \ldots + 1$.

What is the value of $\{3\} \times \{2\}$ Where × is a multiplication operator? **[Jun 2019]**

(a) 116 (b) 210
(c) 263 (d) 478

90. A sum of money doubles at compound interest in 6 years. In how many years will it become 16 times? **[Jun 2019]**

(a) 16 years (b) 24 years
(c) 48 years (d) 96 years

91. If 152 is divide into four parts proportional to 3, 4, 5 and 7, then the smallest part is **[Jun 2019]**

(a) 29 (b) 26
(c) 25 (d) 24

92. During one year, the population of a town is increased by 5% and during the next year, the population decreased by 5%. If the total population is 29,925 at the end of the second year, then what was the population size in the beginning of the first year? **[Jun 2019]**

(a) 25,000 (b) 30,000
(c) 33,000 (d) 36,000

93. The simple interest on a certain sum of money at the rate of 5% per annum for four years is ₹420. At what rate of interest, the same of interest can be received on the same sum after two and half years? **[Jun 2019]**

(a) 4% (b) 6%
(c) 8% (d) 10%

94. In a class, 20% of the boys have blue eyes and 10% of the girls have blue eyes. If the ratio of boys to girls in the class is 4:3, then what is the proportion of the student in the class having blue eyes? **[Jun 2019]**

(a) $\frac{12}{33}$ (b) $\frac{14}{45}$
(c) $\frac{11}{45}$ (d) $\frac{11}{70}$

95. Bangalore is bigger than Jhansi, Satpura is bigger than Chittor, Rajgarh is not as big as Jhansi but is bigger than Satpura. Which is the smallest? **[Jun 2019]**

(a) Banaglore (b) Jhansi
(c) Satpura (d) Chittor

96. If in a certain code, BAT = 23 and CAT = 24, then how you will code BALL? **[Jun 2019]**

(a) 27 (b) 28
(c) 32 (d) 39

97. Choose the missing term out of the given alternatives **[Jun 2019]**

TEF, UGH, ________________, WKL

(a) CMN (b) UJI
(c) VIJ (d) IJT

98. If RED is coded as 6720, then how would GREEN be coded? **[Jun 2019]**

(a) 16717209 (b) 1677209
(c) 9207716 (d) 1677199

99. Among the five friends, Vineet is taller than Monika, but not as tall as Ram. Jacob is taller than Dalip but shorter than Monika. Who is the tallest in their group? **[Jun 2019]**

(a) Ram (b) Monika
(c) Vineet (d) Jacob

100. The sixth number in a sequence of number is 32 and each number after the first number in the sequence is 4 less than the number immendiately proceeding it. What is the third number in the sequence? **[Jun 2019]**

(a) 36 (b) 40
(c) 44 (d) 48

101. Choose the correct alternative. **[Jun 2019]**

Cup is to coffee as bowl is to ________

(a) Dish (b) Soup
(c) Spoon (d) Food

102. In a school, there are five teachers. A and B both are teaching Hindi and English. C and B both are teaching English and Georaphy. D and A both are teaching Punjabi and Hindi. E and B both are teaching History and French. **[Jun 2019]**

Who among the teacher is teaching maximum number of subjects?

(a) A (b) B
(c) D (d) C and E

103. The smallest integer greater than 1, which is simultaneously a square and a cube of certain integers is: **[Dec 2019]**

(a) 8 (b) 9
(c) 36 (d) 64

104. A person buys 3 items for ₹1500 each and 2 items for ₹1800 each from a shopping mall. On the total bill, a discount of 10% is given. What is the average cost of the items? **[Dec 2019]**

(a) 1650 (b) 1458
(c) 1658 (d) 1550

105. A 50 year old man has a son, whose age is $\frac{2}{5}$th of his age. After how many years, the ratio of the age of the man to his son will be $\frac{5}{3}$? **[Dec 2019]**

(a) 10 years (b) 15 years
(c) 20 years (d) 25 years

106. If the length of the side of a square (5.0 cm × 5.0 cm) is increased by 1%, then the area of the square gets increased by what %? **[Dec 2019]**

(a) 1% (b) 2%
(c) 2.5% (d) 4%

107. By selling 70 pencils for ₹90, a person makes a loss of 25%. How many pencils should be sold for ₹234 to gain a profit of 30%? **[Dec 2019]**

(a) 95 (b) 100
(c) 105 (d) 110

108. Given below is a question followed by three statements. Identify the statements that are necessary to answer the question. **[Dec 2019]**

Question: What is the percentage profit gained by a vendor when he sells an article?

Statements:

(i) He gives a 10% discount on the marked price.
(ii) He would have earned 25% profit if he did not give any discount.
(iii) The cost price of the article is ₹8000.

Choose the correct option.

(a) (i) and (ii) only
(b) (ii) and (iii) only
(c) (i) and (iii) only
(d) (i), (ii) and (iii)

109. Out of a total of 10 students, the average weight of 9 students is 60 kg. If the weight of the 10th student is 9 kg more than the average weight of all the 10 students, then the weight of the 10th student would be: **[Dec 2019]**

(a) 61 kg (b) 69 kg
(c) 70 kg (d) 71 kg

110. In what ratio must a vendor mix two varieties of sugar worth ₹60 per kg and ₹78 per kg so that, by selling the mixture at ₹76.8 per kg, the vendor gains 20%? **[Dec 2019]**

(a) 7:4 (b) 7:2
(c) 5:3 (d) 5:2

111. A circle has the same area as that of a diagonal of a square of length 11.0 cm. What is the diameter of the circle? **[Dec 2019]**

(a) ~ 8.7 cm (b) ~ 17.4 cm
(c) ~ 7.8 cm (d) ~ 15.6 cm

112. The two cities P and Q are 360 km apart from each other. A car goes from P to Q with a speed of 40 km/hr and returns to P with a speed of 60 km/hr. What is the average speed of the car? **[Dec 2019]**

(a) 45 km/hr (b) 48 km/hr
(c) 50 km/hr (d) 55 km/hr

A student obtains overall 78% marks in his examination consisting of Physics, Chemistry, Mathematics, Computer Science and General English. Marks obtained and the maximum marks in each subject are indicated in the following table.

Subject	Physics (Maximum marks = 200)	Chemistry (Maximum marks =100)	Mathematics (Maximum marks = 200)	Computer Science (Maximum marks = 200)	General English (Maximum marks = 100)
Marks Obtained	155	80	165	140	X

113. The marks (X) obtained by the student in General English would be: **[Dec 2019]**
(a) 68 (b) 74
(c) 84 (d) 90

114. A shopkeeper sells a refrigerator for ₹22,000 and makes a profit of 10%. If he desires to make a profit of 18%, then what should be his selling price? **[Dec 2019]**
(a) ₹23,600 (b) ₹39,600
(c) ₹36,000 (d) ₹24,600

115. If $x : y = 7 : 9$, then $3x - 5y : 4x + y = ?$ **[Dec 2019]**
(a) $\frac{-24}{37}$ (b) $\frac{-22}{37}$
(c) $\frac{15}{22}$ (d) $\frac{42}{37}$

116. Identify the wrong number in the given series.
3, 13, 43, 53, 63, 83 **[Dec 2019]**
(a) 13 (b) 53
(c) 63 (d) 83

117. A sum of money with compound interest becomes ₹2400 in one year and ₹3000 in two years. Find the principal amount. **[Dec 2019]**
(a) ₹1900 (b) ₹1910
(c) ₹1915 (d) ₹1920

118. The ratio of two numbers a and b is 3:7. After adding 9 to each number, the ratio becomes 9:17. The numbers a and b are: **[Dec 2019]**
(a) 6, 14 (b) 9, 21
(c) 15, 35 (d) 18, 42

119. Identify the term 'X' in the series: 3, 2, 11, 14, 27, 34, 51, X **[Dec 2019]**
(a) 62 (b) 69
(c) 60 (d) 71

120. Which of the following sets of letters would complete the letters series, when they are placed sequentially? **[Dec 2019]**
bb ___ b ___ ab ___ cbba ___ bcbb ___
(a) a c b a c (b) a c b b b
(c) c b b b a (d) a b b b c

121. Determine the term 'X' in the following series.
2, 9, 20, 35, 54, 77, X **[Dec 2019]**
(a) 104 (b) 102
(c) 89 (d) 110

122. *A* is the father of *B* and *C* is the sister of *A*. *D* is the grandson of *C*. How is *D* related to *B*? **[Dec 2019]**
(a) Uncle (b) Nephew
(c) Cousin (d) Grandson

123. If HPU = 9 and JNU = 9, then DU = ? **[Dec 2019]**
(a) 5 (b) 6 (c) 4 (d) 7

124. In a certain code, ENGLAND is written as ULSNYLV. Using the same code, IRELAND will be written as: **[Dec 2019]**
(a) HQUNYLV (b) QHUNYLV
(c) QUHNYLV (d) HUQNYLV

125. Find the missing term in the following series.
2, 4, 6, 12, 10, 36, 14, ?, 18, 324, ...
(a) 50 (b) 72
(c) 108 (d) 18

126. Apoorav is the son of Madhu. Vinod is the brother of Madhu's husband. How is Apoorav related to Vinod? **[Dec 2019]**
(a) Uncle (b) Brother
(c) Nephew (d) Cousin

127. Find the next term of the series, AT, EQ, IN, OK, ... **[Dec 2019]**
(a) UH (b) UP
(c) US (d) UU

128. The average of 70 numbers is 32. If each number is increased by 3, then the new average will become **[2020]**
(a) 31 (b) 33
(c) 35 (d) 37

129. A clock takes 5 seconds to strike 5 times at 5 O'clock. How long will it take to strike 9 times at 9 O'clock? **[2020]**
(a) 9 seconds (b) 10 seconds
(c) 12 seconds (d) 8 seconds

130. A student scores 55, 60, 65 and 70 respectively in English, Physics, Chemistry and Mathematics. If the credits assigned to English, Physics, Chemistry and Mathematics are 2, 3, 3 and 4 respectively then what would be the average mark of the student? **[2020]**
(a) 62.50 (b) 63.75
(c) 64.25 (d) 64.75

131. A shopkeeper sells an item at a discount of 40% on the item's listed price of ₹ 1500.00. He still makes a profit of 20% on the original cost of the item. What is the original cost of the item? **[2020]**
(a) ₹ 500 (b) ₹ 750
(c) ₹ 600 (d) ₹1080

132. A motorist travels to a place 150 kms away at an average speed of 50 km / hour and returns at a speed of 30 km / hour. His average speed for the whole journey is **[2020]**
(a) 35 km/hour (b) 37.5 km/hour
(c) 40 km/hour (d) 42.5 km/hour

133. In the following letter series, the next term is BDF, EGI, HJL, ... **[2020]**
(a) KMO (b) JMP
(c) ILO (d) KNO

134. A man is 30 years older than his son. Five years ago, his age was 6 times the age of his son. The age of the son is **[2020]**
(a) 10 years (b) 11 years
(c) 12 years (d) 15 years

135. A sum of money earning compound interest annually doubles itself after 4 years. What is the rate of interest? **[2020]**
(a) ~14% (b) ~19%
(c) ~18% (d) ~15%

136. What is the next term in the following series?
4, 12, 28, 52, _____ **[2020]**
(a) 76 (b) 84
(c) 98 (d) 104

137. Ayurveda, which deals with indigenous system of medicine, could be traced to: **[2020]**
(a) Rigveda (b) Yajurveda
(c) Samaveda (d) Atharvaveda

138. How many terms are there in the series 168, 175, 182, _____, 266? **[2021]**
(a) 13 (b) 14
(c) 15 (d) 16

139. Which of the following fractions is the smallest? **[2021]**
(a) 11/16 (b) 29/40
(c) 5/8 (d) 65/80

140. A total of 324 coins of 20 paise and 25 paise make a sum of ₹71. The number of 20 paise coins is **[2021]**
(a) 124 (b) 125
(c) 144 (d) 200

141. Given below are two statements **[2021]**
Statement I: The compound interest on ₹280 for 18 months at 10 % per annum is ₹44.3.
Statement II: At 5.6 % rate of simple interest, a certain sum will be doubled in 15 years
In light of the above statements, choose the correct answer from the options given below:
(a) Both Statement I and Statement II are false.
(b) Both Statement I and Statement II are true.
(c) Statement I is false but Statement II is true.
(d) Statement I is true but Statement II is false.

142. The average of ten number is 7. If each number is multiplied by 11, then the average of the new set of numbers is: **[2021]**
(a) 72 (b) 77
(c) 78 (d) 82

143. Given below are two statements **[2021]**
Statement I: The number 89325324 is divisible by 66.
Statement II: The set of natural numbers is also called the set of whole numbers.
In light of the above statements, choose the correct answer from the options given below:
(a) Both Statement I and Statement II are false
(b) Both Statement I and Statement II are true
(c) Statement I is false but Statement II is true
(d) Statement I is true but Statement II is false

144. If the selling price of ₹24 results in a discount of 20% on the list price, what selling price would result in a 30% discount on list price? **[2021]**

(a) 18 (b) 20
(c) 21 (d) 27

145. Which of the following statements are correct? **[2021]**

A. If A's speed is more than B's speed, then to travel the same distance, A will take more time than B
B. Two speeds, 1500 m/min and 90 km/hr are equal
C. By walking at a speed of 18 km/hr, the distance covered in 2 minutes and 30 seconds is 750 meters

Choose the correct answer from the options given below:

(a) A and B only (b) A and C only
(c) B and C only (d) C only

146. How tall is a tree that is 6 meters shorter than a wall that is seven times higher than the tree? **[2021]**

(a) 1 meters (b) 1.25 meters
(c) 2 meters (d) 7 meters

147. What number comes next in this sequence? 6, 4, 2.5, 1.5, ? **[2021]**

(a) 0.5 (b) –0.5
(c) 1 (d) –1

148. The owner of a mobile phone charges his customer 25% more than the cost price. If a customer paid 8,000/- for a mobile phone then what was the cost price of the mobile? **[2021]**

(a) ₹ 5600 (b) ₹ 6000
(c) ₹ 6400 (d) ₹ 7000

149. In the letter series B, H, R, F. What is the next letter? **[2021]**

(a) L (b) Z
(c) P (d) X

150. Given the relationship between variables Y and X $Y = X^2$: if X changes by 6%, What is the percentage change in Y? **[2021]**

(a) ~ 36% (b) ~ 12%
(c) ~ 8% (d) ~ 6%

151. A man travels in a car from point A to point B and covers a distance of 120 km. For the first 40 km, the speed of his car is 50 km/hr and for the rest of journey the speed is 60 km/hr. What is the average speed of his car from point A to point B? **[2021]**

(a) 55 km/hr (b) 54.25 km/hr
(c) 56.25 km/hr (d) 58.25 km/hr

152. In the series, 1, 3, 6, 10, ... What is the next term? **[2021]**

(a) 12 (b) 15
(c) 18 (d) 20

153. What number should replace the question mark? 7, 8, 9, 10, 12, 14, 16, 20, 21, 28, ? **[Dec 2021]**

(a) 27 (b) 36
(c) 32 (d) 29

154. X is as much younger to Y as he is older to Z. If the sum of the ages of Y and Z is 36 years. What is the age of X? **[Dec 2021]**

(a) 16 Years (b) 15 Years
(c) 18 Years (d) 20 Years

155. Two persons are walking in the same direction at rates 3 km/hr and 6km/hr. A train comes running from behind and passes them in 9 and 10 seconds respectively. The speed of the train is **[Dec 2021]**

(a) 33km/hr (b) 22 km/hr
(c) 44 km/hr (d) 35km/hr

156. Given below are two statements: **[Dec 2021]**

Statement I: Between 4 and 5, the minute hand and hour hand of a clock coincide at 20 minutes past 4.

Statement II: Between 4 and 5, the minute hand and hour hand of a clock are at a right angle at 40 minutes past 4.

In light of the above statements, choose the correct answer from the options given below

(a) Both Statement I and Statement II are true
(b) Both Statement I and Statement II are false
(c) Statement I is true but Statement II is false
(d) Statement I is false but Statement II is true

157. Which of the following statements are TRUE ? **[Dec 2021]**

A. If A's salary is 20% more than B, then B's salary is 20% less than A.
B. By selling 28 pens, a man gains the selling price of 4 pens. The gain is 15%.
C. The average of N consecutive natural numbers starting from 1 is $\frac{(N+1)}{2}$

Choose the correct answer from the options given below:

(a) A and C only (b) B and C only
(c) A and B only (d) C only

158. Find the missing term in the series given as: 4, 6, 12, 14, 28, 30, ? **[2022]**

(a) 32 (b) 36
(c) 52 (d) 60

159. In a certain code, O is written as E, A as C, M as I, S as O, N as P, E as M, I as A, P as N and C as S, then how will COMPANION be written in that code? **[2022]**

(a) SEINCPAEP (b) SENCIAPEP
(c) SENCPIAPE (d) SNEIPCAPE

160. In a class of 43 students, Aashman's rank is 16th from the bottom. What is his rank from the top? **[2022]**

(a) 28 (b) 27
(c) 26 (d) 29

161. A pipe can fill a water tank three times as fast as another pipe. If both are used together, these can fill the tank in 36 minutes. How much time will be taken by the slower pipe alone to fill the tank? **[2022]**

(a) 192 minutes (b) 108 minutes
(c) 144 minutes (d) 160 minutes

162. A retailer buys 40 pens at the marked price of 36 pens from a wholesaler. If he sells these pens giving a discount of 1%, what is the profit percentage? **[2022]**

(a) 12 (b) 15
(c) 20 (d) 10

163. In a certain code, '467' means 'leaves are green', '485' means 'green is good' and '639' means 'they are playing', Which digit stands for 'leaves' in that code? **[2022]**

(a) 6 (b) 7
(c) 4 (d) 9

164. The average age of students, in a class was 15 years, When 5 new boys whose average age was 12 years 6 months were admitted in the class, the average age was reduced by 6 months. How many students were there in the class originally? **[2022]**

(a) 15 (b) 20
(c) 18 (d) 16

165. Number of bacteria in a container doubles in every one minute, If the container gets completely filled with bacteria in 30 minutes, then in how many minutes 1/4th of the container shall be filled with bacteria? **[2022]**

(a) 15 minutes (b) 16 minutes
(c) 28 minutes (d) 25 minutes

166. Find the missing number in the series: **[2022]**
2, 10, 30, 68, 130, 222, ?

(a) 350 (b) 352
(c) 194 (d) 104

167. Certain number of birds are sitting on two trees A and B. Birds sitting on tree A, tell to the birds sitting on tree B, that if 2 birds from tree B shift to the tree A then we are equal in number, However, the birds sitting on tree B, tell those sitting on A that if two birds from your side (tree A) shift to our side (tree B), then we become double than you (tree A). How many birds are sitting on the two trees A and B, respectively? **[2022]**

(a) 8,1 2 (b) 10,14
(c) 14,10 (d) 5, 7

168. A fruit seller has some stock of fruits to be sold in three days period. Everyday he sells 50% of the available fruits and 10% of the leftover fruits gets spoiled during every night. If the total number of fruits that got spoiled in three days is 1983, then find how many fruits were there with the seller in the beginning? **[June 2023]**

(a) 22,000 (b) 21,000
(c) 19,000 (d) 24,000

169. The difference between simple and compound interest on certain principal amount, for 2 years at the rate of 5% per annum is `11.25. Find the principal amount. **[June 2023]**

(a) ₹4, 500 (b) ₹5, 500
(c) ₹4, 000 (d) ₹4, 300

170. If $x = 10$ and $y = 0.1$, which of the following expressions has the highest value? **[June 2023]**

(a) $x^2 y^2$ (b) $x^2 - y^2$
(c) $x^{2+} y^2$ (d) x^2/y^2

171. In a certain coding language; Tour is written as 4156, Screw is written as 73698 and Tear is written as 4926. **[June 2023]**

How the word Sweater will be written in that language?

(a) 7849692 (b) 7892694
(c) 7829946 (d) 7892496

172. What number should replace question mark (?) in the below given series: **[June 2023]**
5, 7, 11, 19, 35, 67, ?
(a) 111 (b) 121
(c) 131 (d) 141

173. The monthly income of a person in the year 2020 was ₹65,000 and his monthly expenditure was ₹45,000. In the year 2021 his monthly income increased by 15% and his monthly expenditure by 7%. What is the percentage increase in his savings ? **[June 2023]**
(a) 33% (b) 31%
(c) 35% (d) 28%

174. 5/9 of a number is equal to twenty five percent of a second number. Second number is equal to 1/4 of a third number. The value of the third number is 2960, how much is the 30% of the first number? **[June 2023]**
(a) 9.99 (b) 99.9
(c) 89.9 (d) 88.9

175. A man invested 1/3 of his retirement gratuity at 6% simple interest; 1/4 of his gratuity at 7% and the rest at 8% simple interest. If his annual return on these investments is ₹7012.5, find the total amount of gratuity invested by the man. **[June 2023]**
(a) ₹89,000 (b) ₹99,000
(c) ₹95,000 (d) ₹1,05,000

176. If in a ceratin, coding language, 'Cheater' is coded as 'ejgcvgt', then how 'Preacher' will be coded in that language? **[June 2023]**
(a) 'rtgcejgt' (b) 'qsfbdifs'
(c) 'rtgbdjgt' (d) 'stgbdjgt'

177. What number should replace question mark (?) in the series given below? **[June 2023]**
7, 10, 19, 46, 127?
(a) 202 (b) 192
(c) 173 (d) 370

178. Consider the following number series: 1, 3, 7, 15, 31, ? ...... **[Dec 2023]**
Identify the missing number (?) from the options given below:
(a) 42 (b) 52
(c) 62 (d) 63

179. A sum of ₹ 10,000.00 (ten thousand) is invested at rate of interest 8% per annum compounded half yearly. What will be the maturity amount in 1½ years? **[Dec 2023]**
(a) ₹ 11248.64 (b) ₹ 10816.20
(c) ₹ 11200.00 (d) ₹ 10108.64

180. Consider the following letter series. AA, BD, CI, DP, ?... **[Dec 2023]**
The next term (?) in the series is
(a) ES (b) EV
(c) EY (d) EB

181. In an organisation, there are a total of 40 employees consisting of 5 Executive officers, 15 Senior Staff and 20 Junior staff. The monthly salaries of an Executive officer, a Senior staff and a Junior staff are ₹2,50,000, ₹80,000 and ₹45,000 respectively. What is the average salary of an employee of the organisation? **[Dec 2023]**
(a) ₹1,20,000 (b) ₹90,250
(c) ₹82,750 (d) ₹83,750

182. A train running at a speed of 90 km/hr starts slowing down at a constant rate of decrease in speed of 2.5 m/s^2. What is the distance covered by the train before it comes to a halt? **[Dec 2023]**
(a) 500 m (b) 750m
(c) 250m (d) 125 m

183. The mean and standard deviation of 75 observations are 45 and 10, respectively. If 2 is added to each observation, the new mean and standard deviation will be (This question can also fall under Research Aptitude) **[Dec 2023]**
(a) 47, 12 (b) 47, 14
(c) 47, 10 (d) 46, 12

ANSWER KEY

1. (a)	2. (c)	3. (c)	4. (a)	5. (c)	6. (a)	7. (a)	8. (a)	9. (b)	10. (b)
11. (c)	12. (a)	13. (b)	14. (b)	15. (c)	16. (a)	17. (a)	18. (d)	19. (a)	20. (d)
21. (d)	22. (d)	23. (b)	24. (c)	25. (d)	26. (d)	27. (a)	28. (c)	29. (a)	30. (c)
31. (c)	32. (b)	33. (d)	34. (d)	35. (a)	36. (b)	37. (c)	38. (c)	39. (a)	40. (b)
41. (d)	42. (c)	43. (c)	44. (c)	45. (a)	46. (c)	47. (b)	48. (a)	49. (c)	50. (d)
51. (a)	52. (d)	53. (c)	54. (b)	55. (b)	56. (a)	57. (d)	58. (d)	59. (a)	60. (a)
61. (b)	62. (a)	63. (c)	64. (a)	65. (c)	66. (c)	67. (b)	68. (c)	69. (c)	70. (d)
71. (b)	72. (b)	73. (c)	74. (b)	75. (c)	76. (c)	77. (c)	78. (b)	79. (b)	80. (d)
81. (b)	82. (c)	83. (b)	84. (d)	85. (b)	86. (c)	87. (c)	88. (c)	89. (b)	90. (b)
91. (d)	92. (b)	93. (c)	94. (d)	95. (d)	96. (a)	97. (c)	98. (b)	99. (a)	100. (c)
101. (b)	102. (b)	103. (d)	104. (b)	105. (d)	106. (b)	107. (c)	108. (a)	109. (c)	110. (b)
111. (a)	112. (b)	113. (c)	114. (a)	115. (a)	116. (c)	117. (d)	118. (d)	119. (a)	120. (c)
121. (a)	122. (b)	123. (a)	124. (b)	125. (c)	126. (c)	127. (a)	128. (c)	129. (b)	130. (b)
131. (b)	132. (b)	133. (a)	134. (b)	135. (b)	136. (b)	137. (c)	138. (d)	139. (c)	140. (d)
141. (a)	142. (b)	143. (d)	144. (d)	145. (c)	146. (a)	147. (c)	148. (c)	149. (d)	150. (b)
151. (c)	152. (b)	153. (a)	154. (b)	155. (d)	156. (c)	157. (d)	158. (d)	159. (a)	160. (a)
161. (c)	162. (d)	163. (b)	164. (b)	165. (c)	166. (a)	167. (b)	168. (d)	169. (a)	170. (d)
171. (d)	172. (c)	173. (a)	174. (b)	175. (b)	176. (c)	177. (d)	178. (d)	179. (a)	180. (c)
181. (d)	182. (d)	183. (c)							

HINTS AND SOLUTIONS

1. **(a):** Elimination of choices is required to solve this question.
   Let's try all the options
   (a). For exact amount of 19, no combination fits-we can try all the combinations
   For (b) 10×2 = ₹ 20
   (c) $(8 \times 2) + (7 \times 1)$ = ₹ 23
   (d) $(7 \times 3) + (8 \times 1)$ = ₹ 29
   Thus, option (a) is the answer.

2. **(c):**

Q	U	E	S	T	I	O	N
↓	↓	↓	↓	↓	↓	↓	↓
D	O	M	E	S	T	I	C

Similarly,

R	E	S	P	O	N	S	E
↓	↓	↓	↓	↓	↓	↓	↓
?	M	E	?	I	C	E	M

Only one choice is possible that is matching of last four letters ICEM. Hence, option (c) is the answer.

3. **(c):** Difference of 1, 3, 5 is the pattern. The terms after 22 will be 23, 26, 31, 32, 35...... Hence, 33 is not the term and option (c) is the answer.

4. **(a):** After B we leave 3 and reach to F, similarly after P leaving 3 we get T and one behind that is S. So, the series is completed by TS.

5. **(c):**

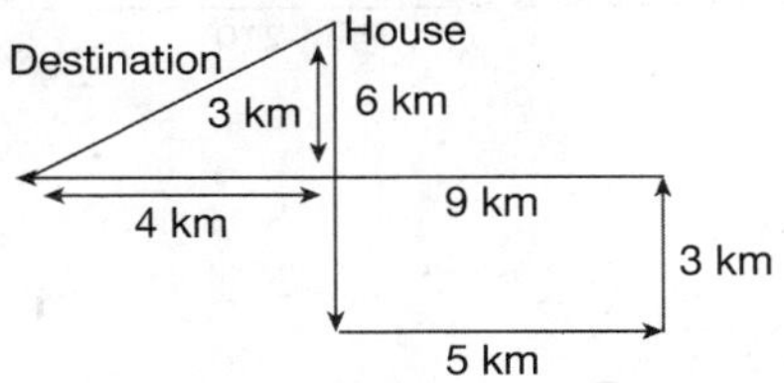

Using Pythagoras theorem (adding squares of 3 and 4, and then taking their square root), the answer is 5 km.

6. **(a):**
   Between
   50 to 59, there are ten numbers
   60 to 69 – ten numbers
   70 to 79 – ten numbers
   80 to 89 – ten numbers
   89 to 99 – ten numbers
   Thus, total numbers from 50 to 99 are 50
   Total numbers with 2 and 7 between 50 to 99 are
   52, 62, 72, 82, 92
   57, 67, 70, 71, 73, 74, 75, 76, 77, 78, 79, 87, 97
   Thus, the above 18 numbers are to be deducted from 50.
   Thus, the exact answer = 50 - 18 = 32
   Alternatively, we can count directly 50, 51, 53, 54, 55, 56, 58.....69, 80, 81, 83.....99

7. **(a):** $1^3 + 1$, $2^3 - 1$, $3^3 + 1$, $4^3 - 1$, $5^3 + 1$ and so on. Hence, the answer is 215.

8. **(a):** B + 2 gives D, D + 1 (and reversing order) gives ED, again D + 4 gives H and so on. Hence, option (a) is the answer.

9. **(b):**

S	T	R	E	A	M	E	R	S
+2	+2	+2	+2		–1	–1	–1	–1
U	V	T	G	A	L	D	Q	R

K	N	O	W	L	E	D	G	E
+2	+2	+2	+2		–1	–1	–1	–1
M	P	Q	Y	L	D	C	F	D

Hence, (b) is the correct option.

10. **(b):**

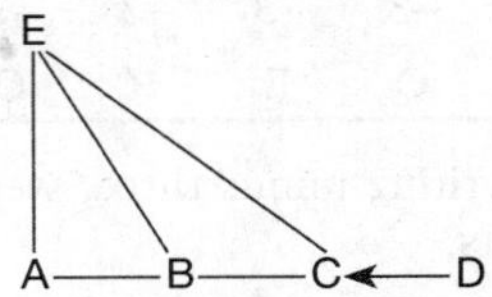

D is the daughter-in-law of E.

11. **(c):** Let's assume that numbers are $3x$ and $5x$.
    According to the statement,
    $$\frac{(3x-9)}{(5x-9)} = \frac{12}{23}$$
    = solving it we get $x = 11$. Hence, the numbers are 33 and 55.

12. **(a):** The total of ages of father and his son = 27×2 = 54 years
    Let the age of father = x years
    Then age of son = $54 - x$ years
    Age of father at the end of 18 years = $x + 18$ years
    Age of son = $54 - x + 18 = 72 - x$ years
    According to question,

$x + 18 = 2\,(72 - x)$

$x + 18 = 144 - 2x$

$x + 2x = 144 - 18 = 126$ years

$3x = 126$ years

$x = 42$ years = Age of Father

Age of son = 54 – 42 = 12 years

13. (b): $\times 2 + 1, \times 2 - 1, \times 2 + 1$ and so on.

$2 \times 2 + 1, 5 \times 2 - 1, 9 \times 2 + 1, 19 \times 2 - 1$ and so on.

14. (b):

Conversion Table		
A = 1	J = 10	S = 19
B = 2	K = 11	T = 20
C = 3	L = 12	U = 21
D = 4	M = 13	V = 22
E = 5	N = 14	W = 23
F = 6	O = 15	X = 24
G = 7	P = 16	Y = 25
H = 8	Q = 17	Z = 26
I = 9	R = 18	

M	A	T	H	U	R	A
–3	–3	–3	–3	–3	–3	–3
J	X	Q	E	R	O	X

Instead of writing minus three, we can assume gap of two alphabets.

Similarly,

H	O	T	E	L	S
–3	–3	–3	–3	–3	–3
E	L	Q	B	I	P

15. (c):

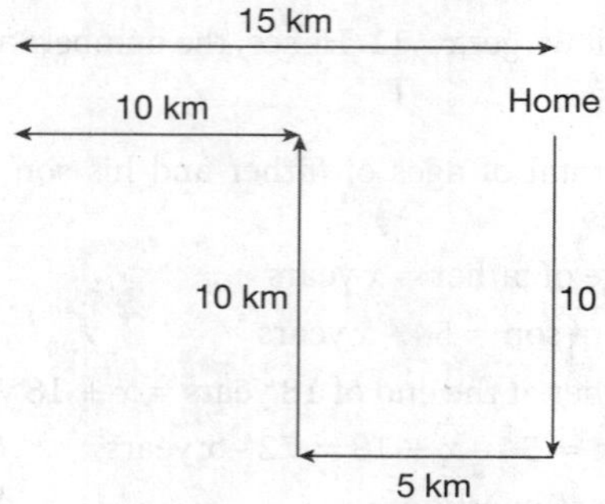

16. (a): The father of the boy's uncle → the grandfather of the boy and daughter of the grandfather → sister of father.

17. (a): Venn diagram for 5 variables is a difficult approach. Let's solve it by method that is usually described under probability topic.

Number of students passed in at least four subjects = Number of students passed exactly in four subjects + Number of students exactly passed in five subjects. ...(i)

But, the number of students passed in four subjects = Number of students failed in one subject only = Failed in English only + ... Failed in Bioscience only = 75 + 145 + 140 + 200 + 157 = 717.

Substituting it in (i), number of students passed in at least four subjects = 5583 + 717 = 6300.

18. (d): Let us assume that present age of person = x years.

Hence, son's age $= \frac{x}{4}$ years.

According to the statement, $\frac{x}{4} = 15 - 3 = 12$ years $\Rightarrow x = 48$ years.

Hence, wife's age = 48 – 3 = 45 years.

Wife's age after 5 years = 45 + 5 = 50 years.

19. (a): +3, +5, +7, +9, ...

20. (d): It is the question of combined arithmetic mean. $X_{12} = \frac{(X_1 N_1 + X_2 N_2)}{N}$, where X_1 and X_2 are arithmetic means of two groups and N_1 and N_2 are their respective frequencies. N is the total number of frequencies.

Here, $N_1 = 70, N_2 = 210 - 70 = 140$

Combined arithmetic mean $= \frac{(60 \times 70 + 78 \times 140)}{210} = 72$

21. (d):

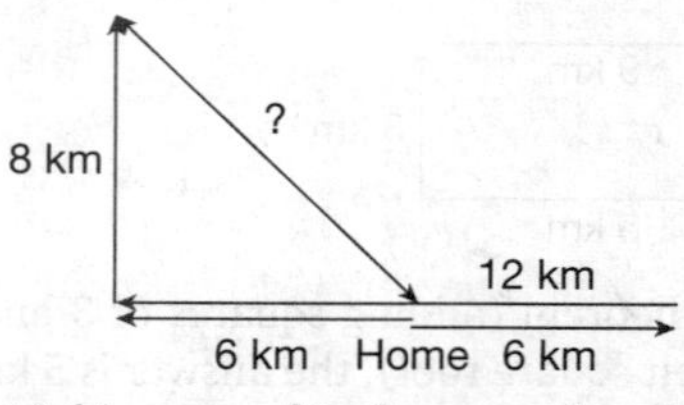

Making use of Pythagoras theorem

$= \sqrt{6^2 + 8^2} = 10$ km

22. (d): B2E, D5H, F12K, H27N, ?

Conversion Table		
A = 1	J = 10	S = 19
B = 2	K = 11	T = 20
C = 3	L = 12	U = 21
D = 4	M = 13	V = 22

E = 5	N = 14	W = 23
F = 6	O = 15	X = 24
G = 7	P = 16	Y = 25
H = 8	Q = 17	Z = 26
I = 9	R = 18	

1. $B \xrightarrow{+2} D \xrightarrow{+2} F \xrightarrow{+2} H \xrightarrow{+2} J$
2. $2 \xrightarrow{\times 2+1} 5 \xrightarrow{\times 2+2} 12 \xrightarrow{\times 2+3} 27 \xrightarrow{\times 2+4} 58$
3. $E \xrightarrow{+3} H \xrightarrow{+3} K \xrightarrow{+3} N \xrightarrow{+3} Q$

Thus, answer is J58Q.

23. (b):

Grandmother	1
Mother	1
Wives	4
Daughters	4 × 2
Total females	14

24. (c):

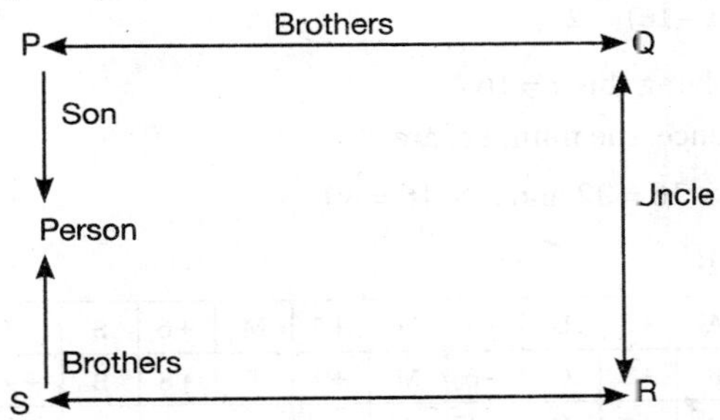

So, P's son, S and R are siblings. Hence, Q is the uncle of R.

25. (d): Let Railway fare from City A to City B = ₹x

And from City A to City C = ₹y

According to question, we get:

$$2x + 3y = 177 \quad \text{(i)}$$

$$3x + 2y = 173 \quad \text{(ii)}$$

Solving equations (i) and (ii), we get x = ₹ 33, which is the required answer.

26. (d):

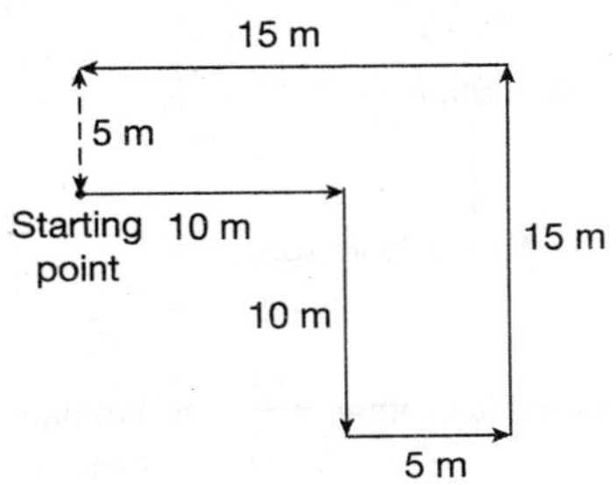

27. (a):

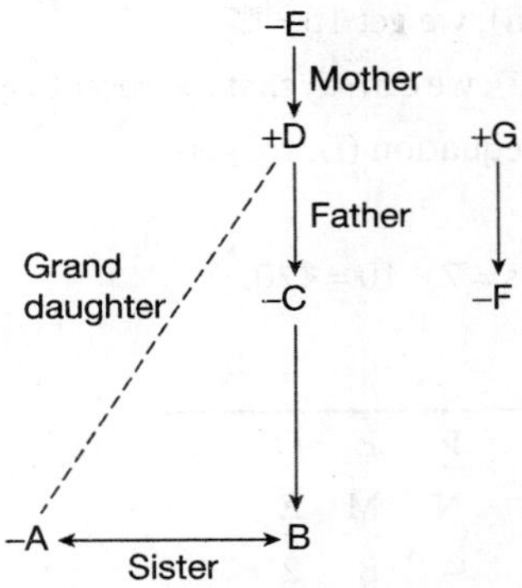

28. (c): The number of alphabets is increasing by 1 and are alternatively being written in reverse order.

AB, EDC, FGHI, NMLKJ, OPQRST

29. (a):

S	E	L	E	C	T	I	O	N
–2	–2	–2	–2	–2	–2	–2	–2	–2
Q	C	J	C	A	R	G	M	L

Similarly,

A	M	E	R	I	C	A	N	S
–2	–2	–2	–2	–2	–2	–2	–2	–2
Y	K	C	P	G	A	Y	L	Q

30. (c): +8, +12, +16, +20, +24 and so on.

31. (c): It's a question of mixed series.

First series: 13, 33, 53, 73, ...

Second series: 22, 42, 62, ...

Thus, 53, i.e., 125 is the right answer.

32. (b): Look at the alphabetic series.

A	B	C	D	E	F	G	H	I	J	K	L	M
1	2	3	4	5	6	7	8	9	10	11	12	13
→												

N	O	P	Q	R	S	T	U	V	W	X	Y	Z
14	15	16	17	18	19	20	21	22	23	24	25	26
→												

33. (d): Let's consider g for glass, p for pencil box and c for cup.

Ali: 1g + 1p + 1c = ₹21 (i)

Rakesh: 1g + 2p + 1c = ₹28 (ii)

Preeti: 2g + 2p +1c = ₹35 (iii)

Comparing (i) and (iii), we get 1p = ₹7

Comparing (ii) and (iii), we can say that the cost of 1g = ₹7

Substituting them in equation (i), we get:

1c = ₹7

So, the cost of 10 cups = 7 × 10 = ₹70.

34. (d)

A	M	N	S	I	P	E	O	C
C	I	P	O	A	N	M	E	S
5	3	6	9	7	4	8	2	1

So, the code for COMPANIES will be SEINCPAMO.

35. (a):

	1		6		15		28		45		66
Difference		5		9		13		17		21	
			+4		+4		+4		+4		

36. (b):

A	+3	D	+4	H	+5	M	+6	S
B	+5	G	+6	M	+7	T	+8	B
D	+7	K	+8	S	+9	B	+10	L

37. (c):

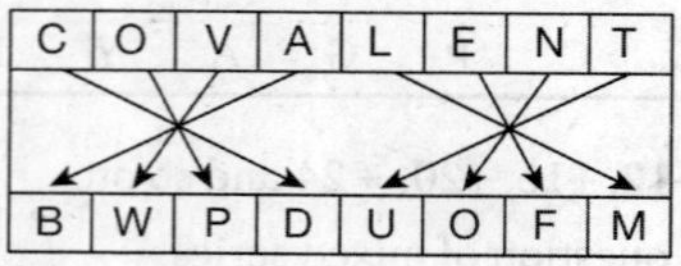

Similarly,

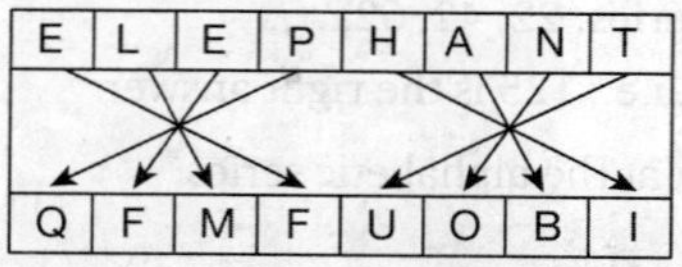

38. (c):

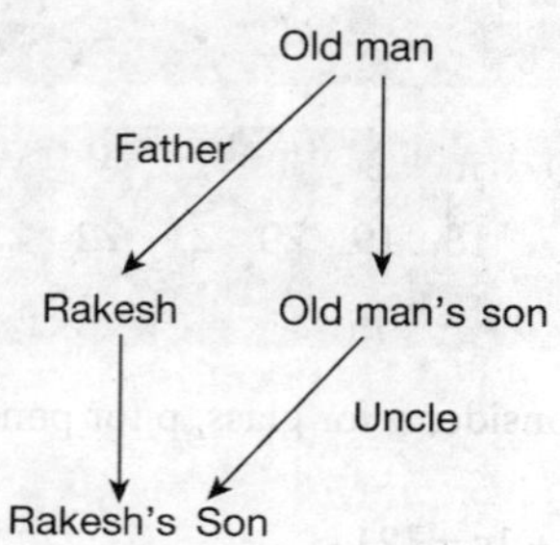

39. (a):

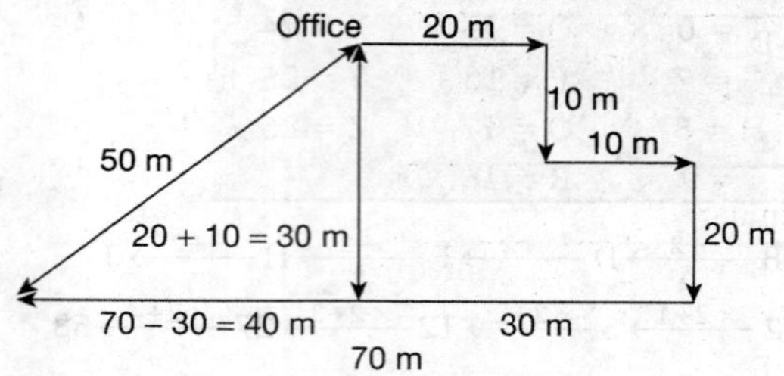

In right-angled triangle on left,

Hypotenuse = $\sqrt{40^2 + 30^2} = \sqrt{2500} = 50$ m

Thus, the distance from office to destination is 50 m.

40. (b): Difference is increasing by 4, so the next difference is 18, and the next term should be 47.

5–(–1) = 6; 15 – 5 = 10, 29–15 = 14

41. (d): Let the numbers be $2x$:$5x$

$$\frac{(2x+16)}{5x+16)} = \frac{1}{2}$$

Solving this $x = 16$

Hence, the numbers are

2 × 16 = 32 and 5 × 16 = 80

42. (c):

A	+3	D	+4	H	+5	M	+6	S	+7	Z
B	+5	G	+6	M	+7	T	+8	B	+9	K
D	+7	K	+8	S	+9	B	+10	L	+11	W

43. (c):

V	A	R	A	N	A	S	I
+1	+2	+3	+4	+5	+6	+7	+8
W	C	U	E	S	G	Z	Q

Similarly,

K	O	L	K	A	T	A
+1	+2	+3	+4	+5	+6	+7
L	Q	O	O	F	Z	H

44. (c):

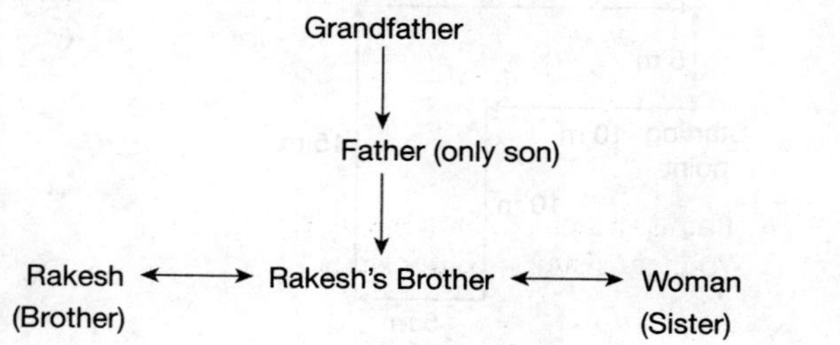

45. (a):

D	I	C	E
+2	+3	+4	+5
F	L	G	J

Similarly,

B	I	T	E
+2	+3	+4	+5
D	L	X	J

So, (a) is the answer.

46. (c): Count the series

7, 11, 19, 35, 67

There are gaps of 4, 8, 16, 32, 64

Thus, missing number = 67 + 64 = 131

47. (b): The next term in the series KB, JH, IM, HQ, GT?

The first terms in the series (if the series is reversed) are F, G, H, I, J, K. Thus F is the first word.

The second letters are increasing in the order of +6, +5, +4, +3, +2 ..... Thus, V will be the second letter.

Thus, FV is the answer.

48. (a):

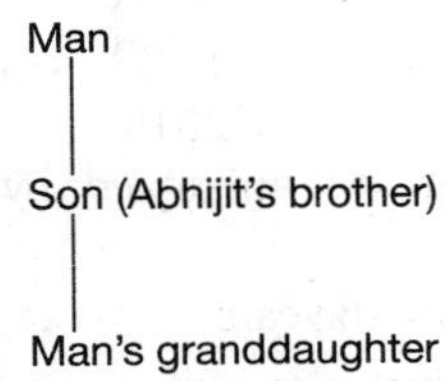

Man is Father of Abhijit

49. (c):

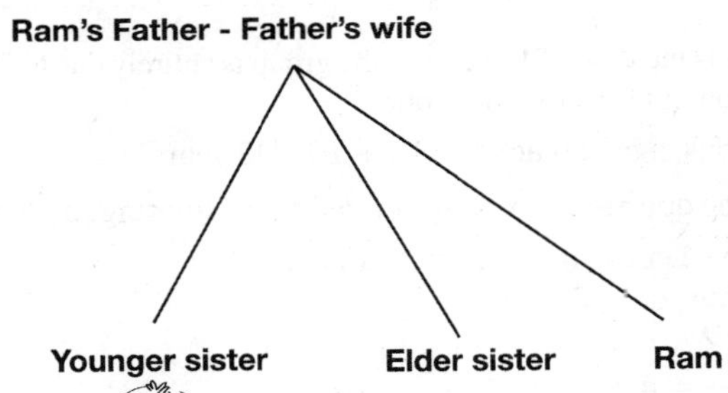

Ram's Father Younger sister   Father's wife Elder sister   Ram

50. (d): We need to add 3, 6, 12, 24, 48 ...

We are doubling 3 at every stage.

51. (a): This can be discussed on the basis of physical characteristics.

52. (d)

We have to add two letters so that we get the letters in the resultant series.

F	A	C	E
+2	+2	+2	+2
H	C	E	G

Similarly,

H	I	G	H
+2	+2	+2	+2
J	K	I	J

53. (c)

English Alphabet–Position Left to Right												
A	B	C	D	E	F	G	H	I	J	K	L	M
1	2	3	4	5	6	7	8	9	10	11	12	13
N	O	P	Q	R	S	T	U	V	W	X	Y	Z
14	15	16	17	18	19	20	21	22	23	24	25	26

Kindly pick the second letter – it's decreasing by one letter if we move from right hand side towards left—U, V, W, X, Y. So we can fix 'T' for the term being asked.

If we pick the first letter, it is increasing by 6, 5, 4, 3, 2, 1 for the rest of letters. It is given in above image directly.

54. (b): Required answer $= 250 \times 4\frac{1}{2} = 1125$ miles

55. (b): First and third letters are in sequence in every term. The middle letter is also simple sequencing in every succeeding term.

56. (a): As the formula for simple interest =

$$\text{Principle} \times \text{Rate} \times \frac{\text{Time}}{100}$$

It means that simple interest is directly proportion to time here.

Thus, interest would vary in the ratio of 9:12, that means 3:4.

57. (d): 345*xy* to be divisible by 90 should have one zero at *y* (unit's) place, and the total of others should be equal to 9. 3 + 4 + 5 = 12, thus, to be divisible by 9, there should be 6 at the place of *x*. Then total will become 18 and the whole number be divisible by 90.

58. (d):

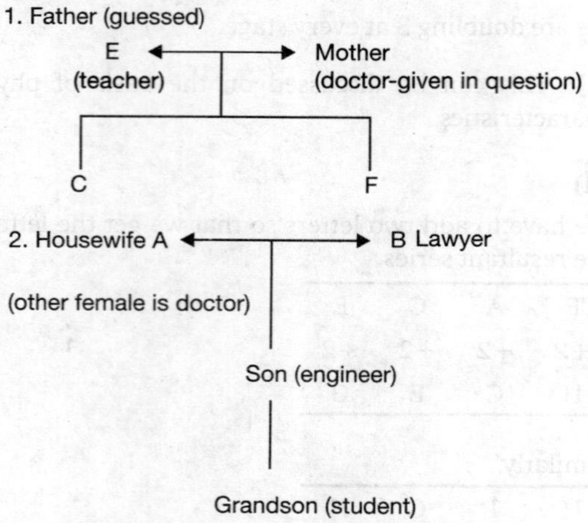

Now, look at choices:

a. No grandfather – as A is female

b. No mother – C has her mother doctor

c. No sister – only sibling, i.e., F

Thus, correct answer is (d).

59. (a):

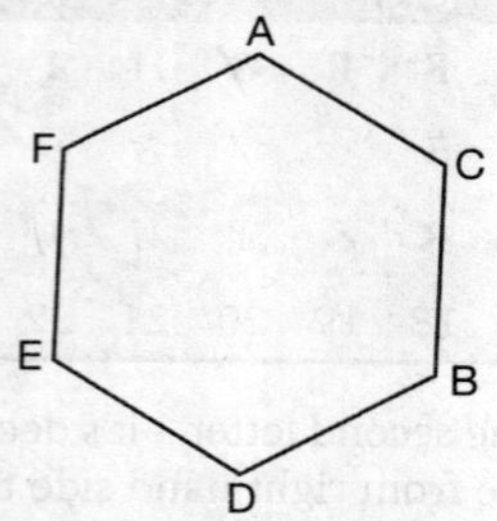

This diagram can be shown in circle also.

60. (a): $\frac{6\cancel{0}}{10\cancel{0}}(a-b)=\frac{4\cancel{0}}{10\cancel{0}}(a+b)$

$6a - 6b = 4a + 4b$

$2a = 10b$

$a = 5b$

Let x % of a is b; So

$\frac{x}{100} \times a = b$

$\frac{x}{100} \times a = \frac{a}{5}$

$x = \frac{100}{5} = 20\,x$

61. (b): Rajan is at 29th position.

Karan is at 9th position.

In between, Divya is at 19th position.

The difference between positions of Rajan and Divya is 10.

62. (a): In the following question, number of alphabet counted is multiplied by 2.

DRIVER= 6 Alphabets = $6 \times 2 = 12$

GOVERNMENT = 10 Alphabets = $10 \times 2 = 20$ BELIEVED = 8 8 alphabets = $8 \times 2 = 16$

BAT = 3 alphabets = $3 \times 2 = 6$

63. (c): Cost price (in case of loss) = $\frac{100}{(100-10)} \times 1800$

= ₹2000

Selling price = $\frac{100+10}{100} \times 2000 =$ ₹2200

64. (a): It is a simple question. When directions of movement are opposite, the speeds will be added up. Thus, effective speed = 9 + 10 = 19 kmph.

Now time = $\frac{\text{distance}}{\text{speed}} = \frac{47.5}{19} = 2\frac{1}{2}$ hours

65. (c): Suppose the required condition will be fulfilled after 'x' number of years.

Thus according to question:

$3.20 + x\left(\frac{50}{100}\right) = 5.30 + x\left(\frac{25}{100}\right) + \frac{40}{100}$

$.25\,x = 2.5$

Thus, $x = 10$ years

Required answer = 2008 + 10 = 2018

66. (c): This question can be attempted by short cut method also.

Average age of students = 18 years

The total number after inclusion of teacher

= 59 + 1 = 60

Total increase = $60 \times \frac{1}{4}$ years = 15 years.

This increase of 15 years to the group is entirely due to inclusion of teacher in the group.

Thus, age of teacher = 18 + 15 = 33 years

The question can be attempted by calculating totals also.

67. (b): Let the numbers be a and b.

Thus, $ab = 2\,(a + b)$

$\frac{1}{2} = a + \frac{b}{ab}$

$\frac{1}{2} = \frac{a}{ab} + \frac{b}{ab}$

$\frac{1}{2} = \frac{1}{b} + \frac{1}{a}$ or $\frac{1}{a} + \frac{1}{b} = \frac{1}{2}$

68. (c): Average $= \frac{\text{Sum total}}{\text{Total number}}$

According to question:

Total age of both groups $= 31 \times 40 + 60 \times 28$
$= 2920$ years

Total number of employees $= 40 + 60 = 100$

Average age $= \frac{2920}{100} = 29.20$ years

69. (c): The speed is on per hour basis. For ease of calculation, let the speed is taken as LCM of 400, 600, 800 and 200 = 2400 kms.
All the sides of square are same.

Time taken for the first side $= \frac{2400}{400} = 6$ hours

For the second side $= \frac{2400}{600} = 4$ hours

For the third side $= \frac{2400}{800} = 3$ hours

For the fourth side $= \frac{2400}{200} = 12$ hours

Total distance $= 4 \times 2400 = 9600$ kms
Time taken $= 6 + 4 + 3 + 12 = 25$ hours

Average speed $= \frac{9600}{25} = 384$ kms/hour

Alternatively, when distances are same, this question can be solved with the help of harmonic mean also. Then there is no need to assume any total distance.

Average speed $= 4/(\frac{1}{400} + \frac{1}{600} + \frac{1}{800} + \frac{1}{200})$
$= 384$ kms/hour

Note: The denominator is 4 as there are four quantities.

70. (d):

Let cost price = 100
Marked price = 100 + 40 = 140
Selling price = 140 – 20% of 140 = 112
Thus, actual profit percentage = 112 – 100 = 12%

71. (b): Given that sum or principle amount is same in both the cases.

$SI = \frac{PRT}{100}$

1 year 3 months $= \frac{5}{4}$ years

8 months $= \frac{2}{3}$ years

Rate of 8 ½ % equals $\frac{17}{2}$%

According to question:

$P \times \frac{5}{4} \times \frac{17}{2} / 100 - P \times \frac{2}{3} \times \frac{7}{100} = ₹45$

$\frac{P}{100} (\frac{5}{4} \times \frac{17}{2} - \frac{2}{3} \times 7) = ₹45$

P = ₹800

72. (b): If one quantity x is 25% higher than other y, it means it is 125/100 or 5/4 of other. Then other quantity y is 4/5 (that is reciprocal of 5/4) of other. It means answer should be 4/5 or 0.80.

73. (c): Let the original inhabitants = 100
The people who died = 5
The remaining inhabitants = 100 – 5 = 95
People who left the village = 20% of 95 = 19
The remaining inhabitants = 100 – 5 – 19 = 76
Now, 76% of original inhabitants = 4750

Original inhabitants $= \frac{4750 \times 100}{76} = 6250$

74. (b): Let the three qualities are mixed as 2, 4 and 3 liters in the order given in the question.

Total quantity = 2 + 4 + 3 = 9 liters
Total cost = 100 × 2 + 40 × 4 + 60 × 3 = ₹540

Cost per liter $= \frac{540}{9} = ₹60$

Selling cost per liter (given) = ₹66
Profit = 66 – 60 = ₹6

Profit percentage $= \frac{6}{60} \times 100 = 10\%$

75. (c): $0.75x = 0.02y$

$\frac{x}{y} = \frac{0.02}{0.75} = \frac{2}{75}$,

$x = 2, y = 75$
Thus,

$\left(\frac{y-x}{y+x}\right) = 75 - \frac{2}{75} + 2 = \frac{73}{77}$

76. (c): Village ⟷ Railway Station
Distance is same both ways.
Total time taken = 5 hours
Let the time taken from village to railway station is t hours and from railway station to village is $5 - t$ hours.
Thus, D = 20 × t = 5 × (5–t) ⇒ t = 1 hour
Distance = 20 × 1 = 20 km.

77. (c):

The sum of five numbers = 5 × 20 = 100

The sum of three numbers = 32

The total of rest of two numbers = 100 – 32 = 68

Average of two numbers = $\frac{68}{2} = 34$

78. (b): Let the Marked Price is be ₹100

Discount on MP = 10% of 100 = ₹10

SP= 100 – 10 = ₹90

Profit = 8 %

Thus, CP = $\frac{100}{(100+8)} \times 90 = ₹\frac{250}{3}$

∴ Price difference is = $\frac{250-100}{3} = ₹\frac{50}{3}$

∴ Percentage of CP (that should be kept above CP)

$= \frac{(50/3)}{(250/3)} \times 100 = 20\%$

This question can be directly solved by taking into account the answer choices and doing small calculations on them.

79. (b): This is a question of weighted arithmetic mean. Let the total number of employees be divided into two groups, the average income of Workers is being denoted by W and that of Executives by E. Their numbers are being mentioned as N_1 and N_2 in the formula. Their numbers are 40 and 60 if their total number is assumed as 100, as given in percentage form also.

Weighted Arithmetic Mean

$= N_1W + \frac{N_2E}{(N_1 + N_2)}$

$= \frac{(40\times39,000 + 60\times42,000)}{100}$

$= \frac{(1,56,0000+2,52,0000)}{100}$

$= \frac{4,080000}{100} = ₹40,800$

80. (d): If E=5 , HOTEL =12 Then, BALM = ??

Let's use the following table:

English Alphabet–Position Left to Right

A	B	C	D	E	F	G	H	I	J	K	L	M
1	2	3	4	5	6	7	8	9	10	11	12	13

N	O	P	Q	R	S	T	U	V	W	X	Y	Z
14	15	16	17	18	19	20	21	22	23	24	25	26

E = 5, Here number of letters = 1

E = $\frac{5}{1} = 5$

HOTEL

H = 8

O = 15

T = 20

E = 5

L=12

8 + 15 + 20 + 5 + 12 = 60

Number of letters in Hotel = 5

HOTEL = $\frac{60}{5} = 12$

Now for BALM

B = 2

A = 1

L = 12

M = 13

2 + 1 + 12 + 13 = 28

Number of Letters in BALM = 4

BALM = $\frac{28}{4} = 7$

81. (b): Let times taken in walking and riding are assumed to be W and R, over a distance.

1 W + 1 R = 40 mins ...(i)

1 W + 1 W = 60 mins

2 W = 60 mins

1 W = 30 mins

Putting 1 W = 30 mins in equation (i)

R = 40 – 30 = 10 mins

Time taken for riding one way = 10 mins

Time taken for riding both ways = 2 × 10 = 20 mins

82. (c): 2/5th of total amount = ₹2000

Total amount = 2000 × $\frac{5}{2}$ = ₹5000

The amount given to Sahil = ₹5000 – ₹2000 = ₹3000

83. (b): Answer is total words minus one.

ACCIDENT has a total of 8 words, so answer is 8 – 1 = 7

84. (d): Time taken by first train from Agra to Delhi = 4 hours

It travels for 2 hours before another train starts.

Time taken by another train from Delhi to Agra = 3.5 hours

Let distance between Delhi and Agra = LCM of 4 and 3.5 = 28 kms

Speed of first train = $\frac{28}{4}$ = 7 kmph

Speed of Second Train = $\frac{28}{3.5}$ = 8 kmph

First train covers (7 × 2) = 14 km by the time another train starts at 7 am.

So, distance between the two trains at 7 am is 28 – 14 = 14 km

Relative speed = 7 + 8 = 15 kmph

Time taken to cross each other

= $\frac{14}{15}$ hours or 56 minutes.

Thus, they meet at 7:56 am.

We must note that:

(1) Distance = Speed × Time

(2) Relative Speed = Sum of individual speeds when two objects move in opposite directions

85. (b): Let such integer is x and its reciprocal is $1/x$.

Thus, $\frac{x+1}{x} = \frac{(x^2+1)}{x}$

Now fitting all answer choices equal to equation, we get $\frac{26}{5}$ as the answer.

86. (c): The total of all numbers = 35 × 18 = 630

The average of first 17 = 17 × 14 = 238

The average of last 17 = 17 × 20 = 340

So, 18th number (that is exactly in the middle) = 630–(238 + 340) = 52

87. (c): Profit or loss is on cost price. Thus, enhancement of price will recover loss of 25% and make profit of 10%

Thus, (10 + 25)% of cost price = ₹175

CP = ₹175 × $\frac{100}{35}$ = ₹500

88. (c): Formula Used:

Expenditure = Price × Consumption

Calculation:

We know that,

Fraction value of 25% = $\frac{1}{4}$

Let the original price be $4x$

Price is increased by 25%

New price = $4x + (\frac{25}{100}) \times 4x = 5x$

Ratio of original price to new price = 4:5

As the expenditure does not change, so price will be inversely proportional to consumption.

Ratio of old consumption to new consumption = 5:4

Decrease in consumption = 5 – 4 = 1 units

Thus, percentage decrease in consumption = $(\frac{1}{5}) \times 100 = 20\%$

89. (b): $\{y\} = 2y + (2y-1) + (2y-2) + \ldots\ldots\ldots\ldots + 1$

Method–1

$\{3\} = 2(3) + (2 \times 3 - 1) + (2 \times 3 - 2) + (2 \times 3 - 3) + (2 \times 3 - 4) + (2 \times 3 - 5)$

$= 6 + 5 + 4 + 3 + 2 + 1$

$= 21$

Similarly,

$\{2\} = 2(2) + (2 \times 2 - 1) + (2 \times 2 - 2) + (2 \times 2 - 3)$

$= 4 + 3 + 2 + 1 = 10$

Thus, $\{3\} \times \{2\} = 21 \times 10 = 210$

Method–2

$\{y\} = 2y + (2y–1) + (2y–2) + \ldots\ldots\ldots\ldots + 1$

This is the sum of first $2y$ positive integers.

Sum of first n positive integers = $\frac{n(n+1)}{2}$

Sum of first $2y$ positive integers = $\frac{2y\,(2y+1)}{2 = y\,(2y+1)}$

$\{3\} = 3\,(2 \times 3 + 1) = 21$

$\{2\} = 2\,(2 \times 2 + 1) = 10$

Thus, $\{3\} \times \{2\} = 21 \times 10 = 210$

90. (b): Here, we should know, in how much time, a principal ₹100 will become ₹1600 at compound rate of interest.

₹100 become ₹200 in 6 years.

The same amount will become ₹400 in 12 years or (6 + 6 years).

And ₹800 in another 6 years, that is in a total time span of 18 years or (6 + 6 + 6 years).

And ₹800 will become double up to 1600 in another six years at the same rate of interest. It means total time will be 18 + 6 = 24 years.

91. (d): The smallest part = $\frac{3}{(3+4+5+7)} \times = 152 = \frac{3}{19} \times = 152 = 24$

92. (b): Let initial population 2 years ago = 100

In case, percentage is of increase and decrease is same, there is always a decrease.

Total percentage decrease $= \frac{52}{100} = \frac{1}{4}\%$

Then population at the end of two years $= \frac{100-1}{4}$

$= \frac{399}{4}$

Now $\frac{399}{4}\%$ of initial population = 29925

Initial population $= 29925 \times 4 \times \frac{100}{39} = 30{,}000$

93. (c): Here Principal and Simple Interest are same in both cases. Even if interest is not given, we can find the answer. R_1 and R_2 are Rates of Interest and T_1 and T_2 are Time Periods for two situations.

$$\frac{P R_1 T_1}{100} = \frac{P R_2 T_2}{100}$$

$$5 \times 4 = R_2 \times \frac{5}{2}$$

$R_2 = 8\%$

94. (d): Let boy and girl ratio = 40:30

Blue eyed boys = 20% of 40 = 8

Blue eyed girls = 10% of 30 = 3

Total Blue eyed = 8 + 3 = 11

Thus, portion of blue eyed $= \frac{11}{70}$

95. (d)

Bangalore

Jhansi

Rajgarh

Satupra

Chittor

96. (a)

As the difference between BAT and CAT is of 1, it means each alphabet should be assigned some number as per its sequencing in the alphabet series.

BAT = 2 + 1 + 20 = 23

CAT = 2 + 1 + 20 = 24

Thus, BALL = 2 + 1 + 12 + 12 = 27

97. (c):

T----------U---------V

E+1------G+1-----I

F+1-------H+1-----J

98. (b)

If we assign a number to all 26 alphabets

Then, A=1, B=2, C = 3, ... Z=26

Thus, R=18, E=5, D=4

In this code,

R = 18 + 2 = 20

E = 5 + 2 = 7

D = 4 + 2 = 6

(2 is added to each code to generate a new code).

RED = D (6); E (7); R (20) = 6720 (order of alphabets and their codes is reversed)

Similarly,

GREEN = NEERG = (14+2) (5+2) (5+2) (18+2) (7+2) = 1677209

99. (a): The sequence of height can be established in the following manner:

Ram

Vineet

Monika

Jacob

Dalip

100. (c): 5th term is 36, 4th is 40 and 3rd is 44.

101. (b): Cup and bowl are two containers for coffee and soup, respectively.

102. (b):

Teachers/ Subjects	Hindi	English	Geography	Punjabi	History	French	Total
A	Y	Y		Y			3
B	Y	Y	Y		Y	Y	5
C		Y	Y				2
D	Y			Y			2
E					Y	Y	2

103. (d): 8 is a cube of 2 but it is not a square of any integer.

9 is a square of 3 but it is not a cube of any integer.

36 is a square of 6 but it is not a cube of any integer.

64 is a square of 8 and a cube of 4.

104. (b): Amount of 3 items = 4500

Amount of 2 items = 3600

Total amount = 8100

Discount given = 10%

$$8100 \times \frac{10}{100} = 810$$

After discount amount = 8100 – 810 = 7290

Average cost of each items = $\frac{7290}{5}$ = 1458

105. (d): Age of man = 50 years

Age of son = $50 \times \frac{2}{5} = 20$ years

According to question,

$$(50 + x) = \frac{5}{3}(20 + x)$$

$$150 + 3x = 100 + 5x$$

$$2x = 50$$

$$x = 25$$

After 25 years, the age of man will be $\frac{5}{3}$ of his son.

106. (b): Length of square = 5.0 cm

Area = 5 × 5 = 25 cm^2

Increase in length = 1% = 0.05 cm

Now length of square = 5.05 cm

Area = 5.05 × 5.05 = 25.5025 cm^2

Difference in area = 25.5025 – 25

= 0.5025 cm^2

% increase in area = $\frac{0.5025}{25} \times 100$

= 2.01

= = 2%

Short Cut Method:

In case two quantities are being multiplied. They are increasing by x and y percentages, then the following formula can be used to find the total percentage increase.

Total increase = $\frac{x + y + xy}{100}$

$= 1 + 1 + \frac{(1 x 1)}{100} = 2.01\%$

107. (c): Let SP of 70 pencils = ₹ 90

According to Question:

$$90 = CP \times \frac{100 - 25}{100}$$

CP = ₹ 120

In 2nd situation, for a SP of ₹ 234 and profit of 30%, the CP is to be found first.

CP = 234 × $\frac{100}{130}$ = ₹ 180

If number of pencils for ₹ 120 is 70, then for CP of ₹ 180, the number of pencils should be one and half times, that is, 70 × 1.5 = 105

108. (a): Let Marked price = ₹ 100

Discount = 10%

Then SP = ₹ 90

If no discount is offered, then profit is 25%. It means SP is ₹ 100.

Thus, CP = $\frac{100 \times 100}{100 + 25}$ = ₹ 80

We have to calculate only 'percentage' profit, so we don't need the third statement.

109. (c): Let the average weight of 10 students = x

Then $10x = [(9 \times 60)] + (x + 9)$

$10x = 540 + x + 9$

$9x = 549$

$x = 61$

Weight of the 10th student = $x + 9$

= 61 + 9 = 70 kg

110. (b): Sale price of 1 kg of the mixture = ₹ 76.8

Gain = 20%

C.P. of 1 kg of the mixture = $\frac{100}{100+20} \times$ ₹76.8

= ₹64

Applying the rule of allegation

Cost of 1 kg sugar of 1st variety Cost of 1 kg sugar of 2nd variety

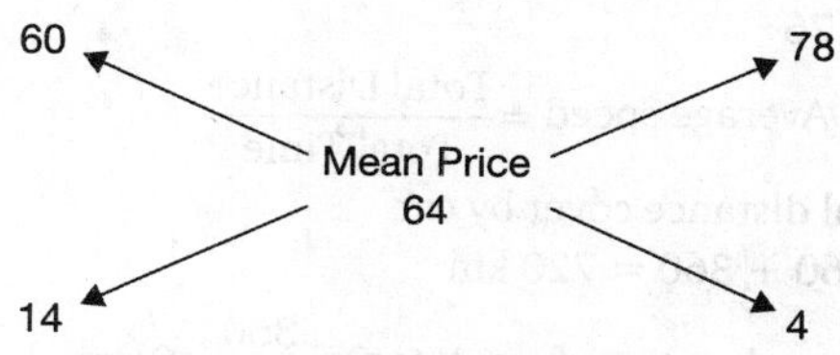

Thus, 14: 4 OR 7:2 is required answer.

111. (a): Given that,

Area of circle = Area of square

Diagonal of square = 11cm

Let side of square = 9 cm

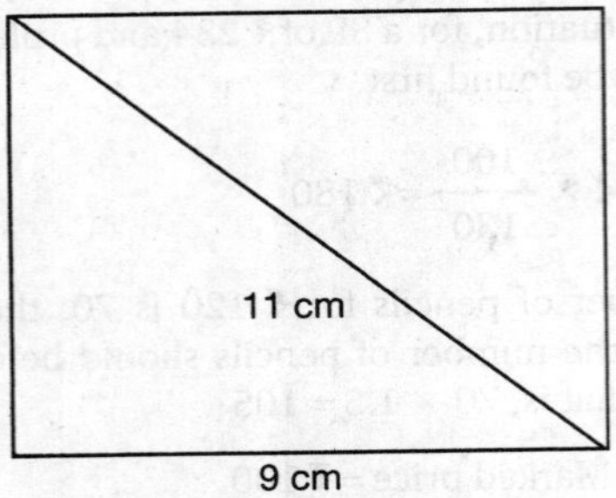

According to Pythagoras Theorem

$c^2 = a^2 + b^2$

$(11)^2 = (a)^2 + (a)^2$

$121 = 2a^2$

$\Rightarrow a^2 = \dfrac{121}{2}$

Area of square $= a^2 = \dfrac{121}{2}$

Now, according to question

Area of circle = Area of square (where in a is the radius of circle)

$\pi r^2 = a^2$

$\pi r^2 = \dfrac{121}{2}$

$r^2 = \dfrac{121}{2\pi}$

Substituting the value of $\pi = 3.142$

$r = \dfrac{121}{2\times 3.14} = 19.25$

$r = \sqrt{19.25} = 4.38$

Diameter of circle $= 2\pi = 2 \times 4.38$

8.76~8.7 cm

= 8.76

112. (b): Average speed $= \dfrac{\text{Total Distance}}{\text{Total Time}}$

Total distance cover by car

= 360 + 360 = 720 km

Time taken to go from P to $Q = \dfrac{360}{40} = 9\text{Hrs}$

Time taken to go from Q to $P = \dfrac{360}{60} = 6\text{Hrs}$

Total time taken – 9 + 6 = 15 Hrs

Average speed $= \dfrac{720}{15} = 48\text{km/hrs}$

113. (c): Total maximum marks = 200 + 100 + 200 + 200 + 100 = 800 marks

Overall percentage marks = 78%

Overall marks $= \dfrac{78}{100} \times 800 = 624$

Total marks obtained = 155 + 80 + 165 + 140 + x = 540 + x

$540 + x = 624$

$x = 624 - 540 = 84$

Marks obtained in English = 84

114. (a): Selling price of Refrigerater = 22000

Profit% = 10

Cost Price $= \dfrac{SP \times 100}{100 + P\%}$

$\dfrac{22000 \times 100}{100 + 10}$

$\dfrac{22000 \times 100}{110} = 20000$

New desired profit = 18%

Selling Price $= \dfrac{(100 + \text{Profit\%})CP}{100}$

$\dfrac{(100+18)}{100} \times 20000$

118 × 200 = ₹ 23600

115. (a): $\dfrac{x}{y} = \dfrac{7}{9} \rightarrow x = \dfrac{7}{9}y$

$\dfrac{3x - 5y}{4x + y} = \dfrac{3\left(\frac{7}{9}y\right) - 5y}{4\left(\frac{7}{9}y\right) + y}$

$\dfrac{\frac{7}{3}y - 5y}{\frac{28y}{9} + y} = \dfrac{\frac{-8}{3}y}{\frac{37}{9}y} = \dfrac{-8}{3} \times \dfrac{9}{37}$

$= \dfrac{-24}{37}$

116. (c): Each of the number except 63 is a prime number.

117. (d): We need to go for reverse calculation. The rate of interest is same in both the calculations.

Interest = 3000 – 2400 = ₹ 600

Principal = ₹ 2400

Time = 1 year

$$R = \frac{I \times 100}{P \times T}$$

R = 25%

The rate of 25% can be applied to earlier year calculation also. This will bring the amount of interest down by 25%. For first year, it will be ₹ 480.

The basic principal amount

= 2400 – 480 = ₹ 1920

118. (d): The ratio of two numbers = a : b = 3 : 7

$$\Rightarrow \frac{a}{b} = \frac{3}{7}$$

$$a = \frac{3b}{7}$$

After adding 9 to each numbers, the ratio becomes 9:17

$$\frac{a+9}{b+9} = \frac{9}{17}$$

$$17a + 153 = 9b + 81$$

$$17a + (-9b) = 81 - 153$$

$$17\left(\frac{3b}{7}\right) - 9b = -72$$

$$\frac{51b}{7} - 9b = -72$$

$$51b - 63b = -504$$

$$-12b = -504$$

$$b = 42$$

$$a = \frac{3b}{7} = 3 \times \frac{42}{7}$$

$$a = 18$$

119. (a): $n^2 + 2, n^2 - 2, n^2 + 2, n^2 - 2$ and so on ... If we put $n = 1$ in $n^2 + 2$, we get $(1)^2 + 2 = 3$, which is the first term.

Similarly, if we put $n = 2$ in $n^2 - 2$ we get,

$(2)^2 - 2 = 2$ (Second term)

$n = 3 = (3)^2 + 2 = 11$

$n = 4 = (4)^2 - 2 = 14$

$n = 5 = (5)^2 + 2 = 27$

$n = 6 = (6)^2 - 2 = 34$

$n = 7 = (7)^2 + 2 = 51$

$n = 8 = (8)^2 - 2 = 62$,

which is the eighth and the required term.

120. (c): The series

bbc| bba |bbc|bba|bbc|bba

The Pattern bbc, bba is repeated.

121. (a):

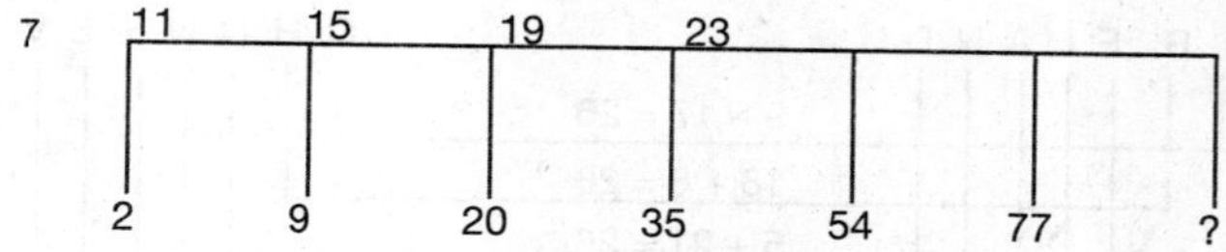

2 + 7 = 9

9 + 11 = 20

20 + 15 = 35

35 + 19 = 54

54 + 23 = 77

77 + 27 = 104

11 is 4 more than 7 and 15 is 4 more than 11 and so on. In this pattern each new number that is 4 more than the last increase and the missing term would be 104.

122. (b):

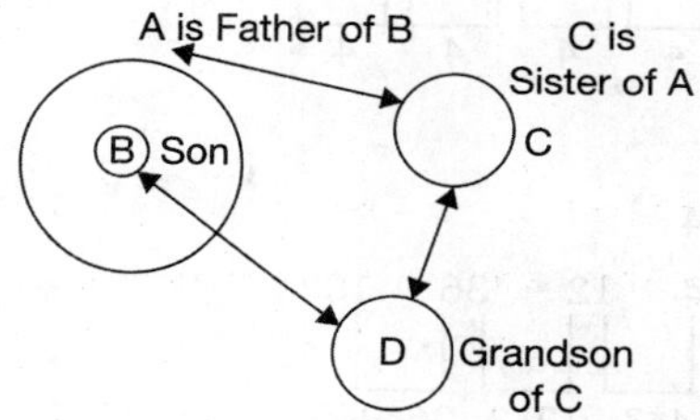

D is the nephew of *B*

123. (a): We need to arrange English alphabets along with their numerical ranks.

A = 1, B = 2, C = 3, D = 4, E = 5, F = 6, G = 7, H = 8, I = 9, J = 10, K = 11, L = 12, M =13, N = 14, O = 15, P = 16, Q = 17, R = 18, S = 19, T = 20, U = 21, V = 22, W = 23, X = 24, Y =25, Z = 26

For HPU, $\frac{8+16+21}{5} = \frac{45}{5} = 9$

For JNU, $\frac{10+14+21}{5} = \frac{24+21}{5} = \frac{45}{5} = 9$

For DU, $\frac{4+21}{5} = 5$

124. (b): The total of pair should stay at 26 that is the total number of alphabets.

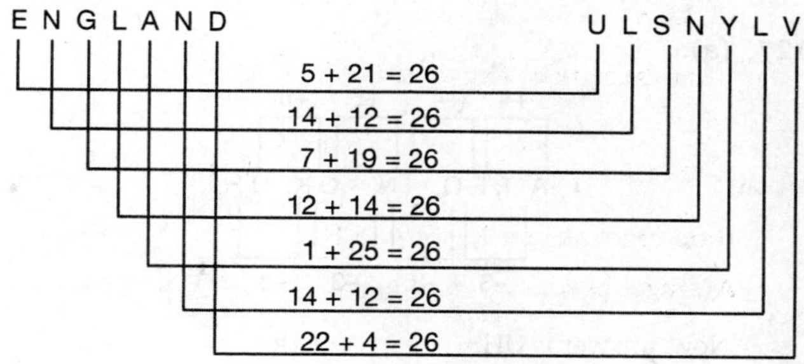

Similarly:

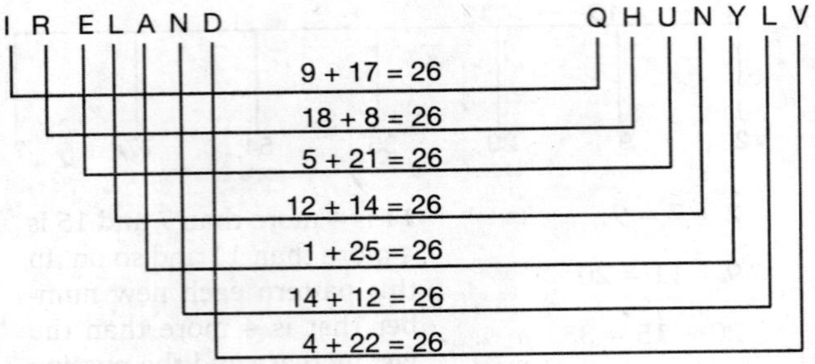

125. (c): 2, 4, 6, 12, 10, 36, 14, ? 18, 32, 4

As we can see, there are two series formed

Series 1

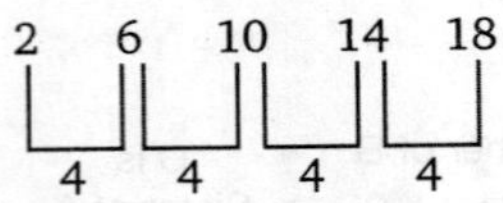

Series 2

4, 12, 36 ? 324

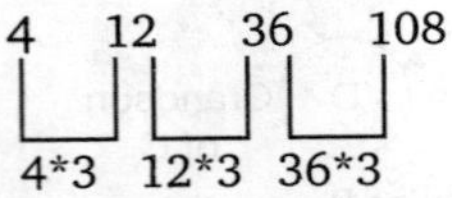

Therefore, 108 is the right answer.

126. (c):

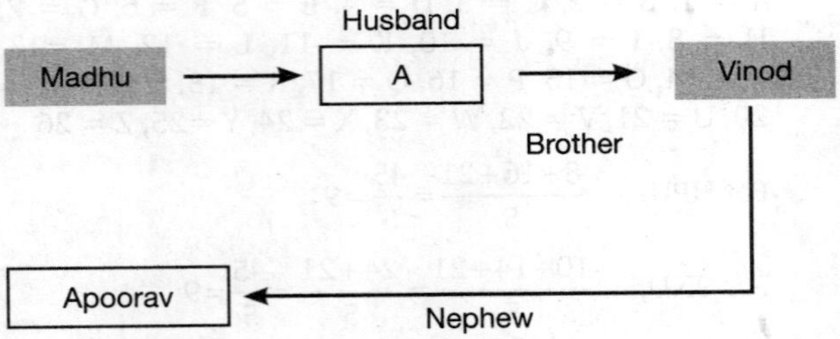

Apoorav is the son of Madhu. Vinod is the brother of Madhu's husband. That means A is the husband of Madhu.

According to this statement, Apoorav is the nephew of Vinod.

127. (a):

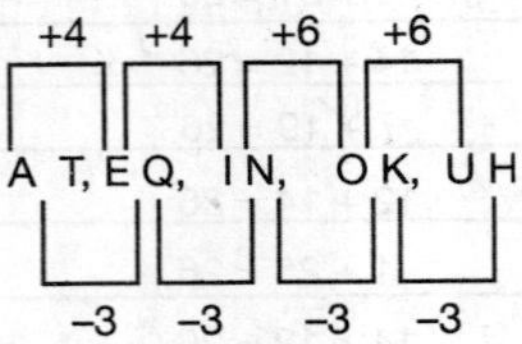

Now, answer is UH.

128. (c):

If each number is increased by the same number such as 3 in this case, their total will increase by multiplication of 3 with 70. Then the total of those numbers is to be divided by 70 to get the answer. Ultimately, we get 32 + 3 (=35) as the answer. Thus, for shortcut, we can directly add the increased number to the given number to get the answer.

129. (b): It needs 5 seconds to strike 5 times.

5 bells $\rightarrow$ 4 intervals = 5 seconds

Thus, to reach at 9 O'clock.

9 bells $\rightarrow$ 8 intervals = 10 seconds

130. (b): The credits can be taken as weights, thus it becomes a question of weighted average.

$$\text{Weighted average} = \frac{\text{Total weighted score}}{\text{Total weights}}$$

Marks	Weights	Weighted score
55	2	110
60	3	180
65	3	195
70	4	280
	12	765

$$\text{Weighted average} = \frac{765}{12} = 63.75$$

131. (b): The net selling price of shopkeeper = (100 – 40) % on 1500 = ₹ 900

Assume that original cost of the item = ₹ x

Profit percentage = 20 %

Selling price $= x + 20\%$ of $x = x + \frac{x}{5} = ₹\,\frac{6}{5}x$

According to question

$$₹\,\frac{6}{5}x = ₹\,900$$

$$x = \frac{900 \times 5}{6} = ₹\,750$$

132. (b): $\text{Average speed} = \frac{\text{Total Distance}}{\text{Total Time}}$

Total distance = 2 × 150 = 300 kms

Time required during first phase $= \frac{150}{50} = 3$ hours

Time required during second phase $= \frac{150}{30} = 5$ hours

Total time taken = 3 + 5 = 8 hours

Thus, average speed $= \frac{300}{8} = 37.5$ kms / hour

Alternatively, this question can be solved directly with harmonic mean.

For the journey where there are equal distances, the average speed can be calculated with help of harmonic mean. (For example, from Chandigarh, Karnal is exactly at middle point while moving to Delhi. Thus, there are two equal distances. In the second option, moving from Chandigarh to Karnal and then coming back constitutes two 'equal phases' of journey).

Harmonic mean / Average speed

$= 2 / [(\frac{1}{x} + \frac{1}{y})]$ where x and y are two speeds

$= 2 / [\frac{1}{50} + \frac{1}{30}]$

$= 2 / [\frac{3+5}{150}]$

$= \frac{2 \times 150}{8} = 37.5$ kms per hour

Here, total distance is not required while finding solution.

133. (a): There is skipping of one alphabet.

B + 2 = D

D + 2 = F

Then, for the first alphabet of second letter series, the letter between D and F is placed.

Thus, fourth series is KMO.

134. (b): Let the age of son = X years

The age of father = X + 30 years

ATQ, five years ago

X + 30 – 5 = 6(X – 5)

X + 25 = 6X – 30

OR 25 + 30 = 6X – X;

5X = 55

X = 55/5 = 11 years

135. (b): Let the principal amount = ₹ 1

Time period = 4 years

Amount = ₹ 2

Then Compound Interest = 2 – 1 = ₹ 1

$1 = 1(1+\frac{R}{100})^4 - 1$

$2 = (1+\frac{R}{100})^4$

$\frac{21}{4} = 1 + \frac{R}{100}$

$1.189 = 1 + \frac{R}{100}$

$1.1892 - 1 = \frac{R}{100}$

$0.1892 \times 100 = R$

R = 18.92 % (apprx)

Thus, 19% seems to be the best possible answer.

136. (b): $1^2 + 3 = 4$

$3^2 + 3 = 12$

$5^2 + 3 = 28$

$7^2 + 3 = 52$

$9^2 + 3 = 84$

Thus, the answer is 84.

137. (c): We can solve this question, by counting all the items with the difference d (i.e 175 – 168 = 182 – 175) Or by using the following formula of Arithmetic Progression

$a_n = 266$, $a = 168$ and $d = 7$

Formula: $a_n = a + (n-1)d$

$266 = 168 + (n-1)7$

$n-1 = \frac{266-168}{7} = \frac{98}{7} = 14$

$n = 14 + 1 = 15$

Thus, (c) is the correct answer.

138. (d)

Ayurveda is an Upaveda of Atharva or Rigveda according to some schools or is a Panchama Veda. It is also considered as Upanga of Atharva Veda i.e. it is not imposed or added from the exterior but is a part and parcel of the main body of the Vedas.

139. (c): The highest denominator in options is 80. We will make every fraction equal to 80.

$\frac{11}{16} \times \frac{5}{5} = \frac{55}{80}$

$\frac{29}{40} \times \frac{2}{2} = \frac{58}{80}$

$\frac{5}{8} = \frac{5}{8} \times \frac{10}{10} = \frac{50}{80}$

$\frac{65}{80}$ – no change required.

Now, every fraction has 80 as denominator, we need to compare only numerators to compare.
Thus, 5/8 is the smallest fraction.

140. (d): Let number of 20 paise coins = X
Then number of 25 paise coins = 324 – X

$$\text{Total value} = X\left(\frac{20}{100}\right) + (324 - X)\frac{25}{100} = ₹\,71$$

$X/5 + (324 - X)/4 = ₹\,71$
$X = 200$

Thus, the number of 20 paise coins is 200.

141. (a): Statement I

$$\text{Amount} = 280\left(1+\frac{10}{100}\right)\left(1+\frac{5}{100}\right)$$

$$= 280\left(\frac{11}{10}\right)\left(\frac{21}{20}\right) = ₹\,323.4$$

Compound Interest = Amount – Principal
= 323.4 – 280 = ₹ 43.4
The given answer is ₹ 44.3.

Statement II

This question is based on simple interest, so interest will be ₹ 5.6 on ₹ 100 every annum. In 15 years, total SI will be 15 × 5.6 = ₹ 84. Thus, amount will not be doubled, but much less than that.

Thus, both statements are not correct.

142. (b): If each averaged number, X, is multiplied by an another number, Y, then new average will be multiplication of those numbers, that is X.Y. Thus, answer to this question will be 7×11 = 77.

143. (d): The number 89325324 is divisible by 66. This is a direct question. Thus, statement I is true.

The set of natural numbers is not same as the set of the whole numbers. The difference between natural numbers and whole numbers is as follows:

Natural numbers include all the positive integers from 1 till infinity (∞) and are also used for counting purpose. The set of natural numbers is represented by the letter 'N'. 0 is not a natural number.

N = {1, 2, 3, 4, 5, 6, 7, 8, 9, 10… and so on }

Whole numbers include all the natural numbers and the number 0. In other words, all natural numbers are whole numbers, but all whole numbers are not natural numbers.

Whole Numbers = {0, 1, 2, 3, 4, 5, 7, 8, 9...}

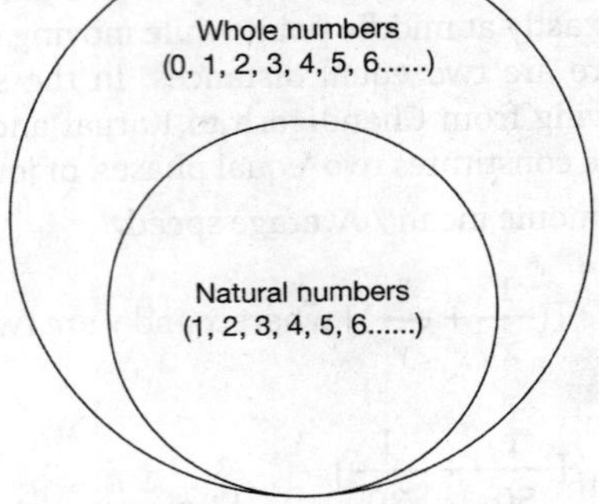

144. (d): The discount offered on the article = 20%
SP = ₹ 24
We can calculate the CP

$$24 \times \frac{100+20}{100} = ₹\,30$$

If 30% discount is offered, then

$$SP = 30 \times \frac{100-30}{100} = 30 \times \frac{70}{100} = ₹\,21$$

145. (c):

(a) If the speed of A is more than that of B, then to travel the same distance, A will take less time than B.

(b) In this statement, the speed is given in different units. We need to convert km/hr to metre/minute.

$$\text{Thus, } 90\text{ km/h} = \frac{90000\text{ m}}{60\text{ min}} = 1500\text{ m/min}$$

Thus, it can be concluded that the two speeds 1500 m/min and 90 km/h are equal. Hence, statement B is true.

$$\text{(c) Speed} = 18\text{ km/h} = \frac{18 \times 5}{18} = 5\text{ m/s}$$

Time = 2 min 30 sec = 150 sec

$$\text{Distance} = \frac{\text{Speed}}{\text{Time}}$$

$= 5 \times 150 = 750$ m

Thus, traveling at the speed of 18 km/h, the distance covered in 2 min and 30 sec is 750 m. Hence, statement C is true.

146. (a): This is a direct question. It can be solved easily by reasoning method.

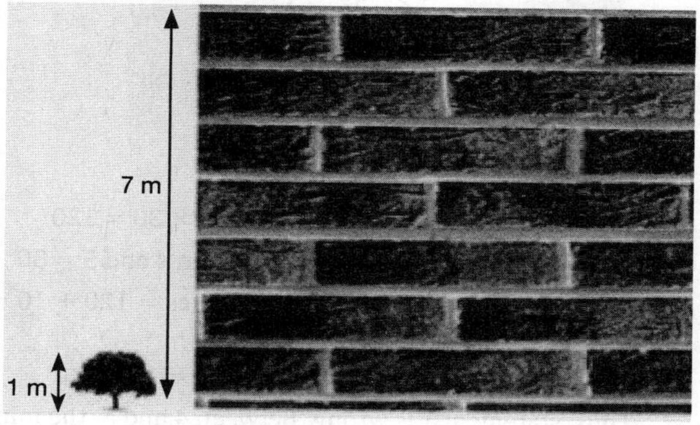

Let the height of tree = x meters

Height of wall = $7x$

$7x - 1x = 6$ meters

$6x = 6$ meters

$x = 1$ meter

147. (c): The series follows a difference pattern cf –2, –1.5, –1, –0.5, and so on.

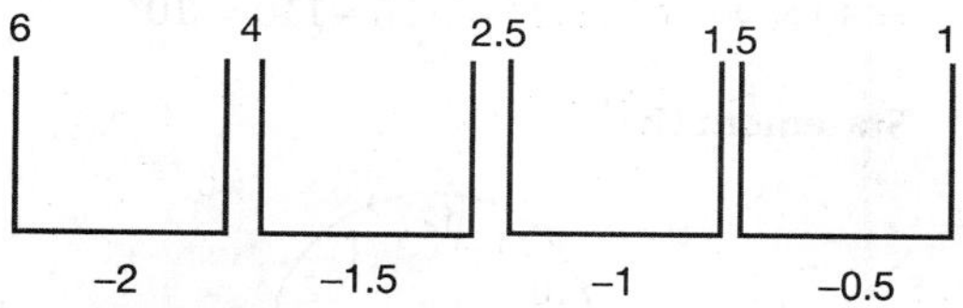

148. (c): Let CP of mobile phone = x

Profit = 25%

SP of mobile phone = ₹8000

$$SP = \frac{CP\,(100 + P\%)}{100}$$

$$8000 = \frac{x\,(100 + 25)}{100}$$

$$x = 8000 \times \frac{100}{125} = ₹6400$$

Thus, the CP of the mobile phone is ₹6400.

149. (d): Given:

B, H, R, F, ……, ……

Calculation:

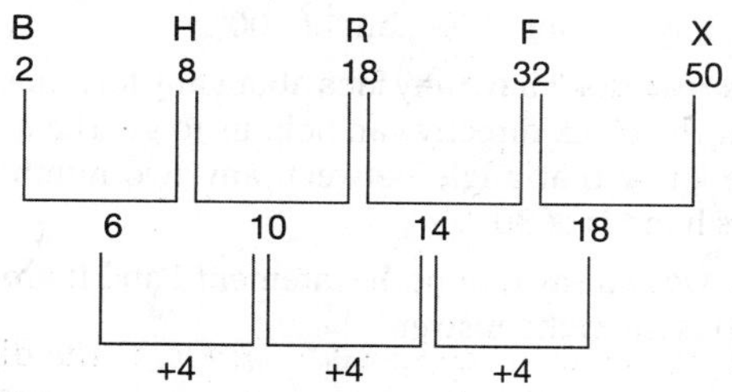

Hence, the next letter in the series is X

150. (b): According to the $Y = X^2$

Let $X = 10$, thus $Y = (10)^2 = 100$

If X changes by 6%,

$$X = 10 + 10 \times \frac{6}{100} = 10 + 0.6 = 10.6$$

$$Y = 100 + (10.6)^2 = 112.36$$

$$\% \text{ change in } Y = 112.36 - \frac{100}{100} \times 100 = 12.36\%$$

Alternatively, we can solve this question by short cut method also.

$$X + Y + XY/100 \frac{6}{100}$$

Given both X and Y are equal to 6%.

$= 6\% + 6\% + 6 \times 6/100$

$= 12 + 0.36 = 12.36\%$

Thus, (b) is the correct answer.

151. (c): Total distance = 120 km

First part of journey = 40 km

The rest of journey = 120 – 40 = 80 km

Time = distance / speed = 120

$$\text{Thus, total time taken} = \frac{40}{50} + \frac{80}{60}$$

$$= \frac{240 + 400}{300}$$

$$= \frac{640}{300} = \frac{32}{15}\text{ km/h}$$

$$\text{Now average speed} = \frac{\text{Total distance}}{\text{Total time taken}}$$

$$= 120 / (\frac{32}{15}) = \frac{120 \times 15}{32}$$

$$= \frac{225}{4} = 56.25\text{ km / hr}$$

152. (b):

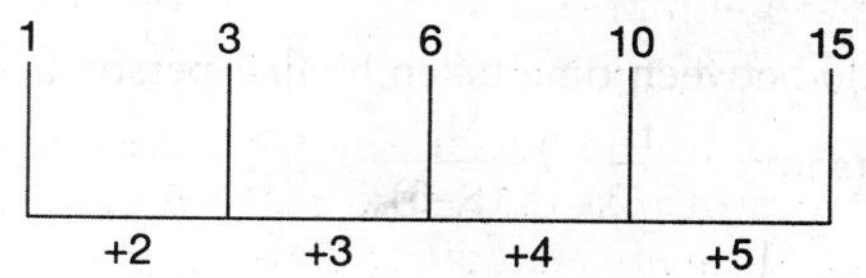

153. (a):

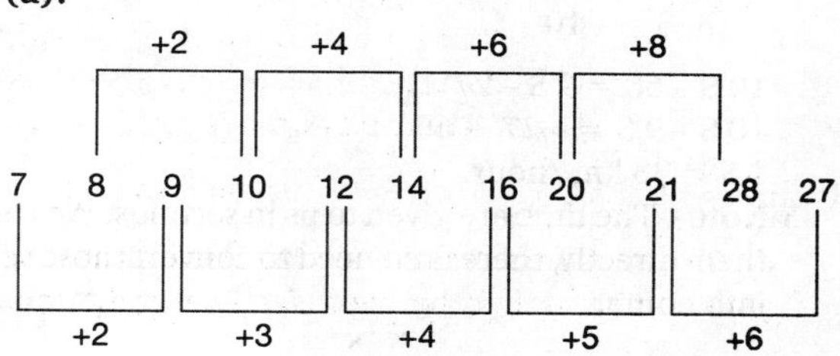

154. (b):

Given that

$y + z = 36$

Now, as per the question

$y - x = x - z$

$2x = y + z$

$2x = 36$

$x = (\frac{36}{2}) = 18$ years

155. (d): We need to work on the following assumptions in this question

1. The person in this question should be assumed to be a point. The time taken by train is actually the time to cover the length of train.
2. The clarity on concept of relative speed is required here. When train and person are moving in the same direction as given in the question, we should take the difference between the two. As the train of speed is higher than that of person, the relative speed of train = S – speed of person.

Here, we assume that the speed of train = S km per hour

3. As both of the persons are moving in the same direction, the time taken by train to cross the person moving with lower speed will be less (given to be 9 seconds in the question).

Let the length of train = L Km

Relative speed of train in context of first person

= speed of train – speed of first person = (S – 3) km / hr

Time taken to cross the first person

$= \frac{\text{Distance}}{\text{Speed}} = \frac{L}{(S-3)}$ hours

Similarly, time taken in case of second person

$= \frac{L}{(S-6)}$ hours

The ratio between time taken by first person and second person $= \frac{L}{(S-3)} / \frac{L}{(S-6)}$

$= \frac{S-6}{S-3} = \frac{9}{10}$

$10\,S - 60 = 9\,S - 27$

$10\,S - 9\,S = -27 + 60$

$1\,S = 33$ km /hour

Note – The time are given to us in seconds. We can take them directly, there is no need to convert those seconds into hours.

156. (c): Statement I

The minutes angle at 20 minutes = 4 × 30 = 120°

The total degrees hour's hand between 4 and 5 = 30°

When timing is 4 hours and 20 minutes = 120 + 10 = 130 degrees

Thus, there is difference of 130 – 120 = 10°

Thus, statement 1 is wrong. Between 4 and 5, the minute hand and hour hand of a clock don't coincide at 20 minutes past 4.

The angle can be calculated with the following short cut formula

$30\text{ Hours} - \frac{11}{2}\text{ (Minutes)}$

$= 30 \times 4 - \frac{11}{2} \times 20 = 120 - 110 = 10°$

Statement II:

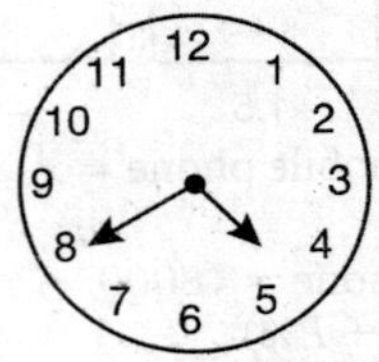

Here, we can calculate the angle between hour hand and minute hand directly with short cut formula

Timing: 4. 40

Formula: $30\text{ (Hour)} - \frac{11}{2}\text{ (Minutes)}$

Substituting values

$30 \times 4 - \frac{11}{2} \times 40$

$= 120 - 220 = 100°$

Thus, angle is not of 90°, but of 100°

In case, we don't have any idea about any formula, looking at the clock directly can help us to get the answer, if we know that angle between any two numbers on hours hand is of 30°.

Thus, we can say that both statement I and II are false, so (b) is the right answer

157. (d): Statement A: If A's salary is 20% more than B, then B's salary is 20% less than A.

Let B's salary be ₹100.

A's salary = $100 + 100 \times \frac{20}{100}$

= 100 + 20 = ₹120

The difference between A's and B's salary = 120 – 100 = ₹20

% difference = $(\frac{20}{100}) \times 100$

= 16.67%.

Thus, statement A is false.

Statement B: Suppose SP of 1 Pen = ₹1

Thus, SP of 28 Pens = ₹28

Gain = SP of 4 Pens = ₹4

CP of 28 Pens = SP – Gain = 28 – 4 = ₹24

Gain % = $\frac{4}{24} \times 100$

= 16.67%.

Thus, statement II is false.

Statement C: Natural numbers are numbers used for counting and ordering. They include all positive integers which starts from 1 and end in infinity. The average of N consecutive natural numbers starting from 1 is $\frac{N+1}{2}$. Thus, statement C is true.

158. (d): 4 6 12 14 28 30 ....

The numbers are in the order of addition of TWO and multiplied by TWO

4 + 2 = 6

6 × 2 = 12

12 + 2 =14

14 × 2 =28

28 + 2 =30

30 × 2 =60

159. (a): Given that

Actual Word	O	A	M	S	N	E	I	P	C
Given Form	E	C	I	O	P	M	A	N	S

Accordingly

Given Word	C	O	M	P	A	N	I	O	N
Coded Form	S	E	I	N	C	P	A	E	P

Thus, (a) is the correct answer.

160. (a): That means that there are 15 students with below ranks in the class and Aashman is 16th student from bottom. Considering his position in the class, there are (43 – 16), that is 27 students above him in the class. Thus, his own position is 28th in the class.

161. (c):

Let the slower pipe alone fill the tank in x minutes. The tank filled by slower pipe in 1 minute = 1/x

Then, faster pipe will fill it in $\frac{x}{3}$ minutes.

The tank filled by faster pipe in 1 minute = $1/x/3$ = $3/x$

$$\therefore \frac{1}{x} + \frac{3}{x} = \frac{1}{36}$$

$$\Rightarrow \frac{4}{x} = \frac{1}{36}$$

$\Rightarrow x = 144$ minutes

162. (d): ATQ, Cost Price of 40 Pens = Marked Price of 36 Pens

Let the Cost Price of 40 Pens = Marked Price of 36 Pens = ₹ 36

Taking them separately,

Cost Price of 40 Pens = ₹ 36

Marked price of 36 pens = ₹ 36

Marked Price of 40 Pens = ₹ 40

Discount is 1% on Marked Price.

Discount = 1% of ₹ 40 = 40 paise

Selling Price = ₹ 40 – 40 Paise = ₹ 39.60

Thus Profit = ₹ 39.60 – ₹ 36 = ₹ 3.60

Profit Percentage = 3.60 / 36 × 100 = 10%

163. (b): 'Leaves are Green' and 'Green is Good' are coded by 467 and 485, respectively. The word Green is there in both sentences and so is 4. Thus, 'Green' is indicated by 4 ....(1)

Similarly, in 'Leaves are Green' and 'They are playing', coded by 467 and 639 respectively, the word 'are' is common. Their codes also have 6 in common................(2)

Comparing (1) and (2) and Leaves are Green with each other, we can say that leaves are indicated by 7.

Thus, (b) is the right answer.

164. (b): Let the original number of students = X

Average age = Total age / Number of students

Total original age = 15X years

New total age = 15X + 5(12.5) = 15X + 62.5 years = 15X + 125/2

New number of students = X + 5

New average age = 15 years – 6 months = 14.5 years = 29/2 years

New average age = 29/2 = (15X + 125/2) / (X + 5)

29/2 (X + 5) = 15X + 125/2

29X + 145 = 30X + 125

X = 145 – 125 = 20

Thus, the original number of students was 20.

Thus (2) is the correct answer.

165. (c): The correct answer is (c).

If the container is completely filled with bacteria in 30 minutes, then at the end of 29 minutes, it was filed by half.

If we move back to 28 minutes, it was filled by ¼ th.

166. (a): We will use the formula: N3 + 1 where N is 1, 2, 3, 4, ...

$1^3 + 1 = 2$

$2^3 + 2 = 10$

$3^3 + 3 = 30$

$4^3 + 4 = 68$

$5^3 + 5 = 130$

$6^3 + 6 = 222$

$7^3 + 7 = 350$

Thus, (a) is the correct answer.

167. (b): Let the number of birds on Tree A = A

And birds of Tree B = B

In first situation – if two birds shift from B to A, then birds on A and B will be equal.

B – 2 = A + 2

A – B = –4 .....(1)

In second situation – If 2 birds shift from A to B, then birds on B will be double than those on A. Here, we are doubling the birds on A so that both on A and B are equal.

2(A – 2) = B + 2

2A – 4 = B + 2

2A – B = 2 + 4 = 6

2A – B = 6 ......(2)

Deducting 2 from 1

A – B – (2A – B) = – 4 – 6

–1A = –10

A = 10

Putting A = 10 in equation (1)

10 – B = –4

–B = –4 –10

B = 14

Now, A=10, B= 14, thus (b) is the answer.

The question can be solved directly from the answer by adding and reducing the values.

168. (d): Let's assume that total number of fruits = 100

On 1st day and night

Number of fruits sold during 1st day = 50%

Fruits left in the evening = 100 – 50 = 50

Fruits destroyed during first night = 10% of 50 = 5

Thus, the story ends with 50 + 5 = 55 fruits.

On 2nd day and night

The number of fruits in the morning = 100 – 55 = 45

The number of fruits sold during 2nd day = 50% of 45 = 22.5

Number of fruits left in the evening = 45 – 22.5 = 22.5

The fruits destroyed during 2nd night = 10% of 22.5 = 2.25

The number of fruits to sold and destroyed during the second day
= 22.5 + 2.25 = 24.75

On third day and night

Number of fruits to be sold in the morning
= 100 – (55 + 24.75) = 20.25

Fruits sold = 50% of 20.25 = 10.125

Fruits destroyed = 10% of 10.125 = 1.0125

After 3 days

Total fruits destroyed = 5 + 2.25 + 1.0125 = 7.26

8.2625% of total fruits = 1983

$$\text{Total fruits} = 1983 \times \frac{100}{8.2625} = 24000$$

Thus, (d) is the correct answer.

169. (a)

Let's assume the principal (for both SI and CI = ₹100, Rate of Interest = 5%, Time Period = 2 years

The absolute interest amount is ₹5 in first year for SI and CI, both are same for the 1st year.

The difference is due to interest during the 2nd year.

Principal amount for CI calculation will be 100 + 5 = ₹105.

For second year, the difference between CI and SI is

$$\text{Difference} = 105 \times 5 \times \frac{1}{100} = 5.25$$

SI for 2nd Year = ₹5

Thus, the difference = 5.25 – 5 = 0.25

If difference is ₹.25, then principal amount = ₹100

If difference is ₹11.25, then principal amount $= \frac{100}{.25} \times 11.25 = ₹4,500$

170. (d): We need to calculate the highest value:

$X^2 = 10 \times 10 = 100$, $y^2 = 0.1 \times 0.1 = .01 = \frac{1}{100}$

Now fitting them into options

(a) $100 \times \frac{1}{100} = 1$

(b) $100 - .01 = 99.99$

(c) $100 + .01 = 100.01$

(d) $100 / \frac{1}{100} = 100 \times 100 = 10000$

Thus, (d) is the correct answer.

171. (d): Making use of codes for 'Tour', 'Screw', and 'Tear':

T	O	U	R
4	1	5	6

S	C	R	E	W
7	3	6	9	8

T	E	A	R
4	9	2	6

From the coding above, we get code for Sweater

S	W	E	A	T	E	R
7	8	9	2	4	9	6

Thus, (d) is the correct answer

172. (c): Take 5 as the starting number:

$5 + 2^1 = 7$; $7 + 2^2 = 11$; $11 + 2^3 = 19$;

$19 + 2^4 = 35$; $35 + 2^5 = 67$; $67 + 2^6 = 131$

Thus, (c) is the answer.

173. (a): ATQ, we will calculate savings for 2021, then take the difference and calculate the percentage increase.

Savings = Income – Expenditure

Savings in 2020 = Income in 2020 – Expenditure in 2020

= 65,000 – 45,000 = ₹20,000

Income in 2021 (with 15% increase over 2020) = 100 + 15% = 115

The actual income with an increase of 15% in 2021

$$= \frac{(100+15)}{100 \times 65000} = ₹74,750$$

Similarly, expenditure in 2021 $= \frac{(100+7)}{100 \times 45,000}$

= ₹48,150

Savings in 2021 = 74,750 – 48,150 = 26,600

Difference in savings = 26,600 – 20,000 = 6,600

Now, percentage Increase in savings =

$$\frac{\text{Difference}}{(\text{Savings in 2020}) \times 100}$$

$$\text{Percentage Increase} = \left(\frac{6,600}{20,000}\right) \times 100 \approx 33\%$$

Thus, (a) is the answer.

174. (b): We need to move in a reverse manner - with third number first to deal with.

Third number is 2960, so 2nd number $= \frac{1}{4}$ of 2960 = 740.

$\frac{5}{9}$ of 1st number = 25% of 740 = 185

1st number $= 185 \times \frac{9}{5} = 333$

30% of 1st number = 30% of 333 = 99.9

175. (b): Let assume the amount of gratuity = ₹300, this figure of ₹300 has been taken as it is easier for the sake of calculation. (we can take any figure such as ₹'X' or ₹1 also).

1st part $= \frac{1}{3}$ of 300 = ₹100

Return on 1st part = 6% of 100 = ₹6

2nd part = $\frac{1}{4}$ of 300 = ₹75

Return on ₹= 7% of 75 = ₹5.25
3rd part = ₹300 – (100 + 75) = ₹125
Return on 3rd part = 8% of 125 = ₹10
Thus, total return = 6 + 5.25 + 10 = 21.25

In case the actual return is ₹7012.5, then total gratuity = $\frac{300}{21.25\times7012.5}$ = ₹99,000

176. (c)

C	H	E	A	T	E	R
+2	+2	+2	+2	+2	+2	+2
E	J	G	C	V	G	T

Similarly

P	R	E	A	C	H	E	R
+2	+2	+2	+2	+2	+2	+2	+2
R	T	G	C	E	J	G	T

177 (d): The series 7, 10, 19, 46, 127 follows a pattern in the differences between consecutive numbers. These differences are 3, 9, 27, and 81 which are actually multiples of 3, specifically 3^1, 3^2, 3^3, 3^4 and lastly 3^5 which is 243.

Thus, the answer is 127 + 243 = 370

178. (d): There are differences of 2, 4, 8, 16, 32 in the number series so that 31 + 32 = 63 is the right answer.

179. (a): We need to consider the timing element in this. The compounding is half yearly, so 1 be divided into three durations. Accordingly, 8% pa is to be halved to 4% six monthly each. Principal is ₹10000.

$A = P(1 + r/100)^n$
$A = 10000(1 + 4/100)^3 = 10000(1 + 1/25)^3$
$= 10000(26/25)^3$
= 175,760,000/15625 = Rs 11,248.64

180. (c): AA, BD, CI, DP, ...

The position of each letter in the alphabet: A = 1, B = 2, C = 3, D = 4, ..., Z = 26.

Now identifying the pattern: 1 × 1, 2 × 2, 3 × 3, 4 × 4, 5 × 5

- AA: A (1) and 1 × 1 = 1, that is 1st alphabet A so AA is the 1st member.
- BD: B (2) and 2 × 2, that is the 4th alphabet D, so BD is the 2nd member.
- CI: C (3) and 3 × 3, that is the 9th alphabet I, so CI as the 3rd member.
- DP: D (4) and 4 × 4 that is the 16th alphabet P, so DP is the 4th member.
- EY: E (5) and 5 × 5 that is 25th alphabet Y, so EY should be the answer.

The answer is (c).

181. (d): The Table has been created for the purpose of better understanding only.

Category	Salary per Person	Number of People	Total Salary
Executive	₹250,000	5	₹1,250,000
Senior Staff	₹80,000	15	₹1,200,000
Junior Staff	₹45,000	20	₹900,000
		Total salary	₹3,350,000.

Total No. of employees = 5 + 15 + 20 = 40
The average salary = 3,350,000/40 = ₹83,750

182. (d): This may be linked with the topic of 'Motion' in Physics also. As the answer options are in 'm' so we convert the figures that way.

We apply the formula, $S = UT + 1/2AT^2$

First change 90 KM/hour into m/s = 90 × 5/18 = 25m/s, that is initial speed called as U.

And V= 0 km/s

Acceleration = - 2.5 m/s^2, as the speed is reducing to zero, it is actually deceleration, so minus sign is put.

Now U = AT, so T = U / A = 25 / 2.5 = 10s

Now $S = UT + 1/2AT^2 = 25 \times 10 + ½(-2.5)10^2$ = 250 – 125 = 125 m

Thus (d) is the answer.

183. (c): The similar question has been solved on page 5.23 in Unit 5. This is based on the principle if values in a series are changed by a constant value such as 2 then any measure of central tendency will change by the same value. Hence, new mean will be 45 + 2 = 47, but the SD will not change, so the answer is (c).

CHAPTER 6

Logical Reasoning

TOPICS OF IMPORTANCE

- **Understand the Structure of Arguments:** Argument Forms, Structure of Categorical Propositions, Mood, and Figure, Formal and Informal Fallacies, uses of Language, Connotations and Denotations of Terms, Classical Square of Opposition.
- Evaluating and Distinguishing Deductive and Inductive Reasoning.
- Analogies
- **Venn Diagram:** Simple and Multiple use for Establishing the Validity of Arguments.
- **Indian Logic:** Means of Knowledge.Pramanas: Pratyaksha (Perception), Anumana (Inference), Upamana (Comparison), Shabda (Verbal Testimony), Arthapatti (Implication) and Anupalabddhi (Non-apprehension).
- Structure and Kinds of Anumana (Inference), Vyapti (Invariable Relation), Hetvabhasas (Fallacies of Inference)

1. 'If a large diamond is cut up into little bits, it will lose its value just as an army is divided up into small units of soldiers, it loses its strength'. **[Jun 2014]**

The argument put above may be called

(a) Analogical (b) Deductive
(c) Statistical (d) Causal

2. Given below are some characteristics of logical argument. Select the code which expresses a characteristic which is not of inductive in character. **[Jun 2014]**

(a) The conclusion is claimed to follow from its premises.
(b) The conclusion is based on causal relation.
(c) The conclusion conclusively follows from its premises.
(d) The conclusion is based on observation and experiment.

3. If two propositions having the same subject and predicate terms can both be true but both cannot be false, then the relation between those two propositions is called **[Jun 2014]**

(a) Contradictory
(b) Contrary
(c) Subcontrary
(d) Subaltern

4. Given below are two premises and four conclusions drawn from those premises. Select the code that expresses conclusion drawn validly from the premises (separately or jointly). **[Jun 2014]**

Premises:

(a) All dogs are mammals.
(b) No cats are dogs.

Conclusions:

(i) No cats are mammals.
(ii) Some cats are mammals.
(iii) No dogs are cats.
(iv) No dogs are non-mammals.

Codes:

(a) (i) only (b) (i) and (ii)
(c) (iii) and (iv) (d) (ii) and (iii)

5. Given below is a diagram of three circles A, B and C interrelated with each other. The circle A represents the class of Indians, the circle B represents the class of scientists, and circle C represents the class of politicians. Here, p, q, r and s represent different regions. Select the code containing the region that indicates the class of Indian scientists who are not politicians. **[Jun 2014]**

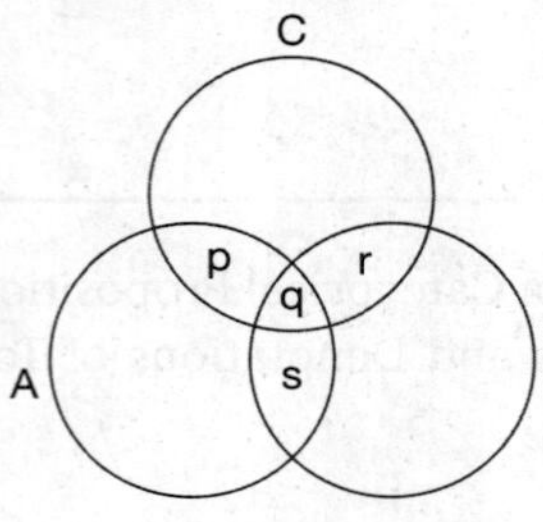

Codes:
(a) q and s only (b) s only
(c) s and r only (d) p, q and s only

6. When in a group of propositions, one proposition is claimed to follow from the others, that group of propositions is called **[Dec 2014]**
(a) An argument
(b) A valid argument
(c) An explanation
(d) An invalid argument

7. Given below is a diagram of three circles A, B and C over-lapping each other. The circle A represents the class of honest people, the circle B represents the class of sincere people and circle C represents the class of politicians. p, q, r, s, U, X, Y represent different regions. Select the code that represents the region indicating the class of honest politicians who are not sincere. **[Dec 2014]**

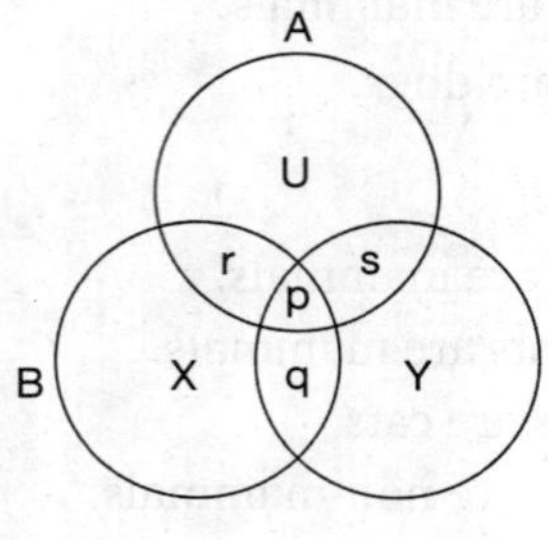

Codes:
(a) X (b) q
(c) p (d) s

8. 'A man ought no more to value himself for being wiser than a woman if he owes his advantage to a better education, than he ought to boast of his courage for beating a man when his hands were tied'. **[Dec 2014]**
The above passage is an instance of
(a) Deductive argument
(b) Hypothetical argument
(c) Analogical argument
(d) Factual argument

9. By which of the following proposition, the proposition 'wise men are hardly afraid of death' is contradicted? **[Dec 2014]**
(a) Some wise men are afraid of death.
(b) All wise men are afraid of death.
(c) No wise men is afraid of death.
(d) Some wise men are not afraid of death.

10. Namita and Samita are brilliant and studious. Anita and Karabi are obedient and irregular. Babita and Namita are irregular but brilliant. Samita and Kabita are regular and obedient. Who among them is/are brilliant, obedient, regular and studious? **[Dec 2014]**
(a) Samita alone (b) Namita and Samita
(c) Kabita alone (d) Anita alone

11. Warrior is related to sword, carpenter is related to saw, farmer is related to plough. In the same way, the author is related to **[Dec 2014]**
(a) Book (b) Fame
(c) Reader (d) Pen

12. If we want to seek new knowledge of facts about the world, we must rely on reason of the type **[Jun 2015]**
(a) Inductive (b) Deductive
(c) Demonstrative (d) Physiological

13. A deductive argument is invalid if **[Jun 2015]**
(a) Its premises and conclusions are all false.
(b) Its premises are true but its conclusion is false.
(c) Its premises are false but its conclusion is true.
(d) Its premises and conclusions are all true.

14. Inductive reasoning is grounded on **[Jun 2015]**
(a) Integrity of nature
(b) Unity of nature
(c) Uniformity of nature
(d) Harmony of nature

15. Among the following statements two are contradictory to each other. Select the correct code that represents them. **[Jun 2015]**

Statements:

(i) All poets are philosophers.
(ii) Some poets are philosophers.
(iii) Some poets are not philosophers.
(iv) No philosopher is a poet.

Codes:

(a) (i) and (ii) (b) (i) and (iv)
(c) (i) and (iii) (d) (ii) and (iii)

16. When the purpose of a definition is to explain the use or to eliminate ambiguity, then the definition is called **[Jun 2015]**

(a) Stipulative (b) Theoretical
(c) Lexical (d) Persuasive

17. Which of the codes given below contains only the correct statements? Select the code: **[Jun 2015]**

Statements:

(i) Venn diagram represents the arguments graphically.
(ii) Venn diagram can enhance our understanding.
(iii) Venn diagram may be called valid or invalid.
(iv) Venn diagram is a clear method of notation.

Codes:

(a) (i), (ii) and (iii) (b) (i), (ii) and (iv)
(c) (ii), (iii) and (iv) (d) (i), (iii) and (iv)

18. Consider the argument given below: **[Dec 2015]**
'Pre-employment testing of teachers is quite fair because doctors, architects, and engineers who are now employed had to face such a testing'.
What type of argument it is?

(a) Deductive (b) Analogical
(c) Psychological (d) Biological

19. Among the following propositions, two are related in such a way that they can both be true although they cannot both be false. Which are those propositions? Select the correct code. **[Dec 2015]**

Propositions:

(i) Some priests are cunning.
(ii) No priest is cunning.
(iii) All priests are cunning.
(iv) Some priests are not cunning.

Codes:

(a) (i) and (ii) (b) (iii) and (iv)
(c) (i) and (iii) (d) (i) and (iv)

20. A cluster of propositions with a structure that exhibits some inference is called **[Dec 2015]**

(a) An inference
(b) An argument
(c) An explanation
(d) A valid argument

21. Consider the following assertion (*A*) and reason (*R*) and select the correct code given below. **[Dec 2015]**

(*A*): No man is perfect.
(*R*): Some men are not perfect.

(a) Both (*A*) and (*R*) are true, but (*R*) does not provide sufficient reason for (*A*).
(b) Both (*A*) and (*R*) are true and (*R*) provides sufficient reason for (*A*).
(c) (*A*) is true, but (*R*) is false.
(d) (*A*) is false, but (*R*) is true.

22. A definition that has a meaning that is deliberately assigned to some symbol is called **[Dec 2015]**

(a) Lexical (b) Precising
(c) Stipulative (d) Persuasive

23. If the proposition 'No men are honest' is taken to be false, then which of the following proposition/propositions can be claimed certainly to be true? **[Dec 2015]**

Propositions:

(a) All men are honest.
(b) Some men are honest.
(c) Some men are not honest.
(d) No honest person is man.

24. Among the following propositions two are related in such a way that one is the denial of the other. Which are those propositions? Select the correct code. **[Jul 2016]**

Propositions:

(A) All women are equal to men.
(B) Some women are equal to men.
(C) Some women are not equal to men.
(D) No women are equal to men.

Codes:

(a) (A) and (B) (b) (A) and (D)
(c) (C) and (D) (d) (A) and (C)

25. Select the code which is not correct in the context of deductive argument with two premises. **[Jul 2016]**

(a) An argument with one true premise, one false premise and a false conclusion may be valid.
(b) An argument with two true premises and a false conclusion may be valid.
(c) An argument with one true premise, one false premise and a true conclusion may be valid.
(d) An argument with two false premises and a false conclusion may be valid.

26. Given below are two premises and four conclusions are drawn from them (taking singly or together). Select the code that states the conclusions validly drawn. **[Jul 2016]**

Premises:
(I) All religious persons are emotional.
(II) Ram is a religious person.

Conclusions:
(A) Ram is emotional.
(B) All emotional people are religious.
(C) Ram is not a non-religious person.
(D) Some religious people are not emotional.

Codes:
(a) (A), (B), (C) and (D) (b) (A) only
(c) (A) and (C) only (d) (B) and (C) only

27. If the proposition 'All thieves are poor' is false, then which of the following propositions can be claimed certainly to be true? **[Jul 2016]**

Propositions:
(a) Some thieves are poor.
(b) Some thieves are not poor.
(c) No thief is poor.
(d) No poor person is a thief.

28. Select the option which is not correct about Venn diagram. **[Jul 2016]**
(a) Venn diagram represents propositions as well as classes.
(b) It can provide clear method of notation.
(c) It can be either valid or invalid.
(d) It can provide the direct method of testing the validity.

29. Consider the following statement and select the correct code stating the nature of the argument involved in it.
To assume that the earth is the only populated world in the infinite space is as absurd as to assert that in an entire field of millet only one grain will grow. **[Jul 2016]**
(a) Astronomical
(b) Anthropological
(c) Deductive
(d) Analogical

30. The following are some characteristics of reasoning. Select the code that states a characteristic that is not a deductive reasoning. **[Jan 2017]**
(a) The conclusion must be based on observation and experiment.
(b) The conclusion should be supported by the premise/premises.
(c) The conclusion must follow from the premise/premises necessarily.
(d) The argument may be valid or invalid.

31. If two standard-form categorical propositions with the same subject and predicate are related in such a manner, i.e., when one is undetermined and the other must be undetermined, then what is their relation? **[Jan 2017]**
(a) Contrary (b) Subcontrary
(c) Contradictory (d) Subaltern

32. Men and women may have different reproductive strategies but neither can be considered inferior or superior to the other, any more than a bird's wings can be considered superior or inferior to a fish's fins. Select the code that states those two propositions. **[Jan 2017]**
(a) Biological (b) Physiological
(c) Analogical (d) Hypothetical

33. Among the following propositions, two are related in such a way that they cannot both be true but can be false. Select the code states those two propositions. **[Jan 2017]**

Propositions:
(i) Every student is attentive.
(ii) Some students are attentive.
(iii) Students are never attentive.
(iv) Some students are not attentive.

Codes:
(a) (i) and (ii) (b) (i) and (iii)
(c) (ii) and (iii) (d) (iii) and (iv)

34. The following are two premised (A) and (B). From those two premises, four conclusions (i), (ii), (iii), (iv) are drawn. Select the code that states the conclusions validly drawn from the premises (taking singly or jointly). **[Jan 2017]**

Premises:

(A) Untouchability is a curse.
(B) All hot pans are untouchable.

Conclusions:

(i) All hot pans are curse.
(ii) Some untouchable things are hot pans.
(iii) All curses are untouchable.
(iv) Some curses are untouchable.

Codes:

(a) (i) and (ii) (b) (ii) and (iii)
(c) (iii) and (iv) (d) (ii) and (iv)

35. If the statement 'None but the brave wins the race' is false, then which of the following statements can be claimed to be true? **[Jan 2017]**

(a) All brave persons win the race.
(b) Some persons who win the race are not brave.
(c) Some persons who win the race are brave.
(d) No person who wins the race is brave.

36. Out of the following four cities, three are alike in some manner while the fourth one is different. Identify the odd one. **[Jan 2017]**

(a) Lucknow (b) Rishikesh
(c) Allahabad (d) Patna

37. Given below are four statements. Among them two are related in such a way that they can both be true but they cannot both be false. Select the code that indicates those two statements. **[Nov 2017]**

Statements:

(A) Honest people never suffer.
(B) Almost all honest people do suffer.
(C) Honest people hardly suffer.
(D) Each and every honest person suffers.

Codes:

(a) (A) and (B) (b) (A) and (C)
(c) (A) and (D) (d) (B) and (C)

38. A deductive argument is invalid if **[Nov 2017]**

(a) Its premises and conclusion are all true.
(b) Its premises and conclusion are all false.
(c) Its premises are all false but its conclusion is true.
(d) Its premises are all true but its conclusion is false.

39. Given below are two premises (a and b). From those two premises, four conclusions (i), (ii), (iii), and (iv) are drawn. Select the code that states the conclusion/conclusions drawn validly (taking the premises singularly or jointly). **[Nov 2017]**

Premises:

(A) All bats are mammals.
(B) No birds are bats.

Conclusions:

(i) No birds are mammals.
(ii) Some birds are not mammals.
(iii) No bats are birds.
(iv) All mammals are bats.

Codes:

(a) (i) only (b) (i) and (ii) only
(c) (iii) only (d) (iii) and (iv) only

40. Just as melting ice-cubes do not cause a glass of water to overflow, melting sea-ice does not increase oceanic volume. **[Nov 2017]**

What type of argument is it?

(a) Analogical (b) Hypothetical
(c) Psychological (d) Statistical

41. Superiority of intellect depends upon its power of concentration on one theme in the same way as a concave mirror collects all the rays that strike upon it into one point. **[Jul 2018]**

(a) Mathematical (b) Psychological
(c) Analogical (d) Deductive

42. Given below are two premises (A and B). Four conclusions are drawn from them. Select the code that states validity drawn conclusion (s) (taking the premises individually or jointly). **[Jul 2018]**

Premises:

(A) Most of the dancers are physically fit.
(B) Most of the singers are dancers.

Conclusions:

(A) Most of the singers are physically fit.
(B) Most of the dancers are singers.
(C) Most of the physically fit persons are dancers.
(D) Most of the physically fit persons are singers.

Select the correct answer from the codes given below:

(a) (A) and (B) (b) (B) and (C)
(c) (C) and (D) (d) (D) and (A)

43. Which one among the following is a presupposition in inductive reasoning? **[Jul 2018]**

(a) Law of identity
(b) Unchangeability in nature

(c) Harmony in nature
(d) Uniformity of nature

44. If the proposition 'domestic animals are hardly ferocious' is taken to be false, then which of the following proposition/propositions can be claimed to be certainly true? Select the correct code. **[Jul 2018]**

Propositions:
(A) All domestic animals are ferocious.
(B) Most of the domestic animals are ferocious.
(C) No domestic animal is ferocious.
(D) Some domestic animals are non-ferocious.

Select the correct answer from the codes given below:
(a) (A) and (B) (b) (A) only
(c) (C) and (D) (d) (B) only

45. Which one of the following statements is not correct in the context of Venn diagram method? **[Jul 2018]**
(a) It is a method of testing the validity of arguments.
(b) It represents both the premises of a syllogism in one diagram.
(c) It requires two overlapping circles for the two premises of a standard-form categorical syllogism.
(d) It can be used to represent classes as well as propositions.

46. Reasoning from a specific case to a general conclusion is known as
(a) Scientific logic (b) Inductive logic
(c) Deductive logic (d) Theoretical logic

47. Two propositions are contradictory when **[Dec 2018]**
(a) Truth of one proposition implies falsity of the other and vice versa.
(b) Truth of one proposition supposes the falsity of the other and vice versa.
(c) Truth of one proposition does not guarantee the falsity of the other.
(d) Truth of one proposition rejects the falsity of the other and vice versa.

48. Among the following, identify the two statements which are in such a relation that the truth of one implies the truth of the other, but not conversely. **[Dec 2018]**

Statements:
(i) All plastics are synthetic.
(ii) Some plastics are synthetic.
(iii) Some plastics are not synthetic.
(iv) No plastics are synthetic.

Options:
(a) (i) and (ii) (b) (i) and (iii)
(c) (i) and (iv) (d) (ii) and (iv)

49. Identify the argument which involves a leap from the known to the unknown. **[Dec 2018]**
(a) Deductive argument
(b) Reductive argument
(c) Inductive argument
(d) Analogical argument

50. Given below are two premises (A and B). Four conclusions are drawn from them. Select the code that states validly drawn conclusion(s) (Taking the premises individually or jointly). **[Dec 2018]**

Premises:
(A) No non-literates are graduates.
(B) All non-graduates are non-teachers.

Conclusions:
(i) All teachers are non-literates.
(ii) All teachers are graduates.
(iii) All non-teachers are non-graduates.
(iv) No non-literate is a teacher.

Options:
(a) (i) and (ii)
(b) (ii), (iii) and (iv)
(c) (iii) and (iv)
(d) (ii) and (iv)

51. The argument which claims that its conclusion is supported by its premises conclusively is **[Dec 2018]**
(a) Analogical argument
(b) Inductive argument
(c) Demonstrative argument
(d) Deductive argument

52. In which of the following instances, deductive argument is invalid? **[Dec 2018]**
(a) When its premises and conclusion are all true.
(b) When its premises are false and conclusion is true.
(c) When its premises and conclusion are all false.
(d) When its premises are true but conclusion is false.

53. The reasoning which would be helpful in seeking new knowledge of facts about the world is
(a) Inductive (b) Speculative
(c) Deductive (d) Demonstrative

54. Among the following statements, two are contradictory to each other. **[Dec 2018]**
Statements:
(i) All men are humans.
(ii) Some men are humans.
(iii) Some men are not humans.
(iv) No men are humans.
Select the code that represents them:
(a) (i) and (iii)
(b) (ii) and (iii)
(c) (i) and (ii)
(d) (i) and (iv)

55. Given below are two premises with four conclusions drawn from them (taking singly or together). Which of the following conclusions could be validly drawn from the premises? **[Dec 2018]**
Premises:
(A) All cats are animals.
(B) Birds are not cats.
Conclusions:
(i) Birds are not animals.
(ii) Cats are not birds.
(iii) All animals are cats.
(iv) Some animals are cats.
Select the correct answer from the codes given below:
(a) (i) and (iii) (b) (ii), (iii) and (iv)
(c) (ii) and (iv) (d) (i), (ii) and (iv)

56. Inductive argument proceeds from **[Dec 2018]**
(a) Particulars to Universal.
(b) Particulars to Particulars.
(c) Universals to Particulars.
(d) Universals to Universals.

57. Choose the word which is different from the rest. **[Dec 2018]**
(a) Paper (b) Wool
(c) Plastic (d) Jute

58. In which of the following argument 'the relation that relation that exists between premises and conclusion is that of logical necessity'? **[Jun 2019]**
(a) Inductive (b) Deductive
(c) Demonstrative (d) Analogical

59. Inference (*anumāna*) in Indian logic is rooted in **[Jun 2019]**
(a) Variable relation between minor term and major term
(b) Invariable relation between middle term and minor term
(c) Variable concomitance between middle term and major term
(d) Invariable concomitance between middle term and major term

60. 'All judge are fairminded' is an example of ____________ proposition. **[Jun 2019]**
(a) Universal affirmative
(b) Universal negative
(c) Particular affirmative
(d) Particular negative

61. The reasoning which would be helpful in finding new knowledge of facts about the world is **[Jun 2019]**
(a) Speculative (b) Inductive
(c) Deductive (d) Analogical

62. Consider the example provided below: **[Jun 2019]**
'This *gavaya* is like my cow'
This is an example of which means of knowledge (pramana).
(a) comparison (b) implication
(c) perception (d) inference

63. Consider the argument provided below: **[Jun 2019]**
'Sound is impermanent because it is invisible'
Identify the fallacy involved in the above argument on the basis of Indian logic
(a) Fallacy of irrelevant reason
(b) Fallacy of wrong assertion
(c) Fallacy of trivial reason
(d) Fallacy of contradictory reason

64. Which of the following statements is true in the case of a test prepared by you as a teacher? **[Jun 2019]**
(a) If a test is reliable, it is objective
(b) If a test is valid, it is reliable also
(c) If a test is reliable, it is valid
(d) If a test is valid and reliable, it is usable

65. All gentlemen are polite **[Jun 2019]**
No criminals are polite
No criminals are gentlemen
Identify the major term in above syllogism
(a) Predicate in the premises
(b) Subject in the premises
(c) Subject of the premise and predicate of the conclusion
(d) Subject of the second premise and subject of the conclusion

66. Consider the argument provided below: **[Jun 2019]**
'Sound is impermanent because it is audible'.
Identify the fallacy involved in the above argument on the basis of Indian logic from the options given below:
(a) Fallacy of trivial reason
(b) Fallacy of irrelevant reason
(c) Fallacy of wrong assertion
(d) Fallacy of contradictory reason

67. Identify the argument under which instantial propositions are inferrable from Universal Proposition **[Jun 2019]**
(a) Deductive argument
(b) Inductive argument
(c) Reductive argument
(d) Analogical argument

68. A perception where we do not have the knowledge of an object characterized by any predicate but an apprehension of some unrelated elements is called as? **[Jun 2019]**
(a) Determinate
(b) Indeterminate perception
(c) Verbal testimony
(d) Implication

69. Since most interactions with other people take place at a highly superficial level, making good____________becomes difficult. **[Jun 2019]**
(a) Course corrections (b) Predictions
(c) Deeds (d) Announcements

70. The proposition 'All leaves are green' is equivalent to which of the following propositions? **[Jun 2019]**
(i) No leaves are green
(ii) No leaves are non-green
(iii) No leaves are in other color than green
(iv) No green is leaf
Select the correct answer from the options given below:
(a) (ii), (iii) and (iv) (b) (i) and (ii)
(c) (ii) only (d) (ii) and (iii)

71. When subject and predicate of both the premises is same but they differ only in quantity, it is known as **[Jun 2019]**
(a) Subaltern (b) Contraries
(c) Subcontraries (d) Contradictories

72. Identify the reasoning in the following argument: 'Writing on paper is similar to writing on the board'. **[Jun 2019]**
(a) Deductive (b) Hypothetical
(c) Analogical (d) Inductive

73. Given below are two premises with four conclusions drawn from them. Which of the following conclusions could be validly from the premises? **[Jun 2019]**
Premises:
(i) All fans are tubes
(ii) Bulbs are not tubes
Conclusions:
(a) Fans are not bulbs (b) All tubes are fans
(c) Fans are bulbs (d) No tube is bulb
Select the correct answer from the options given below:
(1) (a), (b), (c) (2) (a) and (d)
(3) (a) only (4) (b), (c) and (d)

74. If proposition 'All pens are not pencil' is taken to be true then which of the following propositions can be false? **[Jun 2019]**
(a) All pens are pencils
(b) Some pencils are pens
(c) No pen is pencil
(d) Some pens are pencils

75. Inductive argument proceeds from **[Jun 2019]**
(a) Universal to particular
(b) Particular to universal
(c) Universal to universal
(d) Particular to particular

76. Consider the example given below: **[Jun 2019]**
Devadatta is growing fat.
He does not eat food during the day.

Therefore, he must be eating food during the night, other things being equal.

Identify the logic involved in the example provided above by choosing the correct answer from options given below:

(a) Arthapatti (b) Anupalabdi
(c) Anumana (d) Sabda

77. No Musician are Japenese **[Jun 2019]**

All Barbers are Musicians

No Barbers are Japenese

Identify the middle term in the above syllogism

(a) Subject in the first premise and predicate in the second premise
(b) Predicate in the first premise and subject in the second premise
(c) Predicate in the both premises
(d) Subject in the both premises

78. Consider the argument provided below: **[Jun 2019]**

'Sound is permanent because it is a product like the jar'.

Identify the fallacy involved in the above argument on the basis of Indian logic from the options given below:

(a) Fallacy of contradictory reason
(b) Fallacy of wrong assertion
(c) Fallacy of irrelevant reason
(d) Fallacy of trivial reason

79. The proposition 'All birds are cows' is equivalent to which of the following propositions? **[Jun 2019]**

(a) Some cows are birds
(b) Some cows are not non-birds
(c) Some birds are cows
(d) Many birds are cows

Select the correct answer from the options given below:

(i) (a) only (ii) (c) and (d)
(iii) (a), (b), (c) and (d) (iv) (d) only

80. If proposition 'Students are serious' is taken to be false then which of the following propositions can be true? **[Jun 2019]**

(i) All students are serious
(ii) All students are not serious
(iii) Some student are not serious
(iv) Some serious ones are not students

Select the correct answer from the options given below:

(a) (i) only (b) (ii) and (iv)
(c) (iv) only (d) (ii) and (iii)

81. Identify the reasoning in the following argument: **[Jun 2019]**

'Method of teaching in the classroom can be compared to architectural plan of a building'.

(a) Analogical (b) Hypothetical
(c) Inductive (d) Deductive

82. When subject and predicate of both premises is same but they differ in quality as well as quantity, it is known as **[Jun 2019]**

(a) Superaltern (b) Contraries
(c) Contradictories (d) Subaltern

83. Given below are two premises with four conclusions drawn from them. Which of the following conclusions could be validly drawn from the premises? **[Jun 2019]**

Premises:

(a) Some rings are bells
(b) No ring is ornament

Conclusions:

(a) All bells are ornaments
(b) Some ornaments are not bells
(c) No ring is bell
(d) All bells are not ornaments

84. If proposition 'All republics are grateful' is taken to be true which of the following propositions can be false? **[Jun 2019]**

(i) Republics are not grateful
(ii) Some republics are not grateful
(iii) No republics are grateful
(iv) Some republics are grateful

Select the correct answer from the options given below:

(a) (i) only (b) (ii) only
(c) (i), (ii) and (iii) (d) (ii) and (iii)

85. When subject and predicate of both the premises are the same but they differ in quality only, it is known as **[Jun 2019]**

(a) Contradictories (b) Contraries
(c) Subaltern (d) Superaltern

86. Identify the reasoning in the following argument: **[Jun 2019]**

'Pre-active stage of classroom teaching is important just as pre-learning preparation stage of communication'.

(a) Hypothetical (b) Deductive
(c) Inductive (d) Analogical

87. The proposition 'No red is black' is equivalent to which of the following propositions? **[Jun 2019]**

(i) No black is red
(ii) All red are black
(iii) Some red are not black
(iv) Red is not black

Select the correct answer from the options below:

(a) (i), (ii), (iii) and (iv) (b) (iii) only
(c) (i) and (iv) (d) (iv) only

88. Given below are two premises with four conclusions drawn from them. Which of the following conclusions could be validly drawn from the premises? **[Jun 2019]**

Premises:

(i) Some bags are tables
(ii) All bags are chairs

Conclusions:

(i) Some tables are chairs
(ii) No chair is table
(iii) Some chairs are bags
(iv) Some bags are not tables

Select the correct answer from the options given below:

(a) (i) and (iii) (b) (ii), (iii) and (iv)
(c) (i) and (iv) (d) (ii) only

89. 'All republic are grateful' and 'Some republics are not grateful' cannot both be true, and they cannot both be false. This is called as **[Jun 2019]**

(a) Contraries (b) Contradictories
(c) Subaltern (d) Superaltern

90. If the proposition 'Houses are not bricks' is taken to be false then which of the following propositions can be true? **[Jun 2019]**

(i) All houses are bricks
(ii) No house is brick
(iii) Some houses are bricks
(iv) Some houses are not bricks

Select the correct answer from the options given below:

(a) (ii) and (iii) (b) (i) and (iv)
(c) (ii) only (d) (iii) only

91. Given below are two premises with four conclusions draw from them. Which of the following conclusions could be validly drawn from the premises? **[Jun 2019]**

Premises:

(i) No paper is pen
(ii) Some paper are handmade

Conclusions:

(1) All paper are handmade
(2) Some handmade are pen
(3) Some handmade are not pen
(4) All handmade are paper

(a) 1 (b) 2
(c) 3 (d) 4

92. Identify the reasoning in the following argument: 'Use of teaching aids in the classroom to enhance learning is important in a similar way as that the use of ICT for production of knowledge' **[Jun 2019]**

(a) Hypothetical (b) Analogical
(c) Inductive (d) Deductive

93. The proposition 'No historians are non-mathematician' is equivalent to which of the following proposition? **[Jun 2019]**

(a) All historians are mathematicians
(b) No historians are mathematicians
(c) Some historians are mathematicians
(d) Some historians are not mathematicians

94. Consider the example provided below:
'There is no jar now on the ground' **[Jun 2019]**
Identify the means of knowledge (*Pramana*) involved in the example from the options given below:

(a) *Anupalabdhi* (b) *Arthāpatti*
(c) *Pratyakshā* (d) *Anumāna*

95. 'All children are not greedy', is an example of which proposition? **[Jun 2019]**

(a) Universal Affirmative
(b) Universal Negative

(c) Particular Affirmative
(d) Particular Negative

96. Consider the argument given below:
'Sound is permanent because it is audible'. **[Jun 2019]**
Identify the fallacy involved in the above argument on the basis of Indian logic from the options given below:
(a) Fallacy of trivial reason
(b) Fallacy of irrelevant reason
(c) Fallacy of contradictory reason
(d) Fallacy of wrong assertion

97. The argument which claims that its conclusively supported by its premises is called **[Jun 2019]**
(a) Analogical Argument
(b) Inductive Argument
(c) Demonstrative Argument
(d) Deductive Argument

98. Choose the correct alternative. **[Jun 2019]**
Cup is to coffee as bowl is to ____________
(a) Dish (b) Soup
(c) Spoon (d) Food

99. Identify the minor term in the following syllogism :
'Some books are not edifying
All books are interesting **[Jun 2019]**
Therefore, some interesting things are not edifying'
(a) Subject of the conclusion and predicate of the second premises
(b) Predicate of the conclusion and predicate of the first premises
(c) Subject of the both premises
(d) Predicate of the both premises

100. Oar is to rowboat as foot is to **[Jun 2019]**
(a) Running (b) Sneaker
(c) Skateboard (d) Jumping

101. 'In this hospital, some nurses don't wear white dress, some doctors have private practice and medicines prescribed are of high cost. Therefore, treatment in this hospital is of poor quality'. What fallacy does this argument make? **[Dec 2019]**
(a) Fallacy of composition
(b) Slippery slope
(c) Fallacy of accident
(d) Fallacy of division

102. Which of the following is true with reference to *anupalabdhi* as a means of knowledge? **[Dec 2019]**
(a) I do not cognise the pot on the table, therefore it is absent there
(b) I directly perceive the absence of pot on the table
(c) I infer the absence of pot on the table since I do not find it to be there
(d) I know the absence of the pot on the table because I know its similarity with other absences

103. Which one of the following is the characteristic feature of an argument? **[Dec 2019]**
(a) It is either valid or invalid
(b) It is neither valid nor invalid
(c) It is either true or false
(d) It is neither true nor false

104. Consider the following statements. **[Dec 2019]**
(A) Middle term should be distributed in at least one premise.
(B) Middle term should be present in the conclusion.
(C) Both premises can be particular in a valid argument.
(D) Both premises can be negative in a valid argument.
Choose the correct option from the following.
(a) (C) and (D)
(b) Only (C)
(c) Only (A)
(d) (B) and (C)

105. 'If it rains, then the drought will end. The drought has ended. Therefore, it rained'. What kind of fallacy does this commit? **[Dec 2019]**
(a) Deductive fallacy
(b) Inductive fallacy
(c) Abductive fallacy
(d) Informal fallacy

106. Devdatta is fat and he does not eat during the day. Therefore, Devdatta is eating during the night. **[Dec 2019]**
The above example in classical Indian school of logic is a case of:
(a) comparison (b) implication
(c) perception (d) verbal testimony

107. Consider the following statements with reference to the proposition 'Some girls are not students'. **[Dec 2019]**

(i) Subject term students are distributed.
(ii) Predicate term girls are undistributed.
(iii) Predicate term students are distributed.
(iv) Subject term girls are undistributed.

Choose the correct option.
(a) Only (i) and (iii) are correct
(b) Only (ii) and (iii) are correct
(c) Only (i) and (iv) are correct
(d) Only (iii) and (iv) are correct

108. Which one of the following is signified by Udāharaṇa of Anumāna (inference) in Indian logic? **[Dec 2019]**
(a) Statement of reason
(b) Proposition to be proved
(c) Conclusion proved
(d) Universal proposition along with an instance

109. Which one of the following propositions is a contrary to 'All poets are dreamers'? **[Dec 2019]**
(a) Some poets are dreamers
(b) Some poets are not dreamers
(c) No poets are dreamers
(d) No dreamers are poets

110. As per the classical square of opposition, if 'A' proposition is given as true, then which one of the following is correct? **[Dec 2019]**
(a) 'E' proposition is false, 'I' proposition is true and 'O' proposition is false
(b) 'E' proposition is true, 'I' proposition is true and 'O' proposition is true
(c) 'E' proposition is false, 'I' proposition is false and 'O' proposition is true
(d) 'E' proposition is true, 'I' proposition is false and 'O' proposition is false

111. Match List I with List II. **[Dec 2019]**

List I (Values)	List II (Distinguishing Functions)
(A) Sacrifice	(i) Working in a stipulated time
(B) Sincerity	(ii) Confinement of individual mind on action
(C) Self-control	(iii) Showing love and affection
(D) Altruism	(iv) Helping without selfish motives

Choose the correct option.
Code:

	(A)	(B)	(C)	(D)
(a)	(ii)	(i)	(iv)	(iii)
(b)	(iv)	(i)	(ii)	(iii)
(c)	(iii)	(iv)	(i)	(ii)
(d)	(i)	(iii)	(ii)	(iv)

112. The converse of 'All cats are mammals' is: **[Dec 2019]**
(a) some mammals are not cats
(b) no mammals are cats
(c) some mammals are cats
(d) all mammals are cats

113. 'Mr X lives in a slum and is unemployed. Therefore, Mr X deserves to be a minister'.
Which kind of fallacy is committed in this argument? **[Dec 2019]**
(a) Fallacy of composition
(b) Ad misericordiam
(c) Fallacy of division
(d) Fallacy of accident

114. Which among the following terms are distributed in the statement, 'No dogs are reptiles'? **[Dec 2019]**
(a) Only subject term
(b) Only predicate term
(c) Both subject and predicate terms
(d) Neither subject nor predicate term

115. Consider the following with reference to the Indian school of logic. **[Dec 2019]**
(a) It is related to the form of the argument only.
(b) It is related to the content of the argument only.
(c) It is related to the perceptual knowledge alone.
(d) It is related to the presenting analogies alone.

Choose the correct answer from the options given below.
(a) Only (a) (b) Only (b)
(c) Both (a) and (b) (d) Both (c) and (d)

116. Which of the following is not a necessary step when you present an argument based on inference before the others according to the classical Indian school of logic? **[Dec 2019]**
(a) Nigamana (b) Upamāna
(c) Upanāya (d) Udāharaṇa

117. The inference 'A mouse is an animal. Therefore, a large mouse is a large animal' commits which one of the following fallacies? **[Dec 2019]**
(a) Straw man
(b) Slippery slope
(c) Equivocation
(d) Fallacy of composition

118. The term 'yogaja' (intuitive) pertains to which of the following pramānas? **[Dec 2019]**
(a) Perception (b) Inference
(c) Verbal testimony (d) Comparison

119. In which of the following propositions, both can be true simultaneously but cannot be false simultaneously? **[Dec 2019]**
(a) Contrary (b) Contradiction
(c) Subcontrary (d) Subaltern

120. 'All tigers are animals' is an example of which type of proposition? **[Dec 2019]**
(a) Particular negative
(b) Particular affirmative
(c) Universal negative
(d) Universal affirmative

121. The distinction between 'laukika' and 'alaukika' is made with reference to which one of the following pramānas? **[Dec 2019]**
(a) Anumāna (Inference)
(b) Upamāna (Comparison)
(c) Pratyaksha (Perception)
(d) S'abda (Verbal testimony)

122. 'Some students are sincere'—it is an example of which proposition? **[Dec 2019]**
(a) Universal affirmative
(b) Universal negation
(c) Particular affirmative
(d) Particular negation

123. Product of two consecutive integers is divisible by 2. Therefore 4×5 (= 20) is divisible by 2.
This is an example of which type of reasoning? **[Dec 2019]**
(a) Abductive (b) Informal
(c) Inductive (d) Deductive

124. 'All students cleared their examination' and 'Few students did not clear their examination'. This is an instance of: **[Dec 2019]**
(a) contradictories (b) superaltern
(c) subaltern (d) contraries

125. 'Everyone is going to the party. You should go too'. This inference commits which kind of fallacy? **[Dec 2019]**
(a) Ad populum (b) Equivocation
(c) Ad verecundiam (d) Ad ignorantiam

126. Which of the following pramānas is used by classical Indian school of logic to prove the existence of God? **[Dec 2019]**
(a) Arthāpatti (postulation)
(b) Upamāna (comparison)
(c) Pratyaksha (perception)
(d) Anumāna (inference)

127. Given below are two statements: **[2020]**
Statement I: Upamiti is defined as knowledge of the relation between a word and its denotation
Statement II: Verbal testimony is the statement of a trustworthy person and consists in understanding its meaning.
In the light of the above statements, choose the most appropriate from the options given below:
(a) Both Statements I and Statement II are correct.
(b) Both Statements I and Statement II are incorrect.
(c) Statement I is correct but Statement II is incorrect.
(d) Statement I is incorrect but Statement II is correct.

128. Identify the features of Aristotelian syllogism from the following: **[2020]**
(A) It is deductive-inductive and formal material.
(B) It is only deductive and formal.
(C) The major and minor terms stand apart in the premises.
(D) It is verbalistic.
(E) Verbal form is not the essence of inference.
Choose the correct answer from the options given below:
(a) (A), (B) and (C) only
(b) (A), (C) and (E) only
(c) (B), (C) and (D) only
(d) (A), (D) and (E) only

129. When the middle term is both positively and negatively related to the major term, the inference is called **[2020]**
(a) Based on uniformity of co-existence
(b) Kevalanavayi
(c) Kevala vyatireki
(d) Anavaya vyatireki

130. In terms of Indian logic, "This hill has smoke which is invariably associated with fire", is called: **[2020]**
(a) Pratigya or proposition
(b) Universal concomitance together with an example
(c) Upanaya—the application of the universal concomitance to the present case
(d) Conclusion or Nigamana drawn from the preceding proposition

131. From the following identify those which illustrate the fallacy of the unproved middle? **[2020]**
(A) Ashrayasidha (B) Swarupasidha
(C) Vyapyatvasidha (D) Virudha
(E) Badhita
Choose the correct answer from the options given below:
(a) (A), (B) and (C) only
(b) (B), (C) and (D) only
(c) (A), (D) and (E) only
(d) (A), (C) and (D) only

132. Deduction proceeds from **[2020]**
(a) Particular to universal
(b) Universal to particular
(c) Particular to particular
(d) Universal to universal

133. Given below are two statements: **[2020]**
Statement I: When I look deep into myself, I always stumble with one perception or another. I can never catch myself.
Statement II: Self is the logical presupposition of all knowledge. Therefore, the concepts like substance and person cannot be applied to it.
In light of the above statements, choose the most appropriate answer from the options given below:
(a) Both Statement I and Statement II are true
(b) Both Statement I and Statement II are false
(c) Statement I is true but Statement II is false
(d) Statement I is false but Statement II is true

134. Given below are two statements: **[2020]**
Statement I: All knowledge is a recollection. It is true on a certain account.
Statement II: All men by nature, desire understanding.
In light of the above statements, choose the most appropriate answer from the options given below:
(a) Both Statement I and Statement II are true
(b) Both Statement I and Statement II are false
(c) Statement I is true but Statement II is false
(d) Statement I is false but Statement II is true

135. Match List I with List II: **[2021]**

List I	List II
Steps in Inference	Statements
A. Thesis (Pratijñā)	I. Because of smoke
B. Reason (Hetu)	II. Wherever there is smoke, there is fire, as in the kitchen
C. Example (Udāharaṇa)	III. The mountain has fire
D. Application (Upanaya)	IV. The mountain also has smoke accompanied by fire, like the kitchen

Choose the correct answer from the options given below:
(a) A - II, B - I, C - III, D - IV
(b) A - III, B - I, C - II, D - IV
(c) A - III, B - II, C - I, D - IV
(d) A - III, B - IV, C - II, D - I

136. Given below are two statements, one is labelled as Assertion A and the other is labelled as Reason R **[2021]**
Assertion A: According to Naiyāyikas, the fallacy of Savyabhicāra occurs when the middle term leads to different opposite conclusions.
Reason R: When the middle term is irregular, it is distributively not related to the major term.

In light of the above statements, choose the correct answer from the options given below:
(a) A is false but R is true
(b) A is true but R is false
(c) Both A and R are true and R is the correct explanation of A
(d) Both A and R are true but R is NOT the correct explanation of A

137. If 'All men are mortal' is given as True, then which of the following options can be validly inferred from it? **[2021]**
A. 'No men is mortal' is False
B. 'Some men are mortal' is True
C. 'Some men are not mortal' is True
D. 'Some men are not mortal' is False
E. 'Some men are mortal' is False

Choose the correct answer from the options given below:
(a) A, B and D only (b) A, B and C only
(c) A, B, C and D only (d) B, C, D and E only

138. Identify the fallacy committed in the argument:
Some birds are not beautiful creatures. All dogs are beautiful creatures. **[2021]**
Therefore, no dogs are birds.
(a) Fallacy of Exclusive Premises
(b) Fallacy of the Illicit Process of Major Term
(c) Fallacy of the Illicit Process of Minor Term
(d) Fallacy of the Undistributed Middle Term

139. ________ messages have more or less same meaning for the audience. **[2021]**
(a) Abstract (b) Complex
(c) Connotative (d) Denotative

140. Given below are two statements: **[2021]**
Statement I: Truth and Falsehood are predicates of Arguments
Statement II: Validity and Invalidity are predicates of Statements
In light of the above statements, choose the most appropriate answer from the options given below:
(a) Both Statement I and Statement II are correct
(b) Both Statement I and Statement II are incorrect
(c) Statement I is correct but Statement II is incorrect
(d) Statement I is incorrect but Statement II is correct

141. Name the fallacy committed in the argument below: **[2021]**
"All men who understand women are potentially perfect husbands.
All potentially perfect husbands are men of infinite patience.
Therefore, some men of infinite patience are men who understand women."
(a) Exclusive premises
(b) Existential fallacy
(c) Illicit major
(d) Undistributed middle

142. Pick the correct option to represent the given argument. **[2021]**
All artists are egoists
Some artists are paupers
Therefore, some paupers are egoists
Choose the correct answer from the options given below
(a) A II - I figure (b) A II - II figure
(c) A II - III figure (d) A II - IV figure

143. Match List I with List II **[2021]**

List I	List II
A. If 'A' is True	I. 'E' is True; 'O' is True
B. If 'E' is True	II. 'O' is False; 'E' is False
C. If 'I' is False	III. 'A' is False; 'I' is False
D. If 'O' is False	IV. 'E' is False; 'I' is True

Choose the correct answer from the options given below:
(a) A -I , B -II , C -III , D -IV
(b) A -II , B -III , C -I , D -IV
(c) A -III , B -I , C -II , D -IV
(d) A -IV , B -II , C -III, D-I

144. Match List I with List II. **[2021]**

List I	List II
A. Ashrayāsiddha	I. Sound is eternal because it is visible
B. Svarupāsiddha	II. All real are momentory; sound is real; sound is momentory

C. Vyapyatvasiddha	III. All objects are eternal because they are knowable
D. Anupasamhari	IV. Sky lotus is fragrant because it belongs to the class of lotus

Choose the correct answer from the options given below:

(a) A -I , B -III , C -II , D -IV
(b) A -II , B -IV , C -I , D -III
(c) A -III , B -II , C -IV , D -I
(d) A -IV , B -I , C -II , D -III

145. The middle term of the inference is related to the major term neither as a cause nor as an effect but because they are uniformly related to each other in our experience, is known as **[2021]**

(a) Pakshdharmata (b) Purvavat
(c) Samanyatodrshta (d) Sheshavat

146. Which of the following options are true regarding inference with reference to classical Indian system of logic? **[2021]**

(A) It is deductive
(B) It is inductive
(C) It has to be formally valid
(D) It has to be materially true

Choose the correct answer from the options given below:

(a) (A), (B), and (D) only
(b) (A), (B), and (C) only
(c) (A), (C), and (D) only
(d) (A), (B), (C), and (D) only

147. The collection of all the objects to which a term may correctly be applied is called: **[2021]**

(A) The intension of that term
(B) Connotation of that term
(C) The extension of that term
(D) Denotation of that term

Choose the correct answer from the options given below:

(a) (A) and (B) only (b) (B) and (C) only
(c) (A) and (D) only (d) (C) and (D) only

148. "The Daily News carried an article this morning about some local teenagers who were arrested on the charges of drug possession. Teenagers these days are nothing but a bunch of junkies".

Which fallacy is committed in the above statement? **[2021]**

(a) Red Herring
(b) Strawman
(c) Argument against the person (ad hominem)
(d) Hasty Generalization

149. Given below are two statements. One is labelled as Assertion (A) and the other is labelled as Reason (R): **[2021]**

Assertion (A) : The Naiyâyikas did not give separate treatment of the inductive methods as the western logicians have done.

Reasons (R) : According to Nyaya school, universal propostions are obtained from perception itself by one of the forms of extra-ordinary perception.

In the light of the above statements, choose the correct answer from the options given below:

(a) Both (A) and (R) are true and (R) is the correct explanation of (A)
(b) Both (A) and (R) are true but (R) is NOT the correct explanation of (A)
(c) (A) is true but (R) is false
(d) (A) is false but (R) is true

150. Given below are two statements: **[2021]**

Statement I: Sesavata is the inference of what remains (sesa) by elimination of the irrelevant.

Statement II: Sesavata inference corresponds to the method of residues in western inductive logic.

In the light of the above statements, choose the most appropriate answer from the options given below:

(a) Both Statement I and Statement II are true
(b) Both Statement I and Statement II are false
(c) Statement I is true but Statement II is false
(d) Statement I is false but Statement II is true

151. Match List I with List II. **[Dec 2021]**

List I (Proposition in Square of Opposition)	List II (Resultant Proposition)
(A) If 'A' is True	(i) 'I' is false; 'O' is True
(B) If 'E' is True	(ii) 'E' is false; 'A' is undetermined

(C) If 'I' is True	(iii) 'E' and T is undetermined
(D) If 'O' is True	(iv) 'E' is false; 'I' is True

Choose the correct answer from the options given below:

	(A)	(B)	(C)	(D)
(a)	(i)	(iii)	(ii)	(iv)
(b)	(ii)	(i)	(iii)	(iv)
(c)	(iii)	(ii)	(i)	(iv)
(d)	(iv)	(i)	(ii)	(iii)

152. When a middle term does not go further than producing a state of mental oscillation between two opposite views, the case is of: **[Dec 2021]**
(a) Fallacy of Viruddha
(b) Fallacy of Prakaransama
(c) Fallacy of Asiddha
(d) Fallacy of Savyabhichara

153. The Fallacy committed in the argument **[Dec 2021]**
"All textbooks are books intended for careful study. Some reference books are books intended for careful study. Therefore, some reference books are textbooks." is:
(a) Illicit Major
(b) Illicit Minor
(c) Fallacy of four Terms
(d) Undistributed Middle

154. In an illustration of inference that the 'Sun moves, like other moving objects its position changes' represents: **[Dec 2021]**
(a) Purvavat Anumana
(b) Sesavat Anumana
(c) Sämänyatodrsta
(d) Pakshta

155. Pick the incorrect statement. **[Dec 2021]**
(a) 'Truth' and 'Falsewood' may be predicated of propositions but never of arguments.
(b) In the case of deductive argument, the technical terms 'correct' and 'incorrect' are used.
(c) Inductive arguments are neither valid nor invalid but evaluated as better or worse.
(d) The conclusion of a deductive argument follows from its premises necessarily.

156. If the statement 'No birds are mammals' is given as true, what could be immediately inferred from it? **[2022]**
A. 'All birds are mammals' is false
B. 'Some birds are mammals' is false
C. 'Some birds are not mammals' is false
D. 'Some birds are not mammals' is true

Choose the correct answer from the options given below:
(a) A, B and C only (b) A, B and D only
(c) A and D only (d) A and C only

157. "XYZ Home Finance offers best financial product in the country because like a family member and a good friend, XYZ Home Finance fulfills your need to have your own sweet home". Which of the following fallacies is committed in this argument? **[2022]**
(a) Ad Populum
(b) Ad Hominem
(c) Hasty Generalisation
(d) Red Herring

158. Given below are two statements: **[2022]**

Statement I: 'Some S is P' is contrary to 'Some S is not P'.

Statement II: 'Some S is not P' is contradictory to 'All S is P'.

In light of the above statements, choose the correct answer from the options given below:
(a) Both Statement I and Statement II are true
(b) Both Statement I and Statement II are false
(c) Statement I is true but Statement II is false
(d) Statement I is false but Statement II is true

159. Given below are two statements: **[2022]**

Statement I: For the Indian thinkers, inference (anumana) means only a syllogistic inference based on the relation of invariable concomitance between middle term and major term.

Statement II: There should be absence of the middle term wherever there is an absence of the major term.

In light of the above statements, choose the correct answer from the options given below:
(a) Both Statement I and Statement II are true
(b) Both Statement I and Statement II are false

(c) Statement I is true but Statement II is false
(d) Statement I is false but Statement II is true

160. Given below are two statements: **[2022]**

Statement I: According to Classical Indian Logicians (Naiyayikas), the inference from the effect of the cause is called Purvavat.

Statement II: According to Naiyayikas, the inference of cause from the effect is not possible.

In light of the above statements, choose the correct answer from the options given below:

(a) Both Statement I and Statement II are true
(b) Both Statement I and Statement II are false
(c) Statement I is true but Statement II is false
(d) Statement I is false but Statement II is true

161. A wise sage has said, 'The hunger for knowledge is more difficult to remove than the hunger for food, Therefore, one should stick to the food,' Which fallacy is committed in this argument? **[2022]**

(a) Begging the Question
(b) False Dilemma
(c) Ignoratio elenchi (irrelevant conclusion)
(d) Appeal to Emotion

162. 'We should value the Moon more than the Sun because the Moon shines when it is dark whereas Sun shines when there is light anyway,' This statement commits the fallacy of **[2022]**

(a) Appeal to Emotion
(b) Fallacy of False Cause
(c) False Dilemma
(d) Equivocation

163. Given below are two statements, one is labelled as **Assertion A** and the other is labelled as **Reason R** **[2022]**

Assertion A: According to classical Indian Logicians (Naiyayikas), all fallacies are material fallacies.

Reason R: According to Nyaya, Syllogism is deductive-inductive and formal-material.

In light of the above statements, choose the correct answer from the options given below

(a) Both **A** and **R** are true and **R** is the correct explanation of **A**
(b) Both **A** and **R** are true but **R** is NOT the correct explanation of **A**
(c) **A** is true but **R** is false
(d) **A** is false but **R** is true

164. If the statement 'Some plants are not carnivorous' is given as false, then which of the following could be immediately inferred from it? **[2022]**

A. 'Some plants are carnivorous' is true
B. 'Some plants are carnivorous' is false
C. 'No plants are carnivorous' is false
D. 'All plants are carnivorous' is true

Choose the correct answer from the options given below:

(a) B, C and D only (b) A and D only
(c) A and C only (d) A C and D only

165. Which of the following statements are true regarding Nyaya (Classical Indian School of Logic) view of hetra–bha–sa (fallacy) **[2022]**

A. It means that middle term appears to be a reason but is not a valid reason.
B. All fallacies are material fallacies.
C. When an inference is based not on causation but on uniformity of co-existence, it leads to a fallacy.
D. Fallacies occur when any of the five characteristics of a middlle term are violated.

Choose the correct answer from the options given below:

(a) A, B and C only (b) A, B and D only
(c) B, C and D only (d) A, B, C and D

166. Which fallacy is committed in the following argument? **[June 2023]**

'As a society we have an obligation to support the needy, because people who do not have sufficient resources have a right to the resources of the community'.

(a) Begging the question
(b) Equivocation
(c) Fallacy of composition
(d) Appeal to emotion

167. Match List I with List II. **[June 2023]**

List I (Statement)	List II (Logical Equivalent)
A. No fishes are mammals.	I. No fishes are non-mammals.
B. All fishes are mammals.	II. No mammals are fishes
C. Some fishes are mammals.	III. Some mammals are non-fishes

List I (Statement)	List II (Logical Equivalent)
D. Some mammals are not fishes.	IV. Some mammals are fishes.

Choose the correct answer from the options given below:

(a) A-IV, B-I, C-III, D-II
(b) A-II, B-III, C-IV, D-I
(c) A-II, B-I, C-IV, D-III
(d) A-III, B-II, C-IV, D-I

168. If the statement 'Some animals are birds', is given as false, then which of the following statements could be immediately inferred to be true? **[June 2023]**

A. All animals are birds.
B. No animals are birds.
C. Some animals are not birds
D. All birds are animals.

Choose the most appropriate answer from the options given below:

(a) B only (b) A and D only
(c) C only (d) B and C only

169. Which of the following statements are so related that they cannot both be true, although they both may be false? **[June 2023]**

A. All trees have roots.
B. No trees have roots.
C. Some trees have roots.
D. Some trees do not have roots.

Choose the most appropriate answer from the options given below:

(a) C and D only (b) A and B only
(c) B and D only (d) A and C only

170. According to *Nyaya* (classical Indian school of logic) which of the following is an example of Badhit fallacy (non-inferentially contradicted middle)? **[June 2023]**

(a) Sound is quality becuase it is visible.
(b) Sound is eternal because it is produced.
(c) All things are non-eternal because they are knowable.
(d) Fire is cold because it is a substance.

171. Which fallacy is committed in the following argument? **[June 2023]**

'When I called you, you were neither in your class nor in the laboratory. Why are you avoiding me ?"

(a) Circular argument (b) Red herring
(c) Complex question (d) Slippery slope

172. Which of the following statements are logically equivalent? **[June 2023]**

A. Some animals are birds.
B. Some animals are not non-birds
C. Some non-birds are not non-animals
D. Some birds are animals.

Choose the correct answer from the options given below:

(a) B and C only (b) B, C, D only
(c) A, B and D only (d) A, B and C only

173. If the statement "no animals are fishes" is given as false, then which of the following statements can be immediately inferred to be true? **[June 2023]**

A. All fishes are animals.
B. Some animals are not fishes.
C. All animals are fishes.
D. Some animals are fishes.

Choose the correct answer from the options given below:

(a) B and D only (b) A, C and D only
(c) C and D only (d) D only

174. Which of the following propositions are contrary to each other? **[June 2023]**

A. All fishes are mammals.
B. Some fishes are mammals.
C. No fishes are mammals.
D. Some fishes are not mammals.

Choose the correct answer from the options given below:

(a) B and D only (b) A and C only
(c) A and D only (d) B and C only

175. According to Nyaya (Classical Indian School of Logic) Which of the following argument involves the fallacy of Anuspsamhari (non-exclusive middle term)? **[June 2023]**

(a) The hill has smoke because it has fire.
(b) Sound is eternal because it is audible.
(c) All things are non-eternal because they are knowable.
(d) Sound is eternal because it is produced.

176. Given below are two statements, one is labelled as Assertion (A) and other one labelled as Reason (R) **[Dec 2023]**

Assertion (A): As per classical Indian view of logic the argument — 'Sound is quality because it is visible', is fallacious.

Reason (R): As per classical Indian view of logic the argument - 'Sound is quality because it is visible' involves a middle term that cannot by its very nature be present in the minor term.

In light of the above statements, choose the correct answer from the options given below.

(a) Both (A) and (R) are true and (R) is the correct explanation of (A).
(b) Both (A) and (R) are true but (R) is NOT the correct explanation of (A).
(c) (A) is true but (R) is false.
(d) (A) is false but (R) is true.

177. Which of the following propositions are so related that they cannot both be false although they may both be true, as per square of opposition? **[Dec 2023]**

A. Some apes are monkeys.
B. All apes are monkeys.
C. Some apes are not monkeys.
D. No apes are monkeys

Choose the correct answer from the options given below:

(a) B and D only (b) A and B only
(c) A and C only (d) C and D only

178. Which of the following statements are logically equivalent? **[Dec 2023]**

A. Some apes are not non-monkeys.
B. Some monkeys are not non-apes.
C. Some monkeys are apes.
D. Some apes are monkeys.

Choose the correct answer from the options given below:

(a) A and B only
(b) C and D only
(c) B, C and D only
(d) A, B, C and D

179. As per square of opposition, if the statement — 'Some birds are apes' is given as false, then which of the following statements can be immediately inferred to be true? **[Dec 2023]**

A. All birds are apes.
B. Some birds are apes.
C. No birds are apes.
D. All birds are not apes.

Choose the correct answer from the options given below:

(a) C and D only (b) A, C and D only
(c) B and D only (d) B and C only

180. 'It is so obvious that this world was created by an intelligent God. Just look at the amazing degree of organization that the world displays.' Which fallacy is committed in this argument? **[Dec 2023]**

(a) Fallacy of composition
(b) Begging the Question
(c) Straw man
(d) False Cause

ANSWER KEYS

1. (a) 2. (c) 3. (c) 4. (c) 5. (b) 6. (a) 7. (d) 8. (c) 9. (b) 10. (a)
11. (d) 12. (a) 13. (b) 14. (c) 15. (c) 16. (c) 17. (b) 18. (b) 19. (d) 20. (b)
21. (a) 22. (c) 23. (b) 24. (d) 25. (b) 26. (c) 27. (b) 28. (c) 29. (d) 30. (a)
31. (c) 32. (c) 33. (b) 34. (d) 35. (b) 36. (a) 37. (d) 38. (d) 39. (c) 40. (a)
41. (c) 42. (b) 43. (d) 44. (a) 45. (c) 46. (b) 47. (a) 48. (a) 49. (c) 50. (d)
51. (d) 52. (d) 53. (a) 54. (a) 55. (d) 56. (a) 57. (c) 58. (b) 59. (d) 60. (a)
61. (b) 62. (a) 63. (a) 64. (b) 65. (c) 66. (a) 67. (a) 68. (b) 69. (b) 70. (c)
71. (a) 72. (c) 73. (b) 74. (a) 75. (b) 76. (a) 77. (a) 78. (a) 79. (c) 80. (d)
81. (a) 82. (c) 83. (d) 84. (c) 85. (b) 86. (d) 87. (c) 88. (a) 89. (b) 90. (d)
91. (c) 92. (b) 93. (a) 94. (a) 95. (b) 96. (a) 97. (d) 98. (b) 99. (a) 100. (c)
101. (b) 102. (a) 103. (a) 104. (c) 105. (a) 106. (b) 107. (d) 108. (d) 109. (c) 110. (a)
111. (b) 112. (c) 113. (b) 114. (c) 115. (c) 116. (b) 117. (c) 118. (a) 119. (c) 120. (d)
121. (c) 122. (c) 123. (d) 124. (a) 125. (a) 126. (d) 127. (a) 128. (c) 129. (d) 130. (c)
131. (a) 132. (b) 133. (a) 134. (a) 135. (b) 136. (c) 137. (a) 138. (b) 139. (c) 140. (b)
141. (b) 142. (c) 143. (b) 144. (d) 145. (c) 146. (d) 147. (d) 148. (d) 149. (a) 150. (a)
151. (d) 152. (b) 153. (d) 154. (c) 155. (b) 156. (b) 157. (a) 158. (d) 159. (a) 160. (c)
161. (c) 162. (b) 163. (a) 164. (d) 165. (b) 166. (a) 167. (b) 168. (d) 169. (b) 170. (b)
171. (b) 172. (a) 173. (d) 174. (b) 175. (b) 176. (a) 177. (c) 178. (d) 179. (a) 180. (b)

HINTS AND SOLUTIONS

1. (a)

(a) We need to focus on word 'as' in the question statement that establishes link between two similar situations. That word corresponds to analogical inference. The word analogical is derived from the word analogy. Analogical reasoning is different from deductive or inductive reasoning. It is basically a more precise form of conjecture. It is actually the identification of relations valid in one domain of knowledge onto another domain (which is less familiar or unknown to us so far). The relations are identified and their similarity observed in the other domain. The identification of analogical argument depends upon past experience also. For example, 'A shark in the ocean behaves like a wolf in the forest'.

(b) Deductive argument does not apply in this question. Deduction argument applies when we move from general to specific. For example, 'All men are mortal (general). If B is a man (specific), then B is mortal.

Now try to understand these lines below for future questions, we often use inductive argument first in order to move towards deductive argument. Thus, inductive reasoning is more innovative. It means that we move (ascend) from particular to universal and then move (descend) from universal to particular. (The example of inductive argument - 'It often snows in winter. It is winter now. There is a high probability that we'll have snow.' Here, for inductive argument, we should focus on the word 'probability'.)

(c) It is not statistical as we are not talking about any such tool or number here.

(d) A causal argument is the one that talks about cause and effect - how something has caused some particular effect. A causal argument focuses on 'how' or 'why' question. For example, (a) How did things get to be the way they are? (b) Why did something happen? The question statement talks about similarity of two similar situations which are qualitative in nature.

2. (c)

A deductive argument makes the claim that its conclusion is supported by its premises *conclusively*. An inductive argument, in contrast, does not make such a claim. Therefore, if we judge that in some passage a claim for conclusiveness is being made, we treat the argument as deductive; if we judge that such a claim is not being made, we treat it as inductive. Because every argument either makes this claim of conclusiveness (explicitly or implicitly) or does not make it, every argument is either deductive or inductive.

3. (c)

The Easiest Method For 'Square of Opposition'

There is always possibility of one question on square of opposition. Thus, it is being discussed here as a separate topic. These have been discussed in the most easiest manner. First, we need to recall what do we mean by AEIO. This relationship is called as traditional as been put in the form of Aristotle view point.

S and P are respectively called as subject and predicate.

Adrusthartha (अदृष्टार्थ): A sabda that deals with the imperceptible object is called as 'adrsta'. For example, honesty is the best policy. God is one.

Proposition	Letter Name	Quantity	Quality	Terms Distributed
All S are P	A	Universal	Affirmative	S
No S are P	E	Universal	Negative	S and P
Some S are P	I	Particular	Affirmative	None
Some S are not P	O	Particular	Negative	P

S and P are subject and predicate. The word 'are' in the above propositions is called as 'Copula' that joins S and P.

Universal mean 'All' and 'No' are given as subjects in the propositions.

Affirmative means positive, it indicates presence. Negative means 'No' and 'Not' in the above propositions.

Particulars means 'some'.

We have tried to explain the contradictories, contraries, sub contraries and sub alterations. These have been put in the diagram as well. A has relationship with E, I and O. E has relationship with A, I and O. So is the case with I and O. Their network makes up the square of opposition. The square of opposition tells us the relationship between quantity, quality or both.

Distribution

1. In universal proposition, the subject term is distributed whereas in particular proposition subject term is undistributed.
2. In negative proposition, the predicate term is distributed while in an affirmative proposition the predicate term remains undistributed.

Quality and Quantity: Affirmative and Negative refer to Quality. Universal and Particular refer to Particular.

Quality / Quantity	Affirmative	Negative
Universal	All men are honest	No men are honest
Particular	Some men are honest	Some men are not honest

The standard form of categorical proposition having the same subject (S) and predicate (P) but may differ from each other in quality or quantity or both. Such differing has been called opposition. The term opposition is used when there is no apparent disagreement between the propositions.

Traditional Square of opposition

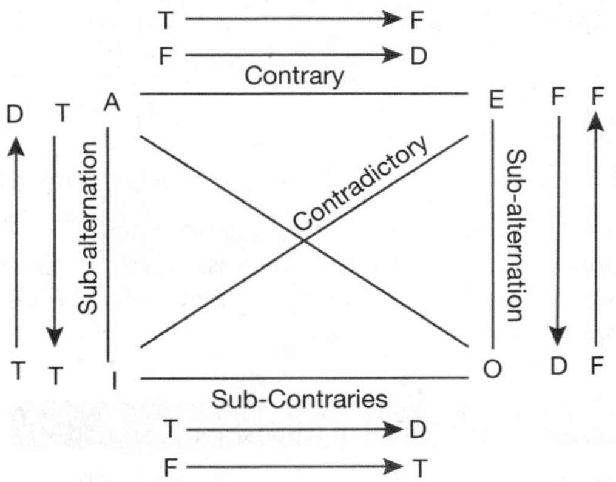

1. **Contradictory:** These categorical propositions differ from each other both in quantity and quality. For example, between A and O, A is Universal Affirmative and O is Particular Negative. Here, Universal and Particular differ in quantity. Also, Affirmative and Negative differ in Quality.

   The same is the case with E (Universal Negative) and I (Particular Positive) that again differs in quantity and quality.

   Two propositions are contradictories if one is denial or negation of the other. They can't both be true OR both be false.

   The contradictories exist in two forms – 1. A and O

   2. E and I

   A ⟶ O E ⟶ I

A	All men are honest	**E**	No men are honest
O	Some men are honest	**I**	Some men are not honest

'X' in the middle of square of oppostion represents contradictories, with opposite truth values. This can be easily remembered.

2. **Contrary:** Two universals (A and E) can't be true together. If A is given to be True, then E is False. If A is given to be false, then O will be doubtful. The vice versa is also applicable.

   A ⟶ E

   A – All men are honest.

   E – No men are honest.

   Since God (or Truth) is assumed to be at the top of diagrams. We assume that God is one, there can't be two Gods. In a similar manner, both of the contraries (A and E) can't be true simultaneously.

3. **Sub-contraries:** Two particulars can't be true together. If I is given to be True, O is doubtful. If I is given to be true, the other will be false. The vice versa is also applicable. It means that both won't be true together.

Further, both terms have the same quantity, both I and O are particular (same quantity). They differ on 'quality' terms only. For example, I is of affirmative quantity, then we know that O is of negative quantity.

I ⟶ O

Example:

Some men are honest.

Some men are not honest.

4. **Sub-alternation:** When two propositions differ only in quantity (one is universal and other is particular), the opposition is called sub alteration.

A ⟶ I

E ⟶ O

Example

A	All men are honest	**E**	No men are honest
O	Some men are not honest	**I**	Some men are not honest

The universals at the top can be equated with the God, and we understand that Truth flows from God (Universal / Top) to the Bottom.

Two propositions are said to stand in the relation of subalternation when the truth of the first (the superaltern) implies the truth of the second (the subaltern), but not conversely. A propositions stand in the subalternation relation with the corresponding I propositions. The truth of the A proposition 'all plastics are synthetic' (A type), implies the truth of the proposition 'some plastics are synthetic (I type). However, the truth of the O proposition 'some rockets are not Made in India products' does not imply the truth of the E proposition 'no rockets are Made in India products.'

Easy Manner to Obtain Results from 'Square of Opposition'

Thus, their recall becomes difficult during the exam. Their relationships have been defined in the following manner. On one diagonal, starting from top of left hand side, we have been given T that stand for Truth. There is F in other diagonal that stands for False.

1. In the first level, there is T F T F. Suppose, A is True, then E is false, I is True and O is False.
2. On the second level, there are F T F T. If E is True, then we will go to the second level, and see that A is F, I is F and O is True. Thus, positions of T and F should be ascertained from the diagonals.
3. If E is False, we should go to the third level where A is D (doubtful), I is True and O is doubtful. If I is true we should look at third level as benchmark (and NOT to level 1).
4. If A is False, then E and I are Doubtful. O is true in that case.

Propositions	A	E	I	O
Level 1	T	F	T	F
Level 2	F	T	F	T
Level 3	D	F	T	D
Level 4	F	D	D	T

Figure 6.1: Truth Table

4. (c)

Let us assume that M stands for mammals, D for dogs and C for Cats.

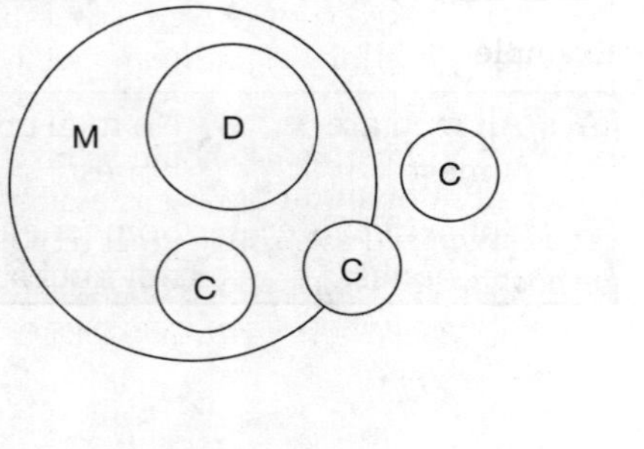

There can be three scenarios for C as shown in the above diagram.

5. (b)

This is very direct question: Indian scientists but not POLITICIANS. So, the answer will be integration between A and B but excludes q.

6. (a)

An argument is a form of communication that tries to persuade its audience to adopt a particular position about a topic. Arguments have three main parts, such as a claim that states the position to be argued, reasons that logically explain why the claim should be accepted;and evidence that supports the reasons with facts, anecdotes, statistics, expert testimony and examples. The statements a writer makes to offer a claim, reasons and evidence can weaken or strengthen an argument.

7. (d)

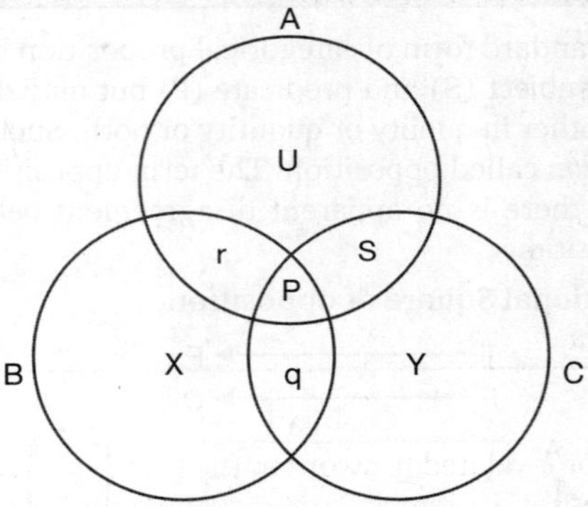

8. (c)

In this question, we are comparing two situations which compares the strength of being wiser. We can focus on the word 'than' in the question statement for the sake of comparison.

9. (b)

It is linked with 'Square of Opposition'.

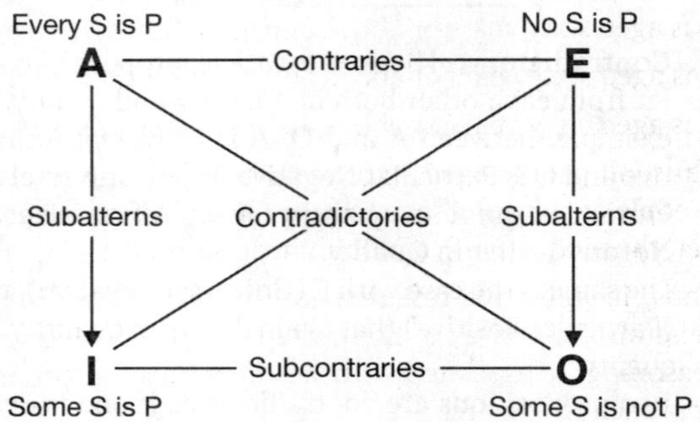

Now putting 'wise men are hardly afraid of death' in the standard format: Some wise men are afraid of death.

All wise men are afraid of death.	All S are P	A
No wise men is afraid of death.	No S are P	E
Some wise men are afraid of death.	Some S are P	I
Some wise men are not afraid of death.	Some S are not P	O

The contradictory terms are 'A and O' and 'E and I'.

Now putting 'wise men are hardly afraid of death' in the standard format: Some wise men are afraid of death. It is contradicted by: All wise men are afraid of death. Thus, (b) is the answer.

10. (a)

	Brillent	Obedient	Regular	Studious
Namita	✓			✓
Samita	✓	✓	✓	✓
Anitha		✓		
Karabi		✓		
Babita	✓			
Kabita		✓	✓	

11. (d)

Warrior is related to sword in the battleground. Carpenter uses saw on wood. Farmer uses his equipment plough in the field. Thus question is about one's instrument. Author uses 'pen' to write a book.

12. (a)

In this question, we are discussing the answer in the forms of inductive and deductive reasoning.

Inductive Reasoning begins with particular instances and concludes with general statements or principles.

A is aged sixty years or above and uses internet.

B is aged sixty years or above and uses internet.

C is aged sixty years or above and uses internet.

Thus, all people aged sixty years or above use internet. (People at sixty or above sixty are less likely to use internet, thus inductive is a probabilistic approach).

Thus, in inductive research, we move from specific to general. Inductive is bottom-up approach. Inductive reasoning is associated with the 'hypothesis generating' approach to research.

Deductive reasoning is mainly associated with the scientific (or positivist) approach to research. The argument moves from general principles to particular instances. Thus, deductive is top-bottom approach. The most importantly, as per question, deductive is linked with the 'hypothesis testing' approach.

All people aged sixty years or above use internet.

A is aged sixty years old.

A does not use computer.

Thus, normally we go from inductive approach to deductive approach. In general, we need to understand that new knowledge emerges from specific instances in society. If that knowledge is true in many cases, then that should be generalized.

Once that is generalized (theorized), this can be used to test other specific instances. Now that will be called as deductive reasoning.

Thus, deductive is a 'deterministic' or 'firmly conclusive approach'.

13. (b)

First of all, we should have an idea about valid and invalid and then true and false. Validity is applicable in context of arguments and true (or false) is applicable in context of prepositions or statements.

Validity is 'formal' in nature and it depends upon correct structure form (such as we follow grammar). It is actually a correct arrangement. True means that premise is assumed to be actually truthful in this world.

We need to see the following example. The premises are true but conclusion is false.

Premise 1: All basketballs are round.

Premise 2: The Earth is round.

Therefore, the Earth is a basketball.

Argument with this form is invalid. The conclusion's truth is not guaranteed by the premises' truth. It could have been possible for the premises to be true and the conclusion false. As this argument is invalid, and all invalid arguments are unsound.

14. (c)

The principle that the future will resemble the past. We can also that when sufficiently similar situations recur, similar effects follow. This principle of uniformity of nature is presupposed in some form in these two situations - scientific prediction as well as certainties of everyday life. The uniformity of nature is justified in inductive inferences.

There is 'unity of nature', it should be taken in the sense of 'continuity of natural law'. It is assumed that all of nature is organized as a single great unit according to a single body of law which operates all the times and at all the places. We can find some examples of unity among plants and animals.

15. (c)

We need to look at 'Square of opposition'.

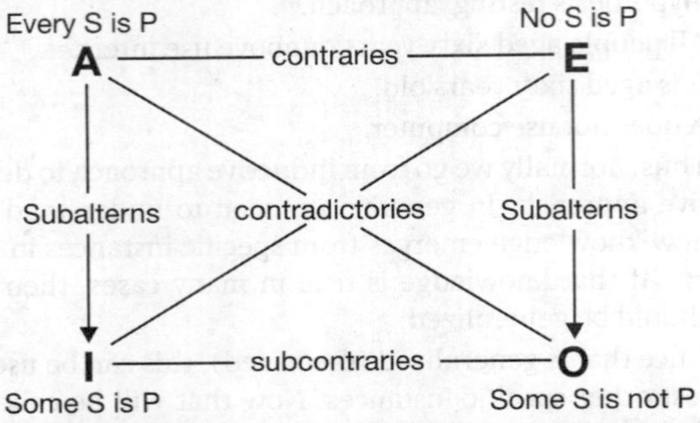

(i)	All poets are philosophers	A	All S is P
(ii)	Some poets are philosophers	I	Some S is P
(iii)	Some poets are not philosophers	O	Some S is not P
(iv)	No philosopher is a poet.	E	No P is S

There is direct matching of A and O as per diagram in the form of contradictories.

16. (c)

Lexical ambiguity is a writing error that occurs when a sentence contains a word that has more than one meaning. This problem, which is also called semantic ambiguity, obscures the writer's intent and confuses the reader. Lexical ambiguity is sometimes used intentionally to create a pun, which is a play on words, often to be funny.

17. (b)

Venn diagrams are basically graphs that employs closed curves and especially circles to represent logical relations between and operations on sets and the terms of propositions by the inclusion, exclusion, or intersection of the curves.

18. (b)

Analogical argument means comparison of two comparable cases. In a sentence, we need to look at word/s that makes such comparison. Here the testing of teachers is being compared with testing of doctors, architects, etc.

19. (d)

We need to refer to square of opposition and truth table. Subcontraries are the propositions, two are related in such a way that they can both be true although they can not both be false. We can look at the position of subcontrary in square of opposition. They actually have I and O propositions.

Among answer choices – the 'I' proposition is addressed by 'some priests are cunning', and 'O' proposition has the statement 'some priests are not cunning'. Thus (d) is the correct answer.

20. (b)

An argument is not merely a collection of propositions. It is a cluster with a structure that captures or exhibits some inference. The conclusion of an argument is the proposition that is affirmed on the basis of the other propositions of the argument.

Two Types of Arguments	
<u>Deductive</u>: Arguments whose conclusions follow, or appear to follow, neccessarily.	<u>Inductive</u>: Arguments whose conclusions follow, or appear to follow, probably.
1. All teachers are funny	1. 90% of all teachers are funny
2. K___ is a teacher	2. K___ is a teacher
∴ K___ is funny	∴ K___ is funny

21. (a)

No man is perfect – E proposition – that is given as Assertion in question.

Some men are not perfect – O proposition – that is given as Reason.

We need to move from O to E, that shows 'sub altern relationship' between the two.

Both statements are true. If O is true (as shown in Level 4 in truth table), E is doubtful. The R does not provide sufficient answer for A.

22. (c)

These definitions have been mentioned in NTA syllabus under the topic language in sixth unit.

Lexical meaning is defined as the meaning of a base or a root word without considering any prefix or suffix which may be attached. An example of lexical meaning is the meaning of the word 'port' in the words import or portable.

A precising definition extends the lexical definition of a term for a specific purpose by including additional criteria that narrow down the set of things meeting the definition.

The direct definition of stipulative is being given in question statement itself.

A 'persuasive' definition is one which gives a new conceptual meaning to a familar word without substantially changing its emotive meaning, and which is used with the conscious or unconscious purpose of changing, by theis means, the direction of people's interests.

23. (b)

'If no men are honest' (particular negative proposition) is false, then 'All men are honest' (universal positive proposition) is true.

If 'All men are honest' is true then its part 'some men are honest' is certainly to be true.

Alternatively, we can look at the truth table in figure 6.1, where FALSE of 'no men are honest' (E-proposition) is given. In that Level-3, only 'I' preposition is given to be true. If 'I' is true, then 'some men are honest' is the answer. Thus (b) is the correct answer.

24. (d)

We need to focus on the word 'related to' in the question statement, and the two propositions which we going to identified among choices must be linked in the manner that one is denial of other. There are three answer choices that start with A. We are going for the identification of propositions.

(A) All women are equal to men - A
(B) Some women are equal to men - I
(C) Some women are not equal to men - O
(D) No women are equal to men – E

Now we are comparing it with Truth Table in diagram.

If 'all women are equal to men' (A) is true then 'some women are equal to men' (I) is also true. Both go in the same direction. So, this A and B can't be the answer.

Then looking at other choices in the same row of truth table tells us that E and O are denial of A (False). Thus, A and C is the right answer.

Similarly, A and D is also the answer.

Thus, there are two right answers –(b) and (d).

Thus, this solving this question has three steps – reading question statement (focusing on words 'related to' and 'denial of other' in that) identification of propositions, their comparison with truth table and getting the right answer. So, we can avoid confusion with the help of truth table.

25. (b)

Deductive argument is based on the claim that the truth of its premises guarantees the truth of its conclusion. The terms valid and invalid are used to characterize deductive arguments. A deductive argument succeeds when, if we accept the evidence as true (the premises), we must accept the conclusion.

An argument is valid if and only if it is necessary that if all of the premises are true, then the conclusion is true; if all the premises are true, then the conclusion must be true; it is impossible that all the premises are true and the conclusion is false.

26. (c)

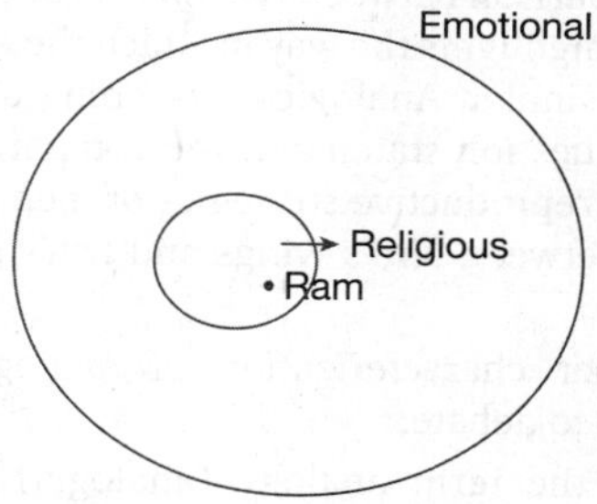

27. (b)

'All thieves are poor' is A proposition. If this statement is false, we can refer to Level 4 of Truth Table in figure 6.1. That level shows only 'O' proposition as the true statement. 'O' proposition means 'some thieves are not poor'. Thus, (b) is the right answer.

To put it in simple terms, we can say that 'All thieves are poor' means 'some thieves are poor'.(Some is also part of All).

If 'All thieves are poor' is false, it means that 'some thieves are not poor' is certainly to be true.

28. (c)

A Venn diagram uses overlapping circles or other shapes to illustrate the logical relationships between two or more sets of items. Often, they serve to graphically organize things, highlighting how the items are similar and different.

29. (d)

The semblance is between earth's features and grain. We need to focus on the word, 'as absurd as to assert' that makes them analogical.

30. (a)

Inductive research, the first point denotes 'observe the different phenomena'. It means first choice in the question is about inductive reasoning and not deductive reasoning.

31. (c)

If we look at the Truth Table, then 'E' and 'I' AND 'A' and 'O' are undetermined. These appear on the 'X' section of 'square of opposition' diagram, thus 'contradictory' is the correct answer.

We can look at square of opposition diagram and Truth Table.

The relation between two standard form categorical propositions with the same subject and predicate are related in such a manner that if one is undetermined the other must be undetermined is contradictory.

32. (c)

An analogy is a comparison between two objects or phenomena events that highlights the way in which they can be thought of to be similar. Analogical reasoning upon an analogy. In the question statement, the comparison is between different reproductive strategies of men and women. And, also between bird's wings and fish's fins. The answer is (c).

However, the proper characterization of analogical arguments is subject to debate.

Aristotle employed the term analogy (analogia). He identified two argument forms, the argument from example (paradeigma) and the argument from likeness (homoiotes).

Analogies play *heuristic roles*, as they help in 'discovery' in a simple manner. Analogy helps in all philosophical investigations and all discoveries, which were not made by mere accident.

33. (b)

First, we need to convert statements (i) and (iii) into standard their forms.

(i) All students are attentive – A

(ii) Some students are attentive – I

(iii) No student is attentive – E

(iv) Some students are never attentive -O

As per question statement – they can't both be true but can be false, we can say that the question is of 'contrary statement'. Contrary covers A and E. Thus, (i) and (iii) applies to the answer. Thus, (b) is the correct answer.

34. (d)

Draw the Venn diagram.

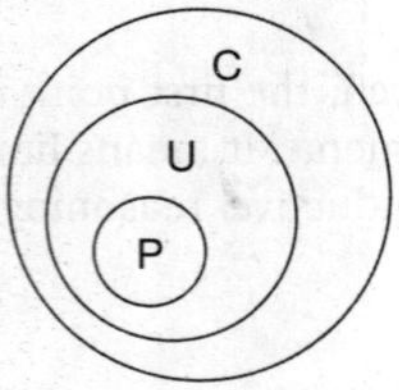

C – Curses

U – Untouchable

P – Pans

Conclusions (i), (ii) and (iv) seems to be valid, but according to official answer key, (d) is the right answer.

35. (b)

Given statement, 'None but the brave wins the race'. We've to reduce this 'exclusive proposition'.

Accordingly, we can write the same statement as:

All brave are winners.

So if this statement is false then

'All brave are not winners', means that 'some person who win the race, are not brave'. Hence, answer is (b).

36. (a)

Lucknow is on the bank of River Gomti, whereas all others are on banks of Holy Ganga.

37. (d)

Refer rules mentioned in chapter in NTA-UGC NET/SET/JRF Paper I—Teaching and Research Aptitude published by Pearson Education to convert these statements into their logical forms. Once that is done, check with 'square of opposition' to answer.

	Given statement	Logical form	Type of proposition
(A)	Honest people never suffer.	No honest person suffers.	E Type
(B)	Almost all honest people do suffer.	Some honest people suffer.	I Type
(C)	Honest people hardly suffer.	Some honest people don't suffer.	O Type
(D)	Each and every honest person suffers.	All honest persons suffer.	A Type

Now, as per question, they can both be true, but they cannot both be false. The propositions are to be subcontrary. I-Type and O-Type makes subcontrary. Thus, (B) and (C) are to be answers. Accordingly, option (d) is the right answer.

38. (d)

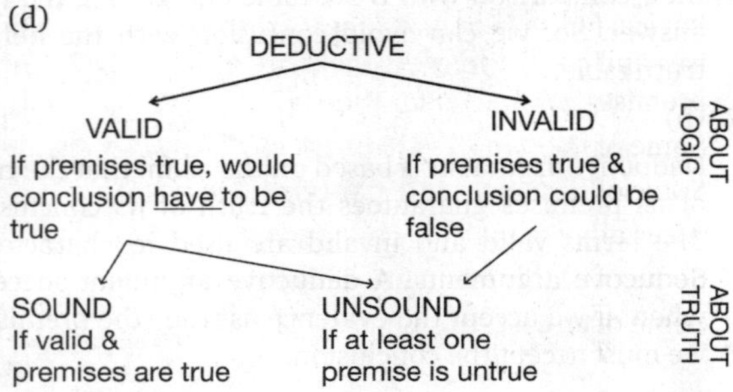

39. (c)

Based upon premises, there can be three Venn diagrams as shown below:

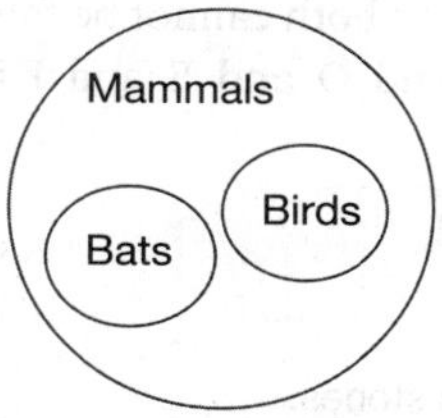

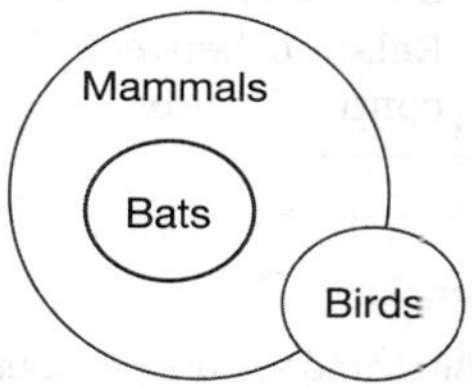

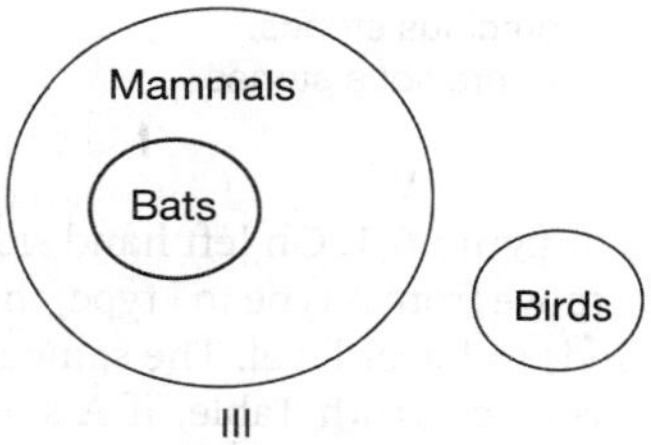

Now looking at all conclusions:

(i) No birds are mammals: May or may not be, so its invalid.

(ii) Some birds are not mammals: May or may not be, so its invalid.

(iii) No bats are birds: Valid

(iv) All mammals are bats: May or may not be, so its invalid.

Thus, only (c) is valid and hence, it is the right answer.

40. (a)

This is a comparative/analogical example to explain an idea.

41. (c)

In the sentence, focus on 'same way', that tells us that we are talking about 'analogical', it means that we are making a comparison.

42. (b)

'Converting Common Language Statements into their Logical forms'. Replace 'Most of the' with 'some' in premises and conclusions. As there are exactly three terms in premises, we can go for their alignment if required.

Some of the dancers are physically fit.

Some of the singers are dancers.

After alignment

Some of physically fit are dancers – (I-Type)

Some of dancers are singers – (I-Type)

I-Type + I-Type – No conclusion.

NET aspirants should note that the alignment of sentences is not of any use in this case as I + I in any case does not give any conclusion.

Thus, (A) some of singers are physically fit and (B) some of physically fit are singers both statements don't apply.

Now we can go for immediate inference by referring tables in chapter of in NTA-UGC NET/SET/JRF Paper I—Teaching and Research Aptitude published by Pearson Education. To check for statements (B) and (C).

Some of physically fit are dancers—(I-Type)

After conversion: Some dancers are physically fit.

Some of dancers are singers—(I-Type)

After conversion: Some singers are dancers.

Thus, (B) and (C) are valid conclusions.

Alternatively, we can try to solve the same question by Venn diagrams also.

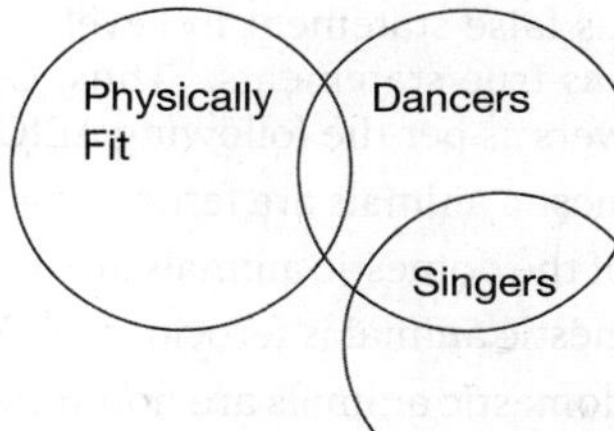

OR

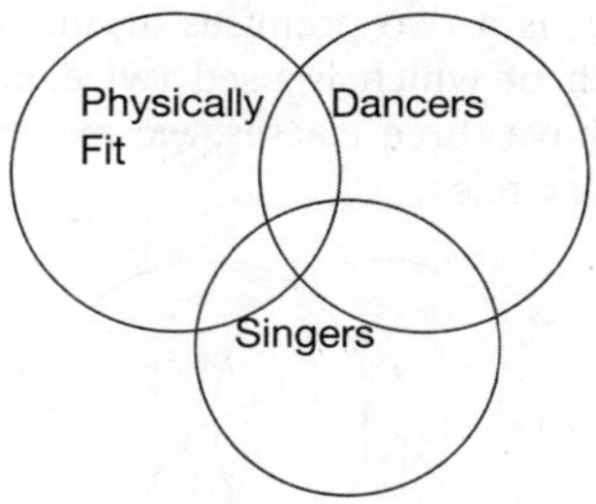

Conclusion (A)—Some of the singers are physically fit. Keeping in view with two possibilities in Venn diagrams may be true or may not be true. In case of doubt, it is not a valid conclusion. Similarly, conclusion (D) is also not a valid conclusion.

Thus, both (B) and (C) apply and hence, (b) is the right answer.

43. (d)

According to John Stuart Mills in his book *'System of Logic'* in 1843 has put the following idea:

(1) A further requirement for induction is that nature is uniform

(2) justification that inductive inferences were grounded on a commitment to the uniformity of nature; that the future will be like the past.

(3) The argument for the uniformity of nature is inductive:

- In the recent past, its near future was like the more distant past, in the more distant past, its near future was like the even more distant past, and so on.
- Therefore, hereafter the future will be like the recent past, the more distant past and the very distant past.

44. (a)

'Domestic animals are hardly ferocious' actually means that 'a very small number of domestic animals are ferocious'. In standard form, we can say that 'some animals are ferocious' (I-type). It is given as a false statement in the question. Now, we can refer to the Truth Table. 'I' is mentioned as false statement in Level 2. 'E' and 'O' are given there as true statements. Thus, C and D are the correct answers as per the following AEIO statements.

(A) All domestic animals are ferocious – A Type

(B) Some of the domestic animals are ferocious – I Type

(C) No domestic animal is ferocious – E Type

(D) Some domestic animals are non-ferocious – O Type

Thus, (c) is the correct answer.

45. (c)

A syllogism is a two premises argument having three terms, each of which is used twice in the argument. Since we have three classes, we expect to have three overlapping circles.

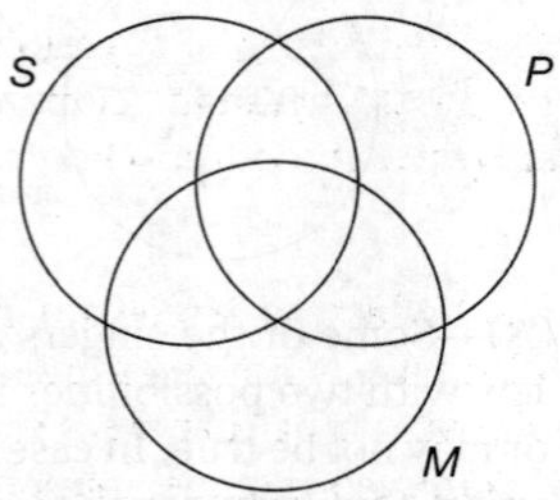

46. (b)

Inductive method is definitely more innovative. Inductive method leads us from known to unknown, particular to general or example to general rule and from concrete to abstract. When a number of concrete cases have been understood, the learner himself is able to attempt for generalization. Thus, inductive method is more useful for the subjects such as mathematics where a lot of drill is required, and there is scope for adoption of different methods.

47. (a)

This is from 'Squares of opposition'.

Contradictories:

(1) Both can not be true and both cannot be false.

(2) Relation between A and O and E and I is called contradictories:

A ⟶ O

E ⟶ I

Example:

A: All diamonds are presious stones.
O: Some diamonds are not precious stones.

E: No diamonds are precious stones.
I: Some diamonds are precious stones.

48. (a)

We need to look at figure 6.1. On left hand side, we discussed that if we move from A type to I type, there is flow of truth (from God) to lower level. The same aspect can be seen from Level I of Truth Table, if A shows truth, then I will also show the truth.

49. (c)

Inductive means moving from specific (known) to general (unknown). Unknown means there can still be exceptions.

50. (d)

This question can be solved with the help of Venn diagram:

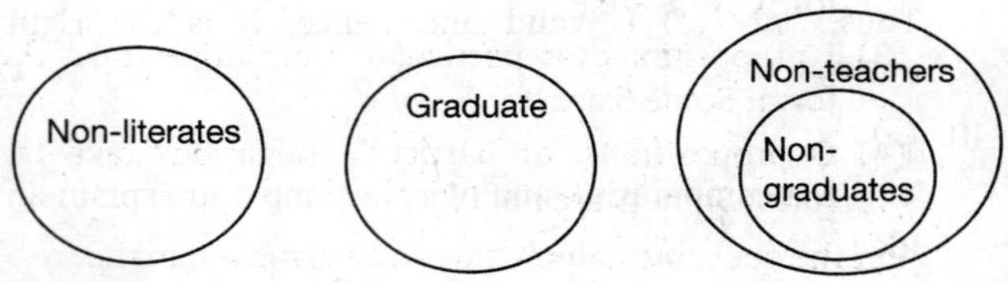

On the basis of above diagrams, we can say that

(ii) All teachers are graduates

(iv) No non-literature is a teacher.

51. (d)

This is direct definition of deductive argument, it means movement from general (theory) to specific.

52. (d)

A valid argument can have false premises; and it can have a false conclusion. But if a valid argument has all true premises, then it must have a true conclusion.

A deductive argument is said to be valid if and only if it takes a form that makes it impossible for the premises to be true and the conclusion nevertheless to be false. Otherwise, a deductive argument is said to be invalid.

53. (a)

This is because inductive reasoning starts with a conclusion and deductive reasoning starts with a premise. Therefore, inductive reasoning moves from specific instances into a generalized conclusion, while deductive reasoning moves from generalized principles that are known to be true to a true and specific conclusion.

54. (a)

This question is basically from 'square of opposition'.

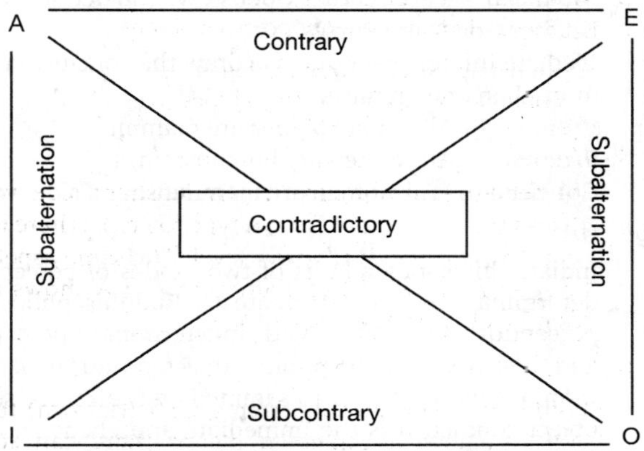

The four corners show the following four situations:

(1) A propositions, or universal affirmatives take the form: All S are P.

(2) E propositions, or universal negations take the form: No S are P.

(3) I propositions, or particular affirmatives take the form: Some S are P.

(4) O propositions, or particular negations take the form: Some S are not P.

Put the question statements can be arranged in the same manner if a learner feels so.

A and O propositions are contradictory, as are E and I propositions. Propositions are contradictory when the truth of one implies the falsity of the other, and conversely.

55. (d)

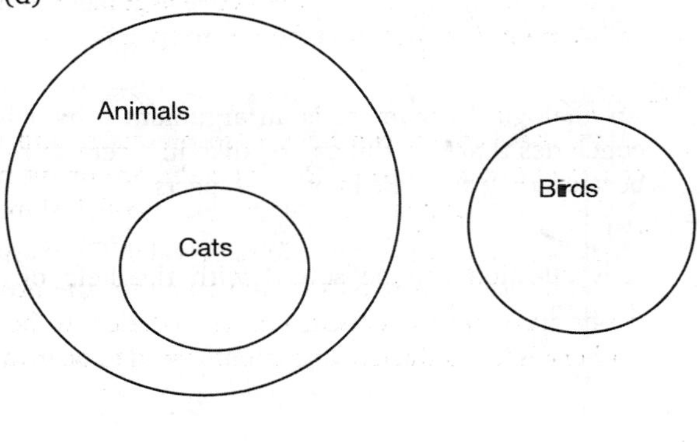

56. (a)

In inductive reasoning, we move from specific instances into a generalized conclusion or say particulars to universal.

57. (c)

Plastic is basically a synthetic material, while others have raw material as their inputs.

58. (b)

The word 'logical necessity' means that relation between premises and conclusion is direct and firm. That happens in case of 'deductive' statements. In inductive, there is scope for 'probability'.

59. (d)

Invariable concomitance is basically *'vyapati'*. *Anumana* requires the knowledge of *Vyapti* as a universal relation between the *Linga* and the *Sadhya* as the middle and major terms respectively. This knowledge of the Linga as middle term is always related to the *Sadhya* which results from the previous experience of their relation to each other.

60. (a)

All of the subject will be distributed in the class defined by the predicate. Example: 'All Judges are fair-minded' This is indicated in diagram 6.1 as well.

61. (b)

New knowledge always comes from specific (individual or particular) instances, and possible collection of such instances will make up the theory. Inductive means from specific to general.

62. (a)

Focus on the word 'like' in the question statement. There is direct mention of *upamana* (comparison) under *Pramanas* under *Nyaya* and other schools.

63. (a)

The answer is 'fallacy of irrelevant reason' where the quality of substance is not mentioned properly, that is different from the point that we see practically in this world. The examples include inappropriate appeal to pity, popular opinion, tradition, authority, etc. Suppose a student fails in an exam, and requests the teacher to pass him in the exam, otherwise 'his parents will be upset'. Since the marks in the exam are given on the basis of performance, but the reason being given is quite irrelevant.

The fallacy of irrelevant reasons has the following forms.

Red herring – This entails distracting the attention of listeners from the topic under discussion.

Appeal to Emotion (argumentum ad populum) – To make use of feelings and prejudices of the people, we don't focus on the reason.

Missing the point (ignoration elenchi) – It is diverting attention from the real point.

Argument from ignorance (argumentum ad ignorantiam) – It is similar to taking advantage of the ignorance of the opponent.

The Straw Man – This is the way to argue against some view by presenting an opponent's position.

Argument against the person (argumentum ad hominem) – that involves attacking the character of the opponent, instead of approving and disapproving the point at issue.

Appeal to force (argumentum ad baculum) – this involves using the force to make opponent to submit.

The appeal to inappropriate authority (argumentum as verecundiam) – Here, we take Godly view of someone's suggestion. If Amitabh Bachchan says that an investment company is the best, we may start investing in that, we may not know about the reputation of that company.

Misericordiam – This is actually an appeal to pity. This method may be used by criminals to escape the punishment.

64. (b)

Validity is a property of the argument (or test) itself. So if a test is valid, it is reliable also. Again, validity refers to how well a test measures what it is supposed to measure. While reliability is necessary, it alone is not sufficient. For a test to be reliable, it also needs to be valid.

65. (c)

We can directly pick (c) as the answer.

In conclusion, we can say that 'No criminals (S / Minor Term) are gentlemen (P / Major term)'.

By definition, Major Term is the predicate (P) of conclusion. Major term lies in the Major Premise.

And Minor Term is the subject (S) of the conclusion. Minor term lies in the Minor Premise.

Middle Term – occurs in both the premises, that is given to be 'polite'.

66. (a)

Fallacy of trivial reasons is an informal logical fallacy where irrelevant and sometimes frivolous objections are made to divert the attention away from the topic that is being discussed. Trivial objections are a special case of red herring.

67. (a)

Here, we can take some idea from the question itself that mentions 'from Universal Proposition', it indicates that proposition is universal in nature. Deductive also says that we move from Universal to Particular (Inductive from Particular to Universal).

In addition, we can say that deductive is of two types - immediate and mediate inference.

Immediate Inference - if we deduce the conclusion from a single premise. For example, from the premise, "Some Purses are Leather Goods", we can deduce "Some Leather Goods are Purses".

Mediate Inference – When we draw the conclusion from more than one premise.

Premise 1 - All human beings are mammals.

Premise 2 - All women are human beings.

Conclusion - All women are mammals.

68. (b)

Indian philosophy admits of two modes of perception- determinate and indeterminate. (In Buddhist philosophy perception is identified with indeterminate perception and determinate perception is rejected outright). Indeterminate perception arises immediately after the sense-object contact. It is the immediate apprehension of an object, without any determination of the name of the object or the class to which the object belongs. It is the direct awareness of an object.

69. (b)

Since there is use of words 'highly superficial level', only prediction fits here.

70. (c)

A proposition asserts that the entire subject class is included in the predicate class ('All S are P'). But it carries the same meaning if the subject becomes negative and so is the predicate.

71. (a)

The answer is mentioned under 'square of opposition'. As discussed there, quantity refers to difference between universal and particular which are given at two levels. They differ in quantity. Thus 'subaltern' is the right answer. (We mentioned God and Devils in that discussion for easy recall).

72. (c)

An analogical argument is an argument in which one concludes that two things are alike in a certain respect because they are alike in other respects.

73. (b)

This question can be solved with the help of Venn diagram.

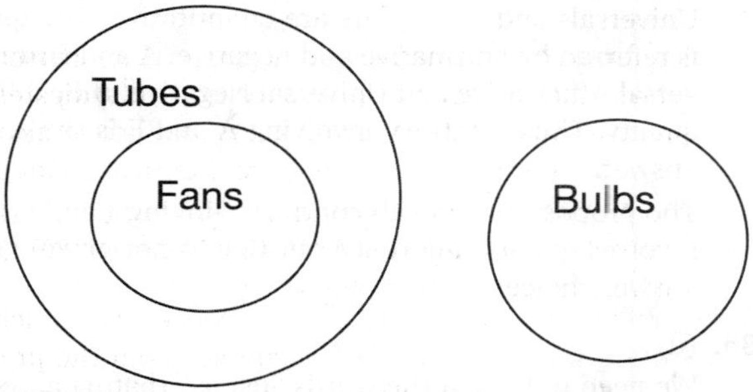

74. (a)

We may attempt this question directly also, by removing 'not' that is affixed before pencils.

If 'all pens are not pencil' is true then we can say that 'all pens are pencils' as false statement.

'All pens are not pencil' can be converted to 'Some pens are not pencils' that is of O type.

Now look at figure 6.1 that shows Truth Table.

Level 4 shows O type as true, then A type is false.

In question, examiner is asking for 'all pens are pencils' as false. In the 'Truth Table (figure 6.1), A type is showing false.

75. (b)

Inductive argument moves from 'Specific to General' or 'Particular to Universal'. An inductive argument is an argument in which it is thought that the premises provide reasons supporting the probable truth of the conclusion. In an inductive argument, the premises are intended only to be so strong that, if they are true, then it is unlikely that the conclusion is false.

76. (a)

Arthapatti is the fifth of the six *pranamas*, with the other five being:

(1) *Pratyaksha*–perception
(2) *Anumana*–inference
(3) *Sabda*–testimony
(4) *Upamana*–comparison
(5) *Anupalabdhi*–non-perception

Arthapatti refers to the way in which knowledge is derived from a set of circumstances.

The central idea is that there is some kind of tension which arises from a new fact being cognized, against the background of another fact, which cannot be resolved without the postulation of third fact. In example given above, the tension is between Devadatta being fat and his not eating during the day.

77. (a)

Premise 1 – No Musician (S) are Japanese (P).
Premise 2 – All barbers (S) are Musician (P)
Conclusion – No Barber (S) are Japanese (P).

Thus, we can get (a) as the right answer.
Musician is the Middle Term here.

78. (a)

Contradictory premises involve an argument (generally considered a logical fallacy) that draws a conclusion from inconsistent or incompatible premises. Essentially, a proposition is contradictory when it asserts and denies the same thing. To be logically committed to the assertion of some statement, S, and it's denial, not-S, at the same time.

79. (c)

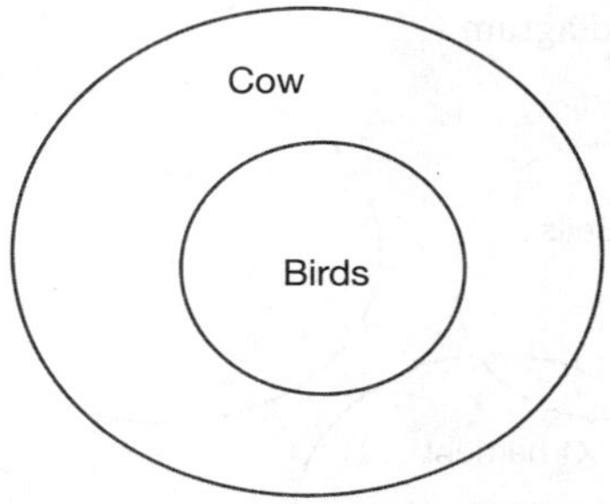

(i) As 'some cows are birds' is true, so is the statement 'birds are cows' also stands true.
(ii) Some cows are not 'non-birds' is also true, as birds are cows.
(iii) From the diagram, we can say that 'some birds are cows' is also true.
(iv) 'Many birds are cows' can be converted into 'some birds are cows'. That has already been put as true, that has been given in diagram as well.

Thus, (c) is the correct answer.

80. (d)

If 'students are serious' is false. Then putting it in standard format, 'All students are not serious' is true. We discussed in answer 16 that 'some' is a part of 'all'.

So, (iii) is also true—'some students are not serious'.

Thus, (ii) and (iii) are correct answers. Hence (d) option is right.

81. (a)

An analogy is a comparison usually either a metaphor or a simile that helps to explain something or make it clearer. Analogical things use analogies or refer to them. A comparison like 'You are quiet as a mouse' or 'My brother was a pig at dinner' is analogical. The Greek root is analogous, 'proportionate.'

82. (c)

We need to look at figure 6.1 for square of opposition.

The two terms given above that are A and E are Universal (in nature, and they are contrary).

The propositions I and O are both particular, and they are sub contraries.

The Sub altern A and I are both affirmative and are qualitative.

Propositions E and O are negative and both are qualitative.

The only option left is contradictories A and O and E and I. A is Universal that is Quantitative and O is Particular but that is Qualitative. Same is the case with E (Universal – Quantitative) and I is (Particular – Qualitative).

Thus, (c) is the correct answer.

83. (d)

Let's go for a Venn diagram

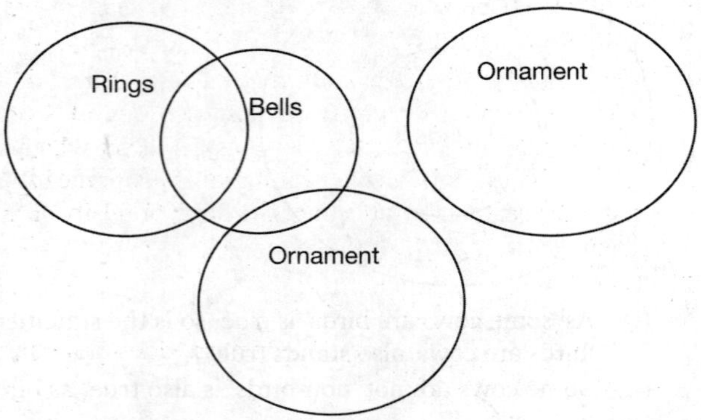

All ornaments can be within bells also, but still not linked with rings.

'All bells are not ornaments' is the right conclusion as we see in the diagram.

84. (c)

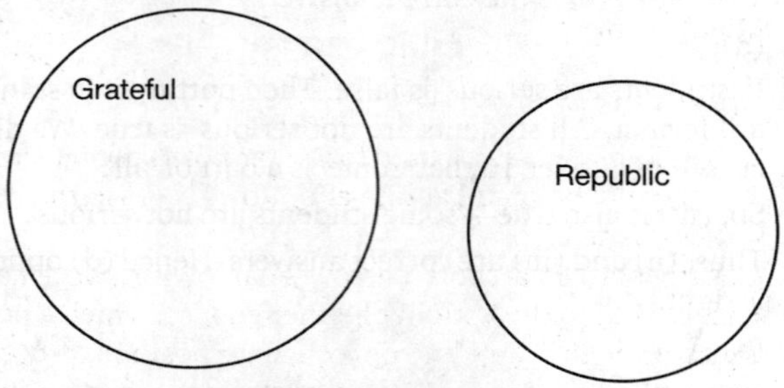

Here we need to assume that some are also part of all. So, first three options are right. Thus, fourth choice does not apply.

'Republics are not grateful' should be out of Venn diagram.

Same is the case with 'some republics are not grateful' and 'no republics are grateful'.

85. (b)

We need to look at figure 6.1 for square of opposition diagram.

Universals and particulars are quantitative. The quality is referred by affirmative and negative. A and E are Universal Affirmative and Universal Negative, they differ in quality. Thus, contrary involving A and E is the correct answer.

The propositions in sub contrary (linking I and O) also involves quality difference but that is not given among answer choices.

86. (d)

We need to look at the words 'just as', that means some comparison is being done. Hence, 'analogical' is the answer.

Analogical terms use analogy and metaphor in assuming that one thing is like and therefore, identical to another thing.

87. (c)

Let's make a Venn diagram:

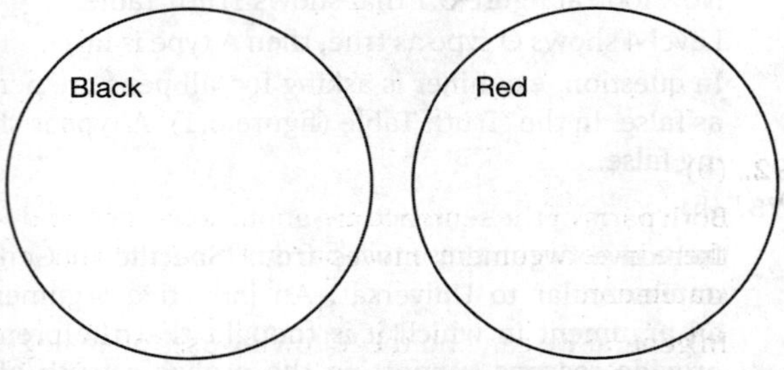

First and fourth statements are right as showed in Venn diagram.

88. (a)

This question can be attempted with Venn diagram:

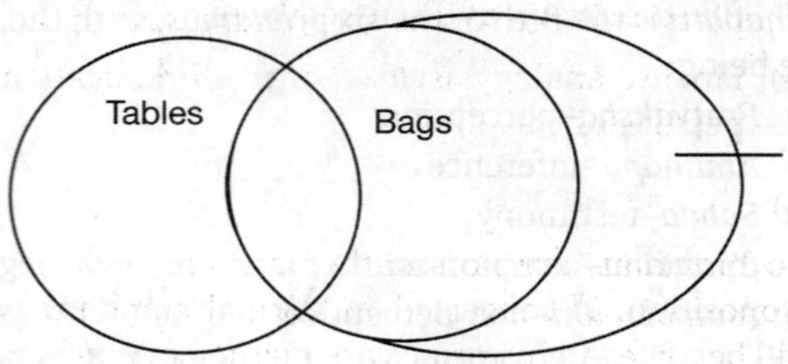

89. (b)

'Every *S* is *P*' and 'Some *S* is not *P*' are contradictories. Some theories of logic consider not only oppositions between propositions but also oppositions between terms ('well' and 'not well'; 'moral' and 'immoral') as contradictories.

Two categorical propositions are contradictories if they are opposed in both quantity and quality; i.e., if one is universal ('every') and the other particular ('some') and one an affirmation and the other a denial.

90. (d)

'Houses are not bricks' is false. Thus, 'houses are bricks' is true. All the houses are bricks is not true as all is not mentioned so we can not take the statement as right. Some is taken as true as it is mentioned in the premise, so 'some houses are bricks' is true.

91. (c)

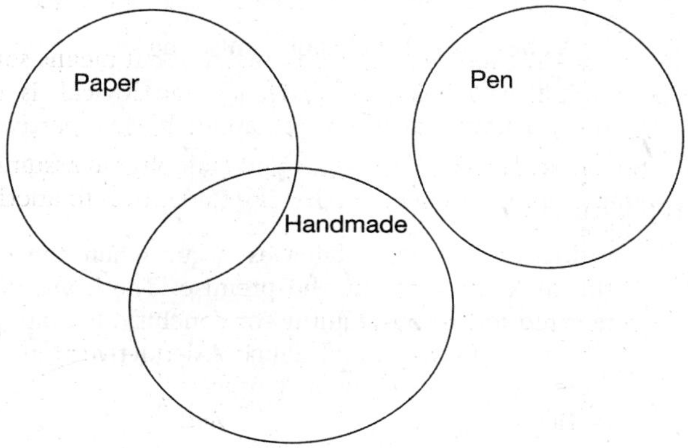

92. (b)

Both parts of the sentence are about some 'use' and 'as' is there in between these two parts. Thus, it is a analogical statement.

In general we can find the following uses of analogy.

(1) Analogies are used in explaining new concepts.

(2) The use of analogy is also in making predictions within domains.

(3) Analogy is also important in creativity and scientific discovery, as discussed later.

(4) Finally, analogy is used in communication and persuasion.

93. (a)

'No historians are non-mathematicians' is a negative proposition. If converted in normal standard way it will become 'All historians are mathematicians'

94. (a)

Indian epistemology accepts six means of knowledge (*pramanas*): perception, inference, verbal testimony, comparison, presumption, and non-cognition. Non-cognition is basically '*Anupalabdhi*'.

Kindly focus on the word, that is 'now' in the statement. It means that jar was there earlier. *Anupalabdhi* (non-cognition) is the only means of the cognition of non-existence. It yields knowledge of absence where an object would be immediately perceived if it were there.

95. (b)

We know that some is always a part of whole. Suppose, we have 26 alphabets and some of them (say vowels – A, E, I, O and U) are part of it.

In the same manner, if I say 'all children are not greedy', I can say that 'some children are not greedy'. If we compare with figure 6.1, then this sentence falls under proposition 'O' that is particular negative. Thus, d is the correct answer.

96. (a)

"No S are P is same as All S are not P" Which is called Universal Negative.

When the sign is unique and resides neither in similar nor in dissimilar locations, for instance, sound is permanent because it is audible. It is a reason which is given in support of a conclusion that is insignificant or a trivial reason in establishing the truth or falsity of the conclusion.

97. (d)

An inductive argument, in contrast, does not make such a claim.

98. (b)

Cup and bowl are two containers for coffee and soup, respectively.

99. (a)

By definition, the subject of conclusion is called as 'Minor Term'.

100. (c)

An oar is an implement used for water-borne propulsion. Oars have a flat blade at one end. Rowers grasp the oar at the other end.

A skateboard is a short narrow board with two small wheels fixed to the bottom of either end, on which a person can ride in a standing or crouching position, propelling themselves by occasionally pushing one foot against the ground.

101. (b)

The slippery slope fallacy is a logical fallacy, where an argument is put forth which asserts that:

(a) A small action will produce a chain of events, which will lead to a negative outcome.

(b) The idea behind slippery slope arguments is that we should not do something such as *A* because *A* will lead to *B* and *B* will lead to *C* and so on until we end up with something bad.

102. (a)

Anupalabdhi or Abhava is a means of knowledge.

Anupalabdhi is a separate independent pramana, which literally means an opinion or an idea on any subject. Non-existence of a thing is apprehended by its non-perception. For example, I do not find the pot on the table. Therefore, it is absent there.

103. (a)

An **argument** is the process by which one explains how a conclusion was reached. **Logic** is the science that we use to explain or represent a consistent argument about a particular topic. There are mainly four ways of presenting an argument – Deductive (with more focus on it), Inductive, Abductive and Analogy.

The argument has premise/s and a conclusion in a combined manner that has valid and invalid features. While true or false is about the statements only - individual premises and conclusion.

Thus, we get (a) as the correct answer.

Specifically, for future questions, we can say that an argument in which the premises do succeed in guaranteeing the conclusion is called a (deductively) *valid argument*. If a valid argument has 'true' premises, then the argument is said also to be sound.

Note that all arguments are either valid or invalid, and either sound or unsound; there is NO middle ground (such as half valid or invalid), such as being somewhat valid.

104. (c)

There are basically six rules of syllogism that must be kept in mind so that (deductive) argument is valid.

1. The middle term must be distributed at least once. (Figures are also based on distribution of Middle term).
2. If a term is distributed in the conclusion, it must also be distributed in its corresponding premise.
3. A categorical syllogism cannot have two negative premises.
4. A negative premise must have a negative conclusion.
5. A negative conclusion must have a negative premise.
6. Two universal premises cannot have a particular conclusion.

105. (a)

Deductive (formula) fallacies occur when the conclusion doesn't follow the premise. These are often referred to as non-sequiturs or conclusions that have nothing to do with initial claims. A deductive argument often follows the following pattern.

i. All dogs have legs.

ii. Tiny is a dog.

Therefore, Tiny has legs.

106. (b)

Let's look at the complete example.

1. Fat Devadatta does not eat during day time.
2. But, he does not lose weight.

These two contradictory statements are reconciled with *arthāpatti pramāa,* that he must be eating during night. *Arthāpatti pramāa* is a Sanskrit term meaning implication. Thus (b) is the right answer.

107. (d)

The review of 'categorical propositions' can help.

Type	Form	Quantity	Quality	Distribution	
				Subject	Predicate
A	All S is P	Universal	Affirmative	Distributed	Undistributed
E	No S is P	Universal	Negative	Distributed	Distributed
I	Some S is P	Particular	Affirmative	Undistributed	Undistributed
O	Some S is not P	Particular	Negative	Undistributed	Distributed

We need to look at statement – 'Some girls are not students'. This statement goes with Type 'O'.

Here, the 'girls' is a subject as we are discussing her as a person or thing, she does something.

Predicate means which tells something about the subject.

108. (d)

Anumana means the method by which knowledge is derived from other knowledge. It is a universal proposition. Udāharan means instance as given in option (d).

109. (c)

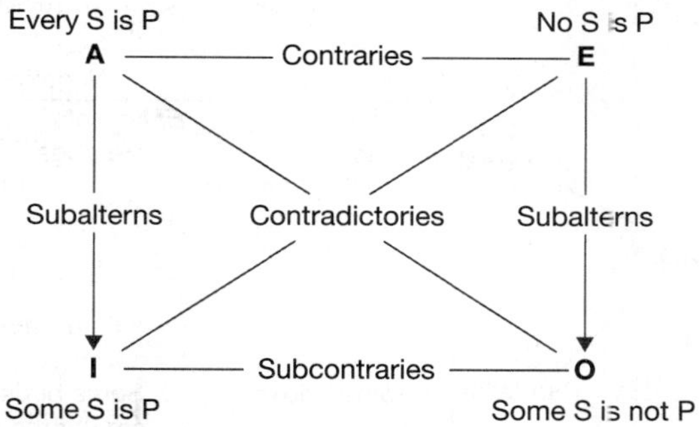

'All poets are dreamers' is 'A-Type'.

'No poets are dreamers' is 'E-Type'.

Contraries are pair of propositions in which both cannot be true but both can be false. 'A' and 'E' are contrary statements.

110. (a)

We need to look at figure 6.1 for Truth Table under square of opposition, and look at Level 1. In that diagram, we have been given that if A proposition is true, then in the same row, E is false, I is true and O is false. Thus, Truth Table is a smart measure to get answers in minimal time. So, remember that.

111. (b)

This is direct question of words and their meanings. They probably fall under the topic of languages.

112. (c)

The converse of a categorical or implicational statement is the result of reversing its two constituent statements. For the implication $P \rightarrow Q$ the converse is $Q \rightarrow P$ for the categorical proposition all S are P, the converse is all P are S is not applicable in universal affirmative. Either way, the statement 'some mammals are cats' can be conversed.

113. (b)

Ad misericordium is an argument based on a strong appeal to the emotions. Also known as argumentum Ad misericordium or appeal to pity of misery.

When an appeal to sympathy as pity is highly exaggerated or irrelevant to the issue at hand, ad misericordium is regarded as a logical fallacy.

Example Mr. X lives in a slum and is unemployed. Therefore, Mr. X deserves to be a minister. It is a strong appeal to the emotions.

114. (c)

Distribution is the status of a term in regard to extension. The subject term is distributed in statement whose quantity is universal and undistributed. The given statement is universal as it includes 'No' with the subject 'Dog' so, the subject is distributed.

In affirmative propositions the predicate term always taken particularly (and therefore in distributed) and in negative propositions the predicate is always taken universally (and therefore distributed). The given statement is a negative proposition so predicate 'are reptiles' is universal and distributed.

115. (c)

(a) It is related to form of the argument only

(b) It is related to the context of the argument only

116. (b)

Upamana is not a step when you present an argument based on inference before the others according to the classical Indian school of logic. Upamana (Sanskrit: Comparison) is one of the pramana of Indian school of logic.

Upamana in Indian school of logic is a pramana or means of having knowledge of something observance of similarities provides knowledge of relationship between the two. It also means getting the knowledge of an unknown thing by comparing it with a known thing.

117. (c)

Equivocation means to slide between two or more different meaning of a word or phrase that is critical to the argument. For an argument to work, the words must have the same meaning throughout the premise and the conclusion.

'A mouse is an animal. Therefore, a large mouse is a large animal.'

This argument illustrates the ambiguous use of a relative word. The word 'large' means different things, depending on the context.

118. (a)

Pramana means proof and means of knowledge.

Perception (Pratyaksha) is that which is before one's eyes. Yogaja is an intuitive and immediate perception of all the objects of the past, present, and future. This form of perception is only possessed by yogis or the liberated souls through the power of meditation. Hence, it is supra-sensuous and supra-relational in nature.

(1) Perception is of two types namely, external perception that arising from the interaction of five senses and worldly objects, and internal perception means the inner sense, the mind.

In Indian philosophy, perception is the first of the five means of knowledge or that helps a person to have correct cognitions of the world.

(2) Inference (Anumāna) means knowing after or measuring along some other thing.

(3) Verbal testimony (Shabda), where we learn mostly by means of words. An oral or written message is a universal mode of communication.

(4) Comparison (Upamāa) is a distinct means of knowledge and cannot be clubbed under Anumāna because a knowledge cannot be gained without the comparison of the two similar.

119. (c)

Subcontrary: Denoting preposition which can both be true but cannot be false.

For example, some *x* are *y* and some *x* are not *y*.

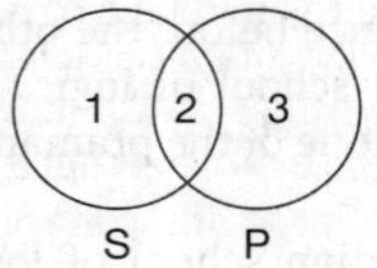

1 = *S* that are not *P*

2 = *S* that are *P*

3 = *P* that are not *S*

120. (d)

We need to look at figure 6.1 for square of opposition. All tigers (S) are animals (P) that is represented by proposition A and is called as Universal Affirmative.

121. (c)

Pratyaksha "that which is before one's eyes," perception is of two types– External – that arising from the interaction of five senses and wordly objects and Internal–perception of inner sense, the mind.

In Indian philosophy, perception, the first of the five means of knowledge, as pramanas, that enable a person to have correct cognitions of the world.

Pratyaksha is of two kinds, direct perception (anubhawa) and remembered perception (smriti).

122. (c)

If the subject category is named S and the predicate category is named P, the four standard forms are:

All students are sincere – (A Form) Universal Affirmative

No students are sincere – (E Form) Universal Negative

Some students are sincere – (I Form) Particular Affirmative

Some students are not sincere – (O Form) Particular Negative

The categorical propositions can be put in the following form also.

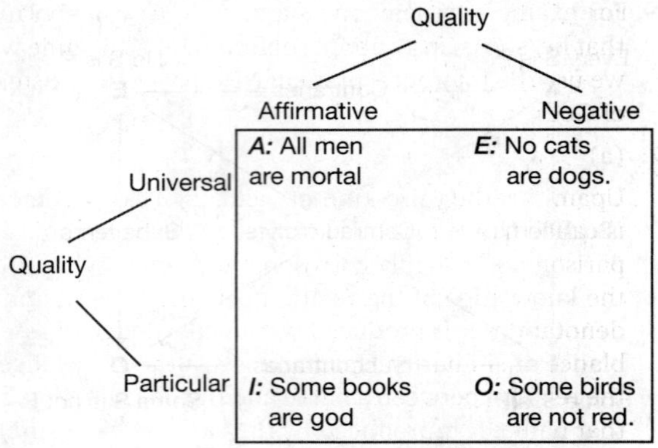

123. (d)

1. Deductive reasoning is a specific conclusion follows a general theory.
2. When we are using deductive reasoning, our conclusions will be correct if all the statements stated by us are correct.

Examples

1. All students in this class play guitar.

Sam is a student of this class. Therefore, Sam plays guitar.

2. Suppose 3 X = 12,

Here, we conclude X = 4

3. If the length of a rectangle is 6 and its width is 5, we conclude its area is 30.

124. (a)

All students clear their examination – A type

Few (some) students did not clear their examination – O type

They are linked as contradictories, so this instance gets reflected in answer (a).

125. (a)

Ad Populum: Also referred as the bandwagon fallacy, the arguer tries to convince the audience to do or believe something because everyone else does.

Ad Populum: Is a fallacious argument that concludes that a proposition must be true because many or most people believe it often concisely encapsulated as "if many believe so, it is so."

Example – An increasing number of people are turning to yoga as a way to get in touch with their inner-being.

126. (d): Anumāna is also known as inference. An inference is an idea or a conclusion that is drawn from an evidence and reasoning. An inference is an educated guess from which we learn about something by experiencing them first-hand but we gain other knowledge by inference—the process of inferring things based on what is already known.

For example, if someone slams a door, you can infer that he/she is upset about something. In the same way, we use the inference 'pramanas' to prove the existence of God.

127. (a)

Upamiti is the third kind of valid cognition, its means is called Upamana. It is knowledge derived from comparison and roughly corresponds to analogy. It is also the knowledge of the relation between a word and its denotation. It is produced by the knowledge of resemblance or similarity. Upamana is just the knowledge of the relation between a name and the object denoted by that name. It is produced by the knowledge of similarity because a man recognizes a wild cow as a 'gavaya' when he perceives its similarity to the cow and remembers the description that 'a gavaya is an animal like a cow'.

Verbal Testimony (Shabda) is a valid source of knowledge in Indian systems.It is the statement of a trustworthy person (aptavakya) and consists in understanding its meaning. A sentence is defined as a collection of words and a word is defined as that which is potent to convey its meaning. The Nyaya states that the power in a word to convey its meaning comes from God. According to later Nyaya, it comes from long established convention. Testimony is always personal. Testimony is of two kinds- Vaidika (spoken by God) and secular (laukika). Thus, vaidika testimony is perfect and infallible because the Vedas are spoken by God.

128. (c)

The Greek philosopher Aristotle is considered the father of deductive reasoning, he discovered deductive reasoning. He wrote the classic example: All men are mortal. Socrates is a man. Therefore, Socrates is mortal.

Aristotle's example is called a syllogism. A syllogism uses deductive reasoning to arrive at a conclusion that is based on two or more propositions that are assumed to be true.

Aristotle is popular for pure verbalism (though Indian logic does not believe much in verbalism).

129. (d)

Like the Aristotelian syllogism, the Indian inference has three terms:

1. minor term : paksha (पक्ष)
2. middle term : linga (लिंग) or hetu (हेतु)
3. major term : sadhya (साध्य)

Example:
If we see smoke in a hill, we conclude that there must be fire in that hill.

minor term paksha : hill

major term sadhya : fire

middle term linga : smoke

Vyapti : smoke is invariably associated with fire The following aspects are important as this question is a combination of our ancient logic system and western logic system.

The first thing to know is anvaya-vyatireki. These words, taken together are parts of vyapati.

1. Anvaya (agreement in presence) can be described in this manner—wherever there is smoke, there ought to be fire (as in the kitchen). It means that the hetu and the sâdhya should agree in being present together. There should not be any case in which one is present and the other is absent.
2. Vyatireka is where there is no fire, there ought to be no smoke (as in a lake or a river). The hetu and the sâdhya should agree in being absent together.

There may be a case where there is a fire, but there is no smoke, like in a red hot iron rod. The fire in the iron rod can be readily experienced by touching it (pratyaksha) and there is no need to resort to anumana there. So even in the absence of smoke, fire is realised. Thus, positively (agreement in presence) and negatively (agreement in absence) terms given in the question are being discussed here. These two steps taken together correspond to Mill's joint method of agreement in presence and in absence in modern theory.

Again, for sake of our repetition. In our inference of the presence of fire in a hill what is the justification of our inference? First, we perceive the presence of smoke which is the mark (the middle term or hetu or paka). This presence of the middle term in the minor term is known as pakadharmatâ. Secondly, we recollect the invariable relation between the middle term (Madhya) and the major term (sâdhya).

130. (c)

Option (c) showing some association, so it should be the answer.

131. (a)

The name 'Asidha' is attached with first three. This is the fallacy of the unproved middle. The middle term must be present in the minor term (pakshadharmata). If it is not, it is unproved. It is of three kinds.

A. Ashraya asidha: The minor term is the locus of the middle term. If the minor term is unreal, the middle term cannot be present in it. For example,'the sky-lotus is fragrant, because it is a lotus, like the lotus of a lake'.

B. Svarupa asidha: Here the minor term is not unreal. But the middle term cannot be its very nature be present in the minor term. For example, 'sound is a quality, because it is visible'. Here visibility cannot belong to sound which is audible'.

C. Vyapyatva asidha: Here Vyapti is conditional (sopadhika). We cannot say,' wherever there is fire there is smoke'. Fire smokes only when it is associated with wet fuel. A red - hot iron ball or clear fire does not smoke. Hence 'Association with wet fuel' is a condition necessary to the aforesaid vyapti. Being conditioned, the middle term becomes fallacious if we say: 'The hill has smoke because it has fire'.

132. (b)

Deduction means moving from universal to particular. Deduction is basically scientific approach to do research as well. It can be identified more with positivism.

133. (a)

Human beings are conscious not only of the world around them but also of themselves: their activities, their bodies, and their mental lives. Thus, they are self-conscious or self-aware. Self-consciousness can be understood as an awareness of oneself.

The second is about Greek maxim – 'know thyself'. That is to know yourself is to know the world.

134. (a)

Statement I: Knowledge is a recollection of facts. Competencies are the person's knowledge and behaviours that lead them to be successful in a job.

Statement II: Understanding is achieved through effective communication.

Thus, both statements are true.

135. (b)

The knowledge through has been classified into

1. svartha – for oneself – one's own inferential knowledge, through linking it with major and minor premises.
2. parartha – through justification of middle term – inferential knowledge for another.
3. **Pararthanumana** – If the motive is for demonstrating the truth of the conclusion to others it is called as Pararthanumana. Here, conclusion is arrived at through justification of the middle term that leads to it. A man having inferred the existence of fire in a hill lays it down as a thesis and proves it as a conclusion following from the major and minor premises and their combination into a third premise. The latter has a five membered syllogism viz., pratijna, hetu, udaharana, upanaya and nigamana.

1st member – **Pratijna** (preposition) — the hill is fiery

2nd member – **Hetu** (reason) — because of smoke

3rd member – **Udaharana** (example) — wherever smoke exists, fire also exists as in kitchen.

4th member – **Upanaya** (application / subsumptive correlative) — there is smoke on the hill.

5th member – **Nigamana** (conclusion) — Hence, the hill is fiery

Apart from above five, the few of the old Naiyayikas speaks of other five members of syllogism:

- Jijnasa — on the desire to know the truth.
- Samsaya — doubt about real nature of a thing.
- Shakyaprapti — the capacity of the pramanas to lead to true knowledge.
- Prayojana — the purpose of making an inference
- Samshaya vyudasa — the removal of all doubts the truth of an inference.

Though Vatsyayana disagreed with the first five and stated them as irrelevant.

136. (c)

This question pertains to irregular behaviour of 'Middle Term'. We can solve other questions, linked directly with Indian philosophy as in the following manner.

The fallacies in Anumana that can be termed as hetvabhasha may occur due to the following:

(i) Asiddha: This fallacy occurs due to unproved hetu. It is also called as Paksadharmata.

(a) Ashrayasiddha: If Paksha (minor term) itself is unreal, then there cannot be locus of the hetu. For example, The sky–lotus is fragrant, because it is a lotus like any other lotus.

(b) Svarupasiddha: It is not possible that Hetu exist in paksa. For example, sound is a quality, because it is visible.

(c) Vyapyatvasiddha: This is termed as **'conditional hetu'**. For example, 'wherever there is fire, there is smoke'. The presence of smoke is because of wet fuel.

(ii) Savyabhichara: This is termed as the fallacy of irregular hetu.

(a) Sadharana: Here, the hetu is considered too wide. It is present in both sapaksa and vipaksa. 'The hill has fire because it is knowable'.

(b) Asadharana: Here, the hetu is considered too narrow. It is present only in the Paksha. It is not present in the Sapaksa and in the Vipaksha. For example, 'sound is eternal because it is audible'.

(c) Anupasamhari

(iii) Satpratipaksa: In this case, one hetu is contradicted by another hetu. In case, both have equal force, then nothing should follow. For example, 'sound is eternal, because it is audible', and 'sound is non–eternal, because it is produced'. The word, 'audible' is counterbalanced by 'produced'. Here, 'audible' and 'produced' carry the equal force.

(iv) Badhita: Here, the another proof (as defined by perception) definitely contradicts and disproves the middle term (hetu). For example, 'fire is cold because it is a substance'.

(v) Viruddha: Here, the virudha, instead of proving something it is proving the opposite. For example, 'sound is eternal because it is produced'.

137. (a)

We need to refer to Truth Table – figure 6.1.

Question statement: All men are mortal – A – given as True

If we look at Level 1, then we get answer for the following statements.

A. No men is mortal – E – given as False
B. Some men are not mortal – I – given as True
D. Some men are not mortal – O – given as False

Thus, correct answer is (a).

138. (b)

Exclusive premise: The fallacy of exclusive premises is a syllogistic fallacy committed in a categorical syllogism that is invalid because both of its premises are negative.

Illicit major: Illicit major is a formal fallacy committed in a categorical syllogism that is invalid because its major term is undistributed in the major premise but distributed in the conclusion.

Premise	Type	Distributed
Some birds are not beautiful creatures.	'O' type (Particular negative)	Only predicate
Therefore, no dogs are birds.	E type (Universal negative)	Both subject and predicate

Thus, in premises 1 some birds (major term / subject) are undistributed. In the conclusion dogs (subject) and the birds (predicate) both are distributed.

Undistributed middle: The fallacy of the undistributed middle is a formal fallacy that is committed when the middle term in a categorical syllogism is not distributed in either the minor premise or the major premise. It is thus a **syllogistic fallacy**.

Illicit minor: the fallacy of illicit minor term is undistributed in the premise but is distributed in the conclusion (but not vice – versa).

139. (c)

The denotative meaning of a word is simply the commonly accepted meaning or the definition that you would find if you were to look up that word in a dictionary.

Typically, the connotative meaning of a word has more of an emotional association and is more likely to trigger an emotional response than the denotative meaning.

140. (b)

Truth and falsehood are predicates of a statement and validity and invalidity are predicates of an argument.

141. (b)

Existential fallacy: In modern times, presupposition that **a class has members is seen as unacceptable.** In 1905, Bertrand Russell wrote an essay entitled, 'The Existential Import of Proposition', in which he called this Boolean approach 'Peano's interpretation'. In an existential fallacy, we presuppose that a class has members even when we are not explicitly told so, that is, we assume that the class has existential import.

Exclusive premise: The fallacy of exclusive premises is a syllogistic fallacy committed in a categorical syllogism that is invalid because both of its premises are negative.

Illicit major: Illicit major is a formal fallacy committed in a categorical syllogism that is invalid because its major term is undistributed in the major premise but distributed in the conclusion.

Undistributed middle: The fallacy of the undistributed middle is a formal fallacy that is committed when the middle term in a categorical syllogism is not distributed in either the minor premise or the major premise. It is thus a syllogistic fallacy.

142. (c)

Mood: Mood depends the type of propositions (A, E, I or O). The mood of a syllogism is determined by the 'quantity' and 'quality' of the three propositions.

Figure: The figure of a categorical syllogism is determined by 'middle term'. It is a number which corresponds to the placement of two middle terms.

Figure 1: When the middle term is on the left in Premise 1 and on the right of Premise 2.

Figure 2: When the middle term is on the right in both premises.

Figure 3: When the middle term is on the left in both premises.

Figure 4: When the middle term is on the right in Premise 1 and on the left of Premise 2.

The following diagram may help to remember the position of figure in a categoral syllogism.

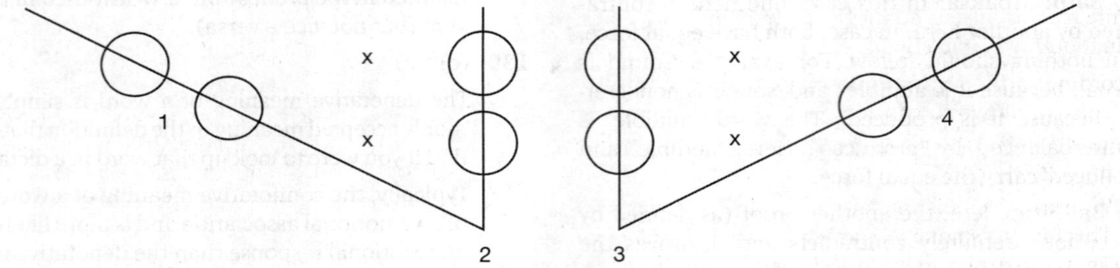

143. (b)

We need to follow the following Truth Table to match List I and List II.

Propositions	A	E	I	O
Level 1	T	F	T	F
Level 2	F	T	F	T
Level 3	D	F	T	D
Level 4	F	D	D	T

Thus, by matching, we can see that (b) is the correct answer.

In this we need to be careful that we pursue True and False in the diagonals. For example, if A is true, we look at Level 1 and see that O is False and E is also False in that level.

144. (d)

The name 'Asidha' is attached with first three. This is the fallacy of the unproved middle. The middle term must be present in the minor term (pakshadharmata). If it is not, it is unproved. It is of three kinds.

A. Ashraya asidha: The minor term is the locus of the middle term. If the minor term is unreal, the middle term cannot be present in it. For example,' the sky-lotus is fragrant, because it is a lotus, like the lotus of a lake'.

B. Svarupa asidha: Here the minor term is not unreal. But the middle term cannot be its very nature be present in the minor term. For example, 'sound is a quality, because it is visible'. Here, visibility cannot belong to sound which is audible.

C. Vyapyatva asidha: Here, Vyapti is conditional (sopadhika). We cannot say,' wherever there is fire there is smoke'. Fire smokes only when it is associated with wet fuel. A red-hot iron ball or clear fire does not smoke. Hence, 'Association with wet fuel' is a condition necessary to the aforesaid vyapti. Being conditioned, the middle term becomes fallacious if we say: 'The hill has smoke because it has fire'.

145. (c)

A. Puravavat inference (a prior): Vatsyayana gives two types of interpretations to purvavat. It is an inference in which the effect is inferred from the cause. The inference of rain seeing a cloud is the example given.

B. Sheshavat inference (a posterior): Here we infer the unperceived cause from a perceived effect.

For example, when we see a river in flood and infer that there was heavy rain. It is case of Sheshavat inference.

C. Samanyatodrista inference (commonly seen): Samanyatodrista refers to the inference based on merely experience. Seeing the Sun in the East in the morning, in the middle in the afternoon and in the west at evening twilight, the movement is inferred.

Psychologically, it has been classified into:

(i) svartha (one's own inferential knowledge) and

(ii) parartha (inferential knowledge of another).

D. Anupsamhari: All matter is eternal, because it is knowable.

Thus, if the cause of the inference is related to the end, neither as a cause nor as an action, but they are equally related to each other in our experience, it is said to be generalisable.

146. (d)

We may refer to answer of question 109 as well.

We need to recall that these personalities played an important role in the development of Indian logic – Anviksiki of Medhatithi Gautama, Sanskrit grammar rules of Pāṇini, Vaisheshika school's analysis of Atomism, Analysis of inference by Gotama (or Gautama), from Nyaya school and the Tetralemma of Nagarjuna.

We must know that an **argument** is the process by which one explains how a conclusion was reached. **Logic** is the science that we use to explain or represent a consistent argument about a particular topic. There are mainly four ways of presenting an argument – Deductive (with more focus on it), Inductive, Abductive and Analogy.

The argument has premise/s and a conclusion in a combined manner that has valid and invalid features. While true or false is about the statements only - individual premises and conclusion.

According to the Nyāya Philosophy, inference for others consists of five constituents.

1. This hill has fire (Pratijnā)
2. Because there is smoke (Hetu)
3. Wherever there is smoke, there is fire (Udāharana)
4. This hill has smoke (Upamāna)
5. Therefore, this hill has fire (Nigamāna)

In this inference, the middle term appears three times, Therefore, it is also known as 'tritiyalinga parāmarsa'. In this inference, if we remove either first two premises or last two premises, the inference will not be an invalid and incorrect one. Hence, for an inference we need three and at least three premises possessing three different terms as its basic requirements. This system is combination of inductive and deductive. The first three propositions (1 to 3) make the inductive system and last three (3 to 5) make the deductive system.

Valid means it should be 'formally' structured.

Materially true means it is assumed to be true in this physical world.

147. (d)

The collection of all those things for which a term can be used correctly is called the extension or the denotation of that term. The meaning of a word is its clear definition as listed in the dictionary. Let us consider the word 'home' as an example. The literal or literal meaning of home is 'the place where one lives' or 'residence'. Home also connotes a place of security, comfort and family. The quote 'Apna ghar apna hota hai' does not refer to the literal meaning of home, but the feelings the word evokes in most of us. This is what is meant by the extension/denotation of a term – it refers to the different meanings that can be correctly associated with that term.

In logic, substantive refers to a correlated word that indicates the context of a word or concept. In contrast, the extension of that term indicates the intrinsic content of a word or concept, which constitutes its formal definition; and 'Vastvartha' indicates the extent of its applicability by naming the particular objects that it represents. The meaning of a word is derived by specifying necessary and sufficient conditions for when an attributive word should be used. For example, the word 'bachelor' has the meaning of an 'unmarried person'.

However, the expression of language comes from another type of word meaning, a meaning or association or set of associations that a word usually comes to mind.

148. (d)

Hasty Generalization: This form of fallacy has two types – direct fallacy and its converse. The fallacy results due to inappropriate use of generalization in both the cases. These fallacies are committed when the differences between normal and special circumstances is ignored. Take a look at the following statement: 'The daily news carried an article this morning about some local teenagers who were arrested on charges of drug possession. Teenagers these days are nothing but a bunch of junkies.' Here, the arrest of the local teenagers does not imply that these days teenagers are bunch of junkies.

Red Herring (Irrelevant Thesis): In the red herring concept, an irrelevant topic or fallacy is introduced in an argument to divert the attention of listeners (or readers) form the original issue. This fallacy is often used in detective or suspense novels. The listeners may be induced to give false examples. For example, a teacher catches a student cheating during an exam. The student replies, 'I know I have made a mistake. Kindly think of my parents. They will feel very bad.' The student used a red herring in his response. He tries to appeal to pity to distract his teacher from the real issue.

Strawmen: The strawmen argument is aptly named after a harmless, lifeless scarecrow. In the strawmen fallacy, one attacks a position of the opponent that does not really hold. It is much easier to defeat your opponent when they are made of straw. For example,

Ad Hominem (Argument Against the Person): The argument of 'X' is good and supported by solid evidence. But at the same time, the personality or character of 'X' has not been generally good. We shift our focus from the premises to the personality of the person putting forth the argument. This fallacy happens rarely in academia, but it is mostly in present in political circles. Usually, rivalry is the reason behind why this fallacy is committed.

149. (a)

Unlike western logic, the Naiyayikas did not give separate treatment to the inductive methods.
According to the Nyaya school, universal propositions are obtained from perception itself, by one of the forms of extraordinary perception.

150. (a)

Sesavat Inference: it is that in which we infer the unperceived cause form a perceived effect. For example, we infer rain that has occurred in the past from the swift, muddy current of water in the river. Sesvata is the inference of what remains (sesa) by elimination of the irrelevant.

Sesvata inference corresponds to the method of residues in western inductive logic. Thus, both the statements are true.

151. (d)

We need to look at question 161.

152. (b)

Fallacy of Viruddha: It is the contradictory middle. The middle term, instead of spreading through the presence of the major term, is spread by the absence of the major term. Instead of proving the existence of the major term in the minor term, it proves its non-existence therein. For example, 'sound is eternal, because it is produced'. Here 'produced', instead of proving the eternality of sound, proves its impermanence.

Fallacy of Prakaransama: This fallacy occurs when a middle term does not go further than producing a state of mental oscillation between two opposite views.

Fallacy of Asiddha: This is the fallacy of the unproved middle. The middle term must be present in the minor term (*pakshadharmata*). If it is not present, it is unproved.

Fallacy of Savyabhichara: This is the fallacy of the irregular middle term in which either the middle term is too broad or too narrow in nature.

153. (d)

Illicit Major: Illicit major is a formal fallacy committed in a categorical syllogism that is invalid because its major term is undistributed in the major premise but is distributed in the conclusion.

Illicit Minor: The fallacy of illicit minor term is undistributed in the premise but is distributed in the conclusion (but not vice-versa).

Undistributed Middle: The fallacy of the undistributed middle is a formal fallacy that is committed when the middle term in a categorical syllogism is not distributed in either the minor premise or the major premise. It is thus a **syllogistic fallacy**.

Fallacy of Four Terms: The fallacy of four terms is the formal fallacy that occurs when a syllogism has four (or more) terms rather than the requisite three, rendering it invalid. For example, no rich person is a vegetarian, and all lawyers are rich people. Therefore, no attorney is a vagabond. There is no logical connection between the term. This is the fallacy of four terms.

154. (c)

Purvavat Anumana: It is the inference in which we surmise the unperceived effect from a perceived cause. For example, we infer future rain from the appearance of dark, heavy clouds.

Sesavat Anumana: It is the inference in which we surmise the unperceived cause from a perceived effect. For example, we infer past rain from the swift, muddy current in the river.

Samanyatodrashta Anumana: It is the inference in which we surmise that 'the sun moves because like other moving objects, its position also changes'.

Pakshata Anumana: It is the inference that refers to the paksha.

155. (b)

We use the terms valid or invalid in case of deductive arguments. An argument in which the premises do succeed in guaranteeing the conclusion is called a (deductively) *valid argument*. If a valid argument has 'true' premises, then the argument is said also to be *sound*. There is no use of words correct or incorrect in case of deductive arguments. Valid means that they should be formally and structurally okay.

Note that all arguments in deductive arguments are either valid or invalid, and either sound or unsound; there is NO middle ground (such as half valid or invalid), such as being somewhat valid.

156. **(b):** As we know, a categorical statement lines up two distinct categories or classes against one another, measuring degrees of comparison, and makes an assertion about the categories. This always involves a subject term and a predicate term:

Universal Affirmative	A	All S are P	All Birds are Mammals
Universal Negative	E	No S are P	No Birds are Mammals
Particular Affirmative	I	Some S are P	Some Birds are Mammals
Particular Negative	O	Some S are not P	Some Birds are Not Mammals

We need to look at traditional square of opposition and the Truth Table.

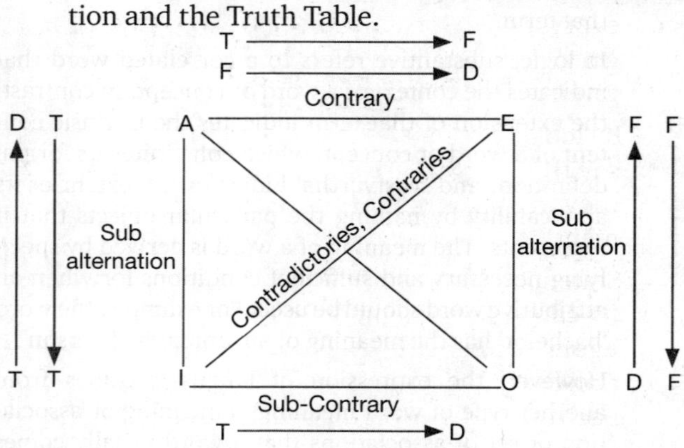

We need to look for separate discussion of contradictories, contraries, sub contraries and sub alternation for questions linked with square of opposition.

A	E	I	O
T	F	T	F
F	T	F	T
D	F	T	D
F	D	D	T

Now look at the question statement – 'No Birds are Mammals' is Universal Negative that is E. As it is given to be true, come to the second row where

A is False–it means that All Birds are Mammals is False.

I is False–it means that Some Birds are Mammals is False

O is True–Some Birds are Not Mammals is True

Thus, as per question A, B and D are part of answer. Thus, option B is the correct answer.

157. (a): Ad Populum: This can also be termed as 'Appeal to Popularity'. This argument supports a position by appealing to the shared opinion of a large group of people such as the majority, the general public.

In this statement, a housemaker, XYZ Home Finance appeals to be like a family member and thus, to fulfil the need to have your own sweet home – most likely by financing through maximum finance, comparatively less rate of interest, long duration and easy to pay system of Equated Monthly Instalments (EMIs).

158. (d): Statement I–'Some S is P' belongs to 'I-category' AND 'Some S is not P' belongs to 'O-category'. That has been explained in the explanation given under question 26.

By looking at first diagram in question 26, we can say that I and O are **sub-contrary** to each other, they are not **contrary** to each other. So, Statement I is a false statement.

Statement II–Again, 'Some S is/are not P' is a **'O-category'** statement and 'All S is P' is a **'A-category'** statement. As given in square of opposition diagram, both O and A are contradictory to each other. Thus, Statement II is a true statement.

Thus, (d) is the correct answer.

159. (a): Statement I–The anumana is basically about attaining inferential knowledge. That is further linked with invariable concomitance or vyapti. Thus, the anumana is based on syllogistic inference that is basically invariable concomitance (vyapti) between middle term and major term. Concomitance means the fact of existing or occurring together with something else.

Thus, we are basically concerned with the definition of Vyapti that is the non-presence of middle term (hetu) in the locus of the non-existence of the major term (sadhya). Vyapti is an invariable and unconditional relation between the middle term and the major term.

For example, the hill is full of fire because it is full of smoke. Here, smoke which is the middle term is absent from all regions outside the region of fire (the major term).

Statement II–Vyapti may also be defined as the co-presence of the middle term with the major term when there is no condition attached to the middle term. Vyapti is the possession of that nature which establishes the connection of the middle term with the major term.

We can show the relation between minor term (paksh), middle term (hetu) and major term (sadhya) with the help of following diagram.

Paksha	Hetu	Sadhya
Minor Term (Mountain) Characteristic-linga	Middle Term (Reason) vyapya (smoke) Factum probans	Major Term (Fire) vyapaka factum probandum

160. (c): Anumana is knowledge that is obtained after a proof. Anumana is not a direct knowledge but it is obtained after some perception, testimony, etc. According to question, we can discuss the following three aspects.

1. **Purvavat**–This is basically cause to effect relationship. This can also be termed as unperceived effect from a perceived cause, thus the perceived cause comes first and thereafter, the unperceived effect (anuman). For example, we can infer the future rain from a present dark clouds.
2. **Sesavat**–An inference in which the unperceived cause is known from a perceived effect.

For example, we come to know about the rain from a muddy flow of water in the river.

3. **Samanyatodrasta Anumana**–There are many universal positions in this world such as different positions of moon around the earth. From these, we can draw inferences.

161. (c): Ignoratio elenchi, is also called as 'ignorance of the refutation'. Refute means overthrow by argument, evidence, or prove to be false or incorrect or controvert. It is broadly defined as any incorrect argument which reaches an evidentially irrelevant conclusion. Historically, the fallacy is also more NARROWLY defined as a counterargument to an argument which does not attempt to prove the contradictory of what was intended to be proved.

In this statement, hunger of knowledge and hunger of food are narrowly linked, without any substantial value. Practically, it functions as a 'catch-all' category. The Traditional Form of Ignoratio Elenchi (fallacy of irrelevancy) is occurring here whenever the conclusion of an argument is irrelevant to its premises. The fallacy of non sequitur is often identified with this version.

162. (b): The fallacy of false cause (non causa pro causa) mislocates the cause of one phenomenon in another that is only seemingly related. The example taken in the question statement are very much natural. The moon is able to shine during the night as it gets light from sun that is reflected back.

163. (a): Material Fallacies

There are five characteristics of a valid middle term; they are as following:

1. **Paksadharmata** - The must be present in the minor term. For example, smoke must be present in the hill.
2. **Sapaksasattva** - It must be present in all positive instances in which the major terms are present. For example, the smoke must be present in the kitchen where fire exists.
3. **Vipaksasattva** - It must be absent in all negative instances in which the major terms is absent. For example smoke must be absent in the lake in which fire does not exist.
4. **Abadhita** - It must be non-incompatible with the minor term. For example, it must not prove the coolness of fire.
5. **Aviruddha** - It must be qualified by the absence of counteracting reasons which lead to a contradictory conclusion. For example, 'the fact of being caused' should not be used to prove the 'eternality' of sound.

Whenever, one of these characteristics is violated, the fallacies take its place. It also says that the validity of an inference depends on the validity of hetu or reason. It is because of this fact that Naiyayikas consider fallacies of inference as fallacies of the reason (hetvabhasa). Fallacies of inference thus are all MATERIAL fallacies.

Fallacies of reason are of five types – Asiddha, Savyabhichara, Satpratipaksha, Badhita and Virudha. They have been discussed as the last topic in Unit 6 of Pearson book.

Material fallacies are also known as fallacies of presumption, because the premises 'presume' too much—they either covertly assume the conclusion or avoid the issue in view.

Reason – The Nyaya system is formal and is deductive-inductive can be understood through the following example

(For such fallacies, we can refer to the last topic of discussion in Unit 6.)

164. (d): This question is quite similar to question number 26 in the previously solved pervious year paper. This is the basic information

Universal Affirmative	A	All S are P	All Birds are Mammals
Universal Negative	E	No S are P	No Birds are Mammals
Particular Affirmative	I	Some S are P	Some Birds are Mammals
Particular Negative	O	Some S are not P	Some Birds are Not Mammals

Now look at the question statement – 'Some plants are not carnivorous', that is basically O – type. This is given to be false.

A. 'some plants are carnivorous' denotes **I-type – given to be True in question.**

B. 'some plants are carnivorous' again denotes **I- type – given to be False**

C. No plants are carnivorous **E-type – given to be False**

D. All plants are carnivorous denotes **A-type – given to be True**

A	E	I	O
T	F	T	F
F	T	F	T
D	F	T	D
F	D	D	T

If O-type is false, then looking horizontally, we can say that

I-type is True – that denotes that option A is a part of answer.

Similarly E as False, that is option C is a part of answer.

A as True, that is option D is also part of answer.

That means that A, C and D are part of answer. Thus overall, (d) is the answer.

165. (b): Basically, criterion of valid knowledge is called as pramana. The inference of one proposition from two premises is called as syllogism. Any error of reasoning is called as fallacy. In nyaya system, it is called as hetvabhasa.

The aspects A and B have been discussed in an earlier question.

C. hetu (causation) is missing, (it may seem more like inductive).

D. Linga paramarsa: The Nyaya syllogism has five terms. Among them, middle term works as a bridge between the major and the minor terms. Therefore, the middle term has main responsibility to prove a syllogism valid or invalid. How a middle term is related to major term is lingaparamarsha. There are five characteristics of a middle term:

1. Paksadharmata - it must be present in the minor term. For example, smoke must be present in the hill.
2. Sapaksasattva - It must be present in all positive instances in which the major terms are present. For example, the smoke must be present in the kitchen where fire exists.
3. Vipaksasattva - It must be absent in all negative instances in which the major terms are absent. For example smoke must be absent in the lake in which fire does not exist.
4. Abadhita - It must be non-incompatible with the minor term. For example, it must not prove the coolness of fire.
5. Aviruddha - It must be qualified by the absence of counteracting reasons which lead to a contradictory conclusion. For example, 'the fact of being caused' should not be used to prove the 'eternality' of sound.

The above five are linked with Hetvabhasa or types of it. In Indian logic a fallacy is called hetvahasa. It means that middle term appears to be a reason but is not a valid reason. All fallacies are material fallacies. We have mentioned the five characteristics of a valid middle term. When these are violated, we have fallacies. Five kinds of fallacies are recognised.

1. Assiddha or sadhyasama - This is the fallacy of unproved middle.
2. Savyabhicara - This is the fallacy of irregular middle.
3. Satpratipaksa - Here the middle term is contradicted by another middle term.
4. Badhita - It is the non-inferentially contradicted middle.
5. Viruddha - It is the contradictory middle.

166. (a) Here, the fallacy is 'begging the question'. We can develop the following scene to prove this.

Premise: People who do not have sufficient resources have a right to the resources of the community.

Conclusion: As a society, we have an obligation to support the needy.

The premise assumes a societal obligation (through the right of the needy to community resources). This premise also leads to conclusion society has an obligation. Thus, there is no independent support for its premise in the argument. Thus, both go in the same direction. This circular reasoning is characteristic of the 'begging the question' fallacy.

(b) **Equivocation:** This fallacy occurs when a term is used ambiguously with different meanings throughout the argument. For, example, the 'resources' in this case.

(c) **Fallacy of composition:** What is true for individual parts of a group is also true for the group as a whole.

(d) **Appeal to emotions:** It is actually some of emotions and more of rights.

167. (b): We can refer to pages 6.17 and 18.

A - II: The statement "No fishes are mammals" (A) is logically equivalent to the statement "No mammals are fishes" (II), because they are contra-positive statements. They are actually formed by negating and interchanging the subject and predicate of a categorical statement. The contra-positive of "No S are P" is "No P are S", and they have the same truth value.

B - III: The statement "All fishes are mammals" (B) is logically equivalent to the statement "Some mammals are non-fishes" (III), because they are obverse statements. This means that they are formed by negating the predicate and changing the quality of a categorical statement. The obverse of "All S are P" is "Some S are not P", and they have the same truth value in every situation.

C - IV: The statement "Some fishes are mammals" is logically equivalent to the statement "Some mammals are fishes" (IV), because they are converse statements. This means that they are formed by interchanging the subject and predicate of a categorical statement. The converse of "Some S are P" is "Some P are S", and they have the same truth value in every situation.

D - I: The statement "Some mammals are not fishes" (D) is logically equivalent to the statement "No mammals are non-fishes" (I), because they are inverse statements. This means that they are formed by negating both the subject and predicate of a categorical statement. The inverse of "Some S are not P" is "No S are P", and they have the same truth value in every situation.

168. (d):

We need to refer to Truth Table again - page 6.15. some animals are birds (I) is given to be false. We need to identify True statement/s as per question.

A. All animals are birds (A) - False.
B. No animals are birds (E) - True
C. Some animals are not birds (O) - True
D. All birds are animals (A) - False.

Thus, B and C are correct, so (d) is the answer.

169 (b): They cannot both be true, although they both may be False, these seem like mutually exclusive statements:

A. All trees have roots.
B. No trees have roots.
C. Some trees have roots.
D. Some trees do not have roots.

Don't going into complications, we can make pairs of them and then see the reality:

A and B: These two cannot both be true at the same time. If all trees have roots, then it cannot be true that no trees have roots. However, they can both be false.

C and D: These two statements can both be true simultaneously (there could be some trees with roots and some without), so they don't fit the criteria.

B and D: Similar to C and D, these statements can be true at the same time (if some trees don't have roots, it doesn't negate the possibility that no trees have roots).

A and C: These statements can both be true simultaneously (if all trees have roots, it's also true that some trees have roots).

Thus, the correct pair is A and B, and (b) is the right answer.

170. (b): Sound is eternal because it is produced. This statement exemplifies the Badhit fallacy in *Nyaya* logic. Badhit fallacy occurs when the middle term in a syllogism is contradicted by a stronger source of knowledge (prama–na). In this case, the middle term is 'produced.'

171. (b): The fallacy committed in the argument is 'Red herring', that brings suspicious or irrelevant information to distract from the main issue or argument.

(a) Circular argument mostly repeats the conclusion as a premise, creating a closed loop of reasoning.
(c) Complex question combines two or more questions into one, making it difficult to answer without accepting one of the implied premises.
(d) Slippery slope means that a small step (may be wrong) in one direction will inevitably lead to a disastrous outcome, often without evidence or justification.

172. (a): This is a question of 'logic equivalence'.

A. Some animals are birds.
B. Some animals are not non-birds, that is equivalent to 'Some animals are birds'.

C. Some non-birds are not non-animals. It does imply that some non-birds are birds.

D. Some birds are animals. This is equivalent to statement A.

Thus, only A, B, and D capture the same logical meaning of 'some animals are birds.'

173. (d): The question is about immediately inferred statements. They are drawn directly from a given statement, without requiring any additional information or reasoning. For shortcut, we can refer to Truth Table under Square of Opposition' in Unit 6. 'No animals are fishes' is E and is false, so we can go Level 3. There I is True which is asked in question - Some animals are fishes.

Alternatively also, The statement "Some animals are fishes" can be immediately inferred to be true based on the given false statement "No animals are fishes".

The correct answer is (d) D only.

174. (b): The correct answer is (b). A and C are contrary to each other, which means that they cannot both be true, but they may both be false. For example, the proposition "All fishes are mammals" (A) cannot be true at the same time as the proposition "No fishes are mammals" (C), but they could both be false if some fishes are mammals and some are not.

The other propositions are not contrary to each other, because they do not have this logical relationship.

B and D are subcontrary to each other. The pairs 'A and D' And 'B and C' are contradictory to each other.

Therefore, A and D are contrary because they both claim something false about fishes being mammals but disagree on the extent (all vs. some). The other statements are either true or not directly incompatible with each other.

175. (b): In addition to question statement, this occurs when the middle term in a syllogism is ambiguous and can refer to different things, leading to an invalid conclusion. We need to look at issues with 'middle term'

(a) **The hill has smoke because it has fire:** The middle term is indicated by 'has fire'. The presence of fire (middle term) exclusively leads to smoke (characteristic being inferred).

(b) **Sound is eternal because it is audible:** Being audible (middle term) is not exclusive to sound being eternal, as many non-eternal things are also audible. This is an example of a non-exclusive middle term.

(c) **All things are non-eternal because they are knowable:** The property of being knowable (middle term) is not exclusive to non-eternal things; eternal things can also be knowable. This could be another instance of a non-exclusive middle term.

(d) **Sound is eternal because it is produced:** The middle term is 'being produced'. This doesn't exclusively lead to it being eternal. Many produced things are non-eternal. This argument also seems to involve a non-exclusive middle term.

Thus, (b) seems to be the clearest result.

176. (a): Both Indian and Western systems recognise the role of middle term in syllogistic reasoning that acts as a bridge between the major and minor premises. A faulty middle term weakens the entire argument.

According to classical Indian system, sound is not visible; it is audible. This type of 'hetvabhasa' is known as 'Asiddha' (असिद्धा - unestablished) in Nyaya. Hetvabhasa is considered as a broader category that takes care of more fallacies related to the middle term.

Reason (R) accurately explains that the middle term 'visible' cannot be naturally present in the minor term 'sound' which is a quality and therefore cannot be directly observed. According to Indian logic, a valid inference requires a middle term that is inherently found in both the major and minor terms.

Thus, (a) is the correct answer.

177. (c): According to traditional square of opposition, this question is about sub-contraries, it should be relationship between I and O. Subcontraries are the pair that can't both be false but may both be true.

In the given statements:

- A: Some apes are monkeys. (I)
- B: All apes are monkeys. (A)
- C: Some apes are not monkeys. (O)
- D: No apes are monkeys. (E)

So, the propositions A (Some apes are monkeys) and C (Some apes are not monkeys) correspond to the I and O forms, respectively. Therefore, the pair that can't both be false, although they may both be true, are A and C. The correct option is (c).

178. (d): A says that 'Some apes are not non-monkeys'. This is O- type proposition. Without double negation, the sentence simply means "Some apes are monkeys." This aligns with option (c): "Some monkeys are apes". This can be taken as an example of obverse statement as per the 'generalised table' comparison on page 6.18 (in Unit 6).

B. Similarly 'Some monkeys are not non-apes' (o) becomes 'Some monkeys are apes' with removal of double negation. That is equivalent to Some monkeys are not apes in D. We can take Pick simple meanings of A and B again. They are actually converse of each other which are logically equivalent.

Thus, all A, B, C and D are logically equivalent of each other and (d) is the answer.

179. (a): Let's move to 'Truth Table' under 'square of opposition' on page 6.15. 'some birds are apes' is I - type proposition. That is given to be False. Now look at table to locate this. This appears in 3rd column of Level 2.

We need to look at true statement as per question.

A. All birds are apes (A) - False.

B. Some birds are apes (I) - False.

C. No birds are apes (E) - True

D. All birds are not apes (O) - True

Thus, C and D are True, so (a) is the correct answer.

180. (b): This fallacy occurs when an argument's premises assume the truth of the conclusion, instead of supporting it. In this case, the statement assumes the existence of an intelligent God (the conclusion) to explain the organization of the world (the premise).

CHAPTER 7

Data Interpretation

TOPICS OF IMPORTANCE

- Sources, Acquisition and Classification of Data
- Quantitative and Qualitative Data
- Graphical Representation (Bar chart, Histograms, Pie chart, Table chart and Line chart)
- Mapping of Data
- Data Interpretation
- Data and Governance

Direction: Read the following table carefully. Based upon this table answer the questions from 1 to 5.

Net area under irrigation by sources in a country (thousand hectares)

Year	Government canals	Private canals	Tanks	Tube wells and other wells	Other sources	Total
1997–98	17,117	211	2593	32,090	3102	55,173
1998–99	17,093	212	2792	33,988	3326	57,411
1999–00	16,842	194	2535	34,623	2915	57,109
2000–01	15,748	203	2449	33,796	2880	55,076
2001–02	15,031	209	2179	34,906	4347	56,672
2002–03	13,863	206	1802	34,250	3657	53,778
2003–04	14,444	206	1908	35,779	4281	56,618
2004–05	14,696	206	1727	34,785	7453	58,867
2005–06	15,268	207	2034	35,372	7314	60,196

1. Which of the following sources of irrigation has registered the largest percentage of decline in net area under irrigation during 1997–98 and 2005–06? **[Jun 2014]**

(a) Government canals
(b) Private canals
(c) Tanks
(d) Other sources

2. Find out the source of irrigation that has registered the maximum improvement in terms of percentage of net irrigated area during 2002–03 and 2003–04. **[Jun 2014]**

(a) Government canals
(b) Tanks
(c) Tube wells and other wells
(d) Other sources

3. In which of the following years, the net irrigation by tanks increased at the highest rate? [Jun 2014]
(a) 1998–99 (b) 2000–01
(c) 2003–04 (d) 2005–06

4. Identify the source of irrigation that has recorded the maximum incidence of negative growth in terms of net irrigated area during the years given in the table. [Jun 2014]
(a) Government canals
(b) Private canals
(c) Tube wells and other wells
(d) Other sources

5. In which of the following years, shares of the tube wells and other wells in the total net irrigated area was the highest? [Jun 2014]
(a) 1998–99 (b) 2000–01
(c) 2002–03 (d) 2004–05

Direction: For a country, (CO_2) emissions (million metric tons) from various sectors are given in the following table. Answer the questions (6 to 11) based on the data given.

CO_2 emissions (million metric tons)					
Sector / Year	Power	Industry	Commercial	Agriculture	Domestic
2005	500	200	150	80	100
2006	600	300	200	90	110
2007	650	320	250	100	120
2008	700	400	300	150	150
2009	800	450	320	200	180

6. What is the percentage (%) growth of CO_2 emissions from power sector during 2005 to 2009? [Dec 2014]
(a) 60 (b) 50
(c) 40 (d) 80

7. Which sector has recorded maximum growth in CO_2 emissions during 2005 to 2009? [Dec 2014]
(a) Power (b) Industry
(c) Commercial (d) Agriculture

8. By what percentage (%), the total emissions of CO_2 have increased from 2005 to 2009? [Dec 2014]
(a) ~89.32% (b) ~57.62%
(c) ~40.32% (d) ~113.12%

9. What is the average annual growth rate of CO_2 emissions in power sector? [Dec 2014]
(a) ~12.57% (b) ~16.87%
(c) ~30.81% (d) ~50.25%

10. What is the percentage contribution of power sector to total CO_2 emissions in the year 2008? [Dec 2014]
(a) ~30.82% (b) ~41.18%
(c) ~51.38% (d) ~60.25%

11. In which year, the contribution (%) of industry to total sectoral CO_2 emissions was minimum? [Dec 2014]
(a) 2005 (b) 2006
(c) 2007 (d) 2009

Direction: Question numbers 12 to 17 are based on the tabulated data given below.
A company has 20 employees with their age (in years) and salary (in thousand rupees per month) mentioned against each of them.

S.No.	Age (In years)	Salary (In thousand rupees per month)
1.	44	35
2.	32	20
3.	54	45
4.	42	35
5.	31	20
6.	53	60
7.	42	50
8.	51	55
9.	34	25
10.	41	30
11.	33	30
12.	31	35
13.	30	35
14.	37	40
15.	44	45
16.	36	35
17.	34	35
18.	49	50
19.	43	45
20.	45	50

12. Classify the data of age of each employee in class interval of 5 years. Which class interval of 5 years has the maximum average salary? [Jun 2015]
(a) 35–40 years (b) 40–45 years
(c) 45–50 years (d) 50–55 years

13. What is the frequency (%) in the class interval of 30–35 years? [Jun 2015]

(a) 20% (b) 25%
(c) 30% (d) 35%

14. What is the average age of the employees? **[Jun 2015]**
(a) 40.3 years (b) 38.6 years
(c) 47.2 years (d) 45.3 years

15. What is the fraction (%) of employees getting salary ≥ 40,000 per month? **[Jun 2015]**
(a) 45% (b) 50%
(c) 35% (d) 32%

16. What is the average salary (in thousand per month) in the age group between 40–50 years? **[Jun 2015]**
(a) 35 (b) 42.5
(c) 40.5 (d) 36.5

17. What is the fraction of employees getting salary less than the average salary of all the employees? **[Jun 2015]**
(a) 45% (b) 50%
(c) 55% (d) 47%

Direction: Given below in the table is the decadal data of population and electrical power production of a country.

Year	Population (Million)	Electrical power production (GW)*
1951	20	10
1961	21	20
1971	24	25
1981	27	40
1991	30	50
2001	32	80
2011	35	100

* 1 GW = 1000 million watt

Based on the above table, answer the questions from 18 to 23.

18. Which decade registered the maximum growth rate (%) of population? **[Dec 2015]**
(a) 1961–71 (b) 1971–81
(c) 1991–2001 (d) 2001–2011

19. Average decadal growth rate (%) of population is **[Dec 2015]**
(a) ~ 12.21% (b) ~ 9.82%
(c) ~ 6.73% (d) ~ 5%

20. Based on the average decadal growth rate, what will be the population in the year 2021? **[Dec 2015]**
(a) 40.34 million (b) 38.49 million
(c) 37.28 million (d) 36.62 million

21. In the year 1951, what was the power availability per person? **[Dec 2015]**
(a) 100 W (b) 200 W
(c) 400 W (d) 500 W

22. In which decade, the average power availability per person was maximum? **[Dec 2015]**
(a) 1981–1991 (b) 1991–2001
(c) 2001–2011 (d) 1971–1981

23. By what percentage (%), the power production increased from 1951 to 2011? **[Dec 2015]**
(a) 100% (b) 300%
(c) 600% (d) 900%

Direction: The following table shows the percentage profit (%) earned by two companies A and B during the years 2011–15. Answer questions 24–26 based on the data contained in the table.

Year	Percentage profit (%)	
	A	B
2011	20	30
2012	35	40
2013	45	35
2014	40	50
2015	25	35

Where per cent (%) Profit =

$$\frac{\textit{Income} - \textit{Expenditure}}{\textit{Expenditure}} \times 100$$

24. In which year, the percentage profit earned by company B is less than that of company A? **[Jul 2016]**
(a) 2012 (b) 2013
(c) 2014 (d) 2015

25. If the total expenditure of the two companies was ₹9 lakh in the year 2012 and the expenditure of A and B were in the ratio 21, then what was the income of the company A in that year? **[Jul 2016]**
(a) ₹9.2 lakh (b) ₹8.1 lakh
(c) ₹7.2 lakh (d) ₹6.0 lakh

26. What is the average percentage profit earned by the company B? **[Jul 2016]**
(a) 35% (b) 42%
(c) 38% (d) 40%

Direction: The following table shows the number of people in different age groups who responded to a survey about their favourite style of music. Use this information to answer the questions that follow. (Question 27–29) to the nearest whole percentage:

Style of music \ Age	Number of people (Years) 15–20	(Years) 21–30	(Years) 31+
Classical	6	4	17
Pop	7	5	5
Rock	6	12	14
Jazz	1	4	11
Blues	2	3	15
Hip-Hop	9	3	4
Ambient	2	2	2

27. What percentage of respondents aged 31+ indicated a favourite style other than classical music? **[Jul 2016]**
(a) 64% (b) 60%
(c) 75% (d) 50%

28. Approximately what percentage of the total sample were aged 21–30? **[Jul 2016]**
(a) 31% (b) 23%
(c) 25% (d) 14%

29. Approximately what percentage of the total sample indicates that Hip-Hop is their favourite style of music? **[Jul 2016]**
(a) 6% (b) 8%
(c) 14% (d) 12%

Direction: The following table embodies data on the sales revenue (₹ in lakhs) generated by a publishing house during the years 2012–2015 while selling books, magazines and journals as three categories of items. Answer questions 30–32 based on the data given in the table.

Item ↓ / Year →	Sales revenue (₹ In lakh) 2012	2013	2014	2015
Journals	46	47	45	44
Magazines	31	39	46	51
Books	73	77	78	78
Total				

30. In 2015, approximately what per cent of total revenue come from books? **[Jan 2017]**
(a) 45% (b) 55%
(c) 35% (d) 25%

31. The number of years in which there was an increase in revenue from at least two categories of items is **[Jan 2017]**
(a) 0 (b) 1
(c) 2 (d) 3

32. If the year 2016 were to show the same growth in terms of total sales revenue as the year 2015 over the year 2014, then the revenue in the year 2016 must be approximately **[Jan 2017]**
(a) ₹194 lakh (b) ₹187 lakh
(c) ₹172 lakh (d) ₹177 lakh

Direction: A university professor maintains data on MCA students tabulated by performance and gender of the students. The data is kept on a computer hard disk, but accidentally some of its data are lost because of a computer virus. Only the following could be recovered.

Gender	Average	Good	Excellent	Total
Male			10	
Female				32
Total		30		

Panic buttons were pressed but to no avail. An expert committee was formed, which decided that the following facts were self-evident.

(i) Half the students were either excellent or good.
(ii) 40% of the students were females.
(iii) One-third of the male students were average.

Answer questions 33–35 based on the data given above.

33. How many female students are excellent? **[Jan 2017]**
(a) 0 (b) 8 (c) 16 (d) 32

34. What proportion of female students are good? **[Jan 2017]**
(a) 0 (b) 0.25
(c) 0.50 (d) 0.75

35. Approximately, what proportion of good students are male? **[Jan 2017]**
(a) 0 (b) 0.73
(c) 0.43 (d) 0.27

Direction: Answer the questions 36 to 40 based on the data given in the table below.

Table: Number of registered vehicles in India and India's population.

Year	Total vehicles (Lakh)	Two wheelers (Lakh)	Cars, Jeeps, Taxis (Lakh)	Buses (Lakh)	Goods vehicles (Lakh)	Others (Lakh)	Population (India) (Million)
1961	6.65	0.88	3.1	0.57	1.68	0.42	439.23
1971	18.65	5.76	6.82	0.94	3.43	1.70	548.15
1981	53.91	26.18	11.60	1.62	5.54	8.97	683.32
1991	213.74	142.00	29.54	3.31	13.56	25.33	846.42
2001	549.91	385.56	70.58	6.34	29.48	57.95	1028.73
2011	1417.58	1018.65	191.23	16.04	70.64	121.02	1210.19

36. The maximum decadal growth in population of India is registered in the period **[Nov 2017]**
(a) 1961–1971 (b) 1991–2001
(c) 2001–2011 (d) 1981–1991

37. In which year the decadal growth (%) in number of cars surpassed that of the two wheelers? **[Nov 2017]**
(a) 1991 (b) 2001
(c) 1981 (d) 2011

38. What was the average decadal growth in the number of cars during 1961–2011? **[Nov 2017]**
(a) ~131% (b) ~68%
(c) ~217% (d) ~157%

39. In the year 2001, out of the total number of vehicles, the number of passenger vehicles (4 wheelers) accounted for **[Nov 2017]**
(a) ~14% (b) ~24%
(c) ~31% (d) ~43%

40. What was the per capita ownership of two wheelers in India in the year 2011? **[Nov 2017]**
(a) ~0.084% (b) ~0.0084%
(c) ~0.84% (d) ~0.068%

Direction: The table given embodies data on the production, exports and per capita consumption of rice in country P for five years from 2012 to 2016. Answer questions 41–45 based on the data contained in the table.

Year-wise production, exports and per capita consumption of rice			
Year	**Production (in million kg)**	**Exports (in million kg)**	**Per capita consumption (in kg)**
2012	186.5	114	36.25
2013	202	114	35.2
2014	238	130	38.7
2015	221	116	40.5
2016	215	88	42

Where, per capita consumption = (consumption in million kg)/(population in million) and consumption (in million kg) = production – exports.

41. The percentage increase in the consumption of rice over the previous year was the highest in which year? **[Jul 2018]**
(a) 2013 (b) 2014
(c) 2015 (d) 2016

42. What is the population of the country in the year 2014 (in million)? **[Jul 2018]**
(a) 2.64 (b) 2.72
(c) 2.79 (d) 2.85

43. The ratio of exports to consumption in the given period was the highest in the year **[Jul 2018]**
(a) 2012 (b) 2013
(c) 2014 (d) 2015

44. In which year, the population of country was the highest? **[Jul 2018]**
(a) 2013 (b) 2014
(c) 2015 (d) 2016

45. What is the average consumption of rice (in million kg) over the years 2012–2016? **[Jul 2018]**
(a) 104 (b) 102.1
(c) 108 (d) 100.1

Direction: The table shows details of expenditure incurred by a tea garden during the years 2008 to 2012. Note that all expenditure reported is in crores.

	Items of expenditure (₹ in crores)				
Year	Salary	Fuel	Bonus	Interest on loans	Taxes
2008	57.6	19.6	0.6	4.68	16.6
2009	68.4	22.4	0.5	6.50	21.6
2010	64.8	20.2	0.76	8.32	14.8
2011	67.2	26.6	0.74	7.28	17.6
2012	84.0	28.4	0.80	9.88	19.6

Answer the following questions based on the data given in the table.

46. The average yearly expenditure on 'Interest on Loans' during the period 2008–2012 was approximately **[Dec 2018]**
(a) ₹6.33 Crores (b) ₹6.88 Crores
(c) ₹8.32 Crores (d) ₹7.33 Crores

47. Bonus as a percentage (%) of salary was highest in the year **[Dec 2018]**
(a) 2008 (b) 2009
(c) 2010 (d) 2011

48. In which year, was the total expenditure (over the five heads of expenditure listed in the table above) the least? **[Dec 2018]**
(a) 2008 (b) 2009
(c) 2010 (d) 2011

49. In which years, the percentage (%) growth of expenditure on salary (as compared to the previous year), was more than 10%? **[Dec 2018]**
(a) 2009 and 2010 (b) 2010 and 2012
(c) 2011 and 2012 (d) 2009 and 2012

50. In which year, the expenditure of taxes and 'Interest on loans', was less than the expenditure on fuel, etc.? **[Dec 2018]**
(a) 2009 (b) 2010
(c) 2011 (d) 2012

Direction: Study the table given below carefully. It shows the number of students appeared, passed and failed in five subjects. The full marks in each subject is also given.

Subject	Total number of students appeared	Number of students who passed	Number of Students who failed	Maximum/ Full marks in the subject
English	600	–	36	600
Mathematics	–	240	60	–
Science	300	216	–	400
Social Studies	360	–	48	400
Computer	–	168	32	400

Some of the cells have missing data. You might need to determine some of the missing data to answer the questions below:

51. What is the difference between the number of failed students in Science and the number of students passed in Social Studies? **[Dec 2018]**
(a) 238 (b) 218
(c) 228 (d) 312

52. Which of the following could be the full marks in Mathematics if the pass marks in Mathematics was 35% and the person who just passed scored 70? **[Dec 2018]**
(a) 400 (b) 600
(c) 500 (d) 200

53. What is the maximum marks that a student can score in all the five subjects together? (You may use the answer of the previous question) **[Dec 2018]**
(a) 500 (b) 1500

(c) 1000 (d) 2000

54. In which subject, was the failure percentage the least? **[Dec 2018]**
(a) Mathematics (b) Social Studies
(c) Science (d) English

55. What is the approximate difference in percentage between the pass % in Social Studies and the pass % in Mathematics? **[Dec 2018]**
(a) 6.5% (b) 26.5%
(c) 2.5% (d) 16.5%

Direction: Read the following passge carefully and answer questions from 56–60.

Consider the following table that shows the distribution of student in two section A and B in a school according to the marks obtained by them. There is a total of 45 student in each of the sections A and B. Answer the questions based on the data contained in the table:

Marks obtained by student		
Marks in class interval	Number of students in Section –A	Section – B
[0 – 9]	2	4
[10 – 19]	5	5
[20 – 29]	10	9
[30 – 39]	4	4
[40 – 49]	8	7
[50 – 59]	4	5
[60 – 69]	7	5
[70 – 79]	5	6

56. How many student in Section–A have obtained 30 or more marks but less than 50? **[Jun 2019]**
(a) 12 (b) 14
(c) 10 (d) 13

57. If the pass mark is 40, approximately what is the percentage of successful students in Section–B? **[Jun 2019]**
(a) 48% (b) 51%
(c) 50% (d) 47%

58. How many student in Section–A and Section–B have obtained 50 or more than 50 marks? **[Jun 2019]**
(a) 23 (b) 43
(c) 32 (d) 34

59. If pass marks is 30, what is the number of failures in both the section together? **[Jun 2019]**
(a) 43 (b) 35
(c) 16 (d) 26

60. How many student in Section–A and Section–B together have obtained marks less than 10? **[Jun 2019]**
(a) 10 (b) 11
(c) 12 (d) 6

Direction: Read the following passage carefully and answer questions from 61 to 65.

The year-wise student strength in a university from different zones of the country in addition to those students who are from foreign countries is shown in table given:

Student strength (in. hundreds)						
Year	North zone	South zone	Central zone	West zone	East zone	Foreign countries
2014	15.1	10.2	6.2	4.0	8.2	1.2
2015	16.2	11.5	5.8	4.1	7.8	1.6
2016	17.2	11.8	6.0	4.5	8.5	1.7
2017	17.4	10.8	6.6	4.8	7.6	1.8
2018	18.0	10.6	6.4	5.4	8.6	2.5

61. During the period 2014–2018, which zone exhibits its cyclic variation? **[Jun 2019]**
(a) East zone (b) West zone
(c) Central zone (d) South zone

62. Which was the year when the students from east zone had maximum representation (%) in the total student strength of the university? **[Jun 2019]**
(a) 2016 (b) 2018
(c) 2014 (d) 2015

63. Which category of students have registered overall maximum growth rate (%) from 2014 to 2018? **[Jun 2019]**
(a) Foreign countries (b) West Zone
(c) North Zone (d) East Zone

64. What is the mean of annual growth rates (%) of the student strength of north zone? **[Jun 2019]**
(a) 6.24 (b) 4.51
(c) 3.86 (d) 4.82

65. What was the percentage (%) of students from for-

eign countries in the year 2018? **[Jun 2019]**
(a) ~4.21% (b) ~3.52%
(c) ~5.24% (d) ~4.85%

Direction: Consider the following table that shows the total number of students and percentage of female and males in five different departments.

Answer the questions based on the data contained in the table:

Department	Percentage of females	Percentage of males	Total No. of students
Physics	45	55	450
Chemistry	35	65	550
English	55	45	300
Hindi	60	40	250
Mathematics	40	60	500

66. Which of the departments has maximum number of female students? **[Jun 2019]**
(a) Physics (b) Chemistry
(c) English (d) Mathematics

67. Which of the department has minimum number of male students? **[Jun 2019]**
(a) Physics (b) English
(c) Hindi (d) Mathematics

68. The total number of students in the Chemistry department forms approximately what per cent of the total number of students in the mathematics department? **[Jun 2019]**
(a) 90% (b) 95%
(c) 105% (d) 110%

69. What is the respective ratio of the number of male students in English department to the number of male students in Mathematics department? **[Jun 2019]**
(a) 9:12 (b) 9:20
(c) 3:5 (d) 45:60

70. What is the total number of females in English and Hindi departments together? **[Jun 2019]**
(a) 315 (b) 325
(c) 335 (d) 345

71. The sum of deviation taken from which of descriptive statistical measure is always equal to zero? **[Jun 2019]**
(a) Mean (b) Median
(c) Mode (d) Percentile

Direction: Read the following passge carefully and answer questions from 72–76.

Consider the following table that shows the total number of ticket sold of five movies P, Q, R, S and T, across two cinema houses A and B on a particular day. In accordance with the table, answer the question that follow

Sale of Movie Tickets Cinema Housewise		
Movies	Cinema	
	A	B
P	200	300
Q	350	400
R	250	350
S	300	350
T	400	250

72. The number of tickets sold of movie T at cinema A is what per cent of the number of tickets of movie P sold at cinema A? **[Jun 2019]**
(a) 220% (b) 200%
(c) 210% (d) 190%

73. What is the difference between the total number of tickets sold of all movies together at cinema A and the total number of tickets sold of all movies together at cinema B? **[Jun 2019]**
(a) 180 (b) 170
(c) 150 (d) 160

74. What is the average number of tickets sold at cinema B for movies T and S together? **[Jun 2019]**
(a) 360 (b) 320
(c) 300 (d) 340

75. What is the total number of tickets sold of movies Q and R together at both the cinemas A and B together? **[Jun 2019]**
(a) 1050 (b) 1200
(c) 1250 (d) 1350

76. What is the ratio of the number of tickets sold of movie P at cinema B to the number of tickets sold of movie Q at cinema B? [Jun 2019]

(a) 2 : 3 (b) 3 : 4

(c) 1 : 2 (d) 3 : 5

Direction: Read the following passage carefully and answer questions from 77 to 81.

Consider the following table that shows the production of fertilizers by a company (in 10000 tonnes) during the year 2011 to 2018.

Answer the question based on the data contained in the table:

Year:	2011	2012	2013	2014	2015	2016	2017	2018
Production of Fertilizers:	35	50	70	55	75	60	85	90

77. What was the approximate percentage increase in production of fertilizers in 2018 compared to that in 2011? [Jun 2019]

(a) 157% (b) 165%

(c) 177% (d) 182%

78. In which year, the percentage increase in production as compared to the previous year was maximum? [Jun 2019]

(a) 2012 (b) 2013

(c) 2015 (d) 2018

79. In how many of the given years was the production of fertilizers more than the average production of the given years? [Jun 2019]

(a) 2 (b) 3

(c) 4 (d) 5

80. What was the percentage decline in the production of fertilizers from 2013 to 2014? [Jun 2019]

(a) 20.4% (b) 21.4%

(c) 22.6% (d) 24.2%

81. The average production of 2012 and 2013 was exactly equal to the average production of which of the following pairs of years? [Jun 2019]

(a) 2011 and 2012

(b) 2011 and 2017

(c) 2012 and 2014

(d) 2015 and 2016

Direction: Consider the following table that shows per cent profit earned by company ABC and company XYZ during the year 2011–2016.

Answer the questions based on the data contained in the table:

Year	Per cent profit earned by company ABC	Per cent profit earned by company XYZ
2011	50	55
2012	70	60
2013	50	45
2014	40	50
2015	60	50
2016	80	75

82. If the amount of profit earned by company XYZ in 2012 was ₹9 lakh, what was the total investment? [Jun 2019]

(a) 12,00,000 (b) 15,00,000

(c) 16,00,000 (d) 18,00,000

83. If the amount invested by the two companies in 2015 were equal, what was the ratio of the total income of company ABC to that of company XYZ in 2015? [Jun 2019]

(a) 5 : 6 (b) 6 : 5

(c) 15 : 16 (d) 16 : 15

84. If each of the companies ABC and XYZ invested ₹20 lakh in 2014, what was the average profit earned by the two companies? [Jun 2019]

(a) ₹8 lakh (b) ₹10 lakh

(c) ₹9 lakh (d) ₹12 lakh

85. If the income of ABC in 2013 and that in 2015 were equal and the amount of investment in 2013 was ₹8, 00,000 then what was the amount invested in 2015? [Jun 2019]

(a) 7,50,000 (b) 9,00,000

(c) 10,50,000 (d) 12,00,000

86. If the profit earned by the company ABC was ₹6,60,000 in the year 2015, what was the total investment of the company in that year? [Jun 2019]

(a) 11,000,00 (b) 14,300,00

(c) 17,600,00 (d) 20,900,00

Direction: Read the following passage carefully and answer questions from 87 to 91.

Consider the following table that shows expenditures of a company (in lakh rupees) per annum over the given years. Answer the questions based on the data contained in the table:

Year	Salary	Transport	Bonus	Interest on Loans	Taxes
	Item of expenditure				
2008	150	90	2.00	20.0	80
2009	180	100	2.50	30.5	95
2010	200	110	2.75	35.5	105
2011	240	115	3.00	40.0	85
2012	250	125	3.25	42.5	100

87. The total amount of bonus paid by the company during the given period is approximately what per cent of the total amount of salary paid during this period? **[Jun 2019]**
(a) 0.9% (b) 1.3%
(c) 1.6% (d) 2.0%

88. The approximate ratio between the total expenditure of the company in the year 2008 and the total expenditure of the company in the year 2009 is **[Jun 2019]**
(a) 57:75 (b) 52:68
(c) 57:68 (d) 68:57

89. The approximate ratio between the total expenditure on taxes for all the years and the total expenditure on transport for all the years is **[Jun 2019]**
(a) 31:40 (b) 25:36
(c) 27:30 (d) 31:36

90. Total expenditure of all the items in 2008 was approximately what per cent of the total expenditure in 2012? **[Jun 2019]**
(a) 66% (b) 69%
(c) 72% (d) 75%

91. What is the average amount of interest per year which the company had to pay (in Rupees) during this period? **[Jun 2019]**
(a) 30.5 Lakh (b) 32.7 Lakh
(c) 33.7 Lakh (d) 35.5 Lakh

Direction: Read the following passge carefully and answer questions from 92–96.

Consider the following table that shows the number (in lakhs) of different sizes of LED television sets sold by a company over the last seven years from 2012 to 2018. Answer the questions based on the data contained in the table:

Year	22"	24"	32"	40"	49"
	Sale of LED Television Sets (in lakhs) of Different Sizes (in inches)				
2012	85	154	124	112	118
2013	100	136	112	94	136
2014	106	124	85	115	145
2015	115	100	160	100	85
2016	100	85	145	85	100
2017	115	70	175	55	130
2018	125	95	170	110	155

92. What was the approximate percentage increase/decrease in the sales of 32–inch LED Television sets in 2017 compared to that in 2013? **[Jun 2019]**
(a) 36% (b) 56%
(c) 57% (d) 64%

93. For which size LED Television sets is the total sales of all the seven year the maximum? **[Jun 2019]**
(a) 22–inch Television
(b) 24–inch Television
(c) 32–inch Television
(d) 49–inch Television

94. For which LED Television sets is the total sales of all the seven year the minimum? **[Jun 2019]**
(a) 22–inch Television
(b) 24–inch Television
(c) 49–inch Television
(d) 40–inch Television

95. What is the difference in the number of 40–inch Television sets sold in 2013 and 2018? **[Jun 2019]**
(a) 1,600,000 (b) 1,500,000
(c) 15,000,000 (d) 16,000,000

96. What is the total sale of Television sets of size 49-inch (in lakhs) over all the seven years? **[Jun 2019]**
(a) 912 (b) 896
(c) 879 (d) 869

Direction: Read the following passage carefully and answer questions from 97–101.

Consider the following table that shows the percentage (%) distribution of population of six cities A–F, ratio of males to females and the percentage (%) adult population in these cities. Total population of these six cities is 24 lakhs. In accordance with table, answer the questions that follow (questions 97–101):

Population City-wise			
City	% of population	male:female	% Adult
A	21	4:3	60
B	18	5:4	64
C	16	5:3	72
D	20	2:3	70
E	10	1:1	75
F	15	3:2	65

97. What is the number of persons of City F who are adult? **[Jun 2019]**
(a) 2,32,000 (b) 2,30,000
(c) 2,34,000 (d) 2,32,000

98. What is the number of persons in City C who are not adult? **[Jun 2019]**
(a) 1,07,520 (b) 1,08,410
(c) 1,09,560 (d) 1,10,800

99. What is the difference between the number of males and the number of females in city B? **[Jun 2019]**
(a) 42,000 (b) 44,000
(c) 45,000 (d) 48,000

100. The number of adult in City E is what per cent of the number of males in City D? **[Jun 2019]**
(a) 82.5% (b) 87.75%
(c) 92.5% (d) 93.75 %

101. What is the total number of male population in City D? **[Jun 2019]**
(a) 1.88 lakh (b) 1.92 lakh
(c) 1.96 lakh (d) 2.04 lakh

Direction: Consider the following table that shows the amount of exports (in crore ₹) from three different companies namely, A, B and C over the years 2012–2018. Based on the data in the table, answer the questions 102–106.

Year-wise Amount of Exports from Companies

	Amount of Exports (In crore ₹)		
Year	A	B	C
2012	40	90	70
2013	70	50	100
2014	50	70	130
2015	80	70	100
2016	110	90	70
2017	60	110	90
2018	130	150	110

102. In how many of the given years, were the exports from company A more than its average annual exports over the given years? **[Dec 2019]**
(a) 2 (b) 3
(c) 4 (d) 5

103. For which of the following pairs of years, the total exports from the three companies, when put together are equal? **[Dec 2019]**
(a) 2014 and 2017
(b) 2015 and 2017
(c) 2016 and 2017
(d) 2014 and 2015

104. What was the difference between the average exports of three companies in 2017 and the average exports of three companies in 2012? **[Dec 2019]**
(a) ₹15.33 crores
(b) ₹18.67 crores
(c) ₹25 crores
(d) ₹20 crores

105. Average annual amount of exports during the given period for company B is approximately what % of the average annual amount of exports for company C? **[Dec 2019]**
(a) 89.64% (b) 91.21%
(c) 94.03% (d) 93.33%

106. In which year, the absolute difference between the exports from companies A and B was the minimum? **[Dec 2019]**
(a) 2013 (b) 2014
(c) 2015 (d) 2016

Direction: The following table presents the data on the number of vehicles of three different types (A, B and C) produced by a company during seven different years, i.e., from 2012 to 2018. Based on the data in the table, answer the questions from 107 to 111.

Year-wise Production of Three Types of Vehicles

Year ↓ / Vehicle →	A Type	B Type	C Type
2012	5000	20,000	15,000
2013	15,000	10,000	22,500
2014	10,000	15,000	30,000
2015	17,500	15,000	23,000
2016	25,000	20,000	15,000
2017	13,000	25,000	20,000
2018	30,000	35,000	25,000

107. In how many years was the production of A type vehicles less than its average production over the given years? **[Dec 2019]**

(a) 2 (b) 4
(c) 3 (d) 1

108. What was the average number of B type vehicles produced by the company over the years? **[Dec 2019]**

(a) 20,000 (b) 25,000
(c) 15,000 (d) 30,000

109. In which of the following years was the total production of all the three types of vehicles was 60,000? **[Dec 2019]**

(a) 2013 (b) 2014
(c) 2015 (d) 2016

110. The number of A type vehicles produced in the year 2014 was what per cent of the number of C type vehicles produced in the year 2016? **[Dec 2019]**

(a) ~33.33% (b) ~66.67 %
(c) 50% (d) 15%

111. What has been the percentage increase of B Type vehicles in the year 2017 over 2016? **[Dec 2019]**

(a) 10% (b) 5%
(c) 20% (d) 25%

Direction: Based on the data in the table, answer the questions that follow.

The table shows the profit percentage earned by the Company A, income of Company B and the expenditure of Company B during the years, 2013–2018 as well as the formula to compute profit percentage.

Year-wise Financial Details (in ₹lakhs)

Year	Profit Percentage of A	Income of B (in ₹lakhs)	Expenditure of B (in ₹lakhs)
2013	40	48.6	36
2014	25	35	25
2015	60	62.4	48
2016	40	77	44
2017	10	80	50
2018	20	72	45

Where,

$$\text{Profit percentage} = \frac{(\text{income} - \text{expenditure})}{(\text{expenditure})} \times 100$$

112. The profit percentage of Company B was maximum in the year? **[Dec 2019]**

(a) 2014 (b) 2015
(c) 2016 (d) 2017

113. What is the difference between profit percentage of Company A and Company B in the year 2013? **[Dec 2019]**

(a) 5% (b) 7%
(c) 12% (d) 15%

114. If the income of Company A in the year 2018 was ₹90 lakhs, then the net profit (in ₹ lakhs) of Company B in 2018 is what percent more than the net profit (in ₹ lakhs) of Company A? **[Dec 2019]**

(a) 30% (b) 60%
(c) 75% (d) 80%

115. If the expenditure of Company A in year 2017 was ₹45 lakhs, then the net profit (in ₹ lakhs) of Company A is what percent of net profit (in ₹ lakhs) of Company B in the same year? **[Dec 2019]**

(a) 15% (b) 25%
(c) 40% (d) 75%

116. If the income of the Company A in the year 2014 happened to be ₹32.5 lakhs, then what was the sum of the net profit (in ₹ lakhs) of Company A and Company B in 2014? **[Dec 2019]**

(a) ₹12.8 lakhs (b) ₹13.2 lakhs
(c) ₹15 lakhs (d) ₹16.5 lakhs

Direction: Read the following passge carefully and answer questions from 117–121.

The following table provides the sales of computers of different types or brands over the years 2001–2007. Based on data, answer the following questions (117–121).

Number of Different Brands of Computers (In Thousands) Sold in Different Years

Years	Types of Computers			
	Lenovo	Acer	IBM	HCL
2001	20	40	50	80
2002	30	25	60	70
2003	50	50	50	55
2004	60	70	40	35
2005	70	85	70	25
2006	80	45	80	20
2007	90	60	100	10

117. The difference in the number of Acer computers sold in 2002 and 2005 is: **[Dec 2019]**

(a) 15,000 (b) 20,000
(c) 45,000 (d) 60,000

118. In which year, the percentage of Acer computers sold as to the total number of computers sold was maximum? **[Dec 2019]**

(a) 2003 (b) 2004
(c) 2005 (d) 2007

119. Name the type or brand of computer, whose sale has continuously decreased over the years, 2001–2007. **[Dec 2019]**

(a) Lenovo (b) Acer
(c) IBM (d) HCL

120. Name the type of computer for which the total sale in all the seven years is maximum? **[Dec 2019]**

(a) IBM (b) Lenovo
(c) Acer (d) HCL

121. The percentage increase in the sales of Lenovo computers in 2007 as compared to sales in 2001 is: **[Dec 2019]**

(a) 200% (b) 250%
(c) 300% (d) 350%

Direction: Read the following passage carefully and answer questions from 122–126.

The following table gives the percentage of marks obtained by five students in five subjects. Maximum marks in each subject are given in the parenthesis below the subject name.

Student	Percentage (%) Marks Obtained				
	Mathematics (100)	Chemistry (150)	Physics (150)	English (100)	Physical Education (100)
A	90	80	95	80	90
B	80	75	90	70	80
C	100	95	95	85	95
D	75	70	60	65	60
E	60	50	65	50	70

122. The aggregate of marks obtained by E is: **[Dec 2019]**

(a) 252.5 (b) 251.5
(c) 353.5 (d) 352.5

123. What is the average percentage of marks obtained by the students in Chemistry? **[Dec 2019]**

(a) 74% (b) 79%
(c) 80% (d) 81%

124. What is the difference between aggregate marks obtained by A and C? **[Dec 2019]**

(a) 40.5 (b) 41.5
(c) 42.5 (d) 43.5

125. The aggregate percentage of marks obtained by C are: **[Dec 2019]**

(a) 92.20% (b) 94.17%
(c) 95.21% (d) 91.17%

126. In which subject, the students have obtained lowest average percentage of marks? **[Dec 2019]**

(a) Chemistry
(b) Physics
(c) English
(d) Physical Education

Direction: Study the data given in the table and answer the questions 127 to 131.

The following table shows the monthly reporting of patients for different diseases to three hospitals in a city:

Disease/Hospital	Hospital A	Hospital B	Hospital C
Heart Attack	320	240	360
Blood Sugar	650	1350	1950
Blood Pressure	700	1400	2100
Kidney Problems	210	420	630

127. What is the average number of patients for the least reported disease? **[2020]**
(a) ~415.2 (b) ~325.4
(c) ~391.7 (d) ~306.6

128. What is the percentage increase in the total number of patients from hospital A to hospital C? **[2020]**
(a) ~120 % (b) ~168.96
(c) ~141 % (d) ~145 %

129. What is the percentage of number of patients reporting for blood sugar compared to the total patients in all three hospitals? **[2020]**
(a) ~25.90% (b) ~38.24 %
(c) ~39.42 % (d) ~35.12 %

130. What is the percentage increase in the number of patients reporting heart attacks from hospital A to hospital C? **[2020]**
(a) 12.5% (b) 13.2%
(c) 11.9% (d) 9.2 %

131. For patients reporting for kidney problems, what is the ratio of the number of patients reporting at hospital A and those reporting at hospital C? **[2020]**
(a) 2:3 (b) 3:4
(c) 1:3 (d) 1:5

Direction: The table below embodies data on the number of candidates who appeared for an interview (I) and got admission (A) in five engineering discipline during the year 2014 to 2019. In accordance with the table, answer the questions 132–136:

Year wise Number of Candidates in Different Engineering Disciplines										
Engineering Discipline →	Chemical		Civil		Aerospace		Petroleum		Electrical	
Year ↓	I	A	I	A	I	A	I	A	I	A
2014	1274	1090	2108	2068	1180	1140	960	935	1216	1194
2015	1165	1065	2050	1980	1260	1180	1004	985	1132	1120
2016	1108	1024	1860	1815	1132	1040	870	855	1260	1246
2017	1230	1180	1996	1948	1060	980	1094	1070	1191	1170
2018	1492	1372	2530	2500	1465	1425	1160	1040	1242	1222
2019	982	930	3488	3448	1640	1590	1020	1010	1362	1342

132. What is the percentage of the total number of candidates admitted to the total number of candidates interviewed for all the years in Chemical Engineering Discipline? **[2020]**
(a) 8.1 % (b) 91.68%
(c) 8.8% (d) 91.86%

133. What is the percentage increase/decrease in the number of candidates admitted in Civil Engineering discipline from the year 2015 to 2016? **[2020]**
(a) 9.09% (b) 8.43%
(c) 8.33% (d) 9.19%

134. What is the average number of candidates who appeared for the in the interview in the year 2016 for admission to all the five engineering disciplines? **[2020]**
(a) 1216 (b) 1314
(c) 1316 (d) 1246

135. What is the difference between the total number of candidates who appeared for an interview over the six years in Aerospace and Electrical Engineering discipline? **[2020]**
(a) 334 (b) 61
(c) 66 (d) 344

136. The ratio of number of candidates who appeared in an interview for admission to Petroleum Engineering discipline in the year 2014 compared to the number of candidates who got admission in Electrical Engineering discipline in the year 2015, is: **[2020]**
(a) 3:5 (b) 6:7
(c) 7:6 (d) 5:3

Direction: Study the table carefully and answer the questions 137 to 141.

In the following table, total Exports and Imports of 5 countries over 4 years (in ₹ Crore) is given. Study the table carefully and answer the given questions. (I-import, E-export)

Year	2017		2018		2019		2020	
Country	I	E	I	E	I	E	I	E
P	25	30	24	32	28	36	22	32
Q	28	26	26	31	29	37	26	34
R	24	32	28	25	32	36	28	34
S	22	28	18	28	16	21	23	32
T	26	31	16	33	12	23	21	28

137. Find out the ratio of export done by country S and T during 2017–2020. **[2021]**
(a) 109/115 (b) 111/115
(c) 108/117 (d) 107/117

138. Which country has the maximum percentage of profit increase from 2019 to 2020? (Profit = Export – Import) **[2021]**
(a) P (b) Q
(c) R (d) S

139. Which year has the minimum average import? **[2021]**
(a) 2017 (b) 2018
(c) 2019 (d) 2020

140. Which year has the maximum exports? **[2021]**
(a) 2017 (b) 2018
(c) 2019 (d) 2020

141. Find out the difference between the average export and average import for the country P. **[2021]**
(a) 7.25 (b) 7.75
(c) 8.25 (d) 8.50

Direction: Study the given table carefully and answer the questions 142 to 146.

Number (N) of candidates (in lakhs) appearing for a University Entrance examination from four different states (A, B, C, D) and the percentage (P) of candidates clearing the same over the years are provided in the table below:

State	A		B		C		D	
Year	N	P(%)	N	P(%)	N	P(%)	N	P(%)
2016	2.31	32	1.64	42	2.60	46	3.3	29
2017	2.02	44	1.72	41	2.45	36	3.1	32
2018	1.98	39	2.02	37	2.20	33	2.9	31
2019	1.85	28	2.10	43	2.50	42	2.7	34
2020	2.20	33	1.90	46	2.55	30	3.0	35

142. Find out the average number of non-qualified candidates in 2019 (from all states). **[2021]**
(a) 135320 (b) 137270
(c) 139870 (d) 144025

143. In which year did the highest number of candidates clear the entrance exam from State B? **[2021]**
(a) 2016 (b) 2018
(c) 2019 (d) 2020

144. Find out the total number of students who have cleared the entrance exam from 2016 to 2020 in State A. **[2021]**
(a) 355460 (b) 358660
(c) 360890 (d) 364420

145. Find out the average number of students who qualified in 2020 (from all states). **[2021]**

(a) 84550 (b) 84580
(c) 85375 (d) 86770

146. Find out the difference between the total number of students who qualified in 2017 and the total number of students who qualified in 2018 (from all states): **[2021]**

(a) 31750 (b) 31880
(c) 32220 (d) 32340

Direction: The following Table-I shows the Sales and Earnings of ABC Corporation in the last years from 2013-2020. and Table-II shows the percentage of Sales in four different categories in the year 2020. Based on the data in the tables, answer the questions.

Table-I: Year-wise Sales and Earnings

Year	Sales (in ₹Billion)	Earnings (in ₹Million)
2013	3	500
2014	6	900
2015	8	200
2016	7	400
2017	5	700
2018	9	800
2019	8	700
2020	10	600

Table-II: Category-wise sales in the year 2020

Category	Percentage (%) of Sales
Computers	25%
TVs	20%
Smartphones	40%
Miscellaneous	15%

147. What is the average (in ₹ billions) of the sales of ABC Corporation for the period 2013-2020? **[2021]**

(a) 5.5 (b) 6.0
(c) 7.0 (d) 8.0

148. For which year was the percentage (%) increase in earnings from the previous year highest? **[2021]**

(a) 2014 (b) 2015
(c) 2016 (d) 2017

149. What was the ratio of earnings to sales in 2015? **[2021]**

(a) 25 : 1 (b) 1 : 4
(c) 1 : 25 (d) 1 : 40

150. Which of the following statements can be deduced from the data given in the Tables I and II? **[2021]**

(A) Sales of Smartphones in the year 2020 exceeded total sales in the year 2013.
(B) Earnings for the year in which earnings were highest were more than the sales for the year in which sales were lowest.
(C) If in the year 2020, the sales of Smartphones had been 10% less, and the sale of Computers had been 10% higher, then the sales of Smartphones would have been less than the sales of Computers.

Choose the correct answer from the options given below:

(a) (A) only (b) (A) and (B) only
(c) (A) and (C) only (d) (C) only

151. What is the sum total (in ₹ millions) of the earnings of ABC Corporation for the period 2013-2019? **[2021]**

(a) 4800 (b) 4200
(c) 4000 (d) 5000

Direction: Study the given table carefully and answer the questions that follow.

In the given table, students enrollment for five different courses in 5 different years are given.

Note: The number in the brackets give the maximum number of seats in each course.

	Courses				
	BTech (60)	MCA (60)	MTech (30)	MPhil (20)	Integrated MTech (30)
2016	45	52	25	16	26
2017	55	56	26	18	24
2018	48	43	21	14	25
2019	53	40	23	15	23
2020	50	46	28	13	27

152. The highest student enrollment was in which year? **[Dec 2021]**

(a) 2019 (b) 2017
(c) 2020 (d) 2016

153. What is the difference between average vacant seats in BTech and average vacant seats in MTech during during 2016-20. **[Dec 2021]**

(a) 4.2 (b) 4-3
(c) 4-4 (d) 4-1

154. Which year had highest number of vacant seats? **[Dec 2021]**

(a) 2019 (b) 2020
(c) 2018 (d) 2017

155. Which course had minimum number of total vacant seats during 2016 to 2020? **[Dec 2021]**

(a) B.Tech (b) MCA
(c) M. Tech (d) M.Phil

156. What is the difference between average enrollment in 2016 and average enrollment in 2017? **[Dec 2021]**

(a) 3.0 (b) 3.3
(c) 3.4 (d) 3.2

Directions for questions 157 to 161: Based on the data in table, answer the five questions that follow:

Consider the following table that shows the percentage distribution of cars and ratio between diesel and petrol engine cars in four different states (A-D).

Total number of cars in all the four states is 1400.

State wise distribution of cars

State	Percentage Distribution of cars	Ratio
		Diesel Engine Cars: Petrol Engine Cars
A	14%	3 : 4
B	28%	5 : 9
C	32%	5 : 3
D	26%	1 : 1

157. What is the difference between the number of diesel engine cars in state 'B' and the number of petrol engine cars in state 'D'? **[2022]**

(a) 24 (b) 42
(c) 56 (d) 68

158. Number of petrol engine cars in state 'C' is what percent more than the number of diesel engine cars in state 'A'? **[2022]**

(a) 100% (b) 125%
(c) 200% (d) 120%

159. If 25% diesel engine cars in state 'C' are Air-Conditioned (AC), then what is the number of diesel engine cars which are non-AC in State 'C'? **[2022]**

(a) 150 (b) 90
(c) 190 (d) 210

160. What is the difference between the total number of cars in State 'C' and the number of petrol engine cars in State 'B'? **[2022]**

(a) 212 (b) 224
(c) 204 (d) 196

161. What is the sum of petrol engine cars in all the states together? **[2022]**

(a) 710 (b) 712
(c) 714 (d) 716

Directions for questions 162 to 166: The following table presents data about the number of men, women and children and percentage (%) of overweight men, overweight women and overweight children in a city during the last six years from 2016 to 2021.

Year-wise Distribution of Population in a city

Year	Number of			Percentage (%) of Overweight		
	Men	Women	Children	Men	Women	Children
2016	27000	19000	7500	15%	36%	30%
2017	37500	32000	10500	7%	35%	28%
2018	31500	30000	6000	30%	25%	35%
2019	33000	27000	8000	16%	30%	30%
2020	35000	34000	10000	12%	27%	32%
2021	39000	37500	22500	37.50%	22%	36%

162. What was the total number of children who were not overweight in the year 2016 and 2017 together? **[2022]**

(a) 4530 (b) 4350
(c) 12810 (d) 14820

163. What was the average of the number of men, women and children who were overweight in the year 2019? **[2022]**

(a) 4812 (b) 5016
(c) 5395 (d) 5260

164. The number of overweight men in the year 2021 was what percent of the number of men who were not overweight in the same year? **[2022]**

(a) 55% (b) 60%
(c) 50.5% (d) 65.5%

165. What was the difference between the number of overweight women and overweight children together in the year 2018 and the number of overweight men in the same year? **[2022]**
(a) 150 (b) 450
(c) 345 (d) 865

166. What was the ratio of the number of overweight women in the year 2018 to the number of overweight men in the year 2020? **[2022]**
(a) 6 : 7 (b) 21 : 65
(c) 15 : 73 (d) 25 : 14

***Directions for questions 167 to 171*:** Based on the data in table, answer the five questions that follow:

The following table shows the distribution of the number of girls enrolled in three schools A, B and C over the years 2017–2021. Based on the data in the table, answer the question:

Year-wise Enrollment of Girls

Years	Enrollment of Girls in Schools		
	A	B	C
2017	200	150	100
2018	150	225	250
2019	275	150	199
2020	250	300	200
2021	300	250	275

167. The ratio between the numbers of girls enrolled in School C in the year 2020 and the total number of girls enrolled in School A and School B together in the same year is **[June 2023]**
(a) 11:3 (b) 3:11
(c) 4:11 (d) 4:7

168. The difference between the number of girls enrolled in the years 2021 and 2017 is minimum in: **[June 2023]**
(a) Only School A
(b) Only School B
(c) Only School C
(d) Both School A and School B

169. Average number of girls enrolled in the year 2019 in all the three schools is: **[June 2023]**
(a) 208 (b) 200
(c) 216 (d) 225

170. Total numbers of girls enrolled in all the three Schools in the year 2017 is ______% of the number of girls enrolled in School C in the year 2020. **[June 2023]**
(a) 44.4 (b) 225
(c) 165 (d) 240

171. Total number of girls enrolled in all the three schools together is the second highest in the year.
(a) 2017 (b) 2019
(c) 2020 (d) 2021

Directions for questions 172 to 176: Based on the data in table, answer the five questions that follow:

The following table presents the findings of a survey into how people travel to work:

Number of People Travelling to Work by			
Cycle	Car	Bus	Walk
72	18	35	55

Note : (a) 1 in 8 of the people who cycled to work were found to be over 65 years of age.
(b) 1 in 3 of the cyclists stated that they travelled to work by bus on rainy days.

Based on the above, answer the question:

172. How many people cycled to work on a rainy day? **[June 2023]**
(a) 24 (b) 48
(c) 72 (d) 64

173. How many respondents indicated that they cycled to work and were over 65 years of age? **[June 2023]**
(a) 12 (b) 9
(c) 8 (d) 7

174. Which of the following statements is true? **[June 2023]**
(a) Slightly fewer than twice as many people indicated that they travelled to work by bus than by car.
(b) Slightly more than twice as many people indicated that they travelled to work by bus than by car.
(c) Slightly more people indicated that they travelled to work by bus than by car.
(d) Slightly fewer people indicated that they travelled to work by car than by bus.

175. The sum of which modes of travelling to work represents half the number of responses represented in the survey? **[June 2023]**

A. Cycle and Car
B. Bus and Car
C. Walk and Bus
D. Walk and Cycle

Choose the correct answer from the options given below:

(a) A and B only (b) A and C only
(c) B and C only (d) B and D only

176. How many more people indicated that they cycled to work compared with those who travelled by either bus or car? **[June 2023]**

(a) 72 (b) 35
(c) 18 (d) 19

The following table shows the percentage (%) distribution of the number of candidates (Boys and Girls) and the number of boys who appeared in an entrance examination from six different cities A – F. A total of 78000 candidates appeared from all the six cities, in which the number of boys was 24000. Based on the data in the table, answer the questions that follow.

City-wise Details of Candidates who appeared in an exam

City	Percentage Distribution	
	Candidates who appeared in the Exam	Boys who Appeared in the Exam
A	17%	23%
B	13.5%	20%
C	15%	17%
D	20%	10%
E	8.5%	21%
F	26%	9%

177. What is the difference between the number of boys and the number of girls who appeared in the exam from City E? **[Dec 2023]**

(a) 3450 (b) 3500
(c) 3550 (d) 3650

178. Number of girls who appeared from City F is approximately ______ % of the number of girls who appeared from all the six cities together. **[Dec 2023]**

(a) 31.55 (b) 32.55
(c) 33.55 (d) 34.55

179. What is the total number of girls who appeared from City A? **[Dec 2023]**

(a) 6420 (b) 6880
(c) 7300 (d) 7740

180. Number of girls who appeared from City C is approximately ______ % of the number of candidates who appeared from City D. **[Dec 2023]**

(a) 45 (b) 49
(c) 54 (d) 57

181. Number of boys who appeared from City A is ______ % more than that from City B. **[Dec 2023]**

(a) 8 (b) 12
(c) 15 (d) 18

ANSWER KEY

1. (c)	2. (d)	3. (d)	4. (a)	5. (c)	6. (a)	7. (a)	8. (a)	9. (a)	10. (b)
11. (a)	12. (d)	13. (d)	14. (a)	15. (a)	16. (b)	17. (c)	18. (a)	19. (b)	20. (b)
21. (d)	22. (c)	23. (d)	24. (b)	25. (b)	26. (c)	27. (c)	28. (c)	29. (d)	30. (a)
31. (c)	32. (d)	33. (a)	34. (b)	35. (b)	36. (a)	37. (d)	38. (a)	39. (a)	40. (*)
41. (b)	42. (c)	43. (a)	44. (d)	45. (d)	46. (d)	47. (c)	48. (a)	49. (d)	50. (c)
51. (c)	52. (d)	53. (d)	54. (d)	55. (a)	56. (a)	57. (b)	58. (c)	59. (b)	60. (d)
61. (a)	62. (c)	63. (a)	64. (b)	65. (d)	66. (a)	67. (c)	68. (d)	69. (b)	70. (a)
71. (a)	72. (b)	73. (c)	74. (c)	75. (d)	76. (b)	77. (a)	78. (a)	79. (c)	80. (b)
81. (b)	82. (b)	83. (b)	84. (c)	85. (a)	86. (a)	87. (b)	88. (c)	89. (d)	90. (a)
91. (c)	92. (b)	93. (c)	94. (d)	95. (a)	96. (d)	97. (c)	98. (a)	99. (d)	100. (d)
101. (b)	102. (b)	103. (d)	104. (d)	105. (c)	106. (c)	107. (b)	108. (a)	109. (d)	110. (b)
111. (d)	112. (c)	113. (a)	114. (d)	115. (a)	116. (d)	117. (d)	118. (c)	119. (d)	120. (a)
121. (d)	122. (d)	123. (a)	124. (c)	125. (b)	126. (c)	127. (d)	128. (b)	129. (b)	130. (a)
131. (c)	132. (d)	133. (c)	134. (d)	135. (a)	136. (b)	137. (a)	138. (d)	139. (b)	140. (d)
141. (b)	142. (d)	143. (c)	144. (d)	145. (c)	146. (d)	147. (c)	148. (c)	149. (d)	150. (c)
151. (b)	152. (b)	153. (c)	154. (c)	155. (d)	156. (a)	157. (b)	158. (a)	159. (d)	160. (d)
161. (c)	162. (c)	163. (d)	164. (b)	165. (a)	166. (d)	167. (c)	168. (d)	169. (a)	170. (b)
171. (c)	172. (b)	173. (b)	174. (c)	175. (b)	176. (d)	177. (a)	178. (c)	179. (d)	180. (b)
181. (c)									

HINTS AND SOLUTIONS

1. (c)

Percentage decline in governmental canals

$= \frac{15268 - 17117}{17117} \times 100 = 10.80\%$

For private canals $= \frac{207 - 211}{211} \times 100 = -1.8\%$ it is decline of 1.8%

For tanks $= \frac{2034 - 2593}{2593} \times 100 = -21.5\%$, hence maximum decline is in case of tanks.

Other sources $= \frac{7314 - 3102}{3102} \times 100$, it is positive, so not to be considered.

Thus, (c) is the answer.

2. (d)

Per cent increase in government canals is

$\frac{14444 - 13863}{13863} \times 100 = 4.02\%$

Similarly,

For tanks $= \frac{1908 - 1802}{1908} \times 100 = 5.55\%$

For other sources $= \frac{4281 - 3657}{4281} \times 100 = 14.5\%$

For tubewells and other wells

$= \frac{35779 - 34250}{34785} \times 100 = 4.27\%$

3. (d)

For 2005–06, required percentage

$= \frac{2034 - 1727}{1727} \times 100 = 17.77\%$ - it shows us the highest increase.

For 2000–01, required percentage

$= \frac{2449 - 2535}{2535} \times 100$ but this is negative (decline)

For 2003–04, required percentage

$= \frac{1908 - 1802}{1908} \times 100 = 5.55\%$

For 1998–99, required percentage

$= \frac{2792 - 2593}{2792} \times 100 = 7.1\%$

4. (a)

Tubewells have shown the increasing trend, other sources and private canals are fluctuating so the maximum negative decrease is in case of government canals.

5. (c)

For 1998–99, required percentage

$= \frac{32090}{55173} \times 100 = 58.1\%$

For 2000–01, required percentage

$= \frac{33796}{55076} \times 100 = 61.3\%$

For 2002–03, required percentage

$= \frac{34250}{53778} \times 100 = 63.68\%$

For 2004–05, required percentage

$= \frac{34785}{58867} \times 100 = 59.09\%$

For year 2002-03, the increase is maximum. Thus, (c) is the correct answer.

6. (a)

Required percentage in power

$= \frac{800 - 500}{500} \times 100 = 60\%$

7. (a)

CO_2 emissions (in million metric tons)

Power = 800 – 500 = 300

Industry = 450 – 200 = 250

Commercial = 320 –150 = 170

Agriculture = 200 – 80 = 120

Thus, (a) is the answer.

8. (a)

Total emissions in 2009 = 800 + 450 + 320 + 200 + 180 = 1950

Total emissions in 2005 = 500 + 200 + 150 + 80 + 100 = 1030

Percentage increase $= \frac{1950 - 1030}{1030} \times 100 = 89.32\%$

9. (a)

Let us calculate first the percentage increase from 2005 to 2006 $= \frac{600-500}{500} \times 100 = 20\%$

Similarly, it can be calculated for other years such 2006–07, 2007–08, 2008–09 for four terms in total.

The total percentage increase

$= \frac{20 + 8.33 + 7.69 + 14.28}{4} = \frac{50.30}{4} = 12.57\%$

10. (b)

Percentage contribution of power sector in 2008

$= \frac{700}{1700} \times 100 = 41.18\%$

11. (a)

Required figure for 2005 $= \frac{200}{1030} \times 100 = 19.41\%$

Required figure for 2006 $= \frac{300}{1300} \times 100 = 23.07\%$

Required figure for 2007 $= \frac{320}{1340} \times 100 = 23.88\%$

Required figure for 2009 $= \frac{450}{1950} \times 100 = 23.07\%$

Thus, 2005 is the answer as the contribution was the minimum in this year.

12. (d)

Classes (Age groups)	Class frequencies	Sum of salaries for different classes (In thousands)	Average group salaries (In ₹) = Sum of salaries/ class frequencies
30–35	= 7	= 2,00,000	28,571
35–40	= 2	= 75,000	37,500
40–45	= 6	= 2,40,000	40,000
45–50	= 2	= 1,00,000	50,000
50–55	= 3	= 1,60,000	53,333

Hence, class 50–55 has the maximum average salary.

13. (d)

Required percentage $= \frac{7}{20} \times 100 = 35\%$

14. (a)

Total of ages (from the question table)
$= 44 + 32 + 54 \ldots 43 + 45 = 806$ years

Average age $= \frac{806}{20} = 40.3$ years

15. (a)

Required percentage $= \frac{9}{20} \times 100 = 45\%$

16. (b)

Required average salary in the age group (40–50) $= \frac{340}{8} = 42.5$ Thousand per month

17. (c)

Average salary of all ages $= \frac{7,75,000}{20} = ₹38,750$

The employees getting salaries less than ₹38,750 are 11 in number.

So, their percentage among total $= \frac{11}{20} \times 100 = 55\%$

18. (a)

Here, we need to calculate the decadal growth: 1951–61, 1961–71, …, 2001–2011.

For example, decadal growth of

1951–61 $= \frac{21-20}{20} \times 100 = 5\%$

For 1961–71 $= \frac{24-21}{21} \times 100 = 14.28\%$

For 1971–81, it is 12.5%

For 1981–91, it is 11.11%

For 1991–2001 = 6.66%, and for 2001–2011, it is 9.375%.

19. (b)

Making use of calculation done in solution for Q No 18, average growth rate

$= \frac{5\% + 14.28\% + 12.5\% \ldots 9.375\%}{6} = 9.82\%$

It is as per available choices, the compound annual growth calculation is most likely to be different.

20. (b)

Here, we have to make use of calculation done in Q No 19 The required answer

$= \left[\frac{(100 + 9.82)}{100}\right] \times 35 = 38.49$ million

21. (d)

The required answer (per capita availability of power)
= 10 GW/20 million

$= \frac{10 \times 1000 \text{ million watts}}{20 \text{million}}$ million = 500 watt.

22. (c)

For the sake of simplification, we need to divide the production by population as we need to get a ratio only for this question.

Average Power Availability of Power
= Average Production / Average Population

(a). Per person availability of electricity during the decade 1981 – 1991:
Average Population during the decade 1981 – 1991
= (27 + 30) = 57 / 2
Average Production of electricity during the decade 1981 – 1991 = (40 + 50) / 2 = 45
Now we can use this formula:
Average Power Availability of Power = Average Production / Average Population
= 45 / (57/2) = (45 × 2) / 57 = (15 × 2) / 19 = 1.578

(b). Similarly for the decade 1991 – 2001:
Average Power Availability of Power = [(80 + 50) / 2] / [(30 + 32)/2]
= 130 / 62 = 65 / 31 = 2.09

(c). Similarly for the decade 2001 – 2011:
Average Power Availability of Power = [(80 + 100) / 2] / [(32 + 35) / 2]
= 180 / 67 = 2.68

(d). Similarly for the decade 1971 – 1981:
Average Power Availability of Power = [(25 + 40) / 2] / [(24 + 27) / 2]
= 65 / 51 = 1.27

Thus, we can say that (c) is the correct option.

23. (d)

The power production in 1951 = 10 GW

Power production in 2011 = 100 GW

Increase = 100 – 10 = 90 GW

Thus, increase in percentage = (90 / 10) × 100 = 900%

Thus, (d) is the correct answer.

24. (b)

It is question of direct observation, it is the only year when profit earned by company B is less than that of company A. There is no need to calculate any percentage.

25. (b)

Total of radios = 2 + 1 = 3.

Expenditure of company A in 2012

$=\frac{2}{3}\times 9 = ₹6$ lakhs

Given that profit of company A in 2012 = 35%
Thus, 35 = [(Income of company A – 6)/6] × 100
Solving, it we get that income of company A = ₹18.10 lakhs

26. (c)

Required percentage

$$=\frac{30+40+35+50+35}{5}=\frac{190}{5}=38\%$$

Here, we calculate this percentage on the basis of assumption that expenditure figure is same for all years. Otherwise, none of the choices is correct.

27. (c)

Required percentage

$$=\frac{5+14+11+15+4+2}{17+5+14+11+15+4+2}\times 100=\frac{51}{68}\times 100$$

$$=\frac{51}{68}=75\%$$

28. (c)

Total sample size = 134

Total of people between ages 21 – 30 years = 33

$$\text{Required percentage} = \frac{33}{134}\times 100 = 25\%$$

29. (d)

$$\text{Required percentage} = \frac{\text{Hip-Hop total}}{\text{Grand total}}\times 10$$

$$=\frac{16}{134}\times 100 = 12\% \text{ (Approximately)}$$

30. (a)

First of all, the total of each column should be done.

2012 – 150, 2013 – 163, 2014 – 169, 2015 – 173

$$\text{Required \% age} = \frac{78}{173}\times 100 = 45\% \text{ (approximately)}.$$

31. (c)

By simple observation, we can find the answer. In 2013, there was an increase in sales in all categories. In 2014, there was an increase in sales in magazines and books in comparison to previous years.

32. (d)

Percentage increase in 2015

$$=\frac{173-169}{169}\times 100 = 2.36\%$$

Now desired sales revenue in 2016 = 173 + 2.36% of 173 = ₹176.97 lakh or ₹177 lakh approximately.

Questions 33–35 are from Data Interpretation

33. (a)

	Average	Good	Excellent	Total
M	163	224	10	482
F	24	8	06	32
T	40	30	105	801

(Good + Excellent = 40)

From statement (b), 40% of total students = 32.
Thus, total students = 32 × 100/40 = 80.
From this, we can say, total of male students = 80 − 32 = 48.
From statement (c), number of male students who are average $= \frac{1}{3} \times 48 = 16.$
Number of male students who are good = 48 − (16 + 10) = 22.
Half the students were either excellent or good

$= \frac{1}{2} \times 80 = 40.$

Thus, the total of excellent students = 40 − 30 = 10.
Thus, the number of female students who are excellent = 10 − 10 = 0.

34. (b)
Proportion of female students who are good

$= \frac{8}{32} = 0.25.$

35. (b)
Proportion of good students who are male

$= \frac{22}{30} = 0.73.$

36. (a): Growth for 1961–1971

$$= \left(\frac{(548.15 - 439.23)}{439.23}\right) \times 100$$

= 24.79 %

Similarly, the growth rate can be calculated for decades given in answer choices.
Here, option (a) is the right answer.

37. (d)
In question, we have to calculate the decadal growth for cars. The same is to be done in case of two wheelers. Students can eliminate choices by doing some approximation.
For year 2011, decadal growth rate of two wheelers

$$= \left(\frac{1018.65 - 385.56)}{385.56}\right) \times 100$$

$$= \left(\frac{633.09}{385.56}\right) \times 100 = 164.40\%$$

For year 2011, decadal growth rate of cars

$$= \left[\frac{(70.58 - 29.54)}{29.54}\right] \times 100$$

$$= \left(\frac{41.04}{29.54}\right) \times 100 = 138.93\%$$

Hence, option (d) is the right answer.

38. (a)
In this question, calculations are to be done for all five decades. Then averaging is done for all of these growth figures.

39. (a)

$$\text{Passenger vehicles} = \frac{70.58 + 6.34}{549.91} \times 100 = 13.9\%$$

40. (*) This question was dropped.
Here, all figures should be converted into lakh or millions. Let's convert them into smaller units, i.e., lakh.
Population = 1210.19 million = 1210.19×10^6
Two wheelers = 1018.65 lakhs = 1018.65×10^5
Per capita availability of two wheelers
= Number of two wheelers/Total population
= $1018.65 \times 10^5/1210.19 \times 10^6 = 0.084$
Answer should not be in percentage as mentioned in question paper. So, each candidate gets 2 marks for the question.

41. (b)
Consumption for different years is given as follows:
2012: 186.5 − 114 = 72.5
2013: 202 − 114 = 88
2014: 238 − 130 = 108
2015: 221 − 116 = 105
2016: 215 − 88 = 127
For year 2013, percentage increase

$$= \frac{88 - 72.5}{72.5} \times 100 = 21.37\%$$

For year 2014, percentage increase

$$= \frac{108 - 88}{88} \times 100 = 22.72\%$$

For year 2015, there is decrease in consumption.

For year 2016, percentage increase

$$= \frac{127 \times 105}{105} \times 100 = 20.95\%$$

42. (c)

Per capita consumption = $\frac{\text{Consumption in million kg}}{\text{Population in million}}$

Or population in million = $\frac{\text{Consumption in million kg}}{\text{Per capita consumption}}$

$= \frac{108 \text{ million kg}}{38.7 \text{ kg}} = 2.79$ million

Note: As population is to be calculated in million, there is no need for conversion of units as consumption is also given in millions. Kg in both numerator and numerators will cancel out each other.

43. (a)

We have already calculated consumption in question

For 2012, desired ratio = 114 : 72.5 = 1.57

For 2013, desired ratio = 114 : 88 = 1.29

For 2014, desired ratio = 130 : 108 = 1.20

For 2015, desired ratio = 116 : 105 = 1.10

For 2016, desired ratio = 88 : 127 = 0.69

44. (d)

Population = $\frac{\text{Consumption (in million kg)}}{\text{Per capita consumption (in kgs)}}$

Population for 2013 = $\frac{88}{35.2} = 2.5$ million

Population for 2014 = 2.79 (already calculated)

Population for 2015 = $\frac{105}{40.5}$

= 2.59 million

Population for 2016 = $\frac{127}{42}$

= 3.02 million

45. (d)

Average consumption

$= \frac{72.5 + 88 + 108 + 105 + 127}{5}$

$= \frac{500.5}{5} = 100.1$ million kg

46. (d) Average interest on loans

$= \frac{4.68 + 6.50 + 8.32 + 7.28 + 9.88}{5} = \frac{36.66}{5}$

= ₹7.33 crores

47. (c) Bonus:

For 2008 = $\frac{0.6}{57.6} \times 100 = 1.04\%$

For 2009 = $\frac{0.76}{64.8} \times 100 = 0.73\%$

For 2010 = $\frac{0.76}{64.8} \times 100 = 1.17\%$

For 2011 = $\frac{0.74}{67.2} \times 100 = 1.10\%$

2010 is the answer.

48. (a) Total Expenditure (In ₹ crores)

For 2008 = 57.6 + 19.6 + 0.6 + 4.68 + 16.6 = 82.48
For 2009 = 68.4 + 22.4 + 0.5 + 6.50 + 21.6 = 119.4
For 2010 = 64.8 + 20.2 + 0.76 + 8.32 + 14.8 = 108.8
For 2011 = 67.2 + 26.6 + 0.74 + 7.28 + 17.6 = 119.42
Option (a) is the right answer.

49. (d) 2009–10 has decrease in the salary.
The calculation can be done in this manner

$= \frac{\text{Difference}}{\text{base year}} \times 100$

50. (c)

Expenditure (in crores)
For 2009 = 6.50 + 21.6 = 28.10
Fuel Expenditure = 22.4
For 2010 = 8.32 + 14.8 = 23.12
Fuel Expenditure = 20.2
For 2011 = 7.28 + 17.6 = 24.88
Fuel Expenditure = 26.6
For 2012 = 9.88 + 19.6 = 29.48
Fuel Expenditure = 28.4
Thus 2011 is the right answer.

Data for questions 52–56

Subject	Total number of students appeared	Number of students who passed	Number of Students who failed	Maximum/ Ful the sub
English	600	564	36	600
Mathematics	300	240	60	200
Science	300	216	84	400
Social Studies	360	312	48	400
Computer	200	168	32	400

51. (c)

Number of students who failed in science = 84

Number of students who passed in social studies = 312

Difference = 312 – 84 = 228

52. (d)

Required answer = 35% of full marks in mathematics = 70

Full marks = 70 × 100/35 = 200

53. (d)

Total marks = 600 + 200 + 400 + 400 + 400 = 2000

54. (d)

We actually need not to calulate each percentage separately. This is can be done directly by an approximation. English has total of 600 students. We can make total number of students for each subject to 600, and then compare.

Subject	Total	Failed
English	600	36
Mathematics	300 × 2 = 600	60 × 2 = 120
Social Studies	360 × 5/3 = 600	48 × 5/3 = 80
Science	300 × 2 = 600	84 × 2 = 168

If number of students is same in each subject, then comparison is easy.
Thus, English is the answer.

55. (a)

Pass percentage in Mathematics

= 240/300 × 100 = 80%

Pass percentage in Social Studies

= 312/360 × 100 = 86.67%

Difference = 86.67 – 80 = 6.67% (approx)

56. (a)

Section–A
(30 – 39) 4
(40 – 49) 8
Thus 4 + 8 = 12 students is the answer.

57. (b)

Passing marks = 40

Twist: People with marks more than 40 are also successful.

Required percentage in Section–B =

$$\frac{\text{Score of 40 and above in Section–B}}{\text{Total candidates in Section–B}} \times 100$$

$$= \frac{23}{45} \times 100 = 51.1$$

58. (c)

	(A)		(B)		
50–59	4		5		
60–69	7		5		
70–79	5		6		
Total =	16	+	16	=	32

59. (b)

Passing marks = 30

Twist: Less than also count under number of failures.

Number of failures

	(A)		(B)		
0–9	2		4		
10–19	5		5		
20–29	10		9		
Total =	17	+	18	=	35

60. (d)

Students scoring less than 10 marks.

	Sec – A		Sec – B	
(0–9)	2	+	4	=6

61. (a)

The question simply asked about cyclical variation which is directly a observation based question, if we see the data of East zone, it shows variation in cycles, 1st decrease then increase and again increase & decrease so the pattern is cyclical in variation.

62. (c)

Percentage representation by East zone

$$= \frac{\text{Strength of East zone}}{\text{Total strength}} \times 100$$

Year

2014: $\frac{8.2}{44.9} \times 100 = 18.2\%$

2015: $\frac{7.8}{47} \times 100 = 16.5\%$

2016: $\frac{8.5}{49.7} \times 100 = 17.1\%$

2017: $\frac{7.6}{48.1} \times 100 = 15.8\%$

2018: $\frac{8.6}{51.5} \times 100 = 16.6\%$

2014 is the right answer.

63. (a)

Increase in North zone $= \frac{18 - 15.1}{15.1} \times 100 = 19.2\%$

West zone $= \frac{5.4 - 4}{4} \times 100 = 35\%$

East zone $= \frac{8.6 - 8.2}{8.2} \times 100 = 4.$

Foreign countries $= \frac{2.5 - 1.2}{1.2} \times 100 = 108\%$

64. (b)

Growth rate over $\frac{2014\text{–}15 = 16.2 - 15.1}{15.1} \times 100 = 7.28\%$

Over 2015–16 $= \frac{17.2 - 16.2}{16.2} \times 100 = 6.17\%$

Over 2016–17 $= \frac{17.4 - 17.2}{17.2} \times 100 = 1.16\%$

Over 2017–18 $= \frac{18 - 17.4}{17.4} \times 100 = 3.44\%$

Thus, mean of annual growth rates

$= \frac{7.28 + 6.17 + 1.16 + 3.44}{4} = 4.51\%$

65. (d)

Percentage of students from foreign countries

$= \frac{2.5}{18 + 10.6 + 6.4 + 5.4 + 8.6 + 2.5} \times 100 = 4.85\%$

66. (a)

Number of female students:

In Physics $= \frac{45}{100} \times 450 = 203$

In Chemistry $= \frac{35}{100} \times 550 = 193$

In English $= \frac{55}{100} \times 300 = 165$

In Mathematics $= \frac{40}{100} \times 500 = 200$

67. (c)

Number of male students:

In Physics = 450 – 203 = 202

In English = 300 – 165 = 135

In Hindi = 40/100 × 250 = 100

In Mathematics = 500 – 200 = 300

Thus, Hindi is the answer.

68. (d)

Required percentage $= \frac{550}{500} \times 100 = 110\%$

69. (b)

Number of male in English = 135

Number of male in Mathematics = 300

Required ratio = 135:300 = 9:20

70. (a)

Number of females in English = 165

Number of females in Hindi = 250 – 100 = 150

Total = 165 + 150 = 315

71. (a)

The sum of the deviations from the mean of a measurement is always equal to 0.

72. (b)

Required answer $= \frac{400 - 200}{100} \times 100 = 200\%$

73. (c)

Difference

= (300 + 400 + 350 + 350 + 250) – (200 + 350 + 250 + 300 + 400)

= 1650 – 1500 = 150

74. (c)

Average $= \frac{250 + 350}{2} = \frac{600}{2} = 300$

75. (d)

The total number of tickets sold of movies Q and R at cinemas A and B

= 350 + 400 + 250 + 350 = 1350

76. (b)

The ratio = 300 : 400 = 3 : 4

77. (a)

Required percentage $= \frac{90 - 35}{35} \times 100 = 157\%$

78. (a)

For 2012, required percentage $= \frac{50 - 35}{35} \times 100 = 42\%$

For 2013, required percentage $= \frac{70 - 50}{50} \times 100 = 40\%$

For 2015, required percentage $= \frac{75 - 55}{55} \times 100 = 36\%$

For 2018, required percentage $= \frac{90 - 85}{85} \times 100 = 5.88\%$

Thus, 2012 is the answer.

79. (c)

Average production

$$= \frac{35 + 50 + 70 + 55 + 75 + 60 + 85 + 90}{8} = 65$$

Thus, production figures of 2013, 2015, 2017 and 2018 were higher than average production.

80. (b)

$$\text{Required percentage} = \frac{55 - 70}{70} \times 100$$
$$= -21.42\ \%$$

81. (b)

We can directly take sum of 2012 and 2013 that comes to be 120. Then look at different such combinations in the answer choices, we can find the answer.

82. (b)

For year 2012:

60% profit of investment = ₹9,00,000

$$\text{Thus, investment} = \frac{900000 \times 100}{60} = ₹15,00,000$$

83. (b)

Let the same equal investment of ₹100 is being made in ABC and XYZ for the year 2015.

ABC: XYZ

Incomes 60% of 100 : 50% of 100

or 60 : 50 = 6 : 5

84. (c)

Total income of both the companies in 2014 = 40% of ₹20 lakh + 50% of ₹20 lakh = ₹18 lakh

$$\text{Average profit} = \frac{\text{Total profit}}{2} = \frac{18}{2} = ₹9 \text{ lakh}$$

85. (a)

According to questions, incomes for 2013 and 2015 were same for company ABC.

50% of ₹8,00,000 = 60% of investment in 2015

$$\text{Investment in 2015} = \frac{50}{100} \times 8{,}00{,}000 \times \frac{100}{60}$$

= ₹6,67,000

86. (a)

Profit percentage on investment = Absolute income in ₹60% on investment = ₹6,60,000

$$\text{Investment} = \frac{660000 \times 100}{60} = ₹11{,}000{,}00$$

87. (b)

Required answer

$$= \frac{2 + 2.5 + 2.75 + 3 + 3.25}{150 + 180 + 200 + 240 + 250} \times 100 = \frac{13.5}{1020} \times$$

100 = 1.32 %

88. (c)

Required answer = 2008:2009

(150 + 90 + 2 + 20 + 80):(180 + 100 + 2.5 + 30.5 + 95)

= 342 : 408

= 57 : 68

89. (d)

Required answer = (80 + 95 + 105 + 85 + 100) : (90 + 100 + 110 + 115 + 125)

= 465 : 540

= 31 : 36

90. (a)

Required answer

$$= \frac{150 + 90 + 2 + 20 + 80}{250 + 125 + 3.25 + 42.5 + 100} \times 100$$

$$= \frac{342}{520.75} \times 100 = 65.6\% \text{ or } 66\% \text{ approx.}$$

91. (c)

Required answer

$$= \frac{20 + 30.5 + 35.5 + 40 + 42.5}{5} = \frac{168.5}{5}$$

= 33.7 lakh

92. (b)

Increase = 175 – 112 = 63

$$\text{Required percentage} = \frac{63}{112} \times 100 = 56.25\%$$

93. (c)

The total sales of LED TV 22" inches over 7 years (in lakhs) = 85 + 100 + 106 + 115 + 100 + 115 + 125 = 746

Similarly, total sales of LED 24" TVs (in lakhs) = 764

Total sales of LED 32" TVs (in lakhs) = 971

Total sales of LED 40" TVs (in lakhs) = 671

Total sales of LED 49" TVs (in lakhs) = 869

Maximum sales is 971 for LED 32" TVs.

94. (d)

Referring solution of 94.

Lowest sale is of 671 in case of 40" LED TVs.

95. (a)

Difference = 110 – 94 = 16 lakhs or 1,600,000

96. (d)

We can again refer to solution of question 94.

Total sales is of 869 for 49" LED Television.

97. (c)

Number of adults in City F

= 65% of 15% of 24,00,000 = 2,34,000

98. (a)

Number of non-adult persons in City C

= (100 – 72)% of 16% of 24,00,000 = 1,07,520

99. (d)

The population of City B = 18% of 24,00,000 = 4,32,000

Difference between ratios = 5 – 4 = 1

Total = 5 + 4 = 9

If total population is 9, then difference = 1

If total population is 4,32,000, then difference

$= \frac{1}{9} \times 4{,}32{,}000 = 48{,}000$

100. (d)

Suppose 75% of 10% of 24,00,000 =

x% of 2/5 of 20% of 24,00,000

The required percentage x

$$= \frac{75\% \text{ of } 10\% \text{ of } 24{,}00{,}000}{2/5 \text{ of } 20\% \text{ of } 24{,}00{,}000} \times 100 = 93.75\,\%$$

101. (b)

Male population in City D = $\frac{2}{5}$ of 20% of 24,00,000 = 1.92 lakh

102. (b)

Total export of company A = 540

Average annual export of company

$$A = \frac{540}{7} = 77.14$$

In 2015, total export is more than its average.

Similarly, in 2016 and 2018, the total export is more than it average = 3 years.

103. (d)

Total export from the three companies in

2014 = 50 + 70 + 130 = 250

2015 = 80 + 70 + 100 = 250

2016 = 110 + 90 + 70 = 270

2017 = 60 + 110 + 90 = 260

Therefore, in 2015 and 2015, the exports are equal.

104. (d)

In 2012, average export of three companies

$$= \frac{40+90+70}{3} = \frac{200}{3} = 66.67$$

In 2017, average export $= \frac{60+110+90}{30}$

$$= \frac{260}{3} = 86.67$$

Difference in average export

= 86.67 – 66.67 = 20 crores

105. (c)

Average annual export of company

$$B = \frac{630}{7} = 90 \text{ crores}$$

Average annual export of company

$$C = \frac{670}{7} = 95.71 = \text{crores}$$

According to question, $\frac{90}{95.71} \times 100 = 94.03\%$

So, B is approximately 94.03% of the average annual amount of C.

106. (c): In 2013, difference between export from company A and B = 70 – 50 = 20 crores

In 2014, difference between export from company A and B = 70 – 50 = 20 crores

In 2015, difference between export from company A and B = 80 – 70 = 10 crores

In 2016, difference between export from company A and B = 110 – 90 = 20 crores

Therefore, in 2015, the difference is minimum.

107. (b)

Average production of A Type over the given year

$$= \frac{115500}{7} = 16500$$

In 2012, 2013, 2014, 2017, production is less than average.

108. (a)

Average number of B Type vehicles produced over the year

$$= \frac{20000 + 10000 + 15000 + 15000 + 20000 + 25000 + 35000}{7}$$

$$= \frac{140000}{7} = 20000$$

109. (d)

Total production in 2016

$= 25000 + 20000 + 15000 = 60000$

110. (b)

Percentage of production of A Type over B Type

$$= \frac{10000}{15000} \times 100 = 66.67\%$$

111. (d)

Percentage Increase in 2017

$$= \frac{25000 - 20000}{20000} \times 100 = 25\%$$

112. (c)

% Profit of company *B* in year 2013 $= \frac{48.6 - 36}{36} \times 100 = 35\%$

% Profit of company *B* in year 2014 $= \frac{35 - 25}{25} \times 100 = 40\%$

% Profit of company *B* in year 2015 $= \frac{62.4 - 48}{48} \times 100 = 30\%$

% Profit of company *B* in year 2016 $= \frac{77 - 44}{44} \times 100 = 75\%$

% Profit of company *B* in year 2017 $= \frac{80 - 50}{50} \times 100 = 60\%$

% Profit of company *B* in year 2018 $= \frac{72 - 45}{45} \times 100 = 60\%$

113. (a)

% Profit of company *A* in year 2013 = 40%

% Profit of company *B* in year 2013 $= \frac{48.6 - 36}{36} \times 100$

= 35%

Difference in Profit = 40 − 35 = 5%

114. (d)

Income of company *A* in year 2018 = ₹90 Lakh

% Profit = 20%

Expenditure of compnay *A* in 2018 $= \frac{90 \times 100}{(100 + 20)}$

$= 90 \times \frac{5}{6}$ = ₹75 Lakh

Net Profit of Company *A* in 2018

= 90 − 75 = ₹15 Lakh

Net Profit of Company *B* in 2018

= 72 − 45 = ₹27 Lakh

Difference in Net Profit = 27 − 15 = ₹12 Lakh

Required % $= \frac{12}{15} \times 100 = 80\%$

115. (a)

Expenditure of Company *A* in year 2017 = ₹45 Lakh

% Profit = 10%

$$\% \text{ Profit} = \frac{\text{Profit}}{\text{Expenditure}} \times 100$$

Profit $= \frac{10 \times 45}{100}$ = ₹4.5 Lakh

Profit of Company *B in* 2017 = 80 − 50 = ₹30 Lakh

Required % $= \frac{4.5}{30} \times 100 = 15\%$

116. (d)

Income of Company *A* in year 2014 = ₹32.5 Lakh

% Profit = 25%

Expenditure of Compnay *A* in 2014

$$= \frac{32.5 \times 100}{(100 + 25)} = \frac{32.5 \times 100}{125} = ₹26 \text{ Lakh}$$

Profit of Company A = 32.5 − 26 = ₹ 6.5 Lakh

Sum of profit of Company *A* and *B* in 2014 = 6.5 + 10 = ₹16.5 Lakh

117. (d)

Computers sold in 2005 = 85,000

Computers sold in 2002 = 25,000

Difference in number of computers

= 85,000 − 25,000 = 60,000

118. (c)

Here, we need not to calculate the total number of computers sold. As a denominator, they may appear everywhere. We should focus on numerator to get the result. So the answer is 85,000 that is (c).

119. (d)

This is a question of simple observation.

HCL computer sale has decreased continuously over the years.

120. (a)

Total sale of IBM (in thousands)

= 50 + 60 + 50 + 40 + 70 + 80 + 100 = 450

Similarly,

Total sale of Lenovo = 400

Total sale of Acer = 375

Total sale of HCL = 295

Therefore, the sale of IBM computer is maximum in all the seven years.

121. (d)

Sale in 2001 = 20

Sale in 2007 = 90

Increase in sale = 90 – 20 = 70

$$\% \text{ increase} = \frac{70}{20} \times 100 = 350\%$$

122. (d)

$$\text{Mathematics} = 60\% = \frac{60}{100} \times 100 = 60$$

$$\text{Chemistry} = \frac{50}{100} \times 150 = 75$$

$$\text{Physics} = \frac{65}{100} \times 150 = 97.5$$

$$\text{English} = \frac{50}{100} \times 100 = 50$$

$$\text{Physical Edu.} = \frac{70}{100} \times 100 = 70$$

Aggregate marks

= 60 + 75 + 97.5 + 50 + 70 = 352.5

123. (a)

Average percentage of marks obtained by students in Chemistry

$$= \frac{80 + 75 + 95 + 70 + 50}{5} = 74\%$$

124. (c)

Aggregate marks obtained by

	A	C
Mathematics	90	100
Chemistry	120	142.5
Physics	142.5	142.5
English	80	85
Physical Education	90	95
	522.5	565

These values have been obtained in the same way as in answer to question number 26.

for example 90% of 150 $= \left(\frac{90}{100}\right) \times 150$

$$= \frac{90 \times 150}{100}$$

$$= \frac{13500}{100} = 135$$

similarly 95% of 150 $= \left(\frac{95}{100}\right) \times 150$

$$= \frac{90 \times 150}{100}$$

$$= \frac{14250}{100} = 142.5$$

Difference in marks obtained

= 565 – 522.5 = 42.5

125. (b)

Aggregate % of marks obtained by C

$$= \frac{565}{600} \times 100 = 94.17$$

Here,

565 = 100 + 142.5 + 142.5 + 85 + 95

600 = 100 + 150 + 150 + 100 + 100

126. (c)

Average percentage of marks in Chemistry = 74% (calculated earlier).

$$\text{In Physics} = \frac{95 + 90 + 95 + 60 + 65}{5} = 81\%$$

$$\text{In English} = \frac{80 + 70 + 85 + 65 + 50}{5} = 70\%$$

$$\text{In Physical Education} = \frac{90 + 80 + 95 + 60 + 70}{5}$$

= 79%

The students have obtained the lowest average percentage of marks in English.

127. (d)

The heart attack is the least reported disease if we do the total of all.

The average number of heart attacks

$$= \frac{320 + 240 + 360}{3} = \frac{920}{3} = 306.67$$

128. (b)

Total number of patients in hospital A

= 320 + 650 + 700 + 210 = 1880

Total number of patients in hospital C
$= 360 + 1950 + 2100 + 630 = 5040$
Increase in number $= 5040 - 1880 = 3160$

Percentage increase in number $= \frac{3160}{1880} \times 100 = 168.96\,\%$

129. (b)

We need to add number of patients in hospital B to those of A and C that have already been calculated.

Total number of patients in hospital B
$= 240 + 1350 + 1400 + 420 = 3410$

Total of numbers in hospitals A, B and C
$= 1880 + 3410 + 5040 = 10330$

Total number of blood sugar patients in all hospitals $= 650 + 1350 + 1950 = 3950$

Required percentage $= \frac{3950}{10330} \times 100 = 38.24\,\%$

130. (a)

Required percentage $= \frac{360 - 320}{320} \times 100$

$= \frac{40}{320} \times 100 = 12.5\%$

131. (c)

Required ratio $= 210 : 630 = 1 : 3$

132. (d)

We need to sort out the total admitted to total interviewed in chemical engineering department.

Total interviewed $= 1274 + 1165 + 1108 + 1230 + 1492 + 982 = 7251$

Total Admitted $= 1090 + 1065 + 1024 + 1180 + 1372 + 930 = 6661$

Required percentage $= \frac{6661}{7251} \times 100 = 91.86\,\%$

133. (c)

Difference $= 1980 - 1815 = 165$

Percentage change $= \frac{165}{1980} \times 100 = 8.33$

134. (d)

Total candidates who appeared in interviews in 2016 $= 1180 + 1860 + 1132 + 870 + 1260 = 6230$

Required average number of candidates which appeared in the interview $= \frac{\text{Sum of observations}}{\text{Number of observations}}$

$= \frac{6230}{5}$

$= 1246$

135. (a)

Total number in Aerospace $= 1180 + 1260 + 1132 + 1060 + 1465 + 1640 = 7737$

Total number in Electrical Engineering $= 1216 + 1132 + 1260 + 1191 + 1242 + 1362 = 7403$

Difference $= 7737 - 7403 = 334$

136. (b)

Ratio $= \frac{\text{Petroleum Engineering interviewed in 2014}}{\text{Electrical Engineering admitted in 2015}}$

$= \frac{960}{1120} = \frac{6}{7}$

Thus, 6 : 7 is the answer.

137. (a)

Exports by country S during 2017–2020 $= 28 + 28 + 21 + 32 = 109$

Exports by country T during 2017–2020 $= 31 + 33 + 23 + 28 = 115$

Thus, required ratio of exports between S and T $= \frac{109}{115}$

138. (d)

As per question, the profit percentage increase by different countries between 2019 and 2020 is to be calculated first.

For Country P

Profit in 2019 $= 36 - 28 = 8$

Profit in 2020 $= 32 - 22 = 10$

Percentage increase $= \frac{10-8}{8} \times 100 = \frac{2}{8} \times 100 = 25\%$

For Country Q

Profit in 2019 $= 37 - 29 = 8$

Profit in 2020 $= 34 - 26 = 8$

Percentage increase $= \frac{8-8}{8} \times 100 = \frac{0}{8} \times 100 = 0\%$

For Country R

Profit in 2019 $= 36 - 32 = 4$

Profit in 2020 $= 34 - 28 = 6$

Percentage increase $= \frac{6-4}{4} \times 100 = \frac{2}{4} \times 100 = 50\%$

As per question, the profit percentage increase by different countries between 2019 and 2020

For Country S

Profit in 2019 $= 21 - 16 = 5$

Profit in 2020 $= 32 - 23 = 9$

Percentage increase $= \frac{9-5}{5} \times 100 = \frac{4}{5} \times 100 = 80\%$

For Country T

Profit in 2019 = 23 – 12 = 11

Profit in 2020 = 28 – 21 = 7

$$\text{Percentage increase} = \frac{7-11}{11} \times 100 = \text{Reduction}$$

Thus, country S has shown the maximum increase in profit.

139. (b)

As every figure is to be divided by 5 (number of years) to calculate average imports, we may get the answer directly by total as well, and thus save time.

The total imports during different years are:

Imports during 2017 = 25 + 28 + 24 + 22 + 26 = 125

Imports during 2018 = 24 + 26 + 28 + 18 + 16 = 112

Imports during 2019 = 28 + 29 + 32 + 16 + 12 = 117

Imports during 2020 = 22 + 26 + 28 + 23 – 21 = 120

Thus, the minimum average imports were in the year 2018. Thus, the answer is (b).

140. (d)

As every figure is to be divided by 5 (number of years) to calculate average exports, we may get the answer directly by total as well, and thus save time.

The total exports during different years are:

Exports during 2017 = 30 + 26 + 32 + 28 + 31 = 147

Exports during 2018 = 32 + 31 + 25 + 28 + 33 = 149

Export during 2019 = 36 + 37 + 36 + 21 + 23 = 153

Export during 2020 = 32 + 34 + 34 + 32 + 28 = 160

The maximum average exports were in the year 2020. Thus, the answer is (d).

141. (b)

The average exports by country P = 30 + 32 + 36 + 32

$$= \frac{130}{4} = 32.5$$

The average imports by country P = 25 + 24 + 28 + 22

$$= \frac{99}{4}$$

Difference = 32.5 – 24.75 = 7.75

142. (d)

Non-qualified candidates (%) = 100 – Number of qualified candidates

State-wise number of non-qualified candidates in the year 2019

$$\text{State A} = 185000 \times \frac{100-28}{100} = 185000 \times \frac{72}{100} = 133200$$

$$\text{State B} = 210000 \times \frac{100-43}{100} = 210000 \times \frac{57}{100} = 119700$$

$$\text{State C} = 250000 \times \frac{100-42}{100} = 250000 \times \frac{58}{100} = 145000$$

$$\text{State D} = 270000 \times \frac{100-34}{100} = 270000 \times \frac{66}{100} = 178200$$

Total non-qualified candidates = 133200 + 119700 + 145000 + 178200 = 576200

$$\text{Required Average} = \frac{\text{Total non-qualified candidates}}{\text{Given number of states}}$$

$$= \frac{576200}{4} = 144025$$

143. (c)

Number of qualified candidates from State B during the given years

$$\text{Year 2016} = 164000 \times \frac{42}{100} = 68880$$

$$\text{Year 2017} = 172000 \times \frac{41}{100} = 70520$$

$$\text{Year 2018} = 202000 \times \frac{37}{100} = 74740$$

$$\text{Year 2019} = 210000 \times \frac{43}{100} = 90300$$

$$\text{Year 2020} = 190000 \times \frac{46}{100} = 87400$$

Thus, in the year 2019, the highest number of candidates cleared the entrance exam from State B.

144. (d)

Number of qualified candidates from State A during the given years

$$\text{Year 2016} = 231000 \times \frac{32}{100} = 73920$$

$$\text{Year 2017} = 202000 \times \frac{44}{100} = 88880$$

$$\text{Year 2018} = 198000 \times \frac{39}{100} = 77220$$

$$\text{Year 2019} = 185000 \times \frac{28}{100} = 51800$$

$$\text{Year 2020} = 220000 \times \frac{33}{100} = 72600$$

Total number of qualified candidates during the years 2016 to 2020 = 73920 + 88880 + 77220 + 51800 + 72600 = 364420

145. (c)

Number of qualified candidates from all the states during the year 2020

State A $= 220000 \times \frac{33}{100} = 72600$

State B $= 190000 \times \frac{46}{100} = 87400$

State C $= 255000 \times \frac{30}{100} = 76500$

State D $= 300000 \times \frac{35}{100} = 105000$

The average number of candidates

$= \frac{72600 + 87400 + 76500 + 105000}{4} = \frac{341500}{4}$

$= 85375$

146. (d)

Number of qualified candidates from all states during the year 2017

State A $= 20000 \times \frac{44}{100} = 88880$

State B $= 172000 \times \frac{41}{100} = 70520$

State C $= 245000 \times \frac{36}{100} = 88200$

State D $= 310000 \times \frac{32}{100} = 99200$

Thus, the total candidates = 88880 + 70520 + 88200 + 99200 = 346800

Number of qualified candidates from all states during the year 2018

State A $= 198000 \times \frac{39}{100} = 77220$

State B $= 202000 \times \frac{37}{100} = 74740$

State C $= 220000 \times \frac{33}{100} = 72600$

State D $= 290000 \times \frac{31}{100} = 89900$

Thus, the total candidates = 72220 + 74740 + 72600 + 89900 = 314460

Thus, difference = 346800 – 314460 = 32340

147. (c)

The sum of sales of ABC corporations during all the years (in billion rupees)

$= \frac{3 + 6 + 8 + 7 + 5 + 9 + 8 + 10}{8} = \frac{56.0}{8} = ₹7.0$ billion.

148. (c)

Year-wise percentage increase during all the years is as follows:

Year 2014 $= \frac{900 - 500}{400} \times 100 = \frac{400}{500} \times 100 = 80\%$

Year 2015 = There is a decrease in earning. We don't need to calculate.

Year 2016 $= \frac{(400 - 200)}{200} \times 100 = \frac{200}{200} \times 100 = 100\%$

Year 2017 $= \frac{(700 - 400)}{400} \times 100 = \frac{300}{400} \times 100 = 75\%$

149. (d)

Total earnings in the year 2015 = 200 million

Total sales in the year 2015 = 8 billion

Required ratio = 200,000,000: 8,000,000,000 = 2 : 80 = 1 : 40

150. (c)

In this question, we need to pay attention to the billion and million characters.

1 million $= 10^6$

1 billion $= 10^9$

Statement a:

Sale of smartphones in the year 2020

$= \frac{10,000,000,000 \times 40}{100} = 4,000,000,000$

Total sales in the year 2013 = 3,000,000,000

Thus, sale of smartphones in the year 2020 exceeds total sales in the year 2013.

Statement b:

Highest earning in the year 2014: 900,000,000

Lowest sale in the year 2013: 3,000,000,000

Highest earning in the year 2014 is less than the lowest sale in the year 2013.

Statement c:

Sale of smartphones in the year 2020 = 3,000,000,000

Sale of computers in the year 2020 = 3,500,000,000

Thus, only statement (a) and (c) are correct.

151. (b)

The sum (in million rupees) of the earning of ABC corporation for the period 2013–2019 is = 500 + 900 + 200 + 400 + 700 + 800 + 700 = ₹4200 millions

152. (b)

Student enrolment for five courses during all the years:

Year 2016 = 45 + 52 + 25 + 16 + 26 = 164

Year 2017 = 55 + 56 + 26 + 18 + 24 = 179

Year 2018 = 48 + 43 + 21 + 14 + 25 = 151

Year 2019 = 53 + 40 + 23 + 15 + 23 = 154

Year 2020 = 50 + 46 + 28 + 13 + 27 = 164

The highest student enrolment was in the year 2017.

153. (c)

Average vacant seats in BTech during 2016–2020

$= \frac{49}{5} = 9.8$

Average vacant seats in MTech during 2016–2020

$= \frac{27}{5} = 5.4$

Difference = 9.8 – 5.4 = 4.4

154. (c)

The total number of vacant seats for five courses during all the years:

Vacant seats = maximum seats – student enrolled

Year 2016 = 15 + 8 + 5 + 4 + 4 = 36

Year 2017 = 5 + 4 + 4 + 2 + 6 = 21

Year 2018 = 12 + 17 + 7 + 6 + 5 = 47

Year 2019 = 7 + 20 + 7 + 5 + 7 = 46

Year 2020 = 10 + 14 + 2 + 7 + 3 = 36

The highest number of vacant seats was in the year 2018.

155. (d)

The total number of vacant seats for five courses during all the years together:

Vacant seats = maximum seats – student enrolled

BTech = 15 + 5 + 12 + 7 + 10 = 49

MCA = 8 + 4 + 17 + 20 + 14 = 63

MTech = 5 + 4 + 7 + 7 + 2 = 27

MPhil = 4 + 2 + 6 + 5 + 7 = 24

Integrated MTech = 4 + 6 + 5 + 7 + 3 = 25

Thus, the minimum number of total vacant seats was in the MPhil course during 2016–20.

156. (a)

Average enrolment in the year 2016 = 45 + 52 + 25 + 16 + 26 = $\frac{164}{5}$ = 32.8

Average enrolment in the year 2017 = 55 + 56 + 26 + 18 + 24 = $\frac{179}{5}$ = 35 .8

Difference = 35.8 – 32.8 = 3.0

From the question 157–161, it seems that we should try to get basic information first of all by making use of some direct or shortcut methods. There are multiple options.

State	Percentage distribution of cars (Total 1400)	Absolute number of cars	Ratio of Diesel and Petrol cars	Diesel cars	Petrol cars
A.	14%	196	3 : 4	3/(3 + 4) of 196 = 84	196 – 84 = 112
B.	28%	392	5 : 9	5/(5 + 9) of 392 = 140	392 – 140 = 252
C.	32%	448	5 : 3	5/8 × 448 = 280	448 – 280 = 168
D.	26%	364	1 : 1	364 / (1+1) = 182	182

Basic calculations which apply in all the questions:

Cars in State A = 14% of 1400 = $\frac{14}{100} \times 1400 = 196$

Cars in State B = 28% of 1400, that means double of 196 = 2 × 196 = 392

Cars in State C = Cars in State B + 4% of 1400 = 392 + 56 = 448

Cars in State D = Cars in State B – 2% of 1400 = 392 – 28 = 364

We can take summation of the numbers to see that it equals 1400

157. (b): The number of diesel engine cars in State B = 182

The number of petrol engine cars in State D = 140

Difference = 182 – 140 = 42

158. (a): The number of petrol engine cars in State C = 168

The number of diesel engine cars in State A = 84

Difference = 168 – 84 = 84

Percentage difference = $\frac{84}{84} \times 100 = 100\%$

159. (d): The number of AC cars in State C = 25% of 280 = 70

The number of non-AC cars = 280 – 70 = 210

160. (d):

The number of total cars in State C = 448

The number of petrol engine cars in State B = 252

The difference = 448 – 252 = 196

161. (c):

The number of Petrol engine cars in all states = 112 + 252 + 168 + 182 = 714

162. (c): The percentage of children who were not overweight in 2016 = 100 – 30 = 70%

Their number = 70/100 × 7500 = 5250

The percentage of children who were not overweight in 2017 = 100 – 28 = 72%

Their number = 72/100 × 10500 = 7560

The total number = 5250 + 7560 = 12810

Thus, (c) is the correct answer.

163. (d): For the year 2019

Number of overweight men = 16% of 33000 = 16/100 × 33000 = 5280

Number of overweight women = 30% of 27000 = 30/100 × 27000 = 8100

Number of overweight children = 30% of 8000 = 30/100 × 8000 = 2400

The total of above three = 5280 + 8100 + 2400 = 15780

Their average = 15780 / 3 = 5260

Thus (d) is the right answer.

164. (b): If we assume that total number of men in 2021 was 100

Then the number of overweight men = 37.5

The number of not overweight men = 100 – 37.5 = 62.5

The required percentage = 37.5 / 62.5 × 100 = 3 / 5 × 100 = 60%

Thus, (b) is the correct answer

165. (a): For the year 2018

The number of overweight women = 25% of 30000 = 25/100 × 30000 = 7500

The number of overweight children = 35% of 6000 = 35 /100 × 6000 = 2100

The total of overweight men and women = 7500 + 2100 = 9600

The number of overweight men = 30% of 31500 = 30/100 × 31500 = 9450

The required difference = 9600 – 9450 = 150

166. (d): The required ratio between overweight women in 2018 and number of overweight men in 2020

= 25% of 30000 : 12% of 35000

= 750 : 420

= 25 : 14

Thus, (d) is the correct answer.

167. (c): We need some basic information to calculate the Ratio of girls in School C in 2020 to Total in A and B in 2020.

Girls in School C in 2020 = 200

Total girls in Schools A and B in 2020 = 250 + 300 = 550

Thus, Ratio = 200 : 550 = 4 : 11

The correct answer is (c).

168. (d): Difference between enrolments in 2021 and 2017:

School A: 300 – 200 = 100

School B: 250 – 150 = 100

School C: 275 – 100 = 175

The minimum difference of 100 occurs in School A and School B.

Thus, the correct answer is (d).

169. (a): Total girls in 2019: 275 + 150 + 199 = 624

Average = $\frac{624}{3} = 208$

Thus, the correct answer is (a).

170. (b): Total girls in 2017 = 200 + 150 + 100 = 450

Thus, the desired percentage = $\frac{450}{200} \times 100$ = 225%

Thus, (b) is the correct answer.

171. (c): Total enrolments for each year:
2017 = 450; 2019 = 624; 2020 = 750; 2021 = 825

The highest enrolment total is 825 in year 2021, and the second highest total in 2020 is 750.

Thus, (c) is the correct answer.

172. (b): The normal number of 'cyclists' on routine days = 72

Given in note that on rainy days, 1 in 3 of the cyclists travel by 'BUS'. That indicates that 2 out of three still use cycle on rainy days.

Thus, the number cyclists on rainy days $= \frac{2}{3} \times 72 = 48$

Thus, (b) is the answer.

173. (b): The normal number of 'cyclists' on routine days = 72

Given in note that 1 in 8 of the people who cycled to work were over 65 years of age.

Thus, their absolute number $= \frac{1}{8}$ of 72 = 9

Thus, (b) is the answer.

174. (c): The comparison is between travellers of car and bus. We need to take basic facts first, and compare the statements against those facts.

The number of people traveling by car = 18

The number of people traveling by bus = 35

Keep in mind that slightly fewer or slightly higher in answer options have not been given any range of numbers. (May be it is due to the fact that it is a survey linked table).

(a) Slightly fewer than twice as many people indicated that they travelled to work by bus than by car: This is not correct because 35 (bus) is not 'slightly fewer than twice' 18 (car). But it is a higher number.

(b) Slightly more than twice as many people indicated that they travelled to work by bus than by car: This is not correct because 35 (bus) is not 'slightly more than twice' 18 (car).

(c) Slightly more people indicated that they travelled to work by bus than by car: This is correct. There are more people who indicated traveling by bus (35) than by car (18).

(d) Slightly fewer people indicated that they travelled to work by car than by bus: This is not correct because there are more people who indicated traveling by car than by bus.

Thus, (c) is the correct answer.

175. (b): ATQ, first calculate the total number of travellers = 72 (Cycle) + 18 (Car) + 35 (Bus) + 55 (Walk) = 180

Half of this 180 $= \frac{1}{2}$ of 180 = 90

Now, look at options whose total matches with 90.

A. Cycle and Car = 72 + 18 =90
B. Bus and Car = 35 + 18 = 53
C. Walk and Bus = 55 + 35 = 90
D. Walk and Cycle = 35 + 72 = 107

Thus, A and C matches 90. Thus, (b) is the answer.

176. (d): Number of people who cycled to work = 72

Number of people who travelled by bus or car = 18 (Car) + 35 (Bus) = 53

The difference between those who cycled and those who travelled by bus or car is 72 – 53 = 19.

Thus, (d) is the correct answer.

177. (a): Basic calculation:

Total No. of candidates = 78000
No. of Boys = 24000
No. of Girls = 78000 – 24000 = 54000

Total candidates from City E = 8.5% of 78000 = 85/1000 of 78000 = 6630
Boys from City E = 21% of 24000 = 21/100 × 24000 = 5040
Girls from City E = 6630 – 5040 = 1590
Difference = 5040 – 1590 = 3450

178. (c): Total candidates from City F = 26% of 78000 =

26/100 × 78000 = 20280
Boys from City F = 9% of 24000 = 2160
Girls from City F = 20280 – 2160 = 18120
Percentage = 18120/54000 × 100 ≈ 33.55%

179. (d): Total candidates from City A = 17% of 78000 = 17/100 of 78000 = 13260
Boys from City A = 23% of 24000 = 5520
Girls from City A = 13260 – 5520 = 7740

180. (b): Total candidates from City C = 15% of 78000 =11700

Boys from City C = 17% of 24000 = 4080

Girls from City C = 11700 − 4080 = 7620

Total candidates from City D = 20% of 78000 = 15600

Percentage = 7620/15600 × 100 ≈ 48.8%

181. (c): Boys from City A = 0.23 × 24000 = 5520

Boys from City B = 20% of 24000 = 4800

Percentage more = (5520−4800) / 4800 of 100

= 720/4800 × 100 = 15%

CHAPTER

8

Information and Communication Technology (ICT)

TOPICS OF IMPORTANCE

- Meaning of Information and Communication Technology
- **ICT:** General Abbreviations and Terminology
- Basics of Internet, Intranet, Email, Audio and Video conferencing
- Digital Initiatives in Higher Education
- ICT and Governance

1. The acronym FTP stands for **[Jun 2014]**
(a) File Transfer Protocol
(b) Fast Transfer Protocol
(c) File Tracking Protocol
(d) File Transfer Procedure

2. Which one of the following is not a/an image/graphic file format? **[Jun 2014]**
(a) PNG (b) GIF
(c) BMP (d) GUI

3. The first web browser is **[Jun 2014]**
(a) Internet Explorer (b) Netscape
(c) World Wide Web (d) Firefox

4. When a computer is booting, BIOS is loaded to the memory by **[Jun 2014]**
(a) RAM (b) ROM
(c) CD-ROM (d) TCP

5. Which one of the following is not the same as the other three? **[Jun 2014]**
(a) MAC address
(b) Hardware address
(c) Physical address
(d) IP address

6. Identify the IP address from the following: **[Jun 2014]**
(a) 300 · 215 · 317 · 3
(b) 302 · 215@ 417 · 5
(c) 202 · 50 · 20 · 148
(d) 202 – 50 – 20 – 148

7. A smart classroom is a teaching space which has **[Dec 2014]**
(i) Smart portion with a touch panel control system.
(ii) PC/Laptop connection and DVD/VCR player.
(iii) Document camera and specialized software.
(iv) Projector and screen.
Select the correct answer from the codes given below.
(a) (i) and (ii) only
(b) (ii) and (iv) only
(c) (i), (ii) and (iii) only
(d) (i), (ii), (iii) and (iv)

8. Symbols A–F are used in which one of the following? **[Dec 2014]**
(a) Binary number system
(b) Decimal number system
(c) Hexadecimal number system
(d) Octal number system

9. Which one of the following is not a search engine? **[Dec 2014]**
(a) Google (b) Chrome
(c) Yahoo (d) Bing

10. CSS stands for [Dec 2014]
(a) Cascading Style Sheets
(b) Collecting Style Sheets
(c) Comparative Style Sheets
(d) Comprehensive Style Sheets

11. Binary equivalent of decimal number 35 is [Dec 2014]
(a) 100011 (b) 110001
(c) 110101 (d) 101011

12. The terms gif, jpg, bmp, png are used as extensions for files which store [Dec 2014]
(a) audio data (b) image data
(c) video data (d) text data

13. Encoding or scrambling data for transmission across a network is known as [Jun 2015]
(a) Protection (b) Detection
(c) Encryption (d) Decryption

14. Which of the following is **not** an output device? [Jun 2015]
(a) Printer (b) Speaker
(c) Monitor (d) Keyboard

15. Which of the following represents one billion characters? [Jun 2015]
(a) Kilobyte (b) Megabyte
(c) Gigabyte (d) Terabyte

16. Which of the following is not open source software? [Jun 2015]
(a) Internet explorer (b) Fedora Linux
(c) Open office (d) Apache HTTP server

17. Which one of the following represents the binary equivalent of the decimal number 25? [Jun 2015]
(a) 10101 (b) 01101
(c) 11001 (d) 11011

18. Which of the following is an instant messenger that is used for chatting? [Jun 2015]
(a) AltaVista (b) MAC
(c) Microsoft Office (d) Google Talk

19. NMEICT stands for [Dec 2015]
(a) National Mission on Education through ICT
(b) National Mission on E-governance through ICT
(c) National Mission on E-commerce through ICT
(d) National Mission on E-learning through ICT

20. Which of the following is an instant messaging application? [Dec 2015]
(i) WhatsApp
(ii) Google Talk
(iii) Viber
Select the correct answer from the codes given below.
(a) (i) and (ii) only
(b) (ii) and (iii) only
(c) (i) only
(d) (i), (ii) and (iii)

21. In a computer, a byte generally consists of [Dec 2015]
(a) 4 bits (b) 8 bits
(c) 16 bits (d) 10 bits

22. Which of the following is not an input device? [Dec 2015]
(a) Microphone (b) Keyboard
(c) Joystick (d) Monitor

23. Which of the following is an open source software? [Dec 2015]
(a) MS Word (b) Windows
(c) Mozilla Firefox (d) Acrobat Reader

24. Which of the following enables us to send the same letter to different people in MS Word? [Dec 2015]
(a) Mail join (b) Mail copy
(c) Mail insert (d) Mail merge

25. The process of copying files to a CD-ROM is known as [Jul 2016]
(a) Burning (b) Zipping
(c) Digitizing (d) Ripping

26. An unsolicited e-mail message sent to many recipients at once is a [Jul 2016]
(a) Worm (b) Virus
(c) Threat (d) Spam

27. The statement 'the study, design, development, implementation, support or management of computer-based information systems, particularly software applications and computer hardware' refers to [Jul 2016]
(a) Information Technology (IT)
(b) Information and Collaborative Technology (ICT)
(c) Information and Data Technology (IDT)
(d) Artificial Intelligence (AI)

28. If the binary equivalent of the decimal number 48 is 110000, then the binary equivalent of the decimal number 51 is given by **[Jul 2016]**

(a) 110011 (b) 110010
(c) 110001 (d) 110100

29. ________ is a type of memory circuitry that holds the computer's start-up routine. **[Jul 2016]**

(a) RIM (Read Initial Memory)
(b) RAM (Random Access Memory)
(c) ROM (Read Only Memory)
(d) Cache Memory

30. An ASCII is a character-encoding scheme that is employed by personal computers in order to represent various characters, numbers and control keys that the computer user selects on the keyboard. ASCII is an acronym for **[Jul 2016]**

(a) American Standard Code for Information Interchange.
(b) American Standard Code for Intelligent Information.
(c) American Standard Code for Information Integrity.
(d) American Standard Code for Isolated Information.

31. Which of the following statement(s) is/are TRUE?
S1: The decimal number 11 is larger than the hexadecimal number 11. **[Jan 2017]**
S2: In the binary number 1110.101, the fractional part has the decimal value as 0.625.

(a) S1 only (b) S2 only
(c) Both S1 and S2 (d) Neither S1 nor S2

32. Read the following two statements. **[Jan 2017]**
I: Information and Communication Technology (ICT) is considered as a subset of Information Technology (IT).
II: The 'right to use' a piece of software is termed as copyright.

Which of the above mentioned statement(s) is/are correct?

(a) Both I and II (b) Neither I nor II
(c) II only (d) I only

33. Which of the following correctly lists the types of the computer memory from highest to lowest speed? **[Jan 2017]**

(i) Secondary storage
(ii) Main memory (RAM)
(iii) Cache memory
(iv) CPU registers

Codes:

(a) (i), (ii), (iii), (iv) (b) (iv), (iii), (i), (ii)
(c) (iv), (iii), (ii), (i) (d) (iii), (iv), (ii), (i)

34. Which of the following is a characteristic of Web 2.0 applications? **[Jan 2017]**

(a) Multiple users schedule their time to use Web 2.0 applications one by one.
(b) Web2.0 applications are focussed on the ability for people to collaborate and share information online.
(c) Web2.0 applications provide users with content rather than facilitating users to create it.
(d) Web2.0 applications use only static pages.

35. With regard to a word processing software, the process of combining static information in a publication together with variable information in a data source to create one merged publication is called **[Jan 2017]**

(a) Electronic mail (b) Data sourcing
(c) Mail merge (d) Spam mail

36. DVD technology uses an optical media to store the digital data. DVD is an acronym for **[Jan 2017]**

(a) Digital Vector Disc
(b) Digital Volume Disc
(c) Digital Versatile Disc
(d) Digital Visualization Disc

37. What is the name for a webpage address? **[Nov 2017]**

(a) Domain (b) Directory
(c) Protocol (d) URL

38. The data storage hierarchy consists of **[Nov 2017]**

(a) Bytes, bits, fields, records, files and databases.
(b) Bits, bytes, fields, records, files and databases.
(c) Bits, bytes, records, fields, files and databases.
(d) Bits, bytes, fields, files, records and databases.

39. Which of the following domains is used for profit businesses? **[Nov 2017]**

(a) .org (b) .net
(c) .edu (d) .com

40. What is the full form of USB as used in computer related activities? **[Nov 2017]**

(a) Ultra Security Block
(b) Universal Security Block
(c) Universal Serial Bus
(d) United Serial Bus

41. Which of the following represents billion characters? **[Nov 2017]**

(a) Terabytes (b) Megabytes
(c) Kilobytes (d) Gigabytes

42. Which of the following statements, regarding the term ICT is/are TRUE? **[Jul 2018]**

P: ICT is an acronym that stands for Indian Classical Technology.

Q: Converging technologies that exemplify ICT include the merging of audio-visual, telephone and computer networks through a common cabling system.

(a) P only (b) Q only
(c) P and Q (d) Neither P nor Q

43. A new laptop has been produced that weighs less, is smaller and uses less power than previous laptop models.

Which of the following technologies has been used to accomplish this? **[Jul 2018]**

(a) Universal Serial Bus Mouse
(b) Faster Random Access Memory
(c) Blu Ray Drive
(d) Solid State Hard Drive

44. Given the following email fields, which of the email addresses will '*swami*' be able to see when he receives the message? **[Jul 2018]**

To ...	ram@test.com
Cc ...	raj@test.com; ravi@test.com
Bcc ...	swami@test.com; rama@test.com

(a) ram@test.com
(b) ram@test.com; raj@test.com; ravi@test.com
(c) ram@test.com; rama@test.com
(d) ram@test.com; rama@test.com; raj@test.com; ravi@test.com

45. Put the following units of storage into the correct order, starting with the smallest unit first and going down to the largest unit. **[Jul 2018]**

(A) Kilobyte (B) Byte
(C) Megabyte (D) Terabyte
(E) Gigabyte (F) Bit

Select the correct answer from the codes given below:

(a) (F), (B), (A), (C), (D), (E)
(b) (F), (B), (A), (D), (E), (C)
(c) (F), (B), (A), (C), (E), (D)
(d) (F), (B), (A), (D), (C), (E)

46. With regard to computer memory, which of the following statement (s) is/are TRUE? **[Jul 2018]**

P: Read Only Memory (ROM) is 'volatile' memory.

Q: Random Access Memory (RAM) is 'volatile' memory.

R: Secondary memory is 'volatile' memory.

(a) P only (b) Q only
(c) P and Q only (d) P and R only

47. Social media platforms have created a **[Dec 2018]**

(a) Society of reactionary opinions
(b) Society of consumables
(c) Society of negativity
(d) Society of networking

48. If the binary equivalent of the decimal number 53 is 110101, then the binary equivalent of the decimal number 50 is given by **[Dec 2018]**

(a) 110011 (b) 110010
(c) 110001 (d) 110100

49. Which one of the following is not part of suite of products of Microsoft Office? **[Dec 2018]**

(a) Microsoft Excel
(b) Microsoft PowerPoint
(c) Microsoft Publisher
(d) Microsoft Windows

50. The internet began with the development of **[Dec 2018]**

(a) USENET (b) Intranet
(c) ARPANET (d) Extranet

51. RFID is an acronym for **[Dec 2018]**

(a) Roaming Frequency Identification
(b) Radio Frequency Identification
(c) Runtime Frequency Identification
(d) Remote Frequency Identification

52. Bluetooth is an example of **[Dec 2018]**
(a) PAN (b) LAN
(c) MAN (d) WAN

53. DNS stands for **[Dec 2018]**
(a) Domain Name Standard
(b) Domain Name System
(c) Distributed Name System
(d) Dynamic Name Standard

54. A terabyte is equal to **[Dec 2018]**
(a) 1024 Megabytes
(b) 1024 Kilobytes
(c) 1024 Gigabytes
(d) 1024 × 1024 Kilobytes

55. The binary equivalent of $(-23)_{10}$ is (2's complement system for negative numbers is used) **[Dec 2018]**
(a) 01001 (b) 10111
(c) 01010 (d) 01000

56. The full form of PDF is **[Dec 2018]**
(a) Portable Data format
(b) Portable Document Form
(c) Portable Document Format
(d) Portable Data Form

57. Which of the given statements are true? **[Dec 2018]**
(i) Modem is a networking device.
(ii) Modem is a voltage stabilizer.
(iii) Modem converts analogue signal to digital signal and vice versa.

Options:
(a) (ii) and (iii)
(b) (i) and (iii)
(c) (i) and (ii)
(d) (i), (ii) and (iii)

58. While sending an e-mail, to differentiate among To:, Cc: and Bcc: fields, which of the following statements is true? **[Jun 2019]**
(a) Recipients in the To: field can see the email addresses that are in the Bcc: and Cc: fields
(b) Recipients in the Cc: field can see the email addresses that are in the To: and Bcc: fields
(c) Recipients in the Bcc: field can see the email addresses that are in the To: and Cc: fields
(d) Only the recipients in the Cc: field can see the email addresses in the Bcc: fields

59. A group's access to digital technology and another group's lack of access to it, will cause a disparity known as **[Jun 2019]**
(a) Internet inequality
(b) Web inequality
(c) Technological imbalance
(d) Digital divide

60. Which one of the following is an educational FM radio network? **[Jun 2019]**
(a) Gyan Darshan (b) Gyan Vani
(c) Gyan Dhara (d) GIAN

61. Software that you can download for free, but have to pay to continue its use after a trial period is called **[Jun 2019]**
(a) Public domain software
(b) Freeware
(c) Open-source software
(d) Shareware

62. Which one of the following computer components is fastest in terms of speed of access? **[Jun 2019]**
(a) USB Drive
(b) Solid State Drive
(c) RAM
(d) Hard Disk Drive

63. SWAYAM refers to **[Jun 2019]**
(a) Study World of Action-Learning for Young Aspiring Minds
(b) Study Web of Active-Learning for Young Aspiring Minds
(c) Student World of Action-Learning for Young Ailing Minds
(d) Study Web of Active-Learning for Youth Awareness Models

64. In internet terminology, what does the acronym WYSIWYG stand for? **[Jun 2019]**
(a) Why You Saw Is What You Got
(b) What You See Is What You Get
(c) Where You See Is Where You Got
(d) What You See Is What You Got

65. Identify the encompassing term that involves the use of electronic platforms to conduct a company's business. **[Jun 2019]**
(a) E-Business (b) E-Commerce
(c) E-Marketing (d) E-Governance

66. Which of the following is generally associated with the domain name of an educational institution? **[Jun 2019]**

(a) .org (b) .edu
(c) .com (d) .inst

67. Which of the following devices enables a computer to transmit data over telephone lines? **[Jun 2019]**

(a) CPU (b) Hub
(c) Switch (d) Modem

68. Which of the following is not considered as a form of secondary storage? **[Jun 2019]**

(a) RAM (b) Floppy Disk
(c) Optical Disk (d) Flash Drive

69. Which of the following is a search engine? **[Jun 2019]**

(a) Flash
(b) Fire fox
(c) Internet explorer
(d) Google

70. The use of Information Technology (IT) to improve the ability of government to address the needs of society is known as__________. **[Jun 2019]**

(a) E–Business (b) E–Administration
(c) E–Governance (d) E–Marketing

71. Joint Photographic Experts Group (JPEG) is used to compress____________. **[Jun 2019]**

(a) Music (b) Video
(c) Image (d) Frame

72. The main two components of CPU are__________ **[Jun 2019]**

(a) Control unit and ALU
(b) ALU and BUS
(c) Control unit and registers
(d) Registers and main memory

73. Which of the following is used to create web pages? **[Jun 2019]**

(a) HTTP (b) URL
(c) FTP (d) HTML

74. Anjali's teacher uses VLE, a software tool designed to deliver courses online. The acronym VLE stands for **[Jun 2019]**

(a) Video Learning Environment
(b) Visual Learning Environment
(c) Virtual Learning Environment
(d) Visual Local Environment

75. Which of the following statement(s) is/are true in respect to ICT? **[Jun 2019]**

P: ICT is an acronym that stands for information and competitive technology.

Q: The effective use of ICT to support learning is the inclusive education exemplifies good teaching for all learners.

(a) P only (b) Q only
(c) Both P and Q (d) Neither P nor Q

76. Which of the following best describe a wiki? **[Jun 2019]**

(a) A system that allows users to add information onto a website but does not change any pre-existing information
(b) A system that allows collaborative modification of its content and structure directly from the web browser
(c) A system that serves as a publically accessible personal journal for an individual
(d) A system that monitors the modification of content within a blog

77. What is the decimal equivalent of binary number 1100110? **[Jun 2019]**

(a) 102 (b) 204
(c) 153 (d) 51

78. One TeraByte (TB) of memory is equal to **[Jun 2019]**

(a) 1024 KB
(b) 1024 × 1024 KB
(c) 1024 × 1024 × 1024 KB
(d) 1024 × 1024 × 1024 Bytes

79. Which of the following is not a/an web browser? **[Jun 2019]**

(a) Internet Explorer (b) Mozilla Firefox
(c) Google Chrome (d) Yahoo

80. In Audio and Video compression, the term RGB means **[Jun 2019]**

(a) Red, Grey, Blue (b) Red, Green, Blue
(c) Red, Green, Black (d) Red, Grey, Black

81. A/An __________ is a computer program that spreads by inserting copies of itself into other executable code or documents. **[Jun 2019]**

(a) Operating System
(b) Computer Virus
(c) Firewall
(d) Anti-virus

82. Match the following. **[Jun 2019]**

Set–I	Set–II
(A) First Generation	(i) Transister
(B) Second Generation	(ii) VLSI microprocessor
(C) Third Generation	(iii) Vacuum tube
(D) Fourth Generation	(iv) Integrated circuit

Select the correct option from the following:

	(A)	(B)	(C)	(D)
(a)	(iii)	(iv)	(i)	(ii)
(b)	(iii)	(i)	(iv)	(ii)
(c)	(iii)	(i)	(ii)	(iv)
(d)	(i)	(iii)	(iv)	(ii)

83. Which of the following hardware was used by the first generation computers? **[Jun 2019]**

(a) Transistors (b) Vacuum tubes
(c) VLSI (d) Integrated circuits

84. Computer uses which number system to store data and perform calculations **[Jun 2019]**

(a) Binary (b) Octal
(c) Decimal (d) Hexadecimal

85. Which of the following mobile payments application is developed by the National Payments Corporation of India based on UPI? **[Jun 2019]**

(a) MYGOV (b) BHIM
(c) UMANG (d) PhonePe

86. What is meant by the term RAM? **[Jun 2019]**

(a) Memory which can only be read
(b) Memory which can only be written to
(c) Memory which is used for permanent storage
(d) Memory which can be both read and written to

87. What is the address specifying the location of a web page? **[Jun 2019]**

(a) URL (b) DNS
(c) HTML (d) HTTP

88. Match Set 'A' with Set 'B' **[Jun 2019]**

A (Media)	B (Transmission/ communication)
(A) Audio	(i) Bandwidth
(B) Advertising	(ii) Linear communication
(C) Internet	(iii) Non-personal communication
(D) Newspaper	(iv) Frequency modulation

Choose the correct answer from the options given below:

	(A)	(B)	(C)	(D)
(a)	(iii)	(iv)	(ii)	(i)
(b)	(i)	(ii)	(iii)	(iv)
(c)	(iv)	(iii)	(i)	(ii)
(d)	(ii)	(i)	(iv)	(iii)

89. SMTP is an acronym for **[Jun 2019]**

(a) Simple Mail Transport Protocol
(b) Simple Mail Terminal Protocol
(c) Simple Mail Transfer Protocol
(d) Simple Mail Transition Protocol

90. Which of the following file format is not a video file format? **[Jun 2019]**

(a) .AVI (b) .MOV
(c) .MP4 (d) .JPEG

91. The convenient place to store contact information for quick retrieval in e-mail is **[Jun 2019]**

(a) Address box (b) Message box
(c) Address book (d) Message book

92. A computer has main memory of 960 KBytes. What is the exact number of bytes contained in this memory? **[Jun 2019]**

(a) 960×8
(b) 960×1000
(c) 960×1024
(d) $960 \times 1024 \times 1024$

93. Select the option that shows the storage devices in order of capacity from lowest to highest. **[Jun 2019]**

(a) CD-ROM, DVD-ROM, Blu-ray
(b) Blu-ray, CD- ROM, DVD-ROM,
(c) CD-ROM, Blu-ray, DVD-ROM,
(d) CD-ROM, DVD-ROM, Blu-ray,

94. Select the true statement about an Operating System (OS). **[Jun 2019]**

(a) An OS controls peripherals, allocates memory and organizes data into fields and records
(b) An OS provided protection against viruses and control peripherals
(c) An OS controls peripheral, and allocates memory and processor time
(d) An OS controls the processor and peripherals and allows the user to connect to the internet

95. Which of the following is a type of malware intentionally inserted into a software system that will set-off a malicious function when specified conditions are met? **[Jun 2019]**

(a) Worm (b) Trojan
(c) Spyware (d) Logic bomb

96. Which one the following pairs least matches in respect of computer? **[Jun 2019]**

(a) 1 Giga Byte : (1024)8 bits
(b) CRT : Cathode Ray Tube
(c) ROM : Rapid Online Memory
(d) CPU : Central Processing Unit

97. Which of the following statement (s) is/are true in respect of Wirless Technology? **[Jun 2019]**

P: Bluetooth is a wireless technology which can connect a head to a mobile phone.

Q: Bluetooth is a long range wireless technology and is a low cost means of data transfer.

(a) P only (b) Q only
(c) Both P and Q (d) Neither P nor Q

98. A virus type that is capable of transferring one computer to another without any ' user interaction' is know as **[Jun 2019]**

(a) Worm (b) Trojan
(c) Key logging (d) Boot sector virus

99. In the context of IT/ICT, which one of the following statements about spamming is true? **[Jun 2019]**

(a) Spamming is posting or e-mailing unsolicited advertising messages to a wide audience
(b) Spamming is sending lines of non-sensical garbage in a chat conversation
(c) Spamming is posting a message that contains graphic description of something offensive
(d) Spamming is a attempt to acquire sensitive imformation for malicious reasons, by masquerading as trustworthy entity

100. Which of the following can be termed as the main benefits of cloud computing ?

(a) Data backup and storage of data
(b) Powerful server capabilities
(c) Cost-effective and time-saving
(d) All of the above

101. Which statementis true about Random Access Memory (RAM) in a computer system? **[Jun 2019]**

(a) RAM is non-volatile and the amount of RAM in a computer system cannot affect its performance
(b) RAM is non-volatile and the amount of RAM in a computer system can affect its performance
(c) RAM is volatile and the amount of RAM in a computer cannot affect its performance
(d) RAM is volatile and the amount of RAM in a computer system can affect its performance

102. You need to use automatic calculations in preparing a budget. Which software application should be used? **[Jun 2019]**

(a) Spreadsheet (b) Presentation
(c) Word processing (d) Desktop publishing

103. What is the binary equivalent of decimal number 75? **[Jun 2019]**

(a) 1101001 (b) 101001
(c) 100101 (d) 1001011

104. What is spyware in respect of computer software? **[Jun 2019]**

(a) Software that aims to gather information about a person without his/her knowledge, and that may send such information to another entity
(b) Legitimate software that allows companies to monitor and supervise the computer of their employees from a central location
(c) Software used to disrupt computer operation or gain access to private computer system
(d) A computer progress hidden within another seemingly harmless program that produces copies of itself and inserts them into another programs or files

105. In analog communication, content is considered to be **[Jun 2019]**

(a) Convergent (b) Static
(c) Physical (d) Ethereal

106. Select the option that includes the file formats suitable for distributing sound files across the internet. **[Dec 2019]**

(a) wmv, mp4, wma, mp3
(b) avi, midi, wav, mp3

(c) avi, mov, wmv, mp3
(d) midi, wav, wma, mp3

107. Which of the following is/are major issues arising out of the growing reliance on information technology? **[Dec 2019]**
(a) Profitability.
(b) Security threats.
(c) Privacy concerns.
Choose the correct option.
(a) Only (a) and (b) (b) Only (a) and (c)
(c) Only (b) and (c) (d) (a), (b) and (c)

108. Which of the following statement(s) is/are correct? **[Dec 2019]**
(a) For the sequence of integers represented in binary as 00111, 01001, 01011, P,...., the next integer P would be represented as 01101.
(b) A byte is a binary number consisting of exactly 8 bits.
Choose the correct option.
(a) Only (a)
(b) Only (b)
(c) Both (a) and (b)
(d) Neither (a) nor (b)

109. Match List I with List II in the context of computer networking. **[Dec 2019]**

List I	List II
(A) VOIP	(i) Makes use of light pulses to transmit data
(B) Fiber optic cable	(ii) Use of internet to make phone calls
(C) URL	(iii) Most appropriate to connect computers in a small building
(D) UTP cable	(iv) Text used by web browsers to locate a web address on the internet

Choose the correct option.

	(A)	(B)	(C)	(D)
(a)	(iv)	(i)	(ii)	(iii)
(b)	(ii)	(i)	(iv)	(iii)
(c)	(ii)	(iii)	(iv)	(i)
(d)	(iv)	(iii)	(ii)	(i)

110. Match List I with List II. **[Dec 2019]**

List I (Digital Initative)	List II (Purpose)
(A) UMANG	(i) G2B services
(B) BHIM	(ii) Learning platform
(C) eBiz	(iii) Unified Payment Interface
(D) SWAYAM	(iv) Single point of access to all government services.

Choose the correct option.

	(A)	(B)	(C)	(D)
(a)	(ii)	(i)	(iii)	(iv)
(b)	(iii)	(ii)	(iv)	(i)
(c)	(iv)	(iii)	(i)	(ii)
(d)	(i)	(iv)	(ii)	(iii)

111. Given below are two statements—one is labelled as Assertion (A) and the other is labelled as Reason (R). **[Dec 2019]**

Assertion (A): A blog is a form of social media.

Reason (R): A blog allows anyone to communicate to a public audience.

In the light of the above statements, choose the correct option.
(a) Both (A) and (R) are true and (R) is the correct explanation of (A)
(b) Both (A) and (R) are true and (R) is not the correct explanation of (A)
(c) (A) is true but (R) is false
(d) (A) is false but (R) is true

112. Select the option that lists components for a cyberspace address (URL) in the correct order from beginning to end. **[Dec 2019]**
(a) Protocol, domain name of the host, path or file
(b) Path or file, protocol, domain name of the host
(c) Protocol, path or file, domain name of the host
(d) Domain name of the host, protocol, path or file

113. Which of the following statements is/are correct? **[Dec 2019]**
(i) Software is loaded into secondary storage from RAM and then it is executed by the CPU.

(ii) A search engine is a software system that is designed to search for information on the World Wide Web.

Choose the correct option.

(a) Only (i)
(b) Only (ii)
(c) Both (i) and (ii)
(d) Neither (i) nor (ii)

114. The main purpose of using ICT for classroom teaching is to: **[Dec 2019]**

(a) make the classroom instructions interesting
(b) divert students' attention in the class
(c) keep students engaged in the class
(d) optimise learning outcomes of teaching

115. Match List I with List II. **[Dec 2019]**

List I (Software)	List II (Description)
(A) Web browser	(i) Prepare written documents
(B) Word processor	(ii) Create and edit web pages
(C) Spreadsheet	(iii) Connect to websites and display web pages
(D) Web authoring	(iv) Analyse and summarise numerical data

Choose the correct answer from the following.

	(A)	(B)	(C)	(D)
(a)	(ii)	(iv)	(i)	(iii)
(b)	(iii)	(i)	(iv)	(ii)
(c)	(iii)	(i)	(ii)	(iv)
(d)	(ii)	(i)	(iv)	(iii)

116. Which of the following statements is/are correct? **[Dec 2019]**

(a) A Local Area Network (LAN) is usually located on one brand of computer.
(b) The acronym 'ISP' stands for Internet Standard Provider.

Choose the correct answer from the options given below.

(a) Only (a) (b) Only (b)
(c) Both (a) and (b) (d) Neither (a) nor (b)

117. Select the option that exclusively contains the text file formats. **[Dec 2019]**

(a) JPEG, MP3, RTF (b) CSV, RTF, TXT
(c) GIF, JPEG, MP3 (d) CSV, MP3, PDF

118. Given below are two statements—one is labelled as Assertion (A) and the other is labelled as Reason (R). **[Dec 2019]**

Assertion (A): The clock speed of CPUs has not increased significantly in recent years.

Reason (R): Software now being used is faster and therefore processors do not have to be faster.

In the light of the above statements, choose the correct option from the following.

(a) Both (A) and (R) are true and (R) is the correct explanation of (A)
(b) Both (A) and (R) are true but (R) is not the correct explanation of (A)
(c) (A) is true but (R) is false
(d) (A) is false but (R) is true

119. Which of the following statements is/are correct? **[Dec 2019]**

(a) The clock speed of a CPU is measured in hertz (Hz).
(b) Bluetooth technology consumes more power than Wi-Fi technology.

Choose the correct answer from the options given below.

(a) Only (a)
(b) Only (b)
(c) Both (a) and (b)
(d) Neither (a) nor (b)

120. The purpose of ICT in education is to: **[Dec 2019]**

(a) attract students
(b) make teaching interesting
(c) optimise learning outcomes
(d) promote technology culture in teaching

121. In computer related activities, which of the following is inappropriate for describing a language translator? **[Dec 2019]**

(a) Assembler (b) Compiler
(c) Interpreter (d) Codec

122. Which of the following terms is related to the digital learning environment for design? **[Dec 2019]**

(a) e-Vidwan (b) e-Acharya
(c) e-Kalpa (d) e-Yantra

123. Which of the following is most suitable for being designated as fourth-generation programming language (4GL)? **[Dec 2019]**
(a) ALGOL (b) Java
(c) C (d) SQL

124. Which of the following is a collaboration tool for providing virtual classroom environment? **[Dec 2019]**
(a) A-Lab (b) A-View
(c) A-Tutor (d) A-Learner

125. Match List I with List II. **[Dec 2019]**

List I	List II
(A) WWW	(i) Volatile memory
(B) JAVA	(ii) Non-volatile memory
(C) RAM	(iii) World Wide Web
(D) ROM	(iv) Programming language

Choose the correct option from the following.

	(A)	(B)	(C)	(D)
(a)	(i)	(ii)	(iii)	(iv)
(b)	(ii)	(iii)	(iv)	(i)
(c)	(iii)	(iv)	(i)	(ii)
(d)	(iv)	(i)	(ii)	(iii)

126. Which of the following is a programming language? **[Dec 2019]**
(a) Deep learning
(b) Machine learning
(c) Artificial intelligence
(d) Python

127. Which of the following is a search engine? **[Dec 2019]**
(a) Internet (b) Bing
(c) Skype (d) Acrobat Reader

128. Given below are two statements—one is labelled as Assertion (A) and the other is labelled as Reason (R). **[Dec 2019]**

Assertion (A): The internet is a collection of interconnected computer networks that are linked by transmission medium such as copper wires, fiber-optic cables, wireless connections, etc.

Reason (R): World Wide Web is a collection of interconnected documents.

From the above two statements, choose the correct answer.
(a) Both (A) and (R) are true and (R) is the correct explanation of (A)
(b) Both (A) and (R) are true but (R) is not the correct explanation of (A)
(c) (A) is true but (R) is false
(d) (A) is false but (R) is true

129. Which description is / are the appropriate among the following for 'E-Governance'? **[Dec 2019]**
(a) To engage, enable and empower the citizens
(b) To provide fair and unbiased services to the citizens
(c) To provide technology driven governance
(d) All of the above

130. Using a website to pour out one's grievances is called **[2020]**
(a) Cyber venting
(b) Web hate
(c) Web anger
(d) Cyber abuse

131. Speed of Internet is measured in **[2020]**
(a) GHz (b) Gbps
(c) GB (d) dpi

132. Which of the following correctly lists computer memory types from lowest to highest speed? **[2020]**
(a) Main Memory, Cache Memory, Secondary Storage
(b) Cache Memory, Secondary Storage, Main Memory
(c) Secondary Storage, Main Memory, Cache Memory
(d) Secondary Stage, Cache Memory, Main Memory

133. What is the full form of the abbreviation GIF? **[2020]**
(a) Graphics Interchange Format
(b) Graphics Interchange File
(c) Global Interchange Format
(d) Graphics Input Format

134. Given below are two statements, one is labelled as Assertion (A) and the other is labelled as Reason (R): **[2020]**

Assertion (A): Machine Learning requires good quality and sufficient data to train and test the algorithm.

Reason (R): For correct classification, good quality data which is free from noise, and sufficient data is required for training and testing of the algorithm.

In light of the above statements, choose the most appropriate answer from the options given below:

(a) Both A and R are correct and R is the correct explanation of A
(b) Both A and R are correct but R is NOT the correct explanation of A
(c) A is correct but R is not correct
(d) A is not correct but R is correct

135. Given below are two statements: One is labeled as Assertion (A) and the other is labeled as Reason (R): **[2020]**

Assertion (A): Random Access Memory (RAM) is volatile and stores data/programs currently in use.

Reason (R): RAM is a storage medium that retains its contents even after the supply of electricity has been turned off.

In the light of the above statements, choose the correct answer from the options given below:

(a) Both (A) and (R) are true and (R) is correct explanation of (A)
(b) Both (A) and (R) are true and (R) is NOT the correct explanation of (A)
(c) (A) is true but (R) is false
(d) (A) is false but (R) is true

136. Consider the following incomplete sentence:

Wi-Fi is short for Wireless Fidelity and it is a set of __________ for using range __________ to allow computing __________ to connect to a LAN or to the Internet. **[2020]**

Complete the above sentence by choosing the correct words in order from the following list:

(A) Standards
(B) Waves
(C) Devices

Choose the correct answer from the options given below:

(a) (C), (B), (A) (b) (C), (A), (B)
(c) (A), (C), (B) (d) (A), (B), (C)

137. Which of the following statement is true in respect of computers? **[2020]**

(a) Software is loaded into secondary storage from RAM and is the executed by CPU.
(b) Software is loaded into RAM from secondary storage and is then executed by CPU.
(c) Software is loaded into RAM from secondary storage and is then executed by motherboard.
(d) Software is loaded into secondary storage from RAM and is the executed by motherboard.

138. Match List I with List II: **[2020]**

List 1 (Computer Terms)	List II (Description)
(A) Operating System (OS)	(I) A service that runs on the internet.
(B) WWW	(II) Software that helps an OS to control a piece of hardware..
(C) Device driver	(III) Software that controls peripherals and allocates memory and processor time.
(D) IP	(IV) Defines network addresses and is used for routing packets.

Choose the correct answer from the options given below:

(a) (A)-(II), (B)-(IV), (C)-(III), (D)-(I)
(b) (A)-(III), (B)-(I), (C)-(II), (D)-(IV)
(c) (A)-(IV), (B)-(I), (C)-(II), (D)-(III)
(d) (A)-(III), (B)-(IV), (C)-(II), (D)-(I)

139. The number of characters in 8 bit ASCII code (American Standard Code for Information Interchange) is **[2021]**

(a) 128 (b) 256
(c) 512 (d) 64

140. INFLIBNET Centre, which is an autonomous Inter-University Centre of the University Grants Commission, maintains **[2021]**

(a) e-Gyankosh (b) e-Pathshala
(c) Shodhganga (d) Swayam Prabha

141. Given below are two statements regarding the Router **[2021]**

Statement I: It enables data packets to be routed between different networks.

Statement II: It works in the Data Link Layer.

In light of the above statements, choose the correct answer from the options given below:

(a) Both Statement I and Statement II are false
(b) Both Statement I and Statement II are true
(c) Statement I is false but Statement II is true
(d) Statement I is true but Statement II is false

142. Match List I with List II **[2021]**

List I	List II
I/O device	Data transfer rate
A. Disk	I. 50 bps
B. Mouse	II. 1 Mbps
C. Laser printer	III. 120 bps
D. Keyboard	IV. 100 Mbps

Choose the correct answer from the options given below:

(a) A - I, B - II, C - III, D - IV
(b) A - II, B - I, C - III, D - IV
(c) A - IV, B - II, C - I, D - III
(d) A - IV, B - III, C - II, D – I

143. The Post Office protocol is **[2021]**

(a) Protocol used for sending emails
(b) Protocol used for transfer of files from one computer to another computer
(c) Protocol used to handle email attachments
(d) Protocol used when receiving emails from the email server

144. mooKIT platform uses, an open source content management system. **[2021]**

(a) DRUPAL (b) JOOMLA
(c) Moodle (d) SAKAI

145. Following are some statements regarding File Transfer Protocol (FTP). Choose the correct statements **[2021]**

A. It is used to access the world wide web (www).
B. It is used to download data from file servers.
C. It is used for very small files.
D. Files are transferred from one device to another.

Choose the correct answers from the options given below:

(a) A and B only (b) A and C only
(c) B and C only (d) B and D only

146. Which of the following statements are true? **[2021]**

A. Simplex data transmission is in two-directions only
B. Half-duplex data transmission is in both directions but not at the same time
C. Full-duplex data transmission is in both directions simultaneously
D. Serial data transmission is when data is sent, 8 bit at a time, over a single wire
E. Parallel data transmission is when one bit of data is sent down over a single wire

Choose the correct answer from the options given below:

(a) A, B and C only (b) B and C only
(c) C and D only (d) C, D and E only

147. What is the World Wide Web (www)? **[2021]**

(a) Collection of webpages stored on websites
(b) Hypertext processor
(c) Interconnected networks
(d) Web browser

148. What is Ethernet? **[2021]**

(a) A collision-detection protocol
(b) A protocol used by many wired LAN's
(c) A protocol used for address translation
(d) A security protocol

149. Given below are two statements. **[2021]**

Statement I: DVDs use a single spiral 'track' to store data working from the centre to the edge.

Statement II: DVDs are Read-only devices

In light of the above statements, choose the correct answer from the options given below

(a) Both Statement I and Statement II are false
(b) Both Statement I and Statement II are true
(c) Statement I is false but Statement II is true
(d) Statement I is true but Statement II is false

150. Match List I with List II. **[2021]**

List I	List II
A. System Software	I. Library Management System
B. Application Software	II. Firewall
C. Security Software	III. Compiler
D. Embedded Software	IV. Automatic fridge

Choose the correct answer from the options given below:

(a) A -I , B -III , C -IV , D -II
(b) A -II , B -IV , C -I , D -III
(c) A -III , B -I , C -II , D -IV
(d) A -III , B -IV , C -I , D -II

151. When a computer is switched on, the BIOS is loaded from: **[2021]**

(a) Hard Disk (b) RAM
(c) ROM (d) CD-ROM

152. Identify the correct order of the following computer storage capacities ranked from largest to smallest capacity. **[2021]**

(A) 100 GBytes
(B) 10 000 000 000 Bytes
(C) 1 TBytes
(D) 1000000 KBytes

Choose the correct answer from the options given below:

(a) (C), (A), (D), (B) (b) (C), (A), (B), (D)
(c) (A), (C), (D), (B) (d) (A), (C), (B), (D)

153. Given below are two statements: **[2021]**

Statement I : Search Engines are websites that help a user to search for information on the worldwide web (www).

Statement II: For any search term, Search Engines provide the exact same results to all the users.

In the light of the above statements, choose the corrrect answer from the options given below:

(a) Both Statement I and Statement II are true
(b) Both Statement I and Statement II are false
(c) Statement I is true but Statement II is false
(d) Statement I is false but Statement II is true

154. With respect to computers, which of the following are random access storage devices? **[2021]**

(A) Magnetic Tape (B) Hard Disk
(C) Pen Drive (D) CDROM

Choose the correct answer from the options given below:

(a) (A), (B), and (C) only
(b) (A), (C), and (D) only
(c) (B), (C), and (D) only
(d) (A), (B), and (D) only

155. Match List I with List II. **[2021]**

List I (Computer Terms)	List II (Description)
(A) Magnetic Tape	(i) Used in digital cameras photo printers and cell phones
(B) Memory Card	(ii) Uses laser beam technology to read or write data
(C) Hard Disk	(iii) Used for data archival purposes but must be accessed sequentially
(D) DVD	(iv) A set of metal disks mounted on a spindle

Choose the correct answer from the options given below:

	(A)	(B)	(C)	(D)
(a)	(iii)	(i)	(iv)	(ii)
(b)	(iv)	(i)	(iii)	(ii)
(c)	(iii)	(iv)	(i)	(ii)
(d)	(ii)	(iii)	(i)	(iv)

156. What is the name of the software application that facilitates building an early accessible bookmark warehouse that becomes searchable to members or the public? **[Dec 2021]**

(a) Social Bookmarking
(b) Database Management System
(c) Enterprise Resource Planning
(d) Reference Management Tool

157. What is Phishing? **[Dec 2021]**

(a) Sending data to a hacker
(b) Some-one sends legitimate-looking emails to users
(c) Search automatically for an iten on the internet
(d) Checking the spelling of websites

158. Given below are two statements. **[Dec 2021]**

Statement I: If the sensor data is outside the acceptable range, then the microprocessor/computer will take action.

Statement II: Sensors in the control application only send data to the microprocessor/computer when something happens.

In light of the above statements, choose the *correct* answer from the options given below

(a) Both Statement I and Statement II are true
(b) Both Statement I and Statement II are false
(c) Statement I is true but Statement II is false
(d) Statement I is false but Statement II is true

159. Which of the following statements are correct? **[Dec 2021]**

A. A WLAN is a wide area network.
B. A hub sends an incoming data packet to the correct device on a network.
C. An IP address is assigned to a device at the manufacturing stage.
D. A network Interface card is needed to allow a device to connect to a network.
E. Routers inspect data packets received over the internet

Choose the correct answer from the options given below.

(a) A and B only (b) B and E only
(c) D and E only (d) B, C and D only

160. Match List I with List II. **[Dec 2021]**

List I	List II
(A) Input device	(i) Traffic light simulator
(B) Output device	(ii) Scanner
(C) Pointing Device	(iii) Speaker
(D) Sensor Device	(iv) Trackerball

Choose the correct answer from the options given below:

	(A)	(B)	(C)	(D)
(a)	(ii)	(iii)	(iv)	(ii)
(b)	(i)	(ii)	(iv)	(iii)
(c)	(iii)	(ii)	(iv)	(ii)
(d)	(ii)	(iv)	(iii)	(i)

161. What are Firewalls? **[Dec 2021]**

(a) Used for address translation in the Network layer.
(b) Used to store the Network Interface Card.
(c) Used for Network congestion control.
(d) Hardware or software that sits between a user's computer and an external computer.

162. Given below are two statements:

Statement I: Policy action and implementation plans require sound database systems at the regional level only.

Statement II: The statistical system should ensure its impeccability with data architecture, security, quality, cleaning and integration. **[2021]**

In light of the above statements, choose the most appropriate answer from the options given below:

(a) Both Statement I and Statement II are correct
(b) Both Statement I and Statement II are incorrect
(c) Statement I is correct but Statement II is incorrect
(d) Statement I is incorrect but Statement II is correct

163. Given below are two statements, one is labeled as Assertion A and the other is labeled as Reason R. **[2022]**

Assertion A: In computer networking a MODEM is considered as both input and output device.

Reason R: MODEM sends data (upload/output) and receives data (download/input) at the same time.

In light of the above statements, choose the correct answer from the options given below:

(a) Both A and R are true and R is the correct explanation of A
(b) Both A and R are true but R is NOT the correct explanation A
(c) A is true but R is false
(d) A is false but R is true

164. Programs that come into a computer system disguised as something else, are called: **[2022]**

(a) Trojan horses (b) Viruses
(c) Web bugs (d) Zombies

165. You have been instructed to install additional RAM into a computer by your teacher. Identify the correct order of the following steps A-C that you should follow to install the RAM safely. **[2022]**

A. Install RAM
B. Isolate computer from the power supply
C. Connect anti-static strap to wrist

Choose the correct answer from the options given below:

(a) A, B, C (b) C, A, B
(c) B, A, C (d) B, C, A

166. Given below are two statements: **[2022]**

Statement I: SWAYAM initiative is a significant step towards providing financial and technical assistance to young start-up entrepreneurs.

Statement II: The tagline of Digilocker logo says "My Documents, Anytime, Anywhere".

In light of the above statements, choose the correct answer from the options given below:

(a) Both Statement I and Statement II are true
(b) Both Statement I and Statement II are false
(c) Statement I is true but Statement II is false
(d) Statement I is false but Statement II is true

167. Match List I with List II. **[2022]**

List I Computer Term	List II Definition
A. Spyware	I. Wireless technology used for transmitting data over short distances
B. Firewall	II. Software that allows the user to gain information about another person's computer activity
C. Bluetooth	III. An attack on a network which involves flooding the network with useless traffic
D. Denial of service	IV. Hardware or software designed to protect a network by controlling what data can and cannot enter

Choose the correct answer from the options given below:

(a) A – III, B – IV, C – I, D – II
(b) A – IV, B – II, C – II, D – I
(c) A – I, B – IV, C – III, D – III
(d) A – II, B – IV, C – I, D - III

168. Which of the following are the principal components of the CPU of a computer system? **[2022]**

A. ALU (Arithmetic-Logic Unit)
B. CU (Control Unit)
C. Processor Registers
D. SSD (Solid-State Drive)
E. VRAM (Video RAM)

Choose the correct answer from the options given below:

(a) A, B and D only (b) A, B and C only
(c) C, D and E only (d) B, C and D only

169. Consider the following spreadsheet: **[2022]**

	A	B	C
1	4	3	
2	5	2	
3	7		
4	8		9
5	9		
6			

If the formula = \$A\$3 + B2 in tell C4 is- copied to cell C5, then what is the value in cell C5?

(a) 9 (b) 8
(c) 7 (d) 17

170. Which of the following is not an essential component required for video-conferencing system? **[2022]**

(a) Video Camera (b) Display Device
(c) Telephone (d) Microphone

171. Many computer users are worried about malware. Which of the following are two examples of malware? **[2022]**

A. Firewall B. Worm
C. Router D. Virus

Choose the correct answer from the options given below:

(a) A and C only (b) A and B only
(c) B and D only (d) C and D only

172. Consider the following in MS-EXCEL spreadsheets: **[June 2023]**

	A	B	C	D	E
	Day	Weather	Temp.	Play Tennis?	Go Running?
1.	Monday	Sunny	High		
2.	Tuesday	Windy	High		
3.	Wednesday	Raining	Medium		
4.	Thursday	Sunny	Low		
5.	Friday	Sunny	Medium		

Suppose the formula = IF (B2 = 'Sunny', IF(C2<> "Low', 'Yes', 'No'),'No') is entered into D2 and then the cell is copied and pasted to D3:D6. On what days does column D report "Yes"?

(a) Monday and Friday only
(b) Monday and Tuesday only
(c) Thursday and Friday only
(d) Monday, Thursday and Friday

173. Which statement best describes data compression? **[June 2023]**

(a) The process of calculating the file size of a saved file.
(b) The process of encoding characters into more than one language.
(c) The process of encoding infomation to try and use fewer bits than the original data.
(d) The process of removing necessary data from a file.

174. Given below are two statements: **[June 2023]**

Statement-I: Twitter is an example of a Web 2.0 application.

Statement-II: Web 2.0 refers to static text-based information websites.

In the light of the above statements, choose the correct answer from the options given below:

(a) Both Statement I and Statement II are true.
(b) Both Statement I and Statement II are false.
(c) Statement I is true but Statement II is false.
(d) Statement I is false but Statement II is true.

175. Which of the following systems use synchronous communication? **[June 2023]**

A. Skype video call
B. Facebook Chat
C. Email
D. Messaging on Snap chat
E. Telephone call

Choose the correct answer from the options given below:

(a) A, B and E only
(b) A, B, D and E only
(c) A, C, D and E only
(d) B and C only

176. Match List I with List II. **[June 2023]**

List I (Storage Device)	List II (Logical Equivalent)
A. Solid State Drive (SSD)	I. Optical media that uses concentric tracks to allow simultaneous read-write operations.
B. ROM	II. Volatile in nature that stores programs and data in current use.
C. DVD-RAM	III. Has no moving part and is therefore a very robust and reliable technology.
D. RAM	IV. Non-volatile in nature that stores firmware

Choose the correct answer from the options given below:

(a) A-I, B-IV, C-III, D-II
(b) A-III, B-IV, C-I, D-II
(c) A-II, B-III, C-I, D-IV
(d) A-IV, B-III, C-I, D-II

177. Consider the following MS-Excel spreadsheets in which the population column represents the city's population in millions of people: **[June 2023]**

	A	B	C	D	E	F
	City	State	Population	Haryana	MP	UP
1.	Patiala	Punjab	8.34			
2.	Sonipat	Haryana	3.86			
3.	Noida	UP	2.71			
4.	Indore	MP	2.16			
5.	Mandi	HP	1.49			
6.	Sagar	MP	1.38			
7.	Panipat	Haryana	1.39			
8.	Gwalior	MP	1.24			

Suppose the formula -IF (\$B2=D\$1,\$A2,0) is entered into cell D2 and then the cell D2 is copied and pasted to D2:F9. How many cells in the range D2:F9 contains 0?

(a) 0 (b) 6
(c) 12 (d) 18

178. Which of the following statements about email security best describes email encryption? **[June 2023]**

(a) This is a self replicating program that can spread by email.
(b) This disguises the content of email messages in order to protect sensitive information.
(c) This consists of sending numerous duplicate mails to the same email address.
(d) The email header is changed so that the message appears to have come from someone else.

179. Given below are two statements about music files: **[June 2023]**

Statement I: A music clip stored in MP3 format would take up more memory than the same clip stored in WAV format.

Statement II: Music files stored in MP3 format are of better quality than files stored in WAV format.

In the lights of the above statements, choose the correct answer from the options given below :

(a) Both Statement I and Statement II are true.
(b) Both Statement I and Statement II are false.
(c) Statement I is true but Statement II is false.
(d) Statement I is false but Statement II is true.

180. Which of the following statements are accurate? **[June 2023]**

A. Web 2.0 is a simple static website without any interaction with its users.
B. Web 2.0 brings people closer together with information using machines.
C. Web 3.0 brings machines closer together using information.

Choose the correct answer from the options given below:

(a) A only (b) B only
(c) B and C only (d) D only

181. Match List I with List II. **[June 2023]**

List I (Output Device)	List II (Description)
A. Inkjet printer	I. Flat panel display that uses the light modulating properties of liquid crystals.
B. LCD screen	II. Flat panel display that uses an array of light-emitting diodes as pixels.
C. LED screen	III. Droplets of ink are propelled onto paper.
D. Laser Printer	IV. Electrically-charged powdered ink is transferred onto paper.

Choose the correct answer from the options given below:

(a) A-IV, B-I, C-II, D-III
(b) A-IV, B-II, C-I, D-III
(c) A-II, B-I, C-III, D-IV
(d) A-III, B-I, C-II, D-IV

182. Given below are two statements: **[Dec 2023]**

Statement (I): An output device that creates an object by building layer upon player of material is called 3D printer. It is widely used in CAD applications.

Statement (II): Laptops can be used even when not plugged into an electricity socket.

In light of the above statements, choose the most appropriate answer from the options given below:

(a) Both Statement (I) and Statement (II) are true.
(b) Both Statement (I) and Statement (II) are false.
(c) Statement (I) is true but Statement (II) is false.
(d) Statement (I) is false but Statement (II) is true.

183. A computer uses RAM and ROM to store data. Which of the following statements describing ROM is/are true? **[Dec 2023]**

A. It stores the programs and data that are currently in use.
B. It is used to boot up the computer when power is turned on
C. Its contents are retained when power is turned off.

Choose the correct answer from the options given below:

(a) A only (b) B only
(c) A and B only (d) B and C only

184. Match List-I with List-II **[Dec 2023]**

List I (Internet Term)	List II (Definition)
(A) HTTP	(i) A unique address given to a device on a network. It is provided by the manufacturer.
(B) URL	(ii) The main protocol that governs the transmission of data using the Internet.
(C) MAC address	(iii) An address given to each device on a network. It is provided by the network.
(D) IP address	(iv) The website address that is typed into the address bar.

Choose the correct answer from the options given below:

(a) (A)–(ii); (B)–(iv); (C)–(i); (D)–(iii)
(b) (A)–(iii); (B)–(iv); (C)–(i); (D)–(ii)
(c) (A)–(i); (B)–(iii); (C)–(ii); (D)–(iv)
(d) (A)–(iv); (B)–(ii); (C)–(i); (D)–(iii)

185. Alisha has agreed to send Khushi a 20-megabyte file. They both have a broadband Internet connection. Alisha has to upload her file to a server and then Khushi needs to download it from the same server. The broadband data transfer rates (speeds) are: 1 megabit per second to upload a file and 8 megabits per second to download a file. If P and Q represent the time taken in seconds to upload and download Alisha's file respectively then (P,Q) = **[Dec 2023]**

(a) (20, 160) (b) (144, 18)
(c) (18, 144) (d) (160, 20)

186. Identify the correct order of the terms A-E to complete the following paragraph about computer devices and technology. **[Dec 2023]**

An ____ allows a user to write on a surface using a pen, and the text and drawings can then be captured and stored for later use. An ____ printer produces a hard copy of a document using ____ and piezoelectric technology. A ____ printer uses a ____ drum, and positive and negative charges, to produce a hard copy of a document.

A. inkjet
B. interactive whiteboard
C. laser
D. rotating
E. thermal bubble

Choose the correct answer from the options given below:

(a) B, E, A, D, C (b) B, A, E, C, D
(c) A, B, E, C, D (d) E, D, C, B, A

ANSWER KEY

1. (a)	2. (d)	3. (c)	4. (b)	5. (d)	6. (c)	7. (d)	8. (c)	9. (b)	10. (a)
11. (a)	12. (b)	13. (c)	14. (d)	15. (c)	16. (a)	17. (c)	18. (d)	19. (a)	20. (d)
21. (b)	22. (d)	23. (c)	24. (d)	25. (a)	26. (d)	27. (a)	28. (a)	29. (c)	30. (a)
31. (b)	32. (b)	33. (c)	34. (b)	35. (c)	36. (c)	37. (d)	38. (b)	39. (d)	40. (c)
41. (d)	42. (b)	43. (d)	44. (b)	45. (c)	46. (b)	47. (d)	48. (b)	49. (d)	50. (c)
51. (b)	52. (a)	53. (b)	54. (c)	55. (a)	56. (c)	57. (b)	58. (c)	59. (d)	60. (b)
61. (d)	62. (c)	63. (b)	64. (b)	65. (b)	66. (b)	67. (a)	68. (a)	69. (d)	70. (c)
71. (c)	72. (a)	73. (d)	74. (c)	75. (b)	76. (b)	77. (a)	78. (c)	79. (d)	80. (b)
81. (b)	82. (b)	83. (b)	84. (a)	85. (b)	86. (d)	87. (a)	88. (c)	89. (c)	90. (d)
91. (c)	92. (c)	93. (a)	94. (c)	95. (d)	96. (c)	97. (a)	98. (a)	99. (a)	100. (d)
101. (d)	102. (a)	103. (d)	104. (a)	105. (b)	106. (d)	107. (c)	108. (c)	109. (b)	110. (c)
111. (a)	112. (a)	113. (b)	114. (d)	115. (b)	116. (d)	117. (b)	118. (c)	119. (a)	120. (c)
121. (d)	122. (c)	123. (d)	124. (b)	125. (c)	126. (d)	127. (b)	128. (b)	129. (d)	130. (a)
131. (b)	132. (c)	133. (a)	134. (a)	135. (c)	136. (d)	137. (b)	138. (b)	139. (b)	140. (c)
141. (d)	142. (d)	143. (d)	144. (a)	145. (d)	146. (b)	147. (a)	148. (d)	149. (d)	150. (c)
151. (c)	152. (b)	153. (c)	154. (c)	155. (a)	156. (a)	157. (b)	158. (c)	159. (c)	160. (a)
161. (d)	162. (c)	163. (a)	164. (a)	165. (d)	166. (b)	167. (d)	168. (b)	169. (c)	170. (c)
171. (c)	172. (d)	173. (c)	174. (c)	175. (b)	176. (b)	177. (d)	178. (b)	179. (d)	180. (c)
181. (b)	182. (a)	183. (d)	184. (a)	185. (d)	186. (b)				

HINTS AND SOLUTIONS

1. **(a):** FTP also known as File Transfer Protocol, is a communication protocol for the simple transmission of files across a network supporting the TCP/IP. This network is generally the Internet, or a local network. FTP is a way of accessing files on another computer.

2. **(d):** GUI stands for 'Graphical User Interface' and is pronounced 'gooey'. It is a user interface that includes graphical elements, such as windows, icons and buttons.

   GIF is 'Graphics Interchange Format.' GIF is an image file format commonly used for images on the web and sprites in software programs.

   PNG (Portable Network Graphics) is a file format for image compression that, in time, is expected to replace the Graphics Interchange Format (GIF) that is widely used on internet.

3. **(c):** The first web browser - or browser-editor rather - was called World Wide Web as, after all, when it was written in 1990 it was the only way to see the web and it is not a synonym for the internet. World Wide Web is a subset of the internet. HTTP is the method used to transfer web pages to our computers.

   Internet Explorer is a World Wide Web browser. It comes bundled with the Microsoft Windows operating system (OS).

4. **(b):** Read Only Memory (ROM) is a type of storage medium that permanently stores data on a PC and other electronic devices. Hence, when a computer is switched on, the BIOS is loaded from ROM. It contains the programming needed to start a PC, which is essential for boot-up it performs major input/output tasks and holds programs or software instructions.

   Random Access Memory (RAM) is the memory or information storage in a computer that is used to store running programs and data for the programs. Data in RAM can be read and written quickly in any order.

5. **(d):** IP stands for internet protocol is a unique address that identifies a device on the internet or a local network. It allows a system to be recognized by other systems connected via the Internet protocol. There are two primary types of IP address formats used are IPv4 and IPv6.

6. **(c):** The IP address space is managed globally by the Internet Assigned Numbers Authority (IANA). An Internet Protocol address (IP address) is a numerical label assigned to each device connected to a computer network that uses the Internet Protocol for communication. An IP address serves two main functions: host or network interface identification and location addressing.

   Internet Protocol version 4 (IPv4) defines an IP address as a 32-bit number. However, because of the growth of the Internet and the depletion of available IPv4 addresses, a new version of IP (IPv6), using 128 bits for the IP address, was developed in 1995.

   An IPv4 address consists of four sets of numbers from 0 to 255, separated by three dots. For example, the IP address of some website is 67.43.14.98. There are three classes of IPv4 address sets that can be registered. The smallest is Class C, which consists of 256 IP addresses (e.g., 123.123.123.xxx where xxx is 0 to 255). The next largest is Class B, which contains 65,536 IP addresses (e.g., 123.123.xxx.xxx). The largest block is Class A, which contains 16,777,216 IP addresses (e.g., 123.xxx.xxx.xxx).

7. **(d):** Smart Classrooms are technology enhanced classrooms that foster opportunities for teaching and learning by integrating learning technology, such as computers, specialized software, audience response technology, assistive listening devices, networking, and audio/visual capabilities.

8. **(c):** A hexadecimal number is a number that uses the letters A-F as well as the digits 0–9.

   To illustrate:

Decimal	Hexadecimal
0	0
1	1
2	2
3	3
4	4
5	5
6	6
7	7
8	8
9	9
10	A
11	B
12	C
13	D
14	E
15	F

9. **(b):**

   (a) **Google Search**: This is a fully-automated search engine that uses software known as web crawlers that explore the web regularly to find pages to add to our index. This engine has acquired almost 70% of the world market. This engine is always evolving to improve the search engine algorithm to provide best results to the end-user.

(b) **Chrome** is not a search engine because it is a web browser that uses the search engine to retrieve and view the information from web pages present on the web servers.

(c) **Yahoo** uses Microsoft's Bing search engine to power results as per deal between Microsoft and Yahoo since 2009.

(d) **Bing or Microsoft's Bing** is a web search engine owned and operated by Microsoft. The service has its origins in Microsoft's previous search engines: MSN Search, Windows Live Search and later Live Search. Bing provides a variety of search services, including web, video, image and map search products.

Search engines such as DuckDuckGo, StartPage, and Swisscows are more suitable if we maintain privacy. Baidu and Yandex may be better options for specific locations.

10. (a):

(1) CSS stands for Cascading Style Sheets.
(2) CSS are a series of instruction that specify how markup elements should appear on a web page.
(3) **Cascading:** Multiple styles can overlap in order to specify a range of style from a whole web site.
(4) **Style:** CSS deals specifically with the presentation domain of designing a web page (Color, Font, Layout, etc.).
(5) **Sheet:** Normally, CSS is a file separate from the HTML file –linked to the HTML file through it.

11. (a): Binary equivalent of 35

$34 = 32\times1 + 16\times0 + 8\times0 + 4\times0 + 2\times1 + 1\times1$

Thus, binary equivalent of 35 = 1 0 0 0 1 1

It can be done in the following manner also.

$\frac{35}{2}=17$ with 1 remainder

$\frac{17}{2}=8$ with 1 remainder

$\frac{8}{2}=4$ with 0 remainder

$\frac{4}{2}=2$ with 0 remainder

$\frac{2}{2}=1$ with 0 remainder

$\frac{1}{2}=0$ with 1 remainder

12. (b): These are basically meant for image data.

JPEG (or JPG, for the file extension; Joint Photographic Experts Group)
PNG (Portable Network Graphics)
BMP (Bitmap)
GIF (Graphics Interchange Format)

13. (c):

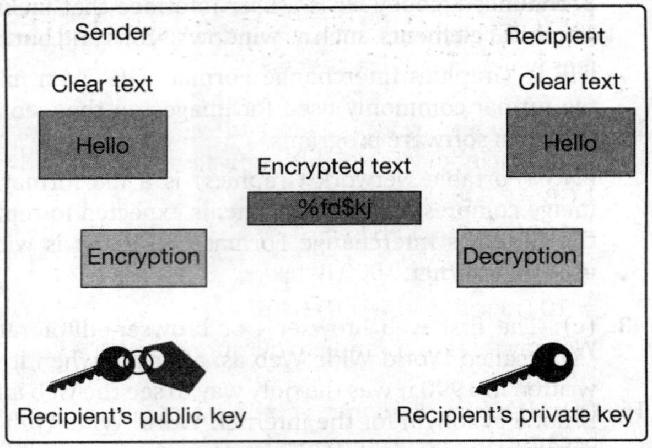

14. (d): We can discuss input and output devices.

Input Devices sends data (or say information) to a computer system for processing.

An output device reproduces or displays the results of that processing. Output devices only receive the output of data from another device.

I/O devices (input/output devices): Some devices can accept input and display output.

Examples of input devices are Keyboard and Mouse, Microphone and Webcam.

The examples of output devices are Monitor, Projector, Speakers etc.

Examples of input/output devices include CD-RW drive and DVD-RW drive, USB flash drive.

(a) **Printer:** This is an external hardware output device that takes the electronic data stored on a computer or other device and generates a hard copy.

(b) **Speaker:** This output hardware device connects to a computer to generate sound. The signal used to produce the sound that comes from a computer speaker is created by the computer's sound card.

(c) **Monitor:** This is basically an output device that displays information in pictorial or text form. A monitor usually comprises a visual display, some circuitry, a casing, and a power supply.

(d) **Keyboard:** A keyboard a key input device that is used for putting information including letters, words and numbers into your computer. QWERTY keyboard is the most popular one.

They are of two types:

1. **Basic keyboard:** this contains 104 keys and is enough to perform all the functions that can be done on a Windows PC.

2. **Extended keyboard:** they may have additional keys. Their design varies among the according to the companies which manufacture them.

15. (c): A gigabyte (GB) is a measure of computer data storage capacity that is roughly equivalent to 1 billion bytes.

1 GB = 1000 Mega Byte

= 1000 × 1000 Kilo Bytes

= 1000 × 1000 × 1000 Bytes

= 10 (raised to power 9) Bytes

We may refer to solution to question number 41.

16. (a): Internet Explorer is not open-source software, because an Open-source software (OSS) is a computer software with its source code made available with a license in which the copyright holder provides the rights to study, change and distribute the software to anyone and for any purpose.

17. (c): This question is quite simple. We have to solve all choices one by one.

16 8 4 2 1

$1\ 0\ 1\ 0\ 1 = 16\times 1 + 8\times 0 + 4\times 1 + 2\times 0 + 1\times 1 = 21$

Similarly, solve for other options also. Option (c) is the right answer.

$1\ 1\ 0\ 0\ 1 = 1\times 16 + 1\times 8 + 0\times 4 + 0\times 2 + 1\times 1 = 25$

Alternatively, we can follow the step by step solution.

Step 1: Divide (25)10 successively by 2 until the quotient is 0:

25/2 = 12, remainder is 1

12/2 = 6, remainder is 0

6/2 = 3, remainder is 0

3/2 = 1, remainder is 1

1/2 = 0, remainder is 1

Step 2: Read from the bottom (MSB) to top (LSB) as 11001.

So, 11001 is the binary equivalent of decimal number 25.

(Students can visit http://www.cimt.plymouth.ac.uk for more examples.)

18. (d):

AltaVista - This was the first search engine that was started in 1995 by Palo Alto. This allowed users to search for things using natural language. Before AltaVista was started, Tim Berners-Lee first created the web and compiled a Virtual Library that was a manual record of all of the websites that users had published. Ultimately, it was bought by Yahoo Inc.

W3Catalog was an early web search engine, first released on September 2, 1993 by developer Oscar Nierstrasz at the University of Geneva.

Mac - The is the short form of series of Macintosh computers made by Apple Inc. since 1984. This was the very first model, starting with it, Apple is largely credited with starting the trend of making computers that are useful for the ordinary people.

Microsoft Office – This is simply called as Office also, it is a family of client software, server software, and services developed by Microsoft. It was first announced by Bill Gates on August 1, 1988, at COMDEX in Las Vegas. The first version of Office contained Microsoft Word, Microsoft Excel (a spreadsheet program), and Microsoft PowerPoint (a presentation program).

Google Talk - Google Talk was an instant messaging service that provided both text and voice communication. The instant messaging service was variously referred to colloquially as Gchat, Gtalk, or Gmessage among its users. Google Talk was also the name of the client applications previously offered by Google to use the service.

19. (a): The National Mission on Education through (NMEICT) has been envisaged as a Centrally Sponsored Scheme to leverage the potential of ICT, in teaching and learning process for the benefit of all the learners in Higher Education Institutions in any time any where mode. This was expected to be a major intervention in enhancing the Gross Enrolment Ratio (GER) in Higher Education by 5 percentage points during the XI Five Year Plan period. NMEICT was launched on 3 February 2009 at Tirupati, Andhra Pradesh.

20. (d): Instant Messaging (IM) is a type of online chat that offers real-time text transmission over the internet.

We have discussed Google Talk earlier.

WhatsApp – This is an internationally available freeware, cross-platform centralized instant messaging and voice-over-IP service owned by US company Meta Platforms. It was developed in 2009.

Viber - This is a secure, private, fun messaging and calling app, connecting over a billion people worldwide. This has been developed by Rakuten, a Japanese company.

21. (b): Byte is the basic unit of information. A byte consists of 8 adjacent binary digits (bits), each of which consists of a 0 or 1.

22. (d): We may refer to solution of question number 14 for definitions and their devices.

(a) Microphone: This device translates sound vibrations in the air into electronic signals and scribes them to a recording medium or over a loudspeaker.

(b) Keyboard: A keyboard is for putting information including letters, words and numbers into your computer. QWERTY keyboard is the most popular one.

They are of two types:

1. **Basic keyboard**–this contains 104 keys and is enough to perform all the functions that can be done on a Windows PC.

2. **Extended keyboard**–they may have additional keys. Their design varies among the according to the companies which manufacture them.

(c) Joystick: This is basically an input device. This can be used for controlling the movement of the cursor or a pointer in a computer device. This is mainly used for gaming and graphics applications.

(d) Monitor: This is basically an output device that displays information in pictorial or text form. A monitor usually comprises a visual display, some circuitry, a casing, and a power supply.

23. (c): Open-source software is any computer software that's distributed with its source code available for modification.

The few browsers have been mentioned below as questions are asked on them. For eg- web browsers:

Firefox, Google Chrome, Microsoft Edge, Apple Safari, Opera, Brave, Vivaldi and DuckDuckgo, etc. A browser is a software application used to locate, retrieve and display content on the World Wide Web, including webpages, images, video and other files.

24. (d): The following diagram shows the basic idea of mail merge.

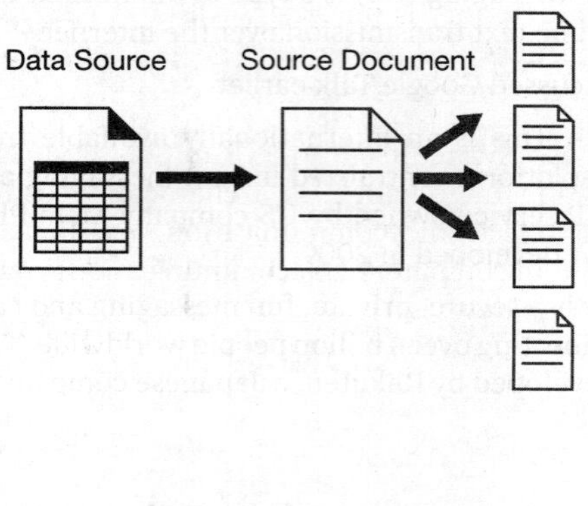

25. (a): The process of copying files to a cd-rom is known as 'burning'. It is a process of recopying the converted files to a recordable DVD or CD. CD drivers use laser to 'burn' the information into a writable CD. This process helps in copying information from computer to a writable disc.

26. (d): Worm: Worms are stand-alone malicious programs which is self-replicating program that can spread throughout a network without human assistance. A computer worm is a subset of the Trojan horse malware.

Virus: This spread from one computer to another inside files. For the virus to be activated, someone has to trigger it with an external action. Viruses must be triggered by the activation of their host.

The damage done by both viruses and worms depends upon the way network is structured. If network consists of many computers connected to each other in a ring formation, then a worm may be a bigger threat than a virus.

Threat: A computer threat is a term that relates to the security of a computer system being compromised.

Spam: This is any kind of unwanted, unsolicited digital communication that gets sent out in bulk. Spam is often sent via email, this can also be distributed via text messages, phone calls, or social media.

27. (a): Information technology is the design and implementation of computer networks for data processing and communication. This includes designing the hardware for processing information and connecting separate components, and developing software that can efficiently and faultlessly analyse and distribute this data.

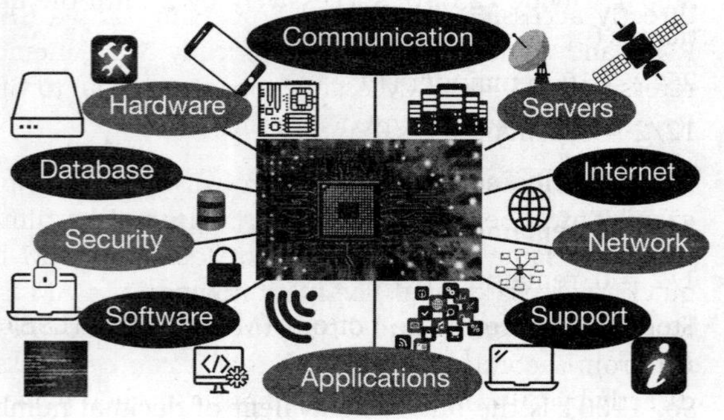

28. (a): As we need binary code for 51, we can find binary code for 3 and add it to that for 48.

Binary for 48 = 110000 (Given)

2	3	1
2	2	1
	0	

So, binary for 3 = 011

Binary for 51 = 110000 + 011
= 110011

Note that in the binary system:

0 + 0 = 0
0 + 1 = 1
1 + 0 = 1
1 + 1 = 0, carry over the 1, i.e., 10

Similar rules for other functions such as subtraction, multiplication, division are given on https://www.calculator.net/binary-calculator.html?d2bnumber1=3&calctype=d2b&x=77&y=23#decimal2binary.

29. (c):

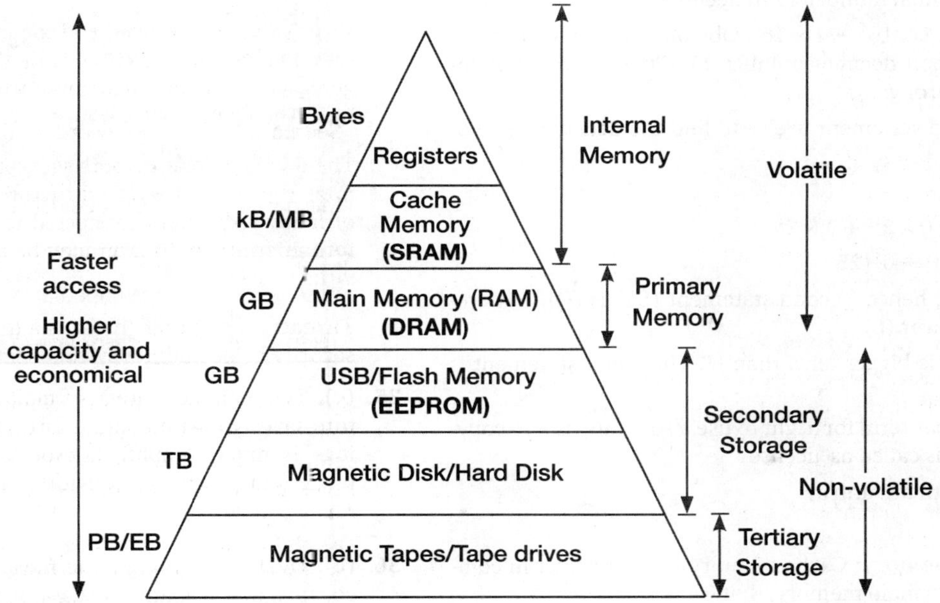

We are starting our discussion with main memory, and then getting into parts.

Main Memory: The memories in the answer options are part of Main memory (primary storage) which are directly accessible by Central Processing Unit – RAM, ROM and sometimes cache. Practically Main memory refers to RAM. Here, accessible means external to CPU. Registers and possibly cache are the part of CPU.

Random Access Memory: When a user opens a program, it must be loaded into the RAM. Its reading almost takes the same time regardless of location. RAM has quick read/write time. The main function of RAM is to load open programs and Operating System currently in use from secondary storage, so that it can be accessed directly by CPU. In this case, data is lost when power is lost. So, it is volatile in nature.

Read Only Memory: This can only be read, so can not be changed once programmed. This is used in small amounts in computers to store essential programmes, such as those needed to be run in order to boot the computer. So, the data is retained when the power is lost, it means that they are volatile in nature. Now most of ROM is being replaced by the more versatile flash storage.

Cache stores copies of frequently used data. Though cache has much lower capacity, it is much faster than RAM. It means that capacity is compromised for the speed. Cache memory is physically closer to CPU. It is checked before RAM is in the fetch stage.There is possibility that browsers and storage have caches.

30. (a): ASCII, abbreviated from American Standard Code for Information Interchange, is a character encoding standard for electronic communication. ASCII codes represent text in computers, telecommunications equipment, and other devices.

31. (b):

Number System	Base	Symbols used
Binary	2	0,1
Octal	8	0,1,2,3,4,5,6,7
Decimal	10	0,1,2,3,4,5,6,7,8,9
Hexadecimal	16	0,1,2,3,4,5,6,7,8,9,A,B,C,D,E,F where A = 10; B = 11; C = 12; D = 13; E = 14; F = 15

Hexadecimal number 11 to decimal

$(11)_{16} = 1 \times 16^1 + 1 \times 16^0$, Obviously this will be much bigger than decimal number 11. Thus, first statement (S1) is wrong.

In second statement, we've to find the decimal value of $(0.101)_2$

So,

$1 \times 2^{-1} + 0 \times 2^{-2} + 1 \times 2^{-3}$

$= 0.5 + 0 + 0.125$

$= 0.625$, hence, second statement (S2) is right. Therefore, answer (b).

32. (b): ICT is bigger term than IT. Thus, first statement is not true.

The proper term for 'right to use a software' is not 'copyright'. It is called as 'license'.

Thus, both are untrue.

33. (c):

Cache memory: Cache memory is much faster in comparison to main memory, that is RAM.

CPU registers: They're part of the Control unit and ALU rather than the memory. Hence, their contents can be handled much faster than any content of memory.

Secondary storage: Operating speed is much slower in comparison to main memory (RAM).

34. (b): The transition of Web1.0 to Web 2.0 is experienced due to rapid speed of the information technology. Web 2.0 is the interactive version of web-based communities and social networking websites like Facebook, Orkut, LinkedIn, etc. It also included video sharing, wikis, blogs, mashups, etc. The second generation of web is commonly referred as Web 2.0. The term 'Web2.0' is commonly associated with web applications that facilitate interactive information sharing, interoperability, user-centered design, and collaboration on the World Wide Web. (http://en.wikipedia.org/wiki/Web_2.0) Examples of Web 2.0 include web-based communities, hosted services, web applications, social networking sites, video sharing sites, wikis, blogs, mashups, and folksonomies.

Let's look at the main technological aspects of Web 3.0 also in comparative terms.

	Base	Symbols used
Communication	Interactive	Engaged/Invested
Information	Dynamic	Portable & Personal
Focus	Community	Individual
Personal	Blogs/Wikis	Lifestreams
Content	Sharing	Curation
Interaction	Web Applications	Smart Applications
Search	Keywords/Tags	Context/ Relevance
Metrics	Cost Per Click	User Engagement
Adcertising	Interactive	Behavioural
Research	Wikipedia	The Semantic Web
Technologies	Flash/Java/XML	RDF/RDFS/OWL

35. (c): The main advantage of mail merge is that the feature saves your time and efforts. Producing mass mailings is much simplified, especially compared to the process of preparing individual letters or envelopes to many people.

36. (c): DVDs are amongst the most common methods of copying and backing up data at home. DVD has very large storage capacity ranging 4.7–9 GB. Their sound and picture quality is excellent, making them ideal for storing films with video and sound.

37. (d): A website address, also known as a URL (Uniform Resource Locator), is an internet or intranet name that points to to a location where a file, directory or website page is hosted.

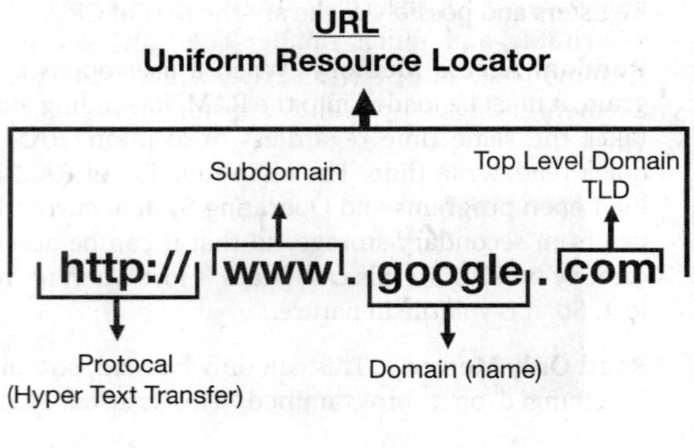

38. **(b): Data Storage Hierarchy**

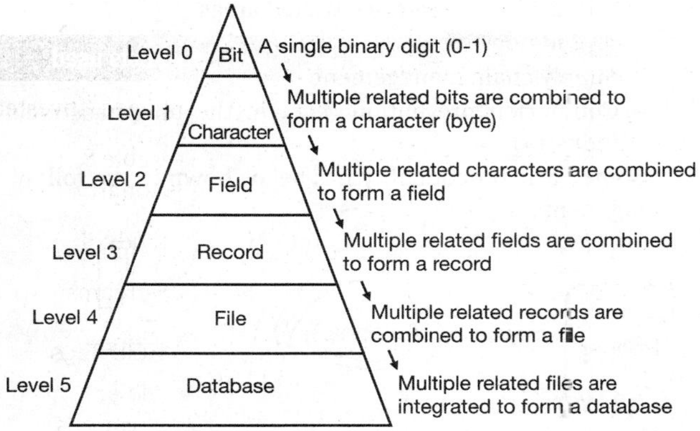

39. **(d):**

Different Domains on the Net	
.com	Commercial/profit business
.net	network
.edu	educational
.org	organization
.net	network
.mil	military
.gov	government

40. **(c):** Universal Serial Bus (USB) is an industry standard that establishes specifications for cables, connectors and protocols for connection, communication and power supply (interfacing) between computers, peripherals and other computers.

A USB flash drive (also called a thumb drive) is a data storage device that includes flash memory with an integrated USB interface. It is typically removable, rewritable and much smaller than an optical disc. Common uses of USB flash drives are for storage, supplementary back-ups, and transferring of computer files.

41. **(d):**

Byte (B)	1	1 byte
Kilobyte (KB)	1,000	1 thousand bytes
Megabyte (MB)	1,000,000	1 million bytes
Gigabyte (GB)	1,000,000,000	1 billion bytes
Terabyte (TB)	1,000,000,000,000	1 trillion bytes

42. **(b):** The definition of ICT is wrong. Different tools are now able to work together and combined to form our networked world—a massive infrastructure of interconnected telephone services, standardized computerized hardware, internet, radio, TV, etc.

43. **(d):** Solid State Drive (SSD) is another type of Hard Disk Drive (HDD). SSD has no moving mechanical components. A conventional hard disk drive has magnetic discs in which data is stored. SSD has an integrated circuit that stores data. The advantages over conventional HDD includes higher speed, shock resistant, security of data, lighter in weight, smaller size, drastic decrease in boot times, much less power consumption.

44. **(b):** swami'(of swami@test.com) will be able to see the above three addresses of ram@test.com, raj@test.com and ravi@test.com but won't be visible to them and also to rama@test.com.

45. **(c):**

A bit is a digit within binary number system.

Tabular representation of various memory sizes

Name	Equal to	Size (In Bytes)
Bit	1 bit	1/8
Nibble	4 bits	1/2 (rare)
Byte	8 bits	1
Kilobyte	1024 bytes	1024
Megabyte	1,024 kilobyte	1,048,576
Gigabyte	1,024 megabyte	1,073,741,824
Terrabyte	1,024 gigabyte	1,099,511,627,776
Petabyte	1,024 terrabyte	1,125,899,906,842,624

46. **(b):** Volatile memory is computer storage that only maintains its data while the device is powered. Volatile memory contrasts with non-volatile memory, which does not lose content when power is lost.

Random Access Memory is volatile. Most RAM (random access memory) used for primary storage in personal computers is volatile memory. Data in the RAM can be read and written quickly in any order. Normally, the random access memory is in the form of computer chips.

47. (d): The networking is basically through Web 2.0.

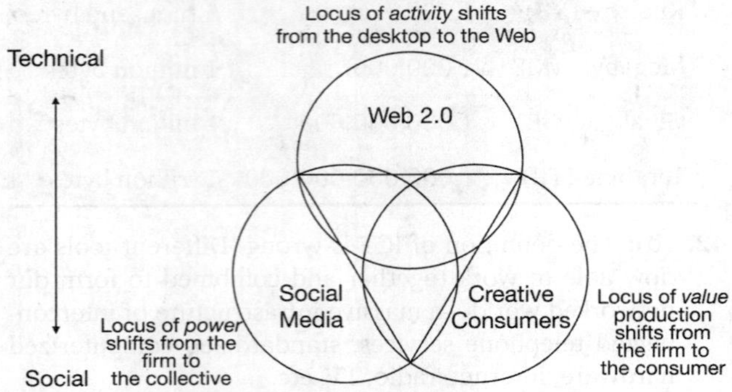

Since 2006, we have moved into Web 3.0 situation that is more participatory in nature. Web 3.0, is basically third-generation internet. It is the next evolution of the World Wide Web. It provides a data-driven Semantic Web. This employs a machine-based understanding of data with the objective of developing a more intelligent and connected web experience for users. The blockchain is an example of it.

48. (b) :

Binary number		*Resistance*
2	50	
2	25	1
2	12	0
2	6	0
2	3	1
2	1	1
	0	

49. (d): Microsoft Office activation keys or product key can be used to activate our trial or limited edition of Office suite. After activating our version of Microsoft Office, we can avail full features of any of office applications including Microsoft Word, Excel, Outlook and PowerPoint.

50. (c): The Advanced Research Projects Agency Network (ARPANET) was an early packet-switching network and the first network to implement the TCP/IP protocol suite. Both technologies became the technical foundation of the Internet. The ARPANET was initially founded by the Advanced Research Projects Agency (ARPA) of the United States Department of Defence.

51. (b): RFID is an acronym for 'radio-frequency identification' and refers to a technology whereby, digital data encoded in RFID tags or smart labels are captured by a reader via radio waves. Few examples of RFID are given below:

- Inventory management
- Asset tracking
- Personnel tracking
- Controlling access to restricted areas
- ID Badging
- Supply chain management
- Counterfeit prevention (e.g., in the pharmaceutical industry)

Some basic functionality has been shown in the following manner.

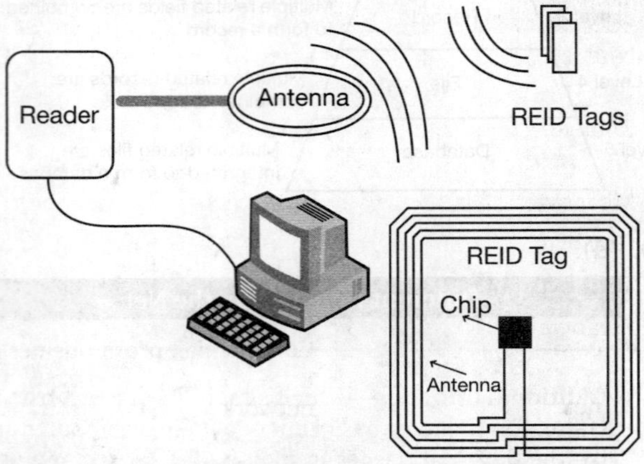

52. (a): Bluetooth is a short-range wireless technology standard that is used for exchanging data between fixed and mobile devices over short distances and building personal area networks.

53. (b): DNS stands for Domain Name System. It is a hierarchical and decentralized naming system for computers, services, or other resources connected to the Internet or a private network. It associates various information pieces with domain names assigned to each of the participating entities. Most prominently, it translates more readily memorized domain names to the numerical IP addresses needed for locating and identifying computer services and devices with the underlying network protocols

Domain Name System delegates the responsibility of assigning domain names and mapping those names to internet resources by designating authoritative name servers for each domain. Network administrators may delegate authority over sub-domains of their allocated name space to other name servers. The Domain Name System also specifies the technical functionality of the database service that is at its core. It defines the DNS protocol, a detailed specification of the data structures and data communication exchanges used in the DNS, as part of the Internet Protocol Suite.

54. (c): The unit symbol for the terabyte is TB. Let's have a comprehensive look at various memory units.

Their typical file media uses have also been given in the table here for future questions.

	Actual Bytes	Approx. Bits	Typical file/ media
1 byte	1	8	Test email, SMS
1 Kilobyte	1024 B = 2^{10}	8×10^3	Word document
1 Megabyte	1024 KB = 2^{20}	8×10^6	Digital photo
1 Gigabyte	1024 MB = 2^{30}	8×10^9	DVD
1 Terrabyte	1024 GB = 2^{40}	8×10^{12}	Hard disk
1 Petabyte	1024 TB = 2^{50}	8×10^{15}	Cloud

Additional Infolines—A bit is simply a 1 or a 0. A true or a false. It is the most basic unit of data in a computer. It's like the dots and dashes in Morse code for a computer. It's also called machine language.

A **byte** is a basic unit of measurement of information storage or transmission that consists of 8 bits.

55. (a): Step by step solution

Step 1: We start with the positive version of the number:

$\Rightarrow |-23| = 23$

Step 2: Divide the number repeatedly by 2, keeping track of each remainder, until we get a quotient that is equal to zero:

$\Rightarrow$ dividend $\div$ divisor = quotient + remainder

$\Rightarrow 23 \div 2 = 11 + 1;$

$\Rightarrow 11 \div 2 = 5 + 1;$

$\Rightarrow 5 \div 2 = 2 + 1;$

$\Rightarrow 2 \div 2 = 1 + 0;$

$\Rightarrow 1 \div 2 = 0 + 1;$

Now we got the quotient 0.

Step 3: Construct the base 2 representation of the positive number, by taking all the remainders starting from the bottom of the list in step 2.

$\Rightarrow 23(10) = 10111(2)$

Step 4: Determine the signed binary number bit length:

The base 2 number's actual length, in bits: 5.

A signed binary's bit length must be equal to a power of 2, as of:

21 = 2; 22 = 4; 23 = 8; 24 = 16; 25 = 32; 26 = 64; ...

First bit (the leftmost) indicates the sign,

1 = negative, 0 = positive.

The least number that is a power of 2 and is larger than the actual length so that the first bit (leftmost) could be zero is: 8.

Step 5: Positive binary computer representation on 8 bits - if needed, add extra 0s in front (to the left) of the base 2 number, up to the required length:

$\Rightarrow 23(10) = 00010111$

Step 6: To get the negative integer number representation on 8 bits, signed binary one's complement, replace all the bits on 0 with 1s and all the bits set on 1 with 0s (reversing the digits):

$\Rightarrow !(00010111) = 11101000$

Step 7: To get the negative integer number representation on 8 bits, signed binary two's complement, add 1 to the number calculated above in step 6:

$\Rightarrow 11101000 + 1 = 11101001$

Conclusion:

Number –23, a signed integer, converted from decimal system (base 10) to a signed binary two's complement representation is –23(10) = 11101001.

In the given Answer last five digits are mentioned i.e. 01001

56. (c): Full form of PDF is Portable Document Format. Portable Document Format is a file format that captures all the elements of a printed document as an electronic image that one can view, navigate, print or forward to someone else. PDF files are created using Adobe Acrobat, Acrobat Capture or similar products.

57. (b): A modem is a network device that both modulates and demodulates analog carrier signals (called sine waves) for encoding and decoding digital information for processing.

Modems (modulators/demodulators) are data communication devices that convert digital signals to analog signals, and vice versa. Modems allow digital transmissions over analog telephone lines. They allow people to connect their computers with other computers, corporate office LANs, and the internet.

58. (c): Difference between CC and BCC :

(Column A) CC	(Column B) BCC
1. It stands for Carbon Copy.	1. It stands for Blind Carbon Copy.
2. In CC, all recipients will be able to see each other mail address.	2. Whereas, in BCC none of the recipient will be able to see each other mail address.
3. Using CC, we can keep management and employees in the loop.	3. Using BCC, we can ensure the privacy of management and employees mail address.
4. Every recipient will get all additional responses to the email.	4. Here recipient will not get any additional responses until we forward the mail to them
5. It permits recipients to know with whom the mail is being shared.	5. Here, recipients don't have any idea with whom mail is being shared.
6. CC is most preferred for keeping the stakeholders informed.	6. BCC is most preferred for keeping the mass emails and email lists.
7. CC makes your email list to be visible to all recipients.	7. BCC makes your email list to be invisible to all recipients.
8.with CC, you can loop everyone into an ongoing thread.	8. With BCC, you can not be included in email responses.

59. (d): Digital divide is a big issue between 'urban and rural areas' and also among rich and poor.

60. (b): Gyan Vani, an educational FM radio station operating in several cities of India. Gyan Vani is heard at 105.4 MHz. It started on air 7 July 2003 at 4 p.m. This channel functions as 'media cooperative' with contributions from many educational institutions, NGOs and other agencies.

61. (d): Public domain software is any software that has no legal, copyright or editing restrictions associated with it. It is released without any conditions upon its use, and may be used without restriction. This type of software generally has the lowest level of support available.

Freeware is also distributed at minimal cost, but in this case the authors do not expect payment for their work. Typically, freeware programs are small utilities or incomplete programs that authors release for their potential benefit to others, but without support. The author of a freeware program may still retain a copyright on its contents and stipulate that others not modify the program or charge significant fees for its use or distribution.

Shareware software is distributed at low (or sometimes no) cost, but usually requires payment and registration for full legal use. Copies are distributed on a trial basis. You are free to test the software, see if it matches your needs, and decide whether it's a good value.

Open-source software is jointly developed software that can be used, shared, borrowed, or changed without restriction

62. (c): RAM is an acronym for random access memory, a type of computer memory that can be accessed randomly; that is, any byte of memory can be accessed without touching the preceding bytes.

63. (b): SWAYAM (Study Webs of Active-Learning for Young Aspiring Minds) MOOC Platform was developed indigenously by AICTE in 2016 to facilitate hosting of online courses which could be accessed by anyone, anywhere at any time free of cost to achieve three cardinal principles of Education Policy viz. access, equity and quality.

64. (b): What You See Is What You Get or WYSIWYG is basically a disambiguation where computer editing software allows content to be edited in a form that resembles its final appearance.

65. (b): We have tried to explain the difference between E-Commerce and E-Business.

Basis for Comparison	E-Commerce	E-Business
Meaning	Trading of merchandise, over the internet is known as E-commerce.	Running business using the internet is knwon as E-business.
What is it?	Subset	Superset
Is it limited to monetary transacions?	Yes	No
What they carry out?	Commercial transactions	Business ransactions
Approach	Extroverted	Ambiverted
Requires	Website	Website, CRM, ERP, etc.
Which network is used?	Internet	Internet, Intranet and Extranet.

66. (b): In the Domain Name System, there is a hierarchy of names. The root of system is unnamed. Internet domain names come in four main types—top-level domains, second-level domains, third-level domains, and country domains.

There are a set of what are called 'top-level domain names' (TLDs). These are the generic TLDs (EDU, COM, NET, ORG, GOV, MIL, and INT), and the two letter country codes from ISO-3166. It is extremely unlikely that any other TLDs will be created.

Second-level domains are the addresses commonly used to host internet applications like web hosting and email addressing.

Third-level internet domain names are created by those that own second-level domains.

For example, for the domain 'mail.twenty.net' the top-level domain is 'net', the second-level domain is 'twenty.net', and the third-level domain is www.twenty.net.

Each country in the world has its own top-level internet domain with a unique alphabetic designation. That is called as 'country domains, for example, .in is for India, .ca is for Canada, .us for United States and so on.

Students can learn more about Internet Corporation for Assigned Names and Numbers (ICANN) that is responsible for allocating IP addresses and managing the domain name system.

67. (a):

(a) We have already discussed about CPU.

(b) A hub (or a network hub) is a common connection point that is used for connection of devices in a network. This functions as a central connection for all the devices that are connected through a hub.

A hub has numerous ports. If a packet reaches at one port, it is able to see by all the segments of the network. This happens as a packet is copied to the other ports.

(c) A switch transmits data from one device to another in form of frames.

(d) A Modem is basically short form of modulator and demodulator. A modem is a box-type device that connects your home/office network directly to the internet.

68. (a): The computer memory is of two types.

1. **Primary storage**: This is a volatile memory which means data is lost as soon as the device loses power and it cannot be retained. The example is of RAM that is also referred as 'working memory'.

2. **Secondary storage**: This is a non-volatile memory which is able to retain data even if the device loses power. The examples are optical media (CDs and DVDs), hard disk drives (HDD), floppy disks, USB flash drives, etc.

69. (d): While Google is the most popular search engine in the world, Baidu is the same for China. It handles almost 75% of such activities in China.

70. (c): E-Governance is directly linked with ability of government to address the needs of society vis-à-vis other choices.

71. (c): The 'Photographic' word is explicitly linked with 'Image'.

72. (a): The two major components of CPU are Control Unit and ALU.

Registers are a type of computer memory used to quickly accept, store, and transfer data and instructions that are being used immediately by the CPU.

The internal bus connects only registers within the CPU.

73. (d):

(a) HTTP (Hyper Text Transfer Protocol): This protocol is foundation of data communication for the World Wide Web. This defines the format of messages through which web browsers (such as chrome, firefox) and web servers communicate. HTTP uses Transmission Control Protocol (TCP) as an underlying transport.

(b) URL (Uniform Resource Locator) is simply the address of a given unique resource on the Web. In theory, each valid URL points to a unique resource. The examples are HTML page, a CSS document, an image, etc.

(c) FTP (File Transfer Protocol) governs how computers transfer files from one system to another over the internet.

HTTP and FTP are both application layer protocols that can allow you to transfer files between two systems.

(d) Hypertext Markup Language (HTML) is the standard markup language for creating web pages and web applications. HTTP forms a triad with CSS and JavaScript for WWW.

74. (c): Virtual Learning Environment (VLE), an online environment of e-resources caters to several disciplines taught at undergraduate and postgraduate level. It is an initiative of the University at Institute of Lifelong Learning.

It was conceived in 2012, DU-VLE hosts quality resources that addresses emerging needs of a diverse teaching and learning community, not only of Delhi University but other universities as well. Drawing from several successful moodle models, the multimedia interactive contents loaded on VLE are categorized discipline-wise.

75. (b): ICT stands for Information and Communication Technology.

Inclusive education proposes all students are provided with equitable access to education within the context of a mainstream educational system and not in a segregated setting.

Specific benefits for students:

(1) Computers can improve independent access for students to education.

(2) Students with special educational needs are able to accomplish tasks working at their own pace.

(3) Visually impaired students using the internet can access information alongside their sighted peers.

(4) Students with profound and multiple learning difficulties can communicate more easily.

(5) Students using voice communication aids gain confidence and social credibility at school and in their communities.

(6) Increased ICT confidence amongst students motivates them to use the internet at home for schoolwork and leisure interests.

Benefits for teachers and non-teaching staff:

(1) Reduces isolation for teachers working in special educational needs by enabling them to communicate electronically with colleagues

(2) Supports reflection on professional practice via online communication

(3) Improved skills for staff and a greater understanding of access technology used by students

(4) Enhances professional development and the effectiveness of the use of ICT with students through collaboration with peers

(5) Materials already in electronic form (for example, from the internet) are more easily adapted into accessible resources such as large print or Braille.

76. (b): A wiki is a knowledge base website on which users collaboratively modify content and structure directly from the web browser. In a typical wiki, text is written using a simplified markup language and often edited with the help of a rich-text editor.

A wiki is run using wiki software, otherwise known as a wiki engine. A wiki engine is a type of content management system, but it differs from most other such systems, including blog software, in that the content is created without any defined owner or leader, and wikis have little inherent structure, allowing structure to emerge according to the needs of the users.

77. (a): $1100110 = (1 \times 2^6) + (1 \times 2^5) + (0 \times 2^4) + (0 \times 2^3) + (1 \times 2^2) + (1 \times 2^1) + (0 \times 2^0) = 102$

78. (c): KB stands for Kilobyte

Megabyte (MB)–1024 kilobyte (KB)

Gigabyte (GB)–1024 MB or 1024 × 1024 kilobytes

Terabyte (TB)–1024 GB or 1024 × 1024 × 1024 kilobytes

79. (d): Internet Explorer' is a type of web browser, made by Microsoft. It's rather old and you probably don't want to use it. Other web browsers include Chrome, Firefox, and Microsoft's replacement, 'Edge'.

Firefox	Mircosoft Edge	Internet Explorer	Google Chrome	Safari	Opera

Yahoo! is an internet portal that incorporates a search engine and a directory of World Wide Web sites organized in a hierarchy of topic categories. The word 'YAHOO' is a backronym for 'Yet Another Hierarchically Organized Oracle' or 'Yet Another Hierarchical Officious Oracle.' The yahoo.com domain was created on 18 January 1995.

80. (b): Video compression is the term used to define a method for reducing the data used to encode digital video content. This reduction in data translates to benefits such as smaller storage requirements and lower transmission bandwidth requirements, for a clip of video content. Audio compression is also defined for the same purpose.

RGB refers to three hues of light that can be mixed together to create different colours.

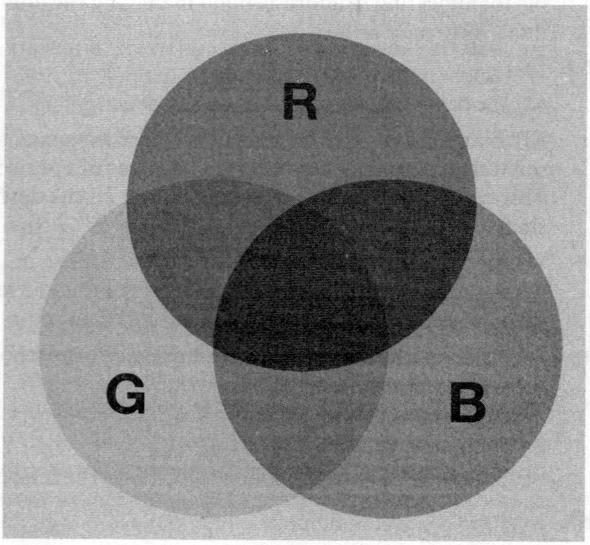

81. (b): The definition of computer virus is given in the question statement itself.

Question may be put on the types of virus as well. The various types of viruses have been mentioned below:

What are the different types of computer viruses?

(1) **Boot sector virus**: This type of virus can take control when you start—or boot—your computer. One

way it can spread is by plugging an infected USB drive into your computer.

(2) **Web scripting virus**: This type of virus exploits the code of web browsers and web pages. If you access such a web page, the virus can infect your computer.

(3) **Browser hijacker**: This type of virus 'hijacks' certain web browser functions, and you may be automatically directed to an unintended website.

(4) **Resident virus**: This is a general term for any virus that inserts itself in a computer system's memory. A resident virus can execute anytime when an operating system loads.

(5) **Direct action virus**: This type of virus comes into action when you execute a file containing a virus. Otherwise, it remains dormant.

(6) **Polymorphic virus**: A polymorphic virus changes its code each time an infected file is executed. It does this to evade antivirus programs.

(7) **File infector virus**: This common virus inserts malicious code into executable files—files used to perform certain functions or operations on a system.

(8) **Multipartite virus**: This kind of virus infects and spreads in multiple ways. It can infect both program files and system sectors.

(9) **Macro virus**: Macro viruses are written in the same macro language used for software applications. Such viruses spread when you open an infected document, often through email attachments.

A Trojan horse, or trojan, is a type of malicious code or software that looks legitimate but can take control of your computer. A trojan is designed to damage, disrupt, steal, or in general inflict some other harmful action on your data or network.

A firewall has the capability of preserving both the software and hardware on the network while an antivirus protects other software as it as an impartial software. A firewall inhibits malicious software from entering into the system while an antivirus removes corrupt files and software from your computer and network.

An operating system (OS) is system software that manages computer hardware and software resources and provides common services for computer programs.

82. (b): 1490–1956: First Generation–Vacuum Tubes. These early Computers used vacuum tubes as circuitry and magnetic drums for memory.

1956–1963: Second Generation–Transistors.

1964–1971: Third Generation–Integrated Circuits.

1972–2010: Fourth Generation–Microprocessors.

2010 onwards: Fifth Generation–Artificial Intelligence.

83. (b): The period of first generation of computers was from 1946–1959. They used vacuum tubes as the basic components for memory and circuitry for CPU (Central Processing Unit). These tubes, like electric bulbs, produced a lot of heat and the installations used to fuse frequently. Therefore, they were very expensive and only large organizations were able to afford it. During this generation, mainly batch processing operating system was used. Punch cards, paper tape, and magnetic tape were used as input and output devices.

84. (a): The electronic circuits, the building blocks of our computer, themselves don't understand anything except that they can be in the on state or off states. A series of on and off signals can be used to represent data - and that's why computers understand binary code.

85. (b): BHIM (Bharat Interface for Money) is a mobile payment App developed by the National Payments Corporation of India (NPCI), based on the Unified Payments Interface (UPI).

86. (d): Random Access Memory (RAM) is the memory or information storage in a computer that is used to store running programs and data for the programs. Data (information) in the RAM can be read and written quickly in any order. Normally, the random access memory is in the form of computer chips.

87. (a): A website address, also known as a URL (uniform resource locator), is an internet or intranet name that points to a location where a file, directory or website page is hosted. Website addresses can represent the home page of a website, a script, image, photo, movie or other file made available on a server for viewing, processing or download. They can also be embedded into the code of web pages in the form of hyperlinks to direct the user to other locations on the internet.

88. (c): Frequency modulation (FM) is the encoding of information in a carrier wave by varying the instantaneous frequency of the wave. FM is used at audio frequencies to synthesize sound. This technique is called as FM synthesis.

Advertising is a non-personal communication that employs an openly sponsored to promote a product, service or idea. Sponsors of advertising are typically businesses wishing to promote their products or services. Advertising is differentiated from public relations in that an advertiser pays for and has control over the message.

Internet is the global system of interconnected computer networks through bandwidths. It uses internet protocol suite (TCP/IP) to link devices worldwide.

Newspaper is a linear communication that is printed on paper on a regular basis. It gives information and opinions about current events and news and many other topics such as political events, crime, business, sports, and opinions.

89. (c): Simple Mail Transfer Protocol, a protocol for sending e-mail messages between servers. Most e-mail systems that send mail over the Internet use SMTP to send messages from one server to another; the messages can then be retrieved with an e-mail client using either POP or IMAP.

90. (d): An AVI (Audio Video Interleaved) file is a sound and motion picture file that conforms to the Microsoft Windows Resource Interchange File Format (RIFF) specification.

MP4 are typically more compressed and smaller in size, while MOV files are often higher in quality and larger in size.

JPEG is basically for image functions..

91. (c): It is basically an address book.

92. (c): 1 KB = 1024 bytes (here in ICT, kilo means 1024 times). Thus, option c is the correct answer.

93. (a): A standard CD-ROM disc can store up to 700 MB of data, or 80 minutes worth of audio.

A standard DVD can hold up to 4.7 GB of data. Dual layer DVDs can hold about 8.5–8.7 GB of data, which is still much less than even the smallest Blu-ray discs.

Blu-ray disc can hold about 25 GB (gigabytes) of data. Dual layer Blu-ray discs can hold as much as 50 GB of data. The larger storage capacity of a Blu-ray disc is a clear advantage over standard DVDs, allowing higher quality of video and audio to be stored.

94. (c): An operating system (OS) is the program that, after being initially loaded into the computer by a boot program, manages all of the other application programs in a computer. The application programs make use of the operating system by making requests for services through a defined application program interface (API).

95. (c): A logic bomb is a piece of code inserted into an operating system or software application that implements a malicious function after a certain amount of time, or specific conditions are met. Logic bombs are often used with viruses, worms, and trojan horses to time them to do maximum damage before being noticed.

96. (c):

(a). Normally 1000 MB is 1 GB.

For computer, the calculations take place in the following manner.

1 Binary Digit (Bit) = 0 or 1

8 Bits = 1 Byte

1024 Bytes = 1Kilo Byte

1024 Kilo Bytes = 1 Mega Byte

1024 Mega Bytes = 1Giga Bytes

(b). **CRT** – This is basically Cathode Ray Tube that is used in traditional computer monitors and televisions. The image on CRT display is created by firing electrons from the back of the tube of phosphorus located towards the front of the screen.

As the electrons heat the phosphorus, they light up, and they are projected on a screen. The colour combination is created by a blend of red, blue and green light.

(c). **ROM** is basically Read Only Memory; it is a type of memory which is non-volatile, permanent data that, normally, can only be read, not written to.

(d). **CPU**– It is basically called as Central Processing Unit, simply it is referred as the processor as well. This portion of a computer that retrieves and executes instructions. The CPU is essentially the brain of a CAD system. It consists of an arithmetic and logic unit (ALU), a control unit, and various registers. The ALU performs arithmetic operations, logic operations, and related operations, according to the program instructions.

97. (a): Bluetooth is mainly used for linking computers and electronic devices in an adhoc way over very short distances, often for only brief or occasional communication using relatively small amounts of data. It's relatively secure, uses little power, connects automatically, and in theory presents little or no health risk.

98. (a): All of these are kinds of malpractices.

Worms are stand-alone software and do not require a host program or human help to propagate.

A trojan horse or simply a trojan is a type of malware that is often disguised as legitimate software. Trojans can be employed by cyber-thieves and hackers trying to gain access to users' systems.

Key-logging is the use of a computer program to record every keystroke made by a computer user, especially in order to gain fraudulent access to passwords and other confidential information.

A boot sector virus is a type of virus that infects the boot sector of floppy disks or the Master Boot Record (MBR) of hard disks (some infect the boot sector of the hard disk instead of the MBR).

99. (a): Spamming is defined as the sending of unsolicited bulk email messages indiscriminately. It is also known as 'junk mail,' unsolicited bulk email (UBE) and unsolicited commercial email (UCE). Benchmark email does not promote or encourage email spam techniques.

100. **(d):** Cloud computing is also called as internet computing. It is basically the on-demand availability of computer system resources, especially data storage (cloud storage) and computing power, without direct active management by the user.

The large clouds often have functions distributed over multiple locations, each location being a data centre. This computing relies on sharing of resources so as to maintain uniformity. It saves cost and investment as it is based on the principle of "pay-as-you-go" model.

101. **(d):** RAM is called 'volatile' memory by analogy because if the computer loses power, all the data stored in RAM (or other volatile memory) is lost or 'evaporates'. Non-volatile memory is memory that keeps its data while the system isn't running.

102. **(a):** Electronic spreadsheets have become powerful management tools for storage and manipulation of data. They are often used as a multipurpose tool for data entry, storage, analysis and visualization. For example, MS Excel is basically a comprehensive spreadsheet program that is available as a stand-alone application or as part of the Microsoft Office suite of software. Excel sheet is used for many personal and professional tasks, most of which need performing simple and complex calculations.

103. **(d):** Divide $(75)_{10}$ successively by 2 until the quotient is 0.

75/2 = 37, remainder is 1

37/2 = 18, remainder is 1

18/2 = 9, remainder is 0

9/2 = 4, remainder is 1

4/2 = 2, remainder is 0

2/2 = 1, remainder is 0

1/2 = 0, remainder is 1

Read from bottom to top, so the $75_{10} = 1001011_2$

104. **(a):** Spyware is unwanted software that infiltrates your computing device, stealing your internet usage data and sensitive information. Spyware is classified as a type of malware—malicious software designed to gain access to or damage your computer, often without your knowledge. Spyware gathers your personal information and relays it to advertisers, data firms, or external users. Spyware is one of the most common threats on the internet. It can easily infect your device and it can be hard to identify. Spyware is a threat to businesses and individual users, since it can steal sensitive information and harm your network.

105. (b)

Analog mass communication is the one way process of transferring message to the receiver, or audience. Here the audience is large so they utilize analog media which was originally used in audio recording that was analogous to the count it was recreating. Here the contents can be only linear and static not dynamic. Our world is analog. Signals are electromagnetic waves which are inherently analog. This can't be changed.

106. **(d)**

MIDI = Musical Instrument Digital Interface

WAV = Waveform Audio File Format

WMA = Windows Media Audio

MP3 = MP3 is a coding format for digital audio

These are audio file formats.

107. **(c):** Security threats and privacy concerns are the major issues out of the growing reliance on information technology.

Security threats can be many like software attacks, theft of intellectual property, identity theft, theft of equipment as information sabotage and information extortion.

Privacy concerns with social networking services is a subset of data privacy involving the right of mandating personal privacy concerning storing, re-purposing, provision to third parties and displaying of information pertaining to oneself via the internet.

108. **(c):**

a. In binary 00111 is 7 in decimal

01001 = 9

01011 = 11

So next term is 13, which is 01101 in binary

$\therefore P = 01101$

b. A binary digit is called a bit. There are two possible states in a bit usually expressed as 0 and 1. A series of eight bits (a string together) makes a byte.

109. **(b):**

a. **VOIP:** Voice Over Internet Protocol also called IP telephony is a method and group of technologies for the delivery of voice communication and multimedia sessions over internet protocol network such as the internet.

b. **Fiber optic cable** also known as an optical fiber cable is an assembly similar to an electrical cable but containing one or more optical fibers that are used to carry light.

c. **URL:** Uniform Resource Locator. It is also known as web address, when it is used with http. URL is a specific character string that is used to access data from the World Wide Web.

d. **Unshielded Twisted Pair (UTP):** is a ubiquitous type of copper cabling used in telephone wiring and local area networks (LANs).

110. (c):

UMANG (Unified Mobile Application for New-age Governance) is envisaged to make e-governance. It is developed by Ministry of Electronics and Information Technology (MeitY) and National e-Governance Division (NeGD) to drive Mobile Governance in India. UMANG provides a single platform for all Indian Citizens to access pan India e-Gov services ranging from Central to Local Government bodies and other citizen centric services.

BHIM (BHARAT INTERFACE FOR MONEY) is an app that lets you make simple easy and quick payment transactions using unified payment Interface. You can make instant bank to bank payment and pay and collect money using just mobile number and virtual payment address. National Payments Corporation of India (NPCI) is an umbrella organisation for operating retail payments and settlement systems in India

eBiz: eBiz is being implemented by Infosys Technologies under the guidance and aegis of Department of Industrial Policy and Promotion, Ministry of Commerce and Industry Govt. of India. The focus of eBiz is to improve the business environment in the country by reducing unnecessary delays in regulatory processes required to start and run business.

SWAYAM: MHRD has started a major and new initiative Project called 'Study Webs of Active Learning for Young Aspiring Minds' (SWAYAM). It is an integrated platform and portal for online courses. This covers all higher education subjects and skill sector courses. The objective is to ensure that the every student in our country has access to the best quality higher education at the affordable cost.

111. (a): Blogs as social media include vlogs, wall postings, emails, instant messaging, music-sharing, crowd sourcing, voice over IP etc.

Blogs is individualized approach to communicate to public audience.

So both 'A' and 'R' are true and R is the correct explanation of (A).

112. (a) The URL consists of three parts: the network protocol, the hostname or address and the file location. A URL is represented as: Protocol://domain_name/directory (file)

1. **Protocol:** Protocol is set of rules, with TCP/IP being the most important one. The protocol declares how your web browser should communicate with a web serve when sending or fetching a web page or document.
2. **Domain name** A domain name is unique reference that identifies a web site on the internet for example doepud.co.uk
3. **Path:** the path typically refer to a file or directory on the web server e.g. Directory file. Php.

113. (b)

(i) The sequence is loading of software from secondary storage into RAM and finally executed by CPU (registers).

(ii) Give direct definition of search engine.

114. (d): Information and communication technology is basically our society's efforts to teach its current and emerging citizens valuable knowledge and skills around computing and communication devices, software that operated them, applications that run on them.

The main purpose of using ICT for classroom teaching is to teach its current and emerging citizens valuable knowledge and skills around computing and communication devices, software that operates them applications that run on them and system that are build with them.

115. (b)

Web Browser: A Web browser is a software program that is used to locate, access, and display web pages. Browsers are used primarily for displaying and accessing websites on the internet as well as other content created using languages such as Hypertext markup language, Extensible Markup Language.

Word processor or word processing program does exactly what the name implies. It processes words. It also processes paragraphs, pages and entire papers. Some examples of word processing programs include Microsoft Word, Word perfect, AppleWorks and openoffice.org

Spreadsheet : A spreadsheet is a computer application for organization, analysis and storage of data in tabular form. Spreadsheets were developed as computerized analogs of paper accounting worksheets. The program operates on data entered in cells of a table.

Web Authoring: Web authoring is the practice of creating web documents using modern web authoring software and tools. Web authoring software is a type of desktop publishing tool that allows users to navigate the tricky environment of HTML and web coding by offering a different kind of graphical users interface.

116. (d): Neither A or B Statement are correct

(a) A local area network is a computer network that interconnects computers network that interconnects computers within a limited area such as a residence, school, laboratories, University Campus or Office Building. By contrast a wide area network not only covers a large geographic distance but also generally involves leased telecommunication circuits. A local area network is usually not located on one brand of computer.

(b) The acronym ISP not stand for Internet standard provides. It stand for Internet standard protocols.

117. (b): CSV, RTF, TXT

CSV (comma-separated values) - a text file which allows data to be saved in a table structured format.

RTF (Rich Text Format) - This file format allows us to exchange text files between different word processors in different operating systems. This was developed by MS Word.

TXT file - This is a standard text document that contains plain text. It can be opened and edited in any text-editing or word-processing program.

118. (c): There was once a time when CPU clock speed increased dramatically from years to years. In the 90s and early 2000s processors increased at incredible speed, shooting from 60MHz Pentium chips to gigahertz – level processors within a decade. Hence it is true.

Software now being used is faster and therefore processors do not have to be faster. It is not true, so R is false.

119. (a): Only 1st statement is correct.

A list of instructions that a CPU can run is a computer program. The clock crate or speed of a CPU's internal parts is measured in Hertz. Modern processors after run so fast that gigahertz is used instead. One GHz is one billion cycles per second.

In the case of computer clock speed, one Hertz equals one tick per second. The usually measured in megahertz or gigahertz.

120. (c): Information and communication technology in education is the mode of education that uses to support, enhance and optimise the delivery of information. Worldwide research has shown that ICT can lead to an improved student learning and better teaching methods.

The main purpose of ICT in education is to enhance the learning in classroom and beyond. It enhances the scope of education by facilitating mobile learning and inclusive education.

121. (d): Codes is a device or a computer program, which encodes or decodes a digital data stream or signals. It is a short form of coder-decoder.

122. (c): e-kalpa is a project on 'Creating Digital-learning Environment for Design'. 'e-kalpa' is sponsored by the Ministry of Human Resources, Government of India as part of the National Mission in Education through .

123. (d): Fourth generation language are Very High-level Languages.

They required a lot of time and effort that affected the productivity of a programmer. The fourth generation programming languages were designed and developed to reduce the time, cost and effort needed to develop different types of software applications.

Advantages of fourth generation languages are:

1. These programming languages allow the efficient use of data by implementing the various database.
2. They require less time, cost and effort to develop different types of software applications.
3. The program developed in these languages are highly portable as compared to the programs developed in the languages of other generation.

Examples: SQL, CSS, coldfusion.

Fifth generation language are basically Artificial Intelligence Language. The examples are mercury, prolog, OPS5.

124. (b): A–view classroom is a framework that provides a rich interactive social environment for e-Learning. It is simple, user-friendly, video conferencing software, which provides a great opportunity to a teacher to teach in a live interactive mode to various geographical locations across India.

125. (c):

(a) **WWW:** The World Wide Web is combination of all resources and users on the Internet that are using the Hypertext Transfer Protocol. A broader comes from the world wide web consortium.

(b) **JAVA:** Java is a general purpose computer programming language that is convenient, class based, object oriented and specifically designed to have a few implementation dependencies as possible.

(c) **RAM:** Random Access Memory is a form of computer memory that can be read and changed in any order, typically used to store working data and machine code. A random access memory device allows data items to be read or written in almost the same amount of time irrespective of the physical location of the data inside the memory. It is volatile memory.

(d) **ROM:** Read only Memory is a type of non-volatile memory used in computer and other electronic devices. Data stored in ROM cannot be electronically modified after the manufacture of the memory device.

126. (d): Python is an interpreted, high-level, general purpose programming language created by Guido Van Rossum and first released in 1991, Python's design philosophy emphasizes code readability with its notable use of significant whitespace. Its language constructs and object-oriented approach aim to help programmers write clear, logical code for small and large scale projects.

127. (b): Bing is a web search engine owned and operated by Microsoft. The service has its origin in Microsoft's Windows Live Search and later Live Search. Bing provides a variety of search services, including web, video, image and map search products. It is developed using ASP.NET.

128. (b): The internet is the global system of interconnected computer networks that uses the internet protocol suit to link devices worldwide. It is a network of networks that consists of private, public, academic, business and government networks of local to global scope, linked by a broad array of electronic wireless and optical networking technologies. The internet carries a vast range of information resources and services such as application of the world wide web, technology and file sharing. It is a true statement.

The world wide web is just one of the ways that information can be disseminated over the Internet. So, web is just a portion of the internet, so, Reason (R) is true but not the correct explanation of A.

129. (d): E-Governance is the application of which transforms the efficiency, effectiveness and accountability of information and transactional exchanges reducing the costs of government citizens and to empower them through access and use of information.

E-Governance is directly linked with ability of Government to address the need of society vis-à-vis other choices.

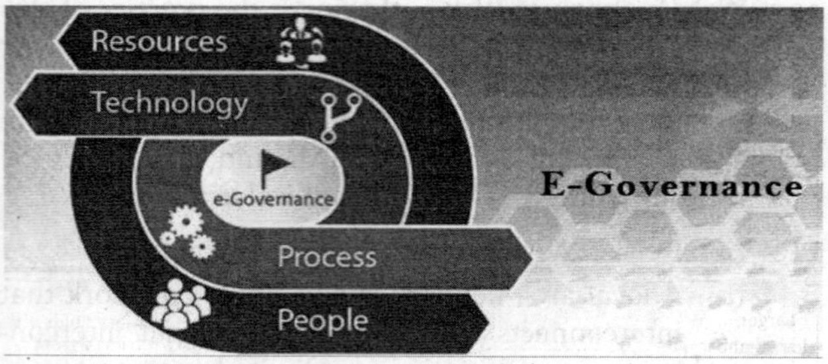

- To build an informed society
- To increase government and citizen interaction
- To encourage citizen participation
- To bring transparency in the governing process
- To make government accountable
- To reduce the cost of governance
- To reduce the reaction time of the government

130. (a): Cyber-venting is the act of bad-mouthing about one's employer, senior executives, colleagues, etc. with the intention of letting off the steam, using websites and making such comments public for all to see them.

131. (b): The speed of Internet is measured in Gbps. Description of all the terms in question are as follows.

GHz: Clock speed is the rate at which a processor executes a task and that is measured in Gigahertz (GHz). A 2.6-Ghz processor, therefore, can run 2.6 billion instructions in a second, while a 2.3-Ghz processor can run 2.3 billion instructions per second.

Gbps: GigaBits or GigaBytes per Second One billion bits or bytes per second. Gbps is a measurement of peripheral data transfer or network transmission speed. The correct abbreviation is "b" for bits and "B" for bytes; however, "b" and "B" are often interchanged.

GB: a unit of information equal to 1000 megabytes or 10_9 (1,000,000,000) bytes. This is gigabyte. A unit for measuring computer memory. megabyte, MB, M - a unit of information equal to 1000 kilobytes or 10_6 (1,000,000) bytes.

dpi (dots per inch): It is a measure of the resolution of a printed document or digital scan. The higher the dot density, the higher the resolution of the print or scan. Typically, dpi is the measure of the number of dots that can be placed in a line across one inch, or 2.54 centimeters.

132. (c):

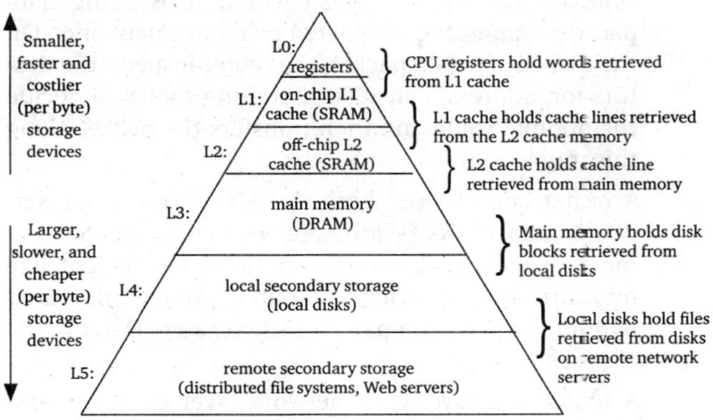

Additional Information:

L1 cache, or primary cache, is extremely fast but relatively small, and is usually embedded in the processor chip as CPU cache. Level 3 (L3) cache is specialized memory developed to improve the performance of L1 and L2. L1 or L2 can be significantly faster than L3, though L3 is usually double the speed of DRAM.

133. (a): GIF is an image file format commonly used for images on the web and sprites in software programs. Unlike the JPEG image format, GIFs use lossless compression that does not degrade the quality of the image.

134. (a): Machine learning is a type of artificial intelligence that allows software applications to become more accurate at predicting outcomes without being explicitly programmed to do so. Machine learning algorithms use historical data as input to predict new output values.

135. (c): The information stored in RAM is lost when the power supply to the PC or laptop is switched off. The information stored in RAM can be checked with the help of BIOS. It is generally known as the main memory, or temporary memory or cache memory or volatile memory of the computer system.

136. (d): Wi-Fi and the internet are two separate things that work together. Think of the internet as a language and Wi-Fi as a method of sending and translating that language. We need a modem, Wi-Fi router and an internet provider to make that happen. LAN is a network that allows devices to connect and communicate.

137. (b): Secondary memory is not accessed directly by the Central Processing Unit (CPU). Instead, data accessed from a secondary memory is first loaded into Random Access Memory (RAM) and is then sent to the Processing Unit. Hence, from this discussion, it is clear that option (b) is correct.

138. (b): Operating System (OS): It is an interface between a computer user and computer hardware. This performs all the basic tasks like file management, memory management, process management, handling input and output, and controlling peripheral devices such as disk drives and printers. Five of the most common operating systems are Microsoft Windows, Apple macOS, Linux, Android and Apple's iOS.

WWW: Tim Berners-Lee, a British scientist, invented the World Wide Web (WWW) in 1989, while working at CERN located in Geneva, Switzerland. The Web was originally conceived and developed to meet the demand for automated information-sharing between scientists in universities and institutes around the world.

Device driver: This is also called as hardware driver that is a group of files that enable one or more hardware devices to communicate with the computer's operating system.

Internet Protocol (IP): It is a suite in relaying datagrams across network boundaries. Its routing function enables internetworking, and essentially establishes the Internet. An IP address serves two main functions: host or network interface identification and location addressing.

Internet Protocol version 4 (IPv4): It defines an IP address as a 32-bit number. A new version of IP (IPv6), uses 128 bits for the IP address that was standardized in 1998. IP addresses are written and displayed in human-readable notations, such as 172.16.254.1 in IPv4, and 2001:db8:0:1234:0:567:8:1 in IPv6.

139. (b): ASCII Code:

Computers work in binary code. Information is coded using 0s and 1s. Each 0 or 1 is called a ***bit***. In the early years of computer development, different computer companies applied the binary system in their own way.

Eventually, a set of standards was developed. Computer manufactures agreed to use one code called the ASCII (American Standard Code for Information Interchange). ASCII is an 8-bit code. That is, it uses eight bits to represent a letter or a punctuation mark. Eight bits are called a byte. A binary code with eight digits, such as $1101\ 1101_2$, can be stored in one byte of computer memory.

Character sets used today are generally 8-bit sets with 256 different characters, effectively doubling the ASCII set.

140. (c):

INFLIBNET – It is abbreviation of Information and Library Network Centre. It is an Autonomous Inter-University Centre (IUC) of UGC. It is located in Gandhinagar, Gujarat. It is a major National Programme initiated by the UGC in March 1991 as a project under the IUCAA, it became an independent Inter-University Centre in June 1996. INFLIBNET is involved in modernizing university libraries in India using the state-of-art technologies for the optimum utilisation of information. INFLIBNET is set out to be a major player in promoting scholarly communication among academicians and researchers in India.

The following institutions and projects are linked with it.

1. **Shodhganga** – A Reservoir of Indian Theses
2. **INDCAT** – Online Union Catalogue of Indian Universities
3. **SOUL** – State-of-art Integrated Library Management System
4. **e-ShodhSindhu** – Consortium for Higher Education e-Resources
5. **ShodhShuddhi** – Provides Plagiarism Detection Software to Institutions
6. **IRINS** – Research Information Management System for Institutions
7. **Vidya-Mitra** – Integrated e-Content Portal
8. **Vidwan** – Expert Database & National Researcher Network
9. **e-PG Pathshala** – an initiative of the Ministry of Education under its National Mission on Education through ICT (NME-ICT) being executed by UGC.
10. **e-Pathya:** It is one the verticals of e-PG Pathshala which is software driven course / content package that facilitates students pursuing higher education (PG level) in distance learning as well as campus learning mode. it also facilitates offline access.
11. **e-Adhyayan (e-Books):** e-Adhyayan is a platform to provide 700+ e-Books for the Post-Graduate Courses. All the e-Books are derived from e-PG Pathshala courses. It also facilitates play-list of video content.
12. **UGC-MOOCs:** It is one of vertical to produce course on Post Graduate subjects in SWAYAM (Online Courses, a Ministry of Education initiative). UGC is one of the national coordinator of SWAYAM, and INFLIBNET is technical partner for UGC-MOOCs.

141. (d): Routers are networking devices. They are responsible for receiving, analysing, and forwarding data packets among the connected computer networks. On the arrival of a data packet, the router inspects the destination address, consults its routing tables to decide the optimal route and then transfers the packet along this route.

A router can be used both in LANs (Local Area Networks) and WANs (Wide Area Networks). Routers are more expensive than other networking devices like hubs,bridges and switches. Routers are manufactured by some popular companies such as Cisco, D-Link, HP, Nortel etc.

A router is a layer 3 or network layer device in OSI Model while data link layer works in the layer 2 of OSI Model. Data link layer is responsible for maintaining the data link between two hosts or nodes.

142. (d): This is a direct question of matching.

143. (d): In computing, the Post Office Protocol is an application-layer Internet standard protocol used by e-mail clients to retrieve e-mail from a mail server. POP version 3 is the version in common use.

The Post Office Protocol provides access via an Internet Protocol (IP) network for a user client application to a mailbox (maildrop) maintained on a mail server.

Thus, the protocol used when receiving emails from the email server.

144. (a):

DRUPAL: Drupal is a free software package that allows an individual or a community of users to easily publish, manage and organize a wide variety of content on a website.

Drupal is used by mooKIT platform for open source content management system.

JOOMLA: This uses to build, organize, manage and publish content for websites, blogs, Intranets and mobile applications.

Moodle: Moodle is a free and open-source learning management system (LMS) written in PHP and distributed under GNU (General Public licence). Moodle is used for blended learning, distance education, flipped classroom and other e-learning projects in schools, universities, workplaces and other sectors

SAKAI: Sakai is a free, community source, educational software platform designed to support teaching, research and collaboration. Systems of this type are also known as Course Management Systems (CMS), Learning Management Systems (LMS), or Virtual Learning Environments (VLE).

145. (d): File Transfer Protocol (FTP): FTP is a standard communication protocol used for the transfer of computer files from a server to a client on a computer network. FTP is built on a client–server model architecture using separate control and data connections between the client and the server. FTP users may authenticate themselves with a clear–text sign–in protocol, normally in the form of a username and password. FTP is often secured with SSL/TLS (FTPS) or replaced with SSH File Transfer Protocol (SFTP) for secure transmission.

146. (b):

1. **Simplex data transmission:** Simplex is the data transmission mode in which the data can flow only in one direction, i.e., the communication is unidirectional.
2. **Half duplex data transmission:** Half duplex data transmission is transmission in both directions but not at the same time.
3. **Full duplex data transmission:** Full duplex data transmission occurs in both directions simultaneously.
4. **Serial data transmission:** Serial Transmission is a form of signal transmission that sends information one bit at a time over a single data channel. Serial interfaces are generally used to connect data communications equipment (DCE) such as modems to data terminal equipment (DTE) such as computers and terminals and for connecting a DCE to a DTE.
5. **Parallel data transmission:** In parallel transmission (e.g., 8 bits) each bit uses a separate wire to transfer data on a parallel link, a separate line is used as a clock signal. This serves to inform the receiver when data is available.

147. (a)

World Wide Web: It is the component of the Internet that combines audio, video and graphics with text is also called the web or simply the WWW. It is a subset of the Internet and is a collection of documents and application residing on the internet and is a collection of documents and applications residing on the Internet servers around the world. Thus, the World Wide Web (WWW) is the collection of webpages stored on websites.

Hypertext Preprocessor (PHP): PHP is a popular scripting language, used to create attractive, user-friendly and interactive web pages. PHP is open-source which means it is well documented and can be easily downloaded for free from the web. It was created in the year 1994 by Rasmus Lerdorf.

Interconnected network: It is a set of computer nodes, including, but not limited to, personal computers, mobile devices, and physical or virtual servers, which are linked together to facilitate the transmission of data between users.

Web Browser: Web browser is an application software to access the World Wide Web. When a user requests a web page from a particular website, the web browser fetches the required content from the web server and then it displays the page on the user's device.

Web browsers are used on a wide variety of devices, including desktops, laptops, tablets, and smartphones. The most used browser is Google Chrome, with 65% of the global market share, followed by Safari at 18%.

A web browser is not the same as a search engine. A search engine is a website that provides links to other websites. However, in order to connect to a website's server and display its web pages, the user must have a web browser installed in the system.

148. (d)

Ethernet: Ethernet is a family of wired computer networking technologies commonly used in Local Area Networks (LAN), Metropolitan Area Network (MAN) and Wide Area Networks (WAN). It was commercially introduced in 1980S. Systems communicating over Ethernet divide a stream of data into shorter pieces called frames. Each frame contains source and destination addresses, and error checking data so that damaged frames can be detected and discarded; most often, higher-layer protocols trigger retransmission of lost frames.

Ethernet is widely used in homes and industry, and interworks well with Wi-Fi technologies. The Internet Protocol is commonly carried over Ethernet, and hence, it is considered one of the key technologies that make up the Internet.

149. (d)

Digital Versatile Disc (DVD): DVD is a digital optical disc data storage format invented and developed in 1995 and released in late 1996. Currently allowing up to 17.08 GB of storage, the medium can store any kind of digital data and was widely used for software and other computer files as well as video programmes watched using DVD player. DVD offers higher storage capacity than compact discs while having the same dimensions.

There were several formats developed for recording video on optical discs before the DVD. Optical recording technology was invented by David Paul Gregg and James Russell in 1963 and was first patented in 1968. Thus, DVDs use a single spiral track to store data working from the centre to the edge.

150. (c)

System software: System software provides the basic functions for computer usage and helps to run the computer hardware and system. Compiler is a type of system software. They convert the source code into another computer language called object code.

Application software: It helps the user to perform singular and multiple tasks. Library management system is an application software.

Security software: Security software is any type of software that secures and protects a computer, network or any computing-enabled device. It manages access control, provides data protection to our PC. Firewall is an example of security software.

Embedded software: Embedded software is a piece of software that is embedded in hardware or non-PC devices. It is written specifically for the particular hardware that it runs on and usually has processing and memory constraints because of the device's limited computing capabilities. Automatic fridge is an example of embedded software.

151. (c): BIOS stands for Basic Input Output System. It is essentially a firmware stored on a small memory chip on the motherboard and is used to provide runtime services for the OS. It instructs the computer to perform basic functions, such as booting and keyboard control. It is also used to identify and configure the hardware in a computer, such as hard drive, floppy drive, optical drive, CPU, memory, and related equipment.

When a computer is switched on, the BIOS is loaded from the ROM, and the OS is loaded into the RAM because it is not volatile – and the OS needs to be on the computer every time it's switched on. Also, the ROM is the ideal place for the OS to be kept until the computer system is switched on.

152. (b): The correct sequence of computer storage capacities ranked from largest to smallest capacity: 1 TBytes > 100 GBytes > 10000000000 Bytes > 1000000 Kbytes.

153. (c): It is a program that searches documents for specified keywords and returns a list of documents where the key words are found. Search engines are websites that help a user to search for information on the internet.

The most popular search engines are Google and Yahoo. Another example of a search engine is Baidu, which was developed by China.

A search term, or search query, is essentially a word or a group of words. A user types the term in the search box. Search engines interpret the search term and show the most relevant results as per the intent of the user. For any search term, search engines do not provide the exact same results to all the users.

154. (c)

Random access Memory (RAM): It is also termed as the main memory. It is the temporary memory, and it is volatile because it allows information to be stored randomly and can be accessed quickly and directly (without the need to go through intervening data).

With respect to computers, the RAM devices are as follows:

I. **Hard Disk:** A computer can both write and read data from the RAM. Every time a user turns on his/her computer, a set of instructions is copied from the hard disk into the RAM. These instructions, which help control the basic computer functions, remain in the RAM until the computer is turned off, following which whatever data is present in the RAM disappears.

II. **USB Flash Drive:** USB flash drives look like a small flat pen. They may have a large storage capacity and can be plugged into any computer with a USB socket. Flash drivers are also commonly referred to as pen drives or memory sticks.

III. **Compact Disc Read-Only Memory (CD-ROM):** The CD-ROM is an optical disc containing audio or software data. A CD-ROM looks much the same as an audio CD but can contain text, sound, pictures and motion video. It can be fixed and rendered unalterable and hence, it is called 'read only'. A CD-ROM drive or optical drive is the device used to read them, not write or erase them.

155. (a)

Magnetic Tape: Used for data archival purpose but must be accessed sequentially

Memory Card: Used in digital cameras, photo printers and cell phones

Hard Disk: Consists of a set of metal disks mounted on a spindle

DVD: Uses laser beam technology to read or write data

156. (a): Social bookmarking is the software application that facilitates building an early accessible bookmark warehouse that becomes searchable to members of the public. It is a central online service that allows users to add, comment, edit and publicly share bookmarks from web documents.

The top social bookmarking sites are:

1. Reddit.com: This is one of the top-rated social bookmarking sites for posting a blog.

2. Mix.com: Mix gets you the perfect platform to store, search and share content.

3. Pinterest.com: Pinterest is a prime source of inspiration for the graphics industry. It's a popular bookmarking site as well, and the fun part is that anyone can use Pinterest.

157. (b): Phishing: Phishing refers to an illicit attempt to trick individuals into handing over personal and confidential information. Phishing scams can comprise legitimate-looking emails to users. For example, they carry an official-looking logo of a known service, like VISA, and may be perpetrated by phone, email or the internet.

158. (c): Statement I: if the sensor data is outside the acceptable range, then the microprocessor/computer will take action. Thus, statement I is true.

159. (c): Network Interface: A network interface is the point of interconnection between a computer and a private or public network. A network interface is generally a network interface card (NIC), but it does not have to have a physical form. An NIC is needed to allow a device to connect to a network.

Router: A router is a device that connects two or more networks, such as one LAN to another LAN that uses the same protocol (ethernet or token ring). A router inspects data packets received over the internet.

IP Address: It is the unique numerical address of a computer on the internet, and it is expressed as four sets of numbers (with a maximum of three digits in each set) separated by dots. For example, 150.237.176.24. Computers on the internet are almost always referred to by more memorable domain names, which are mapped onto their IP addresses by special internet computers known as servers.

Hub: A hub is a place of convergence where data arrives from one or more directions. It is a common connection point for networked computers and other devices. Hubs are used to connect devices in a Local Area Network (LAN).

Wireless Local Area Network: A Wireless Local Area Network (WLAN) links two or more devices using distribution method and provides connection through an access point to a wider internet.

160. (a)

Input Device: It is a device that is capable of loading information into a computer system, for example, keyboard, microphone, mouse, scanner, webcam, etc.

Output Device: It is a device that is meant for anything that comes out of a computer after being processed. Examples of output devices include monitor, headphone, printers, speakers, plotter, Visual Display Units (VDU), etc.

Pointing Device: It is a device that allows the user to control the position of the cursor on a computer screen by physical manipulation of the device in different directions. Examples of pointing devices include tracker ball, joystick, light pen, mouse, etc.

Sensor Device: It is a type of device that detects and then responds according to some input received from the physical environment. The sensor device does some processing on the collected input and generates an output that is in a human-readable format. The input can be in any form, like heat, light, pressure, moisture, motion and other environmental factors. Examples of sensor devices include traffic light simulator, temperature sensor, infrared sensors, smoke detector sensor, etc.

161. (d)

Firewall: A firewall is a software package that acts as a barrier between the computer and the internet connection, keeping an eye on the traffic going to and fro. It also warns the user in case something suspicious appears. Any computer is vulnerable when connected to the internet. It is the hardware or software that sit between a user's computer and an external computer.

162. (c): This question is linked with good governance, so linked with public. Data (statistics) and ICT are also going to be part of it. There seems to be some aberration in statement II.

163. (a): MODEM functions as both – input and output device. MODEM is a contraction of two words - MOdulator / DEModulator which functions simultaneously.

1. When sending communications out of the network, the modem converts (modulates) a digital signal into an analog signal for transmission over analog media such as cable or telephone line.
2. When signals are coming into the modem from the internet, it converts (demodulates) the analog signal back to a digital signal for transmission on the local network.

164. (a):

A. **Trojan Horse**–This is a type of malware that disguises itself as legitimate code or software. Once they get inside the network, these attackers are able to carry out any action that a legitimate user could perform, such as exporting files, modifying data, deleting files or otherwise altering the contents of the device.

B. **Virus**–A computer virus is a type of computer program that, when executed, replicates itself by modifying other computer programs and inserting its own code. If this replication succeeds, the affected areas are then said to be "infected" with a computer virus, a metaphor derived from biological viruses.

C. **Web bug**–This is also known as a Web beacon, is a file object that is placed on a Web page or in an e-mail message to monitor user behaviour.

D. **Zombies**–This is actually a computer connected to the Internet that has been compromised by a hacker via a computer virus, computer worm, or trojan horse program and can be used to perform malicious tasks under the remote direction of the hacker.

165. (d): B, C, A is the correct answer.

Random Access Memory (RAM) – This is essentially a short term memory where data is stored as the processor needs it.

Anti-static Strap – This is a key piece of safety gear that helps to prevent the build up of static electricity near sensitive electronics or other projects where static charge could damage electronics or cause safety issues.

166. (b): Statement 1–Let's look at some basics which have been offered officially.

SWAYAM is basically Study Webs of Active-Learning for Young Aspiring Minds that is part of MOOC Platform. It was developed indigenously by AICTE in 2016 to facilitate hosting of online courses which could be accessed by anyone, anywhere at any time free of cost. The main objective is to achieve access, equity and quality in context of education. This covers subjects from high school onwards till higher education including Skill based courses to ensure that every student benefits from learning material through ICT.

The courses hosted on SWAYAM are in 4 quadrants – video lectures, specially prepared reading material that can be downloaded/printed, self-assessment tests through tests and quizzes and an online discussion forum for clearing the doubts. The objective is to make system inclusive by using audio-video, multimedia and state of the art pedagogy/ technology.

Statement 2–DigiLocker is basically linked with good governance. This Indian digitization online service is provided by Ministry of Electronics and Information Technology (MeitY) under Digital India initiative. This intends to provide services to every Aadhaar holder for accessing driving license, vehicle registration, academic mark sheet in digital format from the original issuers of these certificates. It also provides 1GB storage space for the same.

The structure of DigiLocker includes My Certificates (digital and uploaded documents), My Profile, My Issuer, My Requester and Directories.

167. (d):

A. **Spyware** – This malicious software enters our computer device, gathers data, and forwards it to a third-party without our consent. This legitimate software monitors our data for commercial purposes like advertising.

B. **Firewall** – A Firewall in a computer system is basically a network security system which controls the flow of data between two or more networks, and manages the links between the networks. A firewall can consist of both hardware and software elements. The examples are router (physical firewall), anti virus, Java (software firewall).

C. **Bluetooth** – This is a short-range wireless technology standard that is used for exchanging data between fixed and mobile devices over short distances and building personal area networks.

D. **A Denial of Service** – This form of attack is meant to shut down a machine or network, making it inaccessible to its intended users.

168. (b): Central Processing Unit (CPU): This part of a computer is comprised with digital circuits called arithmetic logic units (ALU) that are capable of performing billions of arithmetic and logic operations every second.

ALU is a digital circuit used to perform arithmetic and logic operations. This makes the fundamental building block of the CPU of a system. The modern CPUs contain powerful and complex ALUs.

Control Unit (CU) - Modern CPUs contain a CU, in addition to ALUs. CU tells the ALU what operation is to be performed on the data. ALU stores the result in an output register. CU moves the data between these registers, the ALU, and memory.

Process Registers – ALUs load data from input registers. A register is a small amount of storage available as part of a CPU.

The information in a computer is stored and manipulated in the form of binary numbers, i.e. 0 and 1 which are managed by Transistor switches which are open or closed.

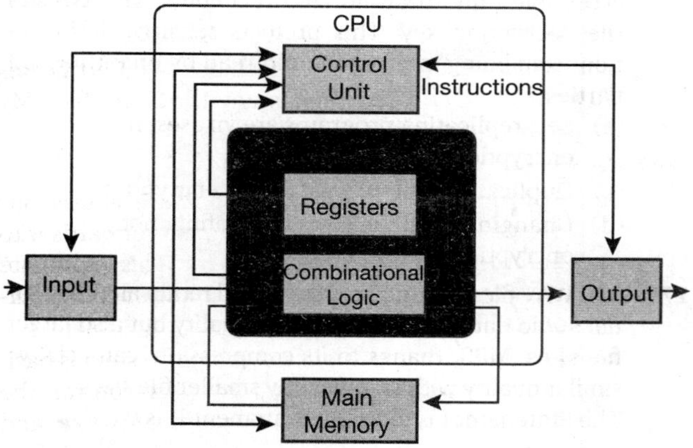

Block diagram of a basic computer with uniprocessor CPU. Black lines indicate data flow, whereas red lines indicate control flow. Arrows indicate the direction of flow.

169. (c): In a spreadsheet application, whenever a cell with a formula is copied over to another cell, any cell references in the formula will shift as per the relative shift in the references of the copied cell and its destination.

The above behaviour can be explicitly disabled by using the '$' character before the column letter or row number or both in the cell references in a formula.

We can take a look at what happens to the formula in cells C3 and D2, when they are copied over from C2.

Example 1 - C2 contain the formula '= A2 + B2'

1. C3 will get the formula '= A3 + B3'
2. D2 will get the formula '= B2 + C2'

Example 2 - C2 contain the formula '= $A2 + B$2'

1. C3 will get the formula '= $A3 + B$2'
2. D2 will get the formula '= $A2 + C$2'

In the above example, the column A in the first reference and row number 2 in the second reference were made absolute using the '$' sign in the original formula of cell C2. Thus, when C2 was copied over to C3 and D2, the absolute part of both cell references didn't change in the formula.

In the given question, the value of the formula in cell C4 is '= A3 + B2'. When this formula is copied over to the cell C5, its value would become '= A3 + B3', as per the behaviour laid out above. Thus, value of C5 comes out to be 7.

170. (c): With video conferencing we can conduct meetings in two or more locations by audio and video transmission. VC specifically uses web cameras, display devices, microphones (for voice communication), high-speed Internet connectivity and personal computers. With VC, those who participate in the meeting can see, hear and speak to one another, regardless of their geographical location. This is useful, can be used both in home and business.

During recent times, the availability of cloud-based services has facilitated the to – do video conferencing with minimal upfront investment. Now there is advantage of rapidly emerging Artificial Intelligence (AI) powered features to improve both the audio and video performance.

171. (c): Malware is actually worrisome, it is any program or file that is intentionally harmful to a computer, network or server. Malware comes in so many variants, there are numerous methods to infect computer systems. The malware includes computer viruses, worms, Trojan horses, ransomware and spyware.

172. (d): The formula can be broken down in the following manner:

- **=IF(B2 = 'Sunny', ...):** To check if the value in cell B2 is 'Sunny'.
- **IF(C2 = 'Low', 'Yes', ...):** If B2 is 'Sunny', it checks if the value in cell C2 is 'Low'. If it is, the formula returns 'Yes'. Otherwise, it goes to the next part.
- **'No', ...):** If B2 is not 'Sunny' or C2 is not 'Low', the formula returns 'No'.

When we copy the formula from D2 to D3:D6, the references change automatically based on the relative position.

Thus, we can see the following:

- D3 checks if B3 is 'Sunny' and, if so, if C3 is 'Low'. Since B3 is 'Windy' and C3 is 'High', D3 returns 'No'.
- D4 checks if B4 is 'Sunny' and, if so, if C4 is 'Low'. Since B4 is 'Raining' and C4 is 'Medium', D4 returns 'No'.
- D5 checks if B5 is 'Sunny' and, if so, if C5 is 'Low'. Since B5 is 'Sunny' and C5 is 'Low', D5 returns 'Yes'.
- D6 checks if B6 is 'Sunny' and, if so, if C6 is 'Low'. Since B6 is 'Sunny' and C6 is 'Medium', D6 returns 'No'.

The formula reports 'Yes' only for Monday (D2), Thursday (D5), and Friday (D6), thus (d) is the answer.

173. (c): Data compression is the process of encoding information to use fewer bits than the original representation. The correct answer is (c) The process of encoding information to try and use fewer bits than the original data.

174. (c): Let's look at the statements:

Statement I: Twitter is indeed an example of a Web 2.0 application, as it allows user interaction and content generation, and also build communities.

Statement II: Web 2.0 refers to the second generation of the World Wide Web which emphasizes user-generated content, usability, and interoperability. It does not refer to static text-based information websites.

Statement I is true but Statement II is false, thus, the correct answer is (c)

175. (b): Synchronous communication is where communication happens in real-time. Among the given options: Skype video call, Facebook Chat, Messaging on Snapchat, and Telephone calls are synchronous.

Email is asynchronous.

Here, A, B, D, and E applies, thus, the correct answer is (b).

176. (b): Solid State Drive (SSD) - III - Has no moving parts and is very robust and reliable (III).

ROM - IV - Non-volatile and stores firmware (IV).

DVD-RAM – I Optical media that uses concentric tracks for simultaneous read-write operations.

RAM – II - Volatile and stores programs and data in current use.

Thus, A-III, B-IV, C-I, D-II and correct answer is (b)

177. (d): This MS- Excel question is quite easy. The formula IF ($B2=D$1, $A2,0) checks if the state in each row matches the state at the top of the current column. If they match, it shows the city name; if not, it shows 0.

1. **Column D (Haryana):**
   - Only Sonipat and Panipat are in Haryana.
   - So, only D3 (Sonipat) and D8 (Panipat) will show city names.
   - All other cells in column D will show 0.
2. **Column E (MP):**
   - Indore, Sagar, and Gwalior are in MP.
   - So, E5 (Indore), E7 (Sagar), and E9 (Gwalior) will show city names.
   - All other cells in column E will show 0.
3. **Column F (UP):**
   - Only Noida is in UP.
   - So, only F4 (Noida) will show the city name.
   - All other cells in column F will show 0.

   Now count the zeros:
   - In column D, there are 6 cells with 0.
   - In column E, there are 5 cells with 0.
   - In column F, there are 7 cells with 0.

Total zeros = 6 (D) + 5 (E) + 7 (F) = 18

So, the answer is 18 cells in the range D2 : F9 contain 0, which is option (d) 18.

178. (b): Email encryption scrambles the content of an email message into an unreadable format, making it accessible only to authorized recipients who possess the decryption key. This protects sensitive information from being intercepted and read by unauthorized parties.

(a) Self-replicating programs are viruses, not encryption.

(c) Duplicate emails are spam, not encryption.

(d) Changing email headers is spoofing, not encryption.

179. (d): WAV files are uncompressed and retain all the original audio data, leading to higher quality but also larger file sizes. MP3, thanks to its compression, can achieve similar quality with significantly smaller file sizes.

The Statement I is false but Statement II is true.

180. (c)

A. This is incorrect. Rather it should be Web 1.0.

B. Web 2.0 technologies have enabled more interactive and social web experiences, connecting people in various ways.

C. Web 3.0 is creating a more connected and intelligent web, where machines can process and analyze data in more human-like ways, leading to more sophisticated and seamless user experiences.

Thus, (c) is the correct answer.

181. (b)

A-IV: Inkjet printers use electrically charged ink droplets, not powdered ink.

B-II: LCD screens utilize liquid crystals for displaying images, not LEDs.

C-I: LED screens rely on arrays of light-emitting diodes as pixels, not modulating light.

D-III: Laser printers transfer electrically charged powdered ink onto paper, not ink droplets.

Thus, (b) is the correct answer.

182. (a): Statement I: This accurately describes a 3D printer. It builds objects layer by layer using specific materials, making it popular in CAD (Computer-Aided Design) applications where virtual designs are translated into physical objects.

Statement II: This is also true. Modern laptops come equipped with batteries that allow them to operate for several hours without being plugged into a power outlet. The exact duration will depend on battery capacity and usage.

Here, (a) is the correct answer.

183. (d): This question is basically about the functions performed by ROM.

Statement A: stores the programs and data that are currently in use. This statement is incorrect. It is actually done by RAM that is a type of volatile memory that is used for temporary storage of data that the CPU needs immediate or frequent access to. When a program is run on a computer, it is loaded into RAM from the hard drive or another storage device.

Statement B: ROM is used to boot up the computer when power is turned on. This is true. ROM typically contains firmware like the BIOS (Basic Input/Output System) in PCs, which is essential for the initial booting process of the computer.

Statement C: Its contents are retained when power is turned off. This is correct. ROM is non-volatile memory, meaning it retains its contents even when the power is turned off. This permanence makes it suitable for storing firmware and other crucial system instructions.

184. (a):

- **HTTP (a):** Stands for HyperText Transfer Protocol. It is the main protocol used for transmitting data over the World Wide Web.
- **URL (b):** Stands for Uniform Resource Locator. It is the address of a resource on the Internet, typically what you enter in a web browser's address bar.
- **MAC address (c):** A unique identifier assigned to a network interface controller for use as a network address in communications within a network segment. It is provided by the manufacturer.
- **IP address (d):** Stands for Internet Protocol address. It is a numerical label assigned to each device connected to a computer network that uses the Internet Protocol for communication.

Thus, the correct match is option (a) that is (a)–(ii); (b)–(iv); (c)–(i); (d)–(iii)

185. (d): Alisha and Khushi need to upload and download the same file from the same server. We are taking megabit as the unit for transfer.

File size = 20 megabytes × 8 megabits/megabyte = 160 megabits

Upload time (P) = 160 megabits/1 megabit/second = 160 seconds

Download time (Q) = 160 megabits / 8 megabits/second = 20 seconds

Therefore, it will take Alisha 160 seconds to upload the file, and Khushi will take 20 seconds to download it. Thus, (d) is the correct answer.

186. (b): There are three paragraphs, the filling of three words in their initial parts may serve the purpose.

1. **First sentence:** This is 'interactive whiteboard', where we can write using a pen, and the information is digitized and stored.
2. **Second sentence:** This mentions an 'inkjet' printer, which uses ink cartridges and piezoelectric technology to produce hard copies.
3. **Third sentence:** This talks about a 'laser' printer, which uses a rotating drum and charges to create hard copies.

The b, a and c at the 1st, 2nd and 4th positions give us the answer. Thus, (b) is the correct answer. We may fill all the words also to get the answer.

CHAPTER 9

People, Development and Environment

TOPICS OF IMPORTANCE

- The Concept of People
- **Development and Environment:** Millennium Development and Sustainable Development Goals
- **Human and Environment Interaction:** Anthropogenic Activities and Their Impacts on Environment
- **Environmental issues:** Local, Regional and Global; Air Pollution, Water Pollution, Soil Pollution, Noise Pollution, Waste (Solid, Liquid, Biomedical, Hazardous, Electronic), Climate Change and its Socio-economic and Political Dimensions
- Impact of Pollutants on Human Health
- **Natural and Energy Resources:** Solar, Wind, Soil, Hydro, Geothermal, Biomass, Nuclear and Forests
- **Natural Hazards and Disasters:** Mitigation Strategies
- Environmental Protection Act (1986), National Action Plan on Climate Change, International agreements/efforts—Montreal Protocol, Rio Summit, Convention on Biodiversity, Kyoto Protocol, Paris Agreement, International Solar Alliance

1. The population of India is about 1.2 billion. Take the average consumption of energy per person per year in India as 30 megajoule. If this consumption is met by carbon-based fuels and the rate of carbon emissions per kilojoule is 15×10^6 kg, then the total carbon emissions per year from India will be **[Jun 2014]**

(a) 54 million metric tons
(b) 540 million metric tons
(c) 5400 million metric tons
(d) 2400 million metric tons

2. Which of the following cities has been worst affected by urban smog in recent times? **[Jun 2014]**

(a) Paris (b) London
(c) Los Angeles (d) Beijing

3. The primary source of organic pollution in fresh water bodies is **[Jun 2014]**

(a) Run-off urban areas.
(b) Run-off from agricultural forms.
(c) Sewage effluents.
(d) Industrial effluents.

4. 'Lahar' is a natural disaster involving **[Jun 2014]**

(a) Eruption of large amount of material.
(b) Strong winds.
(c) Strong water waves.
(d) Strong winds and water waves.

5. In order to avoid catastrophic consequences of climate change, there is a general agreement among the countries of the world to limit the rise in average surface temperature of earth compared to that of pre-industrial times by **[Jun 2014]**

(a) 1.5°C to 2°C (b) 2.0°C to 3.5°C
(c) 0.5°C to 1.0°C (d) 0.25°C to 0.5°C

6. The National Disaster Management Authority functions under the Union Ministry of **[Jun 2014]**

(a) Environment (b) Water Resources
(c) Home Affairs (d) Defence

7. Match List–I and List–II and select the correct answer from the codes given below. **[Jun 2014]**

List–I	List–II
A. Flood	I. Lack of rainfall of sufficient duration.
B. Drought	II. Tremors produced by the passage of vibratory waves through the rocks of the earth.
C. Earthquake	III. A vent through which molten substances come out.
D. Volcano	IV. Excess rain and uneven distribution of water.

Codes:
(a) A-IV, B-I, C-II, D-III (b) A-II, B-III, C-IV, D-I
(c) A-III, B-IV, C-II, D-I (d) A-IV, B-III, C-I, D-II

8. Which one of the following green house gases has the shortest residence time in the atmosphere? **[Jun 2014]**
(a) Chlorofluorocarbon (b) Carbon dioxide
(c) Methane (d) Nitrous oxide

9. Consider the following statements and select the correct answer from the codes given below. **[Jun 2014]**
(i) Rajasthan receives the highest solar radiation in the country.
(ii) India has the fifth largest installed wind power in the world.
(iii) The maximum amount of wind power is contributed by Tamil Nadu.
(iv) The primary source of uranium in India is Jaduguda.

Codes:
(a) (i) and (ii) (b) (i), (ii) and (iii)
(c) (ii) and (iii) (d) (i) and (iv)

10. Which of the anthropogenic activity accounts for more than $\frac{2}{3}$rd of global water consumption? **[Dec 2014]**
(a) Agriculture
(b) Hydropower generation
(c) Industry
(d) Domestic and municipal usage

11. One of the anthropogenic sources of gaseous pollutants chlorofluorocarbons (CFCs) in air is **[Dec 2014]**
(a) Cement industry (b) Fertilizer industry
(c) Foam industry (d) Pesticide industry

12. In terms of total CO_2 emissions from a country, identify the correct sequence. **[Dec 2014]**
(a) USA > China > India > Russia
(b) China > USA > India > Russia
(c) China > USA > Russia > India
(d) USA > China > Russia > India

13. Match List–I and List–II and identify the correct code. **[Dec 2014]**

List–I	List–II
A. World Health Day	I. 16th September
B. World Population Day	II. 1st December
C. World Ozone Day	III. 11th July
D. World AIDS Day	IV. 7th April

Codes:
(a) A-I, B-II, C-III, D-IV (b) A-IV, B-III, C-I, D-II
(c) A-II, B-III, C-IV, D-I (d) A-III, B-IV, C-II, D-I

14. The cyclone 'Hudhud' hit the coast of which state? **[Dec 2014]**
(a) Andhra Pradesh (b) Karnataka
(c) Kerala (d) Gujarat

15. Which of the following is not a renewable natural resource? **[Dec 2014]**
(a) Clean air (b) Fresh water
(c) Fertile soil (d) Salt

16. In which of the countries per capita use of water is maximum? **[Jun 2015]**
(a) USA (b) European Union
(c) China (d) India

17. India's contribution to total global carbon dioxide emissions is about **[Jun 2015]**
(a) ~3% (b) ~6%
(c) ~10% (d) ~15%

18. Two earthquakes A and B happen to be of magnitude 5 and 6, respectively, on Richter scale. The ratio of the energies released E_B/E_A will be approximately **[Jun 2015]**
(a) ~ 8 (b) ~ 16
(c) ~ 32 (d) ~ 64

19. Which of the following combinations represent renewable natural resources? **[Jun 2015]**

(a) Fertile soil, fresh water and natural gas.
(b) Clean air, phosphates and biological diversity.
(c) Fishes, fertile soil and fresh water.
(d) Oil, forests and tides.

20. In the recently launched Air Quality Index in India, which of the following pollutants is not included? **[Jun 2015]**
(a) Carbon monoxide
(b) Fine particulate matter
(c) Ozone
(d) Chlorofluorocarbons

21. The factors that are most important in determining the impact of anthropogenic activities on environment are **[Jun 2015]**
(a) Population, affluence per person and land availability per person.
(b) Population, affluence per person and the technology used for exploiting resources.
(c) Atmospheric conditions, population and forest cover.
(d) Population, forest cover and land availability per person.

22. Inside rural homes, the source(s) of nitrogen oxide pollution may be **[Dec 2015]**
(i) Unvented gas stoves
(ii) Wood stoves
(iii) Kerosene heaters
Choose the correct code from the following.
(a) (i) and (ii) only (b) (ii) and (iii) only
(c) (ii) only (d) (i), (ii), and (iii)

23. Which of the following pollutants can cause cancer in humans? **[Dec 2015]**
(a) Pesticides (b) Mercury
(c) Lead (d) Ozone

24. *Assertion (A):* People population control measures do not necessarily help in checking environmental degradation.
Reason (R): The relationship between population growth and environmental degradation is rather complex. **[Dec 2015]**
Choose the correct answer from the following.
(a) Both (A) and (R) are true, and (R) is the correct explanation of (A).
(b) Both (A) and (R) are true, but (R) is not the correct explanation of (A).
(c) (A) is true, but (R) is false.
(d) (A) is false, but (R) is true.

25. Which of the following phenomena is not a natural hazard? **[Dec 2015]**
(a) Wildfire (b) Lightning
(c) Landslide (d) Chemical contamination

26. As a part of National Climate Change Policy, Indian government is planning to raise the installed capacity of renewable energy by the year 2030 to **[Dec 2015]**
(a) 175 GW (b) 200 GW
(c) 250 GW (d) 350 GW

27. At present, in terms of per capita energy consumption (kWh/year), identify the correct sequence. **[Dec 2015]**
(a) Brazil > Russia > China > India
(b) Russia > China > India > Brazil
(c) Russia > China > Brazil > India
(d) China > Russia > Brazil > India

28. Identify the air pollutant in urban areas which irritates eyes and also respiratory tract of human beings. **[Jul 2016]**
(a) Particulate matter (b) Oxides of nitrogen
(c) Surface ozone (d) Carbon monoxide

29. Which of the following is the largest source of water pollution in major rivers of India? **[Jul 2016]**
(a) Untreated sewage
(b) Agriculture run-off
(c) Unregulated small scale industries
(d) Religious practices

30. Sustainable development goals have specific targets to be achieved by **[Jul 2016]**
(a) 2022 (b) 2030
(c) 2040 (d) 2050

31. Indian government's target of producing power from biomass by the year 2022 is **[Jul 2016]**
(a) 50 GW (b) 25 GW
(c) 15 GW (d) 10 GW

32. *Assertion (A):* Conserving our soil resources is critical to human survival.
Reason (R): Soil is home to many microorganisms and it contains minerals. **[Jul 2016]**

Choose the correct code from the following options.
(a) Both (A) and (R) are correct and (R) is the correct explanation of (A).
(b) Both (A) and (R) are correct but (R) is not the correct explanation of (A).
(c) (A) is true and (R) is false.
(d) (A) is false and (R) is true.

33. World Meteorological Organization's (WMO) objective is to reduce the number of deaths due to hydro-meteorological disasters over the decade 2010–2019 by (with reference to the decade 1994–2003) **[Jul 2016]**
(a) 25% (b) 50%
(c) 75% (d) 80%

34. *Assertion (A):* Sustainable development is critical to well-being of human society. **[Jan 2017]**

Reason (R): Environmentally sound policies do not harm the environment or deplete the natural resources. **[Jan 2017]**

Choose the correct code:
(a) Both (A) and (R) are correct and (R) is the correct explanation of (A).
(b) Both (A) and (R) are correct, but (R) is not the correct explanation of (A).
(c) (A) is true and (R) is true.
(d) (A) is false and (R) is true.

35. The dominant source of pollution due to oxides of nitrogen (NOx) in urban areas is **[Jan 2017]**
(a) Road transport
(b) Commercial sector
(c) Energy use in industry
(d) Power plants

36. Which of the following is not a water borne disease? **[Jan 2017]**
(a) Typhoid (b) Hepatitis
(c) Cholera (d) Dengue

37. The Government of India has set targets for power production from small hydro-projects by the year 2022 is **[Jan 2017]**
(a) 1 Gigawatt (b) 5 Gigawatt
(c) 10 Gigawatt (d) 15 Gigawatt

38. In which country, the recent international agreement on phasing out Hydro Fluoro Carbons (HFCs) was signed? **[Jan 2017]**
(a) Rwanda (b) Morocco
(c) South Africa (d) Algeria

39. Which of the following natural hazards is not hydro-meteorological? **[Jan 2017]**
(a) Snow avalanche (b) Sea erosion
(c) Tropical cyclone (d) Tsunami

40. Which of the following pollutants is the major cause of respiratory diseases? **[Nov 2017]**
(a) Suspended fine particles
(b) Nitrogen oxides
(c) Carbon monoxide
(d) Volatile organic compounds

41. *Assertion (A):* In urban areas, smog episodes occur frequently in winters.

Reason (R): In winters, a lot of biomass is burnt by people for heating purposes or to keep themselves warm. **[Nov 2017]**

Choose the correct answer from the code given below.
(a) Both (A) and (R) are true, and (R) is the correct explanation of (A).
(b) Both (A) and (R) are true, but (R) is not the correct explanation of (A).
(c) (A) is true and (R) is false.
(d) Both (A) and (R) are false.

42. Occurrence of natural hazards is affected by **[Nov 2017]**
(A) Land use changes
(B) Drainage and construction
(C) Ozone depletion
(D) Climate change

Choose the correct answer from the codes given below.
(a) (A), (C) and (D) (b) (A), (B) and (C)
(c) (A), (B) and (D) (d) (B), (C) and (D)

43. Which of the following pollutant gases is not produced both naturally and as a result of industrial activity? **[Nov 2017]**
(a) Chlorofluorocarbons (b) Nitrous oxide
(c) Methane (d) Carbon dioxide

44. Among the following fuels of energy, which is the most environment friendly? **[Nov 2017]**
(a) Ethanol (b) Biogas
(c) CNG (d) Hydrogen

45. 'Fly ash' produced in thermal power plants is an eco-friendly resource for use in **[Jul 2018]**

(A) Agriculture as micro-nutrient

(B) Wasteland development

(C) Dam and water holding structures

(D) Brick industry

Choose the correct answer from the codes given below:

(a) (A), (B) and (D) only

(b) (B), (C) and (D) only

(c) (A), (C) and (D) only

(d) (A), (B), (C) and (D)

46. Which of the following types of natural disasters has no definite beginning and end? **[Jul 2018]**

(a) Earthquakes (b) Landslides

(c) Hurricanes (d) Droughts

47. *Assertion (A):* Indoor air pollution is a serious hazard.

Reason (R): The dispersal of air pollutants is rather limited in indoor environment. Choose the correct answer from the codes given below. **[Jul 2018]**

(a) Both (A) and (R) are true and (R) is the correct explanation of (A)

(b) Both (A) and (R) are true but (R) is not the correct explanation of (A)

(c) (A) is true and (R) is false.

(d) Both (A) and (R) are false.

48. In terms of their contribution to the total power generation in India, identify the correct sequence of energy sources, such as Thermal Power Plants (TPP), Large Hydropower Projects (LHP), Nuclear Energy (NE) and Renewable Energy (RE) which includes solar energy, wind energy, biomass and small hydropower projects. **[Jul 2018]**

(a) TPP > RE > LHP > NE

(b) TPP > LHP > RE > NE

(c) LHP > TPP > RE > NE

(d) LHP > TPP > NE > RE

49. Which of the following is considered as a major source of pollution in rivers of India? **[Jul 2018]**

(a) Unregulated small-scale industry

(b) Untreated sewage

(c) Agricultural run-off

(d) Thermal power plants

50. Recently in Brazil, a bacterium exhibited antibiotic resistance, which was not reported previously **[Dec 2018]**

(a) Pseudomonas species

(b) Salmonella species

(c) Klebsiella species

(d) Streptococcus species

51. One of the following has a positive human influence on the environment? **[Dec 2018]**

(a) Deforestation (b) Over-population

(c) Pollution (d) Conservation

52. *Assertion (A):* The environmental impact of soil erosion can best be mitigated by removing vegetative cover only from the specific site in which construction is to take place.

Reason (R): The environmental impact of soil erosion can also be mitigated by disturbing the vegetation in adjacent areas as little as possible. **[Dec 2018]**

(a) Both (A) and (R) are true and (R) is the correct explanation of (A).

(b) Both (A) and (R) are true but (R) is not the correct explanation of (A).

(c) (A) is true but (R) is false.

(d) (A) is false but (R) is true.

53. *Assertion (A):* Hydropower is an exhaustible energy resource.

Reason (R): The power of falling water would neither diminish nor get exhausted. **[Dec 2018]**

(a) Both (A) and (R) are true and (R) is the correct explanation of (A).

(b) (A) and (R) are true, but (R) is not the correct explanation of (A).

(c) (A) is true, but (R) is false.

(d) Both (A) and (R) are false.

54. In the scheme of life, soil is an essential resource of life, as it plays the following roles. **[Dec 2018]**

(i) It is a reservoir of carbon.

(ii) It is the medium for growth of food and energy for the animal world.

(iii) It provides oxygen to the biotic community.

(iv) It is a natural reservoir for the huge amount of water.

Select the correct answer from the options given above.

(a) (i), (ii) and (iii) (b) (i), (ii) and (iv)
(c) (ii), (iii) and (iv) (d) (i), (iii) and (iv)

55. The biggest hindrance in using biomass as a major energy source is **[Dec 2018]**

(a) Energy yield of low level.
(b) Large amount of land required to grow energy crops.
(c) Technology not well developed for commercialization.
(d) Air pollution due to combustion.

56. An earthquake is rated as 'major' if its magnitude in Richter Scale is in the range of **[Dec 2018]**

(a) 4.0–4.9 (b) 6.0–6.9
(c) 7.0–7.9 (d) 5.0–5.9

57. Plants suitable for bio-monitoring of sulphur dioxide pollution are **[Dec 2018]**

(a) Tomato and lettuce.
(b) Apricot, peach and gladiolus.
(c) Tobacco, grapes and garden bean.
(d) White pine, moss and lichens.

58. Which among the following industries, consumes maximum water in India? **[Dec 2018]**

(a) Engineering
(b) Textiles
(c) Thermal power plants
(d) Paper and pulp

59. *Assertion (A):* Climate change is going to increase social tension in India.

Reason (R): The frequency and intensity of the extreme weather events will have serious consequences for food security. **[Dec 2018]**

(a) (A) is false, but (R) is true.
(b) Both (A) and (R) are true, and (R) is not the correct explanation of (A).
(c) Both (A) and (R) are true, and (R) is the correct explanation of (A).
(d) (A) is true, but (R) is false.

60. One of the main outcomes of the Rio+20 conferences was to develop a set of **[Jun 2019]**

(a) Sustainable Development Goals
(b) Millennium Development Goals
(c) National Development Strategy
(d) National Land Restoration Strategy

61. With increase in temperature, the dissolved oxygen content in a water body **[Jun 2019]**

(a) Decreases
(b) Increases
(c) Remain constant
(d) May increase or decrease depending on the temperature range

62. Oligotrophic lakes are characterized by **[Jun 2019]**

(a) High level of nutrients
(b) Low level of nutrients
(c) Absence of nutrients
(d) High level of organic matter

63. The duration for which of the usable compost generation is 3–6 months? **[Jun 2019]**

(a) Vermicomposting
(b) Semi-automatic waste converter
(c) Pit composting
(d) Automatic waste converter

64. The time frame for the implementation of Millennuim Development Goals was **[Jun 2019]**

(a) 2000–2005 (b) 2000–2015
(c) 2005–2010 (d) 2000–2012

65. Which of the following is the largest sink of CO_2 gas? **[Jun 2019]**

(a) Forests (b) Oceans
(c) Ice sheets (d) Grasslands

66. Which of the following diseases are due to polluted water? **[Jun 2019]**

(i) Giardia (ii) Dengue
(iii) Amoebiasis (iv) Typhoid

Choose the correct answer from the options given below:

(a) (i), (ii) and (iv)
(b) (ii), (iii) and (iv)
(c) (i), (ii), (iii) and (iv)
(d) (i), (iii) and (iv)

67. Choose the set of non-renewable resources **[Jun 2019]**

(a) Uranium, natural gas, soil
(b) Natural gas, uranium, phosphates
(c) Petroleum, uranium, geothermal energy
(d) Shale gas, uranium, soil

68. One of the parameters used to characterize the air quality at a location is PM2.5. Here, the suffix '2.5' refers to **[Jun 2019]**
(a) average number of suspected particles in 1.0 cm^3 of air
(b) size of suspended particles in certain units
(c) concentration of oxides of sulphur and nitrogen
(d) concentration of suspended particles in 2.5 m^3 of air

69. Which of the following is non-vehicular pollutant? **[Jun 2019]**
(a) chlorofluorocarbon
(b) carbon monoxide
(c) hydrocarbon
(d) particulate matter

70. Which of the following is a biological method of disposal of Municipal Solid Waste? **[Jun 2019]**
(a) Land filling (b) Pulverization
(c) Composting (d) Shredding

71. Which of the following pollutants is included in the Air Quality Index in India? **[Jun 2019]**
(a) Carbon dioxide
(b) Chlorofluorocarbons
(c) Sulphur dioxide
(d) Methane

72. Which of the following is are missions under the national action plan on climate change? **[Jun 2019]**
(1) Sustaining the Himalayan ecosystem
(2) Sustainable forest management
(3) Strategic knowledge for climate change
Select the correct answer
(a) (1) and (2) only
(b) (2) only
(c) (2) and (3) only
(d) (1) and (3) only

73. Blue baby syndrome can happen due to excess of which component in water? **[Jun 2019]**
(a) Calcium (b) Magnesium
(c) Nitrates (d) Pesticides

74. The initiative to establish International Solar Alliance was jointly taken by **[Jun 2019]**
(a) USA and India
(b) France and India
(c) Sweden and India
(d) China and India

75. Which one of the following conferences / summit is also known as UN Conference on Sustainable Development (UNCSD)? **[Jun 2019]**
(a) The Stockholm Conference, 1972
(b) The Rio de Janerio Conference, 1992
(c) The Johannesburg Summit, 2002
(d) The Rio+20 Conference, 2012

76. In the formation of surface ozone, which of the following do play an important role? **[Jun 2019]**
(1) Oxides of nitrogen
(2) Oxides of sulphur
(3) Sunlight
(4) Carbon monoxide
Choose the correct answer from the code given below:
(a) (1), (2), (3) (b) (2), (3), (4)
(c) (1), (3), (4) (d) (1), (2), (4)

77. Which of the following belongs to the category of geophysical hazards? **[Jun 2019]**
(a) Infestation (b) Avalanches
(c) Invasive species (d) Diseases

78. Statement–I: The Millennium Development Goals were adopted in the United Nations in the year 2010.

Statement–II: Developing a global partnership for development was one of the Millennium Development Goals. **[Jun 2019]**

Which of the above statements is/are correct?
(a) Only I (b) Only II
(c) Both I and II (d) Neither I nor II

79. Which are the example of potential kinetic energy? Select your answer from the options given below: **[Jun 2019]**
(i) Water that is behind a dam
(ii) Radio singnals
(iii) An airplane idling on the runway
(iv) A satellite before it is launched
(v) A coiled spring
(vi) Heat harnessed from the oceans

Options
(a) (i), (iii), (iv) and (v)
(b) (i), (ii), (iii) and (vi)
(c) (ii), (iii), (iv) and (v)
(d) (ii), (iv), (v) and (vi)

80. The target set by Indian government for generating power from wind energy by the year 2022 is **[Jun 2019]**

(a) 60 GW (b) 50 GW
(c) 40 GW (d) 15 GW

81. Which pollutant is the major source of marine pollution? **[Jun 2019]**

(a) Agricultural run-off
(b) Oil spill
(c) Industrial waste water
(d) Sewage

82. Permafrost is defining characteristic of which biome? **[Jun 2019]**

(a) Taiga (b) Tundra
(c) Grassland (d) Desert

83. Chemical Oxygen Demand in eutrophic water is **[Jun 2019]**

(a) Low (b) Medium
(c) High (d) Extremely low

84. Which of the following statements best explains the concept of sustainable development? **[Jun 2019]**

(a) Use of natural resources minimally
(b) Use of natural resources for our benefit
(c) Use of natural resources judiciously so that they are available for future generations
(d) Preserve our natural resources for our future generation

85. The mangroves exist in **[Jun 2019]**

(a) Fresh water system (b) Temperate areas
(c) Semi-arid areas (d) Saline waters

86. Which of the following is considered as a secondary air pollutant? **[Jun 2019]**

(a) Nitric oxide (b) Ozone
(c) Sulphur dioxide (d) Carbon monoxide

87. Which of the following are features of Paris Agreement? **[Jun 2019]**

(i) The agreement focuses on mitigation measuress for environmental pollution
(ii) The agreement recognizes the principle of equity and common but differentiated responsibilities
(iii) Paris agreement pertains to 2020 climate actions

Select the correct answer:

(a) (i) and (ii) only (b) (i), (ii) and (iii)
(c) (ii) and (iii) only (d) (i) and (iii) only

88. Indian government's target for share of renewable energy in the total installed capacity of electric power in India by the year 2030 is **[Jun 2019]**

(a) 20% (b) 30%
(c) 40% (d) 50%

89. Amongst the following, which is better suited for dumping of nuclear waste? **[Jun 2019]**

(a) Salt mines (b) Deserts
(c) Forests (d) Oceans

90. The long-term effect of cutting down of trees in large areas of rain forests is **[Jun 2019]**

(a) Increased rain fall in those areas
(b) Decreased rain in those areas
(c) Increase in wind speeds in those areas
(d) Increased rate of soil erosion those areas

91. Efficiency of electrical power generation is least amongst the following sources of energy in case of **[Jun 2019]**

(a) Solar (b) Wind
(c) Geothermal (d) Nuclear

92. Montreal protocol aims at **[Jun 2019]**

(a) Reduction in emissions of green house gases
(b) Phasing out ozone depleting substances
(c) Prohibiting transboundary movement of hazardous waste
(d) Enhancing cooperation among UN member states for peaceful uses of nuclear energy

93. In large parts of Eastern India, the ground water is contaminated by **[Jun 2019]**

(a) Arsenic (b) Lead
(c) Mercury (d) Nickel

94. Statement I: Earthquake 'A' is 5 in Richter scale and Earthquake 'B' is 8 on the same scale. Earthquake 'B' has 1000 times the wave amplitude compared to 'A'.

Statement II: The energy released in 'B' is three times that of 'A' **[Jun 2019]**

Choose the correct option:

(a) Statement I is correct and Statement II is incorrect

(b) Statements I and II are correct
(c) Statement II is correct and I is incorrect
(d) Statements I and II are incorrect

95. Taj Mahal is mainly threatened by the deleterious effect of **[Jun 2019]**
(a) Sulphur dioxide (b) Chlorine
(c) Oxygen (d) Hydrogen

96. In the last few years, India has been affected by which of all the following tropical cyclones? **[Jun 2019]**
(a) Gaja, Hudhud, Bhima
(b) Hudhud, Bhima, Ockhi
(c) Gaja, Hudhud, Ockhi
(d) Gaja, Bhima, Ockhi

97. *Assertion (A):* Methemoglobinemia is a condition in which blood is not able to carry and deliver enough oxygen to the body.
Reason (R): Consuming drinking water with high nitrate level may cause methemoglobinemia. **[Jun 2019]**
Choose the correct answer from the options given below:
(a) Both (A) and (R) are true and (R) is the correct explanation of (A)
(b) Both (A) and (R) are true but (R) is not the correct explanation of (A)
(c) (A) is true, but (R) is false
(d) (A) is false, but (R) is true

98. Which of the following are priority areas in relation to the Sustainable Development Goals? **[Jun 2019]**
(i) No poverty
(ii) Zero hunger
(iii) Reducing urbanization
(iv) Peace, justice and strong institutions
Choose the correct answer from the options given below:
(a) (i), (ii), (iii) (b) (i), (iii), (iv)
(c) (ii), (iii), (iv) (d) (i), (ii), (iv)

99. *Assertion (A):* High concentration of ozone in the lower troposphere is desirable.
Reason (R): Ozone present in the atmosphere protects the living organisms on the surface of earth from the harmful ultraviolet radiation of the sun. **[Jun 2019]**
Choose the correct answer from the options given below:
(a) Both (A) and (R) are true and (R) is the correct explanation of (A)
(b) Both (A) and (R) are true but (R) is not the correct explanation of (A)
(c) (A) is true, but (R) is false
(d) (A) is false, but (R) is true

100. Algal blooms in oligotrophic lakes are **[Jun 2019]**
(a) Very frequent (b) Frequent
(c) Very rare (d) Widespread

101. The target set by Indian government for power from roof-top solar installations by the years 2022 is **[Jun 2019]**
(a) 40.0 GW (b) 50.0 GW
(c) 60.0 GW (d) 100.0 GW

102. Which of the following types of energy sources direct energy conversion process to produce electricity? **[Jun 2019]**
(a) Biomass (b) Wind
(c) Geothermal (d) Nuclear

103. Which of the following materials is widely used in solar cell fabrication? **[Jun 2019]**
(a) Nubidium (b) Silicon
(c) Nickel (d) Chromium

104. Biomass fuels have the potential to form a sustainable carbon-neutral energy source because they: **[Dec 2019]**
(a) produce carbon dioxide on combustion as much as they consume when they grow
(b) produce less amount of carbon dioxide on combustion compared to the amount they use during their growth
(c) have carbon content same as fossil fuels
(d) do not produce hazardous emissions on combustion

105. Which among the following natural hazards has relatively slow onset? **[Dec 2019]**
(a) Volcanic eruptions (b) Droughts
(c) Wildfires (d) Land and slides

106. Major sources of oxygen demanding waste in freshwater systems are: **[Dec 2019]**
(A) agricultural runoff (B) food processing
(C) ore mining (D) sewage effluent

(E) landfill sites

Choose the correct option from the following.

(a) (A), (D) and (E) (b) (B), (D) and (E)
(c) (A), (B) and (D) (d) (A), (B), (C) and (D)

107. Under Kyoto protocol, the parties, in the second commitment period, have to reduce their greenhouse gas emissions with reference to 1990 levels by at least: **[Dec 2019]**

(a) 10% (b) 12%
(c) 15% (d) 18%

108. Which of the following is a renewable natural resource? **[Dec 2019]**

(a) Biological diversity (b) Tin
(c) Natural gas (d) Salt

109. How many national parks and wildlife sanctuaries were there in India till March 2011? **[Dec 2019]**

(a) 8 and 421 only
(b) 10 and 75 only
(c) 75 and 421 only
(d) 102 and 515 only

110. Which of the following sequence represents the correct order of soil particles arranged in terms of particle size from the smallest to the largest? **[Dec 2019]**

(a) Gravel, Silt, Clay, Sand
(b) Silt, Clay, Gravel, Sand
(c) Clay, Silt, Sand, Gravel
(d) Silt, Clay, Sand, Gravel

111. Which of the following statements are true about a fuel cell? **[Dec 2019]**

(i) It is a device that uses electrochemical reactions to produce electric current.
(ii) It consists of a positive electrode and a negative electrode separated by an electrolyte.
(iii) Just like batteries, it needs to be recharged with an electric current.

Choose the correct option from those given below.

(a) (i) and (ii) only
(b) (ii) and (iii) only
(c) (i) and (iii) only
(d) (i), (ii) and (iii)

112. Match List I with List II. **[Dec 2019]**

List I (Soil Order)	List II (Description)
(A) Histosols	(i) Soil order that includes soils formed on volcanic ash
(B) Andisols	(ii) Soil order of cold regions including soils underlain by permafrost
(C) Gelisols	(iii) Soil order consisting of soils of dry climates
(D) Aridisols	(iv) Soil order consisting of soils with a thick upper layer of organic matter

Choose the correct option.

	(A)	(B)	(C)	(D)
(a)	(iv)	(i)	(ii)	(iii)
(b)	(ii)	(iv)	(i)	(iii)
(c)	(i)	(ii)	(iii)	(iv)
(d)	(i)	(ii)	(iv)	(iii)

113. Suppose the concentration of Carbon dioxide—a greenhouse gas responsible for climate change, is 400 ppm. What is its concentration in air in terms of percentage? **[Dec 2019]**

(a) 0.04% (b) 0.4%
(c) 0.004% (d) 4.0%

114. Which of the following sequences of disposal options for low hazardous solid waste from industrial and urban sources is in order of increasing desirability? **[Dec 2019]**

(a) Indiscriminate dumping < landfill < incineration < reuse
(b) Composting < landfill < reuse < incineration
(c) Landfill < composting < reuse < incineration
(d) Incineration < composting < reuse < landfill

115. Identify the correct sequence of biomass fuels in terms of their energy content per unit mass. **[Dec 2019]**

(a) Dung (dry) > coconut shells > unsorted domestic refuse
(b) Unsorted domestic refuse > coconut shells > dung (dry)
(c) Wood (dry) > coconut shells > unsorted domestic refuse
(d) Coconut shells > dung (dry) > unsorted domestic refuse

116. Identify the correct group of diseases caused by polluted water. **[Dec 2019]**
(a) Cholera, acute diarrhoea, typhoid and polio
(b) Cholera, typhoid, enteritis and tuberculosis
(c) Typhoid, enteritis and tuberculosis
(d) Cholera, acute diarrhoea, typhoid and tuberculosis

117. National Disaster Management Authority is an agency working under the ministry of: **[Dec 2019]**
(a) Jal Shakti
(b) Home Affairs
(c) Earth Science
(d) Housing and Urban Affairs

118. Biosphere reserves are: **[Dec 2019]**
(i) area comprising terrestrial, marine and coastal ecosystems
(ii) monitored by national governments
(iii) areas where threatened animals and plants are kept in their habitat
(iv) wildlife sanctuaries
Choose the correct statements from the options given below.
(a) (i) and (ii)   (b) (ii) and (iii)
(c) (iii) and (iv)   (d) (i) and (iv)

119. A green building: **[Dec 2019]**
(i) uses minimum amount of energy
(ii) generates waste
(iii) consumes a lot of water
(iv) conserves natural resources
(v) creates space for healthy living
Choose the correct statements from the options given below.
(a) (i), (ii) and (iii)
(b) (i), (iv) and (v)
(c) (ii), (iii) and (v)
(d) (ii), (iv) and (v)

120. At present, in India, the share of which of the following sources of energy in electricity generation is the least? **[Dec 2019]**
(a) Thermal   (b) Solar and wind
(c) Hydro   (d) Nuclear

121. Methane, a greenhouse gas is emitted from: **[Dec 2019]**
(i) landfills   (ii) construction debris
(iii) wetlands   (iv) e-waste
Choose the correct statements from the options given below.
(a) (i), (ii) and (iv)
(b) (i), (iii) and (iv)
(c) (i) and (iii) only
(d) (i) and (iv) only

122. The Montreal Protocol refers to **[Dec 2019]**
(a) Co-operation among UN member countries to combat climate change
(b) Phasing out the consumption and production of ozone depleting substances
(c) Ensuring environmental sustainability
(d) Safeguarding societal quality of life worldwide

123. Identify the Sustainable Development Goals from the list given below. **[Dec 2019]**
(i) Zero hunger
(ii) Quality education
(iii) Universal primary education
(iv) Clean water and sanitation
(v) Green agriculture
(vi) Climate action
Select the correct answer from the options given below.
(a) (i), (ii), (iii) and (iv)
(b) (ii), (iii) (iv) and (v)
(c) (iii), (iv), (v) and (i)
(d) (i), (ii), (iv) and (vi)

124. Match the following two sets. Set I lists the names of states, while Set II indicates state specific missions. **[Dec 2019]**

Set I	Set II
(A) Andhra Pradesh	(i) Mukhyamantri Jal Swavalamban Abhiyan
(B) Gujarat	(ii) Jalyukt Shivar Abhiyan
(C) Maharashtra	(iii) Neeti Samrakshana Udyamam
(D) Rajasthan	(iv) Sujalam Sufalam Jal Abhiyan

Select the correct answer from the options given below.

Code:

	(A)	(B)	(C)	(D)
(a)	(i)	(ii)	(iii)	(iv)
(b)	(iv)	(iii)	(ii)	(i)
(c)	(ii)	(i)	(iv)	(iii)
(d)	(iii)	(iv)	(ii)	(i)

125. As per the provisions of Paris Agreement, the Intended Nationally Determined Contributions (INDCs) are to be reviewed every: [Dec 2019]

(a) 15 years (b) 10 years
(c) 5 years (d) 3 years

126. Average noise levels in heavy traffic zone in major cities of India are generally in which of the following ranges of noise levels? **[Dec 2019]**

(a) 31–40 dBA (b) 41–50 dBA
(c) 70–95 dBA (d) 110–120 dBA

127. Which of the following was not a Millennium Development Goals (MDG)? **[Dec 2019]**

(a) Eradicate extreme poverty and hunger
(b) Improve maternal health
(c) Ensure healthy lives and promote well-being for all at all ages
(d) Ensure environmental sustainability

128. Match List I with List II. **[2020]**

List 1 Categories of Environmental Education Objectives	List II Examples of those objectives
(A) Environmental Awareness	(I) To help social groups and individuals identify and solve environmental problems
(B) Environmental Knowledge	(II) To help social groups and individuals acquire a set of values for the environment
(C) Environmental Attitude	(III) To help social groups and individuals acquire a sensitivity to the total environment
(D) Environmental Skill	(IV) To help social groups and individuals gain a variety of experience in environment and its associated problems

Choose the correct answer from the options given below:

(a) A - II, B - I, C - III, D - IV
(b) A - I, B - III, C - IV, D - II
(c) A - IV, B - II, C - I, D - III
(d) A - III, B - IV, C - II, D - I

129. Noise pollution is measured in decibels (dB) with reference to a standard sound intensity of the following magnitude: **[2020]**

(a) 1 pico watt per m^2
(b) 1 milliwatt per m^2
(c) 1 nanowatt per m^2
(d) 1 microwatt per m^2

130. In a polluted urban area, which one of the following has the highest concentration (ppv) in photochemical smog? **[2020]**

(a) Ozone
(b) PAN
(c) Hydrocarbons (without methane)
(d) Carbon monoxide

131. Match List I with List II. **[2020]**

List 1 Environmental Protocol/Agreement/ Action Plan	List II Provisions
(A) Montreal Protocol	(I) Integrated water resource management
(B) Paris Agreement	(II) Emissions trading
(C) Climate Action Plan	(III) Phasing out ozone-depleting substances
(D) Kyoto Protocol	(IV) Intended Nationally Determined Contributions

Choose the correct answer from the options given below:

(a) A - III, B - II, C- I, D - IV
(b) A - II, B - III, C- I, D - IV
(c) A - II, B - IV, C - III, D - I
(d) A - III, B - IV, C - I, D - II

132. Given below are two statements, one is labelled as Assertion (A) and the other is labelled as Reason (R):

Assertion (A): Lakes are considered to be more susceptible to pollution than rivers.

Reason (R): Water in lakes may take decade(s) to be replaced. [2020]

In light of the above statements, choose the most appropriate answer from the options given below

(a) Both A and R are correct and R is the correct explanation of A
(b) Both A and R are correct but R is NOT the correct explanation of A
(c) A is correct but R is not correct
(d) A is not correct but R is correct

133. Thermal reactors produce energy by fission of the following nuclear fuels **[2020]**

A. Uranium-235 (^{235}U)
B. Uranium-233 (^{233}U)
C. Uranium-238 (^{238}U)
D. Thorium-232 (^{232}Th)
E. Plutonium-239 (^{239}Pu)

Choose the correct answer from the options given below:

(a) A, B, C and E only (b) A, B, C, D and E
(c) A, B, D and E only (d) A, B and E only

134. Contamination of aquatic environment by Polychlorinated Biphenyls (PCBs) can originate from **[2020]**

(A) Sewage effluent
(B) Waste incinerators
(C) Toxic dumps
(D) Thermal power plants
(E) Transport sector

Choose the correct answer from the options given below:

(a) (A), (B), (E) only
(b) (A), (B), (D), (E) only
(c) (B), (C), (D) only
(d) (A), (B), (C) only

135. Which of the following sources of energy on combustion produces maximum carbon dioxide per unit of energy output or heat content? **[2020]**

(a) Coal (sub-bituminous)
(b) Natural gas
(c) Diesel fuel and heating oil
(d) Gasoline (without ethanol)

136. Formulation of long term-low emission development strategies by each country was suggested under **[2020]**

(a) Paris Agreement
(b) Montreal Protocol
(c) International solar alliance
(d) Kyoto Protocol

137. If the intensity of a given noise increase two-fold, the noise level in decibels (dB) increases by **[2020]**

(a) ~ 2 dB (b) ~ 3 dB
(c) ~ 6 dB (d) ~ 10 dB

138. Given below are two statements:

Statement I: Emissions of hydrocarbons and carbon monoxide are inherently very low from diesel vehicles.

Statement II: Diesel driven vehicles are inherently more fuel efficient compared to petrol driven vehicles. **[2020]**

In the light of the above statements, choose the most appropriate from the options given below:

(a) Both Statements I and Statement II are correct
(b) Both Statements I and Statement II are incorrect.
(c) Statement I is correct but Statement II is incorrect.
(d) Statement I is incorrect but Statement II is correct.

139. United Nations Environmental Program (UNEP) was the result of deliberations held during **[2021]**

(a) Earth Summit at Rio de Janeiro in 1992
(b) Human Environmental Conference at Stockholm in 1972
(c) Kyoto Protocol 1997
(d) Montreal Protocol 1987

140. The number of Sustainable Development Goals is **[2021]**

(a) 13 (b) 15
(c) 17 (d) 19

141. Which region of brain is involved in our ability to learn new information, particularly if it is verbal? **[2021]**

(a) Cerebrum (b) Hippocampus
(c) Pons (d) Thalamus

142. According to Urie Bronfenbrenner's biological model of human development, microsystem constitutes ____________. **[2021]**

A. Immediate family B. School
C. Beliefs D. Customs
E. Neighbourhood

Choose the correct answer from the options given below:

(a) A, B and E only
(b) A, B and C only
(c) A, C and E only
(d) C, D and E only

143. Given below are two statements:

Statement I: Small amount of atmospheric Nitrogen dioxide NO_2 is produced from polluting sources

Statement II: Most of the atmospheric NO_2 is produced due to photochemical reactions in the atmosphere **[2021]**

In light of the above statements, choose the most appropriate answer from the options given below:

(a) Both Statement I and Statement II are correct
(b) Both Statement I and Statement II are incorrect
(c) Statement I is correct but Statement II is incorrect
(d) Statement I is incorrect but Statement II is correct

144. Which of the following water borne diseases may be caused by virus, bacteria and protozoa? **[2021]**

(a) Cholera (b) Diarrhea
(c) Hepatitis (d) Typhoid

145. Which of the following state has maximum installed wind power as per MNRE's latest report?

(a) Andhra Pradesh (b) Karnataka
(c) Maharashtra (d) Tamil Nadu

146. In India, according to Niti Aayog's SDG Index (2019-2020), which is the best performing state on SDG-9 (Industry, Innovation and Infrastructure) **[2021]**

(a) Gujarat (b) Karnataka
(c) Kerala (d) Telangana

147. Identify the correct sequence of wind energy potential at 100m above ground level in decreasing order. **[2021]**

A. Karnataka
B. Andhra Pradesh
C. Gujarat
D. Tamil Nadu
E. Andaman and Nicobar Islands

Choose the correct answer from the options given below

(a) A > B > C > E > D
(b) C > A > B > D > E
(c) C > E > B > D > A
(d) D > C > A > B > E

148. Which of the following types of power plants provide electricity consistently running 24 hrs per day, 7 days a week? **[2021]**

(a) Geothermal (b) Hydro
(c) Solar (d) Wind

149. In agricultural regions, groundwater can have significant concentrations of which pollutant? **[2021]**

(a) Cadmium (b) Lead
(c) Nitrate (d) Selenium

150. Which of the following Green House gases were the target gases whose emission was to be covered under the first commitment period of the Kyoto protocol? **[2021]**

A. SO_2 B. CO_2
C. N_2O D. NH_3
E. CH_4

Choose the correct answer from the options given below:

(a) A, B and C only
(b) A, B, C and D only
(c) B, C and E only
(d) B, C, D and E only

151. What will be the resultant of two noise levels of 81 dB and 90 dB generated by two independent sources? **[2021]**

(a) ~ 96 dB (b) ~ 91 dB
(c) ~ 98 dB (d) ~ 118 dB

152. Match List I with List II. **[2021]**

List I	List II
(A) Kyoto Protocol	(i) Clean and Affordable Energy
(B) Montreal Protocol	(ii) Clean Development Mechanism
(C) Paris Agreement	(iii) Nationally Determined Contribution
(D) International Solar Alliance	(iv) Phase out of chlorinated compounds

Choose the correct answer from the options given below:

	(A)	(B)	(C)	(D)
(a)	(ii)	(iv)	(iii)	(i)
(b)	(i)	(iii)	(iv)	(ii)
(c)	(ii)	(iv)	(i)	(iii)
(d)	(iii)	(iv)	(i)	(ii)

153. Given below are two statements: **[2021]**

Statement I : Solar flat plate collectors essentially work on the principle of Green House Effect.

Statement II: Black absorber plat radiates infra-red radiations.

In the light of the above statements, choose the corrrect answer from the options given below:

(a) Both Statement I and Statement II are true

(b) Both Statement I and Statement II are false

(c) Statement I is true but Statement II is false

(d) Statement I is false but Statement II is true

154. Identify the correct sequence in decreasing order of percentage of total world's water in the following locations: **[2021]**

(A) Atmosphere

(B) Rivers and streams

(C) Ground water

(D) Lakes (Fresh water)

(E) Ice caps and glaciers

Choose the correct answer from the options given below:

(a) (E), (C), (B), (D), (A)

(b) (E), (B), (C), (D), (A)

(c) (E), (D), (C), (B), (A)

(d) (E), (C), (D), (A), (B)

155. By the year 2030, Sustainable Development Goal 7 aims at enhancing the global rate of improvement in energy efficiency by a factor of: **[2021]**

(a) Two (b) Three

(c) Four (d) Five

156. According to the Sustainable Development Report (2020), the top-ranked country on the basis of the SDG Index is: **[Dec 2021]**

(a) Bhutan (b) New Zealand

(c) Sweden (d) United Kingdom

157. Which one of the following waterborne diseases does not require direct contact with water but a host to spread? **[Dec 2021]**

(a) Cholera (b) Malaria

(c) Trachoma (d) Schistosomiasis

158. Paris agreement entered into force when the instruments of ratification were deposited by at least 55 countries which accounted for at least: **[Dec 2021]**

(a) 50% of global CO_2 emissions

(b) 55% of global CO_2 emissions

(c) 60% of global CO_2 emissions

(d) 75% of global CO_2 emissions

159. Biogas has a calorific value of about: **[Dec 2021]**

(a) 5000 kcal per cubic meter

(b) 3000 kcal per cubic meter

(c) 2500 kcal per cubic meter

(d) 1800 kcal per cubic meter

160. Under which of the following agreements was it decided to limit the increase in global average temperature to well below 2°C? **[Dec 2021]**

(a) Paris Agreement

(b) Kyoto Protocol

(c) Montreal Protocol

(d) Rio Summit

161. Which of the following air pollutants is known to be a human carcinogen? **[2022]**

(a) Carbon monoxide

(b) Asbestos fiber

(c) Nitrogen dioxide

(d) Sulphur dioxide

162. Which of the following statements about biodiversity are correct? **[2022]**

A. Biodiversity can support ecosystem stability.

B. Human activities have sharply increased species extinctions.

C. Habitat fragmentation has no adverse impact on biodiversity.
D. About 70% of all known species are invertebrates.

(a) A, B and C only (b) A, B and D only
(c) B, C and D only (d) A, C and D only

163. Identify the major sources of methane emissions. **[2022]**

A. Landfills B. Mountain rivers
C. Paddy fields D. Wetlands

Choose the correct answer from the options given below:
(a) A, B and C only
(b) B, C and D only
(c) A, B and D only
(d) A, C and D only

164. Match **List I** with **List II** **[2022]**

List I Objectives/Provisions	List II International Treaties/Agreements
A. Emissions Trading	I. Paris Agreement
B. Sustainable Management of Resources	II. Kyoto Protocol
C. Clean affordable energy	III. International Solar Alliance
D. Intended Nationally Determined Contributions	IV. Rio Summit

Choose the correct answer from the options given below:
(a) A – II, B – IV, C – I, D – III
(b) A – II, B – IV, C – III, D – I
(c) A – I, B – IV, C – III, D – II
(d) A – I, B – IV, C – II, D - III

165. Which among the following pesticides would have the least chance of bioaccumulation in food chains? **[2022]**

(a) Chlordane (b) Aldrin
(c) Carbaryl (d) Endrin

166. Given below are two statements. **[2022]**

Statement I: An ethical framework of sustainable development provides normative guidance regarding our relationship with environment.

Statement II: Anthropocentric model is misleading as evident from its environmental consequences.

In light of the above statements, choose the correct answer from the options given below:
(a) Both Statement I and Statement II are true
(b) Both Statement I and Statement II are false
(c) Statement I is true but Statement II is false
(d) Statement I is false but Statement II is true

167. Which among the following hazards can occur due to anthropogenic causes? **[2022]**

A. Cyclones
B. Nuclear Disaster
C. Floods
D. Volcanoes
E. Forest Fires

Choose the correct answer from the options given below:
(a) A, B and D only
(b) B, C and D only
(c) B, D and E only
(d) B, C and E only

168. Given below are two statements, one is labelled as **Assertion A** and the other is labelled as **Reason R** **[2022]**

Assertion A: Most cyclones cause widespread damage in coastal area.

Reason R: Energy of most cyclones increases after landfall.

In light of the above statements, choose the correct answer from the options given below:
(a) Both **A** and **R** are correct and **R** is the correct explanation of **A**
(b) Both **A** and **R** are correct but **R** is NOT the correct explanation of **A**
(c) **A** is correct but **R** is not correct
(d) **A** is not correct but **R** is correct

169. Arrange the following water bodies in increasing order of the quantity of freshwater they hold: **[2022]**

A. Ice and snow
B. Freshwater lakes and reservoirs
C. Groundwater
D. Rivers and streams

Choose the correct answer from the options-given below

(a) D, B, C, A (b) B, C, D, A
(c) B, D, A, C (d) D, B, A, C

170. Which of the following is envisaged in the Sustainable Development Goals? **[2022]**

(a) By 2020, conserve at least 50% of coastal and marine areas.
(b) By 2030, reduce by one-third of the per capita global food waste at the retail and consumer levels.
(c) By 2030, double the global rate of improvement in energy efficiency.
(d) By 2030, reduce by one-fifth the premature mortality from non-communicable diseases.

171. Chlorination of water is done to **[June 2023]**

(a) remove microbes.
(b) remove hardness.
(c) increase salt contents.
(d) decrease turbidity.

172. What is the average thickness of Ozone layer? **[June 2023]**

(a) > 1 cm (b) < 1 cm
(c) 1 cm to 1 meter (d) > 1 meter

173. Given below are two statements: **[June 2023]**

Statement-I: Ion exchange is an example of tertiary waste water treatment process.

Statement-II: Ion exchange is used for the removal of residual suspended solids.

In the light of the above statements, choose the correct answer from the options given below:

(a) Both Statement I and Statement II are true.
(b) Both Statement I and Statement II are false.
(c) Statement I is true but Statement II is false.
(d) Statement I is false but Statement II is true.

174. Given below are two statements: **[June 2023]**

Statement-I: Montreal Protocol was agreed in 1987 and came into force in 1990.

Statement-II: Kyoto Protocol was agreed in 1997 and came into force in 2005.

In the light of the above statements, choose the correct answer from the options given below:

(a) Both Statement I and Statement II are true.
(b) Both Statement I and Statement II are false.
(c) Statement I is true but Statement II is false.
(d) Statement I is false but Statement II is true.

175. Given below are two statements: **[June 2023]**

Statement-I: Some pollutants such as carbon tetrachloride (CCl4) pesticides and the heavy metals cause liver damage.

Statement-II: Toxic chemicals that cause liver damage are called Hematotoxins.

In the lights of the above statements, choose the correct answer from the options given below:

(a) Both Statement I and Statement II are true.
(b) Both Statement I and Statement II are false.
(c) Statement I is true but Statement II is false.
(d) Statement I is false but Statement II is true.

176. Atmospheric haze is mainly cuased by **[June 2023]**

(a) Ultra fine size particulate matters
(b) Oxides of nitrogen and sulphur
(c) Ozone
(d) Carbon dioxide and Carbon monoxide

177. Given below are two statements: **[June 2023]**

Statement I: Nano scale metallic and bimetallic particles can efficiently remove common water pollutants such as Poly Chloro Benzenes (PCB), Organo chlorine pesticides and halogenated organic solvents.

Statement II: Nano scale metallic bimetallic particles cannot reduce heavy metals such as nickel, arsenic, mercury etc.

In the lights of the above statements, choose the most appropriate answer from the options given below:

(a) Both Statement I and Statement II are correct.
(b) Both Statement I and Statement II are incorrect.
(c) Statement I is correct but Statement II is incorrect.
(d) Statement I is incorrect but Statement II is correct.

178. Given below are two statements: One is labelled as Assertion A and the other is labelled as Reasons R. **[June 2023]**

Assertion A: The change is sea level at any coastal location depends on the sum of global, regional and local factors.

Reason R: Therefore, the global mean sea level rise translates into an uniform rise in sea level around the world.

In the light of the above statements, choose the most appropriate answer from the options given below:

(a) Both A and R are correct and R is the correct explanatin of A.
(b) Both A and R are correct but R is not the correct explanation of A.
(c) A is correct but R is not correct.
(d) A is not correct but R is correct.

179. Oxygen demanding wastes **[June 2023]**
(a) decrease the oxygen level in water.
(b) increase the oxygen level in water.
(c) do not change the oxygen level in water.
(d) increase the temperature of water.

180. Match List I with List II **[June 2023]**

List I [Sustainable Development Goal (SDG) number]	List II [Goal]
A. SDG 2	I. Sustainable cities and communities
B. SDG 3	II. Zero hunger
C. SDG 6	III. Good health and well being
D. SDG 11	IV. Clean water and sanitation

(a) A-I, B-III, C-II, D-IV
(b) A-III, B-II, C-I, D-IV
(c) A-II, B-III, C-IV, D-I
(d) A-II, B-III, C-I, D-IV

181. Match List-I with List-II **[Dec 2023]**

List I Water Category	List II pH Value
(A) Normal Water	(i) < 5
(B) Rain Water	(ii) > 7
(C) Acid Rain Water	(iii) 5 – 6
(D) Ocean Water	(iv) 7

Choose the correct answer from the options given below:
(a) (A)–(iv); (B)–(i); (C)–(iii); (D)–(ii)
(b) (A)–(iv); (B)–(iii); (C)–(i); (D)–(ii)
(c) (A)–(iv); (B)–(iii); (C)–(ii); (D)–(i)
(d) (A)–(iii); (B)–(ii); (C)–(iv); (D)–(i)

182. Given below are two statements: **[Dec 2023]**

Statement (I): Kyoto protocol only binds developed countries and places heavier burden on them.

Statement (II): Kyoto protocol has nothing to do with United Nations Framework Convention on climate change (UNFCCC).

In light of the above statements, choose the most appropriate answer from the options given below:
(a) Both Statement (I) and Statement (II) are true.
(b) Both Statement (I) and Statement (II) are false.
(c) Statement (I) is true but Statement (II) is false.
(d) Statement (I) is false but Statement (II) is true.

183. Leachates are **[Dec 2023]**
(a) Persistent Organic Pollutants
(b) Algae found on eutrophic lakes
(c) Ozone depleting substances
(d) Contaminated liquid draining from landfills.

184. Given below are two statements: **[Dec 2023]**

Statement (I): Exposure to mercury can be either through food chain or in the work place.

Statement (II): Poisoning by inorganic mercury (particularly vapours) results in the damage to the central nervous system.

In light of the above statements, choose the most appropriate answer from the options given below:
(a) Both Statement (I) and Statement (II) are true.
(b) Both Statement (I) and Statement (II) are false.
(c) Statement (I) is true but Statement (II) is false.

(d) Statement (I) is false but Statement (II) is true.

185. Given below are two statements: **[Dec 2023]**

Statement (I): International Solar Alliance's vision: 'Let us together make the sun brighter'.

Statement (II): International Solar Alliance's mission: 'Every home how far away, will have a light at home'.

In light of the above statements, choose the most appropriate answer from the options given below:

(a) Both Statement (I) and Statement (II) are true.

(b) Both Statement (I) and Statement (II) are false.

(c) Statement (I) is true but Statement (II) is false.

(d) Statement (I) is false but Statement (II) is true.

ANSWER KEY

1. (*)	2. (d)	3. (c)	4. (a)	5. (a)	6. (c)	7. (a)	8. (c)	9. (d)	10. (a)
11. (c)	12. (b)	13. (b)	14. (a)	15. (d)	16. (a)	17. (a)	18. (c)	19. (c)	20. (d)
21. (b)	22. (d)	23. (a)	24. (a)	25. (d)	26. (d)	27. (c)	28. (a)	29. (a)	30. (b)
31. (d)	32. (b)	33. (b)	34. (b)	35. (a)	36. (d)	37. (b)	38. (a)	39. (d)	40. (a)
41. (b)	42. (c)	43. (a)	44. (d)	45. (d)	46. (d)	47. (a)	48. (a)	49. (b)	50. (b)
51. (d)	52. (b)	53. (a)	54. (b)	55. (b)	56. (c)	57. (d)	58. (c)	59. (c)	60. (a)
61. (a)	62. (b)	63. (c)	64. (b)	65. (b)	66. (d)	67. (b)	68. (b)	69. (a)	70. (c)
71. (c)	72. (d)	73. (c)	74. (b)	75. (d)	76. (c)	77. (b)	78. (b)	79. (a)	80. (a)
81. (a)	82. (b)	83. (b)	84. (c)	85. (d)	86. (b)	87. (c)	88. (c)	89. (a)	90. (d)
91. (c)	92. (b)	93. (a)	94. (a)	95. (a)	96. (c)	97. (a)	98. (d)	99. (d)	100. (c)
101. (d)	102. (b)	103. (b)	104. (a)	105. (b)	106. (c)	107. (d)	108. (a)	109. (d)	110. (c)
111. (a)	112. (a)	113. (a)	114. (a)	115. (d)	116. (a)	117. (b)	118. (a)	119. (b)	120. (d)
121. (c)	122. (b)	123. (d)	124. (c)	125. (c)	126. (d)	127. (c)	128. (d)	129. (a)	130. (a)
131. (d)	132. (a)	133. (d)	134. (d)	135. (a)	136. (a)	137. (b)	138. (a)	139. (b)	140. (c)
141. (b)	142. (a)	143. (a)	144. (b)	145. (d)	146. (a)	147. (b)	148. (a)	149. (c)	150. (c)
151. (b)	152. (a)	153. (a)	154. (d)	155. (a)	156. (c)	157. (b)	158. (b)	159. (a)	160. (a)
161. (b)	162. (b)	163. (d)	164. (b)	165. (c)	166. (a)	167. (d)	168. (c)	169. (a)	170. (c)
171. (a)	172. (b)	173. (b)	174. (d)	175. (c)	176. (a)	177. (c)	178. (c)	179. (a)	180. (c)
181. (b)	182. (c)	183. (d)	184. (a)	185. (a)					

HINTS AND SOLUTIONS

1. (*) -None of the choices are correct. Marks were given to candidates who attempted this question. Solution is still provided here for the understanding of candidates.

   Population of India = 1.2 billion = 1.2×10^9

   Total energy consumption in India $= 1.2 \times 10^9 \times 30 \times 10^6 = 36 \times 10^{15}$ Joules

   Carbon emission per kilojoule = 15×10^6 kg

   Carbon emission per Joule = $\frac{15 \times 10^6}{10^3} = 15 \times 10^3$ kg

   Total carbon emissions from India = $36 \times 10^{15} \times 15 \times 10^3$ kgs = 540×10^{18} kg

   None of the choices match the answer.

2. **(d)** : Smog is composed of a mixture of air pollutants that reduce visibility. It causes or aggravates health issues such as emphysema, asthma, chronic bronchitis, lung infections, and cancers.

   Beijing's smog conditions can be attributed to a number of factors such as booming economy, an enormous increase in number of vehicles, population growth, manufacturing output (mainly steel industry), surrounding topography and seasonal weather. There is heating of buildings. The pollution levels in Beijing are three times higher in comparison to Los Angeles, the most polluted city in USA.

   The approaches such as closing polluting plants, tighter emissions standards and local government targets have been adopted in recent years to reduce pollution. WHO recommended level for PM 2.5 is 5 micrograms per cubic meter. Beijing had a level of 40.5 micrograms per cubic meter in 2021.

   Beijing Red Alert was issued in Beijing in December 2015. Under China's four-tier warning system for air pollution, red is the most severe followed by orange, yellow and blue, with red alert being the most severe and PM2.5 being alarmingly high that is connected with smog. Beijing has observed a 53% decrease in pollution levels in 2021 when compared with 2015 levels.

3. **(c)** : Organic pollution occurs when an excess of organic matter, such as manure or sewage, enters the water. Water pollution is caused by the dumping of sewage and waste water, marine dumping, industrial waste, and eutrophication.

   Organic pollution, in general, can be split up into three different categories; land pollution, air pollution, and water pollution.

4. **(a)**: Lahar is an Indonesian word which describes a mudflow or debris flow that originates on the slopes of a volcano. Lahar involves a large amount of material, including mud, rock, and ash sliding down the side of the volcano at a rapid pace. These flows can destroy entire towns in seconds and kill thousands of people.

5. **(a)**: We know that climate change and global warming have become real phenomena affecting the earth. According to Intergovernmental Panel on Climate Change (IPCC), global warming uses the reference period 1850–1900 to represent pre-industrial temperature, that now predicts the increase of 1.5°C by 2040.

   Under Paris Agreement in 2015, the nations agreed to cut greenhouse gas emissions so that objective of global temperature increase can be kept well below 2°C above pre-industrial levels. The efforts are required to limit the increase to 1.5°C above pre-industrial levels.

   The global warming reached 0.87°C (±0.12°C) relative to 1850–1900 levels during the decade of 2006–2015. This increase in temperature has happened due to increase in the emission of greenhouse gases in the atmosphere. If global warming is currently increasing by 0.2°C (±0.1°C) per decade, the earth has already achieved increase of 1°C above pre-industrial levels around 2017. At this pace, planet would reach the increase of 1.5°C by 2040. Since 1970s most of the land regions have been warming faster than the global average. Thus, warming in many regions has already exceeded 1.5°C above pre-industrial levels.

   The tipping point indicates the increase in temperature that can't be reversed even through the best of human efforts, so we need to be very careful.

   The Conference of Parties (CoP) that is part of UN Framework Convention on Climate Change discusses such issues every year. The latest Glasgow COP was held in 2021 where India and other nations revised their carbon emission targets. India's focus was on renewable energy sources.

6. **(c)**: National Disaster Management Authority (NDMA), is an agency of the Ministry of Home Affairs whose primary purpose is to coordinate response to natural or man-made disasters and for capacity-building in disaster resiliency and crisis response. It was set in year 2005. Prime Minister is the Chairman of NDMA.

7. **(a)**: A natural hazard is an extreme event that occurs naturally and causes harm to human beings. The harm may be done to other things that we care about, though usually the focus is on humans that may be termed as anthropocentric. A natural hazard may escalate into a natural disaster when an extreme event causes harm in to a huge extent so that people are not able to cope with and respond in an adequate manner.

   In this question, we need to match the direct definitions of natural hazards.

8. (c): The residence time (RT) is a climate change indicator. It depends upon the chemical composition of molecules. It is linked with Global Warming Potential (GWP) also. RT is defined by the time that a gas stays in the atmosphere. For example, carbon dioxide in the atmosphere is defined as the average length of time a molecule of CO_2 remains in the atmosphere before being taken up by the oceans or terrestrial biosphere.

The residence period and Global Warming Potential of the given gases is

GHG	Resi Time	GWP
CO_2	5- 200 years	1
CH_4	11.8 years	27 – 29.8
NO_2	109 years	273
Flourinated (CFCs)	50 to 100s of years	

GWP of sulfur hexafluoride is highest at 25,200

Methane is more than 25 times as potent as carbon dioxide at trapping heat in the atmosphere. Over the last two centuries, methane concentrations in the atmosphere have more than doubled, largely due to human-related activities.

9. (d): Rajasthan receives the highest amount of solar radiation in the country and second-largest in the world. The state is best for solar power generation because its average rainfall is very low. It captures solar radiation of 6-7 kWh/sq-m/day with approximately 325 sunny days per year.

Rajasthan became the first state to cross 10 GW of cumulative large-scale solar PV installations, with over 10 GW installed as of March 2022, and accounts for 24 per cent of the total installations in the country. Jaduguda is the primary source of uranium in India. The Jaduguda mine is a uranium mine located in the Jaduguda village of Purbi Singhbhum district of Jharkhand state.

10. (a): Kindly refer to the following figure by Food and Agriculture Organization for global water consumption.

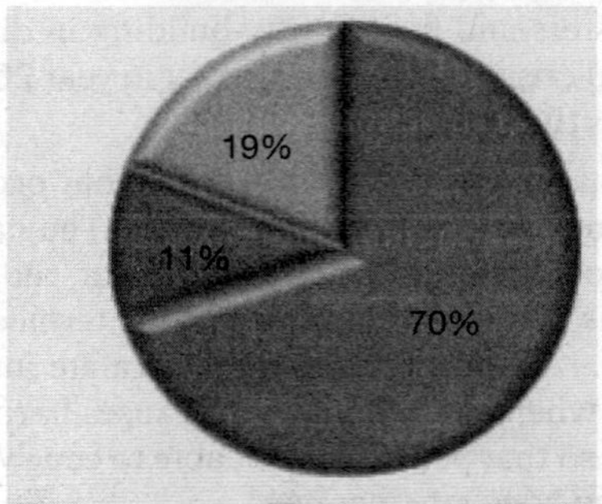

Source: Levels of Teaching l Memory, Understanding and Reflective Level Teaching, http://www.fao.org, accessed on 10 October 2019

11. (c): The foam manufacturing industry in China still uses chlorofluorocarbon (CFC)-11. It is an ozone-depleting substance (ODS) phased out under the Montreal Protocol in 1987. Students can learn more about Kigali agreement for ODS. China uses CFC to save on the higher cost of alternatives.

12. (b): China is currently responsible for more than 27% of total global emissions. The USA accounts for 11% of the global total. India is responsible for 6.6% of global emissions, edging out the 27 nations in the EU, which account for 6.4%. Russia comes after EU.

China is termed as the manufacturing hub of the world. Thus, (b) is the answer.

13. (b): This question is about different days of environment.

1. Word Health Day (April 7): The World Health Organization was established on this day in 1948. The theme of World Health Day 2022 is "Our Planet, Our Health".

2. World Population Day (July 11): UN had established the 'World Population Day' in 1989 after the global population crossed five billion in 1987. In 1990, the day was recognised by the UN General Assembly.

The theme for the World Population Day 2022 is "A world of 8 billion: Towards a resilient future for all – Harnessing opportunities and ensuring rights and choices for all."

In 2011, it had hit the seven billion mark.

3. World Ozone Day (September 16): The ozone layer, a fragile shield of gas, protects the Earth from the harmful portion of the rays of the sun, thus helping preserve life on the planet. This gas gets depleted due to chlorofluorocarbon gases, halons etc. On this day, Montreal protocol was signed. This day is being celebrated since 1994. There was amendment in it under Kigali agreement in 2016. The theme for the year 2022 is 'Montreal Protocol at 35: global cooperation protecting life on earth'.

4. World AIDS Day (December 1): This day was celebrated for the first time in year 1988. This day aims at spreading awareness about global epidemic of AIDS (Acquired Immune Deficiency Syndrome) and spread of HIV (Human Immunodeficiency Virus). The red ribbon has become an internationally recognized symbol for AIDS awareness.

14. (a): The practice of naming storms (tropical cyclones) began in order to help in the quick identification of storms in warning messages because the names are presumed to be far easier to remember than numbers and technical terms. This is mainly taken care of by World Metereological Organization. For details, visit the link https://www.wmo.int/pages/prog/www/tcp/Storm-naming.html.

15. (d): Renewable energy is any energy source that is naturally replenished, like that derived from solar, wind, geothermal or hydroelectric action. Energy produced from the refining of biomass is also often classified as renewable. Coal, oil or natural gas, on the other hand, are finite sources.

Salt does not fall under the category of renewable energy source.

Extremely Severe Cyclonic Storm Hudhud was a strong tropical cyclone that caused extensive damage and loss of life in eastern India and Nepal during October 2014. Andhra Pradesh is the answer here.

16. (a): The US had the world's highest per capita water footprint, at 2,842 cubic meters per annum.

17. (a): The top five nations for Carbon Emissions (in Metric Tonnes) in 2020 have been given as under:

China — 11680.42

United States — 4535.30

India — 2411.73

Russia — 1674.23

Japan — 1061.77

18. (c): Magnitudes are based on a logarithmic scale (base 10). It means that for each whole number you go up on the magnitude scale, the amplitude of the ground motion recorded by a seismograph goes up 10 times. Using this scale, a magnitude 6 earthquake would result in 10 times the level of ground shaking as a magnitude 5 earthquake (and 32 times as much energy would be released).

19. (c): There are two types of energy sources - Renewable and non-renewable. Renewable resources can naturally replenish themselves while non renewable resources cannot. This means that non renewable resources are limited in supply and cannot be used sustainably.

20. (d): Air Quality Index includes eight pollutants—PM10, PM2.5, NO_2, SO_2, CO, O_3, NH_3, and Pb.

AQI was described as 'One Number-One Colour-One Description' for the common man to judge the air quality within his vicinity. The index constituted part of the government's mission to introduce the culture of cleanliness.

It was launched in October 2014, and linked with Swachh Bharat Abhiyaan.

The new Airquality Index (AQI) will use colour-coded table to show air quality and its effect on health. Thus, even common man can understand easily.

Central Pollution Control Board is the main agency to monitor. It is mainly based on the recommendations of IIT-Kanpur.

The air risks will be signified through six levels—good, satisfactory, moderately polluted, poor, very poor, and severe.

AQI	Remark	Color Code	Possible Health Impacts
0-50	Good		Minimal impact
51-100	Satisfactory		Major breathing discomfort to sensitive people
101-200	Moderate		Breathing discomfort to the people with lungs, asthma and heart diseases
201-300	Poor		Breathing discomfort to most people on prolonged exposure
301-400	Very Poor		Respiratory illness on prolonged exposure
401-500	Severe		Affect healthy people and seriously impacts those with existing diseases

In China, Air quality system is divided into four levels: blue, yellow, orange and red to mark each. Beijing city has been the most polluted city.

21. (b): The term anthropogenic designates an effect or object resulting from human activity, we claim that it is being done for development but causes major issues such as carbon emissions, climate change, deforestation and so on. The reasons may also include more reasons such as human reproduction, overconsumption, overexploitation, etc.

22. (d): This question is quite direct. For future questions in NTA Exam, let's learn about effects of nitrogen dioxide (NO_2) on human health.

(1) NO_2 as an irritant affecting the mucosa of the eyes, nose, throat and respiratory tract.

(2) Extreme exposure may result in pulmonary edema and diffuse lung injury.

(3) Development of acute or chronic bronchitis.

(4) Low level NO_2 exposure may result in increased bronchial reactivity, obstructive pulmonary disease, respiratory infections, etc.

23. (a): The term pesticides describe hundreds of synthetic and naturally occurring chemicals designed or naturally produced to deter insects and other agricultural pests including weeds. The main chemicals used as pesticides are arsenic, ethylene oxide and lindane.

24. (a): In this concept, Assertion and Reason is related to Post and Neo Malthus theory. According to that, all countries pass through four stages of demographic evolution. It shows the relationship between population growth and the resources present to them. So, according to that theory, here, both Assertion and Reason are true and Reason is the correct explanation of assertion.

25. (d): Chemical contamination refer to a situation where chemicals are present (where they should not be) or are at higher concentrations. Chemical contamination includes plastics, resins, pharmaceuticals, disinfectants, deodorants, detergents, petroleum products, road run-off, pesticides and biocides, along with the results of land fill and incineration.

26. (d): Indian government has set-up a total of 500 MW power capacity by 2030. The installed capacity for renewable energy will be 350 MW by 2030.

For future questions, look at India's Nationally Determined Contributions (INDC) points, they are closely related with such targets.

(1) A reduction in the emissions intensity of its GDP by 33 to 35 per cent by 2030 from 2005 level.

(2) India has also pledged to create an additional carbon sink of 2.5 to 3 billion tonnes of CO_2 equivalent through additional forest and tree cover by 2030.

(3) India will anchor a global solar alliance, INSPA (International Agency for Solar Policy and Application) for all nations located between Tropic of Cancer and Tropic of Capricorn.

27. (c): These are basically BRICS nations.

According to worldpopulationreview.com, the per capita consumption for electricity in kWh per capita for the year 2022 have been given below.

Brazil – 2620

Russia - 6603

India – 805

China – 3927

These are the latest figures, may help in future questions.

28. (a): The motor vehicles and industrial processes contribute the major part of air pollution. According to the WHO, six major air pollutants include particle pollution, ground-level ozone, carbon monoxide, sulfur oxides, nitrogen oxides, and lead. The exposure to Particulate Matter in air impact respiratory and cardiovascular diseases, neuropsychiatric complications, the eyes irritation, skin diseases, and even cancer.

29. (a): There is a large gap between generation and treatment of domestic waste water in India. The problem is not only that India lacks sufficient treatment capacity but also that the sewage treatment plants that exist do not operate and are not maintained.

The largest source of water pollution is major rivers in India with untreated sewage.

30. (b): Millennium Development (2000–2015) and Sustainable Development (2000–2030) Goals are specifically mentioned in latest NTA syllabus.

The 2030 Agenda for Sustainable Development, adopted by all United Nations Member States in 2015, provides a shared blueprint for peace and prosperity for people and the planet, now and into the future. At its heart are the 17 Sustainable Development Goals (SDGs).

31. (d): India has renewable energy generation target of 175 GW by 2022. Of the target capacity, 100 GW would be from solar power, 60 GW from wind, 10 GW from bio-mass and 5 GW from small hydro power.

For future exams, we need to keep in mind, Global Renewable Energy Investors' Meet (RE-INVEST Meet) programs that is supposed to be organized by Ministry of New and Renewable Energy (MNRE). RE-INVEST is a global platform to explore strategies for development and deployment of renewables. It showcases India's clean energy market and the government's efforts to scale up capacity to meet the national energy demand in socially, economically and ecologically sustainable ways.

For future questions, we need to refer to the latest scene, that is of our commitments at Glasgow, 26th COP meet. These commitments have been given the name of Five Nectar Elements called as PanchAmrit.

1. Reach 500 GW Non-fossil energy capacity by 2030.
2. 50 per cent of its energy requirements from renewable energy by 2030.
3. Reduction of total projected carbon emissions by one billion tonnes from now to 2030.
4. Reduction of the carbon intensity of the economy by 45 per cent by 2030, over 2005 levels.
5. Achieving the target of net zero emissions by 2070.

32. (b): Our soil conservation is vital to human lives on earth. They help in plant growth which provide us food, fuels, clothes, raw material for industry.

Soil provides organic matter, water for such things. Thus, assertion is true.

Reasoning is also true as soil is home to required micro organisms and minerals.

The given assertion and reason are right but not connected with each other.

Thus, overall (b) is the correct answer.

33. (b): First point

WMO originated from the International Meteorological Organization (IMO), which was founded in 1873 to facilitate the exchange of weather information across national borders. Established in 1950 in Geneva (Switzerland), the WMO became a specialized agency of the United Nations in 1951.

World Meteorological Day takes place every year on 23 March to commemorate the creation of World Meteorological Organization in 1950. Students should also keep in mind the organizations such as UN office for Disaster Risk Reduction (UNDRR). There are thirteen (13) UN organizations—FAO, UNDP, UNEP, UNFPA, UNHABITAT, UNICEF, UNOPS, WFP, WMO, WHO, UNESCO, UNV and the World Bank—have prioritized disaster risk reduction in their 2014–2017 strategic work plans.

34. (b): Sustainable development can be defined as development that meets the needs of the present without compromising the ability of future generations. We need to learn MDG (2000–2015) and SDG (2015–2030).

35. (a): Exposure to NO_2 in urban traffic conditions is higher than on suburban roads. It is produced as a result of high temperature conditions.

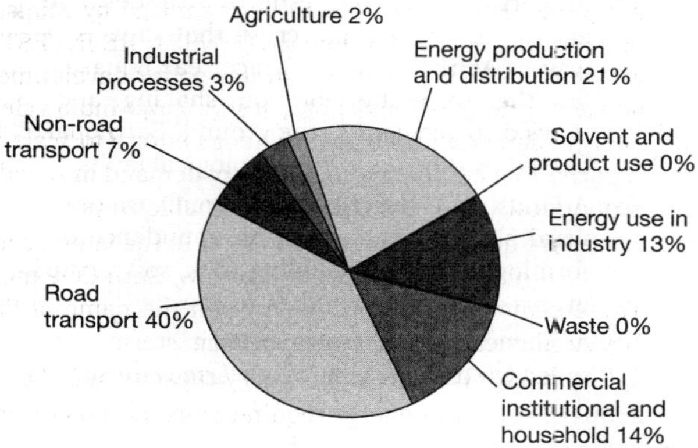

36. (d): What Gives Life, Can Also Take Life. Water borne diseases can be bacterial, parasitic, viral or chemical due to drinking of contaminated water. There are few such diseases.

1. Cholera
2. Typhoid (Enteric fever)
3. Diarrhea
4. Viral Hepatitis A & E

Typhoid fever: This is a bacterial disease spread by drinking or eating contaminated water or food. Typhoid fever is caused by Salmonella typhi bacteria.

Hepatitis: This is basically the inflammation of the liver. The liver is a vital organ that processes nutrients, filters the blood, and fights infections. When the liver is inflamed or damaged, its function can be affected. Heavy alcohol use, toxins, some medications, and certain medical conditions can cause hepatitis.

Cholera is an acute diarrhoeal infection caused by ingestion of food or water contaminated with the bacterium Vibrio cholerae. Cholera remains a global threat to public health and an indicator of inequity and lack of social development.

Viral Hepatitis A and E: It is spread when someone unknowingly ingests the virus — even in microscopic amounts — through close personal contact with an infected person or through eating contaminated food or drink.

Dengue is a viral infection transmitted to humans through the bite of infected mosquitoes. The primary vectors that transmit the disease are Aedes aegypti mosquitoes and, to a lesser extent, Ae. albopictus. The virus responsible for causing dengue, is called dengue virus (DENV).

Among the above, diarrhea is the most widely reported one, followed by typhoid and viral hepatitis. The cases of cholera are very minimal in comparison to these three.

The government wants access of safe drinking water to all. The government launched the National Rural Drinking Water Programme (NRDWP) in 2009, that is now called the Jal Jeevan Mission.

37. (b): The country has set an ambitious target of installing 175 GW of renewable energy capacity by the year 2022, which includes 100 GW from solar, 60 GW from wind, 10 GW from bio power and 5 GW from small hydropower. We need to keep in mind the changes in the form of PanchAmrit that was discussed under question 32.

38. (a): On 15 October 2016, with the United States' leadership, 197 countries adopted an amendment to phase down HFCs under the Montreal Protocol in Kigali, Rwanda. Under the amendment, countries committed to cut the production and consumption of HFCs by more than 80 percent over the next 30 years. The ambitious phase down schedule will avoid more than 80 billion metric tons of carbon dioxide equivalent emissions by 2050—avoiding up to 0.5° Celsius warming by the end of the century—while continuing to protect the ozone layer.

39. (d): Hydrometeorological hazard is 'a process or phenomenon of atmospheric, hydrological or oceanographic nature that may cause loss of life, injury or other health impacts, property damage, loss of livelihoods and services, social and economic disruption, or environmental damage (includes tropical cyclones, thunderstorms, hailstorms, tornados, blizzards, heavy snowfall, avalanches, coastal storm surges, floods including flash floods, drought, heatwaves and cold spells).'

Tsunami is basically related to earthquakes in the sea/oceans.

40. (a): Suspended are basically particulate matters with aerodynamic diameter less than or equal to 10 micrometers, thus also named as PM_{10}. They are produced from combustion processes, vehicles and industrial sources. They get deep into the lungs and cause a broad range of health effects. They cause the following respiratory and cardiovascular problems:

(1) Increasing respiratory symptoms, such as irritation of the airways, coughing, or difficulty in breathing;
(2) Decreasing lung function;
(3) Aggravation of asthma;
(4) Development of chronic bronchitis
(5) Adverse effects on the cardiovascular system; and
(6) Premature death in people with heart or lung disease.

Additionally, there is PM 2.5 which are much more severe.

41. (b): In winter season, the products of incomplete combustion such as PM, VOCs, CO and nitrogen oxides (NOx) load the air. The severity of the resulting winter smog depends on the degree of atmospheric dispersion. The lower the level of atmospheric dispersion, the higher the level of winter smog.

Both A and R are true. However, biomass is mainly used in rural areas. So, option (b) is the right answer.

42. (c): The chlorine and bromine atoms destroy ozone in stratosphere layer. One chlorine atom can destroy over 100,000 ozone molecules. The ozone layer is 15 to 35 kilometres above Earth's surface. The invisible shield of ozone layer protects us from harmful ultraviolet (also called as UV-B) radiation from the sun that is cause of sunburn. UV – C reactions with oxygen increase the amount of ozone in the stratosphere. Stratospheric ozone is called as 'good ozone' while in troposphere, ozone is bad in nature, and is part of pollution.

Thus, we can see that ozone depletion is caused by chlorine, bromine, CFCs, halons etc, that is not a natural hazard.

Land use changes are happening because of urbanization and industrialization.

Climate change refers to long-term shifts in temperatures and weather patterns. The excessive emission of GHGs also play their dubious role.

43. (a): Except chlorofluorocarbons (CFCs), other pollutants in the question are produced naturally. The production of CFCs don't require any natural resource, they are actually produced from various reactions or as a side product. CFCs contain chlorine, fluorine and carbons. They spread out in the atmosphere with the leakage from the refrigeration etc. They deplete ozone layer in the stratosphere. We may refer to answer in question 43 for more details.

44. (d): Hydrogen has the highest calorific value and there is no residue on its burning.

Green hydrogen is defined as hydrogen produced by splitting water into hydrogen and oxygen using renewable electricity. Government has launched National Hydrogen / Ammonia Mission in 2021.

45. (d): Fly ash is the finely divided residue that results from the combustion of pulverized coal and is transported from the combustion chamber by exhaust gases. The most common use of fly ash is as a partial replacement for portland cement used in producing concrete.

46. (d): Drought is the unusual dryness of soil caused by levels of rainfall significantly below average over a prolonged period. Hot dry winds, shortage of water, high temperatures and consequent evaporation of moisture from the ground can also contribute to conditions of drought. Droughts result in crop failure and shortages of water. It has no definite beginning or end.

(a) An earthquake is the result of a sudden release of energy in the Earth's crust that creates seismic waves. At the Earth's surface, earthquakes manifest themselves by vibration, shaking, and sometimes displacement of the ground. Earthquakes are caused by slippage within geological faults.

(b) A landslide is described as an outward and downward slope movement of an abundance of slope-forming materials including rock, soil, artificial, or even a combination of these things.

(c) A hurricane is a large rotating storm with high speed winds that forms over warm waters in tropical areas.

47. (a): The dispersal of air pollutants is rather limited in indoor environment. Indoor sources are associated to anthropogenic activities and the intended use of spaces. In environments a significant role is played by smoking and cooking, followed by heating systems, cleaning, and suspension due to the presence of humans.

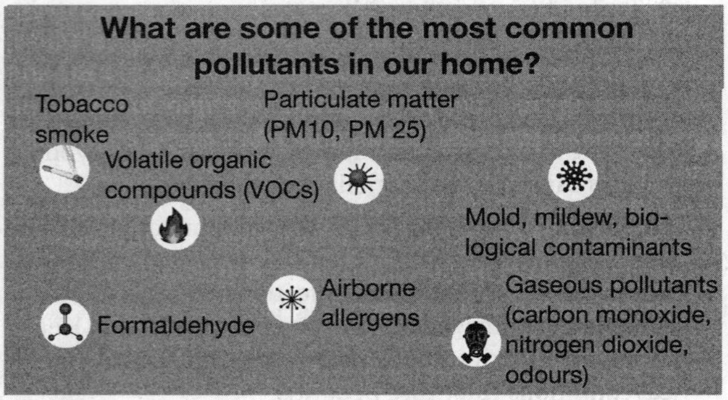

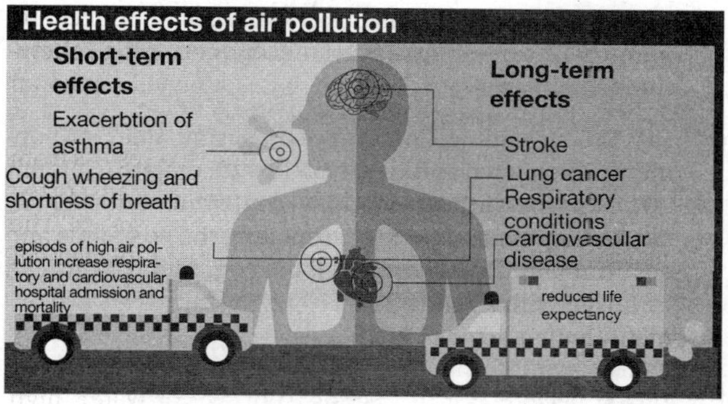

48. (a):

Fuel	MW	% of Total
Total thermal	2,22,693	64.8%
Coal	1,96,958	57.3%
Gas	24,897	7.2%
Oil	838	0.2%
Hydro (Renewable)	45,403	13.2%
Nuclear	6780	2.0%
RES* (MNRE)	69,022	20.1%
Total	343,899	

* **Installed capacity in respect of RES (MNRE) as on 31.03.2018.**

49. (b): Water pollution is major environmental issue in India. The largest source of water pollution in India is untreated sewage. Other sources of pollution include agricultural run-off and unregulated small-scale industry. Most rivers, lakes and surface water in India are polluted dew to industries, untreated sewage and solid wastes.

The most important source of pollution of surface and ground water in India is untreated sewage and there is a large gap between generation and treatment of domestic waste water in India. The problem is not only that India lacks sufficient treatment capacity but also that the sewage treatment plants that exist do not operate and are not well maintained.

50. (b): First discuss something about antibiotic. The overuse of antibiotics in food-producing animals is being blamed for the increase in resistant bacteria, also known as 'superbugs.' When these are passed to humans they can cause serious illness. However, other experts suggest that antibiotic use in food-producing animals poses very little risk to human health.

Infections from common antibiotic-resistant food-borne bacteria, such as Salmonella, can cause more severe health outcomes than infections with bacteria that are not resistant to antibiotics.

51. (d): The main objective of the conservation action is to maintain the essential biological and ecological processes, preserving the genetic diversity, as well as the sustainable use of species and the ecosystem in general.

52. (b): Conserving the environment and preventing soil erosion, desertification, and flooding is essential. Unsustainable farming techniques not only impact natural ecosystems but also ultimately make farming itself impossible.

53. (a): In assertion (A), we can safely assume that exhaustible energy sources include all kinds of non-renewable types of energy generation, such as coal, oil, nuclear or natural gas.

For reason (R), we can use law of conservation of energy. Falling water has in parts both potential energy and kinetic energy.

Additional Information: As question on renewable and non-renewable is important, we need to have a fair idea about them. Please look at the following diagram.

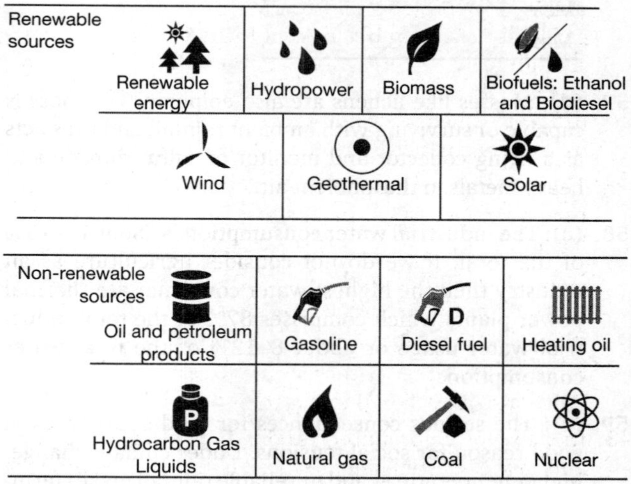

54. (b): After the oceans, the part of soil called as humus, is the largest carbon reservoir. Soils store three times as much carbon as plants and the atmosphere. Soil organic matter such as humus plays a key role in the global carbon cycle as it stores huge amounts of carbon and thus, counters global warming.

Humus, as a part of soil helps in growth of food and energy for the animal food.

Soil acts as natural reservoir of water, it is important part of water cycle or hydrologic cycle or hydrological cycle. It has the continuous movement of water on, above and below the surface of the earth.

55. (b): Some of the most common (and/or most promising) biomass feedstocks are: Grains and starch crops—sugar cane, corn, wheat, sugar beets, industrial sweet potatoes, etc. Agricultural residues—corn stover, wheat straw, rice straw, orchard prunings, etc.

Though biomass is carbon neutral, large amount of land is required for its production. This is dangerous for human beings as crops required for human beings will be replaced for biomass. This may add to food inflation. Ten years back, bout 40% of US corn goes into biofuels. Now 18% of biofuels now used in the UK are made from wheat and corn that are staple foods in the developing world.

56. (c): Earthquakes are classified in categories ranging from minor to great, depending on their magnitude.

Class	Magnitude
Great	8 or more
Major	7–7.9
Strong	6–6.9
Moderate	5–5.9
Light	4–4.9
Minor	3–3.9

57. (d): Mosses like lichens are also epiphyte. The moss is capable of surviving with ambient rainfall and thus acts as a living collector and monitor of sulfur dioxide and heavy metals in the ambient air.

58. (c): The industrial water consumption is about 10–15% of the total. If we do not consider agriculture as an industry then the highest water consumer are thermal power plants which comprises 87% of the total industrial water usage or about 8–12% of the total water consumption.

59. (c): The serious consequences for food security are a good reason for social tensions. Under climate change, higher temperatures and unreliable rainfall makes farming difficult. Climate change not only impacts crop but also livestock, forestry, fisheries and aquaculture, and can cause grave social and economic consequences in the form of reduced incomes, eroded livelihoods, trade disruption and adverse health impacts. The increase in sea level may consume our lands around coastal areas. As per one report, our coastal land may shrink upto 25–30% in coming decades. Intense cyclones such as the recent Fani, Gaja and Hudhud as well as severe floods have caused massive devastation to its coastal states, Odisha, Andhra Pradesh, Tamil Nadu and Kerala, respectively.

In addition to social tensions (food security is an example), there can be upheaval in economic, political tensions as well.

60. (a): United Nations Conference on Sustainable Development, also known as Rio 2012, Rio+20, or Earth Summit 2012 was the third international conference on sustainable development aimed at reconciling the economic and environmental goals of the global community. This can be linked with Agenda 21 of 1992. Sustainable Development Goals started in 2015.

61. (a): Adequate dissolved oxygen is necessary for good water quality. As dissolved oxygen levels in water drop below 5.0 mg/l, aquatic life is put under stress. The lower is the concentration, the greater the stress. Oxygen levels that remain below 1–2 mg/l for a few hours can result in large fish kills.

62. (b): An oligotrophic lake is a lake with low primary productivity, as a result of low nutrient content. These lakes have low algal production, and consequently, often have very clear waters, and abundance of dissolved oxygen with high drinking water quality.

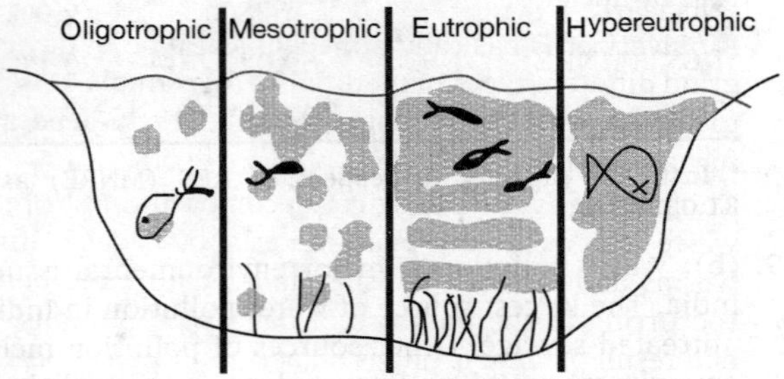

63. (c): Composting is an aerobic method (meaning that it requires the presence of air) of decomposing organic solid wastes. It can therefore be used to recycle organic material. The process involves decomposition of organic material into a humus-like material, known as compost, which is a good fertilizer for plants. Composting organisms require four equally important ingredients—carbon, nitrogen, oxygen and water.

64. (b): Millennium Development Goals are described as a 'roadmap for world development by 2015'. In September 2000, leaders of 189 countries gathered at the UN headquarters to sign MDGs.

65. (b): The main natural carbon sinks are oceans and plants that use photosynthesis to remove carbon from atmosphere and convert it into biomass. Carbon sequestration is also associated with it. More absorption of CO_2 is a 'negative flux', it increases ocean acidification.

Kindly note that colder regions are capable of absorbing more CO_2 than warm regions—Arctic ocean is melting fast and is becoming navigable.

66. (d): Dengue fever is a mosquito-borne tropical disease caused by the dengue virus.

67. (b): Non-renewable energy resources include coal, natural gas, oil, uranium, phosphates etc. Once these resources are used up, they cannot be replaced, which is a major problem for humanity as we are currently dependent on them to supply most of our energy needs.

68. (b): PM means particulate matter, it is a mixture of solid particles and liquid droplets found in the air. $PM_{2.5}$ means fine inhalable particles, with diameters that are generally 2.5 micrometers and smaller.

69. (a): Chlorofluorocarbons were used in aerosols, refrigerators, air conditioners, foam food packaging, and fire extinguishers. Since they deplete ozone layer, they were banned under Montreal protocol (1987). 16 September is International Day for the preservation of the ozone layer.

70. (c): A landfill site is a site for the disposal of waste materials by burial.

A pulverizer is basically a mechanical type of device to grind different types of materials. For example, it is used to pulverize coal for combustion in the steam-generating furnaces of fossil fuel power plants.

Composting is the biological decomposition of organic waste such as food or plant material by bacteria, fungi, worms and other organisms under controlled aerobic (occurring in the presence of oxygen) conditions. The end result of composting is an accumulation of partially decayed organic matter called humus. Composting with worms, also known as vermiculture, results in nutrient-loaded worm castings.

A shredder is a mechanical device used to cut paper or such type of material into either strips or fine particles.

71. (c): Carbon dioxide is basically not a pollutant gas, though carbon monoxide is. We are producing a lot more of carbon dioxide which means that the balance is skewed and the Earth cannot process as much carbon dioxide as it produces. Its production is natural as well as anthropogenic.

The AQI is an index for reporting daily air quality. The AQI is measured on a scale of 0 to 500. The higher the AQI value, the greater the level of air pollution and the greater the health concern. For example, an AQI value of 50 represents good air quality with little potential to affect public health, while an AQI value over 300 represents hazardous air quality.

An AQI value of 100 generally corresponds to the national air quality standard for the pollutant, which is the level Central Pollution Control Board has set to protect public health. AQI values below 100 are generally thought of as satisfactory.

72. (d): National Action Plan on Climate Change (NAPCC) was formally launched on 30 June 2008. They focus on promoting understanding of climate change, adaptation and mitigation, energy efficiency and natural resource conservation.' The specified eight missions are:

(1) National Solar Mission

(2) National Mission for Enhanced Energy Efficiency

(3) National Mission on Sustainable Habitat

(4) National Water Mission

(5) National Mission for Sustaining the Himalayan Ecosystem

(6) National Mission for a Green India

(7) National Mission for Sustainable Agriculture

(8) National Mission on Strategic Knowledge for Climate Change

Government has added National Hydrogen Mission in 2021.

73. (c): Blue baby syndrome can also be caused by nitrates in drinking water leading to methemoglobinemia. Nitrates from polluted drinking water form compounds in the body that change haemoglobin to methemoglobin, decreasing the ability of blood to carry oxygen. In infants, the condition can be fatal.

74. (b): International Solar Alliance (ISA), an alliance of 121 solar resource rich countries lying fully or partially between the Tropics of Cancer and Capricorn. ISA was jointly launched by the Prime Minister, Mr. Narendra Modi, and the then President of France, Mr. François Hollande, on 30 November 2015 in Paris, France on the side-lines of the 21st Conference of Parties (CoP 21) to the United Nations Framework Convention on Climate Change. The ISA Framework Agreement was opened for signature on 15 November 2016 in Marrakech, Morocco, on the side-lines of CoP-22.

75 (d): United Nations Conference on Sustainable Development (UNCSD) – or Rio + 20 took place in Rio de Janeiro, Brazil on 20–22 June 2012. It resulted in a focussed political outcome document which contains clear and practical measures for implementing sustainable development.

76. (c):

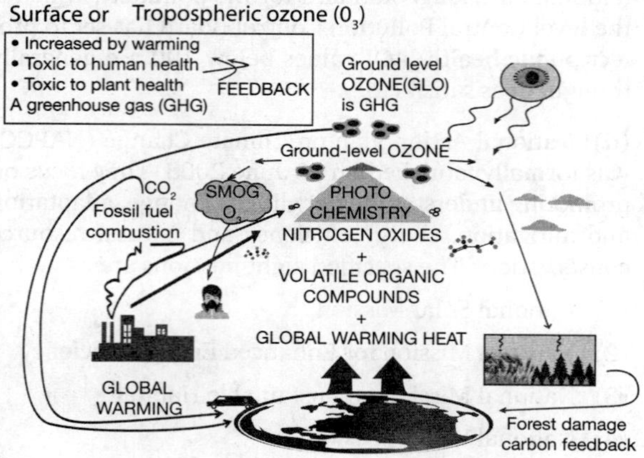

77. (b): Natural hazards are naturally occurring physical phenomena caused either by rapid or slow onset events which can be geophysical (earthquakes, landslides, tsunamis and volcanic activity), hydrological (avalanches and floods), climatological (extreme temperatures, drought and wildfires), meteorological (cyclones and storms/wave surges) or biological (disease epidemics and insect/animal plagues).

Technological or man-made hazards (complex emergencies/conflicts, famine, displaced populations, industrial accidents and transport accidents) are events that are caused by humans and occur in or close to human settlements. This can include environmental degradation, pollution and accidents. Technological or man-made hazards (complex emergencies/conflicts, famine, displaced populations, industrial accidents and transport accidents).

1. **Geological hazards**
   (1) Avalanche
   (2) Earthquake
   (3) Coastal erosion
   (4) Lahar
   (5) Landslide
   (6) Sinkhole
   (7) Volcanic eruption
2. **Meteorological or climate hazards**
   (1) Blizzard
   (2) Drought
   (3) Hailstorm
   (4) Heat wave
   (5) Cyclonic storm
   (6) Ice storm
   (7) Tornado
   (8) Climate change
   (9) Geomagnetic storm
   (10) Flood
   (11) Wildfire

Avalanche: An avalanche occurs when a large snow (or rock) mass slides down a mountainside. An avalanche is an example of a gravity current consisting of granular material. In an avalanche, lots of material or mixtures of different types of material fall or slide rapidly under the force of gravity. Avalanches are often classified by the size or severity of consequences resulting from the event.

78. (b): In September 2000, building upon a decade of major United Nations conferences and summits, world leaders came together at the United Nations Headquarters in New York to adopt the United Nations Millennium Declaration.

The declaration committed nations to a new global partnership to reduce extreme poverty, and set out a series of eight time-bound targets with a deadline of 2015 that have become known as the Millennium Development Goals (MDGs).

79. (a): Kinetic energy is the energy an object has because of its motion. Kinetic energy can be transferred between objects and transformed into other kinds of energy. Potential energy is the stored energy, because of its state of rest.

80. (a): Year 2022 Renewable Energy Targets in India

Source	2022 target (MW)
Wind	60,000
Solar power	100,000
Biomass power (Biomass & Gasification and Bagasse Cogeneration)	10,000
Waste-to-Power	5,000
Small hydropower	175,000

Presently, India has the fourth largest installed wind power capacity in the world.

Currently, Tamil Nadu, Maharashtra, Gujarat, Rajasthan, Karnataka, Andhra Pradesh and Madhya Pradesh are the major states. Wind power accounts for 10% of India's total installed power capacity.

81. (a): Agricultural run-off from farms and lawns is a huge problem for coastal areas. The extra nutrients cause eutrophication, flourishing of algal blooms that deplete the water's dissolved oxygen and suffocate other marine life. Eutrophication has created enormous dead zones in several parts of the world, including the Gulf of Mexico and the Baltic Sea.

82. (b): Arctic Tundra occurs in the far north of the northern hemisphere, north of the Taiga. Characteristically, the subsoil to tundra is usually permafrost, or permanently frozen ground. Any ground remaining at or below 0° C for two or more years is permafrost, it can be from less than one metre to up to 1,000 metres thick.

83. (b): Chemical Oxygen Demand (COD) is the total amount of oxygen required to chemically oxidize the biodegradable and non-biodegradable organic matter. COD is a measure of water and waste water quality. The COD test is often used to monitor water treatment plant efficiency. COD is expressed in milligrams per liter (mg/l).

COD test is often used as an alternate to Biological Oxygen Demand (BOD) due to shorter length of testing time.

84. (c): The definition of sustainable development is given in the question statement itself.

The Sustainable Development Goals (SDGs), also known as the Global Goals, were adopted by all United Nations Member States in 2015 as a universal call to action to end poverty, protect the planet and ensure that all people enjoy peace and prosperity by 2030.

The 17 SDGs are integrated—that is, they recognize that action in one area will affect outcomes in others, and that development must balance social, economic and environmental sustainability.

Through the pledge to 'Leave No One Behind', countries have committed to fast-track progress for those furthest behind first. That is why the SDGs are designed to bring the world to several life-changing 'zeros', including zero poverty, hunger, AIDS and discrimination against women and girls.

85. (d): Mangroves are the only trees that are capable of thriving in salt water. They form unique intertidal forests at the edge of land and sea. The Pichavaram mangroves in Tamil Nadu is India's one of the largest mangrove forests. The Bhitarkanikac Mangroves Forest of Odisha, by the Bay of Bengal, is India's second largest mangrove forest. Other major mangroves occur on the Andaman and Nicobar Islands and the Gulf of Kutch in Gujarat.

86. (b): Let's differentiate between primary and secondary pollutants first.

Primary–Put directly into air from polluting source.

Secondary–When primary combines with other substance in air and creates something more hazardous (acid rain, smong).

Sun often privides energy for these reactions.

Ground level ozone or tropospheric ozone is a colourless and highly irritating gas that forms just above the earth's surface. It is called a 'secondary' pollutant because it is produced when two primary pollutants react in sunlight and stagnant air. These two primary pollutants are nitrogen oxides (NOx) and volatile organic compounds (VOCs).

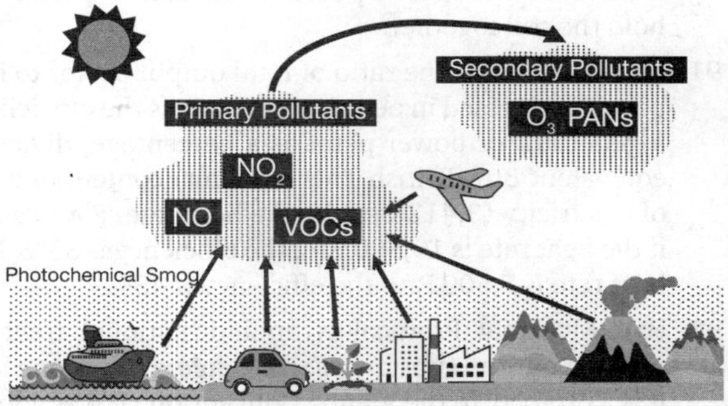

Stratospheric ozone is beneficial as it protects us from some UV related harmful effects from sunlight.

87. (c): (ii) Paris Agreement called for a balance of climate finance between adaptation and mitigation, and specifically underscored the need to increase adaptation support for parties most vulnerable to the effects of climate change, including 'Least Developed Countries and Small Island Developing States'.

(iii) By 2020, we want to see stronger action on climate targets—the Nationally Determined Contributions (NDCs)—of the Paris Agreement. Key to this are a series of events addressing the roadblocks and challenges to bolder climate action, while offering clarity and incentives to scale up ambition. This is the road to 2020, and it requires support from all people, in all countries. We must be 'All in for Climate Action'.

88. (c): Keeping in view our commitment to a healthy planet and our Nationally Determined Contributions as per the Paris Accord on Climate Change, India made a pledge that by 2030, 40% of installed power generation capacity shall be based on clean sources which is approximately 500 GW, it was also determined that 175 GW of renewable energy capacity will be installed by 2022. This includes 100 GW from solar, 60 GW from wind, 10 GW from biopower and 5 GW from small hydropower.

For future questions, students should remember that India has attained global 4th and 5th positions in wind and solar power installed capacities; India is now at 5th global position for overall installed renewable energy capacity.

89. (a): A salt mine is a mine from which salt is extracted. The mined salt is usually in the form of halite (commonly known as rock salt).

Since 1993, ocean disposal has been banned by international treaties.

90. (d): Deforestation is another practice that can greatly increase the rate of erosion in a region. One of the most important barriers to erosion is plant life, as long-lived trees and other species put down roots that literally help hold the soil together.

91. (c): Efficiency is the ratio of total output power to input power, expressed in per cent. To express the efficiency of a generator or power plant as a percentage, divide the equivalent Btu (British Thermal Unit) content of a kWh of electricity (3,412 Btu) by the heat rate. For example, if the heat rate is 10,500 Btu, the efficiency is 33%. If the heat rate is 7,500 Btu, the efficiency is 45%.

92. (b): Montreal Protocol is an international treaty on phasing out the substances that deplete the ozone layer. It is a protocol to the Vienna Convention. It was adopted in Montreal on 16 September 1987.

The main substances meant for complete phasing out are chlorofluorocarbons, halons, carbon tetrachloride, trichloroethane, hydrofluorocarbons (HFCs), hydrochlorofluorocarbons (HCFCs), hydrobromofluorocarbons (HBFCs), and methyl bromide. NET aspirants should remember these names.

93. (a): Arsenic contamination in groundwater in the Ganga- Brahmaputra fluvial plains in India and Padma-Meghna fluvial plains in Bangladesh and its consequences to the human health have been reported as one of the world's biggest natural groundwater calamities to the mankind. In India, seven states namely—West Bengal, Jharkhand, Bihar, Uttar Pradesh in the flood plain of the Ganga River; Assam and Manipur in the flood plain of the Brahamaputra, Imphal river and Rajnandgaon village in Chhattisgarh state have so far been reported affected by arsenic contamination in groundwater above the permissible limit of 10 μg/L. People in these affected states have chronically been exposed to drinking arsenic contaminated hand tube-wells water.

94. (a): Perhaps no seismic subject is as irksome to seismologists as discussions of earthquake size.

First we need to understand wavelength amplitude in statement I and energy in statement II are different concepts. We can try to put them in simple terms.

Statement I is correct. If we move from level 5 to level 6, the wave amplitude (motion) increases by 10 times. If we move from level 6 to 7, wavelength again increases by 10 times. Similarly, it will happen for level 7 to 8. Thus, total wave amplitude will be up by 1000 times, it is by $10 \times 10 \times 10$.

In statement II, when we move from Richter scale 5 to 8, the energy will increase by $32 \times 32 \times 32$ times, and not three times as given in this statement.

95. (a): The air in this place contains serious levels of sulphur oxide and also nitrogen oxide. This is due to the large number of power plants and industries set-up around this area. All these led to acid rain. Acid rain reacted with the marble (calcium carbonate) of Taj Mahal, and causes its yellowing.

96. (c): Cyclone Gaja (2018) hit the Tamil Nadu, Andhra Pradesh and some parts of coastal Puducherry with heavy rainfall in Cuddalore and Pamban.

Cyclone Hudhud (2014) was a strong tropical cyclone, done damage to Visakhapatnam city of Andhra Pradesh. Visakhapatnam or Vizag along with Odisha was mostly affected by Hudhud.

Cyclone Ockhi (2017) from the Arabian Sea affected mainland India along with coastal areas of Kerala, Tamil Nadu and Gujarat.

97. (a): Both assertion and reason are true.

In addition, normally one to two per cent of a person's hemoglobin is methemoglobin; a higher percentage than this can be genetic or caused by exposure to various chemicals and depending on the level can cause health problems known as methemoglobinemia.

Amyl nitrite is administered to treat cyanide poisoning. It works by converting hemoglobin to methemoglobin, which allows for the binding of cyanide and the formation of cyanomethemoglobin.

98. (d): Sustainable Development Goals are a collection of 17 global goals set by the United Nations General Assembly in 2015 for the year 2030.

(1) No Poverty
(2) Zero Hunger
(3) Good Health and Well-being
(4) Quality Education
(5) Gender Equality
(6) Clean Water and Sanitation
(7) Affordable and Clean Energy
(8) Decent Work and Economic Growth
(9) Industry, Innovation and Infrastructure
(10) Reduced Inequality
(11) Sustainable Cities and Communities
(12) Responsible Consumption and Production
(13) Climate Action
(14) Life Below Water
(15) Life on Land
(16) Peace and Justice Strong Institutions
(17) Partnerships to Achieve the Goal

99. (d): In assertion, it should be stratosphere, instead of troposphere, to be true. It helps in Reason (R) so as to be beneficial to us. We can study ozone layer, Montreal protocol for further details.

100. (c): As we can see in the diagram given, algal blooms are least in oligotrophic lakes.

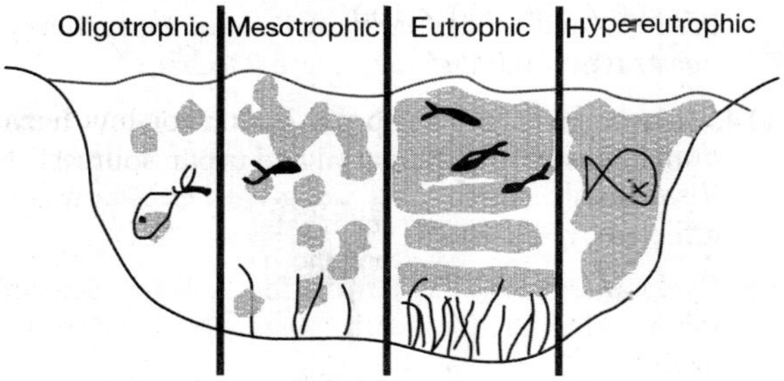

We can look at the following explanation for better idea to attempt such questions in futures.

(1) Oligatrophic–Low levels of organic matter, tend to be deep and clear, oxygen rich bottom supports cold water fish such as trout, phosphrus is limiting.

(2) Mesotrophic–More organic matter, oxygen level in lake bottom is low.

(3) Eutrophic–High levels of organic matter. abundant plant growth, poor clarity'. stratified with oxygen poor bottoms.

(4) A dead zone is an area where oxygen level fall below 2 ppm.

101. (d): India has become the cheapest producer of solar power. In 2010, the total installed solar capacity was 10 MW. In 2016, the installed capacity stood at 6000 MW—a steep climb of 600 times in just 6 years. As of March 2019, the total installed solar capacity stands at 30 GW, accounting for an increase of 5 times in 3 years. Today, solar power has reached 30% of the 2022 target of 100 GW contributing 38% to the renewable energy mix.

The Ladakh region in J&K is colloquially known as the 'solar capital' of India as the city receives solar radiations in its most pristine condition.

102. (b): India's wind energy sector is led by indigenous wind power industry and has shown consistent progress.

The expansion of the wind industry has resulted in a strong ecosystem, project operation capabilities and manufacturing base of about 10,000 MW per annum. The country currently has the fourth highest wind installed capacity in the world with total installed capacity of 35.62 GW (as on 31st March 2019) and

62 Billion Units were generated from wind power during 2018-19.

103. (b): The first practical photovoltaic cell was developed in 1954 at Bell Laboratories. They used a diffused silicon p–n junction. Most practical solar cells are silicon based, because it is cheap and abundant available material.

104. (a): Biomass releases carbon dioxide, a greenhouse gas. However, the plants that are the sources of biomass for energy capture almost the same amount of CO_2 through photosynthesis while growing as is released when biomass is burned which can make biomass a carbonneutal energy source. For example, declaring that biomass energy is carbon neutral because biomass is naturally carbon neutral does not account of GHG emissions released due to management of crops grown for energy production. For example, fertiliser.

105. (b): A drought or drouth is an event of prolonged shortages in the water supply, whether atmospheric (below-average precipitation), surface water or ground water. A drought can last for months or years, or may be declared after as few as 15 days.

106. (c): Agricultural Runoff is water sent from farm fields due to irrigation, rain, or melted snow. This runoff water can contain fertilizers, pesticides, animal waste, or soil particles, which can enter and contaminate sources of drinking water. Agricultural Runoff has been a growing issue for lakes and rivers for oxygen demand.

In food processing industry, organic matter at their places may demand higher oxygen.

Sewage effluents are also rich in organic matter.

107. (d): Under Kyoto protocol, the parties in the second commitment period have to reduce their greenhouse gas emissions with reference to 1990 levels by at least 18%.

108. (a): It is a type of natural resource that can be replenished or takes a rather short period of time for nature to produce to sustain the rate of consumption. This type of natural resource is easier to reproduce or replenish.

109. (d): For future questions, we should try to understand the differences between "National Park' and "Wild-life Sanctuary'.

National Park	Wildlife Sanctuary
A national park Is a more restricted area as compared to wildlife sanctuary. Random access to people is not allowed	Wildlife sanctuary is not a very restricted area. It Is open to general public.
Tickets or permissions are required to enter into a national park.	Tickets or permissions are not required to visit a wildlife sanctuary
A national park has a definite boundary.	A wildlife sanctuary does not have a specific boundary
General public cannot use the park for collecting any materials like fruits, firewood.	General public cannot use the park for collecting any materials like fruits, firewood.
Example: Jim Corbett national park (Gujarat)	Example: Krishna wildlife sanctuary (Andhra Pradesh)

110. (c): The size of soil particles gives texture to the soil. It also determines the amount of air and moisture that exist in the soil. They can be arranged in the following manner, in terms of size.

1. **Clay**: Clay has the smallest particles. A particle measures less than 0.002 mm. It feels sticky when wet. It absorbs water well and it is nutrient rich.
2. **Silt**: Silt particles measures 0.06 to 0.002 mm. Silt's particles are larger than clay particles but smaller than sand particles.
3. **Sand**: Sand particles measures 2.0 mm to 0.06 mm. Sand is the largest type of soil particle. It allows quick drainage and plenty of airflow.
4. **Gravel**: Gravel is a loose aggregation of rock fragments. Gravel is classified by particle size range and Include size classes from granule to boulder size fragments.

111. (a): A fuel cell is an electrochemical cell that converts the chemical energy of a fuel (often hydrogen) and an oxidizing agent (often oxygen) into electricity through a pair of redox reactions. Fuel cells can produce electricity continuously for as long as fuel and oxygen are supplied. Every fuel cell has two electrodes called, respectively, the anode and cathode.

112. (a): The basic definitions have been given in the question itself. There are basically twelve orders of soil. They can be seen in detail at www.globalrangelands.org/topics/rangeland-ecology/twelve-soil-orders

113. (a): Greenhouse gases cause the greenhouse effect on planets. The primary greenhouse gases in Earth's atmosphere are water vapor carbon dioxide, methane, nitrous oxide and ozone.

Concentration of CO_2

= 400 Parts Per Million

$= 400 / 1000000 \times 100$

$= 4/100 = 0.04\%$

114. (a): Sequences of disposal option for low hazardous solid waste from industrial and urban sources.

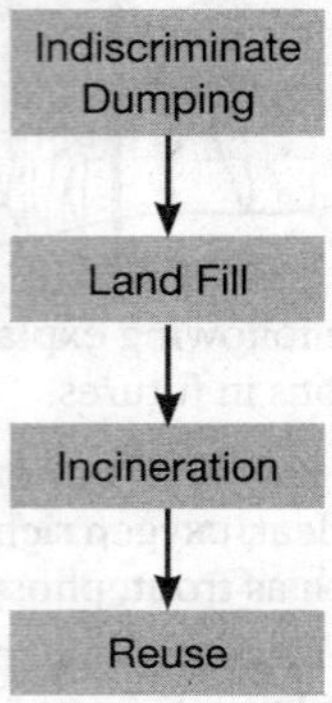

115. (d): Biomass is basically a plant-based material that is used as fuel to produce heat or electricity. The main examples are wood and wood residues, energy crops, agricultural residues, and waste from industry, farms and households.

Calorific value (or heating value or heat of combustion) is a standard that measures the total energy content produced in the form of heat when a substance is combusted completely with air or oxygen.

The coconut shell has scattered hair like structures, dung (dry) is dried in sun light. Unsorted domestic use may not be properly defined.

116. (a): There are following group of diseases caused by polluted water.

1. **Cholera:** Cholera is an infectious disease that causes severe watery diarrhea, which can lead to dehydration and even death if untreated. It is caused by eating food as drinking water contaminated with a bacterium called vibrio Cholera.
2. **Typhoid:** The typhoid bacillus is transmitted by consumption of contaminated food or water. Flies may cause human infection through transfer of the infectious agents to foods. Pollution of water sources may produce epidemics of typhoid fever when large numbers of people use the same source of drinking water.

3. **Enteritis:** It is most often caused by eating or drinking things that are contaminated with bacteria or viruses. The germs settle in the small intestine and cause inflammation and swelling. Enteritis may also cause by: An autoimmune condition, such as crohn disease.
4. **Tuberculosis:** A potentially serious infectious bacterial disease that mainly affects the lungs. The bacteria that cause TB are spread when an infected person coughs or sneezes.

117. (b): National Disaster Management Authority, abbreviated as NDMA is an agency of the Ministry of Home Affairs to considerate response to natural or man-made disasters and for capacity building in disaster resiliency and crisis response.

The National Disaster Management Authority (NDMA) is the apex statutory body for disaster management in India.

The NDMA was formally constituted on 27th September 2006, in accordance with the Disaster Management Act, 2005 with Prime Minister as its Chairperson and nine other members, and one such member to be designated as Vice-Chairperson.

118. (a): Biosphere reserves are areas of terrestrial and coastal ecosystems promoting solutions to reconcile the conservation of biodiversity with its sustainable use. They are internationally recognised, nominated by national government and remain under sovereign jurisdiction of the states, where they are located.

Biosphere reserves help ensure the environmental, economic and social sustainability of the region by encouraging wise use of natural and human resources.

119. (b): Green building refers to both the structure and the application of processes that are environmentally responsible and resource-efficient throughout a building life cycle from planning to design, construction operation maintenance, renovation and demolition.

The common objective of green building is to reduce the overall impact of the build environment on human health and the natural environment by accomplishing the following.

1. Efficiently using energy, water and other resources.
2. Protecting occupant health and improving employee productivity.
3. Reducing wastes, pollution and environmental degradation.

120. (d): Nuclear energy is the fifth-largest source of electricity for India. India also stands at seventh position in terms of the number of nuclear reactors, with over 23 nuclear reactors in 7 power plants across the country which produces 6780 MW of nuclear power.

Nuclear Power Plants at Kaiga (Karnataka), Gorakhpur – Fatehabad, Mahi Banswara (Rajasthan) and Chutka (Madhya Pradesh) are to start power production in 2-3 years.

India is now trying to rely more on Thorium as a nuclear fuel as we have sufficient reserves of it. Unlike uranium, thorium alone cannot be directly used as nuclear fuel in a reactor.

121. (c): Methane (CH_4) is one of the trace gases in the atmosphere that is considered to play a major role in what is called 'greenhouse effect'. There are six major sources of atmospheric methane.

1. Natural wetland.
2. Paddy rice.
3. Emission from livestock production system (including intrinsic fermentation and animal waste).
4. Biomass burning (including forest fires and firewood burning).
5. Anaerobic decomposition of organic waste in landfills.
6. Fossil methane emission during the explanation and transportation of fossil fuels..

122. (b): The montreal protocol on substances that deplete the ozone layer is an international treaty designed to protect the ozone layer by phasing out the production of numerous substances that are responsible for ozone depletion. It was agreed on 16 September, 1987 and entered into Force on 26 August 1989 following a first meeting in Helsinki May 1989.

123. (d): Sustainable development is development that meets the needs of the present without compromising the ability of future generations to meet their own needs.

In September 2015, the UN General Assembly adopted the 2030 Agenda for Sustainable Development that includes 17 Sustainable Development Goals (SDGs). Building on the principle of "leaving no one behind", the new Agenda emphasizes a holistic approach to achieving sustainable development for all.

The 17 SDGs can be seen in solution for question number 99.

124. (c): (a) Andhra Pradesh – Mukhyamantri Jal Swavalamban Abhiyan
(b) Gujrat – Jalyukt Shivar Abhiyan
(c) Maharashtra – Neeti Samrakshana Udyamam
(d) Rajasthan – Sujalam Sufalam Jal Abhiyan

125. (c): Intended nationally determined contributions are (intended) reductions in green house gas emissions under the United Nations framework convention on climate change. All countries that signed that UNFCCC were asked to publish their INDC at the 2013 United Nations climate change conferences held in Warsaw, Poland in November, 2013. The intended contribution was determined without prejudice to the legal nature of the contributions. The term was intended as a compromise between "quantified emissions limitations and reduction objective and "Nationally appropriate mitigation actions" (NAMAs) that the Kyoto Protocol used to describe the different legal obligations of developed and developing countries. As per provisions of Paris Agreement the intended nationally determined contribution are to be reviewed every 5 years.

126. (d)

Aggressive behavior by teachers can cause physical or emotional harm to others. It can involve harming personal property and violates social boundaries.

The three aggression types are – comprised reactive-expressive (verbal and physical aggression), reactive-inexpressive (hostility), and proactive-relational aggression (aggression that can break human relationships, such as spreading rumours).

The use of teachers' assessment is one way of examining individual aggressors, and this is done by analyzing individual abilities, their achievements, inspiration level, and the self-esteem of an individual.

Teachers are trained properly to check the aggressive behaviour so that learning environment stays peaceful for objective learning.

127. (c): The Eight millennium development Goals are:

1. To eradicate extreme poverty and hunger.
2. To achieve universal primary education.
3. To promote gender equality and empower women.
4. To reduce child mortality.
5. To improve maternal health.
6. To combat HIV/AIDS, malaria and other diseases.
7. To ensure environmental sustainability
8. To develop a global partnership for development.

Thus 'ensure healthy lives and promote well being for all at all ages' was not a 'Millennium Development Goal'.

128. (d): The following are basically qualitative concepts about environment:

1. Environmental awareness means being aware about general issues of natural environment. We need to make choices that benefit the earth, rather than hurt it.
2. Environmental knowledge is the information about environment and the ability to understand and evaluate its impact on society and the environment.
3. Environmental attitudes are a psychological tendency expressed by evaluative responses to the natural environment with some degree of favor or disfavor.
4. Environmental skills refer to the knowledge, abilities, values and attitude required to live in, develop and support a society which reduces the impact of human activity on the environment.

129. (a): For sound intensity (the power of the sound waves per unit of area), 0 decibels is equal to 1 pico watt per square meter. This corresponds approximately to the faintest sound that can be detected by a person who has good hearing. A quiet room has a normal sound intensity of around 40 decibels, ten thousand times louder than the faintest perceptible sound, and a thunderclap may have an intensity of 120 decibels, a trillion times louder than the faintest sound.

130. (a): Photochemical smogs are formed by the action of sunlight on oxides of nitrogen, and the subsequent reactions with hydrocarbons. Photochemical smogs were first identified in Los Angeles in the mid-1940s. These smogs act as bronchial irritants and can also irritate the eyes. Among the pollutants involved in photochemical smogs are ozone, nitrogen dioxide and peroxyacyl nitrate (PAN).

131. (d): 1. Montreal Protocol (1987) on Substances that deplete the ozone layer were finalized to control the consumption and production of anthropogenic ozone-depleting substances (ODSs) and some hydrofluorocarbons (HFCs). September 16 is celebrated as World Ozone Day. A UN study 'Scientific Assessment of Ozone Depletion: 2018', has shown that the ozone layer is recovering at a rate of 1-3% per decade. The stratospheric ozone layer protects life on earth from harmful UV radiation.

2. **Paris Agreement** is a legally binding international treaty on climate change. It was adopted by 196 Parties at COP 21 in Paris, on 12 December 2015 and entered into force on 4 November 2016. Its goal is to limit global warming to well below 2, preferably to 1.5 degrees Celsius, compared to pre-industrial levels. Intended Nationally Determined Contributions are (intended) reductions in greenhouse gas emissions declared by different nations so that they are more serious about them.
3. **National Action Plan for Climate Change:** It is a Government of India's programme launched in 2008 to mitigate and adapt to the adverse impact of climate change. The action plan was launched in 2008 with eight sub-missions. Two missions were added later. These missions can be seen in Unit 9.

4. **Kyoto Protocol:** It is an international agreement that aimed to reduce carbon dioxide (CO_2) emissions and the presence of greenhouse gases (GHG) in the atmosphere. It speaks about 'common but differentiated responsibilities'. This protocol required that industrialized nations needed to lessen the amount of their CO_2 emissions to a previous year level. It was signed in 1997 as a part of UNFCCC, and was to be implemented from 2005. The Kyoto Protocol applies to the six greenhouse gases listed in Annex A: carbon dioxide (CO_2), Methane (CH_4), nitrous oxide (N_2O), hydrofluorocarbons (HFCs), perfluorocarbons (PFCs), and sulfur hexafluoride (SF_6).

132. (a): The 'trophic status' of lakes is the central concept in the management of lakes. It describes the relationship between nutrient status of a lake and the growth of organic matter in the lake. Eutrophication is the process of change from one trophic state to a higher trophic state by the addition of nutrient. Agriculture is a major factor in eutrophication of surface waters.

133. (d): The most of nuclear reactors use enriched uranium (U-235) or reprocessed plutonium (Pu-239) as fuel (in the Uranium-Plutonium cycle), and only a handful have used thorium.

Thorium itself will not split and release energy. Rather, when it is exposed to neutrons, it will undergo a series of nuclear reactions until it eventually emerges as an isotope of uranium called U-233, which will readily split and release energy next time it absorbs a neutron. Thorium is therefore called fertile, whereas U-233 is called fissile. China and India both have substantial reserves of Thorium-bearing minerals and not as much Uranium. India has the world's third largest reserves of thorium. As discussed, thorium cannot be used as a fuel in its natural state. It needs to be converted into its usable "fissile" form after a series of reactions.

134. (d): Polychlorinated biphenyls are heavy, syrupy hydrocarbons, they conduct heat but not electricity and are water-insoluble, fire-resistant, and extremely stable in high temperature conditions. They are used to manufacture components in cooling systems and electrical equipment (transformers and capacitors) and also in the composition of sealants, rubber, paints, plastics, inks, and insecticides.

PCBs were banned in 1979, after researchers linked them to cancer and developmental problems in humans. They have an affinity for fat, so they can stay longer to accumulate in living organisms. They become dangerous as increasing as they move up the food chain.

They occur in warehouses, landfills, and even rivers, uncontrolled or abandoned hazardous wastes still remained. To control them, Superfund Program, was created by the Environmental Protection Agency (EPA).

135. (a): Bituminous coal or black coal is a relatively soft coal containing a tarlike substance called bitumen or asphalt. It is of higher quality than lignite and Sub-bituminous coal, but of poorer quality than anthracite. Formation is usually the result of high pressure being exerted on lignite. Carbon content has 60 – 80 percent carbon contents. The ash content is 6 – 12 percent. The higher amount of carbon dioxide is the result of higher carbon contents. The other options don't have that much percentage.

136. (a): Under the Paris Agreement, countries are invited to communicate long-term low greenhouse gas emission development strategies (LEDS), takinginto account their common but differentiated responsibilities and respective capabilities, in the light of different national circumstances.

137. (b): We are given in the question that the ratio of two intensities is 2 to 1. We are then supposed to find out the difference in their sound levels in decibels. We can solve this problem using of the properties of logarithms. The answer is approximately three decibels.

138. (a): Statement 1: Diesel engine, like other internal combustion engines, converts chemical energy contained in the fuel into mechanical power. Diesel fuel is a mixture of hydrocarbons which—during an ideal combustion process—would produce only carbon dioxide (CO_2) and water vapor (H_2O). Common pollutants include unburned hydrocarbons (HC), carbon monoxide (CO), nitrogen oxides (NOx) or particulate matter (PM).

Statement 2: Total concentration of pollutants in diesel exhaust gases typically amounts to some tenths of one percent. Much lower, 'near-zero' levels of pollutants are emitted from modern diesel engines equipped with emission aftertreatment devices such as NOx reduction catalysts and particulate filters.

139. (b): Here, we have taken a broad view to deal with future questions. Since 1972, United Nations Environment Programme (UNEP) has been the global authority to set the environmental agenda, the concept of 'sustainable development' for future generations and an authoritative advocate for the global environment. UNEP is headquartered in Nairobi, Kenya. It has 193 Member States and representatives from civil society, businesses, etc. through the UN Environment Assembly, the world's highest–level decision–making body on the environment.

UNEP's Medium–Term Strategy (MTS) articulates its role in delivering the promises of the '2030 Agenda for Sustainable Development and the United Nations Conference on Sustainable Development (Rio+20) as well as its outcome document, **"The Future We Want**."

Through its campaigns, particularly 'World Environment Day' (June 5), UNEP raises awareness and advocates for effective environmental action. The Day was established in 1972 by the UN at 'Stockholm Conference on the Human Environment' (5–16 June, 1972). This day is connected with the launch of 'UN Decade on Ecosystem Restoration 2021–2030'.

A step further, UNEP can be further linked with UN Framework Convention on Climate Change (UNFCCC), Conference of Parties (COPs), Kyoto Protocol, Paris Agreement and COP26 Glasgow meeting asking for Zero Emissions. World seems to have set Year 2050 as the target year for Zero Emissions and India has set Year 2070 for its own emissions during Glasgow COP26 Meeting.

140. (c): Sustainable Development Goals (SDGs)

SDGs, also known as the Global Goals, were adopted by the United Nations in 2015 as a universal call to action to end poverty, protect the planet, and ensure that by 2030 all people enjoy peace and prosperity.

The 17 SDGs are integrated—they recognize that action in one area will affect outcomes in others, and that development must balance social, economic and environmental sustainability.

The 17 SDGs can be seen in solution for question number 99.

141. (b): Cerebrum: Cerebrum, the largest and uppermost portion of the brain. The cerebrum consists of the cerebral hemispheres and accounts for two–thirds of the total weight of the brain.

Hippocampus: It is a small, curved formation in the brain that plays an important role in the limbic system. It is involved in the formation of new memories and is also associated with learning and emotions.

Hence, the Hippocampus region is involved in our ability to learn new information, particularly if it is verbal.

Pons: It is a portion of the hindbrain that connects the cerebral cortex with the medulla oblongata. It also serves as a communications and coordination centre between the two hemispheres of the brain.

Thalamus: The thalamus functions as a **relay station** in which sensory pathways of the spinal cord and brainstem form synapses on their way to the cerebral cortex. Specific locations in the thalamus are related to specific areas on the body surface and in the cerebral cortex.

142. (a): According to Urie Bronfenbrenner's biological model of human development, microsystem constitutes immediate family, schools and neighbourhood.

143. (a): Statement I: small amount of atmospheric Nitrogen dioxide is produced from polluting sources.

NO_2 is an intermediate in the industrial synthesis of nitric acid. It is largely used in the production of fertilisers also. At higher temperatures, it is a reddish–brown gas. It can be fatal if inhaled in large quantity.

Statement II: Most of the atmospheric NO_2 is produced due to photochemical reactions in the atmosphere.

Nitrogen dioxide, NO_2, present in air is known to be photochemically active due to the presence of an unpaired electron. NO_2 molecule reaches a higher level of energy when it absorbs a photon of light with energy, which converts the ground state molecule to electronically excited state molecule. NO_2, Ozone and PAN show photochemical reactions and photochemical smog is formed.

144. (b): Diarrhoea is a type of waterborne disease which is caused by virus, bacteria and protozoa. The main symptoms of diarrhea are frequent loose, watery stools and a pressing urge to have a bowel movement. The most common causes of acute and persistent diarrhea are infections, travelers' diarrhea, and side effects of medicines. Many viruses cause diarrhea, including norovirus link and rotavirus link. Viral gastroenteritis is a common cause of acute diarrhea.

145. (d): The top six states with installed wind power capacity on 31.03.2019 are: Tamil Nadu, Gujarat, Maharashtra, Karnataka, Rajasthan and Andhra Pradesh

146. (a): In India according to NITI Ayog's SDG Index Gujarat and the Kerala is the best performing state on SDG 9 (Industry, Innovation and Infrastructure).

SDG India Index is an index prepare by the NITI Ayog to measure the progress of the country and that of individual states based on the United Nations initiated Sustainable Development Goals (SDG). The purpose the NITI Ayog index is to estimate the progress of Indian states and UTs through a single measurable index that would serve as a policy tool and initiate action at the state level.

Here, we may talk about Good Governance Index – 2021 as well, under which Gujarat is at the first place. Maharashtra is at second place and Goa at third place. Gujarat has excelled in economic administration, human resource development, public infrastructure and facilities, social welfare and development and judicial and public security.

147. (b): The country currently has the fourth highest wind installed capacity in the world with total installed capacity of 39.25 GW (as on 31st March 2021) and has generated around 60.149 billion units during 2020–21.

Potential of Wind Energy in India

The Government, through National Institute of Wind Energy (NIWE), has installed over 800 wind-monitoring stations all over the country and issued wind potential maps at 50m, 80m, 100m and 120m above ground level. The recent assessment indicates a gross wind power potential of 302 GW in the country at 100 metres and 695.50 GW at 120 metres above ground level. Most of this potential exists in seven windy states given below:

S. No.	State	Wind Energy Potential (1000 m GW)	Wind Potential at 120 m (GW)
1.	Gujarat	84.43	142.56
2.	Rajasthan	18.77	127.75
3.	Maharashtra	45.39	98.21
4.	Tamil Nadu	33.79	68.75
5.	Madhya Pradesh	10.48	15.40
6.	Karnataka	55.85	124.15
7.	Andhra Pradesh	44.22	74.90

Thus, the correct sequence of wind energy potential at 100 m above ground level in decreasing order are as:

Gujarat > Karnataka> Andhra Pradesh > Tamil Nadu > Andaman and Nicobar Islands

148. (a): Geothermal power plants provide electricity consistently running 24 hours per day, 7 days a week, regardless of weather conditions. The power output of a geothermal power plant is highly predictable and stable. The disadvantages of geothermal power plant location is restricted and also runs the risk of triggering earthquakes. This is due to alterations in the Earth's structure as a result of constant digging.

Nuclear power is the only energy source that delivers carbon-free, reliable energy 24 hours a day. Along with wind, solar, and energy storage, nuclear has a vital role in our carbon-free future.

It is a Carbon-Free Energy. We can get 24/7/365 days. The advantages include:

- Nuclear energy is carbon-free.
- Nuclear energy is reliable.
- Nuclear energy is powerful.

149. (c): In agricultural areas, groundwater can contain significant concentration of the nitrate pollutant. When pollutants released on the Earth's surface enter the groundwater, it leads to groundwater pollution. Pollution can result from workplace sanitation systems, landfills, waste from wastewater treatment plants, sewer leaks, petrol filling stations, or overuse of fertilizers in agriculture. Therefore, groundwater in agricultural areas can contain significant amounts of the nitrate pollutant.

Cadmium: Cadmium is a chemical element with the symbol Cd and atomic number 48.

Lead: Lead is a naturally occurring toxic metal found in the Earth's crust. Its widespread use has resulted in widespread environmental pollution, human exposure and public health problems in many parts of the world.

Selenium: Selenium is a toxic element and its high concentration is not only harmful to the environment but also to human health. It causes thyroid disorders, viral infections, preeclampsia (high blood pressure), swelling, etc.

150. (c): Greenhouse gases are atmospheric gases that absorb and emit radiation within the thermal infrared range, thereby, contributing to the greenhouse effect and global climate change. Many different greenhouse gases are produced as a result of human activities, including:

1. Carbon dioxide (CO_2)
2. Methane (CH_4)
3. Nitrous Oxide (N_2O)
4. Hydrofluorocarbons (HFCs)

Perfluorinated compounds:

5. Sulphur Hexafluoride (SF_6)
6. Nitrogen trifluoride (NF_3)
7. Perfluorocarbons (PFCs)
8. Fluorinated Ether (HFE)
9. Per-Flouro Poly Ether (PFPE)
10. Chlorofluorocarbons (CFCs)
11. Hydrochlorofluorocarbons (HCFC)

Even water vapour is a GHG.

At the Rio Earth Summit in 1992, international negotiators adopted the United Nations Framework Convention on Climate Change (UNFCCC). UNFCCC aims to prevent dangerous human interference with the climate system by stabilizing atmospheric concentrations of GHGs at safe levels. The UNFCCC itself has not set any mandatory limits on GHG emissions for individual countries and has no enforcement mechanism. Instead, the UNFCCC provides updates (the 'protocol') that set mandatory emissions limits. The

Kyoto Protocol was adopted in 1997 and came into force in 2005. It set GHG emission reduction targets for a set of industrialized countries. These targets have been implemented in the emission reduction commitment period with the first period from 2008 to 2012 and the second period from 2013 to 2020. More than 190 countries have ratified the UNFCCC and its Kyoto Protocol.

The Kyoto Protocol aims to cut GHG emissions in the developed world by about 5% by 2012 compared to 1990 levels. In India, the Kyoto Protocol was implemented in February 2005. Kyoto Protocol applies to 6 greenhouse gases; Carbon dioxide (CO_2), methane (CH_4), nitrous oxide (N_2O), hydrofluorocarbons (HFCs), perfluorocarbons (PFCs), sulphur hexafluoride (SF_6). The seventh gas nitrogen trifluoride (NF_3) was added at a later stage.

The Intergovernmental Panel on Climate Change (IPCC) has been assisting the UNFCCC in setting national goals to develop a scientific summary of the climate system and the physical basis of climate change. This summary is updated from time to time and published in the IPCC Assessment Report. The Sixth Report (AR6) was published in the year 2021.

The IPCC - AR establishes values for the Global Warming Potential of various green gases. GWP values describe the radiative effect of a given unit of GHG relative to (in comparison to) one unit of CO_2.

According to the latest development, the world has set the year 2050 as the threshold for achieving the Zero Emissions target.

151. (b): Noise is defined as unwanted sound, where it is an irritant and a source of stress. Sound is measured in decibel (dB). It follows a logarithmic scale and not a linear scale. The threshold of hearing is assigned a sound level of 0 decibel.

The resultant of the two noise levels of 81 dB and 90 dB generated by two independent sources is 91 dB.

152. (a): 1. The **Montreal Protocol on Substances that Deplete the Ozone Layer** was finalized in 1987 to control the consumption and production of anthropogenic ozone-depleting substances (ODSs) and some hydrofluorocarbons (HFCs). September 16 is celebrated as World Ozone Day. A UN study titled 'Scientific Assessment of Ozone Depletion: 2018', has shown that the ozone layer is recovering at a rate of 1–3% per decade. The stratospheric ozone layer protects life on earth from harmful UV radiation.

2. The **Paris Agreement** is a legally binding international treaty on climate change. It was adopted by 196 countries at COP 21 in Paris on 12 December 2015 and entered into force on 4 November 2016. Its goal is to limit global warming to well below 2, preferably to 1.5 degrees Celsius compared to pre-industrial levels. Intended Nationally Determined Contributions are (intended) reductions in greenhouse gas emissions declared by different nations so that they are more serious about them.

3. The **International Solar Alliance (ISA)** is an alliance of 121 solar resource-rich countries lying fully or partially between the Tropics of Cancer and Capricorn. The ISA was jointly launched by Prime Minister Narendra Modi, and the then President of France, François Hollande, on 30 November 2015 in Paris, France on the sidelines of the 21st Conference of Parties (CoP 21) at the United Nations Framework Convention on Climate Change. The ISA Framework Agreement was opened for signature on 15 November 2016 in Marrakech, Morocco, on the sidelines of the CoP-22.

4. The **Kyoto Protocol** is a Clean Development Mechanism that aimed to reduce carbon dioxide (CO_2) emissions and the presence of greenhouse gases (GHG) in the atmosphere. It spoke about 'common but differentiated responsibilities'. This protocol required that industrialized nations needed to lessen the amount of their CO_2 emissions to a previous year level. It was signed in 1997 as a part of UNFCCC and was implemented from 2005. The Kyoto Protocol applies to the six greenhouse gases listed in Annex A: carbon dioxide (CO_2), Methane (CH_4), nitrous oxide (N_2O), hydrofluorocarbons (HFCs), perfluorocarbons (PFCs) and sulphur hexafluoride (SF_6).

153. (a): Solar flat plate collectors essentially work on the principle of Green House Effect.

Black absorber plate radiates infrared radiations. Thus, both statement I and II are correct.

154. (d): The correct decreasing order of the percentage of world's water is as follows:

Ice caps and glaciers > ground water > lakes (fresh water) > atmosphere > river and streams

155. (a): Sustainable Development Goal (SDG) 7: Ensure access to affordable, reliable, sustainable and modern energy for all

The targets under SDG 7 by 2030 are:

(a) Ensure universal access to affordable, reliable and modern energy services

(b) Increase substantially the share of renewable energy in the global energy mix

(c) Double the global rate of improvement in energy efficiency

(d) Enhance international cooperation to facilitate access to clean energy research and technology – including renewable energy, energy efficiency and advanced and cleaner fossil-fuel technology, and promote investment in energy infrastructure and clean energy technology

(e) Expand infrastructure and upgrade technology for supplying modern and sustainable energy services for all in developing countries, least developed countries, small island developing States, and land-locked developing countries, in accordance with their respective programmes of support

Thus, by the year 2030, SDG 7 aims at enhancing the global rate of improvement in energy efficiency by a factor of two.

156. (c): According to the Sustainable Development Report 2020, the top-ranked country on the basis of the SDG Index is Sweden with a score of 85.61 ranked 2nd. Finland ranked 1, having an overall score of 85.90. India secured the 120th position with a score of 60.07, and Central African Republic is the worst-performing country. The 2022 SDG Index is topped by Finland, followed by three Nordic countries –Denmark, Sweden and Norway.

The key findings the report are as follows:

1. An estimated 71 million people are expected to be pushed back into extreme poverty in 2020, which indicates the first rise in global poverty since 1998. Lost incomes, limited social protection and rising prices mean even those who were previously secure could find themselves at the risk of poverty and hunger.
2. Underemployment and unemployment due to the crisis mean that some 1.6 billion workers in the informal economy who are already vulnerable – i.e., half of the global workforce – may be significantly affected, with their incomes estimated to have fallen by 60 per cent in the first month of the crisis.
3. More than one billion slum dwellers worldwide are acutely at risk from the effects of COVID-19, suffering from a lack of adequate housing, unavailability of running water at home, shared toilets, little or no waste management systems, overcrowded public transport and limited access to formal healthcare facilities.
4. Women and children are also among those bearing the heaviest brunt of the pandemic's effects. Disruption to health and vaccination services and limited access to diet and nutrition services have the potential to cause hundreds of thousands of additional under-5 deaths and tens of thousands of additional maternal deaths in 2020. Many countries have seen a surge in reports of domestic violence against women and children.
5. School closures have kept 90 per cent of students worldwide (1.57 billion) out of school and caused over 370 million children to miss out on the school meals that they depend on. Lack of access to computers and the internet at home means remote learning is out of reach for many. About 70 countries reported moderate-to-severe disruptions or a total suspension of childhood vaccination services during March and April of 2020.
6. As more families fall into extreme poverty, children in poor and disadvantaged communities are at much greater risk of child labour, child marriage and child trafficking. In fact, the global gains in reducing child labour are likely to be reversed for the first time in 20 years.

157. (b): The various types of waterborne diseases are given as:

1. **Typhoid Fever:** It is a highly contagious disease and generally spreads through unsafe water, contaminated food and poor sanitation.
2. **Cholera:** This disease spreads through contaminated water and causes severe dehydration and diarrhoea. It is more prominent in areas where poor sanitation and poverty are rampant.
3. **Giardia:** This disease is caused by contaminated water, especially water that is found in ponds and swimming pools. It is caused by a parasite.
4. **Dysentery:** It is an intestinal infection caused by severe diarrhoea.
5. **Hepatitis A:** It is a liver infection that occurs when you consume infected food and water.
6. **Malaria:** It is a type of a waterborne disease that does not require direct contact with water but instead uses a host to spread.

158. (b): The Paris Agreement entered into force when the instruments of ratification were deposited by at least 55 countries, which accounted for at least 55 per cent of global CO_2 emissions.

159. (a): Biogas is a mixture of gases that the anaerobic decomposition of organic matter, such as agricultural waste, plant residue, municipal waste, food waste and other wastes, produce. Bacterial action is introduced in digesters with human waste and animal manure. The decomposition of sewage produces methane, which is used for cooking and fuel. Biomass fuel in India accounts for about one-third of the total fuel used in the country, being the most important fuel in over 90 per cent of rural households and 15 per cent of urban households. Biogas has a calorific value of about 5,000 kcal cubic meter. A calorific value represents the amount of heat generated when a fuel burns completely.

THE BIOGAS PROCESS

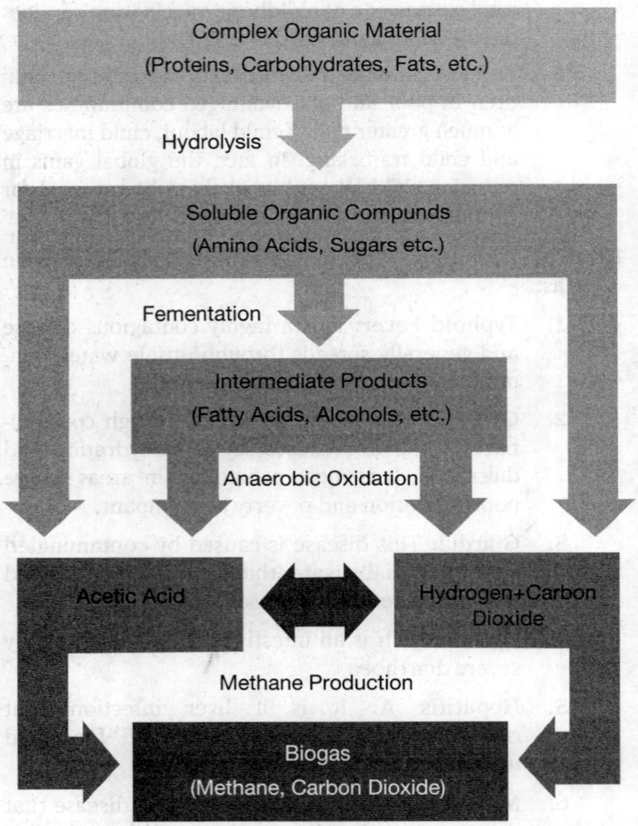

160. (a): In 2015, the Paris Agreement was signed as an international agreement with an aim to reduce global greenhouse gas (GHG) emissions. There are 29 articles in the agreement. The main aim of the Paris Agreement is to keep the rise in the average global temperature of this century well below 2°C above the pre-industrial level. There have to be efforts to limit the temperature increase even further to 1.5°C.

161. (b): Asbestos was nicknamed "the magic mineral" as it has unique chemical and physical properties. The asbestos is used in thousands of products and industries such as roofing, thermal and electrical insulation, cement pipe and sheets, flooring, plastics, textiles, paper, etc. Tiny asbestos fibres collect in the lungs. Asbestos causes mesothelioma, that is a relatively rare cancer of the thin membranes that line the chest and abdomen. It causes cancers of the lung, larynx and ovary. Mesothelioma treatments include surgery, radiation and chemotherapy.

Asbestosis causes permanent lung damage. In **Pleural effusions,** fluid collects around the lungs.

Asbestos deposits are found in Andhra Pradesh, Bihar, Jharkhand, Karnataka, Rajasthan and Manipur.

162. (b):

A. Greater biodiversity in ecosystems, species, and individuals leads to greater stability. For example, species with high genetic diversity and many populations that are adapted to a wide variety of conditions are more likely to be able to withstand weather disturbances, disease, and climate change. In other words, the two key components of ecosystem stability are **resilience and resistance**. Resistance is an ecosystem's ability to remain stable when confronted with a disturbance. Resilience is the speed at which an ecosystem recovers from a disturbance.

B. Extinction is the death of all members of a species of plants, animals, or other organisms. The three types of extinction are mass extinction, background extinction, and human led extinction. Earth could lose 16% of its species if the average global temperature rise exceeds 4.3 °C.
Human activities in the form of anthropogenic activities are basically human interference. The main modern causes of extinction are the urbanisation, industrialisation, loss and degradation of habitat (mainly deforestation), over exploitation (hunting, overfishing), invasive species, climate change, and nitrogen pollution. Our global food system is the primary driver of biodiversity loss, with agriculture alone being the identified threat to 24,000 of the 28,000 (86%) species at risk of extinction.

C. Habitat fragmentation actually leads to withdrawal of support systems to many other species which put their survival at stake.

D.

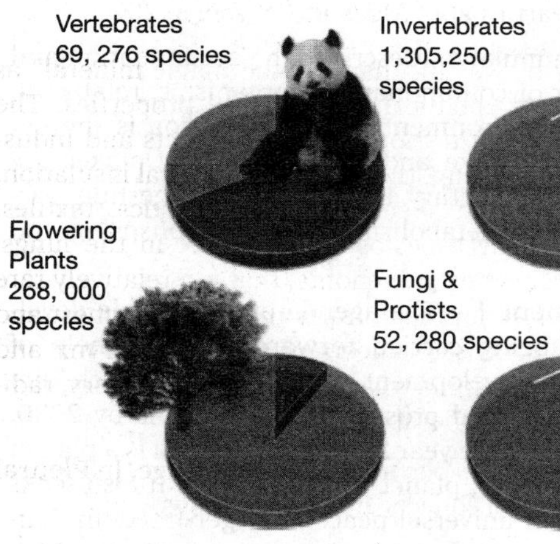

Invertebrates are central to the functioning of ecosystems, and are important part of biodiversity, yet they are underappreciated and understudied. The Red List of Threatened Species of the International Union for Conservation of Nature (IUCN) is an important reference for the threat of species, but it is still heavily biased towards vertebrates, with invertebrates being particularly underrepresented.

163. (d): Landfills–Landfill gases produced during biological degradation of buried organic wastes include methane, which when released to the atmosphere, can contribute to global climate change. This can be taken as a part of manure management.

Methane is the second-most abundant greenhouse gas in the atmosphere, after carbon dioxide.

According to the IPCC, more than 40 per cent of methane emissions come from farms or are an outcome of peatland destruction. A quarter of the global emissions are products of agriculture and land-use changes. The pledge by more than 80 nations, helped by the US and EU, to cut emissions of this GHG (greenhouse gas) by 30 per cent is, therefore, an important step in global warming mitigation efforts. Methane is 80 times more powerful than carbon dioxide in its first 20 years in the atmosphere. While much of the contentious aspects of curbing emissions of this GHG pertain to agriculture, the oil and gas industry — especially natural gas, whose popularity as a relatively cleaner fossil fuel has led to a 50 per cent increase in its use in the past 10 years — is the second-highest emitter of this gas.

THE EMISSIONS SHARE

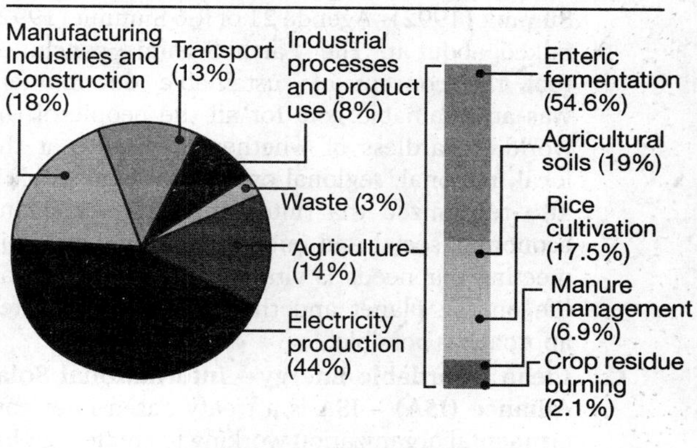

Global Methane Pledge–During Glasgow COP meeting, US and EU floated the idea of Global Methane Pledge so as to contribute towards global temperature rise limit to 1.5°C. Participants joining the Pledge agree to take voluntary actions to contribute to a collective effort to reduce global methane emissions at least 30 percent from 2020 levels by 2030, which could eliminate over 0.2°C warming by 2050. This is a global pledge, and not a national reduction target. Russia, India and China have not signed the Global Methane Pledge.

164. (b):

A. **Emission Trading** – Kyoto Protocol – This protocol was adopted in Kyoto, Japan, on 11 December 1997 and entered into force on 16 February 2005. The main objective of Kyoto Protocol was to reduce the emission of gases. This was put into practice by committing industrialized countries and economies in transition to limit and reduce greenhouse gases (GHG) emissions. The following were the key objectives of Kyoto Protocol.

1. International Emissions Trading
2. Clean Development Mechanism (CDM)
3. Joint implementation (JI)

There were annexed nations for the purpose of reduction of gases. The key concept was 'common but differentiated responsibilities' (CBDR).

The main GHGs were Carbon dioxide (CO_2), Methane (CH_4), Nitrous oxide (N_2O), Hydrofluorocarbons (HFCs), Perfluorocarbons (PFCs); and Sulphur hexafluoride (SF_6).

B. **Sustainable Management of Resources** – Rio Summit (1992) - Agenda 21 of Rio Summit (1992) talked about it. The 'Earth Summit' concluded that the concept of sustainable development was an attainable goal for all the people of the world, regardless of whether they were at the local, national, regional or international level. It also recognized that integrating and balancing economic, social and environmental concerns in meeting our needs is vital for sustaining human life on the planet and that such an integrated approach is possible.

C. **Clean Affordable Energy – International Solar Alliance (ISA)** – ISA is a treaty based inter-governmental organization working to create a global market system to tap the benefits of solar power and promote clean energy applications. This was primarily promoted by India and France. It was started in 30 November 2015.

D. **Intended Nationally Determined Contributions – Paris Agreement** – This agreement was adopted in 2015. They are essence of the Paris Agreement so that they can facilitate the achievement of long-term objectives of emission reduction, better energy measures, forest resources, etc. INDCs embody efforts by each country to reduce national emissions and adapt to the impacts of climate change.

The long term objective is to hold the increase in global average temperature to well below 2°C, to pursue efforts to limit the increase to 1.5°C, and to achieve net zero emissions in the second half of this century. We can get the basic idea of revised goals by studying Conference of Parties 26th Meet at Glasgow in 2021.

165. (c): Bioaccumulation describes the accumulation and enrichment of contaminants in organisms, relative to that in the environment. Bioaccumulation is the net result of all uptake and loss processes. Uptakes are respiratory and dietary. Loss happens by egestion, passive diffusion, metabolism, transfer to offspring and growth.

166. (a): Statement 1 – The agenda of sustainable development is being carried forward with the help of Sustainable Development Goals (SDGs) which aim to bring peace and prosperity to all people by 2030. They started in the year 2015. This Agenda is a plan of action for people, planet and prosperity. It also seeks to strengthen universal peace in larger freedom. Earlier there were Millennium Development Goals which were set for a period between 2000 to 2015.

There are the 17 SDGs which are an urgent call for action by all countries - developed and developing. In simple terms, sustainable development means integrating the economic, social and environmental objectives of society, in order to maximise human well-being in the present, without compromising the ability of future generations to meet their needs.

Statement 2 – Anthropogenic model is the root cause for taking sustainable development agenda more seriously. Anthropogenic activities is the human interruption in nature for the sake of development to make the human life comfortable but these activities bring misery also in the form of pollution, hazards etc. We need to have a look at the following diagram.

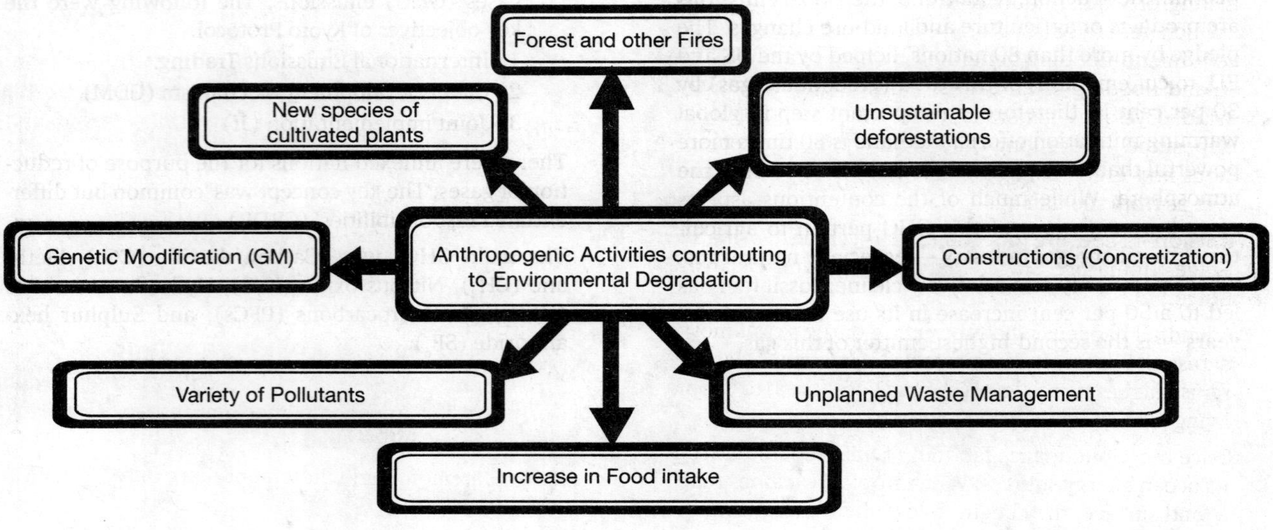

167. (d): Anthropogenic means human interruption in environment for the sake of development. It is basically based on environment possibilism so that humans are to determine which way the environment should go. Earlier there was concept of environmental determinism that said that ultimately the environment should decide its own way.

We need to look at all the events.

Cyclones – They are linked with sea water temperature and pressure conditions. The more about cyclones has been discussed in the earlier paper. The frequency of cyclones has increased during recent decades.

Nuclear Disasters – In a major nuclear disaster, a reactor core is damaged and significant amounts of radioactive isotopes are released which may result in loss of lakhs of lives. The major such examples are Chernobyl disaster in 1986 and Fukushima nuclear disaster in 2011. The largest nuclear power plant in Europe, the Zaporizhzhia Nuclear Power Plant, is located in Ukraine, and has been a major flashpoint for nuclear disaster.

Floods – The frequency of floods has increased during the recent times as the natural way of water has been disrupted due to concretization of natural resources in the form of buildings, roads, factories etc. Deforestation has happened in a big way. There are more and more flash floods which cause more destruction.

Volcanoes – They erupt from within the earth as per the temperature and pressure conditions of the earth, so anthropogenic activities do not play any role in it.

Forest Fires – That is basically burning of forest trees on a massive scale.

168. (c): Assertion – Cyclones cause an amazing rise in the sea level. Cyclones are composite phenomena, consisting of winds, multiple storm waves, storm surges (which generally last from several hours up to a day) and inland flooding generated by heavy rainfall. This inland flooding often causes more fatalities than the wind. Cyclones generally cause massive erosion or deposition – both long- and cross-shore. The forestations and green belts such as mangroves usually protect us from the damage.

Reason – There are four stages of a cyclone - Formative Stage, Immature Stage, Mature Stage and Decaying Stage.

A landfall happens when the centre of the storm moves across the coast. It often carries heavy winds, lashing rains, increasing sea level that can pose threat to people living in the neighbouring region.

Once a cyclone makes landfall, it gets separated from its ocean energy sources. When tropical cyclones reach a land surface, they begin to lose their energy and die out. This is because they are no longer receiving heat energy and moisture from the ocean, which is needed to drive them.

169. (a): Earth is known as 'Water Planet', as our planet has more water than land.

1. In reality, less than three percent of Earth's water is fresh water, and most of that three percent is inaccessible.
2. Over 68 percent of the FRESH WATER on Earth is found in ice and snow (including glaciers).
3. Almost 30 percent of FRESH WATER is found in ground water.
3. Only about 0.3 percent of FRESH WATER is found in the surface water of lakes, rivers, and swamps.
4. In totality, more than 99 percent of Earth's water is unusable by humans and many other living things.

As the question is in the form of increasing quantity, (a) is the correct answer.

170. (c):

Energy is the golden thread that connects economic growth, increased social equity, and environmental sustainability that allows the world to thrive. The indicator for Energy Intensity is in terms of total primary energy supply and GDP at PPP.

Under target number 7 of Sustainable Development Goals, we need to double the global rate of improvement in energy efficiency by the year 2030.

171. (a): Chlorination of water is primarily done to remove or kill microbes. Thus is a water treatment process that disinfects water, that effectively eliminates harmful bacteria, viruses, and protozoa, making the water safe for consumption.

Additionally, chlorine in the water treatment process helps to oxidize impurities such as iron and manganese, improving overall water quality.

Furthermore, chlorination aids in turbidity reduction by settling and removing suspended particles, resulting in clearer and safer water for various uses, including drinking.

172. (b): The average thickness of the ozone layer is less than 1 cm. The correct answer is (b) < 1 cm.

173. (b): Let's look at the statements about Ion Exchange:

Statement I: Ion exchange is not typically categorized as a tertiary wastewater treatment process; it is often a part of the primary or secondary treatment.

Statement II: Ion exchange is used for the removal of ions (like calcium and magnesium), not necessarily for residual suspended solids.

Both Statement I and Statement II are false, so the correct answer is (b)

174. (d):

Statement I: Montreal Protocol was indeed agreed upon in 1987 and came into force on January 1st, 1989. It was not 1990, so this statement is wrong.

Statement II: Kyoto Protocol was agreed upon in 1997 and came into force in 2005. This statement is correct. Thus, (d) is the right answer.

175. (c):

Statement I: It is true that some pollutants, like carbon tetrachloride, pesticides, and heavy metals, can cause liver damage.

Statement II: Toxic chemicals that cause liver damage are called hepatotoxins, not hematotoxins.

Statement I is true but Statement II is false, thus the correct answer is (c).

176. (a)

Atmospheric haze is caused by 'ultra fine particulate matter', that is less than 2.5 microns in diameter (PM2.5). These tiny particles scatter and absorb light, reducing visibility, thus creating haze like conditions. They cause respiratory problems as they get in lung, blood stream and other organs.

Oxides of nitrogen and sulphur contribute to haze formation but are not the main culprit. Ozone can worsen haze but is not the primary cause. Carbon dioxide and carbon monoxide are greenhouse gases but do not directly contribute to haze.

177. (c): Statement I is correct mainly due to their large surface area and unique chemical properties that allow them to adsorb or degrade these pollutants mentioned in the question statement.

Statement II is incorrect as some metallic nanoparticles can be effective against certain heavy metals, others are not and may even exacerbate their toxicity. Not all nano-particles are ineffective against all heavy metals.

178. (c)

Assertion A: That mainly happens due to global average sea level rise due to climate change, regional factors like land subsidence or uplift, and local factors like tides, storms, and riverine input.

Reason R: The impact can vary significantly depending on location. For example, the impact of melting of Arctic and Antarctic oceans can be different.

179. (a): Organic matter in water includes things like plant materials, microorganisms (like bacteria and algae), animal waste, and pollutants from sewage and industry. When these organic materials break down, they use up oxygen in the water. This can be a problem because it reduces the oxygen available for aquatic life, leading to areas with too little oxygen where organisms can't survive. So, organic matter is a main factor in lowering water oxygen levels.

180. (c):

The correct answer is (c) A-II, B-III, C-IV, D-I.

- SDG 2 – II : Zero Hunger
- SDG 3 – III : Good Health and Well-being
- SDG 6 – IV : Clean Water and Sanitation
- SDG 11- I : Sustainable Cities and Communities

181. (b): The values of acidic, neutral, and basic are typically measured on the pH scale, which ranges from 0 to 14 and that indicates the acidity or alkalinity of a solution.

Let's understand the concept in detail for future questions. The pH of a solution is calculated as the negative logarithm of the concentration of hydrogen ions, or $[H^+]$, in moles per litre. The pH value indicates how acidic or alkaline the solution is. For example, a pH of 1 has a large concentration of hydrogen ions and is very acidic, whereas a pH of 13 has a low concentration of hydrogen ions and is very alkaline. If OH^- increases in a solution, then the pH values also increase. This is because OH^- and H^+ are inversely related in a solution. Their total is always 14. A solution with a pH of 5 is ten times more acidic than one with a pH of 6, and a solution with a pH of 3 is a hundred times more acidic than one with a pH of 5.

1. **Acidic:** Solutions with a pH value less than 7 are considered acidic. The lower the pH value, the more acidic the solution is. For example:
   - pH of 0-2 would be strongly acidic (like battery acid). Lemon juice has a pH value of 2-3, tamarind of 2 - 3.5, dahi (yogurt) of 4.5 - 5.5.
   - pH of 3-6 would be weakly acidic (like vinegar or black coffee).
2. **Neutral:** A solution with a pH value of exactly 7 is considered neutral. In case of water the temperature is 25°C. (Some examples of neutral (or almost neutral) are coconut water (7 - 7.5), rainwater (7), sugarcane (6.5 - 7).
3. **Basic (Alkaline):** Solutions with a pH value greater than 7 are considered basic or alkaline. The higher the pH value, the more basic the solution. For example:
   - pH of 8-11 would be weakly basic (like baking soda or ocean water. This is used in Indian dishes also).
   - pH of 12-14 would be strongly basic (like bleach or lye).
   - Soap (9-10.5), Milk of magnesia (antacid medication) has pH of 10.5.

182. (c): Statement (I) is true. Kyoto Protocol was 'legally binding emissions reduction targets' for developed countries. In that Annex B countries (developed nations) have assigned emissions targets and must meet them through domestic reductions or through the Clean Development Mechanism (CDM), which allows them to invest in emissions reduction projects in developing countries. (In comparison, Paris Agreement was cooperative, non-binding emissions reduction commitments as each nation submits a Nationally Determined Contribution (NDC) outlining its intended emissions reductions).

Statement (II): This statement is false. Kyoto Protocol was set through COP3 (3rd Conference of Parties) in 1997 that COP network itself functions through UNFCCC that was adopted on May 9, 1992 in Rio de Janeiro, Brazil, at the Earth Summit. UNFCCC entered into force on March 21, 1994. COP28 was held in Dubai in 2023. UNFCCC (COP29) will be held in Baku, Azerbaijan, from November 11 to 24, 2024.

Thus, (c) is the correct answer.

183. (d):

(a): POPs are organic chemicals, they are persistent, they bioaccumulate in food chains, and pose a risk to human health.

(b): Algae found on eutrophic lakes are a symptom of water pollution caused by excessive nutrients.

(c): ODS contribute to the depletion of the ozone layer in the stratosphere, thus Montreal Protocol was signed to eliminate them.

(d): Leachates are the contaminated liquids that drain from landfills, resulting from the decomposition of waste materials, harmful chemicals, heavy metals etc and thus pose a threat to groundwater and soil.

Thus, (d) is the correct answer.

184. (a): Statement (I): In the food chain, mercury can accumulate in fish and other seafoods, through a process known as bioaccumulation. In workplace (such as industrial settings), this may also happen.

Statement (II): Inorganic mercury, especially in vapor form, is highly toxic and can cause significant damage to the central nervous system, among other health issues. Mercury has a very low boiling point. At room temperature, mercury can evaporate and become a vapor.

185. (a): Both statements fit into the situation. The focus has shifted on renewable energy situation.

CHAPTER

10

Higher Education System

TOPICS OF IMPORTANCE

- Institutions of Higher Learning and Education in Ancient India
- Evolution of Higher Learning and Research in Post-Independent India
- Oriental, Conventional and Non-conventional Learning Programmes in India-Professional, Technical and Skill-Based Education
- Value Education and Environmental Education
- Policies, Governance and Administration

1. Who among the following is the de facto executive head of the Planning Commission? **[Jun 2014]**
(a) Chairman
(b) Deputy Chairman
(c) Minister of State for Planning
(d) Member Secretary

2. Education as a subject of legislation figures in the **[Jun 2014]**
(a) Union List
(b) State List
(c) Concurrent List
(d) Residuary Powers

3. Which of the following are Central universities? **[Jun 2014]**
(i) Pondicherry University
(ii) Vishwa Bharati University
(iii) H. N. B. Garhwal University
(iv) Kurukshetra University

Select the correct answer from the codes given below.

Codes:
(a) (i), (ii) and (iii)
(b) (i), (iii) and (iv)
(c) (ii), (iii) and (iv)
(d) (i), (ii) and (iv)

4. Consider the statement which is followed by two arguments (i) and (ii).

Statement: India should have a very strong and powerful Lokpal. **[Jun 2014]**

Arguments:
(i) Yes, it will go a long in eliminating corruption in bureaucracy.
(ii) No, it will discourage honest officers from making quick decisions.

Codes:
(a) Only argument (i) is strong.
(b) Only argument (ii) is strong.
(c) Both the arguments are strong.
(d) Neither of the arguments is strong.

5. Which of the following universities has adopted the meta university concept? **[Jun 2014]**
(a) Assam University
(b) Delhi University
(c) Hyderabad University
(d) Pondicherry University

6. Which of the following statements are correct about a Central university? **[Jun 2014]**

(i) Central university is established under an Act of Parliament.

(ii) The President of India acts as the visitor of the University.

(iii) The President has the power to nominate some members to the Executive Committee or the Board of Management of the university.

(iv) The President occasionally presides over the meetings of the Executive Committee or court.

Select the correct answer from the codes given below.

Codes:

(a) (i), (ii), and (iv) (b) (i), (iii), and (iv)
(c) (i), (ii), and (iii) (d) (i), (ii), (iii), and (iv)

7. The e-content generation for undergraduate courses has been assigned by the Ministry of Human Resource Development to **[Jun 2014]**

(a) INFLIBNET
(b) Consortium for Educational Communication
(c) National Knowledge Commission
(d) Indira Gandhi National Open University

8. MOOC stands for **[Dec 2014]**

(a) Media Online Open Course
(b) Massachusetts Open Online Course
(c) Massive Open Online Course
(d) Myrind Open Online Course

9. The maximum number of fake institutions/universities as identified by the UGC in the year 2014 are in the State/Union territory of **[Dec 2014]**

(a) Bihar (b) Uttar Pradesh
(c) Tamil Nadu (d) Delhi

10. Which of the following institutions are empowered to confer or grant degrees under the UGC Act, 1956? **[Dec 2014]**

1. A university established by an Act of Parliament.
2. A university established by an Act of Legislature.
3. A university/institution established by a linguistic minority.
4. An institution which is a deemed to be university.

Select the correct answer from the codes given below:

(a) 1 and 2 (b) 1, 2 and 3
(c) 1, 2 and 4 (d) 1, 2, 3 and 4

11. Which of the following are the tools of good governance? **[Dec 2014]**

1. Social audit
2. Separation of powers
3. Citizen's charter
4. Right to information

Select the correct answer from the codes given below:

(a) 1, 3 and 4 (b) 2, 3 and 4
(c) 1 and 4 (d) 1, 2, 3 and 4

12. Which of the following powers, the President has in relation to Lok Sabha? **[Dec 2014]**

1. Summoning
2. Adjournment—*sine die*
3. Prorogation
4. Dissolution

Select the correct answer from the codes given below.

(a) 1 and 4 (b) 1, 2 and 3
(c) 1, 3 and 4 (d) 1, 2, 3 and 4

13. Right to Privacy as a Fundamental Right is implied in **[Dec 2014]**

(a) Right to Freedom
(b) Right to Life and Personal Liberty
(c) Right to Equality
(d) Right against Exploitation

14. Which of the following organizations deals with 'capacity building program' on Educational Planning? **[Dec 2014]**

(a) NCERT (b) UGC
(c) NAAC (d) NUEPA

15. Civil Service Day is celebrated in India on **[Jun 2015]**

(a) 21st April (b) 24th April
(c) 21st June (d) 7th July

16. The South Asia University is situated in the city of **[Jun 2015]**

(a) Colombo (b) Dhaka
(c) New Delhi (d) Kathmandu

17. The University Grants Commission was established with which of the following aims? **[Jun 2015]**

(i) Promotion of research and development in higher education.

(ii) Identifying and sustaining institutions of potential learning.

(iii) Capacity building of teachers.

(iv) Providing autonomy to each and every higher educational institution in India.

Select the correct answer from the codes given below:
(a) (i), (ii), (iii) and (iv)
(b) (i), (ii) and (iii)
(c) (ii), (iii) and (iv)
(d) (i), (ii) and (iv)

18. The Gross Enrolment Ratio (GER) in institutions of higher education in India at present (2015) is about **[Jun 2015]**
(a) 8 per cent (b) 12 per cent
(c) 19 per cent (d) 23 per cent

19. The total number of Central universities in India in April 2015 was **[Jun 2015]**
(a) 08 (b) 14
(c) 27 (d) 43

20. Which of the following are the objectives of Rashtriya Uchchatar Shiksha Abhiyan (RUSA)? **[Dec 2015]**
(i) To improve the overall quality of state institutions.
(ii) To ensure adequate availability of quality faculty.
(iii) To create new institutions through upgradation of existing autonomous colleges.
(iv) To downgrade universities with poor infrastructure into autonomous colleges.

Select the correct answer from the codes given below:
(a) (i), (ii), (iii) and (iv) (b) (i), (ii) and (iii)
(c) (i), (iii) and (iv) (d) (i), (ii) and (iv)

21. The grounds on which discrimination in admission to educational institutions is constitutionally prohibited are **[Dec 2015]**
(i) Religion (ii) Sex
(iii) Place of birth (iv) Nationality

Select the correct answer from the codes given below:
(a) (ii), (iii) and (iv)
(b) (i), (ii) and (iii)
(c) (i), (ii) and (iv)
(d) (i), (ii), (iii) and (iv)

22. Which of the following statement(s) about the Indian political system is/are correct? **[Jul 2016]**
(A) The President is both Head of the State and Head of the Government.
(B) Parliament is supreme.
(C) The Supreme Court is the guardian of the constitution.
(D) The Directive Principles of State Policy are justiciable.

Select the correct answer from the codes given below:
(a) (A), (B), (C) and (D)
(b) (B), (C) and (D)
(c) (B) and (C)
(d) (C) only

23. Which of the following are the fundamental duties? **[Jul 2016]**
(A) To respect the National Flag.
(B) To protect and improve the natural environment.
(C) For a parent to provide opportunities for education to his/her child.
(D) To protect monuments and places of national importance.

Select the correct answer from the codes given below:

Codes:
(a) (A), (B) and (C) (b) (A), (B) and (D)
(c) (A), (C) and (D) (d) (A), (B), (C) and (D)

24. Which of the following statements are correct in respect of NITI Aayog? **[Jul 2016]**
(A) It is a constitutional body.
(B) It is a statutory body.
(C) It is neither a constitutional body nor a statutory body.
(D) It is a think-tank.

Select the correct answer from the codes given below:
(a) (A) and (D) (b) (B) and (D)
(c) (C) and (D) (d) (B), (C) and (D)

25. Which of the following core values among the institutions of higher education are promoted by the NAAC (National Assessment and Accreditation Council)? **[Jul 2016]**
(A) Contributing to national development.
(B) Fostering global competencies among the students.

(C) Inculcating a value system among students and teachers.

(D) Promoting the optimum utilization of the infrastructure.

Select the correct answer from the codes given below:

Codes:

(a) (B), (C) and (D) (b) (A), (B) and (C)
(c) (A), (C) and (D) (d) (A), (B), (C) and (D)

26. The best way for providing value education is through **[Jul 2016]**

(a) Discussions on scriptural texts.
(b) Lectures/discourses on values.
(c) Seminars/symposia on values.
(d) Mentoring/reflective sessions on values.

27. *Assertion (A):* The purpose of higher education is to promote critical and creative thinking abilities among students.

Reason (R): These abilities ensure job placements.

Choose the correct answer from the following code. **[Jul 2016]**

(a) Both (A) and (R) are true and (R) is the correct explanation of (A).
(b) Both (A) and (R) are true but (R) is not the correct explanation of (A).
(c) (A) is true but (R) is false.
(d) (A) is false but (R) is true.

28. Which of the following are the demerits of globalization of higher education? **[Jan 2017]**

(i) Exposure to global curriculum.
(ii) Promotion of elitism in education.
(iii) Commodification of higher education.
(iv) Increase in the cost of education.

Select the correct answer from the following codes:

Codes:

(a) (i) and (iv) (b) (i), (iii) and (iv)
(c) (ii), (iii) and (iv) (d) (i), (ii), (iii) and (iv)

29. Which of the following statements are correct about deemed universities? **[Jan 2017]**

(i) The Governor of the State is the chancellor of deemed universities.
(ii) They can design their own syllabus and course work.
(iii) They can frame their own guidelines regarding admission and fees.
(iv) They can grant degrees.

Select the correct answer from the following codes:

Codes:

(a) (i), (ii) and (iii) (b) (ii), (iii) and (iv)
(c) (i), (iii) and (iv) (d) (i), (ii), (iii) and (iv)

30. The purpose of value education is best served by focussing on **[Jan 2017]**

(a) Cultural practices prevailing in the society.
(b) Norms of conduct laid down by a social group.
(c) Concern for human values.
(d) Religious and moral practices and instructions.

31. Which of the following are the goals of higher education in India? **[Nov 2017]**

(A) Access
(B) Equity
(C) Quality and Excellence
(D) Relevance
(E) Value-based education
(F) Compulsory and free education

Select the correct answer from the codes given below.

(a) (A), (B) and (E) only
(b) (A), (B), (E) and (F)
(c) (A), (B), (C), (D) and (E)
(d) (A), (B), (C), (D), (E) and (F)

32. Which of the following has been ranked the best college in the country (2017) as per the National Institutional Ranking Framework (NIRF)? **[Nov 2017]**

(a) Miranda House, Delhi
(b) St. Stephen's College, Delhi
(c) Fergusson College, Pune
(d) Maharaja's College, Mysore

33. Which of the following universities has received the Visitor's Award for the best Central university in India in February 2017? **[Nov 2017]**

(a) Jawaharlal Nehru University
(b) Banaras Hindu University
(c) Tezpur University
(d) University of Hyderabad

34. Which of the following come(s) within the ambit of the term 'corruption'? **[Nov 2017]**

(A) Misuse of official position.
(B) Deviation from rules, laws and norms.
(C) Non-action when action is required.
(D) Harm to public good.

Select the correct answer from the codes given below.

(a) (A) only (b) (A) and (B) only
(c) (A), (B) and (D) (d) (A), (B), (C) and (D)

35. India has the largest higher education system in the world after **[Jul 2018]**

(A) United States of America
(B) Australia
(C) China
(D) United Kingdom (UK)

Select the correct answer from the codes given below:

(a) (A), (B), (C) and (D)
(b) (A), (B) and (C) only
(c) (A), (C) and (D) only
(d) (A) and (C) only

36. Prime Minister Research Fellowship is for students pursuing Ph.D. programme in **[Jul 2018]**

(a) State and Central universities.
(b) Central universities, IISc, IITs, NITs, IISERs and IIITs.
(c) IISc, IITs, NITs, IISERs, IIITs, State and Central universities.
(d) IITs and IISc.

37. Which of the following statements are correct about gender budgeting? **[Jul 2018]**

(A) It separates budget addressing the specific needs of women.
(B) It assesses the impact of government budget on women.
(C) It is an accounting exercise.
(D) It is another budgeting innovation.

Select the correct answer from the codes given below:

(a) (B) and (D) only (b) (A) and (D) only
(c) (A), (C) and (D) only (d) (A) and (B) only

38. Which of the following are the barriers to citizen-centric administration in India? **[Jul 2018]**

(A) Wooden and inflexible attitude of the civil servants.
(B) Ineffective implementation of laws and rules.
(C) Awareness of rights and duties of citizens.
(D) Lack of job opportunities for the youth.

Select the correct answer from the codes given below:

(a) (A), (B), (C) and (D)
(b) (A), (B) and (C) only
(c) (A), (B) and (D) only
(d) (A) and (B) only

39. In terms of year of establishment, which open university is the youngest among the following (established most recently)? **[Dec 2018]**

(a) Tamil Nadu Open University, Tamil Nadu
(b) Odisha State Open University, Odisha
(c) Krishna Kanta Handique State Open University, Assam
(d) Pt. Sunderlal Sharma Open University, Chattisgarh

40. The institutions of eminence lag granted by the union government in public sector are **[Dec 2018]**

(i) IIT, Delhi
(ii) IIT, Bombay
(iii) Jawaharlal Nehru University, Delhi
(iv) University of Hyderabad
(v) Pondicherry University
(vi) Indian Institute of Science

Options:

(a) (i), (ii), (iv) and (v) only
(b) (ii), (iii), (v) and (vi) only
(c) (i), (ii) and (vi) only
(d) (iii), (iv), (v) and (vi) only

41. Which among the following was launched on 2 October 1978 (the birthday of Mahatma Gandhi)? **[Dec 2018]**

(a) National Adult Education Programme
(b) EduSAT
(c) First educational radio channel
(d) 10 + 2 + 3 Scheme

42. On the recommendations of which commission, 10 + 2 + 3 structure was incorporated in the statement of National Policy on Education, 1968? **[Dec 2018]**

(a) Kothari Commission
(b) Mudaliar Commission
(c) Ramamurti Commission
(d) Mandal Commission

43. University and university-level institutions are categorized into **[Dec 2018]**
(i) Central Universities
(ii) State Universities
(iii) Private Universities
(iv) Deemed-to-be Universities
(v) Institutions of Higher Learning
(vi) Civil Sector Institutions
Options:
(a) (i), (ii), (iii) and (iv)
(b) (ii), (iv), (v) and (vi)
(c) (iii), (iv), (v) and (i)
(d) (i), (iii), (v) and (vi)

44. The Council of Rural Institutes Authority is situated at **[Dec 2018]**
(a) Pune (b) Hyderabad
(c) Ahmedabad (d) Ludhiana

45. The first Open University established in India is at **[Dec 2018]**
(a) Bhim Rao Ambedkar Open University, Hyderabad.
(b) Tamil Nadu Open University, Chennai.
(c) Nalanda Open University, Patna.
(d) Yashwantrao Chavan Maharashtra Open University, Nasik.

46. In 1948, under whose Chairmanship a University Education Commission was set-up to reconstruct University Education in India? **[Dec 2018]**
(a) Sardar Vallabh Bhai Patel
(b) Dr Vikram Sarabhai
(c) Prof. P. C. Joshi
(d) Dr S. Radhakrishnan

47. 'e-Pathshala' is an initiative by **[Dec 2018]**
(a) NCERT (b) UGC
(c) CBSE (d) NCTE

48. The Constitution of India provides right to establish institutions of their choice by all minorities as per **[Jun 2019]**
(a) Article 30(1) (c) Article 29
(b) Article 33 (d) Article 16 (2)

49. During which year the present system of affiliation of collages to the universities was introduced in India? **[Jun 2019]**
(a) 1857 (b) 1948
(c) 1928 (d) 1966

50. Which one of the following report addressed the academic, technical and administrative problems of the examination system? **[Jun 2019]**
(a) Report on Standard of the Educational System (1965)
(b) Report of University Education Commission (1948–49)
(c) Sargent Report (1944)
(d) Hartog Committee Report (1929)

51. Identify the scheme which aims to encourage Social Science Research in Policy relevant areas so as to provide vital inputs in policy formulation, implementation and evaluation **[Jun 2019]**
(a) ICSSR Fellowship
(b) Cognitive Initiatives
(c) ICSSR IMPRESS
(d) ICSSR Research Projects

52. The scheme 'Unnat Bharat Abhiyan' aims to **[Jun 2019]**
(a) Increase strength of students in colleges in India
(b) Link higher educational institution in the country with at least 5 villages
(c) Increase quality in Higher Education
(d) Increase number of colleges in India

53. The purpose of Gurukul system of education is to **[Jun 2019]**
(a) Promote equality and excellence
(b) Minimize stress in learning
(c) Empowering for future learning
(d) Encourage self-help

54. Which of the following commission/committee in the post-independent India has paid attention all the levels of education? **[Jun 2019]**
(a) Radhakrishnan Commission
(b) Mudaliar Commission
(c) Kothari Commission
(d) Acharya Rammurthi Committee

55. NMEICT is an acronym for **[Jun 2019]**
(a) National Massive Education through Information and Communication Technology
(b) National Mission on Education through Information and Communication Technology
(c) National Multipurpose Education through Information and Communication Technology
(d) National Mode of Education through Information and Communication Technology

56. The medium of instruction in the vedic system of education has been. **[Jun 2019]**
(a) Sanskrit (b) Pali
(c) Hindi (d) Urdu

57. The methods of learning in Higher Education in India in the past consisted of **[Jun 2019]**
(a) Memorization, Brainstorming procedure and Seminar
(b) Memorization, Critical analysis and Story telling
(c) Critical analysis, Assignment writing and oral reports
(d) Story telling, Brainstorming procedure and Seminar

58. 'Inspire scholarship' is intended by the finding agency____________. **[Jun 2019]**
(a) Indian Council of Social Science and Research (ICSSR)
(b) University Grants Commission (UGC)
(c) Department of Science and Technology (DST)
(d) National Council of Education, Research and Training (NCERT)

59. National Curriculum Framework was developed by which of the following? **[Jun 2019]**
(a) UGC (b) NCERT
(c) NCTE (d) CBSE

60. Which one of the following forms a necessary component of Conventional Education System in India? **[Jun 2019]**
(a) Learning from books
(b) Learning from the teacher
(c) Learning from thinking
(d) Learning through instructional material

61. The premier organization established in India to deal with capacity building and research in planning and management of education in India and South Asia is **[Jun 2019]**
(a) AIU (b) SAARC University
(c) NUEPA (d) Nalanda University

62. Brain drain problem which was dominant in the middle of 20th century in India is indicative of which one of the following aspects? **[Jun 2019]**
(i) Lack of adequate facilities for advanced study and research in India
(ii) The capacity of the developed nations to buy the talent at a price beyond the means of the developing nations
(iii) Increase of population and under utilization of human research
Choose the correct option from below:
(a) Only (i) and (ii) (b) Only (ii) and (iii)
(c) Only (iii) (d) Only (i) and (ii)

63. GIAN (Global initiative of Academic Networks) has been launched by Government of India in order to **[Jun 2019]**
(a) Encourage Indian scholars to learn abroad
(b) Discourage Indian scholars from researching in India
(c) Encourage global scholars engage with their counter part in India
(d) Encourage global scholars to engage with Indian scholars abroad

64. Which one of the following five year plans of India has given special emphasis on 'Education and Manpower'? **[Jun 2019]**
(a) Third Five Years Plan
(b) Fourth Five Years Plan
(c) Second Five Years Plan
(d) Fifth Five Years Plan

65. The expansion of SANKALP is **[Jun 2019]**
(a) Sanskrit Awareness and Knowledge Acquisition of Language Programme
(b) Skills Acquisition and Karatae Awareness for Livelihood Promotion
(c) Skill Acquisition and Knowledge Awareness for Livelihood Promotion
(d) Sanskrit Awareness and Knowledge Acquisition for Livelihood Promotion

66. In which year the modern Indian University got established? **[Jun 2019]**
(a) 1957 (b) 1857
(c) 1947 (d) 1964

67. The report of which of the following Education Commissions carries the sub title 'Education for National Development'? **[Jun 2019]**
(a) Radhakrishnan Commission
(b) Mudaliar Commission
(c) Calcutta University Education Commission
(d) Kothari Commission

68. In which era given below, higher education in India got a set back? **[Jun 2019]**

(a) British Era (b) Buddhist Era
(c) Mughal Era (d) Post-independence Era

69. Below are given two columns. Column–A represents the stream of courses and Column–B represents the name of courses. Match the two columns **[Jun 2019]**

Column–A (Stream)	Column–B (Name of courses)
(1) Professional	(i) Engineering, Architecture
(2) Academic	(ii) Carpentering, Sewing
(3) Technical	(iii) Medicine, Law
(4) Skill based	(iv) Arts, Commerce

Choose your answer from the options given below:
(a) (1)-(iii); (2)-(ii); (3)-(i); (4)-(iv)
(b) (1)-(ii); (2)-(iii); (3)-(iv); (4)-(i)
(c) (1)-(i); (2)-(ii); (3)-(iii); (4)-(iv)
(d) (1)-(iii); (2)-(iv); (3)-(i); (4)-(ii)

70. Which of the following statements explains the concept of gross enrolment ratio? **[Jun 2019]**
(a) Total number of students divided by the total population
(b) Total number of enrolled students of a particular age group divided by total population of that age group
(c) Total number of students divide by the number of children not admitted to the institution
(d) Total number of students not admitted to the institution divided by the total number children of that age-group

71. Which of the following indicate the pillars of learning contained in the UNESCO Report 1996, 'Learning the Treasure Within'. **[Jun 2019]**
(i) Learning to know
(ii) Learning to be
(iii) Learning to learn
(iv) Learning to understand
(v) Learning to live together
Choose your answer from the options given below:
(a) (i), (ii), (iii) and (iv)
(b) (i), (iii), (iv) and (v)
(c) (ii), (iii), (iv) and (v)
(d) (i), (ii), (iii) and (v)

72. Who is usually the visitor of Central universities in India? **[Jun 2019]**
(a) Prime Minister of India
(b) Minister of Human Resource Development
(c) President of India
(d) Chairman of University Grants Commission

73. Which discipline has the highest percentage of enrolment in the higher education of India? **[Jun 2019]**
(a) Arts
(b) Science
(c) Commerce
(d) Technology and Engineering

74. Which of all the following statements represent the main functions of UGC? **[Jun 2019]**
(i) Recognition of institutions
(ii) Maintenance of quality and standards
(iii) Appointment of Vice Chancellor
(iv) Giving grants to institutions
(v) Making state government responsible for educational development
Choose the correct answer from the options given below:
(a) (i), (ii) and (iii) (b) (i), (iii) and (iv)
(c) (i), (ii) and (iv) (d) (ii), (iii) and (v)

75. Which of the following is a non-coventional learning programme in higher education? **[Jun 2019]**
(a) Swayam
(b) Face-to-face teaching-learning
(c) Tutorial class
(d) Seminar

76. For the day-to-day administration of university, which of the following bodies is responsible? **[Jun 2019]**
(a) Senate
(b) Syndicate/Executive council
(c) Student council
(d) Academic council

77. The main aim of the faculty recharge scheme of UGC was to **[Jun 2019]**
(a) Address the shortage of faculty in higher education institution
(b) Upgrade the teaching skill of the faculty
(c) Upgrade the research infrastructure of the faculty in collage and universities
(d) Strengthen the academia–industry linkage

78. Name the scheme which facilitates academic and research collaboration between Indian institutions and the best institution in the world [Jun 2019]
(a) ICSSR–IMPRESS
(b) Staff Development Scheme
(c) SPARC
(d) Institutional Development Scheme

79. The present form of Inter-University Board that was previously established for promoting cooperation and coordination among universities is [Jun 2019]
(a) UGC (b) AIU
(c) NUEPA (d) ICSSR

80. The Education Commission of India that first took serious note of the problem of brain drain was [Jun 2019]
(a) The Education Commission of India
(b) The University Education Commission
(c) The Calcutta University Commission
(d) The Sargeant Commission

81. In post-independence India, which one of the following Committee/Commission's report deals with all levels of educations in India? [Jun 2019]
(a) Sargeant Commission
(b) Hartog Committee
(c) Kothari Commission
(d) Radhakrishnan Commission

82. Which one of the following institutions was established as a consequence to the closure of Inter-University Board brought in for promotion of cooperation among the Universities in the field of education and allied areas? [Jun 2019]
(a) Associated of Central Universities
(b) University Grants Commission
(c) IIAS, Shimla
(d) Association of Indian Universities

83. Through which Act University Grants Commission came into existence? [Jun 2019]
(a) UGC Act – 1956 (b) UGC Act – 1949
(c) UGC Act – 1944 (d) UGC Act – 1968

84. 'Gyan Darshan' launched by IGNOU refers to which one of the following? [Jun 2019]
(a) Satellite-based education T.V. channel
(b) Educational FM radio network
(c) Global Initiative of Academic Network
(d) Online courses

85. Name the scheme which aims to create research ambience in the institute by promoting research in engineering sciences. [Jun 2019]
(a) E-Shodh Sindhu
(b) Entrepreneurship Development Cell
(c) Research Promotion Schemes (RPS)
(d) Institution Development Scheme

86. In order to meet the demands of market economy and produce competent graduates, who can compete with their counterparts in international markets, the first and foremost change that needs to be introduced in the prevailing system of Indian higher education is related to: [Dec 2019]
(a) admission process
(b) curriculum
(c) educational technology
(d) appointment of teachers

87. Which among the following is the flagship scheme of the Ministry of Skill Development and Entrepreneurship implemented by National Skills Development Corporation? [Dec 2019]
(a) Robotics India
(b) Artificial Intelligence @ schools
(c) Make in India
(d) Pradhan Mantri Kaushal Vikas Yojana

88. Given below are two statements—one is labelled as Assertion (A) and the other is labelled as Reason (R).
Assertion (A): Government of India established higher educational statutory bodies to ensure the quality of education.
Reason (R): There are some educational institutions in India, which do not provide quality education. [Dec 2019]
In the context of the above statements, choose the correct option.
(a) Both (A) and (R) are true and (R) is the correct explanation of (A)
(b) Both (A) and (R) are true but (R) is not the correct explanation of (A)
(c) (A) is true but (R) is false
(d) (A) is false but (R) is true

89. From the following, select the alternative features which make open universities as non-traditional universities. **[Dec 2019]**
(i) Innovative method of teaching and learning.
(ii) Innovative method of admission, curriculum and evaluation.
(iii) Modern communication techniques.
(iv) Teacher's friendly approaches.
Choose the correct option.
(a) (ii), (iii)and (iv) onl
(b) (i), (ii) and (iii) only
(c) (i), (iii) and (iv) only
(d) (i), (ii) and (iv) only

90. Match List I with List II. **[Dec 2019]**

List I (Historic Places)	List II (Discipline)
(A) Taxila	(i) Astronomy
(B) Ujjain	(ii) Buddhism
(C) Sarnath	(iii) Art, Architecture and Painting
(D) Ajanta	(iv) Medicine

Choose the correct option.
Code:

	(A)	(B)	(C)	(D)
(a)	(i)	(ii)	(iii)	(iv)
(b)	(ii)	(i)	(iv)	(iii)
(c)	(iii)	(iv)	(ii)	(i)
(d)	(iv)	(i)	(ii)	(iii)

91. Regarding e-governance, which of the following statements is/are correct? **[Dec 2019]**
(i) Decreasing transparency is an ICT enabled advantage of e-governance.
(ii) E-governance is related to the implementation of ICT in the government processes and functions.
(iii) Common Service Centres (CSCs) help in providing and using e-governance related services.
Choose the correct option.
(a) (i), (ii) and (iii)
(b) (ii) and (iii) only
(c) (i) and (iii) only
(d) (i) and (ii) only

92. Select the period, in which India became a centre of higher learning. **[Dec 2019]**
(a) Gupta period (b) Buddha period
(c) Mughal period (d) British period

93. Which among the following is the statutory function of the UGC? **[Dec 2019]**
(a) To appoint teaching faculty in universities
(b) To control the conduct of examination in universities
(c) To determine and maintain the standards of teaching and research in universities
(d) To develop curriculum for university courses

94. Which among the following recommended the establishment of State Council for Higher Education in each state? **[Dec 2019]**
(a) Report of the Estimates Committee (1965–1966)
(b) Review Committee on UGC (1977), Ministry of Education
(c) National Policy on Education (1986)
(d) Report of the UGC Committee (1990)

95. Who among the following scholars carried back scriptures from Nalanda University and wrote about architecture and learning of this university? **[Dec 2019]**
(a) Kim Huang (Korea)
(b) Jin Tan Yang (Korea)
(c) Xuanzang (China)
(d) Junha Meng (China)

96. The National Skills Qualifications Framework is based on which of the following? **[Dec 2019]**
(a) Competency
(b) Technology
(c) Economic development
(d) Evaluation

97. Which one of the following sequences correctly reflects the evolution of educational technology support in higher education? **[Dec 2019]**
(a) Programmed learning material, textbook support, online and modular material
(b) Textbook supplementation, programmed learning material, modular material and online methods
(c) Modular material, programmed learning, online and textbook supplementation
(d) Online methods, modular material, textbook supplementation and programmed learning material

98. Which of the following emphasised that education needs to be managed in an atmosphere of utmost intellectual rigour, seriousness of purpose and of freedom essential for innovation and creativity? **[Dec 2019]**

(a) National Policy on Education, 1968
(b) National Policy on Education, 1986
(c) NITI Aayog–Three year action Agenda (from 2017–18 to 2019–20)
(d) Draft National Education Policy, 2019

99. What are the current challenges in the field of higher education in India? **[Dec 2019]**

(i) Expansion
(ii) Equity
(iii) Funds
(iv) Examination reforms
(v) Excellence
(vi) Entrance examinations

Select the correct answer from the options given below.

(a) (i), (ii) and (vi) (b) (ii), (iii) and (iv)
(c) (iii), (iv) and (vi) (d) (i), (ii) and (v)

100. Creation of World-Class Universities requires: **[Dec 2019]**

(i) autonomous governance
(ii) focused funding
(iii) control over evaluation mechanism
(iv) independent outcomes
(v) appointment of staff by the state machinery

Select the correct answer from the options given below.

(a) (i), (ii) and (v) (b) (ii), (iii) and (v)
(c) (iii), (iv) and (v) (d) (i), (ii) and (iv)

101. Which of the following modes of admission was prevalent in Nalanda University in ancient times? **[Dec 2019]**

(a) Entrance examination
(b) Interview
(c) Good academic credentials
(d) Peer discussion

102. From the following, identify the organisation that provides a common platform to all universities including institutions of national importance. **[Dec 2019]**

(a) University Grants Commission
(b) Association of Indian Universities
(c) Distance Education Council
(d) Indian Institute of Advanced Study

103. In the age of four vedas, the students were admitted to the vedic schools after the performance of which of the following ceremony? **[Dec 2019]**

(a) Upanayana ceremony
(b) Utsarjana ceremony
(c) Satapatha brahmana ceremony
(d) Dhanurvidya ceremony

104. Which of the following provides the overarching vision that guides research into socially relevant areas? **[Dec 2019]**

(a) ARIIA
(b) IMPRINT
(c) NIRF
(d) SWAYAM PRABHA

105. In which year, the Union Government decided that all cases pertaining to the allocation of grants-in-aid from public funds to the Central Universities and other universities and institutions of higher learning might be referred to the University Grants Commission? **[2020]**

(a) 1952 (b) 1953
(c) 1954 (d) 1956

106. The Chinese scholars, I-Qing and Xuan Zang visited ancient Nalanda University during **[2020]**

(a) 5th century CE (b) 7th century CE
(c) 10th century CE (d) 12th century CE

107. Given below are two statements:

Statement I: Universities are established by Central/State Act under 2(f) of the UGC Act, 1956.

Statement II: Deemed to be University is declared by a Notification of the Central Government, on the advice of the UGC, under section 3 of the UGC Act, 1956. **[2020]**

In light of the above statements, choose the most appropriate answer from the options given below:

(a) Both Statement I and Statement II are true
(b) Both Statement I and Statement II are false
(c) Statement I is correct but Statement II is false
(d) Statement I is incorrect but Statement II is true

108. Which of the following are indicators of external accountability for an institution of higher learning? **[2020]**

(A) Provision for profession development of teachers.

(B) Utilization pattern of library and technical resources.

(C) Relevance of courses to the societal needs.

(D) Performance of students in public examination.

(E) Employment pattern of pass-out students.

Choose the correct answer from the options given below:

(a) (A), (B), (C) only
(b) (B), (C), (D) only
(c) (C), (D), (E) only
(d) (D), (E), (A) only

109. Which statutory body of a University has the power to accord formal approval to the programmes and courses of studies? **[2020]**

(a) Senate (b) Syndicate
(c) Academic Council (d) Board of studies

110. Which of the following types of institution come under the ambit of National Board of Accreditation (NBA)? **[2020]**

(a) Teacher education institution
(b) Technical institutions
(c) Agriculture institutions
(d) Medical institutions

111. Match List I and List II. **[2020]**

List 1 (Concepts)	List II (Schools)
(A) Nirvana	(I) Sankhya
(B) Nihshreyasa	(II) Jainism
(C) Apavarga	(III) Upanishads
(D) Moksha	(IV) Buddhism

Choose the correct answer from the options given below:

(a) A - IV, B - III, C - II, D - I
(b) A - I, B - II, C - IV, D - III
(c) A - II, B - I, C - II, D - IV
(d) A - II B - IV, C - II, D - I

112. In order to transform the regulatory system of Higher Education, the NEP proposes to set up HECI (Higher Education Commission of India). Which of the following are verticals of HECI? **[2021]**

A. NHERC D. NCIVE
B. NAS E. NAC
C. HEGC

Choose the correct answer from the options given below:

(a) A, B and C only (b) A, C and E only
(c) B, C and E only (d) C, D and E only

113. Global Citizenship Education promotes **[2021]**

(a) Common international laws for global citizenship
(b) International public relations
(c) Issues pertaining to citizenship across countries involving VISA
(d) More peaceful, tolerant, inclusive, secure and sustainable societies

114. Match List I with List II. **[2021]**

List I	List II
A. Indian Institute of Advanced Study	I. Noida, UP
B. Indian Biological Sciences and Research Institute	II. Shimla, HP
C. Indian Institute of Soil Science	III. Bhopal, MP
D. Indian Institute of Sugarcane Research	IV. Lucknow, UP

Choose the correct answer from the options given below:

(a) A - I, B - IV, C - II, D - III
(b) A - II, B - I, C - III, D - IV
(c) A - III, B - IV, C - II, D - I
(d) A - IV, B - III, C - II, D – I

115. CBCS is **[2021]**

(a) Choice Based Credit System
(b) Credit Based Choice Scores
(c) Criteria Based Choice System
(d) Criteria Based Creditable Scores

116. University of the ancient period which has been declared by UNESCO as a heritage site is: **[2021]**

A. Mithila B. Vallabhi
C. Pushpagiri D. Takshashila
E. Nalanda

Choose the correct answer from the options given below:
(a) A and B only
(b) B and C only
(c) C and D only
(d) D and E only

117. Match List I with List II. **[2021]**

List I	List II
A. Lay down standards of legal education	I. NCTE
B. Maintaining the quality of technical education	II. AICTE
C. Maintenance of standards in teacher education	III. NMC
D. Access to quality and affordable medical education	IV. BCI

Choose the correct answer from the options given below:
(a) A -I , B -II , C -IV , D -III
(b) A -II , B -III , C -IV , D -I
(c) A -III , B -IV , C -I , D -II
(d) A -IV , B -II , C -I , D -III

118. Which of the following are Central Universities? **[2021]**

A. Dr. Babasaheb Ambedkar Open University
B. Jamia Millia Islamia
C. Panjab University
D. Punjabi University
E. University of Mumbai

Choose the correct answer from the options given below:
(a) A and B only (b) B and C only
(c) C and D only (d) C and E only

119. The first education commission in Independant India is: **[2021]**
(a) National Knowledge Commission
(b) Secondary Education Commission
(c) The Education Commission
(d) University Education Commission

120. Gender Parity Index in higher education in India is: **[2021]**
(a) 0.98 (b) 0.99
(c) 1.1 (d) 1

121. According to NEP-20, the primary activities of the NRF will be to: **[2021]**
(A) Fund competitive peer reviewed grant proposals of all types across all disciplines.
(B) Open new institutions of research and innovation.
(C) Act as a liason between researchers and relevant branches of government as well as industry.
(D) Include research in curriculum at school level.

Choose the most appropriate answer from the options given below:
(a) (A) and (B) only
(b) (A) and (C) only
(c) (B) and (C) only
(d) (C) and (D) only

122. Identify from the following those values which are called "Sattvika Values". **[2021]**
(A) Compassion (B) Jealousy
(C) Respect (D) Falsehood

Choose the most appropriate answer from the options given below:
(a) (A) and (B) only (b) (B) and (C) only
(c) (C) and (D) only (d) (A) and (C) only

123. According to NEP-20, Secondary Education comprises of classes: **[2021]**
(a) VIII-X (b) IX - XII
(c) IX - X (d) IX – XI

124. Prakrit languages have similarities and differences with Sanskrit in many ways. For Prakrit languages, when formalized for literary use, their variation from conventional vedic languages was: **[2021]**
(a) Pali (b) Ardhamagadhi
(c) Apabhramsha (d) Hindi

125. As a result of Wood's Despatch, which of the following Universities were established in 1857? **[2021]**

(a) Calcutta, Bombay and Madras
(b) Bombay, Madras and Delhi
(c) Delhi, Bombay and Calcutta
(d) Madras, Calcutta and Delhi

126. Who among the following is the national coordinator for engineering courses to be launched on SWAYAM platform? **[Dec 2021]**

(a) AICTE (b) NCERT
(c) NPTEL (d) UGC

127. Match List I with List II. **[Dec 2021]**

List I	List II
(A) State with the highest number of universities	(i) Sikkim
(B) State with the lowest number of universities	(ii) Rajasthan
(C) State with the highest GER in higher education	(iii) Bihar
(D) State with the lowest GER in higher education	(iv) Mizoram

Choose the correct answer from the options given below:

	(A)	(B)	(C)	(D)
(a)	(i)	(ii)	(iv)	(iii)
(b)	(ii)	(iv)	(iii)	(i)
(c)	(iii)	(iv)	(i)	(ii)
(d)	(ii)	(iv)	(i)	(iii)

128. The oldest university in India was: **[Dec 2021]**

(a) Nalanda (b) Takshashila
(c) Vikramshila (d) Mithila

129. Central Universities are: **[Dec 2021]**

(A) established by the UGC
(B) established by an act of the Parliament
(C) established by the Department of Education, Government of India
(D) funded by the Central government
(E) Funded by the 'Niti Ayog'

Choose the *correct* answer from the options given below:

(a) A and D only
(b) C and E only
(c) B and D only
(d) B and E only

130. Gross Enrolment Ratio (GER) in higher education calculated as: **[Dec 2021]**

(a) $\frac{\text{Number of enrolments in higher education}}{\text{Total population in the age group of 18 – 23}} \times 100$

(b) $\frac{\text{Number of enrolments in higher education}}{\text{Total population in the age group of 18 – 23}}$

(c) $\frac{\text{Number of enrolments in higher education in the age group 18 – 23}}{\text{Total population in the age group of 18 – 23}}$

(d) $\frac{\text{Number of enrolments in higher education in the age group 18 – 23}}{\text{Total population in the age group of 18 – 23}} \times 100$

131. Choice-based credit system of index graduate level includes: **[Dec 2021]**

(A) Core Course
(B) Elective Course
(C) Ability Enhancement Course
(D) Environment Education Course
(E) English Communication Course

Choose the *correct* answer from the options given below:

(a) A, B, and C only
(b) B, C, and D only
(c) C, D, and E only
(d) A, B, and E only

132. Which region of India experiences the maximum number of cyclones? **[2022]**
(a) East Coast (b) West Coast
(c) Central India (d) Northern India

133. Who is fully credited with the introduction of English education system in India, officially through the necessary order issued by Bentinck, the Governor General of India on 7th March 1835? **[2022]**
(a) Zachary Macaulay
(b) Thomas Babington Macaulay
(c) Alexander Duff
(d) Charles Trevelyan

134. Which University did Xuang Zang and I-Quing visit in India? **[2022]**
(a) Nalanda University
(b) Takshashila University
(c) Banaras Hindu University
(d) Vikramshila University

135. NSSF, as envisaged by the National Knowledge Commission, stands for **[2022]**
(a) National Science and Social Science Foundation
(b) National Scientific and Social Science Foundation
(c) National Scientists and Social Scientists Foundation
(d) National Space Science and Society Forum

136. As per NEP 2020, National Educational Technology Forum (NETF) will have following functions: **[2022]**
A. Provide independent evidence–based advice to central and state government agencies in technology–based interventions
B. Articulate new directions for research and innovation
C. Envision strategic thrust area in the educational technology domain
D. Develop curriculum for technical courses
E. Build intellectual and institutional capacities in educational technology

Choose the correct answer from the options given below:
(a) A, B, C and D only
(b) B, C, D and E only
(c) A, B, C and E only
(d) A, B, D and E only

137. The following are the main objectives of curriculum revision: **[2022]**
A. To align it better with vision and mission of the institution
B. To make it learning outcome based
C. To make it more effective in improving attainment levels against programme outcomes
D. To develop capacities of students for competitive examination
E. To meet the expectations of all stakeholder

Choose the correct answer from the options given below:
(a) A, B, C and D only
(b) A, B, C and E only
(c) A, C, D and E only
(d) B, C, D and E only

138. Some of the most notable universities that evolved during ancient period in India were situated at: **[2022]**
A. Takshashila B. Vikramshila
C. Jagaddala D. Odantapuri
E. Nalanda

Choose the correct answer from' the options given below:
(a) A, B, C, D and E
(b) A, B and E only
(c) A, B, C and E only
(d) A, B, D and E only

139. In pursuance of the National Council of Teacher Education Act,1993, NCTE was established in the year: **[2022]**
(a) 1995 (b) 1993
(c) 1994 (d) 1996

140. Which of the following is NOT correct regarding Digilocker, a key initiative under 'Digital India programme of Government of India? **[2022]**
(a) Indian citizens who sign up for a Digilocker account get a dedicated cloud storage space that is limited to their Aadhar number.
(b) It aims to eliminate the use of physical documents and provide access to their digital documents anytime, anywhere and share it online.
(c) Citizens can self-upload documents and digitally sign them using the e-sign facility.
(d) The slogan of Digilocker is 'My documents, Anytime, Anywhere.'

141. Match List I with List II **[2022]**

List I Concepts	List II Main in Proponent
A. Self-education through development of individuality	I. Sri Aurobindo
B. Integral education	II. Mahatma Gandhi
C. Education to transform human mind	III. Maria Montessori
D. Basic education (Wardha Education System)	IV. J. Krishnamurti

Choose the correct answer from the options given below:

(a) A – I, B – III, C – IV, D – II
(b) A – III, B – I, C – II, D – IV
(c) A – III, B – I, C – IV, D – II
(d) A – I, B – IV, C – II, D – III

142. Which of the following critical dimensions of values and ethics must be focussed for promoting quality Higher Education? **[June 2023]**

A. Accountability
B. Participation
C. Integrity
D. Competency
E. Transparency

Choose the most appropriate answer from the options given below:

(a) A, D and E only
(b) C and E only
(c) B, C and D only
(d) A, B, C, D and E

143. The First Buddhist Council with an aim for education was constituted in **[June 2023]**

(a) Mandalay in 1871 AD.
(b) Vaishali in 383 BC.
(c) Sattapani in 483 BC.
(d) Patliputra in 250 BC.

144. Given below are two statements: **[June 2023]**

Statement-I: National Council for Teacher Education (NCTE) was made a statutory body by the Act of Parliment in 1993.

Statement-II: Dr. S. Radhakrishnan was the Chairman of University Education Commission set up in 1948.

In the light of the given statements, choose the most appropriate answer from the options given below:

(a) Both Statement I and Statement II are correct.
(b) Both Statement I and Statement II are incorrect.
(c) Statement I is correct but Statement II is incorrect.
(d) Statement I is incorrect but Statement II is correct.

145. Which of the following Engineering colleges were there in India in the year 1902? **[June 2023]**

A. Roorkee
B. Sibapur
C. Poona
D. Madras

Choose the correct answer from the options given below: **[June 2023]**

(a) A, B and D only
(b) A, B, C and D
(c) A and D only
(d) A and C only

146. Match List I with List II. **[June 2023]**

List I	List II
A. Shastras	I. Logic
B. Varta	II. Learned disciplines
C. Kavyas	III. Agriculture, trade, commerce and animal husbandry
D. Anviksiki	IV. Imaginative and creative literature.

Choose the correct answer from the options given below:

(a) A-II, B-I, C-III, D-IV
(b) A-II, B-III, C-I, D-IV
(c) A-II, B-III, C-IV, D-I
(d) A-III, B-II, C-IV, D-I

147. What is the full form of 'SPARC'? **[June 2023]**

(a) Standard for Profession of Assessment and Research Communication
(b) Scheme for Promotion of Academic and Research Collaboration
(c) School for Promotion of Assessment and Right to commitment
(d) Social Protection of Advancement and Relationship Complex

148. According to NEP 2020, India will be promoted as a global study destination providing premium

education at affordable costs thereby helping to restore its role as ____. [June 2023]
(a) Economic power
(b) Knowledge Economy
(c) *Vishwa Guru*
(d) *Shiksha Guru*

149. What is the full form of 'NCIVE'? **[June 2023]**
(a) Non-Governmental Course for the Intiation of Vocational Enhancement
(b) National Committee for the Integration of Vocational Education
(c) Non-Governmental Council for the Integration of Veterinary Education
(d) National Commission for the Information of Veterinary Education

150. The Government of India created Department of Science and Technology in the year: **[June 2023]**
(a) 1990 (b) 1985
(c) 1978 (d) 1971

151. The ancient system of education in India included education of which of the following ancient texts? **[June 2023]**
A. Vedas
B. Brahmanas
C. Upanishads
D. Dharma sutras

Choose the most appropriate answer from the options given below:
(a) A and C only
(b) B and D only
(c) A, C and D only
(d) A, B, C and D

152. The policy on higher education during the eighth five-year plan was to encourage **[Dec 2023]**
(a) Expansion of public sector
(b) Involvement of private sector
(c) Establishment of foreign campuses
(d) Entry of foreign Universities

153. Given below are two statements: **[Dec 2023]**

Statement (I): The rating system of higher educational institutions followed in India does not touch the structural diversity of such institutions.

Statement (II): A universal and holistic rating system is not feasible in India.

In light of the above statements, choose the most appropriate answer from the options given below.
(a) Both Statement (I) and Statement (II) are true.
(b) Both Statement (I) and Statement (II) are false.
(c) Statement (I) is true but Statement (II) is false.
(d) Statement (I) is false but Statement (II) is true.

154. Which of the following Indian universities were modelled on the lines of University of London? **[Dec 2023]**
A. Calcutta B. Bombay
C. Madras D. Andhra
E. Mysore

Choose the correct answer from the options given below:
(a) A, B and C only (b) B, C and D only
(c) C, D and E only (d) A, B and D only

155. Which of the following subjects were taught at the University of Navadwip in ancient India? **[Dec 2023]**
A. Archaelogy
B. Physics
C. Logic
D. Literature
E. Tantra

Choose the correct answer from the options given below:
(a) A, B and C only
(b) B, C and D only
(c) C, D and E only
(d) A, B and E only

156. In which of the colleges, the European education was imparted through the medium of mother tongue before independence? **[Dec 2023]**
(a) Mayo College, Ajmer
(b) St. Stephen College, Delhi
(c) St. Xavier College, Calcutta
(d) University College, Lahore

ANSWER KEY

1. (b)	2. (c)	3. (a)	4. (a)	5. (b)	6. (c)	7. (b)	8. (c)	9. (b)	10. (c)
11. (d)	12. (d)	13. (b)	14. (d)	15. (a)	16. (c)	17. (b)	18. (b)	19. (d)	20. (b)
21. (b)	22. (d)	23. (a)	24. (c)	25. (b)	26. (d)	27. (b)	28. (c)	29. (b)	30. (c)
31. (c)	32. (a)	33. (a)	34. (d)	35. (d)	36. (d)	37. (a)	38. (d)	39. (b)	40. (c)
41. (a)	42. (a)	43. (a)	44. (b)	45. (a)	46. (d)	47. (a)	48. (a)	49. (a)	50. (a)
51. (c)	52. (b)	53. (a)	54. (c)	55. (b)	56. (a)	57. (b)	58. (c)	59. (b)	60. (b)
61. (c)	62. (d)	63. (c)	64. (b)	65. (c)	66. (b)	67. (d)	68. (c)	69. (d)	70. (b)
71. (d)	72. (c)	73. (a)	74. (c)	75. (a)	76. (b)	77. (a)	78. (c)	79. (b)	80. (a)
81. (c)	82. (d)	83. (a)	84. (a)	85. (c)	86. (b)	87. (d)	88. (a)	89. (b)	90. (d)
91. (b)	92. (a)	93. (c)	94. (c)	95. (c)	96. (a)	97. (b)	98. (b)	99. (d)	100. (d)
101. (a)	102. (b)	103. (a)	104. (b)	105. (a)	106. (b)	107. (a)	108. (c)	109. (c)	110. (b)
111. (a)	112. (b)	113. (d)	114. (b)	115. (a)	116. (d)	117. (d)	118. (b)	119. (d)	120. (d)
121. (b)	122. (d)	123. (b)	124. (c)	125. (a)	126. (c)	127. (c)	128. (b)	129. (c)	130. (a)
131. (a)	132. (a)	133. (b)	134. (a)	135. (a)	136. (c)	137. (b)	138. (a)	139. (a)	140. (d)
141. (c)	142. (d)	143. (c)	144. (d)	145. (c)	146. (b)	147. (b)	148. (c)	149. (a)	150. (c)
151. (d)	152. (b)	153. (c)	154. (a)	155. (c)	156. (d)				

HINTS AND SOLUTIONS

1. **(b):** NITI Aayog (National Institution for Transforming India)

   The Planning Commission was replaced with more dynamic NITI Aayog in 2014, with key focus on cooperative federalism and competitive federalism. The key objectives of NITI Aayog are

   To evolve a shared vision of national development priorities, sectors and strategies with the active involvement of States.

   To foster cooperative federalism through structured support initiatives and mechanisms with the States on a continuous basis, recognizing that strong States make a strong nation.

   There are concepts such as Think Tank, Knowledge and Innovation Hubs.

   Prime Minister Shri Narendra Modi is ex-officio Chairman of NITI Aayog. Shri Suman Bery is currently Vice Chairperson, NITI Aayog, in the rank and status of a Cabinet Minister. Mr Parameswaran Iyer is the Chief Executive Officer of NITI Aayog.

   Education Vertical of NITI Aayog: The Education Vertical seeks to facilitate a conducive learning environment through policy and programmes so that people can develop to their full potential and contribute towards the socio-economic development of the country.

   The Education Vertical strives to facilitate school readiness, socio-emotional learning, critical and higher-order thinking, and grade-level competency amongst children. It seeks to empower youth with employability skills, research temperament and subject matter expertise through high quality, accessible, equitable, accountable, and affordable education system.

   The Vertical covers:

   1) Pre-primary, elementary, secondary, higher-secondary, higher, technical and teacher education

   2) Formal and non-formal education, including adult literacy

   3) Education of girls, Scheduled Castes (SCs), Scheduled Tribes (STs), minorities, and children with special needs, these are areas with special focus

   The Vertical's key functions include:

   Policy Analysis

   Benchmarking Educational Achievement of States: to track progress and infuse healthy competition among States to improve education.

   Research Studies: to formulate recommendations through extensive research and consultations.

   Programme-Level Intervention: to develop proof of con cept to improve quality of education.

   The Line Ministries in this portal are

   1.Ministry of Education

   2.Ministry of Youth Affairs and Sports

   Project SATH-E: The 'Sustainable Action for Transforming Human Capital-Education', was launched in 2017 to identify and build three 'role model' States for the school education sector. After an elaborate selection process, Jharkhand, Odisha and Madhya Pradesh were chosen. The first phase of SATH-E was completed in March 2020.

2. **(c):** Concurrent list basically deals with the federal aspects of the constitution. This list consists of subjects of common interest to both the Union and the States. Both the Parliament and the State Legislatures can make laws on the subjects included in this list. This list has 52 items which are given in the seventh schedule of the constitution.

   Under Article 42 of the constitution, an amendment was added in 1976 and education became a concurrent list subject which enables the Central government to legislate it in the manner suited to it.

3. **(a):** A central university also known as a union university formed by an act of Parliament. As on August 15, 2022, there are 54 central universities in India.

   Pondicherry University – This university is a collegiate public central university. This was established by an Act of Parliament in 1985. The Vice President of India is the Chancellor of this University.

   Viswa Bharti University – This institution was founded by Guru Rabinder Nath Tagore in Shantiniketan (West Bengal) in the year 1921. This was incorporated as a Central University in 1951 by an Act of Parliament. It is an Institution of National Importance. It is the only university in India where Prime Minister is the chancellor of a university.

   H. N. B. Garhwal University - This university was established in the year 1973 in Srinagar, Uttarakhand. That was converted into a Central University by an Act of Parliament, that is Central Universities Act 2009.

   Kurukshetra University - The university was established in 1956 as a unitary residential University. The foundation stone of the university was laid by late Dr. Rajendra Prasad, the first President of India. It is located in the holy city of Kurukshetra, land of the historical battle of 'Mahabharata' and the great message of Bhagwad Gita.

4. **(a):** Lokpal is a very important term, there can be questions on it in the future also.

   A Lokpal is an anti-corruption authority or ombudsman who represents the public interest. The concept of an ombudsman is borrowed from Sweden.

A person 'Who is or has been a Chief Justice of India, is or has been a judge of the Supreme Court, or an eminent person of impeccable integrity and outstanding ability having special knowledge and expertise of not less than 25 years in the matters relating to anti-corruption policy, public administration, vigilance, finance including insurance and banking, law and management'.

Retired Supreme Court Judge Pinaki Chandra Ghose is the country's first Lokpal. Justice Ghose's name was finalized and recommended by the Selection Committee led by Prime Minister Narendra Modi.

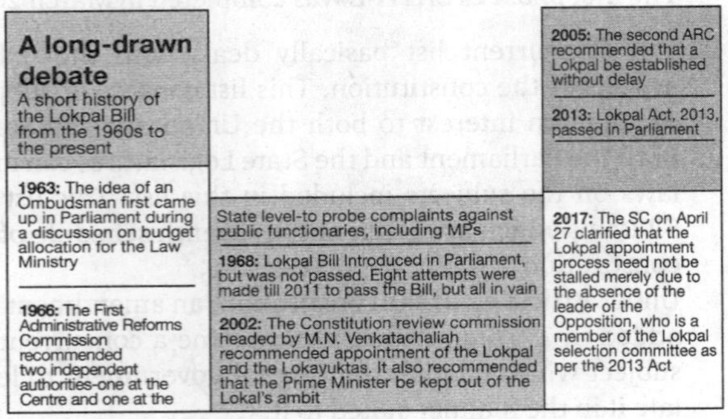

5. **(b):** The concept of Meta University allows the students to increase their flexibility in designing, curriculum, and pursuing subjects of their choice so that their higher education becomes more liberal and accessible to the masses. Thus, it helps students to create new minds conducive to innovation.

   This increases the interaction between students and teachers. Teachers can share teaching material, scholarly publications, research.

   The internet is the most basic communication infrastructure required. A network of universities offers courses in various disciplines that facilitates more collaborative and multidisciplinary learning.

6. **(c):** The President is the Visitor of 161 Central Institutes of Higher Education. The President has the status of visitor of all Central universities, he has no direct role in meetings of Council or Court.

7. **(b):** The Consortium for Educational Communication (CEC) is one of the Inter University Centres set up by the University Grants Commission of India. It has been established with the goal of addressing the needs of Higher Education through the use of powerful medium of Television along with the appropriate use of emerging Information Communication Technology (Information and Communication Technology).

8. **(c):** MOOCs are online courses that offer large-scale interactive participation and provide open access on the Web.

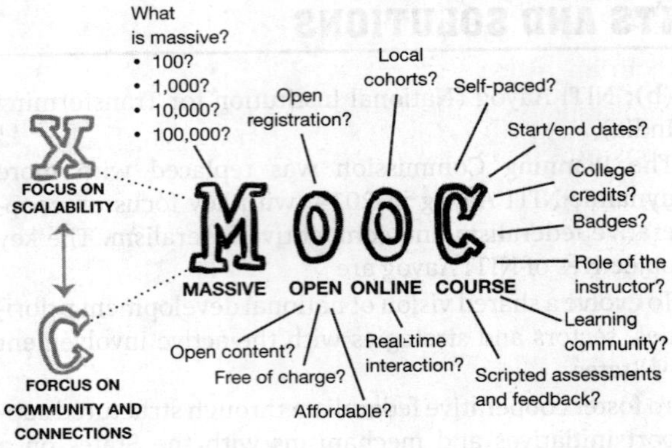

Source: Levels of Teaching l Memory, Understanding and Reflective Level Teaching, https://www.washington.edu/

9. **(b):** The University Grants Commission Act, 1956 under Section 22 (1) provides that a degree can be awarded only by a University established under a Central, State/Provincial Act or an institution deemed to be university under Section 3 of the UGC Act or an Institution especially empowered by an Act of Parliament to confer the degree.

   Universities that offer degrees that are not approved by the UGC are considered to be fake universities in India. UGC releases a list of fake universities in India in the year 2014 U.P. had most fake universities. As in July, 2022, there were 8 fake universities in Delhi, 4 in UP, 2 each in West Bengal and Odisha, 1 each in Karnataka, Maharashtra, Kerala, Puducherry and Andhra Pradesh. The list is available on www.ugc.ac.in website. Every year, UGC releases a list of fake universities ahead of the college admissions.

10. **(c):** Article 30(1) of the Constitution of India gives linguistic and religious minorities a fundamental right to establish and administer educational institutions of their choice. The National Commission for Minority Educational Institutions Act has been enacted to safeguard the educational rights of the minorities enshrined in Article 30(1) of the Constitution. So, minorities can establish institutions but UGC empower universities based on fulfillment of norms and conditions to grant or confer degrees.

11. **(d):** Aadhaar, OMBUDSMAN, Citizen-centric plans, Participatory budgeting, e-governance, Lokpal, Direct Benefit Transfer, Digital India Plans, Maximum Governance, Welfare Government are all parts of good governance.

    Sevottam is an administrative measure to improve the quality of public services in India. The term 'Sevottam' comes from the Hindi words '*Seva*' and '*Uttam*' and means excellence in service delivery.

12. (d): Summoning is the process of calling all members of the Parliament to meet.

Adjournment terminates a sitting.

Prorogation terminates a session.

Dissolution terminates the life of a House.

13. (b): The right to privacy is protected as an intrinsic part of the right to life and personal liberty under Article 21 and as a part of the freedoms guaranteed by Part III of the Constitution.

14. (d):

(a). National Council of Educational Research and Training (NCERT)

This is an autonomous organisation of the Government of India. It was set up in 1961 as a literary, scientific and charitable Society under the Societies Registration Act. It is headquartered in New Delhi. The NCERT helped in the formation National Science Talent Search Scheme (NTSS) in the year 1963. There were changes in NCERT after Kothari Commission recommendations.

University Grant Commission (UGC) - The present system of higher education dates back to Mountstuart Elphinstone`s minutes of 1823. Then, Lord Macaulay's minutes came. Sir Charles Wood`s Dispatch of 1854, called as the `Magna Carta of English Education in India` led to the establishment of the universities of Calcutta, Bombay (now Mumbai) and Madras in 1857, followed by the university of Allahabad in 1887.

In 1925, Inter-University Board (later known as the Association of Indian Universities) was established to promote university linked activities. In 1944, Central Advisory Board of Education recommended Post War Educational Development in India (called as Sargeant Report) recommended the formation of a University Grants Committee that was formed in 1945 to oversee the work of the three Central Universities of Aligarh, Banaras and Delhi, then in 1947, the other existing Universities were added to it.

University Education Commission was set up in 1948 under the Chairmanship of Dr. S Radhakrishnan. It recommended that the University Grants Committee be reconstituted on the general model of the University Grants Commission of the United Kingdom.

In 1952, the Central Government decided that all university linked grants in aids might be referred to the University Grants Commission. Then UGC was recommended on 28 December 1953. But UGC was formally established only in November 1956 as a statutory body of the Government of India through an Act of Parliament for the coordination, determination and maintenance of standards of university education in India.

(c).National Assessment and Accreditation Council (NAAC): This was set up in 1994. NAAC is an independent national accreditation body. NAAC assesses and accredits Higher Education Institutions. The main objective is to maintain the quality of education. This autonomous body is funded by UGC. It is headquartered in Bangalore. It was set up as per recommendations of National Policy in Education (1986) and Programme of Action (1992).

(d). National University of Education Planning and Administration (NUEPA): The NEUPA has its origins in Asian Regional Centre for Educational Planners and Administrators that was set up in 1962. After being taken over by Government in 1965, it was renamed as National Staff College for Educational Planners and Administrators. It was again renamed as National Institute of Educational Planning and Administration (NIEPA) in 1979 and then it became a university as NUEPA. It was conferred the status of Deemed to be University in August, 2006. Like any Central University, NIEPA is fully maintained by the Government of India..

15. (a): Sardar Vallabhbhai Patel, the first Home Minister of Independent India, addressed the probationers of Administrative Services Officers at Metcalf House in Delhi on April 21, 1947, and referred them as the "steel frame of India." The celebration of this day as ' Civil Service Day' started in the year 2006.

16. (c): South Asian University is an international university established by the eight member nations of South Asian Association for Regional Co-operation (SAARC) - Afghanistan, Bangladesh, Bhutan, India, Maldives, Nepal, Pakistan and Sri Lanka. The university started its working from the academic year 2010

17. (b): The question on UGC is always important. The University Grants Commission (UGC) came into existence on 28 December 1953 and became a statutory Organization of the Government of India by an Act of Parliament in 1956, for the coordination,determination and maintenance of standards of teaching, examination and research in university education.

18. (b): Gross Enrollment Ratio (GER) is the ratio of total enrollment in a grade (or standard class) to the population of that officially relevant (eligible) age group. We can multiply that ratio with 100 to get the required percentage. GER in higher education is calculated for the 18-23 age group.

Government makes efforts to increase the GER through Open and Distance Learning, Rashtriya Uchchatar Shiksha Abhiyan (RUSA), ICT based SWAYAM, scholarship schemes etc. GER was used by UN Education index also. As per the New Education Policy, the objective of Government is to take GER in higher education to 50 per cent by 2035. Currently, GER is above 27%.

GER can be calculated for different levels, genders etc. For primary education this GER is 100%, for the secondary, senior secondary and higher education, this is likely to decline.

19. (d): The higher education system in India is provided by public and private universities. Public universities are run by Central and state governments. Universities in India are recognised by the University Grants Commission (UGC), which draws its power from the University Grant Commission Act, 1956. As in July 2022, the number of Central Universities 54.

Kindly take note for future questions that Rajasthan has maximum number of total universities, that is 85. Rajasthan has the most private universities, that is 52.

Tamil Nadu is the state with the most deemed universities, that is 28. West Bengal has the most state universities, that is 35. Delhi has the maximum central universities, that is 7.

20. (b): The Rashtriya Uchchatar Shiksha Abhiyan is the Central government's contribution to further the promise held by the rich expanse of India's state universities. The country's future lies in empowering these campuses with all that it takes to enhance learning, better research and promote innovation. A centrally sponsored scheme, RUSA understands that sometimes the most important lessons of life are learnt outside the classroom. So, whether it is upgrading libraries or computer laboratories, promoting autonomous colleges or clubbing them to consolidate their strength and forming cluster universities, this programme realizes that every institution holds the power to enrich lives through top-class education.

Access, Equity Excellence and Exploration are the objective areas of RUSA.

21. (b): According to Article 29(2): The State shall not deny admission into educational institutes maintained by it or those that receive aid from it to any person based only on race, religion, caste, language, or any of them.

22. (d): President is the head of State and Prime Minister is the head of government. In Indian context, people of the country are sovereign, whereas the Constitution of India is supreme. Parliament is the supreme law making body. The Directive Principles of State Policy are not justiciable.

23. (a): Originally, Constitution of India did not contained any Fundamental Duty. In 1976 , on the recommendation of Sardar Swaran Singh committee 10 fundamental duties were added in the constitution by the 42nd Constitutional Amendment Act of 1976 . One more fundamental duty was added in 2002 by the 86th Constitutional Amendment Act.

Article 51A of the Indian constitution lays down the fundamental duties of citizens in India. The 11 fundamental duties of India are as follows:

(1) To abide by the Constitution and respect its ideals and institutions, the National Flag and the National Anthem.

(2) To cherish and follow the noble ideals which inspired our national struggle for freedom.

(3) To uphold and protect the sovereignty, unity and integrity of India.

(4) To defend the country and render national service when called upon to do so.

(5) To promote harmony and the spirit of common brotherhood amongst all the people of India transcending religious, linguistic and regional or sectional diversities; to renounce practices derogatory to the dignity of women.

(6) To value and preserve the rich heritage of our composite culture.

(7) To protect and improve the natural environment including forests, lakes, rivers and wildlife, and to have compassion for living creatures.

(8) To develop the scientific temper, humanism and the spirit of inquiry and reform.

(9) To safeguard public property and to abjure violence.

(10) To strive towards excellence in all spheres of individual and collective activity so that the nation constantly rises to higher levels of endeavour and achievement.

(11) To provide opportunities for education by the parent the guardian, to his child, or ward between the age of 6–14 years as the case may be.

24. (c): NITI is basically a think tank to guide the nation as per the strategic decision-making. Its resolution says,' The institution will serve as 'Think Tank' of the government, a directional and policy dynamo.

It legal aspects are same as were of Planning Commission, it means that NITI is neither a constitutional body nor it is a statutory body. It has been set-up as a result of 'cabinet resolution'.

NITI is a very important development from examination point of view.

NITI in Hindi or Sanskrit means policy. NITI stands for 'National Institution for Transforming India'. It is the country's premier policy-making institution which is expected to bolster the economic growth of the country. Planning Commission which has a legacy of 65 years has been replaced by the NITI Aayog. Now the time is different when states better and higher role in economic policy making. NITI has adopted a 'bottom-up'approach for states and UTs. It means that where decisions will be taken at the local level and then endorsed at the Central level. It has tried to imbibe the concept of cooperative federalism.

NITI Aayog's creation has two hubs:

(1) **Team India Hub:** It leads the participation of Indian states with the Central government.

(2) **Knowledge and Innovation Hub:** It builds institution's think tank capabilities.

NITI Aayog has seven basic pillars of effective governance. They are:

(1) Pro-people

(2) Pro-activity—to be more responsive towards the needs of citizens

(3) Participation—involvement of citizens

(4) Empowering—specifically women in all aspects

(5) Inclusion of all—irrespective of caste, creed, and gender

(6) Equality—equal opportunity

(7) Transparency—government should be visible and responsive

The NITI Aayog comprises of following:

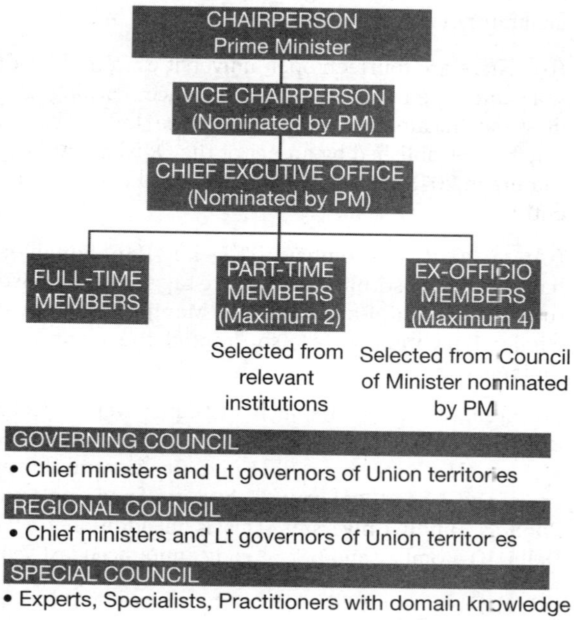

25. (b):

(1) **NAAC (1994) - Headquarters in Bengaluru.**

(2) The National Assessment and Accreditation Council is an autonomous body established by the University Grand Commission (UGC) of India to assess and accredit institutions of higher education in the country.

(3) It is an outcome of the recommendation of the National Policy of Education (NPE)

26. (d): Options (a), (b) and (c) are mostly formal methods . Value education needs more motivation, thus mentoring is required. It needs reflective kind of attitude also, it means that what we have learnt in life so far and how far that can be applied in future situations. It entails with the decision making.

27. (b): Developing critical and creative thinking abilities may not 'ensure' job.

28. (c): Promotion of elitism in education, Commodification of higher education and Increase in the cost of education are the major demerits of globalization of higher education.

29. (b): Who can be the chancellor of a deemed university depends upon the initiator of the institution.

30. (c): Values impact our thoughts, actions and beliefs. They help us in better authentic and proper conduct in a variety of social settings. They have holistic application, they are not specific to a single situation only. The parents, teachers and society have the main task of incorporating values in children. The concept of values have been introduced, even in IITs, IIMs through different subjects.

Value Based Education (VBE) has now been made an integral part of the New Education Policy 2020. The five universal values specifically mentioned in NEP 2020, are "Truth, Peace, Non-violence, Love, Righteous conduct". Value based education is likely to help the nation fight against all kinds of prevailing fanaticism, ill-will, violence, dishonesty, corruption, exploitation and drug abuse.

NCERT has also brought a book "Education for Values in Schools – A Framework". UNESCO has a book: "Learning – The Way of Peace – A Teachers Guide to Peace Education. .

31. (c): Education plays a key role in determining how you spend your adult life – a higher level of education means higher earnings, better health, and a longer life. These goals have been mentioned in our National Education Policies also.

(A) Access – means access to opportunity of education that provides them resources to enable them to achieve their potential. We need to be unbiased as far as providing education to women, different sections of society, divyangs, poor people etc. Government aims to improve Gross Enrolment Ratio.

(B) Equity – personal or social circumstances such as gender, ethnic origin or family background, should not be obstacles to achieve education.

(C) Quality and Excellence – this is a multidimensional concept, we deal with knowledge, skills, creative abilities and moral qualities of individuals in society.

(D) Relevance – so that sections of society are served in a better manner. Pupils become good citizens.

(E) Value-based Education – we may refer to question number 37.

Compulsive and free education may be taken as part of 'inclusive education' which comprises of age group 6 to 14 years under article 21-A. We know that private sector is a big player in higher education.

32. (a): The National Institutional Ranking Framework is a methodology adopted by the Ministry of Human Resource Development, Government of India, to rank institutions of higher education in India. The framework was approved by the MHRD and launched by Minister of Human Resource Development on 29 September 2015.

The following is the latest perspective—courses, criteria of institutions have undergone many changes.

33. (a): The President of India is the Visitor of the Central Universities. For future such questions, the governor of the state, appointed as the union's representative of state by the president, acts as the chancellor of the university. The de facto head of the university is the vice-chancellor.

Hyderabad Central University (2015), Tezpur University (2016) and Jawaharlal Nehru University (2017) received these awards over a period. In 2019, Tezpur University has won the annual Visitor's Award for the 'Best University'. .

34. (d): Norms are behaviours and attitudes that are typical of or approved within a group. Generally speaking, anything that most members of a group consider to be normal, right, correct, proper and/or appropriate is a norm. Rules are guidelines for achieving some goal.

35. (d): India neglected basic education for decades. Subsequently, our Gross Enrolment Ratio is also lower in higher education in comparison to USA and China. India lags behind in research and infrastructure. Only a few Indian institutions have earned global distinction amid shortage of faculty and poor infrastructure.

China has made huge investments in education so its universities rank higher in global rankings. We spent only 4% in education sector despite our target of 6%.

There have been a huge increase in the number of Universities/University level Institutions and Colleges since Independence. Some institutions of India, such as IITs, NITs, IIMs have been globally acclaimed for their standard of education.

36. (d): Prime Minister's Research Fellowship (PMRF) Scheme is aimed at attracting the talent pool of the country to doctoral (PhD) Programs of Indian Institutes of Technology (IITs) and Indian Institute of Science (IISc).

37. (a): The concept of 'Gender Budgeting' , also known as 'Budget for Gender Equity' was introduced in India in 2005–06. It is a powerful tool for achieving gender mainstreaming so as to ensure that benefits of development reach women as much as men. It started with two types of schemes, such as Women Specific Schemes (100% allocation for women) and Pro Women Schemes (at least 30% of the allocation for women).

38. (d): Wooden and inflexible attitude of the civil servants, ineffective implementation of laws and rules are the barriers to citizen-centric administration in India. On the contrary, awareness of rights and duties of citizens is the facilitator of citizen-centric administration in India.

39. (b): There are fourteen open universities in India. Odisha State Open University is a distance learning state university located in Sambalpur, Odisha, India. The university is established by an Act of the Odisha State Legislature in 2015. The University has jurisdiction over the entire State of Odisha.

40. (c): In 2018, IIT-Bombay, IIT-Delhi, IISC Bangalore had received Institute of Eminence tag status. Jio Institute, BITS Pilani, Rajasthan, and Manipal Academy of Higher Education were also granted the Institute of Eminence tag.

This year, in 2019, 14 such institutes were selected under the public institutions category, UGC picked IIT-Madras, IIT-Kharagpur, Delhi University, Central University of Hyderabad, Jadavpur University, Anna University Banaras Hindu University. This is in addition to IIT-Delhi, IIT-Bombay and IISc already announced last year.

41. (a): National Adult Education Programme (NAEP) programme aims at eradicating illiteracy among adults of the age group 15–35.

Following are the objectives of NAEP

(1) Promotion of Literacy–The main sections are economically and socially deprived sections of the society.

(2) Creation of awareness to achieve self reliance

(3) Raising functional capabilities for occupation

(4) Duration is 300–350 hours or 9–10 months

(5) Training of education functionaries

(6) Agencies for coordination

42. (a): National Education Commission, popularly known as Kothari Commission, was an ad hoc commission set-up by the Government of India to examine all aspects of the educational sector in India, to evolve a general pattern of education and to advise guidelines and policies for the development of education in India. On the basis of recommendations of this Commission, a National Policy on Education was set-up in 1968.

43. (a): Central universities are established by an Act of Parliament and are under the purview of the Department of Higher Education in the Union Human Resource Development Ministry.

State universities are run by the state government of each of the states and territories of India, and are usually established by a local legislative assembly act.

Deemed university or 'Deemed-to-be-University', is a status of autonomy granted by the Department of Higher Education on the advice of the UGC, under Section 3 of UGC Act, 1956.

Private universities are approved by the UGC. They can grant degrees but they are not allowed to have off-campus affiliated colleges.

Additional Information—All India Survey on Higher Education (asihe.gov.in) consists of three broad categories; University, College and Stand-Alone Institutions.

44. (b): National Council of Rural Institutes is an independent body which is funded by the MHRD Department of the Government of India which is now, the Ministry of Education (MoE). The headquarter of the institute is at Hyderabad. The main objective behind establishing this body was to promote and facilitate higher education in the rural areas to develop the livelihoods of the rural people.

45. (a): The open universities in India are regulated by the Distance Education Council of India (DEC). It is an organization based in New Delhi which maintains the standards, encourages and organizes the activities of Open and Distance learning in India (ODL). Baba Bhim Rao Ambedkar Open University was set-up in 1982 in India). There are 14 open universities in India.

46. (d): Dr S Radhakrishnan was born on September 5, that is celebrated as National Teacher's Day. He was an Indian philosopher and statesman who served as the first Vice President of India (1952–1962) and the second President of India (1962–1967).

University Education of India: The main recommendations of the committee set up under Dr S Radhakrishnan are as follows.

1. **Faculty in Universities:** The University Education Commission has emphasized that the teacher plays a vital role in the education system; therefore, an adequate faculty with required qualifications are necessary to discharge many types of duties in a university or in a college. The University Education Commission recommended that proper care should be taken in the selection procedure of a teacher for the appointment as a professor, reader, lecturer and an instructor as well as for his or her salaries. Each university should have some research fellows. Besides definite rules regarding the Provident Fund, leave and hours of work should be followed by a university.
2. **Teaching standards:** The most important duty of a university is to maintain the highest standard of its teaching and examinations.
3. **Course of study**
4. **Research and training**
5. **Professional education**
6. **Medium of instruction**
7. **Religious education**
8. **Evaluation system**

47. (a): E-Pathshala has been developed by NCERT for showcasing and disseminating all educational e-resources including textbooks, audio, video, periodicals and a variety of other print and non-print materials through website and mobile app. The platform addresses the dual challenge of reaching out to a diverse clientele and bridging the digital divide (geographical, socio-cultural and linguistic), offering comparable quality of e-contents and ensuring its free access at every time and every place. All the NCERT books have been digitized and uploaded. Currently the e-contents are available in Hindi, English and Urdu. States/UTs are being approached to digitize and share all textbooks in Indian languages through this platform, which will be done in a phased manner.

48. (a): Article 30(1) gives the linguistic or religious minorities the following two rights:

- The right to establish
- The right to administer educational institutions of their choice.

Article 30(2) bars the state, while granting aid to educational institutions, from discriminating against any educational institution on the ground that it is under the management of a linguistic or a religious minority.

49. (a): The process started with three universities established by 1857. The University of Madras, established 1857, is one of the three oldest modern state universities in India, the others being the University of Calcutta and the University of Mumbai.

50. (a): The report of the Standards of University Education Committee,1962, was published by the UGC in 1965, for the promotion and coordination of the university education and for the determination and maintenance of standards of teaching, examination and research in universities.

Examination reforms units were setup, with the commissions support at the universities of Delhi, Baroda, Aligarh and Guwahati.

51. (c): The Indian Council of Social Science Research is the national body overseeing research in the social sciences in India. It was established in New Delhi in 1969 under which- Impactful Policy Research in Social Science (IMPRESS) aims to encourage social science research in policy relevant areas so as to provide vital inputs in policy-formulation, implementation and evaluation.

52. (b): Unnat Bharat Abhiyan is inspired by the vision of transformational change in rural development processes by leveraging knowledge institutions to help build the architecture of an ' Inclusive India'.

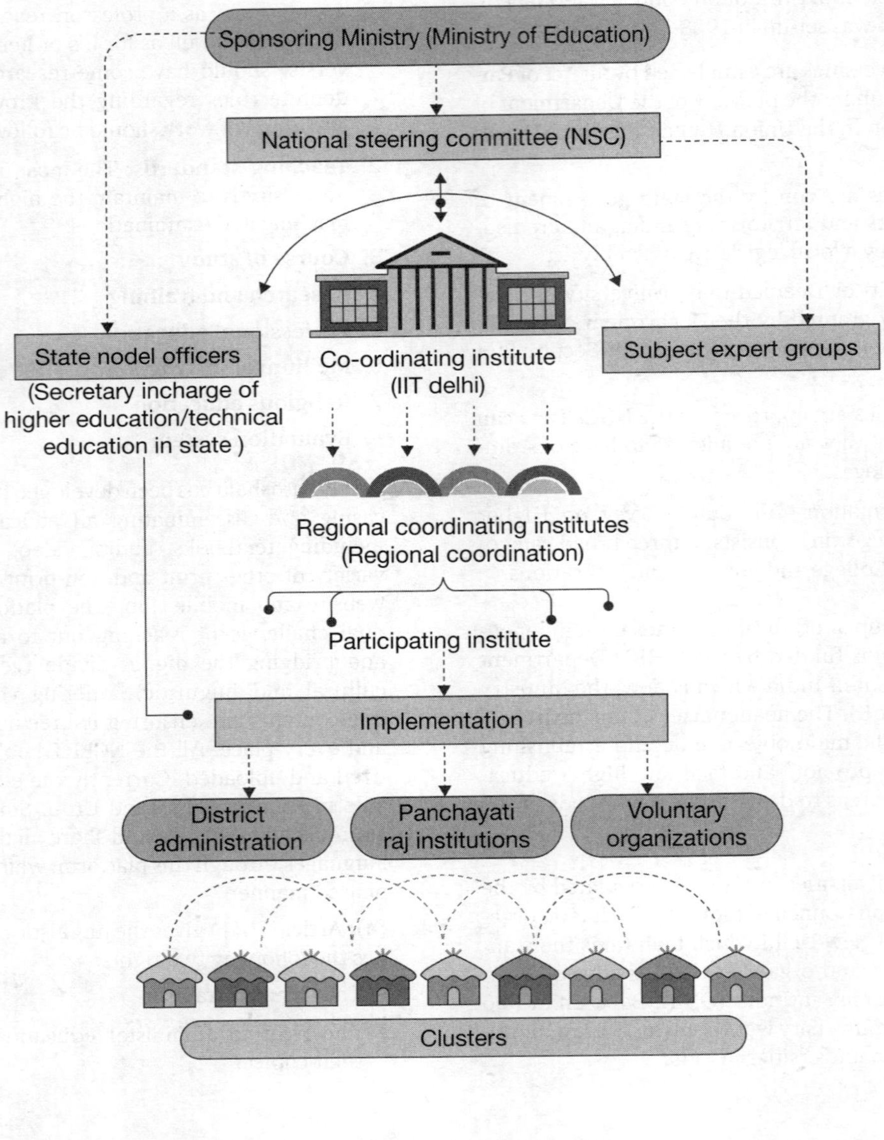

53. (a):

(1) It seems to be the most purposeful approach as all pupils used to live and learn together.

(2) The level of stress not that much prominent during Vedic era.

(3) The focus was more on present capabilities.

(4) Self-help applies only for personal chores.

54. (c): Radhakrishnan Commission was linked with university education, Mudaliar with secondary education and Acharya Rammurthi with the progress of NPE of 1986.

55. (b): The National Mission on Education through Information and Communication Technology (NMEICT) has been envisaged as a Centrally Sponsored Scheme to leverage the potential of ICT, in teaching and learning process for the benefit of all the learners in Higher Education Institutions in any time any where mode. This was expected to be a major intervention in enhancing the Gross Enrolment Ratio (GER) in Higher Education.

The three cardinal principles of Education Policy viz., access, equity and quality could be served well by providing connectivity to all colleges and universities, providing low cost and affordable access-cum-computing devices to students and teachers and providing high quality e-content free of cost to all learners in the country. NMEICT encompasses all the three elements.

56. (a): Sanskrit is traceable to the 2nd millennium BCE in a form known as Vedic Sanskrit, with the *Rigveda* as the earliest known composition.

Buddha's sutras were first written down in Pali.

57. (b): Memorization as per 'Memory Level of Teaching' should come first. What is memorized is 'critically analysed' and then many such instances lead to generalization, a sort of 'story telling'.

58. (c): Innovation in Science Pursuit for Inspired Research (INSPIRE) is an innovative programme sponsored and managed by the Department of Science and Technology for attraction of talent to science.

59. (b): The development of National Curriculum Framework should also be seen in the light of the report, Learning Without Burden (1993). Additionally, the revised National Curriculum Framework (NCF) opens with a quotation from Rabindranath Tagore's essay, Civilization and Progress.

60. (b): Traditional education is also called customary education or conventional education. The main motive of traditional education is to pass on the values, manners skills and the social practice to the next generation which is necessary for their survival. The students simply sit down together and listen to the teacher or another who will recite the lesson.

61. (c): Kindly refer to solution to question number 15.

62. (d): Brain drain is the emigration of highly trained or intelligent people from a particular country.

Reason for India's brain drain:

(1) Unemployment in India

(2) Policies in India

(3) No Value of Talent

(4) Population

(5) Better Lifestyle and Currency Difference

(6) Quality of Higher Education

(7) Wage Gap

63. (c): Government of India approved a new program titled Global Initiative of Academic Networks (GIAN) in Higher Education aimed at tapping the talent pool of scientists and entrepreneurs, internationally to encourage their engagement with the institutes of Higher Education in India so as to augment the country's existing academic resources, accelerate the pace of quality reform, and elevate India's scientific and technological capacity to global excellence.

64. (b): Planning Commission was set-up in March, 1950. The main objective of the government to promote a rapid rise in the standard of living of the people by efficient exploitation of the resources of the country, increasing production and offering opportunities to all for employment in the service of the community.

Under 4th five year plan (1969–74), there was focus on education and manpower.

Priority was to be given to the expansion of elementary education and the emphasis was to be on the provision of facilities for backward areas and communities and for girls.

65. (c): Skills Acquisition and Knowledge Awareness for Livelihood Scheme

(1) Skills Acquisition and Knowledge Awareness for Livelihood (SANKALP) is an outcome-oriented programme of Ministry of Skill Development & Entrepreneurship (MSDE) with a special focus on decentralized planning and quality improvement.

(2) It is a Centrally Sponsored Scheme which is collaborated with the World Bank.

(3) It aims to implement the mandate of the National Skill Development Mission (NSDM).

The main objectives of the scheme are:

(i) **Convergence:** Creating convergence among all skill training activities, both State-led and Government of India funded, at the state level.

(ii) **Quality:** Improving the quality of skill development programs through building a pool of quality trainers, developing model curriculum and content, and standardizing assessment and certification.

(iii) **Evaluation System:** Establishing a robust monitoring and evaluation system for skill training programs.

(iv) **Inclusiveness and Opportunity:** Providing access to skill training opportunities to the disadvantaged sections. Creating industry-led and demand-driven skill training capacity.

66. (b): University Act, 1857 officially called the University Act No II of 1857, was passed by the Indian Legislative Council for the establishment of a university at Calcutta and it received the Governor General's assent on 24 January 1857. The three universities were established at Calcutta, Bombay and Madras.

University of Calcutta (Kolkata) was incorporated on 24th January 1857 while the University of Madras (Chennai) started its operations on the 5th September 1857.

67. (d): Dr S. Radhakrishnan–University Education Commission

Mudaliar Commission–Secondary Education Commission

In 1917 the government appointed the Calcutta University Commission to study and report on the problem of university education. The commission is also known as the Sadler Commission after the name of its chairman Dr Michael E. Sadler, the Vice Chancellor of the University of Leeds.

Kothari Commission, also popular as National Education Commission (1964–1966) Sub title 'Education for National Development' was an ad hoc commission setup by the Government of India to examine all aspects of the educational sector in India, to evolve a general pattern of education and to advise guidelines and policies for the development of education in India.

68. (c): British introduced modern education system but this education was out of reach for majority of Indians.

Mughals ignored scientific and modern education.

During Buddhist period, education was in-built part of our system and was as per requirement of larger masses.

In post-independence era, education was again as per democratic demand conditions. Many government institutions were established.

69. (d): We are aware about all these streams, but we are still mentioning professional stream. Their examples are also quite direct.

Professional stream or skills are career competencies that often are not taught (or acquired) as part of the coursework required to earn your masters or PhD. Professional skills such as leadership, mentoring, project management, and conflict resolution are value-added skills essential to any career.

70. (b): Gross enrolment ratio in Higher Education Total enrolment in higher education, regardless of age, expressed as a percentage to the eligible official population (18–23 years) in a given school year. The GER is widely used to show the general level of participation in and capacity of higher education.

As per All India Survey on Higher Education (AISHE) 2017–18, the Gross Enrolment Ratio (GER) in higher education has increased from 24.5% in 2015–16 to 25.8% in 2017–18. Apart from regular education, open and distance education, SWAYAM, Rashtriya Uchchatar Shiksha Abhiyan (RUSA), etc., also helps in this.

In addition to above, Higher Education Financing Agency (HEFA) was established under the Companies Act, 2013 to leverage funds from market to finance improvement in infrastructure in top institutions of education.

71. (d): The Treasure Within: Learning to know, learning to do, learning to live together and learning to be. Jacques Delors from France is the main proponent of this concept. He stated that lifelong learning is essential for gaining self-esteem and the ability to take control of one's own life.

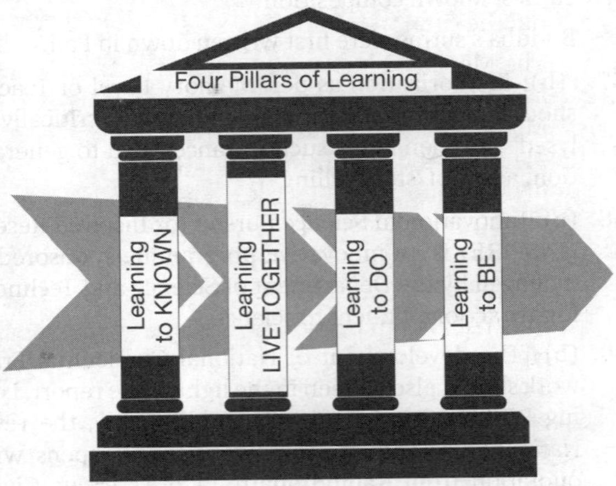

72. (c): Being visitor to an institute of higher level institution means part of regular interactions. The President of India is visitor of Central universities in India.

Central universities in India are established by an Act of Parliament and are under the purview of the Department of Higher Education in the Union Human Resource Development Ministry. In general, universities in India are recognized by the University Grants Commission (UGC), which draws its power from the University Grants Commission Act, 1956.

73. (a): According to All India Survey on Higher Education Report (2017–18), if we look at Undergraduate level, the highest number (36.4%) of students are enrolled in Arts/Humanities/Social Sciences courses followed by Science (17.1%), Engineering and Technology (14.1%) and Commerce (14.1%). B.A. (23.89 Lakh) degree has been awarded to maximum number of students. B.Sc. (11.52 Lakh) is the second highest followed by B.Com. (9.39 Lakh). At Post graduate level, M.A. pass number of students is maximum followed by M.Sc. and M.B.A. Thus, 'Arts' stream has the highest percentage of enrolment in the higher education of India.

74. (c): The main function of UGC in higher education is UGC is the only grant-giving commission in India that is vested with two responsibilities simultaneously.

1. It coordinates, determines, regulates the standards of higher education institutions and

2. To provide funds to these institutions.

In June 2018, the Ministry of Education (then called as Human Resources Development Ministry) proposed its plans to revoke the UGC Act 1956 and come up with a new body, that is Higher Education Commission of India (HECI).

75. (a): Non-conventional education provides opportunites for individuals to continue their educational path without the confines of a classroom and curriculum.

The Ministry of HRD has embarked on a project called as 'Study Webs of Active Learning for Young Aspiring Minds' (SWAYAM), which will provide one integrated platform and portal for online courses. This covers all higher education subjects and skill sector courses. The objective is to ensure that the every student in our country has access to the best quality higher education at the affordable cost.

SWAYAM is a indigenous MOOC covering almost all disciplines. At present about 1550+ courses are listed on SWAYAM out of which 800+ courses are already delivered. About 34 Lakhs students have enrolled in these courses.

76. (b): The day-to-day administration of the university should be in the hands of Syndicate/Executive council of 15 to 20 members presided over by the Vie Chancellor, This could largely be an internal body consisting mainly of academic persons. There could be Deans, School of Studies, 2 Head of the Departments, 2/3 Teachers Representatives of the Principal of the University Colleges, 3 Principals of the constituted or recognized colleges, in addition, the Finance Secretary, Education Secretary/Commissioner and the Chancellor/Chief Rector may nominate 1 or 2 person along with his Secretary as his representative.

The Syndicate/Executive council shall normally meets twice/thrice in a year during its term and consider business brought before it by the Vice Chancellor. The business shall normally consist of administrative matters pertaining to the property of the university, financial transactions, appointments, postings, sanction of expenditure provided for the budget and any other business that would come within the range of day to day administration of the university.

77. (a): The objective of UGC–Faculty Recharge Programme is to induct exceptional candidates with notable record of research in interdisciplinary/frontier areas of science, who will spearhead internationally competitive research programmes along with their teaching responsibilities.

78. (c): The Scheme for Promotion of Academic and Research Collaboration (SPARC) aims at improving the research ecosystem of India's Higher Educational Institutions by facilitating academic and research collaborations between Indian institutions and the best institutions in the world from 28 selected nations to jointly solve problems of national and/or international relevance.

79. (b): The Inter-University Board (IUB) was established in 1925 and was renamed as the Association of Indian Universities (AIU) in 1973.

Let's look at some detailed information for future questions.

Association of Indian Universities (AIU) is an organization and association of major universities in India. It is located in Delhi. Since 1925, it works for the cause of higher education. It assesses the courses, syllabi, standards and credits of foreign universities pursued abroad and equates them in relation to various courses offered by Indian universities. It is mainly concerned with the recognition of Degrees/Diplomas awarded by the Universities in India, which are recognized by the UGC, New Delhi, and abroad for the purpose of admission to higher degree courses in Indian Universities. The main objective of the AIU is to protect and promote the interest of universities and facilitate university activities especially by way of sharing information and increasing cooperation in the field of culture, sports, and allied areas, and help universities in mutual recognition of degrees AIU manages its routine activities through several functional divisions in the AIU Secretariat viz, Administration, Finance, Evaluation, Research, Student Information Services, Sports Division, Library and Documentation, and Publication and Sales Division. Each of these divisions is entrusted with important assignments of national and international level. Affiliation, exchange of views, information bureau and platform for solution of problems are the major functions of AIU.

80. (a): The answer is Education Commission of India. Let's understand—what brain drain does for society? It aggravates the class and income structure for the intellectuals which we have inherited from British rule. This structure has two characteristic features.

1. It places a high premium, both in terms of status and income on the professions vis-à-vis the rest of the society.
2. It has created inordinate inequalities, again in terms of status and income, within the intellectual ranks.

81. (c): Kothari Commission (1964–66) is a very comprehensive system. The title of its report is education and national development. It was third such commission after independence. This Education Commission was appointed by the government of India by a Resolution, dated 14 July 1964, to advise the Government on the national pattern of education and on the general principles and policies for the development of education at all stages and in all aspects.

The commission set-up twelve Task Forces on

(1) School Education
(2) Higher Education
(3) Technical Education
(4) Agricultural Education
(5) Adult Education
(6) Science Education and Research
(7) Teacher Training and Teacher Status
(8) Student Welfare
(9) New Techniques and Methods
(10) Manpower
(11) Educational Administration
(12) Educational Finance.

In addition, it set-up seven Working Groups on

(1) Women's Education
(2) Education of Backward Classes
(3) School Buildings
(4) School–Community Relations
(5) Statistics
(6) Pre-Primary Education
(7) School Curriculum.

These points reflect the scope of policy.

The National Policy on Education in 1968 was also based on this approach.

82. (d): The Inter-University Board (IUB) of India was set-up as an Apex Inter-University Organization on 23 March 1925 to bring together all the universities in India on a common platform through a coordinating body, to protect the interest of the students as well as the universities. Prior to this, having such an organization in India was recommended by the Sadler Commission in 1919 followed by a resolution, made in the Conference of Vice Chancellors of the Indian Universities convened at Shimla in 1924.

The Inter-University Board acquired a legal status with its registration as a Society under the Societies Registration Act, 1860, on September 29, 1967 and was renamed as Association of Indian Universities (AIU) in 1973. Since its inception, AIU is actively engaged in the growth and development of Higher Education. The membership of AIU includes all types of universities.

83. (a): We may refer to solution of question number 15 for detailed idea.

84. (a): IGNOU has the following broadcast channels/programmes:

(1) Gyan Darshan-1
(2) Gyan Darshan-2
(3) Gyanvani
(4) DD-1
(5) Gyandhara
(6) Interactive Radio Counselling (IRC)
(7) IGNOU AIR Broadcast
(8) Sakshat
(9) You Tube Archives

85. (c): Research Promotion Scheme (RPS) aims at to create research ambience in the institutes by promoting research in engineering sciences and innovations in established and newer technologies; and to generate Master's and Doctoral degree candidates to augment the quality of faculty and research.

86. (b): A curriculum is broadly defined as the totality of student experiences that occur in the educational process. The term often refers specifically to a planned sequence of instruction or to a view of the student experiences in terms of the educator or college instructional goals.

87. (d): Pradhan Mantri Kaushal Vikas Yojana is the flagship scheme of the Ministry Of Skill Development and Entrepreneurship implemented by National Skill Development Corporation. The objective of this skill certification scheme is to enable a large number of Indian youth to take up industry relevant skill training that will help them in securing a better livelihood. Individuals with prior learning experience or skills will also be assessed and certified under the recognition of prior learning.

88. (a): Here, we can take example of UGC that is a statutory organization established by an Act of Parliament in 1956 for the coordination, determination and maintenance of standard of university education. They provide funding also.

The institutions have not been able to provide quality education because of lack of resources and supervision as their sheer number is very high. Government has set up other institutions for their grading.

89. (b): Here, non-traditional education means 'Open and Distance Learning' (ODL). It always focus on 'innovative methods' to reach out to prospective learners.

90. (d):

Taxila: Taxila is now located in Pakistan. Taxila University played an important in medicine. But this university functioned under more informal conditions, the education system was flexible. There was no system of examinations. The teachers worked with complete autonomy, forming their own school of learning with their specific set of rules and manner of functioning. Nalanda Univsersity was a formal university and was more structured than Taxila University.

Ujjain - Located on the banks of river Kshipra, this place played an important role in linguistics, astronomy, astrology, arithmetic, classical arts and liberal thinking.

Sarnath - Buddha gave his first sermon in the village of Sarnath, near Banaras. This event is known as Dharma-Chakra-Pravartana (turning of the wheel of law).

Ajanta - The paintings and sculptures in the caves of Ajanta and Ellora are inspired by Buddhism. It was declared as World Heritage Sites by UNESCO in 1983 as the paintings and sculptures of Ajanta had a great influence in the development of art in India.

91. (b):

(i) Increasing transparency is one of the main advantages of e-governance. We usually talk about 'Transparent Government'. RTI, good governance are also parts of it.

92. (a): During Gupta period, the focus was to patronize the centers of higher education at Nalanda, Takshila, Ujjain, Vikramshila and Vallabhi etc. These centres attracted scholars from all parts of India and from several foreign countries.

93. (c): The University Grants Commission of India is a statutory body set up by the Indian Union Government in accordance to the UGC Act 1956 under Ministry of Human Resources Development and is charged with coordination, determination and maintenance of standards of higher education.

Functions of UGC :

1. To enquire into the financial needs of the Universities
2. Allocate and disburse grants to Universities and College for their development and maintenance.
3. Advising central and state Government on the measures for the improvement of university education.
4. To determine and maintain the standards of teaching and research in Universities.
5. Promote and co-ordinate University education.

94. (c): National policy on Education (1986) recommended the establishment of State Council for Higher Education in each state.

The National Policy on Education is a policy formulated by the Government of India to promote education amongst India's people. The Policy covers elementary education to college in both rural and urban India. The first NPE was promulgated in 1968 by the Govt. of Prime Minister Indira Gandhi and the second by Prime Minister Rajiv Gandhi in 1986.

95. (c): Xuan Zang a Chinese scholar carried back scriptures from Nalanda University and wrote about architecture and learning of this University. The best known source of information of that time was through the work of Xaun Zang who carried back many hundred scriptures which were later translated into Chinese. Nalanda was a completely residential University believed to have 2000 teachers and 10000 students.

96. (a): The National Skills Qualifications Framework is a competency based Framework that organizes all qualifications according to a series of level of knowledge, skills and aptitude. These levels, graded from one to ten are defined in terms of learning outcomes which the learner must possess regardless of whether they are obtained through formal, non formal or informal learning. NSQF in India was notified on 27 Dec, 2013. All other frameworks including the NVEQF released by the Ministry of HRD, stand superceded by the NSQF. Under NSQF, the learner can acquire the certification for competency needed at any level through formal, non-formal or informal learning.

97. (b):

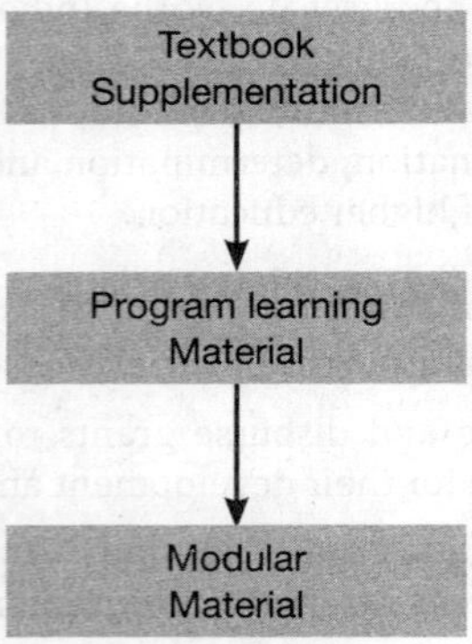

This sequence correctly reflects the evaluation of educational technology support in higher education.

98. (b): Following Kothari Commission recommendations, the first National Policy of Education in 1968 was to be followed by a 'five yearly review to progress and working out of new policies and programmes.' The National Policy of Education of 1986 is the result of such reviews. The main objective was to make education more innovative as per changing needs. Again, a committee was set up under the chairmanship of Acharaya Rammurti in May 1990 to review National Policy of Education (NPE) and to make recommendations for its modifications. To supplement and improve, NPE (1986), a National Programme of Action was launched in 1992. This policy aimed to promote national progress, a sense of common citizenship and culture, and to strengthen national integration. It laid stress on the need for a radical reconstruction of the education system, to improve its quality at all stages, and therefore gave much greater attention to science and technology, the cultivation of moral values and a closer relation between education and the life of the people.

99. (d): There are following current challenges in the field of higher education in India:

(1) Expansion

(2) Equity

(3) Excellence

100. (d):

(i) Autonomous Governance

(ii) Focussed Funding

(iii) Independent Outcomes

These factors require the creation of world class universities.

101. (a): Entrance examination mode of admission was prevalent in Nalanda University in ancient times.

102. (b):

Association of Indian Universities: This is an organisation and association of major universities in India. It is based in Delhi. It evaluates the courses, syllabi, standards and credits of foreign universities pursued abroad and equates them in relation to various courses offered by Indian Universities. The AIU is mainly concerned with the recognition of Degrees/ Diplomas awarded by the Universities in India, which are recognised by the University Grants Commission, New Delhi and abroad for the purpose of admission to higher degree courses in Indian Universities. The AIU is also an implementing agency for the agreements signed under the cultural Exchange Programmes executed between India and other countries in the field of education.

103. (a)

Upanayana is one of the traditional samskaras that marked the acceptance of a student by a teacher or tutor and individual's entrance to a school. This ceremony should be done before the age of 12.

Upanayana is an elaborate ceremony that includes rituals involving the family, the child and the teacher. A boy receives and wears a sacred thread during this ceremony named, 'yajno pavitam'. The yajno pavitam ceremony announces that the child had entered into formal education.

104. (b): Imprint is the first of its kind MHRD supported Pan-IIT + IISc Joint initiative to address the major science and engineering challenges that India must address and champion to enable empower and embolden the nation for inclusive growth and self-reliance. This noval initiative with two fold mandate is aimed at the following.

(a) Developing new engineering education policy.

(b) Creating a road map to pursue engineering challenges.

Imprint provides the overarching vision that guides research into areas that are predominantly socially relevant.

105. (a): Article 282 provides for grants to the States by the union government. This seems to fall under spirit of co-operative federalism where needs of some states (or institutions) are met. This article empowers the Union Government to make grants for a public purpose.

Grants in aids are derived from public funds. These are allocated when government and the legislature decide so. This system of 'grants in aids' was introduced by Wood's Dispatch of 1854 (also known as Magna Carta of English Education in India) that also recommended the setting up universities in British India..

106. (b): Xuanzang (also popular as Hiuen Tsang), born in 602 A.D was the celebrated Chinese traveler. He has been described therefore as the "Prince of Pilgrims."

His visited India during the reign of Harshavardhana. India is much indebted to this Chinese traveler for the valuable accounts he left behind with many details of political, religious, economic, social conditions of those days. The biography of Hiuen Tsang, written by another Chinese, is also another valuable source for Indian history. He remained at the Nalanda University for about five years.

107. (a): The evolution of UGC has been discussed in question number 127.

108. (c): External accountability means contribution towards the society while dealing with external environment. Points A and B are meant for internal purposes.

109. (c): Academic Council is principal academic body of the Universities. They may be subject to the provisions to the Memorandum of Association. They are responsible for the maintenance of standards of education, teaching and training, inter departmental co-ordination, research, etc.

110. (b): Accreditation is a process of quality assurance and improvement, whereby a programme in an approved Institution is critically appraised to verify that the Institution or the programme continues to meet and/or exceed the Norms and Standards prescribed by regulator from time to time. It is a kind of recognition which indicates that a programme or Institution fulfills certain standards.

NBA is one of the two major bodies responsible for accreditation of higher education institutions in India, along with the National Assessment and Accreditation Council (NAAC). NBA was established by the All India Council for Technical Education (AICTE) in 1994 and operated as an autonomous body since 2010. In 2014, it was granted a full membership status in the Washington Accord. NBA accredits technical programmes, such engineering and management programmes, while NAAC accredits general colleges and universities. The NBA accredits programmes and not institutes. These include diplomas, undergraduate and postgraduate programs. The office of NBA is in Delhi.

111. (a)

The words in question, reflect the ultimate goals in life though there is a lot of semblance in these words.

(i) Nihsreyasa (निःश्रेयसम्) is the quest for oneself. It is the search of innate adhyatmikity within oneself. It is said to be the highest goal of mankind.

(ii) Nirvana (निर्वाण) is the goal of the Buddhist path. The literal meaning of the term is "blowing out" or "quenching". Nirvana is the ultimate spiritual goal in Buddhism and marks the soteriological release from rebirths in samsâra.

(iii) The word apavarga means 'liberation.' Pavarga means 'material existence.' In material existence, one always works very hard but is ultimately baffled. One then dies and has to accept another body to work very hard again. This is the cycle of material existence. Apavarga means just the opposite.

(iv) Moksha is the ultimate spiritual liberation.

112. (b): New Education Policy, 2020 proposes a single regulator for higher education institutions across the country, that will be called as Higher Education Council of India (HECI). It will have four verticals for its various roles.

(i) National Higher Education Regulatory Council (NHERC): It will function as the common, single point regulator for the higher education sector including teacher education. It however excludes medical and legal education.

(ii) National Accreditation Council (NAC) – a 'meta-accrediting body'): It will be based primarily on basic norms, public self–disclosure, good governance, and outcomes. It will be carried out by independent accrediting institutions supervised and overseen by NAC.

(iii) Higher Education Grants Council (HEGC): It will look into funding and financing of colleges and universities.

(iv) General Education Council (GEC): It will frame expected learning outcomes for higher education programmes, also referred to as 'graduate attributes'. GEC will formulate a National Higher Education Qualification Framework (NHEQF).

113. (d): Global Citizenship Education: Topics and learning objectives, should be counted as the first pedagogical guidance from UNESCO on global citizenship education. With such education, young people are able to solve problems, make decisions, think critically, communicate ideas effectively and work well with others. This not only helps them personally and educationally, but eventually professionally as well. Thus, a global education in the classroom is paramount.

114. (b):

Indian Institute of Advance Study (IIAS): This research institute is based in Shimla. It was set up by the Ministry of Education in 1964 and it started functioning in 1965.

Indian Biological Science and Research Institute (IBRI): It is located in Noida, UP. IBRI is run by the academicians from different technological fields such as Pharmaceutics, Biotechnology, Bioinformatics, Information Technology and Mathematics. The mandate of IBRI is to undertake research and training from basics to industrial level in biosciences domains.

Indian Institute of Soil Science (IISS): This institute is linked with ICAR (Indian Council of Agriculture Research). ICAR–IISS was established in 1988 at Bhopal with a mandate of "Enhancing Soil Productivity with Minimum Environmental Degradation". IISS has emerged as a leader in basic and strategic research on soils in the country.

Indian Institute of Sugarcane Research (IISR): IISR was established in Lucknow in 1952. It deals with basic issues linked with sugarcane. In 1954, its working was taken care of by Government, then in 1969, it was transferred to ICAR, New Delhi alongwith other central agricultural research institutes.

115. (a): CBCS stands for the choice–based credit system. CBCS grading systems surpass the 'conventional percentage' and grading means to evaluate a student's academic skills. CBCS follows a more standardised way of assessment and examination management. CBCS software grading system is uniform across all educational institutes. It follows the semester pattern and not the annual examination pattern.

UGC also follows a 10–point grading system, with 0 being absent/fail and 10 being outstanding.

Evaluation in choice Based Credit System in Higher Education

Letter Grades	Grade Points
O (Outstanding)	10
A+ (Excellent)	9
A (Very Good)	8
B+ (Good)	7
B (Above Average)	6
C (Average)	5
P (Pass)	4
F (Fail) or Absent (AB)	0

116. (d): UNESCO World Heritage Sites are called special places that are selected by the World Heritage Sites Committee. The purpose of this program is to select and preserve such sites of the world which are important to humanity from the point of view of world culture. For example, forest area, mountain, lake, desert, monument, university, building, city, etc.

Each heritage site is the property of the particular country in which the site is located. It is also in the interest of the international community to preserve them for future generations and for the benefit of humanity. In this way, the responsibility of their protection rests with the whole world community.

In certain circumstances, financial assistance is also given to such places by this committee. So far (as of July 2021) about 1154 sites have been declared as World Heritage Sites all over the world which includes 897 cultural, 218 natural, 39 mixed and 138 other sites.

The ancient Taxila and Nalanda University have been declared as heritage sites by UNESCO.

Nalanda: Nalanda Mahavihar is a world heritage site that is 98 km away from Patna. Nalanda stands out as the most ancient university of the Indian subcontinent. It engaged in the organised transmission of knowledge interrupted period of 800 years. The historical development of the site testifies the development of Buddhism into a religion and the flourishing of monastic and educational traditions.

Takshashila: Takshashila (or Taxila) was an ancient Indian educational centre that was founded in 1000 BCE. This produced some illustrious historical personalities:

(a) Kautilya who wrote Arthashastra

(b) Panini- the compiler of 'Ashtadhyayi' the Sanskrit grammar

(c) Charaka the great Ayurvedic healer (author of Charak Smhita)

(d) Jivaka who once treated Buddha and was the personal physician of the Indian king Bimbisara.

But there was not much formal (or centralized) system of education in Takshashila. It did not award degrees to its students. The education system there was flexible, and was customizable towards students. The faculty here worked with complete autonomy, forming their own school of learning with their specific set of rules and manner.

The manner of functioning of Takshashila differed drastically from Nalanda University that was more structured than Taxila.

By some accounts, the University of Ancient Taxila was considered to be one of the earliest universities in the world.

Pushpagiri: This vihar (or set of monuments) was an ancient Buddhist mahavihara. It is also termed as monastic complex located atop Langudi Hill in Jajpur district of Odisha. The visit of Xuanzang to Pushpagiri vihar indicates that it was an important Buddhist site in ancient India. Like Nalanda, Vikramashila, Odantapuri, Takshashila and Vallabhi, it was a major ancient centre of learning. It progressed between 3rd and 11th centuries CE.

Valabhi: The Valabhi University was an important centre of Buddhist learning. It championed the cause of Hinayana Buddhism between 600 CE and 1200 CE. Valabhi was the capital of the Maitraka empire during the period 480–775 CE.

Mithila: Ancient Mithila University was famous for Nyaya Shastra and logical sciences.

117. (d):

BCI: The Bar Council of India is a statutory body established under the section 4 of Advocates Act (1961) that regulates the legal practice and legal education in India. It prescribes standards of professional conduct, etiquettes, and exercises disciplinary jurisdiction over the bar. It also sets standards for legal education and grants recognition to universities whose degree in law will serve as a qualification for students to enrol themselves as advocates upon graduation.

NCTE: The National Council for Teacher Education, in its previous status since 1973, was an advisory body for the Central and State Governments on all matters pertaining to teacher education, with its Secretariat in the Department of Teacher Education of the National Council of Educational Research and Training (NCERT). The National Council for Teacher Education as a statutory body that came into existence in pursuance of the National Council for Teacher Education Act, 1993 on the 17th August, 1995. The main objective of the NCTE is to achieve planned and coordinated development of the teacher education system throughout the country, the regulation and proper maintenance of Norms and Standards in the teacher education system and for matters connected therewith.

AICTE: All India Council for Technical Education (AICTE) was set up in November 1945 as a national – level Apex Advisory body to conduct a survey on the facilities available for technical education and to promote development in the country in a coordinated and integrated manner.

NMC: National Medical Commission (NMC) is an Indian regulatory body of 33 members which regulates medical education and medical professionals. It replaced the Medical Council of India on 25 September 2020. The Commission grants recognition of medical qualifications, gives accreditation to medical schools, grants registration to medical practitioners, monitors medical practice and assesses the medical infrastructure in India.

118. (b):

Central university: Central universities or union universities in India are established by an Act of Parliament and are under the purview of the Department of Higher Education in MoE. In general, universities in India are recognised by UGC, which draws its power from the UGC Act 1956.

As of August 15, 2022 the list of central universities published by the UGC includes 54 central universities. E.g., Jamia Milia Islamia is a central university.

State universities: State universities are run by the respective state government of the states and union territories of India, and are usually established by a local legislative assembly act. Panjab university is considered both central and state university.

Deemed universities: The Governor of the State is the chancellor of deemed universities. The status of a deemed to be university allows full autonomy in courses, syllabus, admissions and fees. According to the new norms in January, 2019, applicant institution must be in operation for at least 20 years, have 100 teachers and 2,000 students, a minimum teacher-student ratio of 1:20 to get deemed university status. One-third of the students should be pursuing research or post-graduate courses.

Private universities: Private universities are approved by the UGC. They can grant degrees but are not allowed to have off-campus affiliated colleges.

Autonomous institutes: Apart from the above universities, other institutions are granted the permission to autonomously award degrees. These institutes do not affiliate colleges and are not officially called universities but autonomous organisations or autonomous institutes. They fall under the administrative control of the Department of Higher Education, MoE.

These organisations include the Indian Institutes of Technology, the National Institutes of Technology, the Indian Institutes of Science Education and Research, the Indian Institutes of Engineering Science and Technology, the Indian Institutes of Management, the National Law Schools, the All-India

Institute of Medical Science, and other autonomous institutes.

119. (d): Soon after Independence, the University Education Commission was set up in **1948** under the Chairmanship of Dr. S Radhakrishnan "to report on Indian university education and suggest improvements and extensions that might be desirable to suit the present and future needs and aspirations of the country".

120. (d): If we define Gender Parity Index (GPI) in terms of Gross Enrolment Ratio then it shows the ratio for girls (or women) to boys (or men) enrolled in educational institutions. In higher education, it measures the female to male ratio enrolled. It is a measure of relative access to education. If the GPI is less than 1, girls are more disadvantaged than boys in terms of access to the institution. If both are equal then both sexes have the same relative access. A GPI is greater than 1 indicates greater relative accessibility of girls.

The Gender Parity Index (GPI) in higher education is calculated for the age group of 18–23 years. This ratio reflects progress towards gender equality. It also serves as an important indicator of women's empowerment in society. The data provides state-wise gender equality index for all categories including SC and ST.

The All India Survey on Higher Education for the year 2019–20, released in June 2021, showed that India experienced a significant improvement in GPI. With due care, UGC has implemented schemes such as 'Post Graduate Indira Gandhi Scholarship Scheme for Single Girl Child' and Government of India 'Beti Bachao Beti Padhao' which have profound impact on education and society and gender inclusion. Student enrolment increased by 11.4% in the last five years, i.e., from 2015–16 to 2019–20.

There has been an increase of 18.2% in female enrolment in higher education during this period. The government has focused more on girls' education, women empowerment and empowerment of socially backward classes. There has been an increase in the population of women, scheduled castes and scheduled tribes in higher education.

The GPI in higher education in the 2019–20 report is 1.01, which reflects an improvement in relative access to higher education for women in the eligible age group when compared to men, as opposed to 1.00 in 2018–19.

121. (b): The NEP-2020 has a strong emphasis on catalysing and energizing research and innovation across the country in all academic disciplines with a focus on state universities and colleges. At the systemic level, research and innovation make a substantial contribution in enhancing the state-of-the-art research ecosystem of international repute. Such an ecosystem is critical for the HEIs to enhance their research productivity. This is an important consideration for the international and national rating, ranking and accreditation process. At the macro level, such an ecosystem is central to growing and sustaining a large and vibrant knowledge society. Research and innovation at education institutions in India, particularly those that are engaged in higher education, is critical.

To make this a reality, the NEP-2020 envisions establishing a National Research Foundation (NRF). Its overarching goal is to build a culture of research to permeate through the universities. According to NEP-20 the primary activities of the NRF (National Research Foundation) will be to:

i. fund competitive peer-reviewed grant proposals of all types across all disciplines

ii. act as a liaison between researchers and relevant branches of government, as well as the industry

iii. seed, grow and facilitate research at academic institutions, particularly at universities and colleges where research is currently in a nascent stage, through mentoring of such institutions

In summation, the NRF will provide a reliable base of merit-based but equitable peer-reviewed research funding, which will help to develop a culture of research in the country through suitable incentives for the recognition of outstanding research.

122. (d): Sattvika values are compassion and respect. When sattva is dominant, a person pays homage to divine and spiritual values. Strength, respect for gurus, non-violence, meditation, kindliness, silence, self-control and purity of character are the motive force of sattvic action. One of the limitations of sattvic guna is that it binds a person through attachment to happiness and knowledge.

You can excel only when you operate out of your *sattva* when the mind is calm, your intellect is clear and your actions are brilliant. *Sattva* is the pristine state of calm that comes from contemplation and absorption on the higher side. *Rajas* is a state of mental agitation brought about by greed, craving and lust. In *tamas,* the best qualities get shrouded, and your inherent talent lies dormant.

123. (b): According to the NEP-20, secondary education comprises of classes 9 to 12.

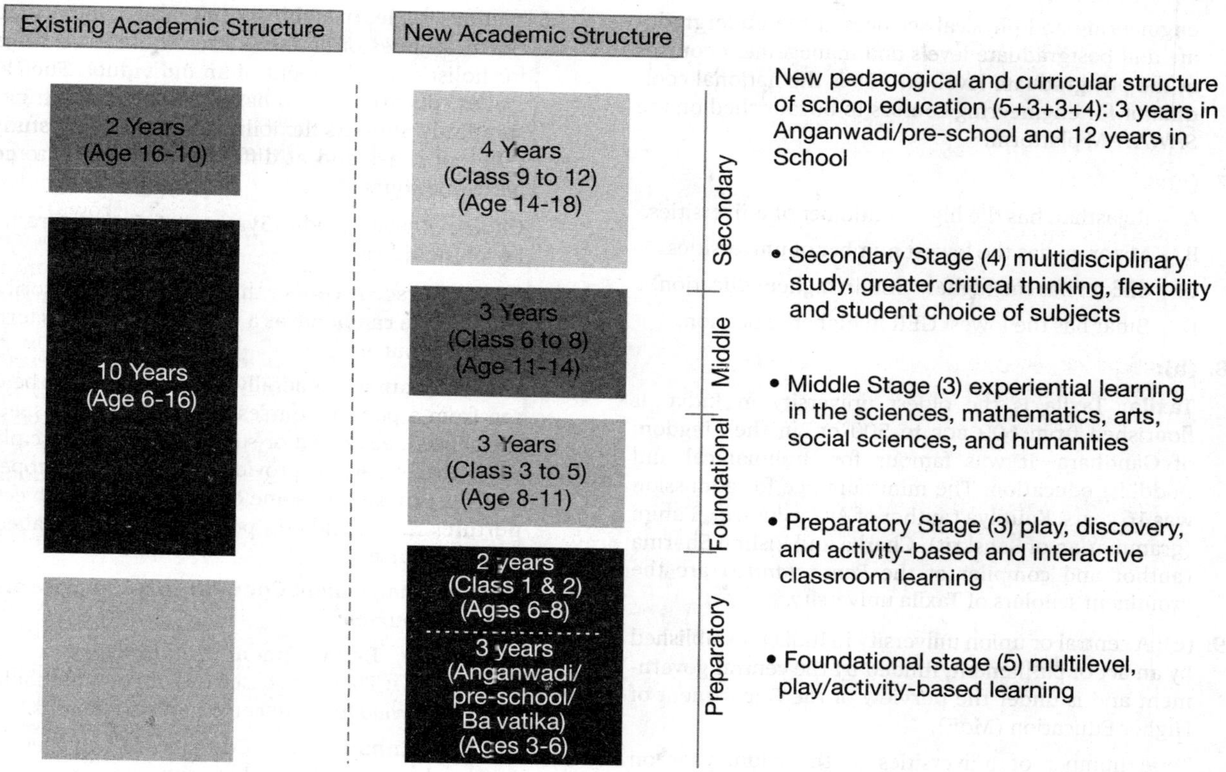

124. (c): The term 'Prakrit' is derived from the word 'Prakriti' which means 'nature' or 'origin'.

Thus, the meaning of Prakrit can be inferred in two ways:

i. A group of languages that were natural, based on the ordinary speech of the common mass.

ii. It may be seen as a group of languages derived from Sanskrit.

Prakrit languages have similarities and differences with Sanskrit in many ways. When Prakrit languages were formalized for literary use, their variations were called Apabhramsa.

Apabhramsa: Apabhramsa was regarded by some grammarians as a dialect of the Prakrit language and was used for religious purposes by Shvetambara and Digambara Jains alike. Works such as the *Harivamsa Purana* and *Bhavishtakaha* fall under the category of Digambara Shauraseni Apabhramsa literature, while *Sanatkumarcharita* and *Kumarapalapratibodha* fall under the group of Shvetambar Maharashtrian Apabhramsa literary works. An Eastern Apabhramsa variety was also found in the Buddhist text *Dohakosha*. However, the use of Apabhramsa was not limited to religious writings. Kalidasa's play *Vikramorvasiya*, fiction such as *Poumkariyu* written by Swayambhudev and messenger poems like 'Sandeshsarsaq 'by Abd-ur Rahman were also composed in Apabhramsa.

125. (a): Sir Charles Wood's dispatch of 1854, also known as the 'Magna Carta of English education in India' recommended creating a properly articulated scheme of education from the primary school to the university level. It sought to encourage indigenous education and the creation of a coherent policy of education.

Subsequently, the following universities were set up in 1857:

(a) University of Calcutta

(b) University of Bombay (now Mumbai)

(c) University of Madras

126. (c): The National Programme on Technology Enhanced Learning **(NPTEL)** is a project of the Ministry of Human Resource Development (MHRD) initiated by seven Indian Institutes of Technology **(Bombay, Delhi, Kanpur, Kharagpur, Madras, Guwahati and Roorkee)** along with the Indian Institute of Science, Bangalore in 2003, to provide quality education to anyone interested in learning from the IITs. The main goal was to create web and video courses in all major branches of engineering and physical sciences at the undergraduate and postgraduate levels and management courses at the postgraduate level. NPTEL is the national coordinator for engineering courses to be launched on the SAWAYAM platform.

127. (c):

A. Rajasthan has the highest number of universities.

B. Mizoram has the lowest number of universities.

C. Sikkim has the highest GER in higher education.

D. Bihar has the lowest GER in higher education.

128. (b):

Taxila: Taxila is the oldest university in India. It flourished from 600 BCE to 500 CE, in the kingdom of Gandhara. It was famous for Brahmanical and Buddhist education. The minimum age for admission was 16 years. Kautilya (author of *Arthashastra*), Panini (grammarian of Sanskrit), Charka and Vishnu Sharma (author and compiler of the *Panchatantra*) are the prominent scholars of Taxila university.

129. (c): A central or union university in India is established by an act of parliament, funded by the central government and is under the purview of the Department of Higher Education (MoE).

Total number of universities in the country as on 25.01.2023 (UGC list) are 1074 as under:

Central universities: 56

State universities: 460

Deemed to be universities: 128

Private universities:430

130. (a): The United Nations Educational, Scientific and Cultural Organization (UNESCO), describes 'Gross Enrolment Ratio' as the total enrolment within a country "in a specific level of education, regardless of age, expressed as a percentage of the population in the official age group corresponding to this level of education".

Gross Enrolment Ratio (GER) in higher education calculated as follows:

$$GER = \frac{\text{Number of enrolment in higher education}}{\text{Total population in the age group of 18–23}} \times 100$$

A high GER indicates a high degree of participation.

131. (a): The Ministry of Education has brought out the New Education Policy (NEP) to bring out reforms in the Indian education system. The Choice Based Credit System (CBCS) is an internationally acknowledged system. It not only offers opportunities and avenues to learn subjects but also explores additional avenues of learning beyond the core subjects for holistic development of an individual. The CBCS makes education broad based and at par with global standards. It offers flexibility for students to study at different times and at different institutions to complete one course.

Choice Based Credit System of Index Graduate Level Includes:

Core Course: A course that should compulsorily be studied by a candidate as a core requirement is termed as a core course.

Elective Course: Generally, a course that can be chosen from a pool of courses and may be very specific, specialized, advanced or supportive to the discipline/subject of study, or provides an extended scope, or enables exposure to some other discipline/subject, or nurtures the candidate's proficiency/skill is called an elective course.

Ability Enhancement Courses: This comprise of two types of courses:

i. **Ability Enhancement Compulsory Courses (AECC):** These are based on the content that leads to knowledge enhancement of participants.

ii. **Skill Enhancement Courses (SEC):** These may be chosen from a pool of courses designed to provide value-based and/or skill-based knowledge.

132. (a): The occurrence of cyclones is a sea linked phenomena so there are no chances of its origin from Northern and Central India. It originates in the seas due to low air pressure conditions. The East coast receives cyclones not only from those that originated in Andaman Sea but also from the Pacific Ocean (typhoons). For transfer of typhoons, there is no big land mass to stop this. The Bay of Bengal receives more rainfall in comparison to west coast. The winds are slower and weaker over the ocean. This part is also fed by rivers Ganga and Brahmaputra.

The surface sea temperature and humidity also play an important part. The average temperature is around 28°C that is intensified by warm air currents.

Odisha state suffers the most from cyclones. The ratio between cyclones from east coasts and west coasts is 4:1.

The tropical cyclones are less in west coast due to dry air intrusion as dry winds flow from west to east. The Arabian Peninsula is already dry. There is a strong wind shear which hampers cyclone development.

The naming of cyclones is done in a schematic manner by World Meteorological Organisation (WMO) that was set up in the year 1950, the roots of which were planted at the 1873 Vienna International Meteorological Congress. WMO maintains rotating lists of names which are appropriate for each Tropical Cyclone basin. If a cyclone is particularly deadly or costly, then its name is retired and replaced by another one.

133. (b): On this day in 1835, Thomas Babington Macaulay successfully westernised education in India; English was made the official language for the government and courts, and was adopted as the official medium of instruction. This point is specifically important in Macaulay Minutes - 'We must at present do our best to form a class of persons, Indian in blood and colour, but English in taste, in opinions, in morals and in intellect'.

134. (a): Nalanda University is the correct answer. Nalanda is an ancient center of higher learning in Bihar from 427 to 1197. Nalanda was established in the 5th century AD in Bihar, India.

A new Nalanda University has been recently developed in Bihar in 2010.

Xuan Zang (or call him Hiuen Tsang) visited Nalanda University in 7th century. He stayed and travelled in India for sixteen years. He translated Buddhist scriptures. He also studied logic, Sanskrit grammar, Yogacara in India. He opposed Samkhya and Vaiseshika that he found to be opposing Budhhist philosophy.

According to I-Quing, there were followers of both "vehicles" - Hinayana and Mahayana. Northern India and most of the islands of the South Seas (such as Sumatra, Java – parts of present Indonesia) practiced Hi –naya –na. The Buddhists in China and Malayu practiced Maha –ya –na.

1. For future questions, note that Fa-Hien was the first Chinese traveller to visit India in the early fifth century. The purpose of his visit was to look for texts sacred to Buddhism.
2. Taxila university was one of the oldest universities of the world.
3. Nalanda University is a public central/union university located in Rajgir in Nalanda district in the state of Bihar. It is designated as an Institute of National Importance (INI) and excellence. This international university is supported by 18 member countries was established by an Act of the Indian Parliament in 2010. The President of India serves as the Visitor to Nalanda University.

135. (a): National Knowledge Commission (NKC) was constructed in 2006 as a high-level advisory body to the Prime Minister of India, with the objective of transforming India into a knowledge society. It was brain child of Sam Pitroda. NKC submitted around 300 recommendations on 27 focus areas. NKC focused on five key areas of the knowledge paradigm – access to knowledge, knowledge concepts, knowledge creation, knowledge application and development of better knowledge services.

NKC has recommended setting up of a National Science and Social Science Foundation (NSSF) for producing research work that can fetch a Nobel Prize for an Indian scientist.

136. (c): National Education Policy, 2020 envisages the setting up of an autonomous body – National Educational Technology Forum (NETF) to provide a platform for free exchange of ideas on the use of technology to enhance learning, assessment, planning, administration and so on, both for School and Higher Education.

Aim of NETF: The aim of the NETF will be to facilitate decision making on the induction, deployment and use of technology by providing to the leadership of education institutions, State and Central Governments and other stakeholders the latest knowledge and research as well as the opportunity to consult and share best practices. The NETF will have following functions:

1. To provide independent evidence-based advice to Central and State Government agencies on technology-based interventions.
2. To build intellectual and institutional capacities in education technology.
3. To envision strategic thrust areas in this domain.
4. To articulate new directions for research and innovation.
5. To lay down standards of content, technology, and pedagogy for online/digital teaching-learning. These standards will help to formulate guidelines for e-learning by States, Boards, Schools, HEIs, etc.
6. To maintain regular flow of authentic data from multiple sources including educational technology innovators and will engage with diverse set of researchers to analyse the data.
7. To conduct multiple regional and national conferences, workshops, etc. to solicit inputs from national and international educational technology researchers, entrepreneurs, and practitioners.
8. To identify technological interventions for the purpose of improving teaching-learning and evaluation process, supporting teacher preparation and professional development, enhancing educational access, and streamlining educational planning, management, and administration including process related to admissions, attendance, assessments, etc.
9. To categorize emergent technologies based on their potential and estimated frame for disruption, and periodically present this analysis to Ministry of Education.

In July, 2021, the Prime Minister stated that National Digital Education Architecture (NDEAR) and National Education Technology Forum (NETF) would be working to make digital and economic framework across the country.

Let us look at the few other initiatives started by Government of India in education sector.

Academic Bank of Credit: This aims to provide multiple entry and exit options for students in Higher education and also the first year Engineering Programmes in Regional Languages and Guidelines for Internationalization of Higher Education.

Vidya Pravesh: The initiative is a three-month play-based school preparation module for Grade 1 students.

Indian Sign Language: The Indian Sign Language has been launched as a subject at the secondary level.

NISHTHA 2.0: This is an integrated programme of teacher training designed by NCERT.

SAFAL (Structured Assessment For Analyzing Learning Levels): SAFAL is a competency-based assessment framework, which has been launched for Grades 3, 5 and 8 in CBSE schools.

Artificial Intelligence Website: A website dedicated to Artificial Intelligence has also been launched.

137. (b): Curriculum revision means to modify the existing curriculum using data from the review. Review and revision are important because they enable teachers to consider the ways curriculum interacts with actual students in a real teaching learning environment. The vision and mission also undergo a change. The social, political, economic and above all the philosophical environment are always at a change so as to make teaching learning process more effective. Thus, there are different stakeholders. The demands of industry also change, so that the curriculum produces more outcome-based citizens.

138. (a): All these universities are actually ancient universities. India is one of the oldest civilizations in the world. It was a centre for higher learning in ancient times. India contributed greatly to the field of Mathematics, Astrology, Astronomy, and other sciences. Vedic science was so advanced that it could be compared with the present day's scientific inventions.

Taxila university was one of the oldest universities of the world but that was not completely centralized. The government has tried to revive the concept of Nalanda University in Bihar.

139. (a): The National Council for Technical Education was enacted in 1993 and was set up in 1995. According to Government sources - the main objective of the NCTE is to achieve planned and coordinated development of the teacher education system throughout the country, the regulation and proper maintenance of Norms and Standards in the teacher education system and for matters connected therewith. It includes the whole gamut of teacher education programmes including research and training of persons for equipping them to teach at pre-primary, primary, secondary and senior secondary stages in schools, and non-formal education, part-time education, adult education and distance (correspondence) education courses.

140. (d): According to Government sources DigiLocker is a flagship initiative of Ministry of Electronics & IT (MeitY) under Digital India programme. DigiLocker aims at 'Digital Empowerment' of citizen by providing access to authentic digital documents to citizen's digital document wallet. The issued documents in DigiLocker system are deemed to be at par with original physical documents as per Rule 9A of the Information Technology (Preservation and Retention of Information by Intermediaries providing Digital Locker facilities) Rules, 2016 notified on February 8, 2017 vide G.S.R. 711(E).

Benefits to Citizens

1. Important Documents Anytime, Anywhere!
2. Authentic Documents, Legally at Par with Originals.
3. Digital Document Exchange with the consent of the citizen.
4. Faster service Delivery- Government Benefits, Employment, Financial Inclusion, Education, Health.

Benefits to Agencies

Reduced Administrative Overhead: Aimed at the concept of paperless governance. It reduces the administrative overhead by minimizing the use of paper and curtailing the verification process.

Digital Transformation: Provides trusted issued documents. Issued Documents available via DigiLocker are fetched in real-time directly from the issuing agency.

Secure Document Gateway: Acts as a secure document exchange platform like payment gateway between trusted issuer and trusted Requester/Verifier with the consent of the citizen.

Real Time Verification: Provides a verification module enabling government agencies to verify data directly from issuers after obtaining user consent.

141. (c):

A. Montessori Method: This was developed by Dr. Maria Montessori (1907) is based on the idea of self-education. The child does not sit still and idle to the lessons taught by the teacher, here, in this system, the child educates himself or herself, but with the teacher as a guide. The child uses hands-on materials and specially prepared classrooms to develop both intellect and character. This type of self-actualization of students is called "normalization." This classroom system is suitable in theory for all ages but mostly practiced by preschoolers and kindergartners. There is respect for feelings of child, the way he/she wants to educate matters.

B. **Integral Education,** as envisioned by the Mother and Sri Aurobindo, regards the child as a growing soul and helps him to bring out all that is best, most powerful, most innate and living in his nature. It helps the child develop all facets of his personality and awaken his latent possibilities so that he acquires
   - a strong, supple, healthy, beautiful body
   - a sensitive, emotionally refined, energetic personality
   - a wide-ranging, lively intelligence and will
   - the subtler spiritual qualities that unify and harmonise the being around the child's inmost Truth or Soul.

The focus and emphasis in Integral Education (IE) is not just information and skills acquisition but also self-development, triggered from within the child and supported and nourished by teachers and parents. Every experience becomes a learning tool for the child in its growth. IE helps the child to integrate with its true Self, its surroundings, its society, its country and humanity; in other words, to become the complete being, the integral being that the child is meant to be.

Answers for Comprehension Passage

142. (d): All the given dimensions (Accountability, Participation, Integrity, Competency, Transparency) are crucial for promoting quality in higher education.

143. (c): The First Buddhist Council was held soon after the death of the Buddha, around 483 BC, at Sattapani cave near Rajgriha (modern Rajgir). The correct answer is (c).

144. (d):

Statement I: The National Council for Teacher Education (NCTE) was indeed established as a statutory body by an Act of Parliament. The year was 1995, not 1993.

Statement II: Dr. S. Radhakrishnan was the Chairman of the University Education Commission set up in 1948.

The correct answer is (d). Statement I is incorrect but Statement II is correct.

145. (c): In 1902, the prominent engineering colleges in India included Roorkee (now IIT Roorkee) and College of Engineering, Pune (then called Poona). The correct answer is (c). A and C only.

146. (b):

A. **Shastras** – II - Learned disciplines

B. **Varta** – III - Agriculture, trade, commerce, and animal husbandry

C. **Kavyas** – IV - Imaginative and creative literature.

D. **Anviksiki** – I - Logic

The correct matching is A-II, B-III, C-IV, D-I, thus answer is (b).

147. (b): SPARC stands for Scheme for Promotion of Academic and Research Collaboration. SPARC aims to enhance research and academic collaborations between Indian institutions and their international counterparts.

148. (c): Vishwa Guru that means World Teacher. NEP 2020 envisions India regaining its historical position as a global leader in education and knowledge.

149. (a): NCIVE stands for National Committee for the Integration of Vocational Education. NCIVE, as outlined in the NEP 2020, is to oversee and facilitate the integration of vocational education into all schools and higher education institutions in a phased manner.

150. (c): The Department of Science and Technology was established in 1978 by the Government of India.

151. (d): All the listed texts - *Vedas, Brahmanas, Upanishads, and Dharma sutras* - were integral parts of the ancient Indian education system. The Vedas served as the foundational texts, Brahmanas provided rituals and practices, Upanishads focused on philosophical inquiries, and Dharma sutras laid down ethical and social codes.

152. (b): Different options have been discussed.

(a): Expansion of public sector happened in earlier plans as per economic policy. Prior to 1991, India had a largely state protected, public sector-dominated economy. That sector still exists in defence, railways, and certain areas of energy etc. But otherwise, the role of government largely shifted from being 'producer' to 'facilitator' and 'regulator'. The LPG became the new rule.

(b): The Eighth Five-Year Plan of India happened between 1992 and 1997. That period almost coincided with economic reforms of 1991 as more requirement of human resources was anticipated in a diversified economy. Then the role of private sector was envisaged to fill the gap. Some opening of economy happened in 1980s' also under Rajiv Gandhi as PM. NEP in 1986) and Programme of Action in 1992 played important role. Janardhan Reddy Committee (1985-86)' recommended self-financing colleges, increased autonomy and flexibility for universities.

(c): A legislation in 2010 and NEP 2020 talked about the role of foreign universities.

153. (c): **Statement (I)**: There is vast variety of institutions in India which includes 1127 universities and almost 43000 colleges as per UGC and AISHE reports. We can see that there is wide structural variety. The institutes may excel in different areas like practical skills development, community engagement, or catering to marginalized communities. NIRF rankings are based on Teaching, Learning and Resources (TLR), Research and Professional Practice (RP), Graduation Outcome (GO), Outreach and Inclusiveness (OI) and Perception (PR) but they don't present a holistic scenario.

Statement (II): acknowledges the inherent difficulty of designing a perfect system. There is no one-size-fits-all rating approach because of diversity of education sector.

154. (a): The three initial universities, Kolkata, Bombay, and Madras were modelled on lines of London University as per Sir Charles Wood's Dispatch of 1854. That era was referred as 'Magna Carta of English Education in India'. They adopted some elements of the British university system, such as the emphasis on research, faculty structure, and academic disciplines. The answer mentioned is (a) though Andhra University was set up at a later stage.

155. (c): This university was founded around 1063 CE. It was located on the Hooghly River in West Bengal, it had connections with both Vaishnavism and Shakta traditions. It is connected with Chaitanya Mahaprabhu, a major proponent of the Bhakti movement during 15th–16th centuries. In this question, it is connected with logic (Tarka), literature (Sanskrit) and Tantra that was a complex set of spiritual practices and rituals.

156. (d): Let's look at some basics of colleges.

(a): Mayo College, Ajmer: This is primarily an English-medium institution. This is not known for European education in the mother tongue.

(b): St. Stephen's College, Delhi: Established by Cambridge Mission, so English based.

(c): St. Xavier's College, Calcutta: Known for Western-style education in English.

(d): University College, Lahore: This is part of the Punjab University that was linked with Calcutta University and followed British education models but Urdu gained prominence after 1913.